Civil War and Reconstruction

EYEWITNESS HISTORY

Civil War and Reconstruction

Rodney P. Carlisle

Facts On File
An imprint of Infobase Publishing

Civil War and Reconstruction

Copyright © 2008 by Rodney P. Carlisle

Maps copyright © 2008 by Infobase Publishing

Facts On File, Inc.
An imprint of Infobase Publishing
132 West 31st Street
New York NY 10001

Library of Congress Cataloging-in-Publication Data
Carlisle, Rodney P.
   Civil War and Reconstruction / Rodney P. Carlisle
      p. cm. — (Eyewitness history)
   Includes bibliographical references and index.
   ISBN 978-0-8160-6347-5 (alk. paper)
   1. United States—History—Civil War, 1861–1865. 2. United States—History—Civil War, 1861–1865—Chronology. 3. United States—History—Civil War, 1861–1865—Personal narratives 4. Reconstruction (U.S. history, 1865–1877) 5. Reconstruction (U.S. history, 1865–1877)—Chronology. 6. Reconstruction (U.S. history, 1865–1877)—Biography. I. Title.
   E468.C245 2007
   973.7—dc22   2006035425

Facts On File books are available at special discounts when purchased in bulk quantities for businesses, associations, institutions, or sales promotions. Please call our Special Sales Department in New York at (212) 967–8800 or (800) 322–8755.

You can find Facts On File on the World Wide Web at http://www.factsonfile.com

Text design by Joan M. McEvoy
Maps by Jeremy Eagle

Printed in the United States of America

VB JM 10 9 8 7 6 5 4 3 2 1

This book is printed on acid-free paper.

CONTENTS

NOTE ON PHOTOS

Many of the illustrations and photographs used in this book are old, historical images. The quality of the prints is not always up to modern standards, as in some cases the originals are damaged. The content of the illustrations, however, made their inclusion important despite problems in reproduction.

AUTHOR'S PREFACE

The Civil War era in American history presents many paradoxes. Probably more literature has been produced on the war, its origins and its aftermath, than on any other period in American history or, for that matter, on any comparable period in the history of the modern world. At the same time, to many 21st-century readers, the events and the issues that divided the nation between 1850 and 1877, and peaked in the bloody war between April 1861 and April 1865, seem increasingly remote from contemporary concerns.

While the war remains fascinating to some history buffs, descendants of participants, visitors to battlefield sites, and many others, for some students and general readers, works on the Civil War appear to represent vast collections of detail, much of it surprisingly trivial. The reasons for the dichotomy in reaction, between fascination with compendia of facts on the one hand and dismayed distress at the complex and often microscopic accounts of the war on the other, reveal aspects of the culture of our own times.

The difference in reaction among modern students of the subject suggests how the study of history fills different purposes for different people. For some, it provides an escape to a different world, peopled by heroes and driven by values missing today. For others, history is interesting for the insights it yields into the causes, structure, and dynamics of the society in which we live. These two different ways of looking at history sometimes lead to completely different approaches to the events of the past. For some, the rich detail evokes the color of the past, firing the imagination. But for those seeking insights and explanations, too much specific detail seems clutter, obscuring the deeper patterns. For both approaches, however, there is no denying that the Civil War represents one of the most intriguing and rich episodes in the history of the United States.

The war was the most disastrous of all American wars in the number of Americans killed and wounded, partly because Americans fought on both sides. The American nation itself emerged from the war as a single nation, since the victory of the Union in effect declared and demonstrated that the perceived right of any state to secede was a constitutional heresy. Although many aspects of states' rights remained in the federal structure, the United States emerged no longer a loose and fragile confederation of sovereign states, but a single nation, with greatly enhanced powers. Socially, the war helped bring the institutionalized slavery of African Americans to an end in the United States and set the stage for the establishment of racial equality, or at least a prologue to liberation. For both these broad reasons, the Civil War is the central turning point in the story of the United States of America. Its causes and outcomes are certainly worthy of serious study and understanding.

For the Civil War history buff, such aspects of larger significance may be of less interest than the specifics: the individual stories of battles, of weaponry, of individual acts of courage and brilliance on the battlefield offset by tales of cowardice and incompetence. So compelling is the desire to relive that era for some that thousands of 21st-century men and women participate in mock battles, dressing in uniforms of the period to march with muskets and rifles in hand across the grassy battlefields of Gettysburg, Antietam, Shiloh, Atlanta, and Perryville. Informed estimates put the number of Civil War reenactors in the United States and abroad (from as far afield as Britain and the Ukraine) at 35,000 to 40,000. Each year there are perhaps as many as 200 small, uniformed demonstrations of skirmishes and battles, with as many as five or six large-scale reenactments of battles, witnessed by hundreds of thousands of friends, relatives, tourists, and the general public. Even without the clash of reenactors, Civil War sites in the state of Virginia alone attract over 500,000 visitors annually.

Some of the attraction of the war years is the fact that the Civil War era marked the end of an age of romanticism and individualism, soon to be replaced by an age of organization, corporations, and countervailing, impersonal forces. The war itself helped bring the age of heroic individualism to an end and ushered in the beginning of a less personal age. The names of Robert E. Lee, Stonewall Jackson, William Tecumseh Sherman, and Ulysses S. Grant among numerous others, have become icons to later generations, representing differing styles of warfare. The names of African-American leaders like Frederick Douglass, Martin Delany, and Robert Smalls have become legendary, as have the contributions of women leaders like Harriet Tubman, the Grimké sisters, and Clara Barton.

That era of heroes and heroines seemed to vanish in the decades following the war. Even the most informed student of American history usually has trouble identifying more than one or two individual American statesmen from the period of the 1880s. The age of great personal achievement on the stage of national affairs seemed to fade. Forces replaced individuals, ideas drove events, and technology and industry took center stage. With the passing of the generation of the Civil War, the glory and romance of history seemed to pass as well.

In the 1860s, generals and common soldiers alike believed that qualities of personal leadership in officers determined the outcome of battles, leading to the personifying of whole events in a way that is simply unheard of in the 21st century. To people at the time, and for generations since, complex military engagements involving hundreds or thousands of men were known as "Stonewall Jackson's" stand, "Pickett's Charge," or "Sherman's March to the Sea," as if victory or defeat could be attributed to the individual officer. The events and leaders were so viewed at the time, and to the delight of their men and to newspaper readers, the exploits of cavalrymen like J. E. B. Stuart, Phil Sheridan, and Jubal Early seemed to capture the dash and brilliance of war as adventure. It is no wonder that the Civil War, at the cusp of change from an age of heroes and villains to an age of class warfare and institutions, continues to be viewed with nostalgia in our age of faceless bureaucracies.

It is natural to try to understand any historical event as an episode in the life of an individual. After all, history happened to people, and it is through people that history can be viewed in its most immediate way. Most of the great historical treatments of the Civil War, by writers ranging from Bruce Catton and Henry Steele Commager through Russell Weigley and James McPherson, are replete with the exploits and foibles of individual generals, naval officers, and political leaders. In fact, unraveling the exact reasons why one side lost or won a particular battle inevitably leads modern analysts, even in questions of strategy or weapons technology, back to the character, intelligence, and decisions of individual officers. Even those who set out to examine the war against theories of operational art, strategy, and tactics usually present the history of battles through the decisions and actions of individual commanders.

Yet behind the adventures and exploits of the men and women of the era, deeper causes and consequences bear study. To understand why several states seceded from the Union, how the leaders of the seceding states believed it was possible to create a separate nation, and why and how the Union suppressed that action, requires exploration of several overlapping issues. Underlying the division was the issue of slavery and the belief on the part of those planters that depended on the slave economy that agitators in other states sought to suppress that institution. In reality a small minority of abolitionists in the North were vocal, committed, and quite certain of the rightness of their cause. In the long view of history they were quite right; later generations have no trouble understanding that slavery was a clear social evil.

To the defenders of slavery in the 1850s, however, it seemed that white abolitionists were simply misguided radicals or, worse, bitter hypocrites, willing to risk bloodshed in order to impose their own interpretation of law and morality on others. Escapes from slavery through the Underground Railroad and a call to outright slave rebellion by John Brown in 1859 won support in churches and newspapers throughout the North. With these developments, the fears of slave-owners and their supporters reached a new pitch.

The efforts to find compromises between regional divisions regarding slavery had persisted through the 1850s, but the social institutions that might have provided forums for rational discussion and quiet resolution of differences all collapsed, apparently incapable of producing a peaceful set of solutions. Historians have explored the breakdown of congressional compromise and of the two-party system, which had been the political institutions holding the nation together. Cultural entities, including religion, the newspaper and book publishing businesses, and colleges and military institutes, sharpened the divisions between the sections rather than healing them. To an extent that is unfamiliar in a world of instant electronic media, the public mind in the 1850s and 1860s was shaped by local sources, such as weekly oratory in churches, public addresses and debates, and small-circulation, local weekly newspapers and magazines, many of them published by religious denominations. All contributed to and reflected the deepening divide.

Because the decisions of individuals did indeed shape the course of events in profound ways in this period, many writers have chosen to present the grand events of the Civil War era through biography. At the core of the conflict were crucial leaders on both sides. In the North, Abraham Lincoln shaped policy regarding the war and slavery, while several of his generals, particularly George McClellan, William T. Sherman, and Ulysses Grant imprinted the tactics and strategy of the war with their own ideas. Similarly, in the South, Confederate president Jefferson Davis, with a stubborn determination that secession was lawful and that the guilt of the war lay with the North, determined much of the course of the war. His generals, especially Robert E. Lee, James Longstreet, Joseph E. Johnston, and John B. Hood, each left the imprint of their decisions on the course of history. Only by contemplating how Lincoln's mind worked is it possible to understand the halting way in which the Union's war goals gradually moved from preservation of the Union to include the abolition of slavery; only by sensing the bitter intensity of Jefferson Davis's beliefs can we grasp the refusal of the Confederacy to bring the war to an end when defeat was clear. Eyewitnesses saw how the war turned from one of gentlemen commenting on the gallantry of their opponents to a murderous conflict by land mine, targeted murder, and intentional destruction of civilian resources.

After the war and even into the 20th century, memoirs and diaries continued to be printed, at first by the participants, then by their descendants and by academic editors. So much material was committed to print on paper that vast quantities of it survive in books, document collections, and in magazine and newspaper files, leaving rich documentation of the tone, the passion, and the views of the contemporary participants and observers.

For those readers who have already studied the Civil War in depth, this volume may offer some departures. I devote the opening two chapters to causes, both political and emotional, that lay behind the growing crisis. The politics of the 1850s and 1860 led to secession of some of the slave-holding states from the United States. Following Lincoln's election and prior to his inauguration, seven Southern states announced their secession, while eight others that had slavery voted to remain in the Union. It was not at all clear, on the inauguration of Lincoln in March 1861, whether the prior secession of seven states and their seizure of federal military facilities on lands granted by the states to the federal government would be regarded as a legal, constitutional action or an act of revolution. That constitutional test became converted to gunfire at Fort Sumter in Charleston Harbor in a series of events that unfolded in the fast-paced early months of 1861.

I have developed two chapters devoted to the maritime side of the Civil War, in many ways crucial to the outcome. The riverine war supported the land conflict, both in the Western and Eastern theaters of the war, while the coastal blockade helped bring the Confederacy to economic ruin. The war on the high seas tied up the Union navy, when a handful of Confederate raiding ships, most of them built abroad, permanently prevented the United States from becoming the world's leading merchant marine power. The naval side of the Civil War, in many ways, shaped the future destiny of the United States, coloring the American view of neutrality and the role of sea power.

Two chapters focus on the process of emancipation that brought slavery in the United States to an end. Emancipation was dictated by the fact that the slaves understood that the war provided a chance to end the institution, and they simply voted with their feet, walking away from plantations to wherever freedom beckoned behind Union military lines or in the collapsing social order of the Confederate states. As the Union struggled to keep up with the broadening self-emancipation of four million slaves, legislation, proclamation, executive order, military rules, state legislatures, and state constitutions hurried to regularize the process in law. Slavery did not end in a single clean legal departure as is so often assumed in the legend of Lincoln, but in more than 30 different ways, depending on locality and timing. A table in Appendix C shows the many ways in which freedom came to different states and regions of the nation. While Lincoln's role in the process was crucial, it was by no means simple. Even though slavery ended, only a few visionary abolitionists and radicals understood that leaving the former slave owners in possession of their landed wealth and leaving the slaves penniless would result in decades of social oppression of the freedmen and their descendants.

In the chapters of this book devoted to the land battles, I focus on only a few of the most crucial of the thousands of military engagements, battles, and raids of the war. In the case of every battle, many excellent works, some of them published in recent years, unravel the decisions, mistakes, and occasional brilliance of the military commanders in great detail. In this volume, my effort has been to concisely depict the broad outlines of the land war through a limited number of the most important battles, showing what happened and detailing crucial consequences of those battles.

Even though the war is often retold as a set of military events divorced from politics, a close look at the elections shows that politics shaped the conduct of the war, emancipation, and the potential reconstruction of the seceded states into the Union in quite crucial ways; at the same time, the news from the battles helped determine the outcome of elections. While radical Republicans tried to force Lincoln to take more punitive measures toward the seceded states and to grant immediate social and political rights to the former slaves, Peace Democrats toyed with secret organizations devoted to supporting the Secession cause and explicitly proclaimed a white racist doctrine. Although most of the party system appeared to vanish in the Confederacy, Jefferson Davis also faced turbulent cross-currents of opposition throughout the war. So one chapter unravels the political campaigns, where the outcomes were told by ballots, not bullets.

Two chapters focus on the end of the war and on the long aftermath of Reconstruction. The myths and legends surrounding Reconstruction left a popular impression that it was a tragic era because the rights of Southern whites were trampled by a vindictive Northern-dominated Congress. More recent scholarship and a less racist view of the events suggests that the tragedy lay in the failure to achieve social justice for the freed slaves. The agony of the postwar years did leave behind seeds of future progress that took a century to germinate.

Some apparently straightforward questions, such as why the war was even fought, why it was so prolonged, and how and why the slaves were freed are fundamental to understanding the unfolding events. To address such basics, the work has a strong focus on causes and consequences, on emancipation, politics, and the connections between policy and events on the ground.

Each period-based chapter has three elements. In order to put contemporary testimony into context, a *narrative* plumbs the deeper issues of causation and presents the unfolding drama of crisis and conflict. A detailed *chronicle of events* covering the same period follows so that the day-by-day and week-by-week happenings are laid out sequentially. Then, each chapter's section of *eyewitness testimony* presents representative comments and observations, not only of political figures and military officers, but also of members of the clergy, journalists, and ordinary men and women, black and white, who left reports, diaries, journals, and letters describing the events they participated in and witnessed. Some of the eyewitness accounts have been previously published in book form, including some long out of print and others only recently uncovered from archives. Also included here are editorials, news accounts, reports, testimony, and dispatches that have not been reprinted in any collection, gathered from contemporary newspapers, investigations, and journals. Many of the selections are long enough to give the eyewitness perspective on a complete episode or incident. At the end of each eyewitness selection is a brief note dating the testimony, explaining who made the observation or comment, and giving the source of the quotation.

Appendix A reproduces crucial documents that illuminate the causes and course of the war, including some official statements by Lincoln and other leaders. Appendix B is devoted to 50 short sketches of individuals that help illuminate how these actors played important parts in the unfolding events. A third appendix presents maps and tables. Notes and a bibliography cite and provide a full listing of the sources used. The various elements of this volume are intended to provide a useful account and a set of tools for those who wish to learn the basic facts of this crucial era as well as those who want to pursue their knowledge in further depth.

1

Ultimate and Proximate Causes
May 1846–November 1860

In 1860, the people of the United States faced the greatest internal crisis that the nation had seen since its founding. That crisis burst into a disastrous civil war in 1861 that lasted four years and took the lives of over 600,000 Americans, more than all other wars in American history combined. The ultimate causes of that war can be traced to divisions over slavery inherent in American society since the 1780s. In that earlier era, the founding fathers worked out compromises and language in the Constitution that balanced the divisions between the regions so they could politically coexist in a single nation. Although tobacco farmers in Connecticut owned slaves, and wealthy Northern merchants and farmers often owned a few household slaves, for the most part, the Northern colonies did not rely on slavery to the extent found in Virginia and the other Southern colonies.

The invention of the cotton gin in 1793 provided a great stimulus to the expansion of cotton plantations, which, in the view of almost all cotton planters, could be worked only with slave labor. By the first decade of the 19th century, the Northern states had either abolished slavery or started a system of gradual emancipation. Meanwhile, the demand for slaves for new cotton plantations spreading into the Old Southwest—Alabama, Mississippi, Northern Florida, and Louisiana—steadily increased. Landowners seeking to profit from cotton, rice, tobacco, and hemp all invested in slaves to plant and harvest the crops. Even as the institution expanded westward, Northern and Southern states agreed to outlaw the importation of slaves from overseas in 1808. The slave-holding states agreed to the prohibition on the slave trade for two reasons. Planters feared that if Afro-Caribbean slaves were brought in, they would bring with them ideas of slave rebellion, spurred by the successes of the Haitian revolutions during the 1790s. Furthermore, the importation of slaves could drive down the domestic price of African-American slaves who had descended from generations imported throughout the colonial period. Slaveholders in the Upper South, particularly Maryland and Virginia, even if they had no need for more slaves on their own tobacco plantations, soon found a ready source of income from the sale of slaves to the expanding cotton regions to the south and west.

Early in the 1800s, as the nation expanded westward, it became clear that maintaining the political balance between Southern states with slavery and Northern states without slavery would be more and more difficult. Congress admitted new states to the Union in the period 1800–20 in pairs, one with slavery and one without, so that a balance would be maintained in the Senate, where each state had equal representation no matter the size of its population. In 1820, the admission of Missouri as a slave state was matched by the division of Massachusetts into two states, with the northern section, Maine, admitted as a free state. Congress extended the line represented by the southern border of Missouri westward through the remaining territory of the Louisiana Purchase. North of this latitude line, 36 degrees 30 minutes, the Missouri Compromise prohibited slavery but permitted it south of that line. This Missouri Compromise line of 36°30', and the debates surrounding it, although preserving a tenuous political balance between the sections, demonstrated how the social and economic division was testing the ability of Congress to maintain compromise between the sections.

Congress had no jurisdiction over conditions and laws regulating slavery within the individual states. However, Congress did exercise jurisdiction over federal territories. If territories developed slavery and later became states, the balance of power in Congress could shift southward. On the other hand, if Congress prohibited slavery in territories and those territories were admitted as free states, the balance would shift to the north.

Issues regarding whether new states and territories should be free or slave flared up intermittently over the next 30 years. The admission of Texas as a state, where Southern American settlers with slaves had established an independent republic by seceding from Mexico, engendered fiery debates in Congress and throughout the nation in 1844–45. Similarly, the war with Mexico, fought over the period 1846–48, was strongly supported in the South but opposed in the North, as many Northerners believed the war would result in continued expansion of slavery and a consequent increase of the representation of slave states in the Congress.

In 1846 the United States settled its boundary dispute with Britain over Oregon Territory by extending the 49th parallel to the Pacific, putting the lands now in Oregon, Washington, and Idaho on the American side of the border. Together with the acquisition of former Mexican provinces won in the war with Mexico in 1848, the nation's size nearly doubled in the 30 years after the Missouri Compromise. With the 1848 discovery of gold in California, the population of that region acquired from Mexico expanded enormously, and the new Californians sought admission to the union as a state. The issue of which of the new lands would include slavery and which would exclude it exploded into a congressional crisis by 1849–50 that threatened to disrupt the nation and all the compromises that had been worked out between the sections.

THE GREAT DEBATE: SLAVERY IN THE TERRITORIES

From the perspective of later generations, the intensity of the debate and the difficulty of finding a compromise solution to the question of which territories would be allowed slavery appear remote, and the difficulties encountered in reaching compromises suggest that the generation dealing with the issue through the 1840s and 1850s was particularly hard-headed or stubborn. After all, several simple solutions were offered. In August 1846, a congressman from Pennsylvania, David Wilmot, introduced a bill that would prevent the existence of slavery in any territory acquired from Mexico, whether by conquest or purchase. The same language had been used during the first years of the republic. Under the Articles of Confederation in 1787, the Northwest Ordinance had excluded slavery north of the Ohio River. The Wilmot Proviso passed in the House of Representatives, but Southerners in the Senate prevented it from coming to a vote and the proviso was not enacted. The Polk administration in 1846, supported by some Southern Democrats, attempted to amend the Wilmot Proviso by having it apply only north of the Missouri Compromise line, extended westward through the new territories acquired from Mexico. However, that measure also failed. The solution of either excluding slavery from all of the new lands, or, as some Southerners preferred, extending the Missouri Compromise line to the Pacific coast to allow it in territories south of the line, both seem in retrospect to be straightforward or simple ways to resolve the issue. But neither measure could muster a majority. A Southern proposal, the Calhoun Resolution, introduced in February 1847, asserted that Congress had no right to exclude slavery from any territory. The deepening and hardening of divisions and fears on both sides prevented any easy compromise between the Wilmot position and the Calhoun position.

The lines of debate stiffened and tempers shortened further by 1849. Representatives of the slaveholding states feared that the rapidly expanding Northern population would create numerous new states without slavery. If that were to happen, the number of senators representing free states would soon become a clear majority. With both houses of Congress dominated by representatives of free states, it seemed to Calhoun and other Southerners that the original geographic check and balance system of the Constitution would collapse. On the other side, Northerners had come to believe that the proslavery factions sought to expand and to dominate in the new territories.

Each side saw the other as engaged in a hostile conspiracy to subvert the underlying regional compromises represented in the Constitution, and the rhetoric of accusation increased in vehemence. Although few Southerners actually expected to extend slavery into the new territories acquired from Mexico, they sought to defend, as a matter of principle, the right to do so. If the North prohibited slavery in some territory gained through military action of the whole nation, Southerners argued, the prohibition would symbolize Northern domination and tyranny over the South. Oddly, Southerners often spoke of such actions as attempts by the North to "enslave" the South.

Nearly all of the Northern members of Congress who opposed slavery in the territories in the 1840s and early 1850s did so not because they sought to abolish slavery or to protect the African American from the conditions of slavery, but because they opposed the political power of the slave states and sought to preserve the power of the free states. A small but vocal minority of abolitionists, who saw slavery itself as a social evil, were themselves divided into a more radical immediatist faction headed by William Lloyd Garrison and a somewhat more moderate faction advocating gradual abolition of slavery, headed by Lewis Tappan and Theodore Dwight Weld. Garrison and his followers disdained the debates in Congress, believing that compromise over the issue of slavery was itself immoral, and that the Constitution represented a compact with evil. The more moderate abolitionists, including Tappan and Weld, held out hope that the political process could be used to begin a process of emancipation. Even so, they shared the view of Garrison that slavery represented a violation of basic human rights and of Christian values, and they sought to persuade others through oratory and print.

Abolitionists like William Lloyd Garrison, Lewis Tappan, and Theodore Dwight Weld and escaped slaves like Frederick Douglass argued that slavery itself represented a barbaric and unethical holdover from the past and that it had no

Northern visitors to the South were sometimes shocked to find slave markets, such as this one in Atlanta. *(Library of Congress, Prints and Photographs Division, LC-B8171–3608)*

place in a modern, 19th-century society. However, most white Americans in both the North and the South had little sympathy for that position. In fact, the Great Debate in Congress over slavery in the territories in 1850 did not echo the concerns of Garrison, Tappan, Weld, and Douglass. Instead the debate and the rhetoric focused on the balance of sectional power.

That balance struck in the Constitution and enforced by the carefully paired congressional admission of states had been awkwardly preserved through the 1830s and 1840s by the political party system. The party system itself began to come under stress from the debates following the war with Mexico.

THE POLITICAL BALANCE

The American constitutional and electoral arrangement had generated a two-party system early in the 19th century. Unlike 20th-century European political parties held together by common commitments to ideologies, 19th century American parties were simply state and local organizations to get out the vote for slates of candidates. Ideas and ideals tended to be reduced to slogans. Even though some individual candidates delivered lengthy and detailed speeches on the issues, there was no strict consistency in positions, even among the candidates of one party in one state and others of the same party in another state. State political parties cooperated at national caucuses or conventions to select candidates for the presidency and vice presidency, and, at the state level, they nominated slates for state government and for representatives in Congress. The state legislatures chose U.S. senators (until 1913), meaning that the party that dominated each state legislature had an interest in cooperating with similar parties in other states to build alliances in the Senate. In reality there were no national political parties, only loose confederations of state parties that assembled at a national convention every four years to choose nominees for the presidency and the vice presidency through a round of interstate horse-trading, promises, and compromises.

By the 1840s, the two loose national alliances of state parties were the Democratic Party and the Whig Party, with several smaller regional or local political parties contesting their dominance. The Democrats and Whigs had organizations in all the states. The only way that either party could hope to control the national presidency was to ensure that, at its conventions held to nominate candidates for national office, the persons chosen would be able to win votes across the nation. Thus the party system had evolved so that candidates would be nationally recognized and conceivably perceived as satisfactory to both North and South. In this way, the party system tended to yield up American presidents who had support of some kind in both North and South and whose party held a majority in one or both houses of Congress. However, if a third party candidate ran for the presidency, with a strong appeal in one section, he could have the effect of disrupting the balance. That is exactly what began to happen by the 1830s and 1840s, with the growth of some of the smaller parties, including the Anti-Masonic Party (with an attack on the perceived domination of a Masonic-based aristocracy), the anti-Catholic and anti-immigrant American or Know-Nothing Party, the Liberty Party, and, sometimes, two factions of Whigs or Democrats. At the state and local level, many other small parties, independent of any of the larger national groups, continually sprang up, sometimes winning municipal and state offices.

In 1844 and 1848, strong antislavery sentiment in the North was a minority position. However, a candidate for the presidency who would be acceptable to Southerners would tend to be disliked by this vocal minority, and that factor influenced the elections. Vehemently antislavery candidates running on third-party tickets had the effect of dividing the Northern vote, thus putting in the presidency a candidate who was more favored in the South. This effect was particularly important in the elections of 1844 and 1848.

The winners, Polk and Taylor in those two years, were acceptable to the South. The Liberty Party and the Free-Soil Party were specifically devoted to ensuring that slavery be excluded from the newly acquired

Henry Clay fashioned the Missouri Compromise and hoped to shape another great compromise between the free and slave states in 1850. *(Library of Congress, Prints and Photographs Division, LC-USZC2–2570)*

territories. In 1844, the candidacy of James Birney prevented the Kentuckian and great compromiser, Henry Clay, from being elected by drawing off crucial votes in New York State. Similarly, in 1848, Martin van Buren drew off more than 120,000 votes in New York to prevent Lewis Cass from winning the Electoral College vote and the election.

THE COMPROMISE OF 1850

With California pressing for admission to the Union as a state in 1850 and with both the Wilmot Proviso and the concept of extending the Missouri Line to the West Coast failing to get a majority in both houses of Congress, a fresh solution was needed. Henry Clay, the 73-year-old senator from Kentucky who had been influential in framing the Missouri Compromise 30 years before, proposed a package of eight resolutions that, together, were intended to resolve the questions dividing Congress over slavery. Although he had expected the resolutions to be packaged together into an omnibus bill, five separate bills were enacted and signed into law in September 1850, each with slightly different alignments of votes. The bills admitted California as a free state, settled the boundary between Texas and New Mexico, assumed the debt of the former republic of Texas, allowed for the organization of the territories of Utah and New Mexico without reference to whether slavery was to be allowed or disallowed there, and outlawed the trade in slaves within the District of Columbia. In addition, the overall five-bill compromise included the Fugitive Slave Act, which immediately became the most controversial feature of the package.

An existing law, passed in 1793, relied on state and local authorities to cooperate in capturing slaves who had run away from their owners. In the South, that law tended to operate more or less effectively, with slave patrols, slave-catchers, and local militias cooperating with sheriffs and municipal police and constables in tracking down runaway slaves and returning them to their owners. However, by the 1830s and 1840s, hundreds of slaves sought freedom in Northern states, where local officials either refused to cooperate or were prohibited from doing so by state or local law. Among the many escapees were several who spoke out against slavery at abolitionist and antislavery meetings. These included Josiah Henson, who escaped to Canada in 1830, Frederick Douglass, who fled to Massachusetts in 1837, and Henry Box Brown and Harriet Tubman, who both escaped to Philadelphia in 1849. Henson, Douglass, and Brown all published book-length narratives telling of their lives in slavery and detailing their escapes, while Tubman soon became active in rescuing others from slavery. An informal network of safe houses and contacts, which was supported by some whites, emerged among the free black community living in both slave states and in the North and came to be known as the Underground Railroad. It helped an unknown number of fugitives from slavery to find their way through Ohio, Pennsylvania, and New Jersey to sanctuary farther north, often in Canada.

The number of slaves who escaped through these routes tended to be exaggerated both by defenders of slavery, as a scandalous breaking of the law, and by opponents of slavery, as tales substantiating the universal human quest for freedom. The census of 1850 concluded that there were about 3 million slaves in the United States, including only about 1,000 fugitives, but, of course, fugitives tended to avoid census takers. In the South, the popular Northern reception given to such notorious escapees as Henson and Douglass and the growing agi-

Henry "Box" Brown escaped from slavery by having himself shipped in a crate to Philadelphia. The story created a sensation. *(Library of Congress, Prints and Photographs Division, LC-USZC4–4659)*

tation by such people and their abolitionist supporters, seemed to give further evidence that the North had abandoned the implicit compromises of the federal constitution. Unsubstantiated estimates by Southern politicians of the number of escapees ran in the tens of thousands, and abolitionists fed the estimate by exaggerated claims of their own. Whether the real number of fugitives who fled to the North and to Canada was as few as 5,000 or as many as 12,000, however, they represented a threat to the system in the South and a heroic group of freedom fighters to many in the North.[1]

To close off the escapes and to force Northern states to accept the legality and permanence of slavery, the Fugitive Slave Act superseded the 1793 law by putting the capture and return of slaves in the hands of federal commissioners. The new law required local authorities to cooperate with the federal agents. Aside from the compulsory nature of the act, it included a provision that awarded judges a fee of 10 dollars for every escaped individual who was declared a fugitive, but only five dollars in cases when the person was declared to be free. Anti-slavery advocates said that, in effect, the federal government had created a system of bribes favoring slaveholders' claims. Defenders of the law argued that the double fee was simply to cover the more costly paperwork involved when a fugitive was to be sent back to the owner. Furthermore, Southern defenders of slavery believed that compliance or non-compliance with the law in the North would demonstrate whether or not the Northern population was serious about preserving the federal union.

Although some Southern politicians advocated in 1850 that the slave states declare their secession from the Union because the right to extend slavery through all the new federal territories had not been explicitly guaranteed, the movement for secession in that year was disorganized. Some argued for immediate individual state action, while other secessionists thought it would be too divisive for the Southern cause if a single state should attempt to secede. Rather, such secessionists claimed they should cooperate with others in a joint action between states. A third faction argued for accepting the compromise and remaining in the Union. After several state conventions met and considered all three courses of action, a resolution was produced in Georgia in December 1850. This Georgia Platform declared that the Compromise of 1850 was final and should be accepted, but that secession should be considered if the Fugitive Slave Act was not enforced or if there was an attempt to abolish slavery in the District of Columbia. The Georgia Platform, with its threat of secession but acceptance of the Compromise of 1850 as a working arrangement, remained more or less the majority doctrine of Southern politicians until 1860. However, the threat of secession had been articulated across the South and was even suggested in the moderate Georgia Platform. In the South, immediate secessionists, interstate cooperationists, and even Unionists all adhered to the theory that the federal union was a compact or contract between states represented by the Constitution. If any state or group of states believed that the compact was no longer being preserved, by this theory, they had a right to withdraw or secede from the Union and to form a new interstate union if they chose. The Georgia Platform also made compliance with the Fugitive Slave Law the explicit condition for continued Southern acceptance of the Union.

The right of secession advanced by Southern leaders in 1850 and threatened throughout the decade was based on a theory of the Constitution that was not widely accepted in the North. Under the secession theory, the federal union represented an agreement or compact, much like a contract, between sovereign states, that had been formed during the American Revolution. The Constitution itself was silent on the question of whether one or more states, once in the Union, could secede. As the Union expanded, new states were formed and then admitted with complete parity under the Union with the original thirteen. In the Union compact, each state consented to delegate its defense, taxing power, and foreign affairs to the federal government. However, under this theory, if, for any reason, one or more states believed that the Union had failed to operate under its original terms, the state or states could revert to independent status by seceding from the Union. Thus, in the view of secessionists, withdrawal from the Union by any state simply required a legal and formal action by a state legislature or a state convention to declare independence from the Union. Secession under this principle had been publicly discussed in 1807 when several New England states considered secession and again in 1832, when South Carolina challenged the federal tariff. However, in the view of most Northern politicians by the 1850s, such an action would constitute a revolutionary act, cloaked in the false appearance of constitutionality. From the perspective of institutional or constitutional theory, the threatened crisis over secession would test which view was correct.

DIVISIONS INTENSIFY

The enforcement of the Fugitive Slave Act brought the issue of slavery and the moral issue of freedom home to many Northern whites who had never seriously thought about whether human rights extended to African Americans. Several states, led by Vermont in 1850, passed new personal liberty laws, which attempted to interpose state authority between the federal commissioners and the individual accused fugitive. Several rescues or attempted rescues of fugitive slaves, some leading to major riots, followed. Among the cases were those of James Hamlet in New York City in 1850, Rachel Parker in Baltimore, and Shadrach and Thomas Sims in Boston in 1851. The African-American community in Christiana, Pennsylvania, resisted slave catchers with firearms in 1851, resulting in the death of a slaveholder, Edward Gorsuch, who attempted to use the law to bring back several fugitives. The rendition of Anthony Burns in Boston in 1854 required the presence of federal troops to protect the federal commissioners from a massed crowd seeking to preserve his freedom. These and other cases engaged hundreds and sometimes thousands of individuals in riots, and reports of the events echoed through the popular press. In these ways, a few episodes came to symbolize for previously uninterested Northern whites the immediate issue of freedom. Even for moderate Southern Unionists, the massive and highly publicized Northern resistance to the Fugitive Slave Act seemed to prove that the North was becoming dominated by radical ideas of abolition and racial equality.[2]

Reading the narrative of Josiah Henson and observing the plight of several escaping slaves through Cincinnati inspired Harriet Beecher Stowe, a 39-year-old writer who had moved to Maine with her husband in 1850. She wrote a serialized novel, *Uncle Tom's Cabin,* which was published over 1851–52 in an antislavery newspaper in Washington, D.C., the *National Era.* The story in installments attracted so much attention that a publisher in Boston brought it out in book form in 1852, and it soon became a massive best-seller, selling over a million copies in a year, more than any book besides the Bible had ever sold before. In addition, an unauthorized version of her novel was produced as a play in August 1852, performed over and over during the next few years.[3]

Challenged as to the authenticity of the scenes described, Mrs. Stowe published in 1853 a *Key to Uncle Tom's Cabin,* providing citations to sources, such as Henson's narrative and newspaper accounts. Because she had used her imagination to reflect for the reader how a mother would react at fear of separation from her children and to describe the situation of slaves in fundamental human terms, rather than as an abstract moral issue, her novel and the dramatized version on stage had a vast and powerful effect in awakening the Northern white conscience about the nature of slavery. The moral side of the issue, which had been understood by only a small proportion of the white population represented by abolitionists, began to influence and shape the nature and vocabulary of the political debate. Increasingly through the 1850s, Northern politicians accused their Southern colleagues of not only seeking to extend political power, but also of supporting an immoral and barbaric institution that was incompatible with Christian morality and the principles of democracy. Southern politicians in return accused Northerners of hypocrisy, using a false or pretended sympathy for the plight of slaves to extend their own power and to attempt to suppress the constitutionally-guaranteed right of slave owners to be secure in their property rights. The Fugitive Slave Law, defenders of slavery argued, simply wrote the constitutional protection of property rights into a piece of legislation, and Northern defiance of the law represented defiance of the Constitution itself.

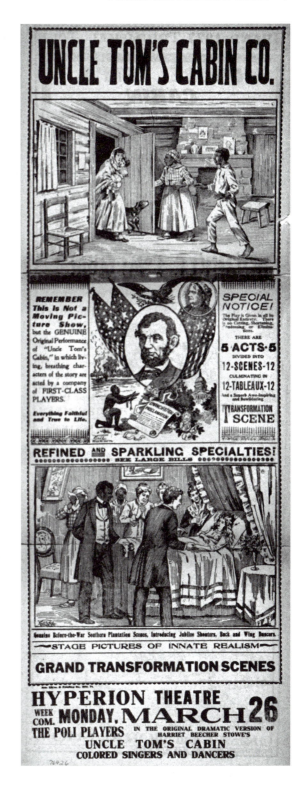

Harriet Beecher Stowe's novel, *Uncle Tom's Cabin,* and the play based on it, helped win sympathy for the plight of slaves among whites in the North. *(Library of Congress, Prints and Photographs Division, [POS-TH-1923. U53, no. 1])*

TERRITORIES AGAIN

Travel to California from the East Coast required either about 90 days by clipper ship around Cape Horn, or a slightly shorter trip by steamer to Panama, by land across the isthmus, and connection to another steamer for the final leg of the trip. The overland trip from the western terminus of the rail lines in Missouri to the West Coast was arduous and dangerous and had to be made in the hot summer months, usually taking much longer than the maritime route. With the growing network of steam railroads linking cities in the eastern part of the United States, it was clear that a transcontinental railroad would shorten the cross-country trip to two weeks or so and would allow the new state to be fully integrated into the American nation. However, there were few towns of any size between Missouri and California, with the exception of Santa Fe in New Mexico. To construct a rail line linking the east and west would be extremely expensive, and there would be little if any business for the line on intermediate points along the way, as the western plains and Rocky Mountains had very few settlements, few mines, no agriculture, and would provide no freight or passengers to sustain the cost of the railroad. Some of the regions were dominated by Native American tribes hostile to any incursion on their traditional lands by settlers or railroad companies.

Federal support for a project to build such a line would be required, and the grant of federal lands not only for a right-of-way, but also as future real-estate assets that could be sold, would be a logical way to give the railroad builders a method of funding. Whether the route was planned through the southern tier of territories from Louisiana and Texas across New Mexico (as favored by Southern politicians) or whether it would have its eastern terminus in Chicago (as advocated by some Northern politicians), the new lands would need to be surveyed and territorial governments would need to settle land claims to make such grants possible.

Stephen Douglas, Democratic senator from Illinois, an advocate of a Northern rail route, hoped to organize the remaining territory, originally acquired in the Louisiana Purchase, that lay between Missouri and the beginning of the Utah Territory that had been established in the Compromise of 1850. The gap of unorganized territory between the western border of Missouri and the edge of Utah Territory (along the crest of the Rockies and now in the middle of the state of Colorado) was about 550 miles. In 1854, Douglas sought support for a bill that would establish territorial government in the region.

Eventually structured to allow for two territories, the Kansas–Nebraska Bill represented an effort by Douglas to finesse the slavery issue. In the Compromise of 1850, Utah and New Mexico had been organized without reference to slavery. This arrangement left the issue of slavery up to the decision of the settlers in the territory, in the parlance of the day, up to "squatter sovereignty." Douglas hoped to use the same principle,

Stephen Douglas advocated popular sovereignty to accept or reject slavery in the new territories of Kansas and Nebraska. His position split the Democratic Party, and his attempt at compromise failed. *(Library of Congress, Prints and Photographs Division, LC-USZ62–135560)*

which came to be known more elegantly as "popular sovereignty," to resolve the question of slavery in Kansas and Nebraska. The problem was that both of these territories lay above the line of 36°30', that is, in territory from which slavery had been excluded under the Missouri Compromise of 1820. In effect, to pass the Kansas-Nebraska Act with a clause allowing popular sovereignty on the slavery issues required that Congress override the Missouri Compromise and open a vast section of territory north of 36°30' to the possibility of slavery, if the settlers in the territories voted to approve it. Douglas saw as one benefit of the bill that it would remove the issue of slavery in the territories from federal jurisdiction almost entirely, laying to rest the issue that had come close to provoking secession in 1850.

Douglas and others supporting his bill argued that slavery was unlikely to take root in the new territories because the climate and conditions there did not favor plantation crops that were suited to cultivation by slaves. By turning the issue over to the settlers themselves, Congress could be relieved of the problem. Furthermore, of course, it would open Kansas to land surveys and land claim settlements that could pave the way for a railroad to link Chicago and San Francisco Bay; and the theoretical opening of the lands to the possibility of slavery might help win Southern votes for the plan. But for many Northern politicians, aware of the growing antislavery sentiment in their home districts or whose own careers had been built upon opposing slavery, opening Kansas and Nebraska, even in theory, to slavery represented an unacceptable compromise with the slave interests. If they voted to approve the bill, they might lose support from those voters who fervently believed slavery was simply evil.

Congress debated the bill over a three-month period, with Douglas whipping votes into line and arguing down his opponents. In the Senate, the bill passed 37 to 14. In the House of Representatives, the debate became even more bitter, with a few congressmen drawing weapons. Some Southern Democrats, under the leadership of Unionist Democrat Alexander Stephens of Georgia, voted in favor of the bill, although the 88 Northern Democrats split 44 in favor and 44 against it. When the bill passed in Congress at the end of May 1854, it did so over the objections of a solid minority of Northern Democrats and Whigs. The House vote was 113 in favor, 100 opposed, and it was immediately signed into law by President Franklin Pierce. Within a month, anti-Kansas Northern Democrats began considering the formation of a new political party.[4]

In July 1854, the Republican Party was born. The party united several factions. It included Northern Democrats who believed the Kansas-Nebraska Act was evidence that the Democratic Party had been taken over by proslavery forces centered in the South. Former Northern Whigs who despaired of the Whig Party recovering strength also joined, as did members of the Free-Soil Party, and some of the other third parties, including some anti-immigrant Know-Nothings. In some areas such as Ohio, Indiana, Connecticut, New Jersey, and Pennsylvania, the new party called itself the People's Party, sending delegates to the national Republican convention in 1856.

Running candidates for Congress and the presidency in 1856, the new party was unlike the early Whig and Democratic parties in that it had organizations and strength only in non-slaveholding states. The Republican candidate for the presidency was John C. Frémont, a military adventurer supported by his father-in-law, Senator Thomas Hart Benton of Missouri. Frémont had faced a charge of mutiny during the war with Mexico for exceeding his authority, but in the Whig tradition, the new party believed his popularity as a military hero might give him a good chance at victory. As it was, Frémont won 1.3 million popular votes to the Democratic candidate James Buchanan's 1.8 million. The anti-immigrant and anti-Catholic party, the American Party or Know-Nothing Party, had grown rapidly among former Whigs in the North. The Know-Nothings ran former Whig Millard Fillmore (and former vice president, who had served out the term as president after Zachary Taylor died in 1850). Fillmore received some 870,000 votes. Clearly, if the Republicans could draw all or most of the Know-Nothing vote, they could have a chance at a popular vote victory for their presidential candidate in the next election scheduled for 1860, even though they were a strictly Northern party, rather than a national one.

Another factor that gave hope to the new Republican Party was the nature of the victory of their opponent, Democrat James Buchanan, in 1856. Buchanan won the presidency with the Electoral College vote of his home state of Pennsylvania, together with the electoral vote of every slaveholding state. He had strong support among conservative, pro-Union Democrats in his home state. Although a Northerner, he had won Southern support because he had been removed from the 1854 debates over Kansas in Congress while serving as U.S. Minister to Britain in the administration of Franklin Pierce. In that post he had joined with other Democratic-appointed ministers to Spain and France in a meeting in Belgium where the three had supported a secret declaration. The document stated that, for the safety of slavery, the United States should acquire Cuba from Spain, either by purchase or by force. Buchanan's support for this Ostend Manifesto had been made public, and even though the document was denounced by Pierce's secretary of state, Buchanan had established himself as a friend of slavery by his support for the manifesto.

Although Buchanan held slavery to be a moral wrong and claimed that the Ostend Manifesto had simply been an effort to support what he and the other ministers believed was settled American foreign policy, he believed the Constitution protected slavery and he supported compromises that would keep the issue from dividing the nation. With Pennsylvania so crucial in the 1856 election, it seemed that if a Northern antislavery Republican who could appeal to Pennsylvania were nominated with Know-Nothing support in 1860, the chances looked very good for a Republican victory in both the popular vote and the electoral college vote in that election. Consequently, Northern Republican senators like William Seward from New York and Charles Sumner from Massachusetts, considered firebrands for their opposition to slavery, were regarded as likely candidates for the presidency in 1860.

However, in May 1856, Sumner, who delivered an extremely hostile speech in the Senate against slavery, was subjected to a brutal attack by a member of Congress from South Carolina, Preston Brooks. Brooks beat Sumner to the floor, breaking his cane over the senator, before being restrained by others present. Brooks claimed that he was whipping Sumner for insulting his father-in-law, Senator Andrew Butler, by alluding to slavery as a "harlot" with whom the senator consorted. Sumner remained incapacitated for nearly three years after the episode, and his empty desk in the Senate served as a reminder of the attack. Northerners saw Brooks's beating of Sumner as evidence of Southern barbarity while Southerners saw it as just punishment for ungentlemanly language and offered congratulations and replacement canes to Brooks. Sumner's inflammatory speech and Brooks' vicious attack in response showed

Congressman Preston Brooks of South Carolina beat Senator Charles Sumner of Massachusetts at his desk in the U.S. Senate on July 14, 1856. Northerners saw it as evidence of Southern brutality, and Southerners saw it as a proper thrashing of Sumner for a speech they regarded as insulting. *(Library of Congress, Prints and Photographs Division, LC-USZ62–38851)*

that Congress, like the party system, was collapsing as a forum for compromise between the sections of the country.

BLEEDING KANSAS

The bill organizing the territory of Kansas not only divided the Democratic Party, giving birth to the Republican Party, but also had more immediate effects on the ground. The exact working of popular sovereignty had never been agreed. The president appointed governors of territories, and territorial legislatures were elected. Whether or not the Kansas territorial legislature, under popular sovereignty, had a right to exclude slavery had not been decided in the act establishing the territory. As a consequence, both proslavery and antislavery organizations attempted to sponsor settlement in the territory to ensure that the majority of the population there would represent their position and elect a legislature in accordance with their views. The Massachusetts Emigrant Aid Society provided funds for antislavery settlers to Kansas, while popular subscriptions for funding in Southern cities financed the migration of some slaveholders and proslavery settlers into the territory. Soon the groups clashed, with gangs of proslavery raiders from Missouri, known as border ruffians, riding in to disrupt antislavery settlements. Antislavery militants organized small paramilitary groups, known as Jayhawkers, to raid into Missouri. Skirmishes between armed forces in November and December 1855 near the antislavery settlement of Lawrence, Kansas, became known as the Wakarusa War. The next summer, raids and reprisals continued, with the number killed in the range of 200. Horace Greeley, the antislavery publisher of the New York *Tribune,* referred to the conflict as "Bleeding Kansas," and the term entered history.

After a group of border ruffians attacked and shot up the town of Lawrence on May 21, 1856, abolitionist John Brown led a small group of his sons and other militia recruits on a reprisal raid. "Captain" Brown and his men dragged five unarmed proslavery settlers and their guests from their homes at Pottawatomie and hacked them to death with swords. This was the first occasion in the conflict in which unarmed individuals had been killed, and the episode became known as the Pottawatomie Massacre.

President Buchanan's appointee as governor arranged for a constitutional convention to get voter approval for a proposed state constitution that would then be submitted to Congress for admission of Kansas as a state. Dominated by proslavery delegates, the Lecompton meeting in 1857 produced a constitution that would allow for a future popular vote on whether slaves could be brought into the state. However, the constitution also had a clause declaring that the slaves already present in the territory and their descendants would remain in slavery. Thus, when the Lecompton Constitution was submitted for a local referendum, the only way to vote against slavery entirely would be to vote for the rejection of the constitution itself. In a fraudulent vote, in which border ruffians swarmed into the territory to cast proslavery votes, the constitution was approved, but the U.S. Congress demanded a new vote, and the constitution was finally voted down in a more legitimate referendum early in 1858. Despite efforts of Buchanan Democrats to line up votes for the Lecompton Constitution, Republicans and many Northern Democrats, even including Stephen Douglas, who saw the fraudulent votes as a perversion of popular sovereignty, fought off approval. Kansas would not be admitted to the Union until early in 1861, as a free state.[5]

By 1858, the bloodshed had declined in Kansas, as settlers there concentrated on issues of land settlement and building up businesses and farms. But the "war" in Kansas indicated how easily the political divisions over slavery could escalate into armed conflict. Further, the problems of elections there showed that popular sovereignty was unable to provide a peaceable solution to the question of whether or not slavery could extend into the territories.

DRED SCOTT AND LINCOLN-DOUGLAS

During the first days of the Buchanan administration in 1857, the Supreme Court reached a decision in a notorious slave case, that of Dred Scott. His owner had taken Scott to a free territory, then returned South to live, keeping Scott as a slave. His case was supported by abolitionists who wanted the courts to decide that once a slave had moved to an area in which slavery was prohibited, he became free. In a complex decision that reflected several different majorities of justices, the Supreme Court ruled that slaves were not citizens and had no right to sue in federal courts. Further, the decision held that Congress had no right to exclude slavery from any territory. Following this line of argument, a majority of justices reasoned that the Missouri Compromise itself was unconstitutional. Even though that compromise had been superseded with the Kansas-Nebraska Act, Northerners were shocked at the decision. For decades, the Missouri Compromise had apparently represented a guarantee of freedom from slavery in the northern West.

Even more shocking, the Court seemed to be saying that Congress had no right to rule on the legality of slavery in any federal territory, and that free blacks living in the North could not have access to federal courts to preserve their freedom. The fact that the Court was dominated by Southerners seemed further proof that slaveholders were using the instruments of the federal government not only to defend the institution of slavery, but also to extend its hold and power.

Census statistics showed that there were only some 320,000 slave owners in the United States. It seemed, through control of Southern state legislatures, through solid votes in the Senate, and through the Court and the presidency, that this minority of 320,000 held the nation in a tight political grip.

Increasingly, antislavery denunciations of the so-called slavocracy held appeal for white Northerners, even those unmoved by appeals to issues of morality or human rights.

In 1858, Stephen Douglas, the Democrat who had worked out the Kansas-Nebraska Act, was up for reelection to the U.S. Senate from Illinois. In the state campaigns for the legislature that would decide the selection of the U.S. senator, Republican Abraham Lincoln challenged him. Lincoln had served one term in the U.S. Congress as a Whig in 1847–49, where he had challenged the justification for the Mexican War. In a series of well-attended debates held throughout Illinois, Lincoln and Douglas met and argued over the issues of the day. Douglas sought to portray Lincoln as being more radical than he was and a defender of equality for African Americans, while Lincoln sought to demonstrate that Douglas had adopted policies that extended slavery into new territories. Repeatedly, Lincoln asked Douglas how it would be possible, under the Dred Scott decision, for voters in a federal territory to exercise popular sovereignty in such a way that they could exclude slavery. A shrewd and accomplished lawyer, Lincoln showed his ability to box in his opponents with logical dilemmas. Lincoln suggested that, if Congress had no right under the Constitution to prohibit slavery in a territory, it would not be constitutional for Congress to delegate such a right to the settlers in a territory. In effect, he pointed out a basic flaw in Douglas's whole theory of popular sovereignty.

Douglas answered the question over and over during the debates, and at Freeport, Illinois, he repeated his point that if the settlers in a territory failed to enact laws that protected the institution of slavery, it would never take root. This so-called Freeport Doctrine, although a stretch of logic, got Douglas out of the Lincoln logic trap. Indeed, the Illinois legislature remained in Democratic hands, and Douglas was chosen by the legislature for another six-year term in the U.S. Senate.[6]

By early 1859, Kansas had quieted down to an extent, as settlers there seemed reconciled to operating under a territorial government and worked on getting land claims straightened out, planting crops, and doing business. Although the Dred Scott case seemed to arm Southern lawyers with increased power to enforce the Fugitive Slave Act, the flurry of rendition cases in the early 1850s had declined. Many fugitives had fled into Canada, beyond the reach of the law, and few owners of fugitives to the North wanted to take on the risk, expense, and notoriety of attempting recapture, even with the aid of federal commissioners and the courts. Then, in 1859, John Brown, already infamous for his part in the Pottawatomie Massacre, put together a scheme for the liberation of slaves through an insurrection that once again plunged the country into heated controversy and division.

JOHN BROWN AT HARPER'S FERRY

In 1858 and 1859, Brown confided to several abolitionists his plans for an uprising, although it remained unclear exactly how much he told them. At least one of his confidants leaked the information, and a warning was sent to the U.S. secretary of war, who discounted the idea as too fantastic to credit. Brown rented a farm near Harper's Ferry, Virginia, and assembled a small force of 18 supporters there. On October 16, 1859, Brown's raiding party seized the armory and rifle works at the U.S. arsenal and gun factory at Harper's Ferry. In the process, his men wounded several residents and killed a black railroad baggage master.

Apparently Brown expected a general uprising of slaves to follow, but he had made no explicit plans on how to notify slaves in surrounding areas that the revolution was afoot. He did send out a group of his own men, who kidnapped two slave owners and brought some of their slaves to the armory, but those slaves refused to participate in any violence. Barricading himself and his supporters in a brick engine house, he began capturing and holding hostages from among the citizens of the town. However, as word of the event spread, militia units streamed toward Harper's Ferry. Within a day, Col. Robert E. Lee arrived with a company of U.S. Marines from Washington, D.C., and established authority over the other military units there. Lee offered Brown a chance to surrender. When he refused, the marines, under Lieutenant J. E. B. Stuart, stormed the fire house and killed most of Brown's men, wounding Brown and taking him prisoner.

The strange affair, known then as John Brown's Raid, was of course an immediate nationwide sensation. The fact that correspondence was found at the rented farm indicating support for Brown among noted abolitionists stirred Southern beliefs that abolitionists would not only support lawbreaking in order to free fugitives, but would also finance and support a slave revolution. Others simply assumed Brown was insane, or as Lincoln himself stated, "peculiar."

John Brown's trial lasted about a month, and he was found guilty of treason against the state of Virginia. He was executed December 2. He made a statement on his capture and a longer one at his trial in which he very calmly declared that he was doing what was right. He remained a bit ambiguous as to whether he had intended slaves to engage in revolution, but since he had with him a planned constitution for a provisional government and since he had more weapons than he could use, including 1,000 spears, it was clear he had expected the slaves in the region to rise in revolution. Southern defenders of slavery were further horrified when, throughout the North, church bells were rung in commemoration of Brown's execution, and thousands of sermons were delivered declaring him a martyr for justice and freedom.

One result of Brown's raid was that Southern states, especially Virginia, began to upgrade and improve their militias out of concern over other possible slave

John Brown's raid on Harper's Ferry, instead of sparking a slave rebellion, led to the killing and capture of Brown's party and the spread of military preparations throughout the slave states. *(Library of Congress, Prints and Photographs Division, LC-USZ62–132541)*

insurrections. As the Southern states organized, trained, and equipped their militias over the next few months, in effect they got a head start over the Northern states in preparing for war.

PROXIMATE CAUSE: ELECTION OF LINCOLN

The divisions in the United States, which had existed since the foundation of the republic, accelerated to a deep, abiding, and hostile controversy by the late 1850s. That division was clearly the ultimate cause of the civil war that followed, especially after Congress was forced to decide how to organize the new territories acquired after the war with Mexico. Very rapidly through the 1850s, the threat of secession and the bitterness over slavery had wracked the nation. The compromises reached in Congress had made the divisions only more severe and the threat to the Union more immediate. The two-party system, which had produced Whig or Democrat presidents more or less acceptable on a nationwide basis, had begun to break down in the 1840s, and by the mid-1850s appeared to have ended as a tool for compromise. The new Republican Party had no strength whatever in the South, and its supporters ranged from mildly antislavery conservatives like former Whig Lincoln, through hot-headed antislavery politicians like William H. Seward of New York, and was supported to varying extents by abolitionists, former anti-Kansas Democrats, and former American Party/Know-Nothing politicians. The latter party, based on opposition to Catholics and immigrants, had reacted against the influx of Catholic Irish immigrants in the period, most of whom voted in the Northern Democratic Party. So in some states with Irish voting strength, it was natural for Know-Nothing Party supporters to turn to the Republican Party when it seemed likely to defeat the Democrats. Even as Republican politicians sought to attract former Northern Know-Nothings, they worked carefully to avoid antagonizing groups, such as German immigrants, who might be offended by Know-Nothing anti-foreign sentiments.

In 1860, four parties emerged. At a convention held in April, Southern Democrats refused to support Stephen Douglas, and the convention adjourned without a presidential nominee. The Democrats reconvened in June and there the Northern wing nominated Douglas. Delegates from the South bolted from that convention, held their own meeting, and nominated Vice President John Breckinridge. Remnants of the Whigs in the South formed the Constitutional Union Party, nominating John Bell for the presidency. The Constitutional Union Party built on earlier Union Party organizations that had emerged among former southern Whigs through the 1850s and absorbed remnants of the Southern branch of the Know-Nothing Party. With strength in Kentucky and the Upper South, the Constitutional Union Party sought compromise to preserve the Union with slavery.

After a tumultuous convention in Chicago, the Republican Party chose on the third ballot to nominate Lincoln for the presidency, defeating those who supported Seward for the post. Lincoln, the more moderate candidate, had repeatedly stated that slavery in slave states was legal and outside the reach of federal law, although not outside the reach of moral suasion. In his opinion, slavery should be excluded from federal territories, and Southerners should begin working toward its gradual elimination. Even though far more moderate than the abolitionists or even the more outspoken antislavery politicians in his own party, Lincoln was clearly the most antislavery of the four major candidates for the presidency. In a speech delivered in New York City, Lincoln made it clear he opposed popular sovereignty and slavery in the territories.

His election in the fall of 1860 was the proximate or immediate cause of secession. In several states, anti-Lincoln forces attempted to nominate a fusion ticket. For the most part that effort failed. Even if all of the anti-Lincoln candidates had worked together on a single candidacy, Lincoln would still have won the electoral college vote, because united opposition to him would have changed the vote only in New Jersey, California, and Oregon for a total of 11 electoral college votes.

Lincoln's victory in the November 1860 election could not be contested constitutionally. However, since the Republican Party represented all those who opposed slavery and because the party had not even been on the ballot in the South, Lincoln's victory weakened the arguing position of Unionists throughout the South. From the point of view of committed Unionists, both North and South, the election of Lincoln, although a political defeat for Southern interests, was not a legitimate reason for seeking some extra-constitutional solution, such as secession. Such Unionists viewed secessionists as hot-headed and irresponsible firebrands, waiting for some simple excuse to act. However, some former Southern Unionists who had supported the Georgia Platform now believed the time for secession had arrived. The crisis that many had feared for a decade or more was suddenly upon the nation.

CHRONICLE OF EVENTS

1846

May 8–9: United States and Mexican forces clash at Palo Alto in northern Mexico (now in south Texas) and at Resaca de la Palma. Both battles are in the disputed territory between the Nueces River and the Rio Grande.

May 13: United States declares war on Mexico. The war is supported by Democrats, opposed by Whigs.

May 18: U.S. forces under Zachary Taylor cross the Rio Grande at Matamoros.

June 10–July 5: Forces under John Charles Frémont assist American settlers in California in the Bear Flag Revolt against Mexican authorities, declaring the Republic of California at Sonoma.

July 7–August 17: U.S. naval forces under Commodore John D. Sloat take Monterey, San Francisco, and Sutter's Fort. Sloat's replacement, Robert Stockton, occupies Santa Barbara and Los Angeles and declares California annexed by the United States.

August 8: Member of Congress from Pennsylvania, David Wilmot, introduces a bill in Congress that would prevent the existence of slavery in any territory acquired from Mexico, whether by conquest or purchase. The Polk administration attempts to amend the Wilmot Proviso by having it apply only north of the Missouri Compromise line of 36°30', but that measure fails. The Wilmot Proviso passes the House, but does not pass in the Senate before the end of the session.

September 22–30: Mexican forces recapture Los Angeles, Santa Barbara, and San Diego in California.

September 25: Taylor's forces capture Monterrey in northern Mexico.

1847

January 10: A mixed force of U.S. troops under Colonel Stephen Watts Kearney that has marched overland from Arkansas through Santa Fe, New Mexico, to San Diego, California, together with volunteers and with sailors from Stockton's ships, completes the reconquest of southern California. A dispute over command eventually results in Frémont's court-martial.

February 8–March 3: An attempt to add the Wilmot Proviso to an appropriation bill passes the House but is defeated in the Senate; the Senate appropriation bill, without the Wilmot Proviso, is finally passed. During the debates, Whigs charge Polk with waging an unconstitutional war.

February 19: Senator John C. Calhoun introduces a four-part resolution declaring that Congress had no right to exclude slavery in the territories.

February 21–March 29: Forces under General Winfield Scott land on the Gulf Coast of Mexico near Vera Cruz.

April 8–August 20: Scott's forces advance via Puebla toward Mexico City.

August 26–September 6: An armistice is declared while the Mexican government considers peace terms brought by Nicholas P. Trist. On refusal of the terms, fighting resumes.

September 8–14: After battles in Chapultepec Park in Mexico City, U.S. forces take the Mexican capital.

November 16: Trist receives an order for his recall but ignores it and continues negotiations.

1848

February 2: The Treaty of Guadalupe Hidalgo is signed. By its terms, Mexico relinquishes all claims to Texas above the Rio Grande and cedes California and New Mexico to the United States. The territory includes, in addition to those states, most of the future states of Utah, Colorado, Arizona, and Nevada. The United States agrees to pay $15 million and to assume claims by U.S. citizens against Mexico amounting to $3.25 million.

February 23–May 30: The Treaty of Guadalupe Hidalgo is ratified in the United States and in Mexico, and ratifications are exchanged on May 30. An attempt to add the Wilmot Proviso to the treaty is defeated in the U.S. Senate. Fourteen Southern Democrats and Whigs oppose the treaty because they support a plan to annex all of Mexico.

August 14: President Polk signs the Oregon bill. During the debates Senator Jesse Bright of Indiana introduces amendments to extend the Missouri Compromise line through the new territories and California to the Pacific; that measure is defeated, and Oregon is organized as a territory with restrictions on slavery. The question of slavery in New Mexico and California (where it had been prohibited by Mexican law) is not resolved by Congress but referred to appeals from territorial courts to the Supreme Court.

September 1–October 13: A convention in California meeting at Monterey adopts a state constitution prohibiting slavery. The constitution will be ratified by a popular vote on November 13.

November 7: Zachary Taylor is elected president and Millard Fillmore is elected vice president, both running as Whigs. New York Democrats, known as Barnburners and supporters of the Wilmot Proviso, refuse to endorse Democratic nominee Lewis Cass, who supports "squatter sovereignty" over the issue of slavery in the territories. The Barnburners nominate former president Martin Van Buren, who is later supported by a new antislavery party, the Free-Soil Party. The New York Van Buren vote is drawn away from Cass, allowing Taylor to win.

December 1–22: Congress enters a temporary deadlock when 15 Free-Soil congressmen prevent the selection of a Speaker of the House by opposing the Whig choice, Robert Winthrop; Southern Whigs oppose him because he refused to pledge opposition to the Wilmot Proviso; Free-Soilers oppose him because he is insufficiently antislavery.

December 20: The state government of California is organized.

1849

February 23: Horace Mann, noted educator and member of Congress from Massachusetts delivers an antislavery address.

March 5: Zachary Taylor is inaugurated as president of the United States.

March 8: Harriet Tubman escapes from slavery in Maryland.

March 29: Henry "Box" Brown has himself mailed in a crate from Richmond to Philadelphia in order to escape from slavery.

July: Henry Bibb, escaped slave, publishes *Narrative of the Life and Adventures of Henry Bibb, An American Slave, Written by Himself.*

July: Josiah Henson, escaped slave living in Canada, publishes *Life of Josiah Henson*. The book will serve as an inspiration to Harriet Beecher Stowe, who will publish her work in 1851 and 1852.

October 13: California convention adopts a state constitution that does not include slavery.

1850

January 29: Henry Clay introduces eight resolutions, linked as an omnibus bill that represents a compromise on the question of slavery in the federal territories.

February 5–April 18: Great debate in Senate over slavery in territories, with speeches by Henry Clay, February 5–6; by John Calhoun (read for him by Senator James M. Mason), March 4; Daniel Webster, March 7; William Seward, March 11; Jefferson Davis, March 13–14; and Salmon Chase, March 26–27. The debate reflects the hardening of sectional lines.

March 12: California applies for admission as a free state.

June 10: The Nashville Convention, representing nine slave states, refuses to endorse the right of secession and recommends the extension of Missouri Compromise line to the Pacific.

July 9: President Taylor dies and is succeeded in office by Millard Fillmore.

September 9–20: The Compromise of 1850 is enacted in five bills promptly signed into law on the following dates:

September 9: California is admitted as a free state.

September 9: The Texas and New Mexico Act is passed. The act settles the boundary between the states, adjusts payment to Texas for lands transferred to New Mexico, and organizes New Mexico Territory but leaves the question of slavery to territorial decision prior to admission as a state.

September 9: The Utah Act is passed. The act organizes territory and leaves the question of slavery to the territory.

September 18: The Fugitive Slave Act, providing for federal commissioners to arrest fugitive slaves, is passed.

September 20: An act abolishing the slave trade in the District of Columbia is passed.

December 13–14: A convention in Milledgeville, Georgia, adopts the Georgia Platform, declaring the Compromise of 1850 final but threatening secession if future acts of Congress modify the Fugitive Slave Law, suppress interstate slave trade, or abolish slavery in the District of Columbia. The Georgia Platform remains the dominant Southern policy through the rest of the decade.

1852

March 20: Harriet Beecher Stowe publishes *Uncle Tom's Cabin* in book form after its previous serialized publication in an antislavery newspaper. It will be presented as a stage play for the first time on August 24. The book sells more than 1 million copies, and the play is widely produced.

November 2: Franklin Pierce, Democrat, is elected president. The Whig and Free Soil parties are both in decline.

1853

January 4: Solomon Northup, after being held 12 years as a slave, is freed in Louisiana by intervention of a New York attorney, who provides proof that Northrup, a free African American, had been kidnapped.

February 10: A bill to organize the territory of Nebraska (including Kansas) is passed by the House of Representatives. In the Senate, the bill will be referred to committee and die there due to Southern votes.

March 4: Franklin Pierce is inaugurated as president of the United States.

March 7: Jefferson Davis is sworn in as U.S. secretary of war. Davis will later serve as president of the Confederate States of America.

June: The play *Uncle Tom's Cabin* opens at the National Theater in Washington.

July: Harriet Beecher Stowe publishes *Key to Uncle Tom's Cabin* that includes documentation to meet the criticism that her novel was entirely a product of her imagination.

November 21–23: Abraham Lincoln and his law partner William Herndon have 34 cases on docket in Sangamon County, Illinois, one of their busiest periods.

December 15: A bill to organize the territory of Nebraska without reference to slavery is introduced in the Senate.

1854

January 23: The Kansas-Nebraska Bill is introduced by Senator Stephen Douglas in an effort to allow for the construction of a transcontinental railroad with a terminus in Chicago. The bill repeals the Missouri Compromise by allowing the two territories to determine whether they would apply for admission as states with or without slavery, incorporating the principle of popular sovereignty.

January 24: Senators Charles Sumner and Salmon Chase sign the Appeal of the Independent Democrats, condemning the Kansas-Nebraska Bill as a violation of the Compromise of 1850, which they incorrectly claim endorsed the Missouri Compromise line.

April 26: The Massachusetts Emigrant Aid Society is organized to support the settlement of antislavery groups in Kansas with the object of organizing it as a state without slavery.

May 30: The Kansas-Nebraska Act is passed and signed.

July 6–13: The Republican Party is founded, incorporating anti-Kansas-Nebraska Democrats, Northern antislavery Whigs, and former Free-Soil Party members. Leaders include Charles Sumner, Salmon Chase, and Edward Bates.

October 18: U.S. ministers to France, Great Britain, and Spain meet at Ostend, Belgium, and issue an aggressive pronouncement that the United States should purchase or acquire Cuba by force from Spain in order to protect slavery. The Ostend Manifesto is disapproved by Secretary of State William Marcy, but its later publication allows Republicans to charge that Democrats support extension of slavery by conquest of more territory.

1855

November 26–December 7: Local conflict along the Wakarusa River near Lawrence, Kansas, between 1,500 border ruffians from Missouri and free-state settlers is known as the Wakarusa War.

1856

May 21–September 15: Civil war in Kansas, called Bleeding Kansas by antislavery newspaperman Horace Greeley, leads to an estimated 200 killings and extensive property damage. Engagements include the sacking of free-state Lawrence by border ruffians on May 21; the midnight execution of five unarmed proslavery settlers by John Brown and seven associates at Pottawatomie on May 24–25; an antislavery raid on the proslavery town of Franklin on August 13; and federal troops dispersing some 2,500 proslavery forces marching on Lawrence on September 15.

November 4: James Buchanan, Democrat from Pennsylvania, is elected president. Formerly U.S. minister to Britain, he had signed the Ostend Manifesto and is thus supported by Southern Democrats. His opponents include Republican nominee Colonel John C. Frémont and American Party (Know-Nothing) candidate Millard Fillmore. The election demonstrates that the Whig Party is dead. Buchanan wins with Pennsylvania votes and Southern votes.

1857

March 4: James Buchanan is inaugurated as president and in his inaugural address he supports popular sovereignty in the territories and asks that there be no further agitation on the slavery issue.

March 6: The Supreme Court delivers its decision in the Dred Scott case, ruling that a slave is not a citizen entitled to sue, that the Missouri Compromise is unconstitutional since it deprives slaveowners of

President James Buchanan, who served from 1857 to 1861, attempted to retain control of some federal facilities in the seceding states while avoiding bloodshed. He was grateful to be able to turn over the problem of secession to President Abraham Lincoln. *(Library of Congress, Prints and Photographs Division, LC-USZ62–116025)*

property rights without due process of law, and that temporary residence of a slave in a free territory does not free him or her.

October 19–December 21: A state constitution for Kansas is drawn up at Lecompton; under its terms, a popular vote would determine whether slavery would be allowed in the future or whether only those slaves already there, and their descendants, would remain in slavery; only a vote against the whole constitution would allow for another constitution without any slavery at all. A fraudulent vote on December 21 approves the constitution with slavery, supported by the Buchanan administration.

1858

January 4: In a new election, the Lecompton constitution is overwhelmingly defeated in Kansas.

February 2: President Buchanan submits the defeated Lecompton constitution to Congress with a recommendation that Kansas be admitted as a slave state.

February 3: Stephen Douglas condemns the Lecompton constitution as a mockery of the principal of popular sovereignty. The Senate approves the Lecompton constitution, but the House votes for a resubmission of the constitution to the voters of Kansas.

May 4: A bill introduced by William English in Congress provides for a popular vote in Kansas on the Lecompton constitution, with a promise of federal lands to be transferred to the state if the constitution is approved.

June 19: In Springfield, Abraham Lincoln delivers his "house divided" speech on accepting the Republican nomination for U.S. Senate.

August 2: The Lecompton constitution is again overwhelmingly defeated by popular vote in Kansas, and Kansas remains a territory.

August 21–October 15: Abraham Lincoln and Stephen Douglas conduct a series of seven debates regarding the institution of slavery and slavery in the territories. Douglas takes the position at Freeport (August 27) that people in a territory can legally bar slavery, costing him any Southern support for the presidential nomination in 1860.

1859

October 4: A free-state constitution for Kansas drawn up at Wyandotte is approved by popular vote in the territory.

October 16–18: John Brown leads a raid with 18 others on the arsenal at Harper's Ferry, Virginia, in hopes of initiating a slave uprising. Ten of Brown's company, one marine, and five local residents are killed. He is captured and held for trial.

October 25–December 2: John Brown is tried, convicted, and hanged for treason.

1860

February 2: Jefferson Davis introduces a Senate resolution, adopted on May 24 after extensive debate on which asserts the right of slave owners to hold slaves in the territories, requests a federal slave code for the territories, and declares state interference in the Fugitive Slave Act inimical to the safety of the nation.

February 27: Lincoln delivers a speech at Cooper Union in New York City opposing popular sovereignty and opposing any extension of slavery in the territories.

April 23–May 3: The Democratic Party holds a convention in Charleston, South Carolina, but fails to agree on a candidate for president, even after delegates from eight Southern states withdraw; Douglas gets a majority but not the required two-thirds of the original number of delegates. The convention adjourns after 57 ballots on May 3.

May 9: A Whig-American Party coalition meets in Baltimore, establishes the national Constitutional Union Party, and nominates John Bell for president. Previously, Southern pro-Union former Whigs had been isolated, some running on Democratic Party tickets or as Southern American Party (Know-Nothing) candidates at the state level. The Constitutional Union Party makes its best showing in Virginia, Tennessee, and Kentucky.

May 16: The Republican Party convention meets in Chicago and nominates Abraham Lincoln for the presidency as a moderate; Senator William Seward of New York, although a leading candidate, is rejected as too radical on the antislavery issue.

June 18: Democrats reassemble in Baltimore and seat a few pro-Douglas delegates from Southern states; remaining Southern Democrats walk out of the convention; Douglas is nominated for president on the basis of two-thirds present.

June 28: Southern Democrats meet in Baltimore and nominate John C. Breckinridge for president.

November 6: In the presidential election, Lincoln wins a clear majority of the electoral college vote with 180 votes; however, he wins none in any slave state. He secures about 39 percent of the popular vote.

EYEWITNESS TESTIMONY

Mr. Wilmot moved an amendment, to add at the end of Mr. McKay's modified bill the following: Provided, That, as an express and fundamental condition of the acquisition of any territory from the Republic of Mexico by the United States, by virtue of any treaty which may be negotiated between them, and to the use by the Executive of the moneys herein appropriated, neither slavery nor involuntary servitude shall ever exist in any part of said territory, except for crime, whereof the party shall first be duly convicted.

The first section of the bill was still under consideration, and after some conversation, the amendment of Mr. Wilmot was received as an amendment to this section.

Report in The Congressional Globe, *August 12, 1846, noting the first introduction of the proposal by Congressman David Wilmot of Pennsylvania, on August 8, 1846, to exclude slavery from the territories acquired from Mexico; later known as the Wilmot Proviso.*

Sir:—I have the honour to acknowledge the receipt of your letter of April 1st. Your name and fame are familiar to me, yet I have not the power to aid in the accomplishment of your wishes. Your African blood would subject you to imprisonment and slavery in this State, as well as in all the other slave States of the American Union. Your genius and reputation could afford you no protection. You belong to a race that has been the slave of the higher and stronger races from time immemorial. If you have read my various speeches and letters, you must be convinced that slavery is an institution ordained by Providence, honoured by time, sanctioned by the Gospel, and especially favourable to personal and national liberty. That it is compatible with Democracy, is evinced by the fact that the slave States are the chief seats of Democracy in this Union, and that we regard the Democratic party here as the main bulwark of the institution.

That slavery is favourable to civilization is demonstrated by the fact, that in this State (South Carolina,) where the slaves are double the number of the whites, refinement of manners is carried to the highest pitch, and Charleston, its capital, is the acknowledged metropolis of American chivalry. It would not avail you in coming here to be invested with a diplomatic character. Necessity knows no law. Self-protection is the first law of society. Though slavery is a benignant institu-

tion, and our slaves are the happiest creatures in the world, yet they might be easily stirred up to rebellion. If free blacks were allowed to come here they might excite their fellow Africans to insurrection. We live, sir, in the midst of a perpetual crisis. We must preserve our throats from butchery, our homes from conflagration, at all hazards. At the same time we must maintain and perpetuate our "peculiar institution." In such a state of things, should you visit Charleston, you would, doubtless, experience no insult, but you would be politely turned out of town by our chivalry, as was lately the case in respect to a public agent sent hither by the State of Massachusetts.

I am, respectfully, yours, J.C. Calhoun

Letter, John C. Calhoun to Alexandre Dumas, dated August 1, 1847, as published in The Friend: A Religious and Literary Journal, *Vol. 21, no. 23 (February 12, 1848), p. 177.*

We must, Mr. Editor, insist that the territory of the nation, whether acquired by treaty, purchase, or conquest, is, and shall be, for the common benefit, and open to the slaveholder and his property; and that we *will* enjoy it, every man, if we choose to go to it, in spite of Federal legislation to the contrary. We deny that Congress has any jurisdiction as to slavery, either in the States or Territories, or in the District of Columbia, or the slave trade between them; and we will not permit any attempted exercise of it. But we assert that the jurisdiction belongs to slaveholders, as forming States or occupying Territories, and to them only. We object to the extension of the ordinance of 1787, or the further application of the Missouri Compromise. They were unwise concessions, having reference only to their special objects, and must not be permitted any force of precedent or further extension. We must concede and compromise *no more.* We claim, and will have, by rights existing before, as well as by the Constitution, *the whole limits and extent of this Federal empire, wherein to assert, every man, his right to his slave, whether in State or Territory, and to his labor, as well as person, in all territory not now embraced in that ordinance and compromise.* We will and must insist that any territory acquired from Mexico, *whatever be the mode or terms,* becomes at once open to slaveholders and slaves, *without the permission or in defiance* of any legislation of Congress; and that the Wilmot Proviso is a nullity as against the jurisdiction of the people of the territory over the matter. This latter is of course subject to the provisions and guarantees of the Constitution. We deny that the Constitution is subject to any amendment interfering with slavery, even by three-fourths of the Congress or the States.

Item, headed "Pro-slavery Democracy—The Demand," from the Correspondent of the Charleston Mercury, *as published in the* National Era, *Vol. 1, no. 38 (September 23, 1847), p. 4.*

I have a large religious society in this town, composed of "all sorts and conditions of men," fugitive slaves who do not legally own the nails on their fingers and cannot read the Lord's Prayer, and also men and women of wealth and fine cultivation. I wish to inform you of the difficulty in which we (the church and myself) are placed by the new Fugitive Slave Law. There are several fugitive slaves in the society; they have committed no wrong; they have the same "unalienable right to life, liberty, and the pursuit of happiness" that you have; they naturally look to me for advice in their affliction. They are strangers, and ask me to take them in; hungry, and beg me to feed them; thirsty, and would have me give them a drink; they are naked, and look to me for clothing; sick, and wish me to visit them. Yes: they are ready to perish, and ask their life at my hands. Even the letter of the most Jewish of the Gospels makes Christ say, "Inasmuch as ye have not done it unto one of the least of these, ye have not done it unto me!" They come to me as to their Christian minister, and ask me to do to them only what Christianity evidently requires.

But *your* law will punish me with fine of 1000 dollars and imprisonment for six months if I take in one of these strangers, feed and clothe these naked and hungry children of want; nay, if I visit them when they are sick, come unto them when they are in prison, or help them, "directly or indirectly," when they are ready to perish! Suppose I should refuse to do for them what Christianity demands. I will not say what I should think of myself, but what you would say. You would say I was a *scoundrel,* that I was *really* an infidel (my theological brethren call me so), that I deserved a gaol for six years! You would say right. But if I do as you must know that I ought, then your law strips me of my property, tears me from my wife, and shuts me in a gaol. Perhaps I do not value the obligations of religion so much as my opponents, of another faith; but I must say I would rather lie all my life in a gaol, and starve there, than refuse to protect one of these parishioners of mine. Do not call me a fanatic; I am a cool and sober man, but I must reverence the laws of God, come of that what will come. I must be true to my religion.

Abolitionist Reverend Theodore Parker, in a letter to President Millard Fillmore, November 21, 1850, as selected in John Weiss, ed., Life and Correspondence of Theodore Parker, *1864, pp. 100–101.*

Some twenty persons have been arrested at Syracuse, on charge of having participated in the recent rescue of a fugitive slave. We observe, however, that they are not accused of *Treason,* but resistance to the law. We fear due notice has not been taken, in Western New York, of the profound legal arguments by which some of our neighbors have settled this question. They do not appear to understand, that, unless these men have committed *treason,* they have done nothing of special importance. They have not apparently felt the overruling necessity which is said to exist, for hanging fifteen or twenty citizens of Syracuse, as enemies of the Union, and for its preservation. They have ventured, at greater risk perhaps than they supposed, to exercise their common sense of this matter,—and to act under its guidance rather than that of partizan fanaticism.

Our readers are aware that we have, from the beginning, denied both the justice and the expediency, of treating, as *treason,* the forcible resistance of legal process in any single case. According to all the authorities, the resistance must be *general,* must extend to all cases; in which the execution of the law is attempted, and must show a purpose to *resist the law itself,* and not merely some particular application of it. All the decisions of high Courts, and all the opinions of distinguished lawyers, which have been quoted upon this subject, have been explicit up on this point; although those who have cited them adroitly evade all allusion to it. Judge Kane himself, in his charge to the Jury in the Christiana case, expressly said that the resistance to the law must be general, or the offence could not be considered treason.

If it were at all necessary, we would willingly quote authorities to show that we are right. But the action of the federal authorities in this Syracuse affair, is quite sufficient. Notwithstanding the earnest and constant efforts of a large portion of the press, the offenders are not to be tried for treason.

The expediency of this course has probably forced itself upon the convictions of those most directly concerned. It is generally deemed desirable that offenses against the law should be punished; and it will be expected that those who resist the law at Syracuse shall suffer the penalty which the law may pronounce. If convicted of *Treason,* they must be hung. Would it conduce to harmony—would it allay agitation, to hang ten or twenty men at Syracuse, for having helped a fugitive slave retain his freedom? Would it reconcile the North to the fugitive slave law, and dispose all Northern men cheerfully and zealously to aid its execution? There can be but one answer to these inquiries. Every Southern man, who has judgment enough to form a rational opinion and coolness enough to exercise it, would deprecate such an execution, as the spark that would arouse the whole North into unquenchable hatred of Slavery and its requirements. Yet, the only alternative would be a pardon or commutation of the sentence; and to this there would be the powerful objection, that the law had not been carried out—that we had statutes which we were willing to enforce—that the whole proceeding had been a mockery of law—and that the authorities, from the outset, did not intend to enforce it. If these men had been tried for treason, they would have evaded punishment. They are to be tried for something of which they were probably guilty, and if they are convicted they will be very likely to undergo the penalty which the law prescribes.

Editorial, entitled "The Slave Rescue at Syracuse," opposing the use of the charge of treason against those who resisted the Fugitive Slave Law, New-York Daily Times, *October 18, 1851, p. 2.*

This story of Mrs. Stowe's is a thorn in the side of the Sunny South. It serves as a test to the popular feeling at the North. Whatever assurances the politician tenders them, they cannot shut their eyes to the fact, that a book, ostensibly written to expose the Fugitive Slave Law to contempt and disregard, has enjoyed a measure of success among Northern readers, that no other American publication ever secured. It has readers everywhere. The avidity with which copies are bought, evinces the satisfaction with which they are read. There cannot be a doubt that the Fugitive Law is what Mr. Brooks, in his maudlin speech to the Caucus, declared it to be—a bitter pill to the North, only submitted to as a condition for preserving peace; and from its very offensiveness, a measure of the devotion which is here entertained for the Union and the Compromises. Mr. Brooks is occasionally right, because, perhaps, in traveling an eccentric orbit, he cannot very well help it. If one hundred thousand copies of the *Log Cabin* [sic] have been sold, it is fair to reason that a hundred thousand families have possessed it, and a half-million

Fugitive slaves became poignant figures as hundreds of prints and cartoons depicted their escape episodes. Patrols tracked them down with dogs and guns. *(Library of Congress, Prints and Photographs Division, LC-USZ62–1286)*

persons have read it. The numeration does not please the *Standard.*

Editorial approving the success of Harriet Beecher Stowe's Uncle Tom's Cabin *in New-York Daily Times, May 31, 1852, p. 2.*

It is alleged also by the friends of the bill that it can do no harm to the North, as slave labor will be unprofitable in the new territories, and Mr. [Edward] Everett [Senator from Massachusetts], by one of those fatal concessions which challenge his claim to broad statesmanship, has given the sanction of his name to this strange theory. We are reluctant to believe in the hypocrisy of the Southern statesmen who have urged this plea, and yet the rapid growth of slavery in Missouri, on the very borders of the new territories, is a direct refutation of their theory. Slavery will go into Kansas, if the Missouri compromise is repealed, and Northern men should look this fact boldly in the face. Some of the southern presses, that are not given to hypocrisy and deception, openly avow the intention of making slave States of these territories. The Charleston Courier says boldly, "Although we hold it clear that the Missouri restriction is unconstitutional, there are a large number who think otherwise, and nothing short of its abolition or removal will have the effect of opening those territories to slaveholders. We have reason to believe, from reliable authority, that, without this measure, a non-slaveholding population would at once occupy those territories, and the slaveholders now there, would have to recede—nay to give way to an emigrant horde of red republicans, in principle, if not in national origin, full of the deadliest hostility to slavery. But remove the Missouri line and restrictions, and Kansas, we are well assured, will be settled by tobacco planters, for the production of which staple the soil and climate are said to be well adapted; and Nebraska will almost necessarily take its social character, and political complexion, and local institutions from Missouri, on which it borders." How can we apologize for the hypocrisy of Northern men, who attempt to hoodwink their constituents by the pretence that slavery cannot go to Nebraska? . . .

Religious men can no longer be indifferent. They have often disclaimed all share in the sin of Southern slavery, on the ground that it was a local institution over which the General Government had no control. The guilt rested alone on the slaveholders, so they have affirmed, not on their fellow citizens of the North. But now the tables are turned. Nebraska is consecrated to freedom, by a national compact held sacred by a whole generation. By southern votes it was consecrated; they have closed the doors against the entrance of slavery, and those doors can be opened only by northern votes, by the assent of the freedmen of the North. If Kansas and Nebraska shall ever re-echo to the lash of the overseer, or be watered by the bondman's tears, the guilt will rest upon the North, and northern Christians cannot evade the condemnation of the civilized world, and the righteous judgments of God. We wait the final issue with hope mingled with alarm. The utterances from many New England pulpits on the approaching Fast-day will be a fitting reply to Senatorial arrogance, and will quicken the tone of moral feeling through the North.

Editorial in the Christian Watchman and Reflector, *entitled "Nebraska and Slavery Extension," arguing against the Kansas-Nebraska Act, Vol. 35, no. 14 (April 6, 1854), p. 54.*

Negotiations were going on for the purchase of Burns, and at eleven o'clock it was confidently stated that he would be purchased by Wendell Phillips and others for $1,200, and that the money had been raised. Wendell Phillips's name seemed to be on every tongue. But the negotiation collapsed and excuses were made. It would be "a covenant with Hell" to admit an ownership in slaves under the shadow of Bunker Hill. "And to plank down the money for it," was another objectionable feature on the tongues of wags.

It turned out that most of the money was raised by the colored people themselves. The negro's owner, Col. Stuttle, was willing to sell but the negotiation fell.

In the evening a mob again gathered around the "slave pen," as it was called, and some stones and bricks were thrown. One of them struck a member of the New England Guards. Many riotous patriots were arrested by the police and locked up in the central station. The excitement was intense on the Sabbath night. But Mr. Taylor, chief of the police, kept cool and preserved the peace without military aid.

Orlando Bolivar Willcox, an army officer who later served as a general on the Union side during the Civil War, describing the rendition of Anthony Burns, May 24, 1854, in his memoir as edited by Robert Garth Scott, in Forgotten Valor: The Memoirs, Letters, and Civil War Journals of Orlando B. Willcox, *pp. 194, 196.*

In the recent contest for a Delegate to Congress, the candidates were Robert P. Flennekin, from Pennsylvania, Gen. Whitfield, late Indian Agent, and a Mr. Wakefield, recently of Iowa. Mr. Flennekin and Mr. Wakefield both avowed themselves against the introduction of Slavery. Gen. Whitfield was the Pro-Slavery candidate. Mr. Flennekin was supported by the Governor and his friends, and by the discreet Anti-Slavery men all over the Territory, including the prominent men of Lawrence. Mr. Wakefield got the ultra Abolition vote. We have not yet received the official returns from the different elections districts, but the entire vote will, in all probability, sum up somewhat in the following proportions. For WAKEFIELD, 175; for FLENNEKIN, 500; for WHITFIELD, 4000. Nothing can be determined by this voting as to the number of Anti-Slavery men at present in the Territory. The whole country was overrun on the day of election by hordes of ruffians from Missouri, who took entire possession of the polls in almost every district, browbeat and intimidated the Judges, forced their own votes into the ballot-box for Whitfield, and crowded out and drove off all who were suspected of being in favor of any other candidate. We are perfectly satisfied that this is the game the ultra Pro-Slavery men of the South intend to play all through in subjecting Kansas to Slavery. We have heard whisperings, for months past, of an extensive secret organization projected by a number of influential Southern leaders, to throw large bodies of voters into this Territory from Missouri at all the elections. An immense fund has no doubt been raised by subscription, through all the Southern States, to carry out the scheme, and if some decided and vigorous measures, equally efficacious, are not resorted to by the friends of freedom, they will find themselves overborne and ruthlessly crushed out of Kansas at the very start, by those mercenary propagandists of Slavery. This is a matter which ought to excite prompt action. I do not know how the development of this desperate expedient of the Pro-Slavery party will affect the honest masses of the American people; but I think it ought to awaken the profoundest indignation throughout the entire country, and call forth the most effectual and conclusive resistance. I am satisfied that no portion of the people of the North can entertain a deeper and more intense hostility to this high handed movement than the Administration Democracy. They concurred in the repeal of the Missouri Compromise in order solely to establish, in the Territories, what they regard as a great principle of popular government. They wanted the people of the Territories to govern themselves. The effort of these Southern leaders to force upon the people of this Territory, by fraud and violence, laws and institutions foreign to their wishes, must, therefore, meet with the earnest condemnation of every honest Democrat in the North. Administration Democrats out here—men who have stood by the Kansas-Nebraska bill from the start—do not hesitate to assert their readiness to abandon all the political attachments they have ever cherished, rather than submit to be overslaughed and trodden under foot by these outside barbarians. If the principle of the Kansas-Nebraska bill cannot be carried out—if in passing from under the authority of Congress, the people of the Territories are to pass under the Government of this or that adjoining State—then we say perish the delusive cry of popular sovereignty, and let Congress resume its reign. Rather than be governed by the slaveholding mobocracy of Missouri, we join the cry for a restoration of the Missouri Compromise.

It is to be hoped that the House of Representatives will not admit Whitfield to a seat as a Delegate from Kansas. The manner of his election should be fully looked into. That "election" was one of the most flagrant outrages ever perpetrated on the rights of a free community. The House of Representatives should pay more respect to its own character, and to the integrity of the laws, than to sanction that outrage by admitting him to a seat. Let us have a full investigation, and decision action. WYANDOT

Selection from "Correspondence of the New-York Daily Times" from a correspondent with the pen name "Wyandot," dated December 5, 1854, as published in the New-York Daily Times, *January 8, 1855, p. 2.*

We think it quite likely . . . that the *Bulletin* is right in saying that a proposition to restore the Slave-Trade would not be sustained by *the people* of the Southern States. But if it should be deemed important and essential to the fortification and perpetuation of the system of Slavery, and to the extension of its political power,—and if it should be pressed upon those grounds by the leading political champions of Slavery at the South, there is very little doubt, judging from past experience, that it would speedily command popular favor and support. The mass of the Southern people are as thoroughly ruled by the 317,525 owners of Slaves among them, as the English people are by the oligarchy that usurps all Government by right of rank and birth;—and whatever these gentlemen may deem essential to the promotion of their own interest, will speedily be made "popular" in the States under their sway. This has been the history of all the aggressive movements of the Slave interest. When Texan annexation was first proposed, it was said to be unpopular at the South; but under the masterly rule of Mr. Calhoun it was very soon made the test of fidelity to Slavery at the South, and of Democracy throughout the Union.

The same thing is true emphatically of the Nebraska bill. The *Bulletin,* with other sensible and judicious journals, insisted from the beginning that not one man in ten at the South cared a straw for the repeal of the Missouri Compromise. Yet, when Senator Dixon of Kentucky proposed it, there were not half a dozen Southern members that dared to oppose it. It was made an essential feature of the general system of Slave propagandism, upon which the leaders of the Slaveholding interest had resolved. And as such, no portion of the South ventured to oppose it; and those at the North who resist and denounce it, are now set down, even by the *Bulletin,* as enemies of the South.

The precedent creates alarm concerning the threatened restoration of the Slave-Trade. That measure is already urged by the *Mercury* and other journals, as essential to the Slaveholding interest,—as affording the only means of filling up Kansas and Nebraska with Slaves, and of thus securing the object aimed at by the repeal of the Missouri Compromise. Henry A. Wise, a Democratic candidate for Governor in Virginia, has openly advocated the scheme—which finds favor, furthermore, with just that class of politicians who have hitherto been the leaders of Southern sentiment in all these measures for Slavery extension. Is it at all strange that the Free States should feel some apprehension as to the result? May they not very fairly fear that this question will soon be presented at the South as a test of fidelity to the interests of Slavery, and at the North as a test of devotion to the Union? And in that case does not experience teach us that it is likely to be successful?

Item, entitled "The Slave Trade and the South," quoting the New-Orleans Bulletin *and the* Charleston Mercury, *on the question of reopening the African slave-trade,* New-York Daily Times, *December 6, 1854, p. 4.*

The Jackson *Mississippian* is in excellent spirits. He has seen Dr. Middleton, one of his neighbors, who has been out to the Kansas Territory to take an observation of its capabilities, and study the signs of its promise. The Doctor found fertile regions and such scenery as is pictured in books for the drawing room. He found just the soil that is needed for raising tobacco and grain. As a hemp-growing country, even Kentucky cannot beat it. The Kansas River runs nearly through the heart of it, while the majestic Missouri takes in washing on its eastern borders.

Then the Doctor finds a social and political promise no less flattering than the physical one. Squatters have taken some thirty or forty thousand claims already. And of the settlers, two to one, he thinks, are pro-Slavery men. The Missourians of course are in for the "Christianizing institution." Large relays of pro-Slavery men are hoped for from Kentucky this Fall, and many of the settlers from Indiana and Illinois he affirms to be in favor of Slavery. Our Jackson editor warms with his genial subject. He says:

"A great object will be achieved should a Slave State spring up on the western borders of Missouri. The West will then be open to us. We will hold in our hands the key to that immense domain, and no power can loosen our hold upon it but an unpropitious climate and an ungrateful soil. With Kansas as a Slave State, the equilibrium of the Union may still be preserved. In the branch of the National Legislature in which all the States are equally represented, without regard to their wealth or population, the South can still maintain equal strength with the North. In the meantime, new accessions to her strength may be made from the territory acquired with Texas; and, mayhap, the gem of the Antilles [Cuba] will glitter, ere long, in the galaxy of Southern States. The recent elections in California indicate a conservative feeling in that quarter on the subject of Slavery; and a proposition is now pending for a division of the State, with a view to the introduction of Slavery."

He expresses great confidence that the Pro-Slavery party will carry the Fall Elections, but fears that, after these, there will be a rush from the Free States sufficient to turn the tide and shape—oh, dire calamity!—the political institutions after the model of Freedom. The elections have resulted as the prophet foretold. Now, let the friends of Freedom profit by his apprehensions, and rush in to save Kansas from the curse.

Item, depicting proslavery advocates as seeking more territory, entitled "Fears and Hopes for Kansas," New-York Daily Times, *December 8, 1854, p. 4.*

The Missouri Compromise prohibited Slavery from Kansas forever. Its repeal permitted its introduction. Apologists for that repeal urged that it could have not *practical* effect,—that is only gave to the people the right to do as they should choose about it,—that the settlers were all opposed to Slavery, and that Kansas would inevitably be a *free* State. Senator Douglas, the nominal author of the movement, said that this would be the result. The election for a Delegate to Congress has resulted in the choice of *a pro-Slavery Democrat* of the Atchison and Douglas school by a large majority. This shows of how little value were the quieting assurances by which the advocates of the Nebraska bill have endeavored to allay the public sentiment against that measure. Of course it has not been brought about without effort; and the character of that effort, and the success which attended it, illustrate forcibly the real nature of the *popular sovereignty* pretext upon which the justification of the bill is based.

The President appointed Gen. Reeder Governor of the Territory. The Governor divided the Territory into sixteen districts, appointed Election Judges for them all, and gave them *instructions to exclude the votes of all who they should have reason to believe* had come into the Territory for the purpose of voting. This gave a single Judge, appointed by a Governor who held office at the will of the President, full power to *disfranchise* voters at his discretion! This is the style of popular sovereignty that prevails in Kansas. Its practical operation is illustrated by the following paragraphs:

From the Parkville, Mo., Luminary

Important Movement—Just before going to press we were informed that immense crowds of Missourians have, within the last two or three days, been going over in Kansas Territory. The numbers are estimated to reach 3,000 or 4,000, most of whom have passed through independence, Kansas City, and Westport. A deputation was sent to Gov. Reeder to request him to open a polling place at the Shawnee Mission; and he was to take the matter into consideration.

From the Washington Correspondence of the Philadelphia Ledger

In July last I wrote you that Kansas would not be a Slave State. I am now of a different opinion. The impertinent and insolent interference of your Eastern fanatics—the colonizing as they have done of hundreds of the lowest class of rowdies to browbeat our voters and prevent a fair expression of the popular will, has brought about this result. They have located themselves near the Kansas River, named their City Lawrence, and number, I am told, some hundreds of voters. I have seen some of them, and they are the most unmitigated looking set of blackguards I have ever laid my eyes on.

Up to late in September, there was no excitement in the Territory on this question. Everybody here and in Missouri believed that Kansas would be a free State; but no sooner did these colonists appear here than all the river counties in Missouri—Andrew, Hold, Buchanan, &c., sent over thousands of their young men to counteract their treasonable schemes. They will be successful.

The colonization from the East referred to above is that of emigrants who go to Kansas as settlers for life. They, of course are excluded from voting. The thousands who go over from Missouri for the purpose of voting, are admitted to the privilege. This is the squatter sovereignty which the present Administration has made the test of democracy, and of fidelity to the Union!

News item favoring free state settlers in Kansas, entitled "Kansas and Slavery," quoting Parkville, Missouri, Luminary, and the Philadelphia Ledger, *as published in the* New-York Daily Times, *December 11, 1854, p. 4.*

These are the points I should make against Commissioner Loring:—

1. He kidnapped a man in Boston who was accused of no offence against any law, divine or human, but who, by the laws of God written in nature, and the constitution and statutes of Massachusetts, and the principles of the Declaration of Independence, was as much entitled to freedom as Mr. Loring himself, or any man in the commonwealth.

2. He was not forced to this, but did it voluntarily. (a) His office did not compel such a wicked service, for Mr. Hallett, in 1850, declined it, and in 1854, Mr. George T. Curtis, who was first applied to for the kidnapping of Mr. Burns, refused the office; in 1851 (in the Sims time) no sheriff or constable of Boston could be found willing to serve the writ of personal replevin, though a fee of five hundred dollars was allowed, and a bond of indemnity to the extent of three thousand dollars more. (b) But if the office, in his opinion, required this, then he ought to have resigned his office, either at once or on the passage of the Fugitive Slave Bill, which "required" such a service of him, or, at least, when called on to steal a man. He cannot plead that the office is any extenuation of so heinous an offence as making a citizen of Massachusetts, accused of no fault, a slave of Virginia.

3. He did not do this hastily, but deliberately, after a week for reflection and consultation with his friends and fellow-citizens.

4. He is not now sorry for the offence, but so justifies it on principle that the act is legal and constitutional, and so professes to understand the tenure of his office of commissioner that he would do the same again if called on; and Massachusetts will, again and again, present to the world the spectacle of a commonwealth, democratic and Christian, which keeps in office, as guardian of widows and orphans, a man who is a professional kidnapper. Is she ready to do that?

5. The manner of the kidnapping was as bad as the matter. I will not refer to the mode of arrest, which he is not responsible for, but, (a.) he advised Mr. Phillips, Burns's attorney, "Not to throw obstacles in the way of his being sent back, as he probably will be"! (b.) He confined him in a Court-house of Massachusetts, contrary to the express words of the statute, and the well-known form of law of his own State. (c.) He decided against the evidence in the case, which proved that the man on trial as a slave in Virginia on a certain time, *was actually at work in Boston at that very time.* (d.) The evidence he relied on for the identity of Burns, the only thing to be proved, as he declared, was the words alleged to be uttered by Mr. Burns, spoken, if at all, under *duresse,* and subsequently denied by him. (e.) He communicated his decision to parties having an

interest adverse to Mr. Burns, twenty-four hours, at least, before it was given in open court.

6. He knows the stealing of a man is wrong. This is not merely matter of inference from his education and position, but from the fact that he declined the fee, ten dollars, his "legal" and "official" recompense for stealing a brother man. This he does, it is supposed, not from general charity towards men-stealers, or from special friendship for Mr. Suttle in this case; but because the money is the price of blood paid for treachery to the Constitution of Massachusetts, and to the natural, essential and unalienable rights of man.

7. He is the first judicial officer of Massachusetts, since 1776 who had kidnapped a man. Had he stolen Mr. Dana or Mr. Ellis, counsel for Mr. Burns, charged with no crime, and delivered them up to the Algerines or Carolinians, he would not more have violated the principles of natural justice and the precepts of the Christian religion. Nay, the offence is worse when committed against a poor man, an unprotected and a friendless man of a despised race, than if committed against rich, educated, and powerful gentlemen, who have material and personal means of defence. Now, the Legislature of Massachusetts is the guardian of the lives and the character of her citizens. If she detains a kidnapper in her high office of Judge of Probate, in her own capital city, she says to the world, "I acknowledge that it is a glory to steal a man, and so will make the kidnapper also guardian of widows and orphans, giving him a better opportunity to crush those who are ready to perish without his oppression!" Is that the lesson for guardians of public morals to teach to the youth and maidens of Massachusetts—to teach in the hearing of Fanueil Hall, in sight of Bunker Hill, over the graves of Hancock and Adams?

8. There are 2038 colored persons in the county of Suffolk; they must do public business at his office. Is it fair for Massachusetts to force them, in their affliction, to come before a judge who is the official enemy of their race—who kidnaps men of this nation? It adds new terrors to the bitterness of death.

9. If there were no law of God, no conscience in man declaring what is right, no golden rule of religion, bidding "Whatsoever ye would that men should do unto you, do ye even so to them," then it might be enough to plead the law of the United States allows him to steal a man. But as there is a law of God,

a conscience, a golden rule, recognized guides of conduct against men, Massachusetts cannot detain in such an office a man who on principle will send his innocent brothers into eternal bondage.

Abolitionist Reverend Theodore Parker, in a letter to Charles Ellis, February 8, 1855, condemning the actions of a federal fugitive slave commissioner, as selected in John Weiss, ed., Life and Correspondence of Theodore Parker, 1864, *pp. 144–146.*

This Supreme Court has made many righteous decisions. It now makes one horribly wicked. Shall we repudiate the court? If so we might as well have none, which would be a greater evil.

1. We ought to oppose and dispose the decision. The several States must as far as possible nullify it.

2. We ought to prepare for the crisis coming. The oligarchs of slavery are waxing bolder and bolder, more and more insulting. There are now no free colored men in the North. Soon they will see that our free labor interferes in some way with their progress, and will begin to interfere with that. The next step now will probably be the purchase of Cuba, after which without any special act, the foreign slave trade with Africa will be open. The act of Congress in pronouncing the slave trade piracy, and abolishing it is unconstitutional. Congress had no right to pass such a quixotic act. Everything protecting the colored man is unconstitutional—everything interfering with the slaveholder is unconstitutional. The bogus legislature in Kansas is not unconstitutional; the free legislature is. And so on throughout.

3. Now every man, North and South, who has any regard for right, should solemnly vow to himself and God, with all the solemnity of an oath, that he will never vote for a man for any office in State or the United States, who is not openly and reliably opposed to all slavery; and who will not make use of all means to cripple, abolish, and extirpate it.

4. Again as Christians we have a special duty. Our church is not of God unless she shakes off this curse and sin with the deepest indignation. This injustice to the black man she shall not connive at. She ought to say and preach that the black man has a right to his liberty everywhere. He has. The United States has no right to deny him citizenship. He has a right, and is bound to obey God rather than man. Liberty is natural, and slavery is not even an exception—there is no exception; the master is

always and must be a sinner; guilty, too, of one of the deepest of crimes. All apparent exceptions are not exceptions. They are not only transitional passages as rapid as possible from a great evil to good.
5. Lastly, we ourselves must declare our freedom; our freedom from party in State and in Church. There are some who will assent to anything if done by their party; and there are some Christians who think more of what they call the peace and quiet of the church than they do of the cause of God. Such men sin and lead others to sin, and the exigences of the times now loudly call them to repent.

There is only one ray of light, and that is—the insanity of strong defenders excites a more determined opposition. Anti-slavery progresses. When the final conflict comes, which it would seem will be not far hence, if God is in favor of justice and the power of truth is not a chimera, slavery will be crushed to the earth and liberty be universal.

Extract from editorial entitled "The Late Decision of the Supreme Court of the United States," decrying the Dred Scott decision, in Zion's Herald and Wesleyan Journal, *Vol. 28, no. 11 (March 18, 1857), p. 42.*

In regard to John Brown, you want me to curse him. I will not curse John Brown. You want me to pour out execrations upon the head of old Ossawatomie. Though all the slaveholding Balaks in the country fill their houses with silver and proffer it, I will not curse John Brown. I do honestly condemn what he did, from my standpoint, and with my convictions I disapprove of his action, that is true but I believe that his purpose was a good one; that so far as his own motives before God were concerned, they were honest and truthful; and no one can deny that he stands head and shoulders above any other character that appeared on the stage in that tragedy from beginning to end; from the time he entered the armory there to the time when he was strangled by Governor "Fussation." [General laughter.]

He was not guilty of murder or treason. He did unquestionably violate the statute against aiding slaves to escape; but no blood was shed, except by the panic-stricken multitude, till Stevens was fired upon while waving a flag of truce. The only murder was that of Thompson, who was snatched from the heroic protection of a woman, and riddled with balls at the railroad bridge. Despotism has seldom sacrificed three nobler victims than Brown, Stevens, and Hazlitt.

As I remarked, Mr. Chairman, this brings us to confront slavery, and ask what right this Caliban has upon earth? I say no right. My honest conviction—and I do not know why gentlemen need take offense; they need not unless they choose—my honest conviction is, that all these slaveholding laws have the same moral power and force that rules among pirates have for the distribution of their booty; that regulations among robbers have for the division of their spoils; and although I do not believe gentlemen have behaved very handsomely to me, I am going to add notwithstanding, that I do not mean to say that gentlemen who are slaveholders would be guilty of these particular things—that is not the point—I am talking about this matter in the court of conscience, in the court of right and wrong; and I insist that any laws for enslaving men have just the same moral force as the arrangement among robbers and pirates for distributing their spoils.

I want to know by what right you can come and make me a slave? I want to know by what right you can say that my child shall be your slave? I want to know by what right you say that the mother shall not have her child, given to her from God through the martyrdom of maternity?

Abolitionist Owen Lovejoy, speech delivered in April 1860, supporting John Brown, from the Congressional Globe, *as reprinted in Edwin Rozwenc,* Slavery as a Cause of the Civil War, *p. 25.*

The New York, Michigan, and Wisconsin delegations sat together and were in this tempest very quiet. Many of their faces whitened as the Lincoln *yawp* swelled into a wild hosanna of victory.

The convention now proceeded to business. The most significant vote was that of Virginia, which had been expected solid for Seward, and which now gave him but eight and gave Lincoln fourteen. The New Yorkers looked significantly at each other as this was announced. Then Indiana gave her twenty-six votes for Lincoln. This solid vote was a startler. The division of the first vote caused a fall in Seward stock. It was seen that Lincoln, Cameron, and Bates had the strength to defeat Seward, and it was known that the greater part of the Chase vote would go for Lincoln.

The convention proceeded to a second ballot. Every man was fiercely enlisted in the struggle. The partisans of the various candidates were strung up to such a pitch of excitement as to render them incapable of patience, and the cries of "Call the roll" were fairly hissed through their teeth. The first gain for Lincoln was in New Hampshire. The Chase and the Frémont vote from that state were given him. His next gain was the whole vote of Vermont. This was a blighting blow upon the Seward interest. The New Yorkers started as if an Orsini bomb had exploded. And presently the Cameron vote of Pennsylvania was thrown for Lincoln, increasing his strength forty-four votes. The fate of that day was now determined. New York saw "checkmate" next move and sullenly proceeded with the game, assuming unconsciousness of her inevitable doom. On this ballot Lincoln gained seventy-nine votes. Seward had one hundred and eighty-four and a half votes, Lincoln one hundred and eighty-one . . .

While this ballot was taken amid excitement that tested the nerves, the fatal defection from Seward in New England still further appeared, four votes going over from Seward to Lincoln in Massachusetts. The latter received four additional votes from Pennsylvania and fifteen additional votes from Ohio. It was whispered about: "Lincoln's the coming man—will be nominated this ballot." When the roll of states and territories had been called, I had ceased to give attention to any votes but those for Lincoln and had his vote added up as it was given. The number of votes necessary to a choice were two hundred and thirty-three, and I saw under my pencil as the Lincoln column was completed the figures 232 ½—one vote and a half to give him the nomination. In a moment the fact was whispered about. A hundred pencils had told the same story. The news went over the house wonderfully, and there was a pause. There are always men anxious to distinguish themselves on such occasions. There is nothing that politicians like better than a crisis. I looked up to see who would be the man to give the decisive vote. In about ten ticks

The four-way presidential election of 1860, depicted in this cartoon, resulted in an Electoral College sweep for Abraham Lincoln. *(Library of Congress, Prints and Photographs Division, LC-USZC4–12942)*

of a watch, Cartter of Ohio was up. I had imagined Ohio would be slippery enough for the crisis. And sure enough! Every eye was on Cartter, and everybody who understood the matter at all knew what he was about to do. He said: "I rise (eh), Mr. Chairman (eh), to announce the change of four votes of Ohio from Mr. Chase to Mr. Lincoln." The deed was done. There was a moment's silence. The nerves of the thousands, which through the hours of suspense had been subjected to terrible tension, relaxed, and as deep breaths of relief were taken, there was a noise in the wigwam like the rush of a great wind in the van of a storm—and in another breath, the storm was there. There were thousands cheering with the energy of insanity.

*Newspaperman Murat Halstead, May 18, 1861
reporting the nomination of Lincoln at the Republican
Party convention, in the* Cincinnati Commercial,
from Caucuses of 1860, *as selected in Henry Steele
Commager, ed.,* The Blue and the Gray, *p. 3.*

This notorious agitator and skeptic held forth at City Hall, last Sabbath, in defense of his peculiar views. Large audiences were present.

In the afternoon he descanted upon the Bible, denying its authenticity and inspiration, and claiming that it should be accepted as truth only in so far as it accorded with the opinions of the individual. The discourse, though marked by considerable ability, accredited its author as the possessor of an erratic and unbalanced mind.

But the evening lecture was *the* feature of his performance. Slavery was his topic, and he fulfilled his promise to unfold the character of Garrisonian Abolitionism. He claimed with truth that his principles were identical with those of the Republicans, the only point of difference being that *he* boldly followed out Republican ideas to the logical conclusion, while *they* timidly shrank therefrom. He conceded that the indignities offered their opposition to slavery, were occasioned by the agitation on "higher law" grounds, arguing that slavery being wrong, it was a duty to eradicate it, regardless of consequences. He threw a bomb-shell into the Republican ranks when he said that if slaves were rightfully held as property in the States, they were held with parity of right in the Territories.

The whole lecture was of the "fire-eating" order, after the fashion of the *Liberator,* and disgusting to all right-thinking and loyal citizens. He advocated the utopian and fatal idea of immediate emancipation—an idea impossible of itself and were it possible, full of disaster

for white and black alike. The Union he looked upon as "a covenant with death and an agreement with hell," and prayed for its dissolution. Slaveholders were abused with more violence and vulgarity than were exhibited in Sumner's defamatory oration, and all "doughfaces" were severely flagellated. To our minds exhibitions of this sort on the Sabbath are improper and disgraceful. . . . The large majority of those who met to listen to Garrison . . . went in the same spirit as they would visit a theater or other place of amusement. . . . We would not interfere with Mr. Garrison in the expression of his vagaries. They are so violent and extravagant, that in an intelligent community no harm can come of them. But in the name of a decent propriety we protest against the use of the Sabbath for such performances as were transacted in our City Hall last Sunday evening.

Editorial, Lawrence *[Massachusetts]* Sentinel, *July 7,
1860, regarding a speech by William Lloyd Garrison,
delivered July 1, 1860, as published in George M.
Frederickson, ed.,* William Lloyd Garrison,
pp. 114–115.

But I tell you here, today, that the institution of slavery must be sustained. The South has made up its mind to keep the black race in bondage. If we are not permitted to do this inside of the Union, I tell you that it will be done outside of it. Yes, sir, and we will expand this institution; we do not intend to be confined within our present limits; and there are not men enough in all your borders to coerce three million armed men in the South, and prevent their going into the surrounding territories. Well, sir, you ask me if we can preserve this institution out of the Union? That question is very frequently asked. I do not know what the result will be. I believe we can. I believe that, although fanaticism is rampant at the North, there is still good sense enough among the people to hold abolitionism in check, and prevent it from making personal war upon us whenever we make up our minds to secede peaceably from this Confederacy.

The gentlemen from Pennsylvania Mr. [HICKMAN] said the other day that they would coerce us. I would like to know if he will head the force that comes down for that purpose? He will remember that Mississippi acquired some character in the war with Mexico. He will recollect that we had a regiment of riflemen there, headed by JEFFERSON DAVIS, who still lives to lead, it may be, a southern army in defense of her rights. I would remind him, also, that there was Palmetto regiment from Southern Carolina that did some good service in the Mexican war. Other southern

States were represented there, and gained an immortality of renown. If he will but cast his eye back to these things, and then recollect that everything we have, and everything that we hold sacred and dear on earth, will be staked upon the issue, he must see at once that any attempt upon the part of the North to coerce us must result in bloodshed—I might say knee-deep—upon our borders. No, the North will never attempt to coerce us. Whenever the South makes up her mind to remain no longer in the confederation of States, we will say to you, "We want no bloodshed; we have nothing against you, if you will let us alone, we will shake hands with you, and walk out of this Confederacy bidding you God's blessing, and wishing that you may prosper; we will leave you in peace, and intend to make no war upon you." But if you undertake to make war upon us, first look well to the consequences. I believe there is still sufficient conservative feeling left in the North to prevent this state of things. Not only that, but I believe there are men upon this floor, from the North, over whose dead bodies you will be compelled to walk before you ever reach the South. But you will not attack us. You will not send down an army, and spend millions of dollars, for the purpose of reducing us to a condition worse than that of our slaves.

Otho Robards Singleton, speech during congressional campaigns of 1860, threatening a vigorous defense of the South if force is used, from Congressional Globe, *November 1860, as selected in Edwin Rozwenc,* Slavery as a Cause of the Civil War, *p. 21.*

2 Secession, Border States, and First Battles
December 1860–December 1861

In the weeks between the election of Abraham Lincoln to the presidency in November 1860 and his inauguration on March 4, 1861, the crisis that had been impending for at least a decade culminated in seven slave states making good their threat to secede. Lincoln's election precipitated the secession from the United States, first of South Carolina in December 1860, then of five more states between January 9 and February 1, 1861. The six states—South Carolina, Mississippi, Alabama, Florida, Georgia, and Louisiana—then sent delegates to a convention in Montgomery, Alabama, over the period February 4–9, to write a constitution and select a provisional president for the Confederate States of America. Texas seceded later in February and joined the Confederacy in early March.

SECESSION OR UNION

In retrospect, the secession of the seven states and the formation of the Confederacy can be stated succinctly as a straightforward set of events. At the time, however, as the news of the actions of separate states went by telegraph to daily and weekly newspapers across the country, no one could predict the outcome of the crisis and whether all or just a few of the slave states would declare secession. In Washington, congressional committees struggled unsuccessfully with ideas for compromise, including a constitutional amendment that would guarantee the continued existence of slavery. Some optimists suggested that the wisest course would be to let the hot-headed states of the Gulf South make their declarations, but to ignore them. Eventually, they argued, the movement for secession might run down and the states that had declared themselves out of the Union would one by one rejoin.

In 1861, there were only a few ways in which the federal presence was felt at the local level. Once a state recalled its senators and representatives from Washington, the only federal connections remaining between a state and the central government were the offices known as customs houses devoted to collecting tariffs on imported goods, U.S. post offices, and military installations such as arsenals, forts, and navy yards. In most cases, such facilities were staffed by very small detachments made up mostly of local citizens, so that if they agreed with the secession of their state, they could simply resign their federal positions and report to new local officials or turn over the keys, files, and weapons to new local appointees. In the army and navy, officers held commissions without expiration dates; they were free to resign at any time. Thus, if an officer from a seceding state wished to follow his state, he could simply resign his federal commission, and if his state or the new Confederacy wished to accept his offer of services, he could enlist for a similar or higher rank in either a state militia or in the provisional army or navy of the Confederate States of America after that government organized in February. For all of these reasons, secession was at first a bloodless action, represented by the departure of representatives from Washington, local seizure of federal military facilities, resignation of military officers from their posts, and the changing of the bureaucratic structure of the post offices and customs houses. If secession was an act of revolution, it was at first a revolution on paper, without gunfire, and done with all the dressings of legality rather than violence.

Even so, the acts of secession by state conventions called during these weeks were usually heated affairs, some held behind closed doors. Only in South Carolina did the convention vote unanimously to secede, on December 20. Elsewhere in the slave states, there were sizable minorities preferring to remain in the Union, and in several of the 15 slave states that view was represented by respectable majorities. Secessionists were discouraged at the size of the pro-Union vote in Georgia and Alabama, at the fact that Sam Houston, governor of Texas, refused to support a call for a state convention to secede, and that a secession convention had to be convened extra-legally there. Furthermore, the state legislature of Delaware firmly voted for remaining in the Union, and referenda called in Tennessee, Arkansas, and Missouri through mid-February all rejected secession.

In the states that voted for secession, secessionists themselves divided between *immediate* secessionists and *cooperationists*. On the surface, this difference meant that immediate secessionists argued for the action of their own single state without waiting for the formation of a confederation or joint action, while cooperationists believed that a state should secede only after there had been an interstate convention agreeing on joint action among a number of slave states. Immediatists accused cooperationists of being conservative, cowardly, or even of hiding their unionist sympathies behind a cloak of delay. Further, the immediatists argued that the right of individual states to secede could be constitutionally defended, but the formation of a group effort by states already in the Union could be construed as an illegal act of treason against the United States by individuals and states who had not already renounced that citizenship and the Union. To strengthen their arguments by presenting the conventions with a *fait accompli,* immediatists in some states, with support from militia officers and governors, acted before the conventions in taking over federal military facilities. Such prior seizures in Georgia, Alabama, Florida, and Louisiana made it difficult for cooperationists to prevail in those states. Nevertheless, convention members holding out for delay racked up respectable minorities in both Alabama and Georgia.

As the seven seceding states made good on their proclamations, they withdrew their congressmen and senators from Washington. With a firm free-state majority in the Senate after the departure of eight senators from South Carolina, Mississippi, Alabama, and Florida, the U.S. Senate passed the bill admitting Kansas as a free state, a bill that had been languishing in committee for a year since its introduction. President Buchanan signed that bill into law on January 29. Even with the departure of a few slave-state senators, it was clear that the federal government would be committed to, and take action on, the free-state positions advocated by Republicans over the previous few years. Among those resigning were Senator James Chesnut from South Carolina, whose wife Mary would leave a diary that became a classic of American literature, and Robert Toombs of Georgia, who was later defeated by former senator Jefferson Davis of Mississippi for the position of president of the Confederacy.

Thus, by mid-February, it appeared the movement for secession, although successful to an extent, had run into serious barriers, winning out only in seven of the 15 slave states, with one of its most notable effects being the sudden preponderance of antislavery voting strength in the Senate. In Texas, Governor Sam Houston continued to argue that the secession action in his state was illegal. Votes in referenda and conventions continued to run against secession in Missouri and Arkansas and, in late February, in North Carolina. Only in South Carolina, Georgia, and the four Gulf of Mexico states was secession more or less regularized by the action of a legally called state convention. From the point of view of president-elect Lincoln and other Republicans, even those regularly called conventions acted illegally when they voted for their states to secede from the Union. Their theory of secession, Lincoln and other Republicans believed, was based on an ingenious but specious argument. In Lincoln's view, the states were the creation of the United States during the American Revolution, and the argument that the states could invoke their own sovereignty to withdraw from the federal union was simply illegal and unconstitutional. Realizing that when Lincoln took office, he would be obliged by his own logic to attempt to enforce his views, the seceding states made military preparations for that event.

FORTS AND ARSENALS

In the seceding states, the governors activated state militia, often reenforced by the resignation from their commissions of officers in the U.S. Army. These forces took over various arsenals and forts throughout the Gulf states, in some cases as noted, even before the state declared its secession, as hotheads hoped to commit their more conservative and cooperationist colleagues. Takeovers in early 1861 included Fort Pulaski in Georgia on January 3, the Mount Vernon arsenal and local forts in Alabama on January 4 and 5, the Apalachicola arsenal in Florida on January 6, the Pensacola Navy Yard in Florida on January 15, the Augusta arsenal in Georgia on January 24, and all the federal forts and facilities in Texas by February 18.

Even with these military resources, the seven states of the Confederacy did not represent a very formidable nation, since those states were not the richest, most populous, or most developed part of the slaveholding South. The act of secession and formation of a new confederacy was viewed by some in the North as an irresponsible bluff in the weeks before the inauguration of Lincoln, one doomed to failure on economic grounds. Northern editorialists noted the marked lack of support for the Confederacy in Europe.

For outgoing president Buchanan or incoming president Lincoln to call the bluff with force, however, might tip the balance in the Upper South. Even many pro-unionists or cooperationists in the states of Tennessee, Arkansas, North Carolina, and Virginia believed that if the federal government took steps to coerce the Gulf states into giving up their acts of secession, such steps would require moving federal troops across their territory of the Upper South. If those Upper South states were to face such an invasion, many argued, the act of coercion would force them to join with their seceding sister states. Such sentiments were also shared by the governors of Missouri and Maryland, if not by majorities of the populations in those states. By mid- and late February, no one could predict with certainty how the crisis would evolve.

From the beginning of the secession crisis in December 1860 with the action of South Carolina, President James Buchanan had faced a crucial military question in that state. In the harbor of Charleston, federal forts were held by U.S. troops, serving under Major Robert Anderson, a Kentuckian who had no intention of resigning his commission. Quietly, on December 26, Anderson moved the garrison from Fort Moultrie on Sullivan's Island (easily reached by bridges) near the entrance of the harbor to the more isolated harbor island that housed the partially-completed Fort Sumter. For a period, Anderson could continue to purchase food and other supplies in the markets of Charleston, but Buchanan realized that Anderson's position was tenuous. On January 6, 1861, well before the organization of the Confederacy, when only South Carolina had taken any official action to secede, Buchanan ordered the navy to charter a ship and to send it with supplies, ammunition, and 200 troops to reinforce Anderson at Sumter. The departure of the *Star of the West* was an ill-kept secret, with newspapers describing how 200 marines remained belowdecks to conceal themselves. Consequently, when the steamer approached Charleston harbor on January 9, it was driven off by threatening shell fire from South Carolina batteries at Morris Island and Fort Moultrie that registered a few hits. Buchanan chose not to regard the firing on the private ship under navy charter as an act of war or rebellion by South Carolina, and these first shots of the Civil War faded almost unnoticed into history.

However, Fort Sumter remained an issue to be faced by the incoming president. If Lincoln were to emulate Buchanan's effort by sending in arms and men to the forts that remained in federal hands in the South, secessionists throughout the wavering states might see that as an act of coercion. If he did nothing, however, it seemed that Anderson would be starved out and that then the seceding states would be able to claim that they had established control over nearly every significant military installation within their territories, giving proof to the world that they had indeed established a separate sovereignty without opposition from the federal government. Some strong Union supporters in the North argued that the wise course would be to take no overt coercive act, thereby giving no cause for secession to the slave states that had not yet seceded. Others argued that a good slap would make the seceding states recognize they had been foolish to believe they could peacefully carve a separate nation out of the United States and that the place to do that would be in Charleston harbor.

The crisis over Fort Sumter would be only one of many dilemmas faced by Lincoln as he contemplated what he would do after his inauguration. He had time to consider such issues as he traveled by a roundabout route from Springfield, Illinois, to Washington over a two-week period in mid-February, giving speeches to welcoming crowds. Through Indianapolis, Cincinnati, Columbus, Cleveland, Pittsburgh, several towns in upstate New York, New York City then Trenton, Philadelphia, and Harrisburg, he did some thinking aloud about what he intended to say at his inaugural address, sometimes using the very phrases that would later appear in the carefully crafted speech delivered on March 4. Some of his statements contradicted others he made, as if he were testing out their logic in his own mind and before various audiences.

FROM BALLOTS TO BULLETS

During Lincoln's 12-day long railroad trip, the secession drama continued to unfold. Lincoln received word on February 13 that the Electoral College vote had been counted and that he was duly elected. Meanwhile, the Confederacy's organizing convention in Montgomery went ahead to select Jefferson Davis as provisional president of the Confederate States of America, and he was inaugurated to that position on February 18. The same day, elections in Arkansas and Missouri rejected secession. On February 22, Lincoln took a side trip from Philadelphia to Harrisburg, Pennsylvania, for his last address before proceeding to Washington. He heard rumors, forwarded to him from Allan Pinkerton, the head of a private detective agency, that plotters in Baltimore planned to kidnap or murder him; similar warnings came from General Winfield Scott, general in chief of the army. Taking the warnings seriously, Lincoln quietly rode in the express car of a night train through Baltimore, arriving in Washington at six in the morning. Whether or not the plotters were capable of carrying out such a scheme was much debated then and later, but in that unsettled situation when harebrained ideas could sometimes turn into action, probably Lincoln's caution was well-advised, even if it did cause him some embarrassment from hostile cartoons that showed him sneaking into Washington like a thief in the night. Before he was inaugurated March 4, word came that both Missouri (once again) and North Carolina had rejected secession. Unionists in North Carolina prayed that Lincoln would do nothing to discredit their position.

This cartoon depicts Seward losing the presidential nomination to Lincoln because of the machinations of Horace Greeley. *(Library of Congress, Prints and Photographs Division, LC-USZC2–2641)*

On March 4, Lincoln took the oath of office and delivered an address in which he condemned secession and pledged to hold federal properties. The crafting of his passage on federal properties was quite careful, and he modified his original strong position on advice from Senator Seward (soon to be his secretary of state) and others. However, Lincoln also made a point in his address that showed his fundamental grasp of the logical problem of secession. He denied the right of a minority to decide that it would not concur with a majority in a democracy. The very logic of secession relied on such a supposed right, and he pointed out that a nation premised on that principle would soon begin to come apart as minorities within it inevitably refused to concur in majority decisions. Indeed, whether the newly formed Confederacy could continue to exist when each state within it held the decision as to how much and even whether it would contribute to the joint effort, did in fact remain a central issue over the following four years. In one sense, Lincoln's inaugural speech foretold an underlying flaw in the theory of the Confederacy that in the end would be a central factor in its downfall.

Through the next weeks, as Lincoln organized his administration and dealt politely with suggestions from Secretary of State Seward, who indicated that he would be willing to run the government, the crisis at Fort Sumter continued to simmer. A secession convention elected in February met in Virginia and seemed inclined to follow the pattern of the other states in the Upper South, rejecting secession. However, the Virginia convention sought some assurance that Lincoln would not employ coercion against the seceding states and remained in session through the first weeks of his administration to watch events.

On April 6, Lincoln decided on a modified version of Buchanan's plan to assert control over Fort Sumter by sending a supply ship. This time, however, Lincoln did not attempt a secret mission, but instead openly notified the governor of South Carolina, Francis Pickens, and Confederate general Pierre Gustave Toutant Beauregard of the ship's orders. On March 1, Beauregard had resigned his U.S. Army commission and accepted a position as brigadier general in the Confederate army, and he was in charge of organizing secession military forces in Charleston. Beauregard and Pickens received Lincoln's notification on April 8 that he was sending a supply ship, without troops or ammunition, to Fort Sumter; by telegram they questioned Jefferson Davis in Montgomery as to what action, if any, should be taken. Davis and his cabinet faced a problem that had been created by Lincoln's notification of his plans, one of the many dilemmas that Lincoln had a knack in creating for those who opposed him. If Davis and his cabinet did nothing, the United States would have demonstrated that it could send a naval ship into Charleston Harbor, the heart of the Confederacy, and the federal fort would remain as proof that the Confederacy did not control its own territory. On the other hand, if the secession government waited for the ship to arrive and then opened fire on it, it would be undertaking an act of war, making it clear that its actions were not merely legalistic and constitutional niceties. Davis chose a third course, to demand immediately that Major Anderson abandon the fort or face bombardment. If he consented, the Confederacy would have made good its control without gunfire. It was a gamble.

On April 10, Beauregard received his instructions from Montgomery and delivered his ultimatum to Major Anderson on the 11th. Anderson refused to surrender, although he indicated that he would run out of supplies in a few more days and be forced for that reason to leave the fort. However, acting under his orders from Montgomery, Beauregard ordered the shore batteries to open fire on the fort at 4:30

On April 12, 1861, the firing on Fort Sumter converted a constitutional crisis into an act of armed rebellion. *(Library of Congress, Prints and Photographs Division, LC-USZC4–528)*

in the morning on April 12, 1861, and he watched the bombardment from a house still standing on the waterfront of Charleston. Thus began the war. After 34 hours of bombardment, Anderson surrendered the damaged and partially burned fort. There were no casualties except for one man killed when a gun accidentally exploded during the honorary gun salute ordered by Anderson as the troops marched out of the fort. Although the bombardment had not killed or wounded anyone, the outbreak of the war is dated from the morning of April 12. From the perspective of the Confederate states, war had broken out between two established nations; from the perspective of the Union, the Confederates had undertaken an act of rebellion.[1]

THE BORDER STATES

The nature of the decision and action was crucial in determining the course of action in the rest of the slave states. Although Delaware had already voted firmly to reject secession, and several other slave states had held either elections or conventions that refused to join in secession, the episode of Fort Sumter altered the situation. In most of the North, and to varying extents in the wavering border states, some saw the firing on Fort Sumter as a clear act of rebellion. Lincoln himself saw it that way, and issued a call for 75,000 volunteers for the army. In Virginia, Lincoln's call for volunteers was perceived as an act of intended coercion, and secessionists won the day. The Virginia convention declared cooperation with the Confederacy on April 17 by a two-thirds majority, and secession itself was confirmed a month later by a popular vote of about three to one. New votes in Arkansas for secession on May 6 and in Tennessee for cooperation with the Confederacy on May 7 put those states on the side of the Confederacy. North Carolina, the last to secede, did so on May 20. In Missouri, Governor Claiborne Jackson favored secession, but the legislature and federal authorities stymied his effort to take over the federal arsenal in St. Louis. Jackson fled with a group of supporters to Neosho in southern Missouri. There a rump legislature voted to secede and join the Confederacy, but Missouri remained largely under federal control throughout the next few years.

Although by the end of May 1861 it had become clear that 11 states had seceded and joined the Confederacy, the specifics of how they reached the decision, in several cases after votes for remaining in the Union, showed that the political foundation of the Confederacy was on shaky ground. Despite the rhetoric of the more hot-headed secessionists, the step-by-step and reluctant secession of Tennessee, Virginia, North Carolina, and Arkansas and the divisive debates between immediatists and cooperationists in the Gulf states reflected the basic constitutional difficulties faced by the Confederacy. Perhaps most importantly, each state had acted independently in severing its ties with the Union; as a consequence, the Confederacy was not quite a single sovereign nation, but a confederation or alliance of 11 states each claiming its own sovereignty, and each claiming the right to make its own independent decisions. Over the next four years, as the Confederacy fought the Union, political leaders in the South struggled simultaneously over whether and to what extent to convert the Confederacy into a single nation.[2]

In the North, the question of the status of three of the four slave states, the border states, still seemed anomalous. The Delaware legislature had voted to remain in the Union, so that situation seemed clear enough, even though several local militia units in that state formed with the intent of supporting the Confederacy. Kentucky would at first vote to remain neutral in the conflict, but after facing an invasion of Tennessee troops, the Kentucky legislature reluctantly supported the Union cause. Missouri, torn by internal civil war, was occupied with federal troops. Its Southwestern counties bordering on Kansas and Arkansas continued to harbor units of the former border ruffians who had invaded Kansas during the 1850s. Several bands of these irregulars organized and grew, fighting

The town of Lawrence, Kansas, suffered from a devastating raid by William Quantrill and his guerrillas in 1863. It had earlier been attacked by border ruffians from Missouri. *(Library of Congress, Prints and Photographs Division, LC-USZ62–132750)*

Confederate sympathizers in Baltimore rioted and attacked U.S. troops on their way to Washington. *(Library of Congress, Prints and Photographs Division, LC-USZ62–133073)*

on the Confederate side, raiding pro-Union settlements in Kansas and Missouri, and running attacks against Union army patrols. The most notorious of these guerrilla forces was led by William Quantrill. Quantrill's force, numbering as few as 20 and as many as several hundred at its peak, sometimes slaughtered unarmed civilians or Union soldiers attempting to surrender, and he was eventually treated by the Union as a wanted outlaw.[3]

Maryland was the most crucial of the border slave states that had not seceded. With the U.S. capital carved out of Maryland on its Potomac River border with Virginia, in the District of Columbia, access to the national capital depended on transit through this slave state. Although western Maryland was firmly unionist, and the state capital, Annapolis, was strongly in Union hands with the Naval Academy located there, southern tobacco counties like Charles County and the city of Baltimore harbored strong pro-Confederate elements. The governor, the mayor of Baltimore, and several state legislators were open Confederate sympathizers, as were some leaders and units of the state militia.

As federal troops of the 6th Massachusetts Regiment traveled through Baltimore on their way to Washington on April 19, they had to move through the streets of the city from one train station to another. There, local pro-secession mobs tore up the paving blocks, constructed barricades, and attacked the troops. In the ensuing gunfire and hand-to-hand clashes with bayonets and knives, four soldiers and 12 locals were killed and dozens more were wounded. On the approval of the mayor and the governor, elements of the state militia began burning railroad bridges to prevent further transit of Union forces to Washington, excusing their actions on the grounds that they sought to avoid future riotous disturbances. With such support from the mayor of Baltimore, it appeared in mid-April that the action of Marylanders might cut off Washington, surrounding it with Confederate sympathizers and bringing an early victory to the secessionists. However, federal troops began arriving in Annapolis by ship, then used uncut rail lines that ran from Annapolis to Washington and bypassed Baltimore.

FIRST BLOODSHED

As troops poured into Washington, the presence of Confederates directly across the Potomac River in Alexandria, Virginia, presented a potential threat. Embarrassingly, Confederate flags flew prominently over several buildings there, quite visible from the Washington side of the Potomac. Finally, on May 24, a unit of volunteers, the brightly uniformed 11th New York Zouaves, recruited by a rising and ambitious young politician, Colonel Ephraim Ellsworth, marched into Alexandria to take the city for the Union. Ellsworth, who had previously clerked in Lincoln's law office in Springfield, Illinois, had led a campaign to recruit troops, and he had popularized the concept of troops dressed in uniforms matching the zouave outfits of the French in North Africa, with baggy red trousers and a bright blue jacket. Ellsworth had accompanied Lincoln on the long train trip from Springfield to Washington, acting as a sort of travel manager. Ellsworth's flair for publicity had earned him repute in the North as a future Napoleon and in the South as a recruiter of rowdies from among the notoriously tough New York firemen. Although he had no real military training or experience, he had become a national figure through his colorful recruiting and his personal association with Lincoln.

Ellsworth proceeded directly to the Marshall House hotel, which flew a large Confederate flag from a tall pole on its roof. He rushed to the roof, hauled down the flag, and brought it downstairs. There he was met by the proprietor of the hotel, James T. Jackson, who shot him dead with a shotgun. Almost instantly, one of Ellsworth's privates shot and killed Jackson. Ellsworth was the Union's first notable casualty, and Jackson was the Confederacy's first martyr. Lincoln openly mourned the death of the Zouave colonel, ordering that Ellsworth's body be laid in state in the White House before being taken to upstate New York for burial.

In the North, Ellsworth was a tragic symbol of the national cause, while in the South, the hotel proprietor was viewed as a defender of Southern rights against ruthless invaders. Although troops had been killed in Baltimore a month before, the death of four enlisted men at the hands of a mob did not resonate with the public as much as the death of a well-known officer while in the symbolic act of removing a Confederate flag. News items North and South focused on Ephraim Elmer Ellsworth, little realizing that his death and that of James Jackson would be followed by more than 600,000 others. Alexandria was secured for federal occupation, with Union pickets on the roads out of town warily eyeing Confederate outposts in the Arlington hills beyond, toward Warrenton and Manassas.

MERRYMAN

In late April, Lincoln issued an order allowing military arrests without trial of civilians engaged in any attempt to disrupt the remaining communication lines through Maryland. In Baltimore, General George Cadwalader,

Colonel Elmer Ellsworth was the first Union officer to die in the Civil War, shot at the Marshall House Inn in Alexandria as he removed the Confederate flag from the building. This print shows Corporal Frank Brownell immediately shooting Ellsworth's assailant, hotel proprietor James Jackson. Ellsworth was hailed as a martyr in the Union cause, and Jackson as a martyr in the Confederate cause. *(Library of Congress, Prints and Photographs Division, LC-USZC2–2231)*

based at Fort McHenry, soon found himself in the midst of a major confrontation over this order, which suspended the writ of habeas corpus.

Under the U.S. Constitution, an individual cannot be held in prison in the United States without a hearing before a judge, in which the authorities are to produce in court both the accused individual and the charges against him. If a person is arrested and not brought before a judge within a short period, he can ask a judge to secure a writ of habeas corpus, that is, an order from the judge to bring the person and the charges to court. In this way, if the charges are regarded by the judge as not based on sufficient cause, the judge can release the accused from custody at the court. The privilege of a writ of habeas corpus was one of the few rights specifically enumerated in the Constitution itself, in Article I, rather than in the amendments constituting the Bill of Rights. The wording in Article I of the Constitution, however, states that the privilege can be suspended in cases of rebellion or invasion when the public safety may require it. The Constitution does not specify whether the power to suspend resides with the president or Congress. Faced with the uprising in Baltimore and evidence of support for secession elsewhere in states that had not yet seceded, Lincoln ordered General Winfield Scott, general in command of the army, to suspend the writ as necessity demanded.

John Merryman, a leader in the Maryland Horse Guards, had been recruiting pro-Confederate Marylanders and had used his force to tear down telegraph lines and burn bridges during the April confrontation over sending federal troops through Maryland. Arrested on order of a Pennsylvania officer, Merryman was locked up in Fort McHenry. His lawyer petitioned Judge Roger Taney, Chief Justice of the Supreme Court and head of the federal court in Baltimore, for a writ. Taney, outraged at what he saw as Lincoln's usurpation of power, ordered Merryman produced in court. General Cadwalader refused, and Taney sat down to write an opinion condemning the suspension of the writ, *Ex parte Merryman,* which did not have the effect of releasing Merryman, but which became a classic document of civil liberties. Cadwalader simply ordered the guards at Fort McHenry to refuse entry to representatives of Taney's court. Several months later, the military authorities turned Merryman over to the civil courts; he then posted bail, and his case never came to trial.[4]

Roger B. Taney, Chief Justice of the Supreme Court, ruled in the *Merryman* case that the president did not have the power to suspend habeas corpus. Nevertheless, Lincoln continued to order arrests without trial of known and suspected Confederate sympathizers, especially in Maryland *(Library of Congress, Prints and Photographs Division, LC-USZ62–107588)*

THE LINES ARE DRAWN, FIRST BATTLES

With Maryland increasingly under Federal control with U.S. troops and some militia units coming in from Pennsylvania, the line between the Confederacy and the Union began to be clearer. The Confederate Congress adjourned in May, voting to reassemble in July in Richmond, Virginia, making it the new national capital of the 11-state Confederacy. Lincoln and his advisers were well aware that the South was severely divided over the question of secession, and that in a stretch of counties through the southern Appalachian Mountain chain, the absence of slaveholders and long-standing resentment at the domination of the states by powerful plantation interests could work in favor of the Union. From western Virginia in the North, southward in a broad sweep through eastern Tennessee, western North Carolina and into the hill country of northern Alabama and Georgia, unionist voters and non-slaveholding farmers held the potential for splitting the Confederacy. One early effort to tap this potential succeeded.

Under General George McClellan and later General William Rosecrans, Union troops moving in from Ohio drove Confederate forces out of West Virginia, in the small but important battles of Philippi, June 3, and Rich Mountain, July 11. In a constitutionally peculiar procedure, a convention met in Wheeling, in western Virginia, declared itself the legislature of the whole state of Virginia, rescinded the secession of the state, declared that secession illegal, and then authorized the formation of a new state, West Virginia, consisting of 50 counties in the mountainous, largely non-slaveholding part of the state. Under Article IV, section 3 of the U.S. Constitution, no new state could be formed out of an existing state without the permission of that state's legislature, hence the necessity of formally declaring a Virginia government before creating the new state. This process of secession within secession was later recognized by Congress, admitting West Virginia to the Union in 1863. The Wheeling action was affirmed by a federal court in 1870, ruling that as a practical and technically constitutional procedure, the process had been legitimate. In this fashion, West Virginia became a fifth loyal border state, one that retained slavery but sided with the Union.[5]

The two victories securing West Virginia for the Union were the last Union army victories of any consequence for many months. Over summer and fall 1861, Confederates stood off several minor attempts and one major attempt at a Union advance into Virginia. The Union held Fortress Monroe near Norfolk, Virginia. Under General Benjamin Butler, a former Massachusetts politician, Union forces attempted to move inland and were turned back in a skirmish at Big Bethel. Butler was removed from command for the failure, but would restore his reputation later that summer when his troops aboard naval ships were present when Confederates were driven from two forts in Hatteras Inlet in North Carolina. Such seacoast positions became quite useful in enforcing a blockade of the seceding states, announced by Lincoln in April. Other naval forces secured Ship Island off the Gulf Coast of Mississippi in September, while another expedition took Port Royal, off Georgia, in November. Facilities in these locations helped extend the blockade.

Meanwhile, in a major debacle, Union troops under General Irvin McDowell suffered a defeat at Manassas in Virginia on July 20–21, known in the North as the First Battle of Bull Run. There, after some initial advances, federal troops ran into stiff resistance on Henry House Hill by Confederate troops under Brigadier General Thomas J. Jackson, who refused to move his men. There his brigade stood like a stone wall, commented Confederate Bernard Bee before dying of his wounds, apparently bitter that Jackson's troops did not move to support his own retreating brigade. Henceforth, General Jackson was known as Stonewall Jackson, in North and South, and his brigade, the 1st Virginia, became known as the Stonewall Brigade. Civilians from Washington had expected an easy victory and many, including some members of Congress, had ridden out to the battlefield in carriages with picnic baskets to view the event. Stunned, they fled, helping to

The First Battle of Bull Run, also known as First Manassas, destroyed the reputation of the Union's General Irwin McDowell and established the legend of Stonewall Jackson. *(Library of Congress, Prints and Photographs Division, LC-USZ62–5454)*

choke the roads with their vehicles as wounded troops and disorganized units stumbled back to Centreville, Washington, and safety. To rebuild and better train the Union army, Lincoln replaced McDowell with General George McClellan, fresh from his West Virginia victory at Philippi.

Although about 18,000 troops on each side faced each other at Manassas, the Union lost about 2,700 killed, wounded, and missing, while the Confederacy lost less than 2,000 in all three categories. Colonel William T. Sherman tried to rally his troops, and, as he marched with them back to camp, he had to threaten to shoot one junior officer in order to prevent him from simply going home. While the battle represented a Confederate victory, Southern forces were too badly disorganized to follow up with an attack on Washington. As later analysts have noted, the pattern of failure to follow up on a victory recurred over and over through the war, usually because the surviving soldiers on the victorious side were as physically and morally exhausted as the losers.

In a second debacle, in October, Colonel Edward Baker of the 71st Pennsylvania Infantry, a former Republican politician, attempted to lead a federal force across the Potomac River above Washington to cut into Virginia and take Leesburg. He made several miscalculations, however. He did not understand the difficulty of crossing the river, and he choose a terrible spot for his advance against Confederate troops holding high ground at Ball's Bluff on the Virginia side. Baker was killed, along with some 48 of his troops. Over 700 of his men were missing and presumed drowned or captured, and another 158 wounded. The misadventure had been ordered by General Charles Stone, who soon found himself in trouble with Congress. Stone had set a policy of returning slaves to their owners when he found them escaping to his lines and camps, and word of this practice, together with the overall failure at Ball's Bluff where he had not ordered reserve troops to go to Baker's aid, gave Congress reason to believe he was pro-Southern. Congress formed a special group, the Committee for the Prosecution of the War, and that committee urged the secretary of war to arrest Stone.

BALANCE OF POWER

The army on both sides had expanded rapidly, with commissions going to many inexperienced leaders, either selected by state governors or elected by their units. As a consequence former state and national legislators, with very little background or understanding of the military art, found themselves facing decisions as generals that would have tremendous ramifications for operations. Recruiters like Ellsworth and elected militia officers, with some experience as political leaders but completely ignorant of military discipline and tactics, accounted for dozens of poor decisions that led to confusion, lost battles, tangled communications, and botched battles on both sides. Morale declined as inexperienced officers had the troops repeatedly go through close order drill exercises that seemed to the recruits to have little practical value, frequently under miserable conditions of excessive heat, deep sand, or slashing rain and deep mud. Unlike inexperienced officers, trained officers understood the necessity of keeping units together and firing their weapons correctly, as communication by word of mouth between officers and men on the firing line was crucial and depended on maintaining discipline. In the first months of the war, troops from both sides marched long distances or traveled by freight cars, often arriving to find no provision for an encampment, no food, shelter, or even drinking water available. Under these conditions, thousands fell sick and hundreds died before the first battles.

Both the Union and Confederate armies had dozens of officers, graduates of West Point, Virginia Military Institute, or the Citadel in Charleston, and some of them veterans with experience in the war with Mexico. Even so, not all trained West Point or other academy graduates and veteran officers measured up to the demands of the war. Eventually, as the war ground on and incompetents either got themselves killed or demoted for their failures, a process of selection slowly tended to produce more effective officers on the Northern side. On the Southern side, some of the best officers were killed in the first two years of the war. Yet professional West Point training and Mexican War experience did not always yield an understanding of how the war had to be fought. At West Point, Professor Dennis Hart Mahan drilled students according to the tactics of Napoleon, which had become somewhat outmoded by rifled muskets, more effective artillery, railroad transportation, and other developments.

Some Northern editorialists believed at the time that the Confederacy had little or no chance to succeed militarily against the Union. Knowing in retrospect that the Confederacy lost, historians and students for generations have pondered the issue of why Southern leaders believed they could win. Some contemporary observers and many later analysts thought a Northern victory was such an obviously foregone conclusion that it made the Confederate effort seem irrational or foolhardy from the beginning. Others have dug deeper into the issue, and have pointed out that despite some surface appearances of superior Northern strength, there were several logical reasons for Confederate leaders to believe they had a chance to win the conflict.

Certainly the North seemed stronger in industrial capacity, population, and in statistics such as miles of completed and functioning railroad track and numbers of railroad engines and cars. Several factors made that preponderance deceptive, however. Some of the population in the free states lived in the west, in California, Oregon, and Washington. Although units from these and other areas of the mountain West fought on the Union side, the distance of the region from the conflict limited their numbers and the involvement of the economies of those regions. Furthermore, the presence of more than 3 million slaves in the South turned out to represent an asset to the Confederacy, especially in the first two years of the conflict. Slave labor continued to work farms and plantations, freeing a higher proportion of the white population to participate in the conflict. Although the industrial capacity of the North was far greater than the South, the weapons technology of the period did not require a sophisticated industrial base. Muskets, powder, bullets, and horse-drawn smoothbore cannon could be manufactured readily in existing and newly-built Southern facilities, and many weapons were captured from Union forces. Close analysis of all the land battles during the war revealed that the Confederates never lost a battle because of lack of ammunition, powder, shot, or shell, although their lack of other supplies, such as food, transport equipment, shoes, and clothing often weakened their position.

On the broadest level, the task of the Confederates was easier in some respects than that of the Union forces. All the Confederates had to do to make their point of establishing national independence was to fight a defensive war, holding territory and falling back as needed until the federal forces were worn down and recognized the existence of the new nation. By contrast, the Union had to invade and conquer the entire Confederacy. Weapons and tactics of the era tended to favor the defense. Furthermore, as Northern troops advanced into the South, they would be occupying hostile territory, which would require leaving behind garrisons and troops to police against domestic uprising and to protect lines of transport and supply from raids, decreasing the numbers available for engagement on the advancing front. For such reasons, from a strictly military or balance of forces point of view, the chances for victory of the Confederacy were not an empty fantasy.

Furthermore, while the South faced discontent and pro-unionist sentiment in Appalachia with varying degrees of non-cooperation, the North harbored large-scale sympathy for the South in the border states and Copperhead, or pro-Southern, sections of Ohio, Illinois, and Indiana. Even more crucial was the fact that slave states, Kentucky, Missouri, Maryland, and Delaware, and the newly severed West Virginia, were strongly divided. Even committed unionists in those states remained angry at more radical Republicans who saw the Civil War as a chance to bring slavery to an end. Lincoln had campaigned for the presidency on a platform committed to allowing slavery to exist where it was already legal. Thus his support among radical Republicans in Congress was tempered by concern that he would show too much consideration to slaveholders; his support in the border states was tempered by fear that the radicals would convince him to take actions against the institution of slavery. He walked a fine line on this question, and Confederates recognized the political challenges he faced. All such issues were the subject of numerous editorials, news items, and public discussions.

The recruitment and retention of troops in the North ran into trouble, with soldiers who signed up for a three-month commitment expecting to walk away, as the officer under Sherman attempted to do. Indications that the North employed despotic methods such as suspension of rights that could stir discontent and weaken Northern morale, together with early Southern victories on the field of battle, gave Confederates further causes for optimism that were not entirely unrealistic. For the Union to win would require not only improved military command, but also intelligent political leadership, difficult but correct decisions, and staying power.

CHRONICLE OF EVENTS

1860

December 20: South Carolina convention unanimously declares secession.

December 26: Major Robert Anderson (USA) spikes the guns at Fort Moultrie and moves his garrison from there to Fort Sumter in Charleston harbor.

December 28: South Carolina commissioners demand from President James Buchanan that U.S. troops be removed from Charleston harbor and that all U.S. military installations in South Carolina be turned over to the state.

December 30: South Carolina troops take over the U.S. arsenal at Charleston.

December 31: President Buchanan refuses to cede federal forts to South Carolina.

1861

January 2: The lower house of the Delaware legislature unanimously rejects secession; upper house endorses rejection 5 to 3.

January 3: Georgia troops east of Savannah take over Fort Pulaski.

January 4: Alabama troops take over the Mount Vernon arsenal in Alabama.

January 5: Alabama troops take over Fort Morgan and Fort Gaines.

January 5: At the orders of President James Buchanan, the chartered supply ship *Star of the West* steams from New York to Fort Sumter with 200 troops aboard.

January 6: Florida troops take over the Apalachicola arsenal.

January 7: Florida troops take over Fort Marion in St. Augustine.

January 9: *Star of the West* is repulsed by South Carolina batteries from Morris Island and Fort Moultrie; this action is not treated by the U.S. government as an act of war or rebellion.

January 9: A Mississippi state convention declares secession by a vote of 85 to 15.

January 10: Florida state convention declares secession by a vote of 62 to 7.

January 10: Louisiana troops take the Baton Rouge arsenal and barracks.

January 11: Alabama convention declares secession by a vote of 61 to 39.

January 15: Joint Alabama and Florida troops take over the U.S. navy yard at Pensacola, Florida, and nearby Fort Barrancas; no shots are fired.

January 19: Georgia convention declares secession by a vote of 208 to 89.

January 21: Six U.S. senators, from the states of Florida, Mississippi, and Alabama, depart from the Senate because of the secession of their states.

January 21: The Senate, after departure of a total of eight Southern senators (including two from South Carolina), now approves a bill previously submitted by Senator Seward in February 1860, admitting Kansas as a free state to the Union under the October 1859 Wyandotte Constitution. The House of Representatives had passed a similar bill admitting Kansas as a free state in April 1860.

January 24: Georgia troops take the Augusta arsenal.

January 26: A Louisiana state convention declares secession by a vote of 113 to 17.

January 28: The House of Representatives passes the bill as amended by the Senate admitting Kansas as a free state and sends the act to the president.

January 29: President Buchanan signs the bill admitting Kansas as a free state. Statehood is proclaimed.

February 1: An irregularly called state convention in Texas declares secession by vote of 166 to 8, over objections of Governor Sam Houston. (The act of secession is confirmed by a popular vote held on February 23.)

February 1: The U.S. Mint and Customs House in New Orleans is taken by state authorities.

February 4–9: Representatives of six seceding states meet in a convention in Montgomery, Alabama; they establish a constitution of the Confederate States of America; elect Jefferson Davis as provisional president and Alexander Stephens as provisional vice president.

February 4: A convention is called in Virginia to consider secession, but it holds off action.

February 7: The Choctaw Nation in Indian Territory adheres to the Confederacy.

February 8: Arkansas troops take over the arsenal at Little Rock.

February 9: A state referendum in Tennessee rejects a call for a convention to consider secession, by a vote of 69,387 to 57,798.

February 11–23: Lincoln's trip from Springfield to Washington proceeds via Indianapolis, Cincinnati, Columbus, Cleveland, Pittsburgh, Buffalo, Rochester, Syracuse, Albany, Troy, New York City, Trenton, Philadelphia, and Harrisburg.

February 13: Lincoln receives word that the Electoral College vote declaring him president has been officially counted.

February 16: Texas troops take the San Antonio arsenal.

February 18: All U.S. military posts in Texas are surrendered to the state.

February 18: Jefferson Davis is inaugurated as provisional president of the Confederacy.

February 18: In Arkansas a secession convention elects a majority of Unionists.

February 18: An election in Missouri selects a pro-Union slate of delegates to a state convention.

February 22: Lincoln is warned by Allan Pinkerton and others of a plot to kidnap or assassinate him in Baltimore; he travels incognito on a night train.

February 23: Lincoln arrives in Washington, D.C., at 6 A.M.

February 23: A Texas referendum endorses secession 44,317 in favor, 13,020 opposed.

February 28: A Missouri convention meets and rejects secession.

Founder of a still extant private detective agency, Allan Pinkerton set up an espionage unit known as the Secret Service. After retirement, Pinkerton wrote dime detective novels, and this portrait was made during his career as a writer. *(Library of Congress, Prints and Photographs Division, LC-USZ62–117576)*

February 28: A North Carolina referendum defeats a call to a secession convention.

March 1: The president of the Confederate States takes control of military affairs in seven states: Alabama, Florida, Georgia, Louisiana, Mississippi, South Carolina, and Texas.

March 2: Texas is formally admitted to the Confederacy.

March 4: Lincoln is inaugurated as president of the United States; in his inaugural address he denounces secession and pledges to hold federal properties.

March 5: Another convention in Texas approves joining the Confederacy, which had already admitted Texas three days earlier.

March 18: Governor Sam Houston of Texas, who opposes secession, is dismissed from office; Lieutenant Governor Edward Clark succeeds him.

March 22: An abortive effort is led by Governor Claiborne F. Jackson to have Missouri secede from the United States and join the Confederacy.

April 6: Lincoln notifies Governor Pickens of South Carolina and General Beauregard that he is sending a ship on the way to provision Fort Sumter, but that it has no troops or arms aboard.

April 8: Governor Pickens and General Beauregard receive Lincoln's notification of intent to resupply Fort Sumter that was sent on the 6th.

April 9: Jefferson Davis and his cabinet at Montgomery, Alabama, receive Lincoln's notification and decide that Fort Sumter should be taken before the relief ship arrives.

April 10: General Beauregard receives his orders from Davis.

April 11: South Carolina requests that Major Anderson surrender Fort Sumter; he refuses, but notes that he will have to abandon the fort in a few days, after exhausting his supplies.

April 12: Shore batteries open fire on Fort Sumter at 4:30 A.M.; the Civil War begins at this date and hour.

April 13: Major Anderson surrenders Fort Sumter at 2:30 P.M. after 34-hour bombardment; 5,000 artillery shells are fired with no casualties.

April 14: Major Anderson marches out of Fort Sumter; during the honorary gunfire salute, one soldier is killed and several others wounded by an accidental gun explosion.

April 15: Lincoln declares insurrection; he calls for 75,000 volunteers.

April 17: The Virginia convention by a vote of 103 to 46 agrees to cooperate militarily with the Confederacy on the basis of Lincoln's call for volunteers and seeks a referendum on secession.

April 19: Lincoln declares a blockade of seceded states: South Carolina, Georgia, Alabama, Florida, Mississippi, Louisiana, and Texas.

April 19: A mob attacks the 6th Massachusetts Regiment passing through Baltimore: four are killed, 36 wounded; 12 Marylanders are killed in the encounter. Members of the pro-Confederate state militia destroy rail lines and bridges.

April 20: Robert E. Lee declines General Winfield Scott's offer of Union command and resigns his U.S. Army commission.

April 27: Lincoln authorizes General Winfield Scott to suspend habeas corpus in certain circumstances and to make arrests to protect the rail line from Annapolis to Washington. Under suspension of writ of habeas corpus, the mayor of Baltimore and 19 state legislators are arrested over the next few weeks.

April 27: Lincoln extends the blockade to include Virginia and North Carolina.

May 1: Governor Isham Harris of Tennessee calls upon the state General Assembly for a vote of alliance with the Confederacy.

May 6: Arkansas secedes despite an earlier vote to remain in the Union.

May 7: Tennessee legislature approves military liaison with the Confederacy despite an earlier vote on February 9, in an action similar to that in Virginia; Tennessee calls for a referendum on official secession.

May 7: Virginia is admitted to the Confederacy.

May 9: The British government receives William Yancey and Pierre Rost, Confederate commissioners.

May 10: Captain Nathaniel Lyon, leading Union troops, takes Camp Jackson on the outskirts of St. Louis, Missouri.

May 13: Britain declares neutrality but recognizes the belligerent status of the Confederacy.

Jefferson Davis shifted the members of the Confederacy's cabinet in and out of office several times. *(Library of Congress, Prints and Photographs Division, LC-USZ62–132563)*

May 20: North Carolina secedes despite the February 28 vote; the four states of the Upper South have seceded (or offered to cooperate militarily with the Confederacy) on the grounds that the Union had attempted to "coerce" the seven states of the Gulf. Secession of North Carolina makes it the 11th and last state to join the Confederacy; later popular votes in Virginia (May 23) and Tennessee (June 8) confirm actions already implemented by the state governments.

May 20: The Kentucky legislature votes to remain neutral.

May 21: The Confederate Congress adjourns in Montgomery, Alabama, and plans to reconvene two months later at Richmond, Virginia, making that city the capital of the Confederacy.

May 21: Charles Francis Adams, U.S. minister to Britain, protests the British position of recognition of belligerent status of the Confederacy; Britain pledges not to receive Confederate commissioners again.

May 23: A Virginia referendum approves secession by a vote of 96,750 in favor, 32,134 opposed.

May 24: A unit of Union troops, New York Fire Zouaves, led by Colonel Ephraim Ellsworth, takes Alexandria, Virginia, across the Potomac from Washington; Ellsworth is killed, the first Union officer killed in the war, when he attempts to take down a Confederate flag at the Marshall House hotel. Ellsworth's body is laid in state at the White House.

May 25: Pennsylvania troops arrest John Merryman, lieutenant in the Maryland Horse Guards, who had actively led the resistance of Marylanders to Union forces in April.

May 27: Merryman's application for a writ of habeas corpus to Chief Justice Roger Taney results in Taney ordering Merryman to be produced in court.

May 28: An attempt by court officials to obtain release of Merryman from imprisonment in Fort McHenry is rebuffed by military guards. General George Cadwalader refuses to obey the court order. Taney issues the opinion *Ex Parte Merryman* denying that the president has the power to suspend habeas corpus. Merryman will be transferred to civil courts on July 13; he will be granted bail and his case eventually dropped.

June: The Confederate government moves to Richmond.

June 1: Britain forbids the navy of either side in the American Civil War from bringing prize ships to British ports.

June 3: General McClellan leads troops who successfully clear Confederates from the Valley of the Kanawah at the Battle of Philippi, West Virginia.

June 8: A Tennessee referendum, or plebiscite, approves an act of secession by 104,913 to 47,238 votes; opposition to secession is concentrated in eastern Tennessee, which will try unsuccessfully to secede from Tennessee over the following months.

June 10: Union forces under General Benjamin Butler march from Fortress Monroe inland to a skirmish at Big Bethel where they are repulsed by Confederates. Butler is relieved of his command for the failure.

June 11–June 19: A convention at Wheeling, West Virginia, meets to organize a Union state government, declaring the secession of Virginia void on June 17 and selecting Francis Pierpont as governor on June 19. West Virginia, consisting of 50 northwestern counties of Virginia, will be admitted as a state to the Union, June 20, 1863.

July 4: Lincoln sends a message to Congress describing secession as an ingenious sophism and outlining his response to it, including his decision to suspend habeas corpus.

July 5: Attorney General Edward Bates issues an opinion supporting suspension of habeas corpus by Lincoln following the firing on Fort Sumter. About 18,000 individuals are arrested under the suspension throughout the North, including some 13,000 in Maryland.

July 11: General William Clarke Rosecrans leads a Union victory at Rich Mountain, West Virginia.

July 17: Confederate troops under General Joseph E. Johnston move by rail on the Manassas Gap Railroad to Bull Run, the first strategic movement of troops by train in history.

July 20–21: First Battle of Bull Run/Manassas is fought, resulting in Confederate victory. Confederates under Thomas J. Jackson resist the Union advance; his resistance earns him the name "Stonewall."

July 24: Union general Irvin McDowell, whose forces were defeated at Bull Run, is replaced by General George McClellan.

August 7: U.S. Navy authorizes the construction of seven ironclad gunboats.

August 10: A battle is fought at Wilson's Creek, Missouri, in which Union general Nathaniel Lyon is killed.

August 16: Lincoln forbids U.S. trade with states in secession.

August 27–29: Union forces under Benjamin Butler and navy flag officer Silas Stringham take forts Clark and Hatteras, North Carolina, in the Battle of Hatteras Inlet.

September 3: Confederate troops under Major General Leonidas Polk cross from Tennessee into Kentucky, taking Hickman and Columbus.

September 6: Union troops under Grant occupy Paducah, Kentucky.

September 11: The Kentucky legislature demands Confederates leave the state.

September 18: The Kentucky legislature raises troops to expel Confederates.

October: Pro-secession legislators meet in Neosho, southwest Missouri, and declare secession. Some 109,000 troops in Missouri fight on the Union side; about 30,000 on the Confederate side.

October 21: Union forces are defeated at Ball's Bluff, on the Potomac River above Washington. As a consequence, General Charles P. Stone is imprisoned in February 1862 on suspicion of treason and held without charges for six months.

November 1: General Winfield Scott retires, and he is replaced by George McClellan as general in chief.

November 7: Union forces take Port Royal, South Carolina.

November 18: At a convention at Russellville, Kentucky, troops in the Confederate army adopt an ordinance of secession for the state of Kentucky.

December 20: The Joint Committee on the Conduct of the War, led by radical Republicans, presses Lincoln for more action, including the imprisonment of General Charles P. Stone for the debacle at Ball's Bluff.

EYEWITNESS TESTIMONY

Throughout the city yesterday the greatest excitement prevailed in relation to the news from Forts Moultrie and Sumter. As early as 8 o'clock in the forenoon the rumors of the destruction of the former of these military posts, and the occupation of the latter by the forces of the United States was circulated. It was at first currently reported and believed, that Fort Moultrie had been laid in ruins; that the guns were spiked, and the carriages, &c., together with the baraacks [sic], burned, and that the post had been entirely abandoned. The reports spread like wildfire, and soon gained currency in every part of the city. Crowds of citizens anxiously inquired of each other the latest intelligence in relation to the affair; squads collected on every corner of the streets, and in front of the public resorts, to canvass the subject.

The newspaper offices were besieged, the hotel halls were thronged, and even the grave and serious gentlemen composing the State Convention shared in the general excitement. On all hands anger and indignation were expressed at the supposed perfidious conduct of the Federal authorities, at whose instance it was at first thought the movement was made. The people were greatly incensed at the idea of a willful *breach of those assurances of non-action which had been volunteered by the Government at Washington,* and upon which so much reliance and confidence had been placed by the entire population, that every impulse to take the necessary precautions for their own safety had been restrained.

Instinctively men flew to arms.

Report from the Charleston Courier *of December 28, 1860, "The Question of the Forts," describing South Carolina's reaction to Major Anderson moving to Fort Sumter, in the* New York Times, *January 1, 1861, p. 10.*

Wilmington, Del., Thursday, Jan 3.

The Legislature of Delaware met at Dover, on Wednesday, and organized by choosing Dr. Martin, of Sussex, Speaker of the Senate, and Mr. Williamson, of Newcastle, Speaker of the House.

Hon. H. Dickenson, Commissioner from Mississippi, was received to-day, and addressed both Houses in a strong Southern speech, taking ground in favor of South Carolina and secession, and inviting Delaware to join in a Southern Confederacy. He claimed the right of the Southern States to secede, and said that if they were not allowed to do so, war was inevitable.

The speech of Mr. Dickenson was greeted with applause and hisses.

After the speech the House adopted unanimously the following resolution, in which the Senate concurred by a majority:

Resolved, That having extended to Hon. H. Dickenson, Commissioner from Mississippi, the courtesy due him as a representative of a sovereign State of the Confederacy, as well as to the State he represents, we deem it proper and due to ourselves and the people of Delaware to express our unqualified disapproval of the remedy for the existing difficulties suggested by the resolutions of the Legislature of Mississippi.

Report of the January 2, 1861, meeting of the Delaware legislature to consider secession, entitled "The Delaware Legislature, Reception of the Secession Commissioner from Mississippi," in the New York Times, *January 4, 1861, p. 8.*

The agitation of feeling under which this community has been laboring for some time past, has been precipitated into action in a quite unforeseen manner. No sooner was the news of the evacuation of Fort Moultrie received here, than the public mind was turned to the consideration of what might be deemed necessary to do with regard to the fortifications of Mobile Bay, and the Arsenal at Mount Vernon; but the general opinion soon settled down to the conclusion that it was inexpedient, at least, to interfere with them until the ordinance of secession should be passed, it being taken for granted that that act would not be long delayed when the Convention should assemble, as it will to-morrow. But on Thursday, a great excitement was occasioned by the intelligence that the United States steamer *Crusader* had arrived in the Bay, and it was readily surmised that her visit was connected with some purpose of garrisoning Fort Morgan, to protect it from a *coup de main.* The only occupants of the Fort, heretofore, have been an Ordnance Sergeant and two or three laborers. It was soon reported that the object of the Steamer's visit was to cash a draft for prize-money due the crew for the capture of a slaver; but while there is no doubt of the truth of this, yet it was very natural, in the present state of things, to imagine that it merely [served as] a convenient pretext for her presence here.

The news of the *Crusader's* arrival was telegraphed without delay to Gov. Moore, who, believing that it involved a necessity for immediate action, dispatched orders to the Colonel of the Volunteer Regiment of the city to take possession of the fort and the arsenal. The order was promptly obeyed, four companies being embarked for the fort at 11 o'clock at night, and three for the arsenal. Both parties arrived at their destinations before day, and took possession as directed.

Report, entitled "From Mobile—the Alabama Secession Flag—Sentiment of the People, etc.," describing the seizure of fortifications near Mobile prior to secession in Alabama, dated January 6, 1861, as published in the New York Times *of January 15, 1861, p. 1.*

The Senators and Representatives from the seceding States have again changed their tactics. Having lost the control of the Executive Government, they concluded to abandon the purpose of factiously embarrassing the Legislative Department, and will retire immediately.

Senator Toombs [of Georgia] and family left today. He is anxious to be present at the meeting of the Georgia Convention.

The Mississippi Senators, notwithstanding the telegram requesting them to remain for the purpose of mischief, will withdraw to-morrow, if Mr. Davis is well enough to be in the Senate. He is quite ill tonight with a severe affection of the throat.

The Alabama Senators and Members will retire on Tuesday if the ordinance of secession is ratified to-morrow, as is anticipated, unless the act is made to take effect on the 4th of February, when the ordinance recommends the holding of a Southern Convention.

The Florida delegation expect to retire on Tuesday.

Extract from news item, entitled "Our Washington Dispat[c]hes," datelined January 13, 1861, in the New York Times, *reporting on the departure of senators and representatives of the seceding states from Congress, January 14, 1861, p. 1.*

The South have wrapped themselves up in dreams; they are in a state of mental ecstacy [sic] from self-glorification. The nonsense can be taken out of them only in one way—*by practical experience of the results of secession,* which, instead of being the state of exaltation they picture, is humiliation, destruction, and death. What South Carolina is tasting all must drink to the very lees. Nothing but a feeling of complete immunity and protection could have given Southern people such airs of superiority and insolence as they have displayed, or induce them to rush madly into the vortex of disunion. They unfortunately forgot one element in the calculation—that producing a staple [cotton] they could nei-

A key to the spread of cotton agriculture was the development of the large-scale cotton gin, such as the steam-driven one in this photo in the building with the smokestack. *(Library of Congress, Prints and Photographs Division, LC-USZ62–120480)*

ther eat, drink nor wear, and nothing else, it was more important for them to *sell* than for others to *buy.* . . .

The South, in the frame of mind described, must, at the reception they have encountered from the friends who were to lend them their Armies, and blockade for them the Ports of New-York and Boston, have been overwhelmed with a stupor as excessive as was our own at the outset of their mad career. The English are not such ignoramuses as not to know that any disturbance of the kind reduces the price of cotton and puts money in their own pockets. They are quiet as lambs at the very moment the South supposed they would be rushing to their rescue with ship-loads of gold. They have several months' supply of cotton on hand, and well know that in due time hunger will send forward the new crop. About this they do not borrow a moment's anxiety. They have had to deal with insolent and turbulent fellows themselves, and understand well the difference between passion and necessity. But there is one thing about which they are as excited as ourselves—the monstrous impudence, assumption and lawlessness of the Cotton States, and the revolting doctrines upon which their new Confederacy is to be based. They speak with an indignation and earnestness at which the most rampant Secessionists must quail. Cotton or no cotton, Englishmen are not afraid to call infamous things by their right names, or hurl their execrations at those who outrage humanity and the moral sense of mankind.

If the South could have had the experience it has gained within these two months before committing the acts that led to it, they never would have taken the first step. It is not pleasant to brave the common sense of mankind, or to be an outlaw to the great family of nations. It is still worse, if possible, to be cut off from all commercial relations with it, by which property is destroyed, social order subverted, and distress and squalor take the place of abundance and elegance. This is not the haven to which our Southern brethren set sail. They thought they were clearing for a very different one. Still less will they like the compliment of being saluted as madmen, and of being treated as such by the great family of mankind.

> *Extract from an editorial, suggesting that the British are likely to denounce secession, entitled "The Ideas on Which Secession is Based," reacting to an article in DeBow's Southern Review by Major W. H. Chase, itself entitled "Southern Secession—its Status and Advantages," in the New York Times, January 15, 1861, p. 4.*

Mr. Toombs told us a story of General Scott and himself. He said he was dining in Washington with Scott, who seasoned every dish and every glass of wine with the eternal refrain, "Save the Union; the Union must be preserved." Toombs remarked that he knew why the Union was so dear to the General, and illustrated his point by a steamboat anecdote; an explosion, of course. While the passengers were struggling in the water a woman ran up and down the bank crying: "Oh, save the red-headed man!" The red-headed man was saved, and his preserver, after landing him, noticed with surprise how little interest in him the woman who had made such moving appeals seemed to feel. He asked her, "Why did you make that pathetic outcry?" She answered: "Oh, he owes me ten thousand dollars." "Now, General," said Toombs, "the Union owes you seventeen thousand dollars a year!" I can imagine the scorn on old Scott's face.

> *Mary Chesnut, planter-class diarist, in her diary, reporting a conversation between Senator Toombs and General Winfield Scott, in her entry for February 19, 1861, in A Diary from Dixie, p. 5.*

The nation still very sick, but no worse. Secession has run its course and reaction has set in. Missouri votes strongly for the Union. Even Arkansas tends the same way. There would no doubt be like symptoms in the Gulf States but for the reign of terror there, and had they not committed themselves so deeply in the first hot stage of secession fever. It would certainly come, sooner or later, in South Carolina itself, but before it can have time to develop itself, a collision is inevitable. That will postpone the return of common sense indefinitely. Fort Sumter cannot long be left without reinforcement, and

federal revenue must be collected at Southern ports. Unless these things, and others, be done, we virtually confess and declare that our national existence is a mere name, without the power of self assertion that gives national dignity to the smallest German Grand Duchy. If the federal government have no constitutional power to repress the treason of a minority, it may as well disintegrate at once and let the counterfeit sovereignty, "the likeness of a kingly crown," that has imposed on all the powers of Christendom so long, be swept into the rubbish bin of history at once, as a detested and acknowledged humbug. Though the original secession epidemic has, I think, exhausted itself, we have yet to see what Virginia, Tennessee, and other states will do when the contest begins between the federal government and the rebellious slave states. Which side will they take???

> *George Templeton Strong, New York philanthropist, commenting on secession of several states, in his diary entry for February 20, 1861, from Allan Nevins, ed., Diary of the Civil War, 1860–1865, pp. 100–101.*

All the particulars of Mr. Lincoln's visit here, and journeyings elsewhere, have been chronicled at painful length. His public entry on Tuesday was witnessed by myriads of spectators. So far as we observed it personally in Broadway, his reception was respectful, not enthusiastic. . .

We have watched with much anxiety the words that have fallen from time to time from the lips of the President Elect, hoping to gather therefrom some clue to his policy, some key to the destinies of this anxious and agitated country. In vain. As with Louis Napoleon, it is doubtful whether there be more mystery in Mr. Lincoln's silence or in his speech. Observe how he sways to and fro, as though to take back to-day what he said yesterday, and prevent too strong an impression for the morrow.

At Indianapolis, he palpably laid down his views of "coercion," which, according to him, would *not* consist in holding and "retaking" the forts and other property, and collecting the duties on foreign importations. We thought that the South, and lookers-on in general had precisely thus interpreted the term.—At Cleveland, and again at Philadelphia Mr. Lincoln held that the panic, the crisis, the anxiety of the country, are artificial. How glad we should be, if it were so—Replying to Mayor [Fernando] Wood, of this city, the President Elect, using the common illustration of the Ship of State, alluded to the possibility of finding it needful to throw passengers and cargo overboard, in order to save the vessel; declaring also that the principles on which the Union is based are better worth preserving than the Union itself. Further, he entirely coincided with the Mayor's intimation that the restoring of fraternal relations between the States can only be accomplished by peaceful and conciliatory means.—Finally, to the House of Assembly at Trenton, N.J., Mr. Lincoln announced that it might be "necessary to put the foot down firmly."

Whoever can reconcile these various hints, or can deduce from them any inkling as to what the doctrines of the White House will be, must have great skill in putting together the pieces of a Chinese puzzle. We only cite them as an excuse to one or two correspondents, who have accused us of being "Meager" in our accounts and comments. The latter we certainly shall not undertake; but in the difficult position which we occupy, we can at least most heartily re-echo Queen Victoria's wish, that all "differences may be susceptible of a satisfactory adjustment."

Extract from an editorial entitled "North and South" from the New York journal Albion, A Journal of News, Politics, and Literature, *discussing the mixed messages given by president-elect Abraham Lincoln on his trip from Springfield, Illinois, to Washington prior to his inauguration, Vol. 39, No. 8, (February 23, 1861), p. 90.*

In the hotel parlor we had a scene. Mrs. Scott was describing Lincoln, who is of the cleverest Yankee type. She said: "awfully ugly, even grotesque in appearance. The kind who are always at corner stores sitting on boxes, whittling sticks, and telling stories as funny as they are vulgar." Here I interposed to sigh: "But Douglas said one day to Mr. Chesnut 'Lincoln is the hardest fellow to handle I have ever encountered yet.'" Mr. Scott is from California. He said: "Lincoln is an utterly American specimen, coarse, rough and strong. A good-natured, kindly creature, and as pleasant tempered as he is clever. And if this country can be joked and laughed out of its rights, he is the kind-hearted fellow to do it. Now if there be a war and it pinches the Yankee pocket, instead of filling it—" Here a shrill voice came from the next room (which opened upon the one we were in, by folding doors thrown wide open). "Yankees are no more mean and stingy than you are. People at the North are as good as people at the South." The speaker advanced upon us in great wrath. Mrs. Scott apologized and made some smooth, polite remarks, though evidently much embarrassed; but the vinegar face and curly pate refused to receive any concession. She said: "That comes with a very bad grace after what you were saying," and she harangued us loudly for several minutes. Someone in the other room giggled outright. We were quiet as mice. Nobody wanted to hurt her feelings; she was one against so many. If I were at the North I should expect them to belabour us, and should hold my tongue. We separated from the North because of incompatibility of temper. We are divorced, North from South, because we have hated each other so. If we could only separate politely, and not have a horrid fight for divorce.

Mary Chesnut, planter-class diarist, in her entry for March 14, 1861, reporting on discussions about Lincoln's character, in A Diary from Dixie, *pp. 19–20.*

This Convention has deprived the people of a right to know its doing by holding its sessions in secret. It has appointed military officers and agents under its assumed authority. It has declared by ordinance, that the people of Texas ratify the Constitution of the Provisional Government of the Confederate States, and has changed the State Constitution and established a TEST OATH of allegiance to the Confederate States, requiring all persons now in office to take the same, or suffer the penalty of removal from office; and actuated by a spirit of petty tyranny, has required the Executive and a portion of the other officers at the seat of Government to appear at its bar at a certain hour and take the same. It has assumed to create organic laws and to put the same in execution. It has overthrown the theory of free government, by combining in itself all the Departments of Government, and exercising the powers belonging to each. Our fathers have taught us that freedom requires that these powers shall not be all lodged in, and exercised by any one body. Whenever it is so, the people suffer under a despotism.

Fellow-Citizens, I have refused to recognize this Convention. I believe that it has derived none of the powers which it has assumed either from the people or from the Legislature. I believe it guilty of an usurpation, which the people cannot suffer tamely and preserve their liberties. I am ready to lay down my life to maintain the rights and liberties of the people of Texas. I am ready to lay down the office rather than yield to usurpation and degradation.

Texas governor Sam Houston in a proclamation regarding the Texas convention declaring secession, issued March 16, 1861, two days before he was deposed, as reproduced in Henry Steele Commager, Fifty Basic Civil War Documents, *p. 27.*

Part of the fleet was visible outside the bar about half-past ten A.M. It exchanged salutes with us, but did not attempt to enter the harbor, or take part in the battle. In fact, it would have had considerable difficulty in finding the channel, as the marks and buoys had all been taken up. It was composed originally of the frigates *Pawnee,* under Commodore Rowan; the *Pocahontas,* under Captain Gillis; the *Powhatan,* under Captain Mercer; the steam transport *Baltic,* under Captain Fletcher; and, I believe, the steam-tugs *Yankee, Uncle Ben,* and another, which was not permitted to leave New York. The soldiers on board consisted of two hundred and fifty recruits from Governor's Island, under the command of First Lieutenants E. M. K. Hudson, of the Fourth, and Robert O. Tyler, of the Third Artillery, and Second Lieutenant A. I. Thomas, of the First Infantry. This expedition was designed by Captain [Gustavus Vasa] Fox, in consultation with G. W. Blunt, William H. Aspinwall, Russel Sturges, and others. After the event much obloquy was thrown upon the navy because it did not come in and engage the numerous batteries and forts, and open for itself a way to Charleston; but this course would probably have resulted in the sinking of every vessel.

As far back as December I had written to New York that it was very difficult for a gun on shore to hit a small boat dancing on the waves in the day-time, and at night it is almost impossible. I suggested, therefore, that we might be re-enforced and provisioned by means of a number of small boats, supplied from several naval vessels as a base of operations. The same idea had occurred to Captain Fox; and on the present occasion he had brought thirty launches to be used for this purpose. They were to be manned by three hundred sailors, and in case they were assailed, the fleet was to protect them as far as possible by its guns. Unfortunately, the different vessels did not reach the rendezvous together. The *Pawnee* and *Pocahantas* arrived on the 12th, but lost a great deal of time in waiting for the *Powhatan,* which contained the launches and other arrangements, without which a boat expedition could not be organized. The *Powhatan* never appeared, having been unexpectedly detached, by order of the President, at the solicitation of Secretary Seward, and without consultation with the Navy Department. I think the *Baltic* was detained by running upon Rattlesnake Shoal. The steam-tug *Uncle Ben* was driven into Wilmington by a storm, and the *Yankee* did not make its appearance until the 15th. The expedition was thus an utter failure.

Nevertheless, a passing schooner was purchased and loaded up with provisions and soldiers, and an attempt would have been made to run in on the night of the 13th, but by that time it was too late. The fort had surrendered.

Abner Doubleday, Union army captain, later general, recounting the effort to relieve Fort Sumter with a naval expedition on the day that the Confederate batteries opened fire on the fort, April 12, 1861, as recounted in his memoir, Reminiscences of Forts Sumter and Moultrie, in 1860–61, *pp. 149–151.*

Steamship *Baltic,* Off Sandy Hook, April 18, 1861
Hon. S. Cameron, Secretary of War, Washington, D.C.—

Sir: Having defended Fort Sumter for thirty-four hours, until the quarters were entirely burned, the main gates destroyed by fire, the gorge wall seriously injured, the magazine surrounded by flames, and its door closed from the effects of the heat, four barrels and three cartridges of powder only being available, and no provisions but pork remaining. I accepted terms of evacuation, offered by General Beauregard, being the same offered by him on the 11th inst., prior to the commencement of hostilities, and marched out of the fort Sunday afternoon, the 14th inst., with colors flying and drums beating, bringing away company and private property, and saluting my flag with fifty guns.

Robert Anderson,
Major First Artillery

Major Robert Anderson, Union commander at Fort Sumter, filing his official report on the fall of Fort Sumter, April 13–14, 1861, in a dispatch sent April 18, 1861, as quoted in Henry Steele Commager, Fifty Basic Civil War Documents, *p. 22.*

My dear Sister: I am grieved at my inability to see you. . . . I have been waiting for a "more convenient season," which has brought to many before me deep and lasting regret. Now we are in a state of war which will yield to nothing. The whole South is in a state of revolution, into which Virginia, after a long struggle, has been drawn; and though I recognize no necessity for this state of things, and would have forborne and pleaded to the end for redress of grievances, real or supposed, yet in my own person I had to meet the question whether I should take part against my native State.

With all my devotion to the Union and the feeling of loyalty and duty of an American citizen, I have not been able to make up my mind to raise my hand against my relatives, my children, my home. I have therefore resigned my commission in the Army, and save in defense of my native State, with the sincere hope that my poor services may never be needed, I hope I may never be called on to draw my sword. I know you will blame me; but you must think as kindly of me as you can, and believe that I have endeavoured to do what I thought right.

To show you the feeling and struggle it has cost me, I send you a copy of my letter of resignation. I have not time for more. May God guard and protect you and yours, and shower upon you everlasting blessings, is the prayer of your devoted brother,

R. E. Lee

Former U.S. general Robert E. Lee, to his sister, Mrs. Anne Marshall, on April 20, 1861, explaining his resignation from the U.S. Army, from Henry Steele Commager, Fifty Basic Civil War Documents, *p. 24.*

The Alabama crowd are not as confident of taking Fort Pickens as we were of taking Fort Sumter. Baltimore is in a blaze. They say Colonel Ben Huger is in command there. General Lee, son of Light Horse Harry Lee, has been made General in Chief of Virginia. With such men to the fore we have hope. The New York Herald says, "Slavery must be extinguished, if in blood." . . .

Wigfall is black with rage at Colonel Anderson's account of the fall of Sumter. Wigfall did behave so magnanimously, and Anderson does not seem to see it in that light. "Catch me risking my life to save him again," says Wigfall. "He might have been man enough to tell the truth to those New Yorkers, however unpalatable to them a good word for us might have been. We did behave well to him. The only men of his killed, he killed himself, or they killed themselves, firing a salute to their old striped rag."

Mary Chesnut, planter-class diarist, in her entry for April 27, 1861, commenting on Confederate reaction to Major Anderson's report of the firing on Fort Sumter, in A Diary from Dixie, *pp. 45–46.*

The regiment proceeded to disembark by companies Company E having the honor to be the first on shore, Company A following immediately after them, Col. Ellsworth being at the head of his men. I landed with Company A, and immediately ran forward and offered my services to Col. Ellsworth as his aid, which were accepted. I was sent to find the Adjutant, and he was ordered to form the regiment into line, which he accomplished. Capt. Leverich, with his company (E), was dispatched to the depot, to tear up the tracks, leading south, which was done as only Zouaves could do

it. Col. Ellsworth then started post haste for the telegraph, to stop the communication with Richmond by that way. I volunteered to accompany him, and off we started, accompanied by our Chaplain, G. W. Dodge, in uniform, and E. H. House, of the Tribune . . . Col. Ellsworth then called for a file of men from Company A, to follow him in double quick time, and the whole party started up the street toward the telegraph office. On our way, we had occasion to pass the Marshall House kept by one J. W. Jackson, who had flaunted out a secession flag upon our arrival in the town. Col. E. spied this, and remarked to me that he must have that flag. We entered the hotel; in the front room we found one white man, (the proprietor,) and a negro. Col. E. asked him who raised that flag. He replied that he was one of the boarders, and did not know. He then went up stairs, and reaching the skylight, Col. E. ascended the ladder, myself after him. Handing me his revolver, I handed him my knife, with which he cut the halliards, and hauled the flag down. We now proceeded to descend, private Francis E. Brownell being first, Col. E. next, House next, with his hands on Ellsworth's shoulder, myself being last. As we rounded a turn in the hall to go down stairs, the proprietor, (the pretended boarder) stood at the foot of the stairs, with a double-barreled gun in his hands, and aimed at our party, and more particularly at the one in advance. Brownell threw up his piece to ward off the gun which Jackson aimed at him. Jackson, however, discharged his gun, the contents lodging in the heart of the Colonel, who fell forward on his face, his life's blood perfectly saturating the secession flag, which the Colonel was carelessly rolling up as he descended the stairs. Quick as lightning Brownell discharged his piece, killing Jackson immediately, hitting him between the eyes, and finished the job by thrusting his sword bayonet into the breast. The sudden shock only for an instant paralyzed us; recovering, we turned the Colonel on his back, washed his face with water, and endeavored to revive him, but to no effect. I immediately stationed guards about the house, forbidding any one to leave it, threatening myself to shoot the first man of the rebels that dared to move.

Account by Lieutenant H. J. Winser, one of the eyewitnesses to the killing of Colonel Ellsworth, in a letter dated May 26, 1861, entitled: "The Death of Col. Ellsworth, Full Particulars of the Assassination by an Eye-Witness—The Zouaves Swear that they will be Revenged—Singular Coincidences," New York Times, *May 26, 1861, p. 8.*

Most of the seceded slave States are much divided. Eastern Tennessee, Northern Alabama, Western Virginia, are wholly in favour of the Union. Kentucky has expressly refused to go out. Tennessee is still balancing; Missouri cannot go. Maryland, now that her mob has been suppressed, speaks and acts the language of Union, and she is encouraged to it by the presence of Pennsylvania forces in Baltimore and overhanging her western counties, which at the same time are known to be faithful, thoroughly Union. It is the slave-selling and slave-working parts of the South that have alone desired to break away,—by no means all of these, nor any considerable part of them but through delusion, venality, or terror. How can the North and West withhold their effort to suppress the terror which has enchained so many? It is their sacred duty under the Constitution. We have, therefore, both duty and right to confirm us in the effort. It will, I have not doubt whatever, be strenuously made. We have no reason to doubt, from either the purposes we entertain, or the motives which actuate us, or the means we shall apply, that God will help us.

> Horace Binney, a Philadelphia lawyer, commenting on divisions within the South, in a letter to Sir J. T. Coleridge, dated Philadelphia, May 27, 1861, from Life of Horace Binney, as selected in Henry Steele Commager, The Blue and the Grey, pp. 41–42.

Every segment of line we succeeded in forming was again dissolved while another was being formed; more than two thousand men were shouting each some suggestion to his neighbor, their voices mingling with the noise of the shells hurtling through the trees overhead, and all words of command drowned in the confusion and uproar. It was at this moment that General Bee used the famous expression, "Look at Jackson's brigade! It stands there like a stone wall"—a name passed from the brigade to its immortal commander. The disorder seemed irretrievable, but happily the thought came to me that if their colors were planted out to the front men might rally on them, and I gave the order to carry the standards forward some forty yards, which was promptly executed by the regimental officers, thus drawing the common eye of the troops. They now received easily the orders to advance and form on the line of their colors, which they obeyed with a general movement; and as General Johnston and myself rode forward shortly after with the colors of the Fourth Alabama by our side, the line that had fought all morning, and had fled, routed and disordered, now advanced

General P. G. T. Beauregard resigned his U.S. Army commission and took command of Confederate troops in Charleston before the firing on Fort Sumter. *(Library of Congress, Prints and Photographs Division, LC-DIG-cwpb-05515)*

again into position as steadily as veterans. . . . We had come none too soon, as the enemy's forces, flushed with the belief of accomplished victory, were already advancing across the valley of Young's Branch and up the slope, where they had encountered for a while the fire of the Hampton Legion, which had been led forward to the Robinson house and the turnpike in front, covering the retreat and helping materially to check the panic of Bee's routed forces.

> General P. G. T. Beauregard, describing the Battle of Bull Run, July 20–21, 1861, from Robert Underwood Johnson and Clarence Clough Buel, eds., Battles and Leaders of the Civil War, Vol. I, p. 210.

We witnessed sights we had never seen before. The horrors of a battle field. As we marched in sight the cowardly villains were retreating, we could see their guns glittering among the bushes as they moved off. We heard that the 4th Ala was surrounded at one time by the overwhelming forces of the enemy and cut up terribly. General Bee was badly wounded. Heard that Col. Jones was killed, Lieut. Col. Law and Major Scott badly wounded. Syd May was in the fight but came off unhurt. It is said that the enemy came up with a Confederate flag, and our men thinking they were friends did not fire upon them, but as soon as they got within an hundred and fifty yards of our troops, turned loose both artillery and musketry, mowing them down like grass before a scythe. It was the bloodiest battle ever fought on the continent. We lost a great many in killed and wounded. Their loss was tremendous. The enemy were completely routed, losing fifty pieces of artillery, ten thousand stands of arms and a great many prisoners. The Virginians did excellent fighting. They charged their famous Shermans battery. . . . The number of killed cannot yet be accurately ascertained. Both sides lost heavily. . . .

John Henry Cowan, soldier of the Greensboro (Alabama) Guards, describing his participation in the Battle of Bull Run in his diary entry of noon, July 21, 1861, as published in G. Ward Hubbs, ed., Voices From Company D: Diaries of the Greensboro Guards, Fifth Alabama Infantry Regiment, Army of Northern Virginia, *pp. 22–23.*

I found myself in a crowd of men; among them was an officer, who said: "Colonel, I am going to New York today. What can I do for you?" I answered: "How can you go to New York? I do not remember to have signed a leave for you." He said, No; he did not want a leave. He had engaged to serve three months, and he had already served more than that time. . . . I noticed that a good many of the soldiers had paused about us to listen, and knew that, if this officer could defy me, they also would. So I turned on him sharp, and said: "Captain, this question of your term of service has been submitted to the rightful authority, and the decision has been published in orders. You are a soldier, and must submit to orders till you are properly discharged. If you attempt to leave without orders, it will be mutiny, and I will shoot you like a dog! Go back into the fort *now* instantly, and don't dare to leave without my consent". . .

That same day, which must have been about July 26th, I was near the riverbank . . . when I saw a carriage coming by the road that crossed the Potomac River at Georgetown by a ferry. I thought I recognized in the carriage the person of President Lincoln. . . . I was in uniform, with a sword on, and was recognized by Mr.

Lincoln and Mr. Seward, who rode side by side in an open back. I inquired if they were going to my camps, and Mr. Lincoln said: "Yes, we hear that you had got over the big scare, and we thought we would come over to see the 'boys.'". . .

At last we reached Fort Corcoran. The carriage could not enter, so I ordered the regiment, without arms, to come outside, and gather about Mr. Lincoln, who would speak to them. . . . In the crowd I saw the officer with whom I had the passage at reveille that morning. His face was pale, and lips compressed. . . . The officer forced his way through the crowd to the carriage, and said: "Mr. President, I have cause of grievance. This morning I went to speak to Colonel Sherman, and he threatened to shoot me." Mr. Lincoln, who was still standing, said, "Threatened to shoot you?" "Yes, sir, he threatened to shoot me." Mr. Lincoln looked at him, then at me, and stooping his tall, spare form toward the officer, said to him in a loud stage-whisper, easily heard for some yards around: "Well, if I were you, and he threatened to shoot, I would not trust him, for I believe he would do it." The officer turned about and disappeared, and the men laughed at him. . . . I explained the facts to the President, who answered, "Of course I don't know anything about it, but I thought you knew your own business best."

U.S. Colonel (later, general) William T. Sherman, describing his threat to shoot an officer for desertion after the retreat of his forces from the Battle of Bull Run, on July 26, 1861, from Memoirs of William T. Sherman, *as quoted in T. J. Stiles,* In Their Own Words: Civil War Commanders, *p. 16.*

Several prominent men, and my friends, had entered with spirit into the work of raising recruits and forming companies when one day Levi P. Coman, a lawyer stepped into my office and spoke to me saying he had understood that I had contemplated enlisting and wished to know if I was ready now and if I would join his company. I was busy writing at my desk, but dropped my pen and told him that I was ready to go and that I would as soon enlist with him as with any other. Then and there, he swore me into the service of the United States, October 18, 1861.

As soon as I could arrange my business affairs, I entered into the work of enlisting recruits. This was a task which required a great deal of tact and perseverance and there was such competition among the many recruiting officers that to persuade the men who were inclined to enlist that our company was "the best" made it necessary to use much cunning argument. The willing ones had become scarce as the first calls had carried off the most enthusiastic. I thought it no stretch of duty to get up in the night and ride twenty miles if I had heard of one man who was likely to enlist. Of course, we were subjected to many disappointments, as often the men would waver in their minds. My field of work was in the Southwestern part of the county, and in the North of Fairfield County where I had acquaintances and influence obtained through my business connections there.

Charles Dana Miller, Ohio grain merchant and Union army brevet major, in his memoirs, recalling his recruitment on October 18, 1861, in Stewart Bennett and Barbara Tillery, eds., The Struggle for the Life of the Republic: A Civil War Narrative by Brevet Major Charles Dana Miller, 76th Ohio Volunteer Infantry, *pp. 4–5.*

From the beginning of the battle a steady stream of wounded men had been trickling down the zig-zag path leading to the narrow beach, whence the boats were to convey them to the Island. As it happened the two larger bateaux were just starting with an overload when the torrent of terror-stricken fugitives rolled down the bluffs—upon them. Both boats were instantly submerged, and their cargoes of helpless human beings (crippled by wounds) were swept away to unknown graves! The whole surface of the river seemed filled with heads, struggling, screaming, fighting, dying! Man clutched at man, and the strong, who might have escaped, were dragged down by the weaker. Voices that strove to shout for help were stifled by the turbid, sullen waters of the swollen river and died away in gurgles. It is strange how persons about to drown turn to their fellows for strength; they may be in mid-ocean, with no hope for any, yet will they grasp one another and sink in pairs. Captain Otter, of the First California, (an apposite name for a swimmer,) was found a few days later with two men of his company clutching his neckband. Had he attempted to save them, or had they seized him and dragged him down? One officer was found with $126 gold in his pocket; it had cost his life.

Randolph Abbott Shotwell, then a private in the 8th Virginia Infantry Regiment, commenting on the debacle at Ball's Bluff, October 21, 1861, in his autobiography Three Years in Battle, *quoted in Henry Steele Commager,* The Blue and the Gray, *p. 119.*

The total white population of the eleven states now comprising the Confederacy is 6,000,000, and therefore, to fill up the ranks of the proposed army (600,000) about ten per cent of the entire white population will be required. In any other country than our own such a draft could not be met, but the Southern States can furnish that number of men, and still not leave the material interest of the country in a suffering condition. Those who are incapacitated for bearing arms can oversee the plantations, and the negroes can go on undisturbed in their usual labors. In the North the case is different; the men who join the army of subjugation are the laborers, the producers and the factory operatives. Nearly every man from that section, especially those from the rural districts, leaves some branch of industry to suffer during his absence. The institution of slavery in the South alone enables her to place in the field a force much larger in proportion to her white population than the North. . . . The institution is a tower of strength to the South, particularly at the present crisis, and our enemies will be likely to find that the "moral cancer" about which their orators are so fond of prating, is really one of the most effective weapons employed against the Union by the South. Whatever number of men may be needed for this war, we are confident our people stand ready to furnish.

Montgomery Advertiser, *November 6, 1861, as quoted in James M. McPherson,* The Negro's Civil War, *pp. 38–39.*

3

From Slavery to Freedom: Battlefield Emancipation and Contrabands
May 1861–June 1862

The original seven states of the Confederacy that announced their secession and the formation of a new nation did so explicitly because of the election of Lincoln as a purely regional candidate who opposed the institution of slavery. The four states that joined the Confederacy, after varying degrees of reluctance, did so because Lincoln had used military force in his attempt to preserve the Union. Thus from the beginning of the war, two intertwined issues explained secession and the outbreak of hostilities: slavery and the constitutional nature of the Union.

For political reasons, neither Lincoln nor Davis at first construed the war as an attack upon, or a defense of, the institution of slavery although each had supporters who did. Even though the institution of slavery and views about that institution had generated the political crisis that led to secession, the war itself was at first presented and politically defended by both sides as being over the issue of secession. Lincoln at first insisted that the war was fought to preserve the Union, especially because it was essential that he not lose the tenuous, at best, support of the slaveholding border states of Maryland, Kentucky, and Missouri. Similarly, Jefferson Davis and most leaders of the Confederate states perceived the war and presented it as one to defend their rights, including the right to secession, against a usurpation of power by the North, not perceiving or arguing for the war as a defense of the institution of slavery. After all, slave owners constituted a small minority of the Southern white population, less than 320,000 of the 5.5 million whites in the South. Although the planter class held a firm grip on the political leadership of the South, the population that would be called upon to provide most of the troops and much of the monetary sacrifice held no slaves.

Yet on both sides, committed minorities took stronger positions more explicitly related to slavery. In the North, particularly in upstate New York, New England, and in mid-western states remote from the border with slavery, such as Wisconsin, Minnesota, and Michigan, antislavery sentiments among whites ran strong. A small but vocal group of black spokesmen, including clergymen and journalists, hoped the war would lead to the end of slavery. White politicians, journalists, and clergymen in those upper-North states who had built their careers on antislavery positions saw the war as an opportunity to bring down the slave power of the Southern planter class by ending the institution of slavery. Several periodicals voiced these views, including the radical Republican newspaper edited by Horace Greeley, the *New York Tribune,* and *The Liberator,* founded and edited by the abolitionist, William Lloyd Garrison, and *Douglass' Weekly,* published by former slave Frederick Douglass. Such publications represented only the extremes of public opinion, while more conservative newspapers throughout the North, such as the *New York Times,* held to the view that preservation of the Union was far more important than liberating slaves. That view was shared by committed Unionists such as George Templeton Strong, one of the founders of the Sanitary Commission, devoted to providing aid to Union soldiers, and a staunch defender of Lincoln. Strong and some others like him moved gradually to a more antislavery position during the war years.

Even in the South, the deep diversity of views on the role of slaves, whether they could be relied upon to remain loyal and whether they should be armed and freed, continued to divide the army, the state governments, and the Confederate government itself. Planters saw the preservation of slavery as key to the survival of a way of life, although gradually more military leaders and others were willing to recruit slaves into the army and free them, if the independence of the Confederacy could be preserved in no other way. From 1861 until early in 1865, the Confederate army leased slaves and used them not only in constructing fortifications but in serving as ammunition handlers for artillery and as teamsters and other workers at and near the front lines. Such service, however, did not entail arming the slaves, nor did it involve any promise of liberation as a reward for work. Southerners opposed to arming and freeing slaves in defense of Confederate independence believed that such an action would remove the whole basis for their claim to uniqueness. If slavery were to be ended, they pointed out, there was no need for secession. In the South as well as the North, opinions on the issue of slavery varied with the region and the political and economic status of the individual. And, as in the North, the views of individuals evolved with the unfolding of events.

Even the positions of strong antislavery spokesmen and politicians in the North varied in their sources and their premises. Many Northerners who had opposed slavery in the territories did so not because they saw slavery itself as immoral, but simply because they wanted western territories to be open exclusively to free white settlers. Thus it was that the territory of Oregon excluded not only slaves but also settlement by free blacks, by law in 1849 and by state constitution in 1857. Other Northern states and territories and numerous individual Northern counties and cities had excluded black immigration, although such laws were intermittently enforced. Black exclusion laws had been passed in the states of Connecticut (1784), New Jersey (1786), Ohio (1802), Illinois (1819, 1829, and 1853), and Indiana (1831 and 1852), and in the territories of Michigan (1827) and Iowa (1839). Illinois, Indiana, and Oregon included black exclusion laws in their constitutions. In 1862 in the midst of the war, in a popular referendum in Illinois, both Republicans and Democrats supported maintaining the prewar racial exclusion law. African Americans were excluded from juries in all states prior to 1860. These facts, together with a history of segregation and maltreatment of African Americans throughout the Northern states, demonstrated that Northern opposition to slavery, even where a majority might support an end to slavery, did not derive from majority white support for racial equality. In fact, it was not inconsistent for a white Northerner to be explicitly opposed to slavery and at the same time to be openly a white supremacist or bigot. Such people found it perfectly logical to oppose both slavery and slaves.

Lincoln clearly believed that slavery was unethical and that all men had a right to freedom, but he, like strong majorities of whites throughout the North, also strongly favored racial segregation, even to the point of supporting the deportation of freed blacks entirely out of the United States. Whether or not and how slaves in the Confederacy should be freed was no clear choice for Lincoln, and he opposed several early actions of Union army generals to emancipate slaves, partly on the grounds that the United States and its armies had no legal or constitutional authority to do so. While his views evolved, so did those of his generals and political supporters, all at differing rates.

Furthermore, while some Northern whites could see the value of ending slavery as a wartime measure or even as a humanitarian act, almost all, including most abolitionists and committed radical Republicans, shared the values and prejudices of the day. Even those commissioned to recruit black troops, to operate relief and supply distribution to black refugees, and those setting up employment opportunities for the newly freed slaves reflected attitudes of racial stereotyping, patronizing condescension, or simple prejudice.

FROM CONTRABAND TO CONFISCATION

For the Union, the question of the status of slaves and how that status would bear on the war arose within a few weeks of its outbreak and to an extent remained unresolved throughout the war. Policy evolved sometimes by accident, sometimes by concerted policy decision. From the beginning, a few Northern antislavery politicians and abolitionists sought to end slavery as a war measure directed at the rebellious states, but how to accomplish it within the framework of law was not a simple matter. By constitutional interpretation and established law, including the Fugitive Slave Law of 1850, slaves were legally held to servitude, whether or not it seemed unethical. For a government pledged to uphold the law, such considerations were binding. Politically, the fact that slaveholders in Maryland, Kentucky, and Missouri could vote and exert power in those crucial states during the war years meant that any measures against slavery had to be carefully constructed so as not to erode support in those quarters. The Union hold was tenuous in all three states, and, despite the inclinations of abolitionists, a move to strike at slavery could immediately affect the strategic situation, a view held not only by Lincoln, but also by many of his advisers and supporters.

For the Union, one pathway through these dilemmas began to emerge in May and June 1861, within a few weeks after the war's start. As slaves heard of the advance of Union troops in their neighborhoods, or as Union troops overran territories where slaveowners had abandoned both their slaves and their plantations, the Union was confronted with a dramatic development: African-American fugitives from slavery walked singly, in family groups, and, in some areas, by whole plantation workforces, to areas under the jurisdiction of the U.S. Army. When civilian slaveholders appeared to reclaim the slaves as their property, the slaves' legal status needed to be defined.

On May 23, 1861, about six weeks after the first shot upon Fort Sumter, Union general Benjamin Butler was holding Fortress Monroe in Virginia when three slaves who had run away from their plantation appeared at the gates of the fort. Shepard Mallory, Frank Baker, and James Townshend explained that they were about to be shipped to North Carolina to work on defensive Confederate fortifications there. Their owner was Confederate colonel Charles K. Mallory, of the 115th Virginia Militia. He sent, under a flag of truce, Major M. B. Carey to obtain the release of the three men. General Butler refused to turn over the slaves and then offered a couple of innovative explanations. According to some reports, he pointed out that the Fugitive Slave Act of 1850 did not impose any obligations to a foreign country, which Virginia claimed to be. Furthermore, he indicated that any slave employed by the enemy to build fortifications represented contraband of war. There was a nice irony in his position, for by calling slaves contraband, he used the slaveholders' own legal logic against them. He did not deny that the slaves were legally regarded as property, rather than as persons, but he held that they represented a class of property that prevented their return, that of contraband of war, similar to arms, transport equipment, or livestock that could be employed for warlike purposes.

Butler's approach immediately caught the imagination, not only of the press and Northern observers, but also of the slaves themselves, who soon willingly appeared at Union camps, claiming status as contrabands. The idea that a human being could be a type of contraband was such an ironic concept and such an appropriate way of exploiting the slaveholders' own view of the slave, that journalists, political cartoonists, and politicians all started using the word. Within weeks, the term *contraband* had taken on a new meaning and was widely applied in the press, in conversations, and in evolving policy papers at the War Department. Butler himself would later express ambivalence over the claim of contraband status, perhaps embarrassed at its identification of African Americans as a type of property, yet somewhat pleased that his almost offhand justification became a precedent for much of the liberation of slaves during the war. Butler's solution attracted the attention of Simon Cameron, Lincoln's first secretary of war, who quickly endorsed it, and of the U.S. Congress. When the Confiscation Act of 1861 was passed on August 6, the law regularized Butler's action, declaring that slaves employed in arms or labor against the United States could be confiscated as contraband of war and were free. Although the word *free* was not defined to indicate any group of rights, and although it left unclear to what extent, if at all, the protections of law and the Constitution extended to this class of people, to be free certainly meant that a slave's status as property had ended. Increasingly after August 1861, such a contraband was called a freedman. The term *freedman* was carefully applied and distinguished from the term *free man,* which referred to a black person born to freedom or manumitted by individual action of a slaveholder in the prewar period.[1]

To clarify the position of army officers who were confronted by either loyal or rebel owners demanding

General Benjamin Butler earned fame for his policy of declaring fugitive slaves fleeing to Union lines as contraband of war. His later methods of administration in occupying New Orleans earned him the nickname "Beast Butler" throughout the Confederacy. *(Library of Congress, Prints and Photographs Division, LC-B8172–1406)*

The Union army employed former slaves declared contraband of war as construction laborers and in other noncombatant roles long before allowing them to serve as troops. *(Library of Congress, Prints and Photographs Division, LC-USZ62–106352)*

the return of their slaves, in March 1862 Congress passed a law prohibiting the army from enforcing the Fugitive Slave Law or from returning any fugitives at all under penalty of dismissal from the service. Even though freedmen could not be returned to servitude, however, their status was far from established. Treatment at the contraband camps varied. At Fortress Monroe and other locations, young black men were offered paid employment by the army as construction laborers and teamsters, while some of the women were hired as cooks and laundresses. The elderly and children were provided with rations, but in some of the camps, ration deliveries were so irregular and health conditions so miserable, that mortality rates climbed rapidly. Contraband camps were clearly temporary expedients in the nature of refugee holding areas. The War Department admitted that support of the wives and children of contrabands employed in the war effort by the Union was indeed an army responsibility. All of these developments were followed quite closely in the abolitionist press, such as *The Liberator,* in radical newspapers such as Horace Greeley's *New York Tribune,* and in more conservative publications, such as the *New York Times.*[2]

Some generals announced abolition of slavery well before Lincoln was willing to make such a gesture, and on two occasions that were publicly well known and reported, Lincoln rescinded such battlefield declarations of wider emancipation. On August 30, 1861, General John C. Frémont, who had run for president as the Republican nominee in 1856, issued a proclamation declaring that the slaves belonging to any Missourian who took up arms against the United States were freed. Lincoln quickly modified the decree to conform to the 1861 Confiscation Act, so that only those slaves who had been employed by forces in rebellion were affected. When General David Hunter declared slaves in Florida, Georgia, and South Carolina to be freed as of May 9, 1862, Lincoln had the secretary of war countermand the order 10 days later.[3]

THE POLITICS OF EMANCIPATION

The obvious advantages to the war effort of emancipating slaves and of recruiting them to serve in the Union army became forceful arguments for the more radical Republican supporters of the president, many of them former antislavery politicians. Nevertheless, Lincoln and his more conservative supporters understood that any such moves would have to be taken carefully, so as not to alienate the sizable population of slaveholders in the loyal border states. Furthermore, a true antislavery attitude was really prevalent only in the upper North. The states that bordered those with slavery—Pennsylvania, New Jersey, Ohio, Indiana, and Illinois, as well as New York City itself—were far less inclined to support any measure that would link the war goals to liberation of the slaves, although some individual congressmen from those states were ardent radicals.

There were several reasons for the greater hostility to liberation in the more Southerly states on the Union side of the line. Politically, the Democratic Party was strong in those regions. Socially, whites there apparently dreaded the possibility that freed blacks would immigrate in large numbers to their regions despite exclusion laws, and their racial prejudice on this point surfaced in many ways. White workingmen in those states feared the influx of former slaves as competitors for jobs who would drive down wages, mixing economic motivation with simpler racial hostility. Among the immigrant and working class, prejudice against blacks was fueled by fear that freedmen would compete for low-paying jobs, would act as strike-breakers, and would be patronized by the economic elites.

It was clear that Lincoln himself shared the view that African Americans and whites should live separately, and he said as much to a visiting delegation of black spokesmen representatives on August 14, 1862. At that meeting he surprised his guests by strongly endorsing the idea of deportation and colonization abroad, as reported in Greeley's *New York Tribune*.

In the interview Lincoln asserted that African Americans suffered greatly by living among whites and that whites suffered by their presence. He stated that white Americans were unwilling for free African Americans to remain in the United States. He did not propose to discuss this attitude, but it was a fact that had to be dealt with, he said, and he could not alter it, even if he tried.

When the meeting was reported in the *Tribune* and other papers, African-American spokesmen and meetings roundly denounced the colonization idea. Among those objecting were black abolitionists from Philadelphia, Isaiah Wears and Robert Purvis; the internationally-known black abolitionist Frederick Douglass; writers for the black newspaper *Anglo-African;* and numerous petitioning groups organized among Northern free men. Garrison's *Liberator* staunchly opposed Lincoln's plans for colonization; Garrison and his followers had long fought against plans for the colonization of Liberia in West Africa by individually manumitted slaves and free African Americans on the grounds that slaves should be liberated and granted full U.S. citizenship rather than face deportation.

DEPORTATION AND COLONIZATION

Colonization was an established idea, ever since its endorsement by the prosperous black shipowner from Massachusetts, Paul Cuffe, in 1816 and the formation of the American Colonization Society (A.C.S.) in 1821. Under the A.C.S. plan, Northern and Southern white supporters provided funds that were used to establish a settlement in West Africa that became Liberia to which some 12,000 free blacks emigrated over the four decades before the Civil War. In addition, smaller organizations in Maryland and Mississippi sponsored settlements on the nearby coast of Africa, later incorporated in the nation of Liberia. Liberia, although not internationally recognized with diplomatic representation, was proclaimed a self-governing republic in 1848. While the majority of black leadership in the United States had rejected emigration and colonization, the idea still attracted a small following up to and during the Civil War, with advocates like James T. Holly and James Redpath, who endorsed plans to emigrate from the United States to Haiti, and Martin Delany, who advocated African emigration and visited Nigeria to consider settlement there, before returning to the United States to serve in the Union army as a medical officer with the rank of major. The United States officially established diplomatic recognition of both Liberia and Haiti in 1862.

Colonization and deportation had won support among whites who believed slavery should be ended, but who shared the white majority's opposition to the presence of a free black population anywhere in the United States. In August 1861, the first Confiscation Act endorsed the concept that blacks who had been employed in the rebellion could be classified as contraband and declared free. But the bill also included a provision, Section 12, that authorized the president to negotiate with some tropical country for the deportation and colonization of the newly freed slaves. The bill provided limited funds for the purpose, and in December Lincoln requested Congress to increase the funding. Plans and proposals were developed for several nations and colonies around the Caribbean region over the next year and were seriously considered by the State Department and the cabinet.

Lincoln looked at one proposal to set up a black colony in the Chiriqui province of Colombia, now in western Panama near the border with Costa Rica. A real estate promoter by the name of Ambrose Thompson held a claim to land there that he had tried to develop as a coaling station, and he secured support from the Colombian government for the concept of a colony of African-American freedmen. Thompson's land grant included some two million acres, and he had incorporated the Chiriqui Improvement Company to set up coal mines on the land. He offered coal to the U.S. Navy at a discount if the government would provide him with African-American laborers to work the mines. Lincoln suggested to the delegation of African-American spokesmen who visited him in August 1862 that they bend their efforts to recruiting workers for the coal operation. However, when Lincoln presented the plan to his cabinet, it was roundly disapproved, partly because of complaints from the Costa Rican government. The Costa Ricans apparently believed that the Colombians would use the settlement as a base from which to launch cross-border insurrectionary expeditions. Furthermore, scientist Joseph Henry of the Smithsonian Institution reported that the coal deposits in the Chiriqui province were not worth exploiting, and some members of the cabinet questioned whether Ambrose held clear title to the land he claimed. The plan was rejected in October 1862, even though Thompson claimed he had applications from thousands of potential settlers.

Another proposal did get off the ground. A shady promoter by the name of Bernard Kock saw an opportunity for a fortune and proposed a settlement on an island in the Caribbean that would include a plantation employing 1,000 freed slaves. Kock arranged a 10-year contract with the Haitian government to develop a 25-square-mile island off the coast of Haiti, Île à Vache, or as Horace Greeley disparagingly called it in English, Cow Island. Lincoln had Kock investigated and rejected his proposal, but when it was presented again with the endorsement of two New York financiers in October 1862, Lincoln approved the plan, with a limit of 500 freedmen to be colonized. The financiers recruited Kock to manage the plantation, and a shipload of 468 settlers departed for the island in April 1863. When Lincoln heard that Kock had been put in charge, he had him dismissed. As it turned out, no provisions had been made for housing, schools, or other facilities on the brush-covered island, and the experiment was a total failure. The surviving settlers were brought back to the United States in March 1864. Although other sites were offered and investigated, including lands in Ecuador, the Virgin Islands, British Honduras, and the Dutch colony of Surinam on the northern coast of South America, Secretary of State Seward rejected all these offers on the grounds of inadequate preparation and protection of the rights of the freedmen. Lincoln's support for colonization, whether from genuine conviction or simply as a temporary gesture to gain wider white support for the possibility of emancipation, soon faded as the practical difficulties and diplomatic objections to deportation and resettlement mounted.[4]

James Redpath had established a newspaper, *Pine and Palm,* and worked as an agent of the Haitian government to encourage emigration through the period 1861–63. Although Garrison and other abolitionists disapproved of the deportation connotations of Lincoln's plans, they were a bit more ambivalent regarding the voluntary emigration plans of African-American leaders like Holly and Redpath, expressing some relief when Redpath dropped the plan but refraining from criticizing the motives of the black advocates of voluntary emigrationism. The distinction between voluntary emigrationism, endorsed by a few black leaders, and colonization, endorsed by white leaders, was quite clear to observers at the time who followed these issues, because the two different concepts sprang from very different motives. Voluntary emigrationism reflected a concept of self-sufficiency and self-determination; colonization drew support from whites who saw the continued presence of freed African Americans in the United States as a troublesome issue and hoped to sidestep the whole question of the future status of freed African Americans simply by removing them from the United States.

The Liberator continued to argue for emancipation and the establishment of civil liberties and civil rights for African Americans as citizens in the United

Cotton plantations, some quite small and others with hundreds of slaves, spread through the Gulf states to Texas by 1860. *(Library of Congress, Prints and Photographs Division, LC-USZ62–121658)*

States. Somewhat naively, from the perspective of later generations of black and white civil rights advocates, Garrison and some of his followers tended to believe that racial prejudice would simply vanish with the abolition of slavery.

REFORM EXPERIMENTS

While Lincoln and his cabinet were considering the colonization efforts, events on the ground continued to demand more practical and immediate resolutions. In mid–1861 it was still possible to believe that the war might end soon, with much of slavery in place and the number of contrabands limited in number. As the war dragged on, the issue of African-American status grew in magnitude. When Union forces arrived on the Sea Islands off the coast of South Carolina, the planters, overseers, and almost all the rest of the white population simply evacuated the area, abandoning the plantations and the estimated 10,000 slaves to the Union forces. After the islands were taken by the Union navy in November 1861 and occupied by the army, the Treasury and the War Departments of Lincoln's government vied for developing a response to the massive new responsibility. Whatever practice they established could be an example, perhaps suitable for extension as other areas were conquered. Secretary of the Treasury Salmon Chase (who later resigned under pressure and was appointed to the Supreme Court by Lincoln) dispatched a friend and associate, Edward L. Pierce, to investigate conditions there. Pierce had already served as General Butler's superintendent of contrabands at Fortress Monroe. Pierce reported back in March 1862 with a plan calling for federal administration of the plantations. Simon Cameron, still serving as secretary of war in December 1861, recommended the straightforward emancipation of the slaves in the region, although Lincoln deleted Cameron's suggestions for emancipation from the War Department report for the year. Abolitionists saw the sudden presence of thousands of former slaves within Union lines as an opportunity to demonstrate that African Americans could successfully adjust to a life of freedom, something defenders of slavery had claimed was impossible. Thus the government handling of the Sea Islands, in the eyes of some abolitionists, would not only test the government response, but would also serve to demonstrate that the newly freed slave could adjust promptly to the new status. Such a test or example was clearly implied by the constant reference to resolution of the status of the Sea Island freedmen s an "experiment."[5]

Pierce's plan was put in effect on the Sea Islands. However, instead of turning the plantations over to the freed slaves as individuals or arranging for transfer of title to groups of them, Pierce believed that the lands should be retained by the government and be operated as businesses with white leadership. Superintendents were hired and the plantations began operation as government enterprises, with small compensation to the individual laborers. Pierce's superintendents tended to regard the workers as still legally slaves, simply abandoned by their owners, and treated them as such, enforcing discipline, often at gunpoint, and distributing supplies and food much as the former slave owners had done. Even though the superintendents were drawn from abolitionist supporters in New York and Boston, they shared the prevailing white sentiment that African Americans needed to be instructed on how to operate the plantations on which they had lived all their lives and that they had to be guided by whites in their transition to freedom. The superintendents' paternalistic values turned out to be little different from those of the former plantation masters. Pierce found it ironic that he, a staunch Republican from Massachusetts, had to play the role of slave overseer, first at Fortress Monroe and later in South Carolina, yet he viewed the contrabands with condescension. The other superintendents and teachers from the North shared Pierce's attitudes toward the local Sea Island freed people.

The operation of the Sea Island lands was shifted to army control under General Rufus Saxton in April 1862. Saxton tended to favor the idea that the freedmen could operate the lands by themselves, with the plantations cut up into smaller units run by families, and he was finally able to arrange some transfer of land at sales for unpaid taxes so that black ownership of land was established. However, the original superintendents continued to argue for large-scale operations under white supervision, and some of the land was purchased and run by New York–funded companies. One of the large land-holding companies was headed by Edward Philbrick, a former government-appointed superintendent. Whether paternalistic capitalism, as set up by Philbrick, or government-sponsored yeoman peasantry would prevail, was fought out by the government administrators. Despite the public attention paid to the Sea Island experiment, the settlements provided no long-range solutions for the future.

In April, General David Hunter requested permission to arm black troops in the Sea Islands. When no response came, he began accepting volunteers into a regiment that he called the First South Carolina Volunteers. Before the troops saw any action, however, he received orders to disband the unit, which he did by August, but he retained one company that formed a nucleus of a regiment a year later when the policy of arming black units was approved.

Lincoln meanwhile continued to work toward some form of legalized emancipation. Congress passed and Lincoln signed a bill to provide financial aid to any state that would set up a plan for gradual and compensated emancipation. None of the border states responded despite the fact that Lincoln urged them to do so. In another move, Congress abolished slavery in the District of Columbia, setting

This 1866 print shows a freedman plowing his own land. *(Library of Congress, Prints and Photographs Division, LC-USZ62–134227)*

up a fund for compensating the owners, and also providing further funding for the planned deportation scheme. Through the summer of 1862, however, Lincoln hesitated to take more direct steps.

In an act that could have been applied more widely, Congress modified the revenue laws. At the time, direct federal taxes were imposed on property. With an amendment passed on June 7, the government was empowered to confiscate lands on which the owners had been delinquent in tax payments. Some challenged the law on the grounds that it appeared to violate the constitutional provision against imposing penalties on later generations for the crimes of ancestors. Lincoln himself criticized it on those grounds. If the act had been widely applied, most of the plantations in the Confederacy could have been confiscated, title acquired, and distribution made to former slaves and poor whites in a land reform system.

Thus by the summer of 1862, tentative steps at land reform in the Sea Islands had been tried and had bogged down in inter-departmental controversy. Radical generals like Frémont and Hunter had been prevented from declaring abolition. Lincoln's first ideas of deportation of contrabands and state-enacted gradual emancipation appeared to be going nowhere. The contraband policy could be applied clearly only in cases in which slaves had been directly employed in working on Confederate military projects, such as gun emplacements and fortifications. Congress was ready to extend that law, and Lincoln began to consider proposals to use his war-making power to further spread emancipation. Meanwhile, the war on land and sea heated up through 1862.

CHRONICLE OF EVENTS

1861

May 23: Three fugitive slaves appear at Fortress Monroe, asking sanctuary.

May 25: General Benjamin Butler rules that slaves escaping to his lines at Fortress Monroe in Virginia are contraband of war; he refuses to return them to their masters.

August 6: The Confiscation Act of 1861 is signed into law, providing for the emancipation of slaves employed, with the knowledge of their owners, in arms or labor in support of the rebellion, confirming General Butler's policy set at Fortress Monroe. The law explicitly provides for escaped slaves to be returned to their owners if the owners can demonstrate their loyalty to the Union. Section 12 of the act empowers the president to open negotiations with "some tropical territory beyond the limits of the United States" for transportation, colonization, and settlement of the former slaves.

August 30: General John C. Frémont issues a proclamation declaring that slaves of Missourians in rebellion are free.

September 1: Mary Chase, a freedwoman from Alexandria, opens a school for contrabands.

September 11: After Frémont refuses to modify his order to conform to the Confiscation Act of 1861, Lincoln rescinds the order and removes Frémont from command in Missouri.

September 17: Mary Peake, a free black woman from Hampton, Virginia, opens a school for contrabands at Fortress Monroe.

November 7: The U.S. Navy occupies Port Royal and adjacent Sea Islands off South Carolina.

December: Lincoln requests funds to purchase lands outside the United States for deportation and colonization of freedmen.

December: Secretary of the Treasury Salmon Chase sends Edward L. Pierce, formerly General Butler's superintendent of contrabands at Fortress Monroe, to Port Royal to organize the labor of contrabands in the Sea Islands.

Cotton planting, cultivating, and picking were labor-intensive until late in the 20th century. *(Library of Congress, Prints and Photographs Division, LC-USZ62–120752)*

December 1: Secretary of War Simon Cameron proposes emancipation for abandoned slaves in response to the evacuation of the Sea Islands by planters who abandoned both slaves and plantations. Lincoln orders the deletion of passages in Cameron's annual report advocating emancipation of former slaves and their enlistment in the army.

1862

March: After an inspection visit by Pierce to the Sea Islands, plantation superintendents recruited in Boston and New York begin to arrive to organize the labor of the abandoned slaves there. Pierce's superintendents regard the workers as still legally slaves, abandoned by their masters.

March 6: Lincoln urges the border states to gradually abolish slavery, with compensation to slave owners. He indicates that the cost of the war will exceed the fair value of all the slaves.

March 13: Congress as an additional article of war, prohibits U.S. Army officers, under pain of dismissal from the service, from enforcing the Fugitive Slave Act or returning any "fugitives from labor."

April: Secretary of War Stanton directs General Rufus Saxton to take charge of abandoned plantations and the overseeing of labor in the Sea Island area.

April 3: General David Hunter requests permission to arm black troops in the Sea Islands.

April 10: Congress pledges to provide financial aid to any state that undertakes gradual, compensated emancipation.

April 16: Lincoln signs the act abolishing slavery in the District of Columbia, with a fund for compensating owners. The average compensation is $300 per slave. The bill also appropriates $600,000 to support deportation and colonization of the freedmen, in response to Lincoln's earlier request for funding.

April 25: Major General David Hunter declares slaves in Florida, Georgia, and South Carolina to be freed May 9.

Tobacco cultivation employed slaves in Maryland, Virginia, and North Carolina. *(Library of Congress, Prints and Photographs Division, LC-USZ62–120795)*

May: Receiving no response to his April 3 request, General David Hunter recruits a black regiment at the Sea Islands, but it is not sanctioned by the War Department and it is disbanded (but for one company) by August.

May 19: Lincoln rescinds General Hunter's order freeing slaves in the region.

May 19: Lincoln again urges the border states to enact gradual, compensated emancipation laws.

June 7: Congress passes the Direct Tax Act, which provides for the forfeiture to the federal government of lands on which the owners fail to pay tax; this law is a mechanism for the confiscation of plantation lands. It is only sparingly employed, however.

June 19: Congress prohibits slavery in all federal territories; the act does not provide compensation to slave owners.

EYEWITNESS TESTIMONY

Fortress Monroe, Saturday, May 25, 5 P.M.—Three fugitive slaves, the property of Col. Mallory, commander of the rebel forces near Hampton, were brought in by our picket guard yesterday. They represented that they were about to be sent South, and hence sought protection. Major Corry came with a flag of truce, and claimed their rendition under the Fugitive Slave Law, but was informed by Gen. Butler, that, under the peculiar circumstances, he considered the fugitives contraband of war and had sent them to work inside the Fortress, and Col. Mallory was politely informed that so soon as he should visit the Fortress and take a solemn oath to obey the laws of the United States, his property would promptly be restored. Another party came in this morning with a flag of truce, but with no better success. On their return, it is supposed they set fire to Hampton bridge, an immense volume of smoke being now visible in that direction.

It is reported that large numbers of slaves continue to arrive at Fortress Monroe, desiring to be set at work. On Tuesday over forty arrived, and are held as contraband of war.

Untitled article regarding the first decision to treat fugitive slaves as contraband of war, datelined May 25, 1861, as published in the abolitionist weekly newspaper, The Liberator, *Vol. 31, No. 22 (May 31, 1861), p. 87.*

"Sir,—Your action in respect to the negroes who came within your lines from the service of the rebels is approved. The department is sensible of embarrassments which must surround officers conducting military operations in a State, by the laws of which slavery is sanctioned. The government cannot recognize the rejection by any State of its Federal obligations; nor can it refuse the performance of the Federal obligations residing upon itself.

Among these Federal obligations, however, no one can be more important than that of suppressing and dispersing armed combinations formed for the purpose of overthrowing its whole constitutional authority; while, therefore, you will permit no interference by the persons under your command with the relations of persons held to service under the laws of any State, you will, on the other hand, so long as any State within which your military operations are conducted is under the control of such organizations, refrain from surrendering to alleged masters any persons who may come within your lines.

You will employ such persons in the services to which they may be best adapted, keeping an account of the labor by them performed, of the value of it, and of the expense of their maintenance. The question of their final disposition will be reserved for future determination.

Simon Cameron, secretary of war, in a letter to General Benjamin Butler, dated May 31, 1861, quoted in an article entitled "Important Decision of the Government— Slaves of Rebel Owners Contraband of War," endorsing Butler's decisions regarding contrabands, reprinted in the abolitionist newspaper, The Liberator, *Vol. 31, No. 23 (June 7, 1861), p. 91.*

The contrabands are curious as to what shall be their fate. One or two told me that after working on our intrenchments it would go hard with them if their masters returned. One inquired suspiciously why his master's name was taken down. All hope that, some how or other, they will soon be free, and that their fugitive masters will never return. They call me by various titles, as boss, massa, general, &c. The post of an overseer of negroes in Virginia is certainly a new one for a pretty earnest Massachusetts Republican to occupy, and as your correspondent addressed them, there was one message which he then wished he could deliver to them, and that was that the hour of their emancipation had come. Indeed, in conversation with one or many, I tell them all that they are as much entitled to their freedom as I am to mine.

And will the Government be so false as ever to fail to protect every negro who has ever served our officers or men, helped to build our defences, or in any way aided our cause? If it shall ever be so base and treacherous as that, it will deserve to be a thousand times overthrown, and be forever accursed among the nations. Whatever may be our general duty to this oppressed race, to such as we have thus employed, our national faith and our personal honor are pledged. The code of a gentleman, to say nothing of the grander law of rectitude, at least necessitates protection to that extent.

Yesterday I was at the Fort for the purpose of inquiring whether rations could be furnished to the negroes on account of their wives and children—it being manifest justice to provide for their families, whom they could not labor to support while so employed. This suggestion was cordially responded to, and rations ordered for them. This morning I inquired of each man whether he had a wife and children. In some instances the melancholy answer was given that he had had a wife, but she had been sold and carried off. . . .

Your readers will, I trust, not complain that I have so much to say about the negroes. They are the main feature of interest here. This is our first introduction to slave-life in Virginia, and we are now summoned to confront the gravest question of the war. God grant that we may have the courage and forecast to meet it! The anxious student of passing events cannot fail to find in the slave society, which is now presented, objects for perpetual reflection.

Letter to the Boston Traveller *regarding the situation of contraband slaves at Fortress Monroe, signed "P.," probably Edward Pierce, civilian supervisor of the contrabands appointed by General Butler, dated July 10, 1861, included in an article entitled "The Contraband at Fortress Monroe," as published in the* New York Times, *July 20, 1861, p. 2.*

Are these men, women, and children slaves? Are they free? Is their condition that of men, women, and children or of property, or is it a mixed relation? What their status was under the Constitution and laws, we all know. What have been the effect of rebellion and a state of war upon that status? When I adopted the theory of treating the able-bodied negro fit to work in the trenches as property, liable to be used in aid of rebellion, and so contraband of war, that condition of things was in so far met, as I then and still believe, on a legal and constitutional basis. But now a new series of questions arise. Passing by women, the children certainly cannot be treated on that basis; if property, they must be considered the incumbrance, rather than the auxiliary of an army, and of course, in no possible legal relation, could be treated as contraband. Are they property? If they were so, they have been left by their masters and owners, deserted, thrown away, abandoned, like the wrecked vessel upon the ocean. Their former possessors and owners have causelessly, traitorously, rebelliously, and to carry out the figure, practically abandoned them to be swallowed up by the Winter storm of starvation. If property, do they not become the property of the salvors? But we, their salvors, do not need and will not hold such property and will assume no such ownership; has not, therefore, all proprietary relation ceased? Have they not become thereupon men, women, and children? No longer under ownership of any kind, the fearful relics of fugitive masters, have they not by their masters' acts, and the state of war, assumed the condition, which we

hold to be the normal one, of those made in God's image? Is not every constitutional, legal, and moral requirement, as well to the runaway master as their relinquished slaves, thus answered? I confess that my own mind is compelled by this reasoning to look upon them as men and women. If not free born, yet free, manumitted, sent forth from the hand that held them, never to be reclaimed.

General Benjamin Butler, in a letter of July 20, 1862, to Secretary of War Simon Cameron, as published under the title "General Butler on the Contraband Question," in the abolitionist newspaper, The Liberator *1, no. 32 (August 9, 1861), p. 127.*

The war now prosecuted on the part of the Federal Government is a war for the Union, for the preservation of all the Constitutional rights of the States and of the citizens of the States in the Union, hence no question can arise as to fugitives from service within the States and territories in which the authority of the Union is fully acknowledged. The ordinary forms of judicial proceedings must be respected by the military and civil authorities alike, for the enforcement of legal forms. . . .

A more difficult question is presented in respect to persons escaping from the service of loyal masters. It is quite apparent that the laws of the State under which only the service of such fugitives can be claimed, must needs be wholly or almost wholly suspended, as to the remedies, by insurrection and the military measures necessitated by it; and it is equally apparent that the substitution of military for judicial measures for the enforcement of such claims must be attended by great inconvenience, embarrassments, and injuries.

Under these circumstances, it seems quite clear that the substantial rights of local [sic-loyal] masters are still best protected by receiving such fugitives, as well as fugitives from disloyal masters, into the service of the United States, and employing them under such organizations and in such occupations as circumstances may suggest or require. . . .

After tranquility shall have been restored upon the return of peace, Congress will doubtless properly provide for all the persons thus received into the service of the Union, and for a just compensation to loyal masters. In this way only it would seem, can the duty and safety of the Government and just rights of all be fully reconciled and harmonized. . . .

You will, however, neither authorize nor permit any interference by the troops under your command with the servants of peaceable citizens in a house or field, nor will you in any manner encourage such citizens to leave the lawful service of their masters, nor will you, except in cases where the public good may seem to require it, prevent the voluntary return of any fugitive to this service from which he may have escaped.

Union secretary of war Simon Cameron, in a letter to General Benjamin Butler, August 11, 1861, providing instructions on the treatment of fugitive slaves, reported under the title, "The Contraband Question," in the abolitionist newspaper, The Liberator, *31, no. 32 (August 16, 1861), p. 131.*

The letter of Mr. Cameron, Secretary of War, to Gen. Butler, at Fortress Monroe, indicates the policy of the Government in regard to the treatment of slaves who shall escape from citizens of rebel States and seek protection in the armies of the United States. The ground taken seems eminently prudent and sound, and cannot fail, we think, to give satisfaction to the country.

The slaves that escape from the citizens of rebel States are of two classes. First, those that escape from rebel masters; and secondly, those that escape from loyal citizens. None of either class are to be returned by the intervention of the military authorities. The remanding of fugitive slaves can only be ordered by a judicial tribunal of the United States; but inasmuch as in the rebel States where our armies are, the authority of the National Government is denied, and its officers expelled, it follows that no delivery of a fugitive slave to his master can be made according to law. If there be any State law, as doubtless there is in all slave-holding States, for the recovery of fugitives, it may be enforced by the State authorities. On this point, Mr. Cameron says that the State law, if the State is in rebellion against the General Government, must needs be wholly or almost wholly suspended, in the presence of the Union armies where the negroes have taken refuge. . . .

The Government [of the United States] needs their labor, and has a right to impress it. And, so far as rebel masters are concerned, the Government has a right to strip them of all chance of recovering their fugitives, and so does well to keep the "contrabands" in the public service. In the end the National Government may either return fugitive slaves to loyal masters, or provide to pay for them, if by the nation's will or negligence they are lost to their rightful owners. . . . we begin to see now the stupendous fatuity of Secessionism, which under the color of protecting Slavery by dissolving the Union, is causing Slavery to melt from the land as snows under a summer's sun.

Editorial in the New York Times, *commenting on Secretary of War Simon Cameron's development of contraband policy, entitled "Government Policy on Slavery in the Seceded States," August 13, 1861, p. 4.*

Leaving the Jersey ferry boat this afternoon, we met the distinguished Charles Sumner. He says he knows the instructions given to General Sherman as to his relations with the contrabands of the district he is to occupy and all the secret history of their discussion and settlement in the Cabinet, and that they are equivalent to *Emancipation.* We shall see. I put no great faith in Sumner, and we may as well effect our landing and secure our foothold before we consider that question. I observe that the word "contraband" has established itself in a new sense as designating a class of biped mammalia. This we owe to General Butler. "Secesh" is another novelty that may become classical English.

George Templeton Strong, New York philanthropist and businessman and co-founder of the U.S. Sanitary Commission, commenting on how the word contraband *has taken on a new meaning, in his diary entry for November 8, 1861, from Allan Nevins, ed.,* Diary of the Civil War, 1860–1865, *p. 192.*

I am tired of this state of tension, which has now lasted a year.

But we have gained something already. Emancipation in the District of Columbia has passed both Houses by more than two to one, and unless Lincoln veto the measure, which is unlikely, the nation has washed its hands of slavery. Only the damnedest of the "damned abolitionists" dreamed of such a thing a year ago. Perhaps the name of abolitionist will be less disgraceful a year hence. John Brown's "soul's a marching on," with the people after it.

George Templeton Strong, in his diary entry for November 8, 1861, commenting on the spread of emancipation procedures, from Allan Nevins, ed., Diary of the Civil War, 1860–1865, *p. 216.*

Lincoln has signed the [District of Columbia] Emancipation Bill. Has any President, since this country came into being, done so weighty an act? The federal government is now clear of all connection with slaveholding.

George Templeton Strong, commenting on Lincoln's decision to sign the bill freeing slaves in the District of Columbia, on April 16, 1862, in Allen Nevins, ed., Diary of the Civil War, 1860–1865, *p. 217.*

I find a great many of the people about here who really believe that Northern people intend to sell the negroes of rebels, and all they can get. The wily master points his slave to this returned fugitive and the other, and says—"Now Jim, Sambo, Dick, don't you see these people are opposed to letting you go free? If I was a rebel they would take you and sell you to some outlandish place. Which would you rather do—stay with me or go with them?" The poor slave, who always dreads the auction block, gives the desired answer. If you ask him of what party his master is, Union or Rebel, he will say Union. How can they know the truth, when they see the Northern troops doing the dirty work of their masters, which a gentlemanly Confederate would scorn to do, and they see the Northern troops arresting supposed rebels, and guarding their slaves until executive clemency releases them. For instance about the time our [Hooker's] Division marched down here, the Indiana cavalry arrested a man by the name of Big Dick Posey. This is his universal cognomen. He is the king rebel of Charles county. As soon as the arrest was made, his slaves were placed under guard . . . There is not a slave or free man within twenty miles that does not know that this man is in collusion with the enemy, and they see the Union troops holding his slaves while he undergoes the form and ceremony of government arrest. It is hard to convince these people that we are on the side of freedom.

George E. Stephens, African-American newspaper correspondent, to the editor of the Weekly Anglo-African, *commenting on the difficulty of convincing slaves in southern Maryland to denounce their masters as pro-Confederate, on November 30, 1861, as quoted in Donald Yacovone,* Voice of Thunder, *pp. 145–146.*

[President Lincoln] told us a lot of stories. Something was said about the pressure of the extreme antislavery party in Congress and in the newspapers for legislation about the status of all slaves. "Wa-al," says Abe Lincoln, "that reminds me of a party of Methodist parsons that was travelling in Illinois when I was a boy thar, and had a branch to cross that was pretty bad—ugly to cross, ye know, because the waters was up. And they got considerin' and discussin' how they should get across it, and they talked about it for two hours . . . till at last an old brother put in, and he says, says he, 'Brethren, this here talk ain't no use. I never cross a river until I come to it.'"

New York philanthropist George Templeton Strong, recounting a discussion with Lincoln regarding the need for a policy on emancipation, on January 28, 1862, as recorded in his diary on January 29, 1862, in Allen Nevins, ed., The Diary of George Templeton Strong, *pp. 204–205.*

There was quite an exciting time in one of the camps this morning. The slave hunters did not come for "Jim, the negro spy," on last Saturday as they said they would do, but they put it off until this morning. I suppose they thought they would by this little delay, put him off his guard, but no, no, it seems that these fellows who have serious objections to serving a master, have learned intuitively that "Eternal vigilance is the price of liberty." When a man's limbs have been bruised by the galling chains, he knows how sweet it is to be able to step forth free and unencumbered, and he will run fast and kick hard should any one attempt to reinvest him with those chains. Well about twelve o'clock three Maryland magnates—slave hunters—rode into camp, provided with abundant dingy looking papers. A crowd was of course assembled in double quick time, without any regard to either right or left dress. There stood James, looking on in calm dignity. One asked, "Why don't you take him?" "I want the officer to let me take him," stammered the frightened hunter.

"Why you fool, there is not an officer in this whole division that dare give this man to you as a slave."

"Put 'em out! Put 'em out! Ride 'em on a rail!" went up from every quarter. In a twinkling of an eye they were in their saddles. Groans, hisses, and snowballs were showered on their devoted heads, and the last that was seen of them was when they were making Maryland mud fly in ignoble style.

George E. Stephens, African-American newspaper correspondent, to the editor of the Weekly Anglo-African, *reporting an incident in Charles County, Maryland, when slave hunters attempted to retrieve a runaway from Hooker's Division, on February 6, 1862, as quoted in Donald Yacovone,* Voice of Thunder, *p. 176.*

It does not belong to the military to decide upon the relation of master and slave. Such questions must be settled by the civil courts. No fugitive slaves will, therefore, be admitted within our lines or camps, except when specially ordered by the General commanding.

General Henry Wager Halleck in Order No. 13, clarifying his policy in Missouri of not admitting fugitive slaves to Union lines, issued February 23, 1862, as quoted in Horace Greeley, The American Conflict, *p. 241.*

It has come to my knowledge that slaves sometimes make their way improperly into our lines; and in some instances they may be enticed there; but I think the number has been magnified by report. Several applications have been made to me by persons whose servants have been found in our camps; and in every instance that I know of, the master has recovered his servant and taken him away.

I need hardly remind you that there will always be found some lawless and mischievous persons in every army; but I assure you that the mass of this army is law-abiding, and that it is neither its disposition nor its policy to violate law or the rights of individuals in any particular.

Union general Don Carlos Buell, in a note to J. R. Underwood, chairman of the Military Committee in Frankfort, Kentucky, stating Buell's policy of refusing sanctuary to fugitive slaves in Tennessee, March 6, 1862, as quoted in Horace Greeley, The American Conflict, *p. 244.*

I deprecate this nascent Colonization Party, not because I fear its success. When slavery shall be abolished, (and we are on the eve of its abolition,) the party will die. Hatred of the blacks, which is the pabulum and soul of the party, gets all its life and virus from slavery. Slavery dead, and the desire to colonize the blacks would also be dead. You and Senator [James R.] Doolittle [of Wisconsin] would find no more sympathy with your scheme. Nay, you would yourselves have no more sympathy with it. And if slavery shall live, even the slaveholders will not consent on any terms to the colonization of the mass of the blacks, either those in or those out of slavery. They will, as were the slaveholders of Maryland, be found valuing the labor of black men too highly to consent to their expulsion from the country. Nor do I deprecate the party, because the first actual attempt to drive five millions of useful, innocent people out of the nation would begin a war of races, in which the dozen millions of blacks in this hemisphere, and the whole civilized world in addition, would be against us; for there will never be this first actual attempt. When the time for it shall have come, the daring and the disposition will both be lacking.

It is for other reasons that I deprecate this Colonization movement. Its tendency will be to hold back the Government from striking at the cause of the war; and to produce hesitation, diversion, compromise, at a moment when the salvation of the country calls for blows, immediate, united, and where, at whatever damage to whatever other interest, they will fall most effec-

"STAND UP A MAN!"

The freeing of slaves by advancing Union troops changed the war from the suppression of rebellion to a war for liberation. *(Library of Congress, Prints and Photographs Division, LC-USZC4–2520)*

tively. Not its least lamentable tendency is to foster in the American people that mean pride of race, and that murderous spirit of caste, by which they have outraged and crushed so many millions, and for which they are now, in the righteous providence of God, called to an account so appalling.

Gerrit Smith, abolitionist leader, writing to Montgomery Blair, postmaster general and leading Republican, arguing against the proposal to colonize freed slaves abroad, in a letter published in the Liberator *32, no. 16 (April 18, 1862), p. 64.*

4

Blockade Ships and River Gunboats

January 1861–December 1862

The naval and maritime side of the Civil War tends to hold a lesser place in public memory than the conflict between the armies on land. Part of the reason may lie in the fact that battles in ever-shifting waters are difficult to commemorate with monuments, statues, and reenactments. Yet even though they are less celebrated, the struggles on the water were as crucial to the defeat of the Confederacy as those on land and were as well-documented. River and sea battles, like those on land, were the subject of thousands of reports and hundreds of memoirs and diaries. Naval engagements generated a rich literature that traditionally tended to focus on the decisions and actions of officers and the episodic battle outcomes as ships clashed with each other or with land fortifications. The broad outline of the naval war, like the course of the war on land, sometimes seems obscured by the very richness of the mass of minute detail, the volumes of heroic anecdote, the exploits of gallant officers, and the mistakes and cowardice of pure poltroons.

The broader outline of the first two years of the maritime war can be seen in two theaters: the azure-blue offshore waters of the Gulf and Atlantic coasts, where the Union sought to blockade the Confederacy, and the muddy brown waters of the inland rivers, where gunboats clashed and battered gun emplacements ashore. It was only later in the war that the Confederates began in earnest to take on the Union navy with high-seas cruisers and with novel submarines, the subject of a later chapter in this volume.

The maritime Civil War not only helped decide the ultimate Union victory, it also left a technical legacy whose impact stretched far beyond North America. As with the battles on land, the war on water saw many new developments in weaponry, representing turning points in the terrible technology of destruction. Out of the ingenuity of inventors, engineers, and entrepreneurs came a wide range of innovations—in ironcladding, rotating turrets, mines, submarines, and ship-borne ordnance—that changed the nature of warfare on and under water. Steam supplemented sails at sea and sometimes completely replaced sails in rivers and estuaries.

STAFFING UP

Even before the war began, leaders of the Confederacy were well aware that their actions might need to be defended militarily. Among the first steps that the seceding government took was the establishment of a navy, drawing from among the officers who resigned their commissions in the U.S. Navy to form the core of the new service. Before the formation of the Confederacy, Captain Raphael Semmes of the U.S. Navy, born in Maryland and an adopted son of Alabama, offered his services and some political advice to Howell Cobb, who would chair the Confederation convention at Montgomery. Among his other points, Semmes suggested that U.S. military officers resigning their commissions be given the same rank in the new service.[1]

Before Lincoln's inauguration, the Confederacy's provisional president, Jefferson Davis, appointed Stephen R. Mallory, former senator from Florida, to serve as secretary of the navy. Mallory had previously chaired the U.S. Senate Naval Committee and was as well-qualified as any Confederate politician to serve in this cabinet position. Mallory immediately saw that the Confederacy, with no navy whatsoever, had to adopt radical methods, and he was quick to support several: the development of ironclads that could wreck havoc among the Union's entirely wooden fleet; the dispatch of commissioners to Europe to buy modern war vessels that could harry American merchant and naval shipping on the high seas; and capitalization on the numerous advances in technology that would make it possible to remotely detonate mines, or torpedoes, as they were known. Mallory's willingness to try out such initiatives shaped much of the maritime conflict.

A week after Davis appointed Mallory, Lincoln chose Gideon Welles as his secretary of the navy. Welles, a former Democratic politician turned Republican journalist, had little direct experience, having once served in a minor patronage position in the procurement offices of the Navy Department. Nevertheless, Welles turned out to be one of Lincoln's best cabinet appointments, with a steady administrative hand, a fairly good ability to judge character, and with intelligent and analytical views on numerous strategic and policy questions bearing on the war and the navy. Like Mallory, Welles tended to be more forward-looking and willing to change with the times than many of the officers in command of ships and men.

In another lucky early appointment, Lincoln chose Augustus Vasa Fox in May 1861 to serve as chief clerk of the navy; later, Fox was appointed to the new position of undersecretary of the navy. Although his duties were not rigidly defined, Fox was able to take on a role somewhat like that of a later chief of naval operations, working closely on strategic plans. He was handicapped in that position by holding a civilian rather than a military post; nevertheless, his abilities combined with those of Welles to make the Navy Department quite efficient in comparison to the much more chaotic War Department that oversaw the Union army's operations.

FROM BLOCKADE TO ANACONDA

Within a week after the firing on Fort Sumter, Lincoln declared a blockade of the original seven states of the Confederacy, soon extended to Virginia and North Carolina. Overland commerce to the two landlocked states of the Confederacy, Arkansas and Tennessee, was also prohibited. By declaring a blockade of the ports of the Confederate states, Lincoln revealed two fundamental aspects of the rebellion. First, he recognized that the war would at least in part be one of economics, and he intended to cut off both the import and export trade of the Confederacy with the rest of the world. Second, although he wanted to regard the actions of the Southern rebels as those of individuals in rebellion against their government, by blockading Southern ports he made it clear to the world that in some ways at least, he would treat the Confederacy as a belligerent power, not simply as a collection of individual rebels.

At first, the blockade was only a notion, as the U.S. Navy had a total of 14 effective and available ships with which to enforce it. However, step by step over the following months and years, the blockade was strengthened. By the end of the war Secretary Welles had added more than 600 vessels to the Union navy by construction and purchase. The blockade required that naval vessels tediously patrol off major Southern harbors and inlets, an intensely boring service only occasionally enlivened by the sighting of a blockade runner or, even more rarely, by a Confederate attempt to sortie out to do battle. The blockade ships had to be close enough to the port or inlet to intercept incoming and outgoing ships, but had to operate beyond the range of shore batteries, usually limited in those days to about three to five miles. There they would steam back and forth, attempting to stop any inbound or outbound commercial vessels they encountered to ensure that they carried no contraband.

At first it seemed that the North might have trouble mounting an effective blockade against the Confederacy's 3,549–mile coast. However, on closer examination, the task became simpler. Much of the Southern coast was blocked by sandbars. Some ports that had deep enough harbors to accommodate ocean-going ships had no rail connections to the interior; numerous smaller ports could be accessed only by shallow-draft coastal and river vessels. When such considerations were reviewed, it was clear that a blockade could be quite effective by focusing first on a limited number of ports: Wilmington, North Carolina; Charleston, South Carolina; Mobile, Alabama; and New Orleans. Although ports like Beaufort, South Carolina; Fernandina, Florida; and Galveston, Texas, had potential, they were underdeveloped. Pensacola, a fine harbor, could be readily blockaded by the Union-held Fort Pickens at the western tip of Santa Rosa Island. Soon, the Union's few ships, supplemented by commandeered coastal steamers, had effectively bottled up the South from much of its international trade. From June 1861 to August, no international steamers whatsoever entered or departed Confederate-held harbors. Some 86 sailing ships, mostly schooners, entered the ports in that period, but only two of them carried any foreign goods. By fall 1861, prices of imported commodities in the Confederacy had already begun to climb. Even so, in these first months, Confederate leaders believed that Britain, once it began to suffer from the failure to obtain cotton imports, would swing to the Confederate side. Politicians, merchants, and newspapermen even supported an official Confederate export embargo on cotton in hopes that it would force the British hand. Britain, however, had stockpiles of cotton in storage from the previous year, and began to develop other sources in Egypt and India.

David Farragut had served in the navy since his youth. After the battle of Mobile Bay, he was the first U.S. officer to be promoted to the rank of admiral. *(Library of Congress, Prints and Photographs Division, LC-USZ62–103590)*

Soon the business of blockade-running by daring private operators began, supplemented by state and Confederate-owned operations. Although the majority of blockade-runners were able to slip past the patrols, their high fees to offset the risks they ran contributed to inflation of prices. Another consequence was that the blockade led to the military and diplomatic isolation of the Confederacy as well as its slow economic strangulation. Shortages of imported items, ranging from coffee to whalebone stays for corsets, together with the general inflation of currency, brought the conflict home to civilians, even those with no family involved in the shooting war itself. The blockade also meant that the Confederacy had to develop, in a short period, facilities for the manufacture of cannon, powder, shot, and small arms and had to devote scarce manpower to these new enterprises.

As director of the Confederacy's Ordnance Bureau, Major Josiah Gorgas began to implement a plan for domestic production; at the same time, to meet immediate needs, he sought to import weapons by way of blockade-runners. The first of these to arrive with a significant cargo of cannons, ammunition, small arms, and other valuable items such as shoes and blankets was the iron-hulled screw merchantman, *Bermuda,* which arrived in Savannah, Georgia, on September 18, 1861. Soon private companies began shipping needed supplies in smaller, shallow-draft steamers from ports in Cuba and the Bahamas for some of the unguarded inlets and ports in Florida, Georgia, and the Carolinas.

The Union's blockade ships needed facilities for repair, coaling, and restocking. So, early in the war, naval forces seized selected off-shore islands and ports to serve as military bases and depots. Through mid- and late 1861 the Union had three successes in these efforts. On August 28, 1861, a combined force of naval ships commanded by Flag Officer Silas Stringham and troops under the command of General Benjamin Butler took Fort Hatteras and Fort Clark in the Hatteras Inlet. It was the first real Union victory of any kind, with about 670 Confederate prisoners, and the loss of one man from the Union forces. Then, on September 17, 1861, the Union navy seized Ship Island off the coast of Mississippi, which would prove to be a key to later naval strategies in the western Gulf. Even more significantly, on November 7, 1861, the navy took without opposition Port Royal, South Carolina, the surrounding Sea Islands, and the small port of Beaufort. Beaufort provided deep-water access but had no rail connection to the interior.

As the war went on, naval expeditions mounted from Boston, New York, Philadelphia, and the Chesapeake Bay continued to pick off forts and islands, which served to enforce and tighten the blockade. In a few cases the captured points became launching sites for further invasions of the interior. On February 7, 1862, a squadron of 100 ships carrying troops under General Ambrose Burnside took Roanoke Island, North Carolina; a smaller naval operation under Captain Samuel Du Pont, on March 3, 1862, captured Fenandina, Florida, effectively cutting Florida off from much further participation in the war.

In June 1861, the U.S. Navy established the Commission of Conference, also known as the Strategy Board or Blockading Board. The commission or board was chaired by Du Pont. Working from ideas proposed by Winfield Scott, this Strategy Board made the Anaconda policy an official objective, intended to choke off the Confederacy like a giant snake squeezing a person's body. The blockade of the coast would be logically administered with separate sections controlled by separate squadrons under separate commands and with clearly defined boundaries. The Atlantic Blockading Squadron covered from the Chesapeake to the tip of Florida, and the Gulf Blockading Squadron covered from that point in Florida around the Gulf Coast to the Rio Grande border between Texas and Mexico.

In September 1861, the Atlantic Blockading Squadron was split into northern and southern sections, with the dividing point at Wilmington, North Carolina. Partly as a cover for the planned operation to attack New Orleans, the Gulf Squadron was divided into an eastern and western command, with the western command operating out of Ship Island, and the eastern command covering from Pensacola eastward and around Florida to Cape Canaveral, where the South Atlantic Blockading Squadron's jurisdiction ended.

In November 1861, then captain David Porter was able to meet with Gideon Welles to put before him a plan for the seizure of New Orleans. Welles took Porter and his idea to Lincoln, and then all three met with General McClellan to see how many troops could be spared from the army to assist in the operation. Despite efforts at secrecy, word of the plans soon leaked. There is evidence that Welles and Lincoln had already discussed the concept of a seaborne invasion to seize New Orleans when Porter began to advocate it. As the South's largest port city and commanding the outlet of the Mississippi River to the Gulf, New Orleans was certainly an obvious objective to anyone who glanced at a map of the Confederacy. Nevertheless, specific planning appeared to get underway only after Porter's meeting with Welles.[2]

To head the expedition as flag officer, Lincoln and Welles chose the 60-year-old officer David Farragut, who had served in the navy since he was a teenager. Although born in Tennessee, he was intensely loyal to the Union cause. In addition, he was level-headed, as well as an inspiring leader, and he was willing to leave detailed staff work, which he found tedious, to competent officers in his command. Porter was given the task of organizing a mortar-fleet that would bombard forts Jackson and St. Philip that lay across from each other on the lower Mississippi River, guarding the approach to New Orleans.

Ship Island, off the state of Mississippi, was chosen as a staging ground for the New Orleans attack, scheduled to begin in April 1862. If the attack were successful, Lincoln and Welles visualized that Union forces could move down the Mississippi River from bases in Illinois and Kentucky and north up the river from New Orleans to divide the western South from the eastern South. Combined with the coastal blockade, control of the Mississippi, when completed, would completely encircle the heartland of the Confederacy in an ever-tightening, anaconda-like grip. The plan to take control of the Mississippi River was a good one, but it took far longer to accomplish than Porter and Lincoln's other advisers had hoped. Meanwhile, the blockade of Atlantic and Gulf coasts of the Confederacy continued to tighten.

ASSESSING THE BLOCKADE

Altogether, some 500 ships participated in the blockade during the war years, with the number on patrol at any one time running at about 150 once the blockade got underway. Although all statistics are approximate, the patrols captured or destroyed about 1,500 ships attempting to run the blockade. Steamers, especially those built with blockade-running in mind, were more successful than sailing ships in outrunning the steam-powered blockade ships of the Union navy. Of 1,300 attempts to run the blockade with a steamer, more than 1,000 succeeded.

Records show that, over the course of the war, some 400,000 rifles and rifled muskets came in through the blockade and about 3 million pounds of lead, or about one-third of all that was consumed by the Confederacy. So, while effective in some senses, the blockade did not entirely prevent the Confederacy from obtaining important war materiel from overseas.

On average, a Union blockade ship might see about one blockade runner a month and capture only one or two a year. An incentive for these officers and men alike was the promise of prize money from ships captured, amounting to half the value of the ship and its contents distributed among officers and crew, with the other half sent to the Treasury Department. The profit motive helped offset the boredom. As the blockade tightened in 1862, with only a handful of Southern ports remaining open, the chase became more difficult for both sides.

Blockade runners tended to be fast steam-powered ships, built especially for the purpose in Britain. Experienced blockade-running captains would choose foggy or moonless nights for their quick passes, operating out of Cuba, the Bahamas, or Bermuda into the ports of Wilmington, Charleston, or Mobile, still held by the Confederates. On the inbound trips they carried not only war materiel also but luxury goods in short supply. Eventually the Confederate government would establish rules that outlawed the import of such luxuries as corset stays and would require that at least half the cargo be given over to supplies for the war, at established government rates. On the outbound trips, after an initial effort on the part of the Confederate government to limit cotton exports, the primary cargo was cotton.

Over 80 percent of blockade runners got through the blockade without being captured, but, more importantly, the blockade had the effect of limiting the total number of ships attempting to reach Southern ports. Some estimates suggest that the blockade cut trips in and out of Southern ports from 20,000 in the period 1856–60 to about 8,000 during the four years of the war. Furthermore, successful blockade runners were built to be fast, with limited

This captured blockade runner, used to transport goods to and from the Confederacy, was typical of the class, as demonstrated by its raked masts. *(Library of Congress, Prints and Photographs Division, LC-B8171–7416)*

cargo space. The consequence in shortages, psychological isolation, and, perhaps most important, inflation of prices, had a severe effect on the Confederate war effort. However, that effect was probably felt more on the homefront than on the battlefield, where Confederate industries supplemented by imports were able to supply the troops with weapons, powder, and shot, if not always new uniforms and shoes.

EPISODE: THE TRENT AFFAIR

The day after a naval squadron under Samuel Du Pont took Port Royal, South Carolina, the U.S. ship *San Jacinto* fired a gun across the bows of the British packet steamer *Trent,* which had departed from Havana, Cuba, on November 7. The captain of *San Jacinto,* Charles Wilkes, brought the *Trent* to a halt and sent a young lieutenant, Donald Fairfax, aboard *Trent* with orders to arrest two Confederate emissaries to Europe, James Mason and John Slidell, and to seize the ship. Fairfax later claimed that he had argued against the action, fearing it would engage the United States in a dispute with Britain that could lead to war. Even so, he carried out the arrest order, over the objections of the master of the ship and many of its Confederate civilian passengers. The two emissaries put up a show of resistance and had to be forcibly taken from the ship by armed sailors from *San Jacinto.* Fairfax made it clear, that he would not seize the ship, despite the order to do so. Wilkes apparently also thought better of taking the ship and simply declared that he had seized the two messengers, together with their families and personal luggage. However, Mason and Slidell did not bring off the ship any documents showing their commissions or instructions. Since they carried unwritten instructions from a belligerent party, Wilkes claimed that Mason and Slidell were themselves contraband of war, a very dubious claim under international law. If Fairfax had seized the ship, or at least any incriminating instructions and documents along with the two emissaries, it might have been a stronger case.[3]

When the news reached England, those who favored the Confederacy thought they had a chance to unite public opinion behind their cause. Cooler heads prevailed, however, as an exchange of notes proceeded. In the United States, the press and public alternately blamed or praised Charles Wilkes for the impetuosity or bravado of the seizure of Mason and Slidell from aboard a British ship. Eventually, Lincoln and his advisers decided that the intelligent thing to do was to back down, and to surrender Mason and Slidell back to the British, releasing them on New Year's Eve, 1861. Officially, they chided Wilkes for exceeding his instructions, and admitted to the British that the seizure would have been legal only if the ship and all its contents, including incriminating documents, had been brought into an American port for condemnation proceedings. In effect, the U.S. position was that, if the ship had been properly confiscated, the action would have been legal, but since Mason and Slidell had no physical contraband with them and since the ship had not been condemned, they would be released. The British were caught in something of a dilemma over this position. If they accepted the American line of thinking, they would be agreeing that confiscation on the high seas without taking a ship to port was illegal, which had been their own practice and one that contributed to American grievances leading up to the War of 1812. On the other hand, if the British held that such a seizure at sea was legal, they would have to admit that their protest against the action of Wilkes had been poorly based. Their reaction was simply to note the release without comment, accepting the statement and the release as a diplomatic way out of the crisis.

Some analysts have seen the fine hand of Lincoln himself in this resolution of the matter. He may have once again used his knack for placing his opponents on the horns of a dilemma, as displayed in the Lincoln-Douglas debates at Freeport, in the decision to announce his intention to supply Fort Sumter, in the preliminary Emancipation Proclamation, and in many other stratagems of politics and diplomacy. In all of these situations, Lincoln's actions created what in the modern era would be called a win-win situation for his side of the conflict. Others have credited American ambassador to Great Britain Charles Francis Adams with handling the *Trent* crisis with discretion, softening the sometimes harsh stand taken by Secretary of State William Seward.[4]

Despite the fact that the Union government officially disavowed the action of Wilkes, he was praised in much of the press and in Congress for standing up to the British. The fact that Lieutenant Fairfax's hesitation to take the ship as a prize had at once confused the issue and provided a convenient way out of the diplomatic dilemma tended to be forgotten, and Wilkes became the object of credit or blame. In Britain, after the announced release of Mason and Slidell, a temporary British embargo on sending saltpeter to the Du Pont powder works in Delaware was lifted, and public opinion began shifting in favor of the Union.

CLASH OF IRON

The Union faced far more crucial maritime issues with the loss of the U.S. naval yard at Norfolk, Virginia, to Confederate forces upon the secession of Virginia. Although departing Union officers tried to destroy ships and facilities that would fall into Confederate hands, the base and several ships proved a powerful threat to the Union once Confederate forces took over. Situated at the mouth of the Chesapeake, a strong Confederate presence at Norfolk could control access to Baltimore, Annapolis, and Washington, as well as to many minor ports on the mainland of Maryland and its eastern shore. Confederates, strapped for cash, hastily refitted the partially destroyed *Merrimac* and rechristened it *Virginia*. With inadequate funds to purchase ship timber, the ship was armored with train rails and iron plate, making it the first ironclad of the Civil War. With its armor, the new vessel soon demonstrated the validity of Secretary Mallory's thesis that innovative Confederate methods would be required to offset Union numbers. As the fitting went forward, word spread in the North. Although the effectiveness of *Virginia* was untested, Americans had read of the fact that newly launched British and French ironclad vessels appeared impregnable against wooden ships. As *Virginia* was readied for war, the Union navy sought bids for the construction of vessels to oppose her.

John Ericsson, a Swedish designer and inventor of the ship propeller, did not submit a bid at first; but, on the urging of Cornelius Bushnell, a personal friend of Gideon Welles, Ericsson finally turned over a cardboard model and plans for a fully ironclad ship that could meet the need. Lincoln himself looked at the model; while naval officers were skeptical, the contract was set up, with the ship to be built in 90 days. On October 25, 1861, the keel of the new ship, known during construction as the *Ericsson Battery,* was laid at the Brooklyn Navy Yard. Ericsson himself coordinated the manufacture by dozens of shops and factories of all parts, including the engines, and the ship was completed, much to the chagrin of later generations of naval contract managers, almost exactly on time and on budget. It was launched late in January 1862, outfitted with guns, and given several practice runs before being towed through the winter Atlantic to the mouth of the Chesapeake. After being nearly swamped at sea, the strange craft that looked like a cheesebox on a raft showed up in Chesapeake Bay late on the evening of March 8, 1862, almost too late to save Washington from bombardment. The *Virginia,* with its railroad iron cladding, was quite capable of steaming unopposed up Chesapeake Bay and then the Potomac River directly to the capital.

Earlier on March 8, *Virginia* (the former *Merrimac*) destroyed the USS *Cumberland,* rammed the USS *Congress,* and ran the USS *Minnesota* aground off Hampton Roads. It was the greatest single day's loss of U.S. naval ships by enemy action until December 7, 1941. As word of the destruction reached Washington, members of Lincoln's cabinet were in panic, expecting to see *Virginia* steam up the Potomac and begin shelling the city. Newly appointed secretary of war Edwin Stanton, chosen by Lincoln to replace Simon Cameron, paced frantically, actually going to the window in expectation of seeing shells hit government buildings in the District of Columbia from *Virginia's* cannon. Navy Secretary Welles maintained a cool demeanor, believing that the *Ericsson Battery,* renamed by Ericsson himself as *Monitor,* would save the day.

Meanwhile, the *Monitor* had just arrived at the mouth of the Chesapeake. On the morning of March 9, Lieutenant John L. Worden, in command, ordered *Monitor* tied up next to the grounded *Minnesota* in order to protect the ship from further attack. Later that morning the two ironclad ships, the *Virginia* and the *Monitor,* met, firing at each other at close range, causing some dents and minor damage. *Virginia* was briefly driven onto the shoals. Following instructions not to load the guns with full powder charges, *Monitor's* 175-pound missiles nevertheless cracked open *Virginia's* armor in a few spots. One shot from *Virginia* wounded Lieutenant Worden with a shell that exploded immediately in front of the viewing slot through which he was observing the action. Blinded, he turned

The importance of the clash between the Union *Monitor* and the Confederate *Virginia* (former *Merrimac*), the first battle between two ironclad ships, was immediately recognized. *(Library of Congress, Prints and Photographs Division, LC-USZC4–1752)*

over command to Lieutenant Samuel Dana Greene, who exchanged a few more shots with *Virginia*. After several hours, with crews exhausted and the ships limping from damage to smokestacks and deck gear, both retired from the action. Worden later recovered vision in one eye, but bore the gray imprint of black powder and iron particles on his face the rest of his life. Southern papers reported a *Virginia* victory, while the Union counted the battle as a success and continued to describe the clash as a conflict between the *Monitor* and the *Merrimac,* insisting on retaining the Union name for the ship that had threatened to sink the whole Union fleet.

Although the battle might justly be termed a draw in its outcome, it had the effect of driving *Virginia* back to Norfolk for repairs, where she remained confined over the next few months. Facing Union land forces, the Confederates evacuated the navy yard and blew up *Virginia* on May 10, 1862, rather than let her fall into Union hands. Although *Monitor* made a few more patrols, the innovative ship was lost at sea on December 31, 1862, while being towed South. The revolving turret design of USS *Monitor* had proven effective, even though the application was flawed in that it was hard to stop the turret once it began to revolve. The turret concept together with the low profile of *Monitor* was soon replicated by the construction of dozens of single- and double-turret monitors by the Union. Almost immediately after the clash of the ironclads, American and European editorialists and commentators saw the battle as a historic engagement, with deeper implications for the future of naval warfare, and they were right.

THE CAPTURE OF THE *PLANTER*

Early on the morning of May 13, 1862, Robert Smalls, a slave employed as a pilot aboard the Confederate steamer *Planter,* quietly steered the ship through the harbor of Charleston. The cotton steamer had been converted to serve as a dispatch boat, and it was loaded with some 200 pounds of ammunition and carried four guns. Smalls had aboard eight fellow slaves and their wives and children, including Robert's brother, John Smalls, who served as assistant engineer. Robert Smalls had been planning the escape since he had heard of the Union capture of his hometown, Beaufort, South Carolina, and the recruiting of black troops at Port Royal. Working with his brother, he had quietly laid plans for the escape, waiting for a night when the white officers were ashore on leave and when the ship was loaded with a valuable cargo. When the Confederate officers left on the evening of May 12, they instructed Smalls to get ready for the next day's trip out to Forts Sumter and Ripley with a supply of powder. Smalls sent for his friends and family, and they were ready to steam out before dawn.

The ship passed the Confederate forts, including Sumter, where Smalls gave an innocent blast of his signal whistle, and then sped out of the harbor and approached the blockade ship, *Onward.* Before the startled Union sailors could ready a gun for firing, Smalls hoisted a small white flag, which, because it was so dirty,

After leading a daring seizure of the small Confederate ship *Planter* and turning it over to blockading Union forces off Charleston Harbor, Robert Smalls served in the Union navy. By act of Congress, the navy awarded prize money to Smalls and his group. *(Library of Congress, Prints and Photographs Division, LC-USZ62–117998)*

was at first not recognized as a signal. Steaming closer, Smalls shouted over, offering the ship and her guns, pointing out that they belonged rightfully to the U.S. government. As the slaves danced on deck and shook their fists back at the Confederate fortifications, *Onward* took the prize.

The *Planter* was no great capture, but the courage and daring of Smalls and his fellows immediately caught the imagination of the Northern press. Congress reacted by insisting that the half-share of the value of the ship usually awarded to blockade ship crews be distributed among Smalls and his crew. Even some Northern editorialists who doubted whether emancipation was a good idea believed that Smalls had at least demonstrated that slaves were not docile and happy under the paternalistic system and that he had proven the abolitionists' claim that the desire for freedom was universal.

Smalls later enlisted in the U.S. Navy and helped Union crews track down and defuse emplanted torpedoes in the Charleston area. Later he served as pilot on the monitor *Keokuk* in an attack on Fort Sumter in September 1863. He was promoted to the rank of captain for heroism in that attack and received the command of *Planter*. In a postscript to his exploits, Smalls, capitalizing on his well-earned notoriety, entered politics after the war, serving first in the South Carolina state constitutional convention in 1868, and then in the state legislature from 1868 to 1872. He served as a delegate to the national Republican conventions in 1872 and 1876, and he was elected to Congress as a representative from South Carolina for several terms, 1875–79, 1882–83, and 1884–87.

The gunboat *Planter* was captured by Robert Smalls and delivered to the Union navy off of Charleston. *(Library of Congress, Prints and Photographs Division, LC-USZ62–117998)*

ANACONDA IN BROWN WATER

Many of the battles throughout the whole course of the war were combined operations of army troops and naval vessels operating under joint command. Working out such cooperation between the services was not at all easy. On the Union side, the army believed the navy should have no jurisdiction over interior waterways, and thus river ships through 1862 were manned by mixed crews of naval officers, civilians, and soldiers assigned to river duty, serving under the War Department. Such a cumbersome arrangement left the naval commanders of the river boats without clear authority to build, arm, supply, and man the vessels; several even had to provide their own funds in order to get started. Confusion over the same issue of jurisdiction was even worse on the Confederate side. Private armed ship operations and state navies or naval militias compounded the complexity for rebel commanders, who often had to patch together *ad hoc* command structures on the spot. In several notable situations, Confederate naval and army officers and state officers completely refused to cooperate with each other.[5]

Early in 1862, in the West, Union forces began moving down the Mississippi River from Cairo, Illinois. Crucial to the battles in this region, especially in the upper Mississippi River, in Tennessee, and in Alabama, were newly-designed gunboats, built low to the water and entirely ironclad. These city-class gunboats

J. B. Eads of St. Louis constructed seven ironclad gunboats for the Union in the period from August 1861 to January 1862. *(Library of Congress, Prints and Photographs Division, LC-DIG-cwpbh-05219)*

(because each was named after a city on an inland river) were built by naval constructor Samuel Pook and were also known as Pook's Turtles; they were the first ironclads introduced by the Union.

Samuel Pook understood that river vessels could be designed along entirely different lines than traditional oceangoing craft. Steam-propelled and shallow-draft, they would not require the sleek lines of sailing vessels, he argued. Instead, he developed a hull that was shaped like a shingle or bread-slice. The turtles were 175 feet long and broad in the beam at 51 feet, and were rated at just over 500 tons. The flat-bottomed craft drew only six feet, and in still water were supposed to be able to make eight knots, or something better than nine miles an hour. The speed of a flowing river, of course, would either add or detract from that speed, over ground, depending on whether the ship steamed downriver or upriver. Casemates, or armored gun emplacements, were protected with iron slabs 2 ½ inches thick, with three heavy guns aimed forward, four smaller ones on each side, and two pointed to the rear. The paddlewheel was mounted in a protected well inside the rear armored casemate. However, much of the small boat was left unarmored, which proved to be a serious flaw in battle. Although the Confederates had already armored wooden vessels in 1861, such as *Virginia* and a wooden tug, *Manassas,* construction on *St. Louis,* the first of Pook's Turtles designed from the start as an ironclad, began on September 27, 1861, fully two months before Ericsson laid the keel of *Monitor.* Designed by Pook, the work was contracted to a St. Louis engineer, James Eads, who worked his crews around the clock, seven days a week, to get the gunboats into service. Seven gunboats were commissioned in mid-January 1862: *Cairo, Carondelet, Cincinnati, Louisville, Mound City, Pittsburg,* and *St. Louis. St. Louis* was later renamed *Baron de Kalb.* The Pook-designed and Eads-built craft soon made headlines and history.

The turtles saw decisive action on February 4, 1862, at Fort Henry on the Tennessee River. Conventional wisdom held that wooden warships had to mount five times as much ordnance as a shore emplacement or fort in order to have an equal battle, but the ironclads demonstrated that new calculations would be required. With *Cincinnati* as flagship, Captain Andrew Hull Foote commanded the fleet, while General Ulysses S. Grant accompanied the expedition aboard the partially armored *Essex,* under the command of David Porter's brother, "Dirty" Bill Porter. *Essex* was a casemated gunboat, meaning that the guns were protected behind armor. It was converted from a river ferry and mounted four guns. After witnessing a shell from Fort Henry pass directly through *Essex,* Grant made the decision to march his troops overland rather than attempt to approach the forts by river.

Shelling from *Carondelet* and *Cincinnati* penetrated the earthen protection of the gun emplacements at Fort Henry like .45 slugs through a thin piece of wood, knocking out the fort's guns one by one. *Carondelet* was hit several times, but kept fighting, while aboard the then wooden-armored *Essex,* a 32-pound cannonball blew up one of the boilers, scalding the crew and officers with steam. *Cincinnati,* carrying the flag of the squadron leader, was also the object of careful aim from the fort. At about four in the afternoon, after a full day of gunfire, Confederate general Lloyd Tilghman surrendered. The Confederate losses at the fort included 21 killed, wounded, or missing, while 94 survivors of the rear guard that had stayed to man the guns were taken prisoner. Most of the garrison, some 2,600 troops, had retreated overland to Fort Donelson. Following the battle, Foote ordered the fleet up the Tennessee River, seizing Confederate ships loaded with military equipment and taking as a prize the steamer *Eastport,* which the Confederates were in the process of outfitting as an ironclad ram.

The Fort Henry battle was followed by an attack on Fort Donelson on February 13. Under the command of Henry Walke, *Carondelet* was towed from Paducah, Kentucky, to the fort. Walke ordered a bombardment so that Grant's forces, marching overland from Fort Henry, would know he had arrived. While awaiting the rest of the flotilla under the command of Foote, Walke ordered the attack to continue even after one lucky shot from the fort had wounded several men and splintered some of the oak and iron armor. The rest of the fleet arrived on February 14, carrying a division of troops under General Lew Wallace (later, the author of *Ben-Hur*). Four of the turtles, *Pittsburg, St. Louis, Louisville,* and *Carondelet,* lined up about a half-mile from the fort and blasted the defending gun emplacements. However, as they approached within a few hundred yards, high fire from the bluffs began to rain down on the un-armored upper decks of the turtles. *Pittsburg, St. Louis,* and *Louisville* were all damaged, and only *Carondelet* moved in for a face-to-face shooting match with the guns ashore. After receiving some disastrous hits, and following orders, Walke retreated with Foote. *Carondelet* had lost one rudder, six men killed or mortally wounded, and 13 wounded. The gunboat had been hit 35 times, but still managed to limp back with the flagship from the battle.[6]

Nevertheless, the Union controlled the river downstream from the fort, and Grant's troops approached on the landward side, almost entirely cutting off Fort Donelson on land and water. After an attack by Confederates, Grant's counterattack on Donelson went forward under covering fire from *St. Louis* and *Louisville.* The Confederate officers at Donelson debated who should surrender. Brigadier General John B. Floyd was at the time under indictment by a grand jury in Washington for corruption and mismanagement of funds in his earlier job as secretary of war under President Buchanan and feared being captured. Gideon Pillow, second in command, had a long-standing personal animosity to the third in command, General Simon Bolivar Buckner. When defeat came, Floyd and Pillow evacuated quietly, taking only selected troops with them by river, while Nathan Bedford Forrest slipped away with 700 of his cavalrymen through an ice-crusted slough formed by a backwater of the river. Left to offer the surrender, General Grant's old classmate, S. B. Buckner, was shocked at the ungentlemanly terms offered by Grant; "unconditional surrender," but he had no choice. The fort officially fell to Union forces on February 16. Grant's career was launched and the beginning of the slow collapse of the Confederacy in the west was under way. The press and the public liked the tone of "unconditional surrender," and it entered the lexicon of American warfare, as well as redounding to Grant's reputation. The combined operation of land and river forces had worked well.

The turtles and other Union ironclads continued the fight down the Mississippi and up its eastern tributaries through the late winter and early spring

Union gunboats helped secure Island No. 10 for the Union. *(Library of Congress, Prints and Photographs Division, LC-USZC2–1985)*

of 1862. They participated from February 28 to April 8, 1862, in the extended battles for Island No. 10. That island is about 60 miles by river below Columbus, Kentucky, and it was the Confederate strong point against any Union advance southward along the river. The nearby town of New Madrid on the Missouri side of the river was a weak point of the Confederate defense. On February 28, General John Pope, commanding the Union Army of the Mississippi, marched his troops overland from Commerce, Missouri, toward New Madrid. After struggling through swamps, the force arrived outside New Madrid on March 3 and laid siege to the town. After an ineffectual defense, the Confederates pulled back from New Madrid to Island No. 10 and Tiptonville, a village on the Tennessee side of the river, leaving New Madrid to Pope's troops who occupied it on March 14. The next day, Captain Andrew Foote arrived just upstream with a flotilla of gunboats, including turtles. On the night of April 4, 1862, *Carondelet* passed the Confederate guns emplaced at Island No. 10, and *Pittsburgh* ran past two nights later. Together, the two ironclad turtles blocked the Confederate escape route to the south; on April 8, Confederate general William W. Mackall surrendered Island No. 10 to the Union. Step by step, around the tortuous curves and islands of the Mississippi, the Union had extended its control down from the section where Kentucky, Tennessee, and Missouri share the river, all the way to Fort Pillow, Tennessee, about 40 miles north of Memphis.

Nevertheless, Confederate forces continued to hold key positions along the stretch of the Mississippi River from Memphis, Tennessee, south about 300 miles by river to Vicksburg, Mississippi, and up the Yazoo River tributary that joins the Mississippi at Vicksburg. The Yazoo flows for hundreds of miles through the rich delta lands from Yazoo City and other territory then firmly in Confederate hands. With guns ashore in fortifications at Memphis and along the high bluffs of Vicksburg, armored Union ships would face a withering fire if they tried to pass.

On instructions from Richmond, Confederate captain Isaac Brown was hard at work at Greenwood, 160 miles upstream on the Yazoo River from Yazoo City, outfitting a ship that would play a crucial part in the river wars of the West, the ironclad ram *Arkansas*. Salvaging iron rails from the river and scrounging parts and supplies, Brown worked to get his vessel in shape through the early spring of 1862. A fully casemated ram with two powerful steam engines, the ship was armed with two 8-inch guns, two 32-pounder smoothbore guns, and two 6-inch rifled cannon. The gun carriages were constructed locally, by carpenters who had never seen a ship's gun carriage before; they would later serve quite well.

NEW ORLEANS AND MORE RIVER BATTLES

On April 18, 1862, flag officer David Farragut ordered the bombardment of forts Jackson and St. Philip on the Mississippi River below New Orleans. Farragut had not expected the bombardment to destroy the strongly embedded shore batteries but consented to the plan and operation headed by Captain David Porter. Over six days of steady bombardment, an estimated 16,800 shells rained down on Fort Jackson. The mortar ships were anchored around a bend in the river below the fort, with trees and foliage tied to their masts for camouflage, fairly sheltered from counter-bombardment. Fort Jackson, an old, low-lying and star-shaped fort with heavy earthen walls, was battered by some 1,400 direct hits, which blew holes in the roofing, knocked down a levee that resulted in flooding of the center of the fort, and set fire to flammable wooden structures. The constant bombardment demoralized the Confederate defenders, although the number of casualties inside the heavily casemated walls was slight. After six days, Porter reported the fort afire and his mortar ammunition running low.

Farragut decided to run past the forts, despite their still being able to fire on his ships. Further delay, he believed, would only allow the Confederates more time to prepare their defenses and further exhaust the Union's own supplies and ammunition. On April 24, Farragut's forces succeeded in cutting a line of blockading ships bound together with chain and fought their way past the forts and defending Confederate ships in a spectacular night battle lit by gunfire, burning ships, and blazing rafts piled high with pine knots and pitch and sent downstream by Confederate defenders. The *Manassas,* a tug that had been lightly armored and fitted out as gunboat and ram on a private venture, had been seized by the Confederate navy. She succeeded in ramming the Union steamers *Mississippi* and *Brooklyn* during the struggle. The *Mississippi* in turn attempted to run down the low-lying *Manassas,* narrowly missing her but driving her ashore. After *Mississippi* fired several shots through the thin plating on *Manassas,* her crew jumped ship; *Manassas* broke loose from the mud, drifted a few hundred yards, and exploded.

After a furious engagement with other defending ships and the shore batteries, 13 of Farragut's 17 ships got through, losing 37 men killed and 147 wounded.

The Confederate ram *Manassas* attacked the Union ship *Richmond* at the Southwest Pass during the advance on New Orleans. *(Library of Congress, Prints and Photographs Division, LC-USZ62–109732)*

The scorched and damaged survivors moved upriver and anchored off the city of New Orleans on April 25. Union sailors and marines gingerly ventured into the city. Although no Confederate military officials remained, the mayor and other civilian officials refused to surrender the city. Nevertheless, operating in the face of a hostile mob, Farragut's marines finally raised the U.S. flag over federal facilities in the city on April 29. Word of the fall of New Orleans began to reach both Porter and his mortar fleet as well as the remaining Confederate troops at the downriver forts.

The forts fought on for two more days. The Confederates were wracked by dissension, weakening their resistance. At the moment when Captain Porter was securing signatures on a surrender of Fort St. Philip and Fort Jackson, whose troops had mutinied against their command, the partially completed Confederate ironclad *Louisiana* was set afire and drifted down with the current and onto Porter's mortar fleet and the *Harriet Lane,* where the surrender papers were laid out on a table for signature. Porter thought the attack by a fire ship during a surrender discussion a rather sharp practice and complained to the Confederate fort commanders while they examined the surrender conditions. The Confederate army officers explained to Porter that they had no jurisdiction to arrange a surrender by naval forces and had no responsibility at all over ships under state command or private jurisdictions. Fortunately for all parties, *Louisiana* exploded before reaching the *Harriet Lane. Louisiana* had been similar in design to *Virginia* and a potentially powerful threat to the invading fleet, but her captain, Commander McIntosh, later claimed that he had ordered the ship fired, not with the intention of attacking during the truce and surrender discussions, but in order to prevent the ship from falling into Union hands. In fact, he had dispatched a messenger to warn Porter that the ship, while afire, might burn through its hawsers and drift downriver. Although the Confederates had made an effort to flood the powder magazine, the ship still blew up. Disputes about whether a particular action had represented a *ruse de guerre* of doubtful ethics, a simple accident, or a departure from gentlemanly conduct characterized the maritime war as much as they did the war on land. Some of the disputes continued for years, with charges and counter-charges published well into the 20th century.

Over the period of May and June 1862, as army troops under General Butler occupied New Orleans, Farragut ordered his fleet to steam farther up the Mississippi, taking both Baton Rouge, Louisiana, and Natchez, Mississippi. On June 6, Union forces moving down the river captured or destroyed seven out of eight Confederate gunboats defending Memphis, and that city surrendered to Union forces. Finally, at Vicksburg in June, ships approaching from the North met Farragut's fleet pushing upstream from New Orleans. Altogether, the turtles and gunboats from the north and Farragut's steamers from New Orleans mounted more than 200 guns and 23 mortars. However, the city of Vicksburg, built on the bluffs above the east bank of the river, had the advantage of height. In addition to the gun emplacements on the 200-foot-high cliffs, the city was defended by some 10,000 troops under Confederate general Earl Van Dorn. While Farragut hoped to dig a channel that would divert the river to the west of the city, the river refused to cooperate due to the summer's dropping water level. Meanwhile, his ships and men withered in the Mississippi heat, the men suffering from dysentery and malaria. Before Farragut could withdraw, Isaac Brown arrived after an adventurous trip down the Yazoo from Greenwood, with the newly completed *Arkansas,* commissioned on May 26, 1862.

Aboard *Arkansas* one engine kept dying while the other continued to drive its separate propeller, sending the ship in frustrating, complete circles until the recalcitrant engine would kick in again. Mounting 10 guns and resembling its model, the *Merrimac-Virginia,* the ship could be a formidable opponent despite the balking engines. On his trip down the Yazoo, Brown encountered *Carondelet,* the Union turtle that had fought so notably at forts Henry and Donelson and at Island No. 10. At Memphis, *Arkansas* hit and drove off the smaller *Carondelet.* Surprising the Union fleet at Vicksburg, *Arkansas* pulled in among them, firing in every direction simultaneously, damaging several of the Union craft, including *Queen of the West* and *Essex,* before pulling up under the safety of the Vicksburg bluffs. After a few attempts to sink *Arkansas,* Farragut ordered his fleet downriver, leaving Confederates in control of a crucial reach of the Mississippi from Vicksburg South to Port Hudson, just North of Baton Rouge. Even though Natchez, about halfway between Vicksburg and Port Hudson, had already surrendered to Union control, Confederates could freely ferry across the river both North and South of Natchez for a hundred river miles in each direction.

Encouraged by the Confederate success at Vicksburg, General Van Dorn decided to try to retake Natchez and ordered *Arkansas* to assist in the operation. However, *Arkansas* arrived too late. After an attack by *Essex,* Brown pulled the balky ironclad onto the shoals, ordered everyone aboard to flee into the swamps, and then fired the ship. It blew up behind him, on August 6. Even with the defeat of Van Dorn at Natchez and the loss of *Arkansas,* Vicksburg and a vital stretch of the river remained in Confederate hands through the fall and winter of 1862.

David Porter took credit for conceiving the idea of attacking New Orleans from the sea, although Lincoln and some of his advisers had already toyed with the notion. *(Library of Congress, Prints and Photographs Division, LC-USZ62–113173)*

IMPROVISED INGENUITY

The Confederacy resorted to several innovative methods to make up for its paucity of naval forces. These methods included a wide range of ingenious attempts to address the maritime inferiority of its navy when compared to the large and growing Union naval contingent. As on the Union side, passenger and freight river steamers, tugboats, and harbor craft were armored. Where ironcladding or thin boiler iron was unavailable, ships were sometimes stiffened with timber, or built to act as rams, even without any guns aboard. Some were loaded with bales of cotton and known as "cotton-clads." In unlikely upriver locations like Greensboro, Alabama, conversion and construction hurried forward. As the war stretched on into 1862, new designs of blockade runners appeared, with shallow draft and sleek lines, often with smokestacks raked back, and steam vented underwater to reduce noise. Hundreds of the craft were built in yards in England, Scotland, Ireland, and Canada especially for the purpose; hundreds more, built in New York, Philadelphia, or some other Northern port before or during the war were converted in Southern yards to their new functions. Some of the sleek craft were owned by agencies of various Confederate state governments, some by the Confederate government; the vast majority were owned by private firms engaged in the highly speculative and often highly profitable blockade-running business.

The maritime war in its first two years also saw the development of a range of innovative weapons, including spar torpedoes, emplanted clockwork and electric torpedoes or mines in rivers and harbors, and submarine vessels. Both sides began to consider designs for submarines. A major problem confronting submarine designers in this period was how to propel the ship, since it was impossible to move them by steam power when submerged, for lack of oxygen. The fact that the Confederacy considered and experimented with torpedoes and submarines, weapons of stealth, reflected the realization in the South of the desperate position of the Confederacy when it came to maritime power. Like Germany in World Wars I and II, the Confederacy was at a great naval disadvantage compared to its enemy. And, like Germany, the Confederacy was quick to break with the conventions of the past, resorting to methods that, even as they were employed, caused Confederate sailors to question the ethics of their actions. For a generation that prided itself on gallantry in warfare and the avoidance of *ruses* such as false surrenders or firing of weapons after a flag of truce was shown, the use of weapons that destroyed without fair warning seemed to verge on criminality. Nevertheless, like other nations and peoples at other times in history who fought from a position of weakness, the motivation was strong to resort to methods that violated existing norms of warfare.

Innovation was not the monopoly of the Confederacy, however, as *Monitor* and the western river turtles demonstrated. Such new vessels entirely changed the look of warships from the graceful lines of wooden ships that mounted dozens of weapons in broadside, to new mechanical monsters, belching black coal smoke and steam, with a few heavy guns partially or fully protected behind iron casemates. The change did not come all at once, and during the war many oceangoing warships, powered by both sail and steam, reflected characteristics of both the earlier era and the later one. By December 1862, the beginnings of the revolution in naval warfare could be glimpsed, to be further advanced in the later years of the war.

CHRONICLE OF EVENTS

1861

January 26: U.S. naval officer Raphael Semmes resigns his commission and offers to join any planned Confederate navy.

February 19: The Confederate Provisional Congress creates a Navy Department.

February 28: Stephen R. Mallory of Florida, former chair of the U.S. Senate Naval Committee, is appointed Confederate secretary of the navy.

March 7: Lincoln appoints Gideon Welles as secretary of the navy.

March 16: The Confederacy establishes the Confederate States Marine Corps.

April 19: Lincoln proclaims a naval blockade of seven states of the Confederacy; due to ships being overseas, in repair, or unseaworthy, only 14 U.S. naval ships are available to enforce the blockade. Over the next four years the U.S. Navy will purchase 418 ships and build another 208. The navy will increase from 8,500 officers and men to 58,000 officers and men by the end of the war.

April 27: Lincoln extends the blockade to Virginia and North Carolina. Through four years of war, five out of six ships that attempt it, get through the blockade. Britain and other maritime powers recognize the blockade as legal and effective. The Union navy captures and destroys some 1,500 blockade runners, including intra-coastal ships.

May 9: Augustus Vasa Fox is appointed chief clerk of the U.S. Navy.

May 23: Lloyd J. Beall is appointed commandant of the Confederate States Marine Corps.

June: The Commission of Conference (Blockading Board or Strategy Board), chaired by Captain Samuel Du Pont, establishes a blockade plan to strangle the Confederate economy with two blockading squadrons, Atlantic and Gulf.

August 1: Augustus Fox is promoted from chief clerk to assistant secretary of the navy.

August 28–29: Union ships take Fort Hatteras and Fort Clark at Hatteras Inlet.

September: The Atlantic Blockading Squadron is split into the North Atlantic Blockading Squadron (NABS) and the South Atlantic Blockading Squadron (SABS). NABS covers Chesapeake Bay to Wilmington, North Carolina; SABS blockades from Wilmington to Cape Canaveral.

September 6: Flag Officer Andrew Hull Foote arrives in St. Louis to take command of the western river flotilla.

September 17: The Union takes Ship Island off the Gulf coast of Mississippi; the island becomes one of the bases for the Gulf Blockading Squadron.

September 18: The first blockade runner with a cargo of arms for the Confederacy, *Bermuda*, arrives in Savannah, Georgia. Included in the cargo are 6,500 Enfield rifles, 20,000 cartridges, and at least 18 rifled field cannon.

September 18: Flag Officer Samuel Francis Du Pont is placed in charge of the South Atlantic Blockading Squadron.

October 25: The keel of the ironclad *Monitor*, designed by John Ericsson, is laid; construction is completed within about 90 days, in late January 1862.

November 6: Two wooden gunboats, *Tyler* and *Lexington*, assist General U.S. Grant in the battle at Belmont, Missouri, preventing further losses during the Union retreat.

November 7: A U.S. naval squadron under Flag Officer Samuel Francis Du Pont takes Port Royal, South Carolina, and surrounding islands. Port Royal becomes the headquarters for the South Atlantic Blockading Squadron.

November 7: U.S. gunboats on the Mississippi engage in the Battle of Belmont.

November 8: USS *San Jacinto* detains the British mail steamer *Trent*, which had departed Havana, Cuba, on November 7; Union sailors remove James Mason and John Slidell, Confederate envoys on their way to Europe.

November 14: A blockade runner, *Fingal*, arrives at Savannah from West Hartlepool, England, with a cargo of weapons and supplies. Trapped at Savannah, the ship is later clad with iron and converted to a warship, *Atlanta*.

1862

January 1: Mason and Slidell are released by the U.S. government, defusing the *Trent* affair.

January 9: Flag Officer David Farragut takes command of the West Gulf Blockading Squadron, with the objective of taking New Orleans.

January 16: The United States commissions seven armored gunboats for the Mississippi. The seven are *Cairo, Carondelet, Cincinnati, Louisville, Mound City, Pittsburg,* and *St. Louis;* they are nicknamed Pook Turtles for their designer, Samuel Pook. Known as the

City class gunboats or Cairo class, these are the first Union ironclads, 512 tons, 175 feet long, draft of six feet, protected with 2.5-inch iron armor.

January 20: The Gulf Blockading Squadron is divided into the East Gulf Blockading Squadron (EGBS) and West Gulf Blockading Squadron (WGBS). EGBS operates out of Key West and covers the area from Pensacola to Cape Canaveral; WGBS covers Pensacola to the Rio Grande, operating out of bases in Pensacola and Ship Island, Mississippi, and is first commanded by Flag Officer David Farragut.

February 4–16: The Union mounts combined naval and army attacks on Forts Henry and Donelson on the Tennessee River in western Tennessee; U.S. Grant commands army forces and Flag Officer Andrew Foote commands riverine forces, under War Department rather than Navy Department orders.

February 7: A squadron of almost 100 widely assorted ships under the command of Flag Officer Louis Goldsborough, with troops under the command of General Ambrose Burnside, takes Roanoke Island in North Carolina.

February 25: USS *Monitor* is commissioned.

February 28–April 8: The river battle of Island No. 10 on the Mississippi River.

March 3: Naval forces under Flag Officer Samuel Francis Du Pont take Fernandina, Florida.

March 8: The ironclad CSS *Virginia* (formerly the *Merrimac*) and accompanying ships destroy the USS *Cumberland* and USS *Congress* and force the USS *Minnesota* aground off Hampton Roads, Virginia. This engagement is hailed in the Southern press as a great Confederate victory.

March 9: In the first battle between two ironclads, CSS *Virginia* and USS *Monitor* clash for four hours off Hampton Roads; although the battle is inconclusive, *Virginia* retires.

March 22: The twin-bladed screw steamer *Oreto* is secretly taken from Liverpool to Nassau in the Bahamas. There it is smuggled out on August 17, armed, and becomes the commerce raider CSS *Florida*.

April 4: The Union gunboat *Carondelet* gets past the Confederate batteries on Island No. 10 at New Madrid, Missouri.

April 18: Under Admiral Farragut, the U.S. fleet begins a six-day bombardment of Fort Jackson on the Mississippi River below New Orleans.

April 24: Farragut's fleet runs past the forts, destroys several enemy ships, and advances toward New Orleans.

April 25: Federal warships anchor at New Orleans, and naval officers attempt to arrange a surrender of the city.

May 9–10: Confederates evacuate the Norfolk-Gosport naval yard in Virginia.

May 10: USS *New Ironsides* is launched in Philadelphia; a steam frigate, the ship is mostly ironclad with 4.5-inch iron and carries 16 11-inch Dahlgren guns. The ship becomes the flagship of Rear Admiral Samuel F. Du Pont off Charleston.

May 10: Union forces take Pensacola, Florida.

May 11: Confederates evacuate and blow up CSS *Virginia* off Craney Island in the James River.

May 12: In a daring exploit, a party of eight African-American slaves led by Robert Smalls, together with their wives and children, takes over the Confederate steamer *Planter* and delivers it with its ordnance to the U.S. blockade ship *Onward* off Charleston. Smalls is proclaimed a hero, and the U.S. Senate orders that half the proceeds of the sale of the *Planter* be distributed to Smalls and his crew.

May 15: The Confederate navy establishes a naval school at Drewry's Bluff, Virginia, under William H. Parker.

June 6: The Battle of Memphis on the Mississippi River is fought; of eight Confederate ships, four are captured and three destroyed; the gunboat *Van Dorn* retreats. Memphis is taken by Union forces.

June 28: Farragut takes his fleet past the Vicksburg batteries and initiates attempts to dig a channel to divert the Mississippi River.

July 1: Naval forces help in the transfer of the Army of the Potomac to Harrison's Landing on the James River in Virginia.

July 5: The U.S. Navy establishes several new bureaus. Dividing the responsibilities formerly covered by the Bureau of Construction, Equipment and Repair, two new bureaus are established: Bureau of Steam Engineering, headed by Benjamin F. Isherwood, and Bureau of Equipment and Recruiting, headed first by Andrew H. Foote. The Bureau of Ordnance is split from the Bureau of Ordnance and Hydrography and will be placed under the direction of John A. Dahlgren on July 22, 1862; the Bureau of Navigation will also be organized on this date.

July 14–22: The CSS *Arkansas*, ironclad, fights down the Yazoo River, damaging the Union's *Carondelet* and *Queen of the West* and joins Confederate forces at Vicksburg; *Arkansas* clashes with the *Essex* and the *Arkansas* survives. Union ships retire north and south

As Union gunboats ran the gauntlet of fire to New Orleans, the battle lit the night. *(Library of Congress, Prints and Photographs Division, LC-USZC2–1917)*

from Vicksburg for the season. Confederates maintain control of the river from Vicksburg south almost to Baton Rouge, Louisiana.

July 16: The U.S. Congress approves the creation in the navy of the rank of rear admiral; prior to this date the highest rank was that of captain; officers in charge of squadrons were designated flag officers.

July 30: The first flag officer to be granted the rank of rear admiral is David Farragut; his appointment is dated back to July 16, the date of creation of the rank, in honor of his victory at New Orleans in April.

August 6: The Confederate gunboat *Arkansas* is damaged in naval engagement with three Union vessels at Baton Rouge on the Mississippi; the crew scuttle and destroy the gunboat.

August 21: The ironclad Union frigate *New Ironsides* is commissioned.

October 1: Union gunboats on the Mississippi, previously operating directly under the War Department, are officially put under the navy command of David Dixon Porter.

November 22: The blockade runner *Fingal* is recommissioned as the Confederate casemate ram, CSS *Atlanta,* based at Savannah.

December 12: The 512–ton Union gunboat *Cairo* is destroyed on the Yazoo River by an improvised torpedo implanted under the direction of Confederate captain Isaac Brown, former commander of the *Arkansas.*

December 29: The USS *Monitor* is lost off Cape Hatteras while being towed during a storm.

EYEWITNESS TESTIMONY

Permit me to remind you of the conversation we had just before you left Washington. I think States enough have gone out to determine me as to the course I shall pursue. If invited by the Confederacy of the Cotton States I will accept service in its navy and abandon my present position. The chances are that Maryland (my native State) and all the other border slave states will speedily follow you, but whether they do or not I will cast my destiny with yours if you will permit me. I am in some sort claimed as a citizen of Alabama, having resided in that state several years before I was ordered to Washington upon my present duty, and it is probable that my nomination to the new executive for a post in the navy of the new Confederacy will be made by Gov'r Fitzpatrick and other friends from that State. However this may be, may I ask you also to perform this service for me and to inform me promptly of your action and that of the new President in the premises? . . . As you are a delegate to the convention to form the new Government I may perhaps not inappropriately say a word or two to you on the subject of the organization of your army and navy. The Southern States being planting and agricultural States and but little engaged in commerce and navigation (though doubtless their separation from the North will make them more commercial and navigating than they have hitherto been), they will require but a small naval force for several years to come; and it strikes me also that it will be bad policy to establish a large army. I would advise therefore that both your navy and army lists be kept within very small compass. I mean the regular forces of each, or such as are to be kept on foot as well in peace as in war. If a war ensue, which I do not anticipate, your regular military establishment can be temporarily increased to meet the emergency by appointments and enlistments to continue during the war and by the commissioning of privateers and other irregular maritime forces to serve during the same period. This will enable you at the end of the war to dismiss, as a matter of course and without complaints, all the personnel of both services excepting only the small army and navy lists before referred to. I have said that I do not think we shall have a war and these are my reasons for the opinion. If the border slave states join you the old confederacy [the Union] will be split nearly in half, and the idea of coercion would be simply ridiculous; if they do not join you, being retained by compromises that will satisfy them, they will be a barrier and a safeguard to you and will

hold the hands of the Vandals who might otherwise be disposed to make war upon you. No slave state could possibly be an ally of the free states in a war upon slave states upon the slave question. Be cool therefore in organizing your military and naval establishments and do not consent to place too great burthens upon the shoulders of the people. It is easier to make armies and navies than to get rid of them when made, and the people will not and ought not to submit to exhorbitant taxation to support large establishments for which they ordinarily have no use. One word more and I shall have done.

Your naval officers I suppose will be taken from the present navy list of the old government. Preserve their relative rank in their new relations. You know rank is of essence with military and naval men, and the rule I suggest to you is not only just and proper and will work well but it will put an end to all jealousies, rivalries and heart-burnings. May I ask the favor of a line in reply?

Raphael Semmes, commander, U.S. Navy, to Howell Cobb, then president of the Confederate Provisional Congress, January 26, 1861, offering unsolicited advice on matters of state and organization of the naval service of the Confederacy, as published in U. B. Phillips, The Correspondence of Robert Toombs, Alexander H. Stephens, and Howell Cobb, *pp. 533–535.*

U. S. Steamer *San Jacinto.* At sea, Nov. 8, 1861. Sir: You will have the second and third cutters of this ship fully manned and armed and be in all respects ready to board the steamer *Trent,* now hove to under our guns.

On boarding her you will demand the papers of the steamer, her clearance from Havana, with the list of passengers and crew.

Should Mr. Mason, Mr. Slidell, Mr. Eustis, and Mr. McFarland be on board, you will make them prisoners and send them on board this ship immediately, and take possession of her as a prize.

I do not deem it will be necessary to use force, that the prisoners will have the good sense to avoid any necessity for using it; but if they should they must be made to understand that it is their own fault.

They must be brought on board.

All trunks, cases, packages, and bags belonging to them you will take possession of, and send on board this ship; any dispatches found on the persons of the prisoners, or in possession of those on board the steamer, will be taken possession of, examined, and retained if necessary.

I have understood that the families of these gentlemen may be with them; if so, I beg you will offer some of them in my name a passage in this ship to the United States, and that all the attention and comforts we can command are tendered them and will be placed in their service.

In the event of their acceptance, should there be anything which the captain of the steamer can spare to increase the comforts in the way of necessaries or stores, of which a war vessel is deficient, you will please to procure them; the amount will be paid for by the paymaster.

Lieutenant James A. Greer will take charge of the third cutter which accompanies you, and assist you in these duties. I trust that all those under your command in executing this important and delicate duty will conduct themselves with all the delicacy and kindness which become the character of our Naval Service.

I am, very respectfully, your obedient servant, Charles Wilkes, Captain. To Lieutenant D. M. Fairfax, USN Executive Officer, *San Jacinto.*

Orders of Captain Charles Wilkes to Executive Officer, Lieutenant D. M. Fairfax, regarding arrest of Mason and Slidell from the Trent, *including his orders to take the ship as a prize, November 8, 1861, as included as a footnote to Fairfax's own report of the incident, in Robert Underwood Johnson and Clarence Clough Buel,* Battles and Leaders of the Civil War, *Vol. II, p. 136.*

I was impressed with the gravity of my position, and I made up my mind not to do anything unnecessary in the arrest of these gentlemen, or anything that would irritate the captain of the *Trent,* or any of his passengers, particularly the commissioners—lest it might occur to them to throw the steamer on my hands, which would necessitate my taking her as a prize.

Executive Officer, Lieutenant D. M. Fairfax, regarding his handling of the arrest of Mason and Slidell from the Trent, *November 8, 1861, in Fairfax's own report of the incident, in Robert Underwood Johnson and Clarence Clough Buel,* Battles and Leaders of the Civil War, *Vol. II, p. 136.*

On the 9th of November, 1861, I arrived at New York with the *Powhatan* and was ordered to report to the Navy Department, which I did on the 12th. In those days it was not an easy matter for an officer, except one of high rank, to obtain access to the Secretary of the Navy, and I had been waiting nearly all the morning at the door of his office when Senators Grimes and Hale came along and entered into conversation with me concerning my service on the Gulf Coast. During this interview I told the senators of a plan I had formed for the capture of New Orleans, and when I had explained to them how easily it could be accomplished, they expressed surprise that no action had been taken in the matter, and took me in with them at once to see Secretary Welles. I then gave the Secretary, in as few words as possible, my opinion on the importance of capturing New Orleans, and my plan for doing so. Mr. Welles listened to me attentively, and when I had finished what I had to say he remarked that the matter should be laid before the President at once; and we all went forthwith to the Executive Mansion, where we were received by Mr. Lincoln.

My plan, which I then stated, was as follows: To fit out a fleet of vessels-of-war with which to attack the city, fast steamers drawing not more than 18 feet of water, and carrying about 250 heavy guns; also a flotilla of mortar-vessels, to be used in case it should be necessary to bombard Fort Jackson and St. Philip before the fleet should attempt to pass them. I also proposed that a body of troops should be sent along in transports to take possession of the city after it had been surrendered to the navy. When I had outlined the proposed movement the President remarked:

"This should have been done sooner. The Mississippi is the backbone of the Rebellion; it is the key to the whole situation. While the Confederates hold it they can obtain supplies of all kinds, and it is a barrier against our force. Come, let us go and see General McClellan.". . .

[Lincoln] then explained to the general the object of his calling at that time, saying: "This is a most important expedition. What troops can you spare to accompany it and take possession of New Orleans after the navy has effected its capture? It is not only necessary to have troops enough to hold New Orleans, but we must be able to proceed at once toward Vicksburg, which is the key to all that country watered by the Mississippi and its tributaries. If the Confederates once fortify the neighboring hills, they will be able to hold that point for an indefinite time, and it will require a large force to dislodge them."

Admiral D. D. Porter, recalling the decision to attack New Orleans, taken at a meeting November 12, 1861, in Robert Underwood Johnson and Clarence Clough Buel, Battles and Leaders of the Civil War, *Vol. II, pp. 23–24.*

When the *Carondelet,* her tow being cast off, came in sight of the fort [Donelson] and proceeded up to within long range of the batteries, not a living creature could be seen. The hills and woods on the west side of the river hid part of the enemy's formidable defenses, which were lightly covered with snow; but the black rows of heavy guns, pointing down on us, reminded me of the dismal looking sepulchers cut in the rocky cliffs near Jerusalem, but far more repulsive. At 12:50 P.M., to unmask the silent enemy, and to announce my arrival to General Grant, I ordered the bow-guns to be fired at the fort. Only one shell fell short. There was no response except the echo from the hills. The fort appeared to have been evacuated. After firing ten shells into it, the *Carondelet* dropped down the river about three miles and anchored. But the sound of her guns aroused our soldiers on the Southern side of the fort into action; one report says that when they heard the guns of the *avant-courrier* of the fleet, they gave cheer upon cheer, and rather than permit the sailors to get ahead of them again, they engaged in skirmishes with the enemy, and began the battle of the three days following. On the *Carondelet* we were isolated and beset with dangers from the enemy's lurking sharpshooters.

On the 13th a dispatch was received from General Grant, informing me that he had arrived the day before, and had succeeded in getting his army in position, almost entirely investing the enemy's works. "Most of our batteries," he said, "are established, and the remainder soon will be. If you will advance with your gun-boat at 10 o'clock in the morning, we will be ready to take advantage of any diversion in our favor."

I immediately complied with these instructions, and at 9:05, with the *Carondelet* alone and under cover of a heavily wooded point, fired 139 70-pound and 64-pound shells at the fort. We received in return the fire of all the enemy's guns that could be brought to bear on the *Carondelet,* which sustained but little damage, except from two shots. One, a 128-pound solid, at 11:30 struck the corner of our port casemate, passed through it, and in its progress toward the center of our boilers glanced over the temporary barricade in front of the boilers. It then passed over the steam-drum, struck the beams of the upper deck, carried away the railing around the engine-room and burst the steam-heater, and glancing back into the engine-room, "seemed to bound after the men," as one of the engineers said, "like a wild beast pursuing its prey." I have preserved this ball as a souvenir of the fight at Fort Donelson. When it burst through the side of the *Carondelet,* it knocked down and wounded a dozen men, seven of them severely. An immense quantity

of splinters was blown through the vessel. Some of them, as fine as needles, shot through the clothes of the men like arrows. Several of the wounded were so much excited by the suddenness of the event and the sufferings of their comrades, that they were not aware that they themselves had been struck until they felt the blood running into their shoes. Upon receiving this shot we ceased firing for a while.

Henry Walke, commander of Carondelet, *describing the opening of the battle of Fort Donelson, February 12 and 13, 1862, in Robert Underwood Johnson and Clarence Clough Buel,* Battles and Leaders of the Civil War, *Vol. I, p. 431.*

Our gunners kept up a constant firing while we were falling back; and the warning words, "Look out!" "Down!" were often heard, and heeded by nearly all the gun-crews. On one occasion, while the men were at the muzzle of the middle bow-gun, loading it, the warning came just in time for them to jump aside as a 32-pounder struck the lower sill, and glancing up struck the upper sill, then, falling on the inner edge of the lower sill bounded on deck and spun around like a top, but hurt no one. It was very evident that if the men who were loading had not obeyed the order to drop, several of them would have been killed. So I repeated the instructions and warned the men at the guns and the crew generally to bow or stand off from the ports when a shot was seen coming. But some of the young men, from a spirit of bravado or from a belief in the doctrine of fatalism, disregarded the instructions, saying it was useless to attempt to dodge a cannon-ball, and they would trust to luck. The warning words, "Look out!" "Down!" were again soon heard; down went the gunner and his men, as the whizzing shot glanced on the gun, taking off the gunner's cap and the heads of two of the young men who trusted to luck, and in defiance of the order were standing up or passing behind him. This shot killed another man also, who was at the last gun of the starboard side, and disabled the gun. It came in with a hissing sound; three sharp spats and a heavy bang told the sad fate of three brave comrades. Before the decks were well sanded, there was so much blood on them that our men could not work the guns without slipping.

Henry Walke, commander of Carondelet, *describing action during withdrawal from the battle of Fort Donelson, February 14, 1862, in Robert Underwood Johnson and Clarence Clough Buel,* Battles and Leaders of the Civil War, *Vol. I, p. 435.*

Just before sunset I took a ramble through the grounds and encampments of the rebels. It is impossible to describe the scene. The rebels were falling into line preparatory to embarking upon the steamers. Standing upon a hill beyond the village, I had at one view almost all their force. Hogarth never saw such a sight; Shakespeare, in his conceptions of Falstaff's tatterdemalions, could not have imagined the like. I do not mean that they were deficient in intellect, for among them were noble men, brave fellows, who shed tears when they found that they were prisoners of war, and who swore with round oaths that they would shoot Floyd as they would a dog, if they could get a chance, but for grotesque appearance they were never equaled, except by the London bagman and chiffoniers of Paris.

There were all sorts of uniforms, brown colored predominating, as if they were in the snuff business and had been rolled in tobacco dust. There was sheep gray, iron gray, blue gray, dirty gray, with bed blankets, quilts, buffalo robes, pieces of carpeting of all colors and figures, for blankets. Each had his pack on his shoulder. Judging by their garments, one would have thought that the last scrapings, odds and ends of humanity, had been brought together. I do not write this as impeaching at all their bravery, but to show the straitened condition of the Southern Confederacy that can only give its troops such an outfit.

Crossing a ravine I came upon three guns of the battery attached to Floyd's brigade, which had become stuck in the mud, when with his command he silently stole away. The horses had been cut from the traces, the harnesses left in the road and were trampled in the mud. Beyond, picketed in the village grave yard, were several hundred horses and mules. Arms, equipments, blankets were scattered over the ground and trampled in the mud—all indicating the immense waste of property, and loss to the rebels.

Passing through a ravine, I came upon a negro trudging under a heavy load. He said that he was a free man; that he lived in Tennessee, and had been impressed into the service to cook, and dig intrenchments. I noticed many others. He said that some were slaves, servants to the officers, and that others had been impressed. . . .

I mingled freely with the prisoners, officers and men, to ascertain, if possible, their views and feelings. There is a marked difference between those from Mississippi, Arkansas and Texas, from the Kentuckians and Tennesseans. Those from the Gulf States were sour, not inclined to talk as a general rule; or if talk-ative, they at once commenced about the negro, and were defiant.

The Tennesseans, I think, or a majority of them, were not much sorry that the result was as it was. I heard one Mississippian express his utter contempt of the Tennesseans. The Mississippi Colonel informed me that if compelled to retreat from Nashville it wold be given to the flames, and if we moved South we should find all the cities and towns destroyed, and if at last we conquered, we should find a destroyed country. It is not easy to understand such insanity.

Extract from an account by an eyewitness to the surrender of the Confederates at Fort Donelson, originally published in the Boston Journal, *as reproduced in the* New York Evangelist, *under the title "The Scene after the Surrender of Fort Donelson," 32, no. 10 (March 6, 1862), p. 7.*

C. S. Steam Battery Virginia [former Merrimac]
Off Sewell's Point, March 8, 1862
Flag-Officer: In consequence of the wound of Flag-Officer Buchanan, it becomes my duty to report that the *Virginia* left the Yard this morning at 11 o'clock A.M., steamed down the river past our batteries, and over to Newport's News, where we engaged the frigates *Cumberland* and *Congress* and the batteries ashore, and also two large steam-frigates, a sailing frigate, and several small steamers armed with heavy rifled guns. We sunk the *Cumberland,* drove the *Congress* ashore, where she hauled down her colors and hoisted the white flag; but she fired upon us with the white flag flying, wounding Lieut. Minor and some of our men. We again opened fire upon her, and she is now in flames. The shoal water prevented our reaching the other frigates. This, with approaching night, we think, saved them from destruction. Our loss is two killed and eight wounded. Two of our guns have the muzzles shot off; the prow was twisted, and armor somewhat damaged; the anchor and all flag-staffs shot away, and smoke-stack and steam-pipe were riddled. The bearing of officers and men was all that could be wished, and in fact it could not have been otherwise, after the noble and daring conduct of the Flag-Officer, whose wound is deeply regretted by all on board, who would kindly have sacrificed themselves in order to save him. We were accompanied from the yard by the *Beaufort,* Lieut. Parker, and *Raleigh,* Lieut. Alexander, and as soon as it was discovered up the James River that the action had commenced, we were joined by the *Patrick Henry,* Commander Tucker, the *Jamestown,*

Lieut. Barney, and the *Teaser*, Lieut. Webb, all of which were actively engaged, and rendered very efficient service. Inclosed I send the surgeons' report of the casualties. I have the honor to be, Sir, very respectfully, your obedient servant. Catesby Ap R. Jones, Ex. and Ord. Officer.

Catesby ap R. Jones to Flag Officer F. Forrest, reporting on initial victories of the Virginia (the Confederate ironclad rebuild of the Merrimac) on March 8, 1862, as quoted in an article entitled, "The Naval Battle in Hampton Roads. Official Rebel Report of the Engagement," in the New York Times, March 14, 1862, p. 8.

Early in the morning the Ericsson Battery, now called the *Monitor*, was discovered off Newport's News Point, she having gone up there during the night. A sharp encounter soon took place between her and the *Virginia*, during which time they were frequently not more than 30 or 40 yards apart. Unfortunately the *Virginia* ran aground and the *Ericsson* using her advantage, poured shot after shot into her, but without doing any serious damage. In a short while, however, the *Virginia* succeeded in getting off, and putting on full head of steam, ran her bow into the *Ericsson*, doing, as it is thought, great damage.

We are rejoiced to say that notwithstanding the firing was much heavier than on Saturday, there were no casualties on either of our vessels—not a man being in the least injured by shots from the enemy or otherwise.

Several of the enemy's gunboats being within range, they were favored with a shell or two from the *Virginia* with telling effect, and in every case disabling or sinking them. One of these laying alongside the *Minnesota* had a shell thrown aboard of her, which on bursting tore her asunder and sent her to the bottom.

Having completely riddled the *Minnesota*, and disabled the *St. Lawrence* and *Monitor*, besides, as stated above, destroying several of the enemy's gunboats—in a word, having accomplished all that they designed, and having no more material to work upon, our noble vessels left the scene of their triumphs and returned to the yard, where they await another opportunity of displaying their prowess.

News report, entitled "The Great Naval Victory," portraying the clash of ironclads as a Confederate victory, from The Norfolk Day Book of the 10th, as reported in the New York Times, March 14, 1862, p. 8.

This terrible battle of the ships—*Monitor, Merrimac*, etc. All hands on board the *Cumberland* went down. She fought gallantly and fired a round as she sank. The *Congress* ran up a white flag. She fired on our boats as they went up to take off her wounded. She was burned. The worst of it is that all this will arouse them to more furious exertions to destroy us. They hated us so before, but how now?

In the naval battle the other day we had twenty-five guns in all. The enemy had fifty-four in the *Cumberland*, forty-four in the *St. Lawrence*, besides a fleet of gunboats, filled with rifled cannon. Why not? They can have as many as they please, the whole boundless world being theirs to recruit in. Ours is only this one little spot of ground—the blockade, or stockade, which hems us in with only the sky open to us. For all that, how tender-footed and cautious they are as they draw near.

Mary Chesnut, planter-class diarist, commenting on Monitor-Merrimac clash in her diary entries of March 11 and 12, 1862, in Ben Ames Williams, ed., A Diary from Dixie, p. 198.

. . . The wonderful duel between the *Monitor* and the *Merrimac* has still an infinity to teach us. Important as was the naval action that took place in Hampton Roads, on Saturday and Sunday, regarded as an event in the war, its special interest is already swallowed up in the vast proportions of the problem which it opens to the world. At one stroke a blow is aimed at the rebellion, and a new chapter added to science. A problem on which the nations of Europe have for ten years lavished all the resources of their wealth and skill, to arrive at no satisfactory result, is suddenly taken up in the shock of war, put to the crucial test, and pushed far on toward a definitive solution. For the first time, iron-clad vessels have met in battle, and the engagement between the *Merrimac* and the *Monitor* has given us all we practically know of this new and terrible enginery of war. Of course, the whole world will look with intense interest for full and accurate details.

Editorial entitled "The Exploit of the Monitor-A Scientific Comment" in the New York Times, March 13, 1862, p. 4.

The first act of Farragut was to send Captain Henry H. Bell, his chief-of-staff, up the river with the steamers *Kennebec* and *Wissahickon*, to ascertain, if possible, what preparations had been made by the enemy to prevent the passage of the forts. This officer reported that the obstructions seemed formidable. Eight hulks

The clash of the *Monitor* and *Merrimac* was the subject of numerous prints and paintings. *(Library of Congress, Prints and Photographs Division, LC-USZC2–1319)*

were moored in line across the river, with heavy chains extending from one to the other. Rafts of logs were also used, and the passage between the forts was thus entirely closed.

The Confederates had lost no time in strengthening their defenses. They had been working night and day ever since the expedition was planned by the Federal Government. Forts Jackson and St. Philip were strong defenses, the former on the west and the latter on the east bank of the Mississippi. . . .

Fort Jackson was built in the shape of a star, of stone and mortar, with heavy bomb-proofs. It set back about one hundred yards from the levee, with its casemates just rising above it. I am told that the masonry had settled somewhat since it was first built, but it was still in a good state of preservation. Its armament consisted of 42 heavy guns in barbette, and 24 in casemates; also 2 pieces of light artillery and 6 guns in water-battery —in all, 74 guns. The last was a very formidable part of the defenses, its heavy guns having a command-

ing range down the river. The main work had been strengthened by covering its bomb-proofs and vulnerable part with bags of sand piled five or six feet deep, making it proof against the projectiles of ordinary guns carried by ships-of-war in those days. The fort was also well supplied with provisions and munitions of war, which were stowed away in a heavily built citadel of masonry situated in the center of the works. Altogether, it was in a very good condition to withstand either attack or siege. Fort Jackson was under the immediate command of Lieutenant-Colonel Edward Higgins, formerly an officer of the United States navy, and a very gallant and intelligent man.

Fort St. Philip was situated on the other side of the river, about half a mile above Fort Jackson, and, in my opinion, was the more formidable of the two works. It covered a large extent of ground, and although it was open, without casemates, its walls were strongly built of brick and stone, covered with sod. The guns were mounted in barbette, and could be brought to bear on any vessel going up or down the river. There were in all 52 pieces of ordnance. One heavy rifled gun bore on the position of the mortar fleet, and caused us considerable disturbance until the second or third day after the bombardment commenced, when it burst.

Admiral D. D. Porter, in a memoir written in 1872, describing the defenses of forts St. Philip and Jackson below New Orleans before commencing the attack on New Orleans, about March 18–20, 1862, in Robert Underwood Johnson and Clarence Clough Buel, Battles and Leaders of the Civil War, *Vol. II, p. 29.*

I informed the officers and crew of the character of the undertaking, and all expressed a readiness to make the venture. In order to resist boarding parties, in case of being disabled, the sailors were well-armed, and pistols, cutlasses, muskets, boarding-pikes, and hand-grenades were within reach. Hose was attached to the boilers for throwing scalding water over any who might attempt to board. If it should be found impossible to save the vessel, it was designed to sink rather than burn her. During the afternoon there was a promise of a clear moonlight night, and it was determined to wait until the moon was down, and then to make the attempt whatever the chances. Having gone so far, we could not abandon the project without an effect on the men almost as bad as failure.

At 10 o'clock the moon had gone down, and the sky, the earth, and the river were alike hidden in the black shadow of a thunder-storm, which had now spread itself over all the heavens. As the time seemed favorable, I ordered the first master to cast off. Dark clouds now rose rapidly over us and enveloped us in almost total darkness, except when the sky was lighted up by the welcome flashes of vivid lightning, to show us the perilous way we were to take. Now and then the dim outline of the landscape could be seen, and the forest bending under the roaring storm that came rushing up the river.

With our bow pointing to the island, we passed the lowest point of land without being observed, it appears, by the enemy. All speed was given to the vessel to drive her through the tempest. The flashes of lightning continued with frightful brilliancy, and "almost every second," wrote a correspondent, " every brace, post, and outline could be seen with startling distinctness, enshrouded by a bluish white glare of light, and then her form for the next minute would become merged in the intense darkness." When opposite Battery No. 2, on the mainland, the smoke-stacks blazed up, but the fire was soon subdued. It was caused by the soot becoming dry, as the escape-steam, which usually kept the stacks wet, had been sent into the wheel-house, as already mentioned, to prevent noise. With such vivid lightning as prevailed during the whole passage, there was no prospect of escaping the vigilance of the enemy, but there was good reason to hope that he would be unable to point his guns accurately. Again the smoke-stacks took fire, and were soon put out; and then the roar of the enemy's guns began, and from Batteries Nos. 2, 3, and 4 on the mainland came the continued crack and scream of their rifle-shells, which seemed to unite with the electric batteries of the clouds to annihilate us.

While nearing the island or some shoal point, during a few minutes of total darkness, we were startled by the order, "Hard a-port!" from our brave and skillful pilot, First Master William R. Hoel. We almost grazed the island, and it appears were not observed through the storm until we were close in, and the enemy, having no time to point his guns, fired at random. In fact, we ran so near that the enemy did not, probably could not, depress his guns sufficiently. . . . Having passed the principal batteries, we were greatly relieved from suspense, patiently endured, however, by the officers and crew. But there was another formidable obstacle in the way—a floating battery, which was the great "war elephant" of the Confederates, built to blockade the Mississippi permanently. As we passed her she fired six or eight shots at us, but without effect. One ball struck the coal barge, and one was found in a bale of hay; we found also one or two musket-bullets. We arrived at New Madrid about midnight with no one hurt, and were most joyfully received by our army. At the suggestion of Paymaster Nixon, all hands "spliced the main brace."

Henry Walke, commander of Carondelet, *describing the run past Island No. 10 on April 4, 1862, in Robert Underwood Johnson and Clarence Clough Buel,* Battles and Leaders of the Civil War, *Vol. I, pp. 442–445.*

The vessels now being in position, the signal was given to open fire; and on the morning of the 18th of April the bombardment fairly commenced, each mortar-vessel having orders to fire once in ten minutes.

The moment that the mortars belched forth their shells, both Jackson and St. Philip replied with great fury; but it was some time before they could obtain our range, as we were well concealed behind our natural rampart. The enemy's fire was rapid, and finding that it was becoming rather hot, I sent Lieutenant Guest up to the head of the line to open fire on the forts with his 11-inch pivot. This position he maintained for one hour and fifty minutes, and only abandoned it to fill up with ammunition. In the meantime the mortars on the left bank (Queen's division) were doing splendid work, though suffering considerably from the enemy's fire.

I went on board the vessels of his division to see how they were getting on, and found them so cut up that I considered it necessary to remove them, with Farragut's permission to the opposite shore, under cover of the trees, near the other vessels, which had suffered but little. They held position however, until sundown, when the enemy ceased firing. At 5 o'clock in the evening Fort Jackson was seen to be on fire, and, as the flames spread rapidly, the Confederates soon left their guns. There were many conjectures among the officers of the fleet as to what was burning. Some thought that it was a fire-raft, and I was inclined to that opinion myself until I had pulled up the river in a boat, and by the aid of a night-glass, convinced myself that the fort itself was in flames. This fact I at once reported to Farragut.

> *Admiral D. D. Porter, describing the shelling of Fort St. Philip, New Orleans, April 18, 1862, in Robert Underwood Johnson and Clarence Clough Buel,* Battles and Leaders of the Civil War, *Vol. II, p. 35.*

When the fleet had passed the forts, and it was certain that they were ascending the river, the troops evacuated with the exception of one regiment, who threw down their arms and would not leave. The mob took the place of the city troops, and commenced to burn all the cotton they could find, (from 10,000 to 15,000 bales,) rolling the sugars into the river, knocking in the heads of molasses casks, and doing whatever damage they could. . . .

The next morning after the ships arrived, an immense crowd assembled on the levee, of both sexes and all ages; a murmur of applause in the crowd drew the attention of the worst of these people, who fired their pistols, killing upward of seventy-five and wounding others. This is referred to by Commodore Farragut in his dispatch to the Mayor. One of the parties killed was an Englishman of the name of Moody, whose body was awfully cut and shot, and was hanging to a telegraph pole in front of his door, upon which hung his sign, "Get your shirts at Moody's." This man had lived fourteen years in New-Orleans, had acquired a handsome property and was a good citizen. Many then fled on board the ships, fearing outrages; and the parties who directed Capt. Bailey to the City Hall, were chased to the levee where they escaped to the boats of the United States fleet. Thirty men attempted to board one of the United States vessels; seven were killed by firearms, and others drowned in the attempt of this desperate act. Houses were set on fire, and the narrator says it was the most awful night he ever passed, and the next morning he took his family to Mobile from their house in New-Orleans, for safety. On the 1st May there was not a soul in the streets; the stores, hotels, and every place of business was closed, and the city appeared dismal.

> *Extract from an eyewitness account of incidents surrounding the arrival of Union naval forces at New Orleans, originally published in the New York* Journal of Commerce *and republished in the* New York Times, *May 25, 1862, p. 2.*

Here, for instance, is Robert Small, pilot of the *Planter,* who with his companions, ran that steamer out from Charleston, under the guns of Fort Sumter. They must have been allowed to be very "idle hands" to have perpetrated such a piece of mischief as that. It would have required no small amount of skill and courage, even in white men, to have planned and carried out such an undertaking, whose only chance of success was its boldness, and where failure would have made death, and that in its most horrible shapes, the inevitable lot of all. And yet these eight colored men ran such a risk as that for the purpose of escaping from this patriarchal institution—of running away from the ranks of those happiest of laborers—away from all the blessings of being "taken care of."

We consider this action of Small and his fellows as one of the boldest deeds of the whole war. It should be recognized as such, and we believe it will be by the nation; and it is one of the cases which pinch very close those who argue the ultra-conservative side of the question, How shall we treat the slaves? It may be all very well for Gen. Halleck to make orders forbidding the entrance of fugitive slaves within his lines, but we do not believe that even he would turn back a company of fugitives who come bringing with them six cannon of large calibre, and other property from the rebels to the value of some $30,000. No man can help admitting that for such a case Gen. Hunter's order is more appropriate treatment than Gen. Halleck's. We could almost wish that the President in his proclamation, in reference to the order of Gen. Hunter, had especially excepted this case of Robert Small and his fellows. It would not have made that proclamation less acceptable to the people if it had contained such a reservation. The Senate, as we all know, promptly passed a bill to give the men one-half of the value of the *Planter* and her cargo, and this is all very well. But it was not for money that these men did this bold deed. It sprang from love of freedom first and love of country next. They ran these tremendous risks that they might be free, and the most appropriate return which our government could make them would be to secure to them the freedom they sought. We sympathized not at all with Gen. Hunter's order. But we should certainly applaud the Government for giving this once the lie to those who charge the proverbial ingratitude of rulers upon Republics.

> *Extract from an editorial,* New York Times, *May 25, 1862, entitled "The Planter and its Colored Captors," praising the action of Robert Smalls in delivering the* Planter *to Union hands on May 12, 1862, p. 4.*

On the 28th of May, 1862, I received at Vicksburg a telegraphic order from the Navy Department at Richmond to "proceed to Greenwood, Miss., and assume command of the Confederate gun-boat *Arkansas,* and finish and equip that vessel without regard to expenditure of men or money." I knew that such a vessel had been under construction at Memphis, but I had not heard till then of her escape from the general wreck of our Mississippi River defenses. Greenwood is at the head of the Yazoo River, 160 miles by river from Yazoo City. It being the season of overflow, I found my new command four miles from dry land. Her condition was not encouraging. The vessel was a mere hull, without armor; the engines were apart; guns without carriages were lying about the deck; a portion of the railroad iron intended as armor was at the bottom of the river, and the other and far greater part was to be sought for in the interior of the country. . . . Our engines' twin screws, one under each quarter, worked up to eight miles an hour in still water, which promised about half that speed when turned against the current of the main river. We had at first some trust in these, not having discovered the way they soon showed of stopping on the center at wrong times and places; and as they never both stopped of themselves at the same time, the effect was, when one did so, to turn the vessel round, despite the rudder. Once in the presence of the enemy, we made a circle while trying make the automatic stopper keep time with its sister-screw.

The *Arkansas* now appeared as if a small sea-going vessel had been cut down to the water's edge at both ends, leaving a box for guns amidships. The straight sides of the box, a foot in thickness, had over them one layer of railway iron; the ends closed by timber one foot square, planked across by six-inch strips of oak, were then covered by one course of railway iron laid up and down at an angle of thirty-five degrees. The ends deflected overhead all missiles striking at short range, but would have been of little security under a plunging fire . . .

> *Captain Isaac Brown, CSN, recalling the outfitting of the Confederate steamer,* Arkansas, *May–June 1862, as published in Robert Underwood Johnson and Clarence Clough Buel,* Battles and Leaders of the Civil War, *Vol. I, pp. 576–578.*

The morning of the 6th of June we fought the battle of Memphis, which lasted one hour and ten minutes. It was begun by an attack upon our fleet by the enemy, whose vessels were in double line of battle opposite the city. We were then at a distance of a mile and a half or two miles above the city. Their fire continued for a quarter of an hour, when the attack was promptly met by two of our ram squadron, *Queen of the West* (Colonel Charles Ellet) leading, and the *Monarch* (Lieutenant-Colonel A. W. Ellet, younger brother of the leader). These vessels fearlessly dashed ahead of our gun-boats, ran for the enemy's fleet, and at the first plunge succeeded in sinking one vessel and disabling another. The astonished Confederates received them gallantly and effectively. The *Queen of the West* and *Monarch* were followed in line of battle by the gun-boats, under the lead of Flag-Officer Davis, and all of them opened fire, which was continued from the time we got within

This Mississippi River gunboat, the USS *Fort Hindman,* was typical of the class. *(Library of Congress, Prints and Photographs Division, LC-USZ62–113172)*

good range until the end of the battle—two or three tugs keeping all the while a safe distance astern. . . . The [*General*] *Price, Little Rebel* (with a shot-hole through her steam-chest), and our *Queen of the West,* all disabled, were run on the Arkansas shore opposite Memphis; and the *Monarch* afterward ran into the *Little Rebel* just as our fleet was passing her in pursuit of the remainder of the enemy's fleet, then retreating down the river. The *Jeff. Thompson,* below the point and opposite President's Island, was the next boat disabled by our shot. She was run ashore, burned, and blown up. The Confederate ram *Sumter* was also disabled by our shell and captured. The *Bragg* soon after shared the same fate and was run ashore, where her officers abandoned her and disappeared in the forests of Arkansas. All the Confederate rams which had been run on the Arkansas shore were captured. The *Van Dorn,* having a start, alone escaped down the river. The rams *Monarch* and *Switzerland* were dispatched in pursuit of her and a few transports, but returned without overtaking them, although they captured another steamer.

The scene at this battle was rendered most sublime by the desperate nature of the engagement and the momentous consequences that followed very speedily after the first attack. Thousands of people crowded the high bluffs overlooking the river. The roar of the cannon and shell shook the houses on shore on either side for many miles. First wild yells, shrieks, and clamors, then loud, despairing murmurs, filled the affrighted city. The screaming, plunging shell crashed into the boats, blowing some of them and their crews into fragments, and the rams rushed upon each other like wild beasts in deadly conflict. Blinding smoke hovered about the scene of all this confusion and horror; and as the battle progressed and the Confederate fleet was destroyed, all the cheering voices on shore were silenced. When the last hope of the Confederates gave way, the lamentations which went up from the spectators were like cries of anguish.

Boats were put off from our vessels to save as many lives as possible. No serious injury was received by any one on board the United States fleet. Colonel Ellet received a pistol-shot in the leg. . . .

Henry Walke, describing the Battle of Memphis, June 6, 1862, as published in Robert Underwood Johnson and Clarence Clough Buel, Battles and Leaders of the Civil War, *Vol. I, pp. 450–452.*

As the sun rose clear and firey out of the lake on our left, we saw a few miles ahead, under full steam, three Federal vessels in line approaching. These, as we after-ward discovered, were the iron-clad *Carondelet,* Captain Henry Walke, the wooden gun-boat *Tyler,* Lieutenant William Gwin, and a ram, the *Queen of the West,* Lieutenant James M. Hunter. Directing our pilot to stand for the iron-clad, the center vessel of the three, I gave the order not to fire our bow guns, lest by doing so we should diminish our speed, relying for the moment upon our broadside guns to keep the ram and the *Tyler* from gaining our quarter, which they seemed eager to do. I had determined, despite our want of speed, to try to ram our iron prow upon the foe, who were gallantly approaching; but when less than half a mile separated us, the *Carondelet* fired a wildly aimed bow gun, backed round, and went from the *Arkansas* at a speed which at once perceptibly increased the space between us. The *Tyler* and ram followed this movement of the iron-clad, and the stern guns of the *Carondelet* and the *Tyler* were briskly served on us. . . . We soon began to gain on the chase, yet from time to time I had to steer first to starboard, then to port, to keep the inquisitive consorts of the *Carondelet* from inspecting my boiler-plate armor. . . . While our shot seemed always to hit his stern and disappear, his missiles, striking our inclined shield, were deflected over my head and lost in air. I received a severe contusion on the head, but this gave me no concern after I had failed to find any brains mixed with the handful of clotted blood which I drew from the wound and examined. A moment later a shot from the *Tyler* struck at my feet, penetrated the pilot-house, and cutting off a section of the wheel, mortally hurt Chief Pilot Hodges and disabled our Yazoo River pilot, Shacklett, who was at the moment much needed, our Mississippi pilots knowing nothing of Old River. . . .

Aided by the current of the Mississippi, we soon approached the Federal fleet—a forest of masts and smoke-stacks—ships, rams, iron-clads, and other gun boats on the left side, and ordinary river steamers and bomb-vessels along the right. To anyone having a real ram at command, the genius of havoc could not have offered a finer view, the panoramic effect of which was intensified by the city of men spread out with innumerable tents opposite on the right bank. We were not yet in sight of Vicksburg, but in every direction, except astern, our eyes rested on enemies. I had long known the most of these as valued friends, and if I now had any doubts of the success of the *Arkansas* they were inspired by this general knowledge than from any awe of a particular name. It seemed at a glance as if a whole navy had come to keep me away from the heroic city—six or seven rams, four or five iron-clads, without including one accounted for an hour ago, and the fleet of Farragut generally, behind or inside of this fleet. . . .

At the moment of collision, when our guns were muzzle to muzzle, the *Arkansas's* broadside was exchanged for the bow guns of the assailant. A shot from one of the latter struck the *Arkansas's* plating a foot forward of the forward broadside port, breaking off the ends of the rail-road bars and driving them in among our people; the solid shot followed, crossed diagonally our gun-deck, and split on the breech of our starboard after-broadside gun. This shot killed eight and wounded six of our men but left us still half our crew. What damage the *Essex* received I did not ascertain, but that vessel drifted clear of the *Arkansas* without again firing, and after receiving the fire of our stern rifles steamed in the face and under the fire of the Vicksburg batteries to the fleet below. Had Porter at that moment of the collision thrown fifty men on our upper deck, he might have made fast to us with a hawser and with little additional loss might have taken the *Arkansas* and her twenty men and officers. . . .

Thus closed the fourth and final battle of the *Arkansas,* leaving the daring Confederate vessel, though reduced in crew to twenty men all told for duty, still defiant in the presence of a hostile force perhaps exceeding in real strength that which fought under Nelson at Trafalgar. . . . If the *Arkansas* could not be destroyed, the siege must be raised, for fifty ships, more or less, could not keep perpetual steam to confine one little 10–gun vessel within her conceded control of six miles of the Mississippi River. It was indeed a dilemma, and doubtless the less difficult horn of it was chosen. Soon after our contribution to the *Essex's* laurels, and between sunset and sunrise, the lower [Union] fleet started for the recuperative atmosphere of salt-water, and about the same time the upper fleet—rams, bombs, and iron-clads—steamed for the North. Thus was dissipated for the season the greatest naval force hitherto assembled at one time in the New World.

Captain Isaac Brown, CSN, recalling the participation of the Confederate steamer, Arkansas, *in lifting the siege of Vicksburg, July 15, 1862, as published in Robert Underwood Johnson and Clarence Clough Buel,* Battles and Leaders of the Civil War, *Vol. III, pp. 576–578.*

The Confederate ram *Arkansas* is blown up by its crew to avoid capture by the approaching Union gunboat *Essex* on August 4, 1862. *(Library of Congress, Prints and Photographs Division, LC-USZC2–2253)*

Under the double orders of two commanders-in-chief to be at Baton Rouge at a certain date and hour, Stevens could not use that tender care which his engines required, and before they completed their desperate run of three hundred miles against time, the starboard one suddenly broke down, throwing the vessel inextricably ashore. This misfortune, for which there was no present remedy, happened when the vessel was within sight of Baton Rouge. Very soon after, the *Essex* was seen approaching under full steam. Stevens, as humane as he was true and brave, finding that he could not bring a single gun to bear upon the coming foe, sent all his people over the bows ashore, remaining alone to set fire to his vessel; this he did so effectually that he had to jump from the stern into the river and save himself by swimming; and with colors flying, the gallant *Arkansas,* whose decks had never been pressed by the foot of an enemy, was blown into the air.

Captain Isaac Brown, CSN, recalling the destruction of the Arkansas *near Baton Rouge, December 1862, as published in Robert Underwood Johnson and Clarence Clough Buel,* Battles and Leaders of the Civil War, *Vol. III, p. 579.*

5

Two Bitter Years
January 1862–December 1863

Throughout 1862 and 1863, the Civil War increased in intensity, with numerous battles and heavy casualties that convinced both sides they were in for a long and bitter war. Although many factors would come together to shape the outcome of a particular battle, the tendency at the time, and for many historians since, was to give credit or blame to individual officers. The dismissal of less competent officers, and numerous casualties among both competent and incompetent, saw several very astute military leaders eventually emerge.

In the South, Robert E. Lee soon acquired a reputation for daring, the taking of calculated risks, and winning battles. His successes and ability to anticipate the tactics and errors of his opponents convinced President Jefferson Davis and much of the Confederate leadership and public that he could win the war, particularly through his initial successes in defending Richmond in early 1862.

On the Northern side, Lincoln kept searching for competent leadership through 1862 and much of 1863, dismissing and appointing leaders in repeated efforts to subdue the Confederacy by seizing its capital at Richmond. Although he recognized that U.S. Grant tended to win battles in the western theater of the war in 1862, Grant's personal enemies spread rumors of his ungentlemanly behavior and alcoholism. Despite Grant's detractors, Lincoln and Secretary of War Stanton came to believe that General Grant was willing to commit troops to battle and could win, using well calculated plans, overwhelming force, and a dogged willingness to push on his troops.

By the end of 1863, the North had found in Grant a general to match Lee, not with the same skills that Lee had but with a record of victory. With the victories of the Union in mid–1863 at Vicksburg under Grant and at Gettysburg under General Meade and then with Grant's successes in Tennessee in November, the hopes of the South for international recognition and for successfully defending secession dimmed. With the victories of November 1863, Grant and his officers felt that the war could be won in 1864.

There were literally hundreds of battles, engagements, and skirmishes during these two years, but by focusing on just a few major campaigns and key battles, the broad sweep and pattern of what transpired in the war on land during 1862 and 1863 can be discerned. The most significant of the numerous battles and campaigns of these two years can be summarized in four very broad sweeps. The first was the attempt to take Richmond by the Union in the Peninsular Campaign of early 1862 and the later Union attempts stopped by Lee at Fredericksburg and Chancellorsville. The second was the Confederate victory at Second Bull Run and Lee's two attempts through Maryland and Pennsylvania to the heart of the Union, stopped at Antietam in September 1862 and at Gettysburg in July 1863. The third was Grant's victory at Shiloh, Tennessee, in April 1862 and his final victory at Vicksburg in July of 1863 that put an end to Confederate plans to move through Kentucky to the Ohio River. The fourth was the Confederate defeat of the Union advance at Chickamauga Creek in northern Georgia, and then the bottling up of Union forces in Chattanooga and their relief by forces under Grant in late 1863. Through hesitancy, errors, blunders, and oversights, many generals fell into disfavor, including, on the Union side, McClellan, Pope, Burnside, Hooker, and Rosecrans, among others. For this reason, the individual careers of officers represented a crucial part of the larger story, affected by and affecting the outcome of campaigns.

Details of the battles show that the brilliance or mistakes of individual officers often determined the outcome, but sometimes bad luck, miscommunication, or other factors beyond anyone's control were crucial to one or the other side's defeat. Given the chances of war, many attributed results to divine providence. Often, good or faulty intelligence shaped the course of battle, and both sides experimented with means to get better information.

ESPIONAGE AND INTELLIGENCE

To gather reliable information, the Confederate army instigated a series of espionage and counterespionage measures in the field. These included appointing provost marshals to guard against infiltration by Unionists, questioning Union deserters, and using civilian and partisan units to gather information in areas occupied by the Union army. Reconnaissance in force with cavalry units often yielded excellent information while at the same time inflicting casualties and disrupting rear areas of the enemy.

Surprisingly for modern students of the subject, one of the best sources for data regarding the Northern armies were publicly available Northern newspapers, which could be readily obtained and sent back over the lines. For example, before First Bull Run, Southern officers could get detailed accounts of which Union regiments were stationed around Washington simply by reading the *Washington National Republican*. Confederate newspapers tended to be more circumspect in reporting unit strengths and dispositions.

On the Union side, General George McClellan relied on an espionage outfit created by the founder of a Chicago detective agency, Allan Pinkerton. General McClellan hired Pinkerton (who had worked for him in civilian life) as his intelligence chief. Pinkerton coordinated reports from some two dozen spies who interrogated prisoners, contrabands, and refugees. Pinkerton's agents very rarely tried to penetrate even the porous Confederate lines, and, using secondhand information of dubious reliability, they reported greatly exaggerated figures for Confederate strength, partly accounting for McClellan's hesitancy to advance during the Peninsular Campaign. After the eventual removal from command of McClellan, the Union turned away from Pinkerton's agents and attempted to build intelligence offices within the army structure.[1]

One of Pinkerton's agents, and apparently the only one who actually did any scouting, as distinct from interviewing, was John C. Babcock. He drew accurate maps of Confederate dispositions; after McClellan's dismissal, Babcock served as intelligence chief under Provost Marshal Marsena R. Patrick. When, in early 1863, Major General Joseph Hooker assumed command of the Army of the Potomac, Babcock wrote a paper describing a proposed secret service department of the army. The document became a basis for the Bureau of Military Information, established and at first operated by Colonel George Henry Sharpe.

Colonel Sharpe's Bureau of Military Information began to provide more reliable military information, partly because he sent out active spies to penetrate behind enemy lines. Sharpe also contacted and received information from volunteer pro-Union spies in the south like Elizabeth Van Lew. Regarded as a harmless eccentric by her neighbors in Richmond, Elizabeth Van Lew was a committed abolitionist. By visiting Union prisoners in Richmond prisons on errands of mercy, she gathered valuable information about Confederate troops. Furthermore, she planted a former slave of her own family, Mary Elizabeth Bowser, in the home of Jefferson Davis. Bowser carefully noted the content of dinner conversations, then relayed information back to Van Lew, who in turn forwarded details to Sharpe in Washington. However, the significance of such dinner conversations may have been exaggerated in romantic accounts of wartime espionage, which tended to surround the exploits of individual spies, especially women, with an aura of legend and adventure.

Both sides were aided by such volunteer spies as Van Lew and Bowser, some of whom developed quite professional methods of gathering information and transmitting it through trusted couriers and intermediaries. A number of such amateurs turned professional worked in the Southern cause. Belle Boyd was only 17 when the war broke out. She warned Stonewall Jackson that Union troops planned to destroy a bridge, and he was able to advance rapidly before they struck, based on her information. She seemed to delight in long night rides to convey information. She was arrested some six or seven times, and imprisoned twice, once in the Old Capitol Prison in Washington, D.C. She developed a reputation for spending the night in the tents of officers of both sides, scandalizing well-bred Confederate ladies.

A few actors and actresses turned their skills to espionage and conspiracy, including a minor actress, Pauline Cushman, who worked for the Union. Born in New Orleans, she had run away from home at age 18 to New York, where she married an actor, Charles Dickenson. Dickenson joined the Union army as a musician and died in 1862. Cushman went on stage to earn a living and was performing in Louisville, Kentucky, which was under Union control in late 1862 and early 1863. There, two paroled Confederate officers bribed her to offer a toast to Jefferson Davis during a performance. She informed Union officers that she would do it, and, as a consequence, she became notorious as a pro-Confederate heroine, even though her true sympathies were with the North. In March 1863, she began to follow the Confederate army through Kentucky and Tennessee, giving performances and at the same time gathering information she relayed back to the advancing Federals. She was arrested on order of Confederate general Braxton Bragg, tried as a spy, and sentenced to hang. Before the sentence could be carried out, however, Union troops overran the position and Cushman was freed. At this point, her cover was blown. She traveled to Washington, personally received an honorary commission as major in the army from President Lincoln, and went on a lecture tour in uniform to tell her story.

A unique aspect of the Civil War was the fact that it was fought between Americans who shared the same language and culture. Since both sides understood each other's habits and mannerisms so well, it was extremely easy to gather and transmit military or strategic intelligence. Both sides exploited intelligence, sometimes quite wisely. Often, however, the commanders were so flooded with data, rumor, good information, mistaken estimates, and intentional disinformation that many battles were needlessly fought and tens of thousands of soldiers needlessly perished. In no other war in all of modern history did the enemies so closely share culture, language, and training and thus facilitate the use of intelligence to the same degree. Although mistakes were made by both sides in gathering and interpreting information, several Confederate officers seemed to display a greater intuitive understanding of the use of battlefield information than did many of their Union counterparts.

Accounts of the four broad campaigns through 1862 and 1863 in the eastern and western theaters of the war and the battles within them demonstrate the interplay of factors that accounted for victory or defeat. The personalities of leaders, the accidents of war, the question of available intelligence, and sometimes such factors as weather, terrain, and outright mistakes shaped specific outcomes.

PENINSULAR CAMPAIGN

In the first half of 1862, Union forces, commanded by General George McClellan, attempted to move west through Virginia from Fortress Monroe to take Richmond, the capital of the Confederacy. The land from Fortress Monroe to Richmond lies between the York and James Rivers, forming a peninsula that is spotted with swampy sections. This long set of battles became known as the Peninsular Campaign, and lasted from March 1862 through August 1862.

General McClellan moved a massive army of about 105,000 men by ship from around Washington, D.C., to Fortress Monroe near the tip of the peninsula. McClellan reasoned that the superior number of his advancing forces would preclude attack on its flanks, with water on both sides, and would batter the defensive line of the Confederates, commanded by Major General John B. Magruder. With command of the rivers once established by Union gunboats, his flanks would be protected. However, because of faulty intelligence received through his reliance on Pinkerton, McClellan vastly overestimated the strength that General Magruder commanded. Coupling that overestimate of enemy strength with his horror at seeing his men wounded and killed, McClellan developed a very gradual, cautious, and step-by-step strategy. In fact Magruder had only about 17,000 men to defend Richmond at first, until his forces were strengthened by the arrival of a Confederate army under General Joseph E. Johnston. Despite the leakage of detailed information from behind the lines, McClellan did not believe indications that his forces outnumbered the Richmond defenders by more than five to one at the beginning of his campaign.

In May, McClellan began his grand assault, advancing slowly and enforcing his lines every night with new fortifications. When he finally reached Johnston's first lines of defense, he found them abandoned. As McClellan advanced and Johnston retreated, both armies became bogged down in mud. After an engagement at Williamsburg, Johnston abandoned the whole eastern section of the peninsula, yielding the Norfolk Navy Yard back to the Federals. There, Confederates abandoned and burned the *Virginia*. Union navy vessels in support of McClellan's advance were stopped on May 15 at Drewry's Bluff, about seven miles from the outskirts of Richmond, by obstructions placed in the river. Despite the navy pleading with McClellan to dispatch a small force of soldiers by land to dislodge the Confederate fortress there, Fort Darling, McClellan preferred to delay that effort, hoping that army forces would be able to take Richmond without further naval aid.

On May 31 and June 1, 1862, General Johnston, together with James Longstreet's corps, attempted to destroy two Union corps detected not far from Richmond, near the villages of Seven Pines and Fair Oaks. However, the Confederate attack there was indecisive and confused, partly because verbal orders rather than written ones left intentions and plans for exact movements unclear. For decades, Confederate officers debated exactly where they had been located and what orders had reached them. In this case the information about their own forces was flawed and contributed to the mixed results. Johnston was wounded twice in the battle. The leadership of the defense of Richmond fell to Lee after the wounding of General Johnston on May 31. Lee had already been noticed by Jefferson Davis as a brilliant strategist and had served as a military adviser in Richmond. Lee's rise to the position of preeminent Confederate officer began with his taking over the Richmond defense from the disabled Joseph Johnston.

At the Battle of Seven Pines (known as Fair Oaks to Union commanders), the North suffered 5,031 casualties, while the South suffered 6,134. While the battle was a tactical and slight numerical victory for McClellan's forces, he did not capitalize on it; to many it seemed the deaths had left no clear result for either side.

A few days later, General J. E. B. Stuart led a cavalry division in a reconnoitering ride completely around McClellan's forces. The reconnaissance revealed valuable intelligence that McClellan's right flank was unsecured; on the other side, the ride also confirmed McClellan in his mistaken understanding that he faced vastly superior numbers. The "ride around McClellan," as it came to be known, was treated in the Confederate press and lore as a great feat.

At a series of engagements known as the Seven Days battles, between June 25 and July 1, 1862, Lee outsmarted McClellan. Leaving only 25,000 troops to defend Richmond against an attack, Lee moved some 47,000 men into a daring offensive against McClellan's exposed right flank. McClellan withdrew after the battle at Gaines's Mill. After an engagement at Malvern Hill, McClellan abandoned the Peninsular Campaign altogether. Lee had hoped to destroy the Union army, but McClellan extracted the remaining forces by the end of July. On the Confederate side, Lee won the support of the Southern populace and political leadership by his outmaneuvering of McClellan and by his defense of Richmond, even though he had taken severe losses in several engagements.[2]

SHILOH (PITTSBURG LANDING)

While McClellan planned his attack on Richmond via the peninsula, the Union commander of the western theater of the war, Henry ("Old Brains") Halleck, planned advances through Tennessee in early April 1862. Under the overall command of Halleck, Generals U.S. Grant and Don Carlos Buell marshaled strong forces to move into central Tennessee. Grant had some 39,000 men disembarked at Pittsburg Landing on the Tennessee River, while Buell commanded about

36,000 at Nashville. Halleck ordered Buell to join with Grant for a grand assault on the Confederate position at Corinth, Tennessee.

Meanwhile, Confederate general Albert Sidney Johnston had assembled a strong force of about 44,000 men at Corinth by the end of March. Johnston hoped to engage Grant's forces before Buell could join up with Grant. On April 3, 1863, Johnston led his men out of Corinth for what should have been a one-day march northwestward toward Grant's position at Pittsburg Landing. His inexperienced troops were slowed by thickly wooded country and heavy rains and did not reach their destination until the afternoon of April 5. Although some officers, especially General P. G. T. Beauregard, argued for withdrawal because of the loss of momentum and the exhausting advance, Johnston insisted on an attack the next morning.

Early on Sunday morning, April 6, Johnston's skirmishers encountered a division of Union troops under the command of General William Sherman, near a log church called Shiloh. After attacking Sherman's division, another commanded by General Benjamin Prentiss, and a third under the command of General John B. McClernand, the Confederates finally overran the Union position. In the advance and in the confusion of battle, however, Confederate units became mixed together, and it became increasingly difficult for officers to direct the movement of their units. Meanwhile, Grant, who was several miles back from the battle, ordered General Prentiss to hold a line against the Confederate advance at all costs. Prentiss established a strong defensive stand along a sunken road concealed by heavy brush. As Confederates threw troops at this position, charge after charge fell before withering fire, until the spot earned the name "the Hornet's Nest." In the attacks, Confederate general Albert S. Johnston was mortally wounded.

General Pierre Beauregard took command of the Confederate forces and battered the Union defensive line with artillery fire. After several hours, Prentiss

The Battle of Shiloh stunned both the Union and Confederacy, as the number of casualties in this one battle exceeded those of all Americans in all previous American wars. *(Library of Congress, Prints and Photographs Division, LC-USZC4–1910)*

called an end to the slaughter, surrendering with about 2,000 survivors. The defense of the Hornet's Nest, however, had given Grant enough time to fortify a position along a ridge farther back toward the river landing point, and Beauregard called off the assault.

That evening, more Union forces began to arrive to support Grant, including a division under General Lew Wallace and most of the force led by General Don Carlos Buell. With these reinforcements, Grant decided to take the offensive, and on the morning of April 7, the larger Union forces began to push back the Confederate troops, supported by gunboats *Tyler* and *Lexington* on the river. After realizing that he confronted fresh troops, Beauregard ordered a retreat back to Corinth.

The casualties from the two days of battle reached figures that shocked leaders and the public on both sides. The Union lost 1,754 dead, 8,408 wounded, and 2,885 taken prisoner. The Confederates lost 1,723 killed, 8,012 wounded, and 959 missing. Even though the Union losses were staggering, Grant had pushed back past the Shiloh church, and his counterattack after the first day's initial defeat solidified his reputation as a dogged and determined officer. Grant's determination had overcome Johnston and Beauregard's gamble, with the aid of mud, terrain, confused Confederate lines of communication, the sacrifice of thousands of lives, and the timely arrival of reinforcements. Albert Sidney Johnston paid with his own life. Shiloh represented even more of a turning point in the western theater than the earlier Union victories at Forts Henry and Donelson; the Confederates were now clearly on the defensive in Tennessee. The more than 23,000 total casualties proved that the war was to be bloody, desperate, and drawn-out.[3]

SECOND MANASSAS (BULL RUN)

After driving McClellan off from his attempt on Richmond, Confederates moved again toward the critical rail and road junctions west of Washington, D.C., at Manassas junction, near the stream, Bull Run, where Federals had been routed in the opening months of the war in 1861. General John Pope, who had led Union troops successfully in the battle for Island No. 10 on the Mississippi in 1861, commanded Union forces at the Second Battle of Bull Run, on August 29, 1862. Despite his earlier successes, his reputation was destroyed at Second Bull Run, and he and others were discredited as incompetent officers. Pope blamed the failure at Second Bull Run on the fact that many of his officers remained loyal to General McClellan and had resisted Pope's orders.

At Second Bull Run, on August 29 and 30, 1862, General Pope hoped to intercept and stop Stonewall Jackson after he had raided and burned federal facilities at Manassas junction. Believing the Confederates had retreated, Pope ordered Fitz-John Porter to move against a position strongly held by Confederate troops under General Longstreet. Porter reported strong forces in front of him, but Pope insisted he push ahead. Porter's advance was met by artillery fire and then by a rebel infantry charge. Instead of throwing in a large force, Pope sent in smaller units one by one, throwing them against a strong Confederate position behind an abandoned railway embankment that ran from Sudly Springs to the southwest. Although Pope blamed Porter, both officers were discredited by the defeat. Total Union casualties were almost double those of the Confederates, with 16,000 killed, wounded, and missing, out of some 60,000 engaged. The Confederate losses amounted to about 9,200 of some 50,000.

ANTIETAM (SHARPSBURG)

With Confederates holding the area to the west of Washington in Virginia and with raids through the Shenandoah Valley farther to the west, the way seemed clear for Lee to attempt an invasion of the North. The victory at Second Bull Run further cleared the way for Lee to attempt an invasion of Maryland, with the stated purpose of providing Marylanders an opportunity to join the Confederacy, in September 1862. He hoped not only to recruit Marylanders to the cause, but also to convince the Union that the war would be too costly to continue, especially since it would begin to be fought on the Union side of the line.

To implement his plan, Lee forded the Potomac River in early September and marched his troops through the countryside to the west and northwest of Washington, through Frederick, Maryland, and was planning to move on to Pennsylvania if recruits could be found. Lee sent Jackson to take the federal arsenal at Harpers Ferry. Ever daring, Lee divided his forces in the attack, communicating detailed plans in his Order 191. A copy of the order, wrapped around cigars, was discovered near Frederick by Union troops occupying a camp recently abandoned by Confederate forces. The order was sent to McClellan, and it was soon confirmed as authentic, both through the handwriting of the order and the discovery of some Confederate troops in the assigned positions detailed in the document. Lee learned that the order had been found, but made a fateful decision to stay and fight, rather than to retreat back across the Potomac. He left a division under General Daniel Harvey Hill to delay McClellan at South Mountain and took up a position near the village of Sharpsburg, Maryland, where Antietam Creek stood between his forces and the route that would be taken by the superior federal forces. The crucial clash in this campaign, on September 17, 1862, came to be known as the Battle of Sharpsburg (to the South) or the Battle of Antietam (to the North).

Although Jackson took over 10,000 prisoners and some 73 artillery pieces at Harpers Ferry and then advanced to support Lee, the Confederates remained

Burnside's Bridge still stands as a memorial at Antietam. Union troops could have waded across the creek, but instead they captured the bridge at the cost of heavy casualties. *(Library of Congress, Prints and Photographs Division, LC-USZC4–1768)*

greatly outnumbered, with some 47,000 holding the position at Sharpsburg against McClellan's more than 70,000. Confederates fell in great numbers, fighting at several locations, near the Dunker church, in a cornfield, and in a sunken road. In the attack, General Burnside led his division to the creek and finally, at three o'clock on the afternoon of September 17, 1862, his troops funnelled across a small stone bridge, thereafter known as Burnside's Bridge. The battle was considered by some to be the bloodiest ever fought on a single day during the war, with total casualties on both sides amounting to 4,700 dead, over 18,000 wounded, and more than 3,000 missing. The one-day battle certainly ranks in casualties with the later two-day battle at Chickamauga in which there were some 36,000 wounded and dead on both sides. After Antietam, Lee retreated back across the Potomac, as the river began to rise.

The outcome of the battle was that Lincoln now had the victory that his advisers had suggested must come if he were to issue his preliminary emancipation proclamation. Without such a victory, they had warned, the proclamation would seem to be a desperate measure of a government facing defeat. Lincoln dismissed McClellan on November 7 and promoted Burnside in his place. Lee's attempt to carry the war onto Union territory had been stopped, at least for 1862.

With the dismissal of McClellan, Allan Pinkerton's agency fell into disuse. The National Detective Service, under Lafayette Baker who reported directly to Secretary of War Edwin Stanton, began secret police work in Washington. With Babcock, one of Pinkerton's agents, serving as intelligence chief of the Army of the Potomac, the Union army gradually moved in the direction of a regular intelligence service within its own structure.

FREDERICKSBURG

Burnside, as the new commander of the Army of the Potomac, planned a new offensive against Richmond. He established three "grand divisions," under Generals William Franklin, Joseph Hooker, and Edwin Vose Sumner. Burnside's plan was to approach Richmond by marching straight toward it by way of Warrenton and Fredericksburg, Virginia, and to cross the Rappahannock River at Fredericksburg with the use of pontoon bridges.

Lee set up two corps for defense, one under General Longstreet called in from Culpepper, the other under Jackson, brought down from the Shenandoah at Winchester. Lee had in these two corps some 75,000 men, and he planned to defend Fredericksburg at Marye's Heights, with lines along a sunken road and stone wall fronted by an open plain about two miles wide that lay south from the edge of the town.

Burnside was able to march his force fairly quickly to Falmouth, across the Rappahannock from Fredericksburg, arriving with 130,000 men by November 19, 1862. However, due to bureaucratic delays, the pontoons needed for crossing the river did not arrive until November 25, giving Lee plenty of time to prepare the defense. Burnside had the bridges laid directly across from the town of Fredericksburg, where they were met by sniper fire from buildings on the other side. In retrospect, it certainly seemed an unwise crossing point. Using artillery to suppress the snipers, the Union army began crossing on five pontoon bridges on December 12, 1862, with Franklin on the left, Sumner on the right, and Hooker in a reserve position in the middle. Longstreet's force stopped Sumner's advance of some 50,000 men as they attempted to move over a mile of open plain toward

A Currier and Ives print of the Battle of Fredericksburg, December 13, 1862, shows Union troops advancing by ranks into murderous fire. *(Library of Congress, Prints and Photographs Division, LC-USZ62–1649)*

the fortified hills to the south of town. At the base of the hill was a steeply-walled creek that also prevented Union forces from approaching Lee's dug-in forces defending Marye's Heights. Dropping in ranks on the frozen ground, the advance faltered under withering fire from well-positioned Confederate troops on the heights, while Jackson's force behind railroad embankments of the Fredericksburg and Potomac line held back the advance of Franklin on the Union left. The Union forces lost some 12,600 killed, wounded, and missing to Confederate losses of about 5,300. The consequence of the battle was that, once again, Lee had demonstrated excellent generalship and held off an attack by superior numbers. Walt Whitman's brother was an enlisted man in the Union forces and wrote home of the horror of these advances. Wounded Union soldiers lay exposed in the no-man's-land below Marye's Heights, slowly dying of thirst and their injuries.

In an attempt to redeem himself, Burnside ordered a follow-up attack on Fredericksburg in mid-January 1863. He planned to march the Army of the Potomac several miles west of Fredericksburg to Bank's Ford and cross the Rappahannock there. The forces moved out on January 19; almost immediately, a driving rainstorm turned the advance into a struggle against liquid mud, with wagons, guns, troops, horses, and portable pontoon bridges stalled along miles of back roads. Defeated by the weather on this Mud March, Burnside was replaced by General Hooker on January 26, 1863.

CHANCELLORSVILLE

The Union did not abandon the effort to take Richmond, and Lincoln hoped that Joseph Hooker would be able to achieve what McClellan and Burnside could not. Hooker planned a new massed assault. Again, numbers seemed to favor the Union side, with Hooker commanding some 134,000 troops against about 60,000 available to Lee for defense. Hooker planned to move to Lee's left and rear, enveloping his forces near Fredericksburg. Lee, in what many analysts believe was one of the most brilliantly executed strategies of the war, divided his forces and responded quickly to the changing situation in the battles of May 1–4, 1863, at Chancellorsville to the west of Fredericksburg.

Hooker put 75,000 troops across the Rapidan and Rappahannock Rivers, and another 40,000 under General Sedgwick approached Fredericksburg a little farther east. Lee left only 10,000 soldiers under Jubal Early to face Sedgwick, and he marched the remainder west to meet Hooker.

Confronted by an advancing Confederate army, Hooker apparently lost his nerve, pulled back into a tangled woods west of Chancellorsville known as the Wilderness, abandoning the attack and yielding the initiative to Lee. Although Hooker learned of a flanking maneuver by Stonewall Jackson's forces through the Wilderness and warned O. O. Howard, his commander on his right flank, Howard apparently ignored the warning and his troops were caught unsuspecting and panicked. While returning from reconnoitering at night, Jackson was wounded by fire from his own Confederate troops and died a few days later. Lee realized that the small force he had left behind at Fredericksburg was falling back in front of Sedgwick along Plank Road, which connected Fredericksburg and Chancellorsville. So Lee dispatched a small force to stop Sedgwick at a defensible line on the road at the Salem church. Then, Early counterattacked from the South. Sedgwick, with his flank and rear under attack, wisely retreated north across the Rappahannock at Bank's Ford. Meanwhile, Stuart, who had taken over Jackson's corps after he was wounded, moved 50 cannon into a position at Hazel Grove near Chancellorsville, and Hooker also withdrew.

Lee's strategy of dividing his forces from a center position and applying them where needed against advance from more than one direction had worked again. While Confederate losses of 13,000 were greater in proportion than the Union losses of 17,000, Lee had once again saved Richmond from a Union advance. However, his loss of Stonewall Jackson was like the loss of his own right arm, he claimed. Like McClellan, Burnside, and Pope before him, Hooker was discredited by the Union defeat.[4]

GETTYSBURG

Lee attempted another campaign into the North in 1863, marching his troops well into Pennsylvania, with units moving through Mechanicsburg and to the shores of the Susquehanna River opposite the state capital at Harrisburg in late June. A Confederate infantry brigade, moving east on the Chambersburg pike, accidentally encountered two Union infantry brigades west of Gettysburg. Union general John Buford realized that Gettysburg was strategically placed, as seven different roads converged on the town. Buford's men were armed with new repeating Spencer rifles, and when they dismounted and fought back against Confederates under General Henry Heth, they held them back on July 1.

The accidental skirmish developed into a major set of battles along a 7-mile front over three days. A corps of Union troops under General John F. Reynolds came to support Buford's dismounted cavalry. A Confederate sharpshooter killed Reynolds, and the Union forces fell back to the south of Gettysburg. The Union troops were then joined by General Oliver Howard's XI Corps, while more Confederates assembled. Although neither General Meade on the Union side nor General Lee on the Confederate side had anticipated a battle, both began sending troops to the scene.

On July 2, Union troops held strong defensive positions south and east of the town of Gettysburg, ranging from Culp's Hill to Cemetery Hill, and then south along Cemetery Ridge and the Taneytown Road to Little Round Top, in a front that looked like a fishhook when viewed on a map. Lee ordered Longstreet to attack at the south end or left of the Union position at Little Round Top. After marching to a good attack position, fighting broke out in several locations to the south of town, later famous for all the slaughter at these spots: the Peach Orchard, the Wheatfield, the rocky gorge known as Devil's Den, and farther to the north, Culp's Hill.

The battle continued into a third day, July 3. Meade expected a major attack at the center of his position on Cemetery Ridge, and Lee planned just such a push. After battering Culp's Hill in the morning, a major assault of 13,000 Confederates in four brigades marched out of the woods on Seminary Ridge toward Cemetery Ridge from the west. Crossing the Emmitsburg Road, the Confederates, under Major General George Pickett, advanced into artillery and rifle fire. Although some of the Confederates planted their flags on the ridge, they were driven back.

Eyewitnesses struggled to find the words to describe the slaughter. Casualties on both sides were terrible, but the numbers were greater on the Confederate side, partly because they had been attacking defended positions. Over the three days of fighting, the Union lost 3,155 killed, 14,529 wounded, and 5,365 missing. The Confederates suffered 3,903 killed, 18,735 wounded, and 5,425 missing. The battle put an end to Lee's effort to take the war to the North, although later raids into Union states threw scares into defenders there.[5]

VICKSBURG

Grant began operations against Vicksburg, in the second campaign to take that city, in March 1863. Success eventually came because Grant was able to coordinate several large movements of troops, surrounding Vicksburg on the east and north and isolating the force under General John C. Pemberton from possible support from Confederate troops farther to the east near Jackson, Mississippi, under the command of General Joseph E. Johnston. In April, Union naval vessels under Admiral Porter slipped south past the Vicksburg batteries, and at the same time a large force under General Benjamin Grierson moved down the Yazoo delta territory to the east of Vicksburg to attack Baton Rouge, Louisiana. This force drew off some of Pemberton's defenders. Diversionary attacks by Grant's forces north of Vicksburg drew still others away from the city. Grant received information from a local slave that an ideal landing place south of Vicksburg could be had at Bruinsburg, and he acted on the information. He landed two corps, under McClernand and McPherson, to the east side of the Mississippi just south of Vicksburg on April 30. Grant sent word east to Sherman to march from Jackson, and Sherman's force joined up with Grant's two corps on May 8. With Pemberton's defending forces distributed through the region, and with Sherman and Grant cutting off Johnston's Confederates at Jackson, Union forces began to close in on Vicksburg from the north and east. After two failed assaults on the city in late May, Grant settled in to besiege and bombard the city through June 1863. Pemberton's garrison, reduced to 20,000 men, suffered from starvation and illness, while city residents took refuge in caves carved out of the clay embankments along city streets and roads. Finally Pemberton surrendered unconditionally to Grant on July 4, and Grant immediately paroled the captured prisoners, on the grounds that feeding and transporting them would entail too great a drain on Union resources. Many of the paroled troops actually went home, but others moved east to fight again at Chattanooga.

With the Confederate surrender of Vicksburg and the loss of 20,000 prisoners there to Grant on July 4, as well as the defeat of Lee at Gettysburg, the Union had a great morale boost from two near-simultaneous victories. Over the next two weeks the news of the victories at Gettysburg and Vicksburg began gradually to offset the reaction to the newly instituted Union draft, but not before riots in New York and other Northern cities revealed the intensity of Northern dissension. The drama of Pickett's charge to Cemetery Ridge was recognized almost immediately; in time, it was seen as the high-water mark of the Confederate effort and was marked with a monument at the very spot where the advance had stopped. Within months, Gettysburg came to be seen as a decisive battle, and Lincoln commemorated the burial ground there in his classic Gettysburg Address, delivered in November 1863.

The grand struggle at Gettysburg is probably the most studied battle of the war. Although Lee's forces had penetrated far into Pennsylvania on this second major foray to the North, reaching the outskirts of the state capital at Harrisburg, the defeat at Gettysburg finally put an end to Lee's plans to carry the war to the Union through western Maryland and into central Pennsylvania. Combined with the victory at Vicksburg, the two battles marked a clear turning point in the war. Although the Confederacy would fight on for another 20 months, the Confederates could no longer hope that they would win by conquering Philadelphia or Washington to force a Union acceptance of Confederate independence. After the failure of Pickett's charge, Confederates could only hope that, with the weapons and tactics of the era favoring the defense, they would be able to draw out the war for so long that the North would eventually concede Confederate independence. The Confederates continued to look for the political resistance to Lincoln's administration and the active dissent in the North to wear down the resolve of the Union.

CHICKAMAUGA AND CHATTANOOGA

In fall 1863 the Union attempted to penetrate into Georgia from Tennessee. Having divided the Confederacy by the Mississippi River with the conquest of Vicksburg, the Union plan was to divide the eastern half again, driving across Tennessee to eastern Tennessee and thence to the Atlantic Coast near Charleston and Savannah. This grand drive was halted at Chickamauga in Northern Georgia, and Union troops were pushed back and then besieged in Chattanooga. The lifting of the siege of Chattanooga, and then decisive battles there in late November 1863 that broke the Confederate hold on the high ground around the city, seemed to spell the end of the Confederacy.

Union general William Rosecrans sought to move his Army of the Cumberland from Tennessee into northern Georgia in mid-September 1863. In a series of engagements, Confederate general Braxton Bragg took advantage of the terrain and also the fact that Rosecrans did not position his troops well. Bragg's forces were reinforced with five brigades of Virginia troops, with his total strength at 66,000. In a struggle that lasted all day on September 19, through woods and clearings along the roads near Chickamauga Creek in northern Georgia, both sides fought to a standstill. Then, on the 20th, Rosecrans believed that a gap had formed in his line, and he ordered General Thomas Wood to move troops from the right of the line to fill the gap. Confederates under Longstreet seized the moment and poured through the opening left by Wood's redeployment, sweeping Rosecrans and his forces back. Union general George H. Thomas fought a rear-guard action, holding Snodgrass Hill and later a position on the road that led to Rossville Gap and the way back to Chattanooga, allowing the defeated Union forces to retire. Bragg's forces followed them and took up besieging positions on the high ground surrounding the city. As in many other Civil War battles, the offense took more casualties, and, ironically, the side that lost more men was regarded as the victor. Confederate losses were 2,312 dead, 14,674 wounded, and 1,468 missing; Union losses were 1,657 dead, 9,756 wounded, and 4,757 missing. But the advance of the Union into Georgia had been stopped at Chickamauga, and Bragg was hailed as brilliant for seizing the opportunity presented by Rosecrans's error and for driving the Union army back into Tennessee.

Retreating from Chickamauga, Union forces fled through Rossville Gap to Chattanooga, Tennessee. The outcome of the battle was that the Union advance into Georgia had been stalled. With the siege of Chattanooga, and with Union rations cut back, it appeared that, within weeks, the rest of the Army of the Cumberland under Rosecrans might be forced to surrender.

General Bragg followed the Union troops into Tennessee and was able to take high ground in an arc to the South and east of Chattanooga. At that city, Rosecrans waited behind trench lines for relief; Lincoln sent Joseph Hooker and considered removing Rosecrans, while Braxton Bragg tried to starve out the Federals. Lincoln appointed Grant as commander of the Military Division of the Mississippi. On his arrival, Grant relieved Rosecrans and then approved a plan to open a combined river and overland route that would bring in food and supplies. The so-called Cracker Line was opened in October, when rations for the troops in Chattanooga were down to two or three days' worth.

With the addition of troops under Hooker, Grant had some 70,000 troops facing the besieging force of 50,000 under Bragg. Longstreet took two divisions and two artillery battalions off to Knoxville, Tennessee. Adopting a subterfuge, by having Sherman's fresh troops march as if on parade, Grant was able to send out a powerful reconnaissance in force to Orchard Knob on November 23. Then, on November 24, Hooker led three divisions that fought their way all morning up Lookout Mountain, through fog and mist. Troops remaining down in Chattanooga could not tell the progress of the battle until the blue Union uniforms showed late in the afternoon, causing the engagement to become known as the Battle Above the Clouds.

Also on November 24, Union forces under Sherman fought their way up Missionary Ridge, seizing the Confederate artillery on the crest and turning several pieces on the retreating Confederates, routing them from their trenches and works along the high ground. Despite the desperate fighting, the casualties were not as heavy as the earlier engagement along Chickamauga Creek. The Confederates lost 361 dead, 2,160 wounded, and 4,146 missing. The Federal losses were 753 dead, 4,722 wounded, 349 missing. Bragg's failure to hold the high ground at Lookout Mountain and Missionary Ridge, as well as his failure to destroy Rosecrans and his forces when he had a chance, put an end to his career (although Jefferson Davis trusted him enough to make him his personal military adviser in Richmond).

The Battle of Chattanooga was fought on the ridges surrounding the city. *(Library of Congress, Prints and Photographs Division, LC-USZC4–2382)*

On the Union side, the Battle of Chattanooga solidified Grant's reputation, and Lincoln felt justified in later promoting him to command all Union armies. With the victory at Chattanooga, it seemed, the way would be clear to march through Georgia to Atlanta and then to the sea, cutting the remaining core of the Confederacy across its waist.

CHRONICLE OF EVENTS

1862

January 10–19: In battles at Middle Creek and Mill Springs, the Union temporarily firms up its control of eastern Kentucky.

February 8: The Union wins control of Roanoke Island, North Carolina.

March–June: In a series of engagements in the Peninsular Campaign, Union general George McClellan attempts to take Richmond by marching his troops overland from Fortress Monroe up the peninsula formed by the York and James Rivers. The battles of Yorktown, Williamsburg, Seven Pines, Stuart's Ride around McClellan, and the Seven Days fighting are all part of the Peninsular Campaign.

March 14: Union forces take the city of New Bern, North Carolina, closing one of the Confederacy's few deep water ports that have rail connections to the interior.

April 5–May 3: The battle of Yorktown is fought.

April 6–7: After the Union victories at forts Henry and Donelson, Union general Don Carlos Buell occupies Nashville, Tennessee, and Union general Ulysses S. Grant works his troops South to Pittsburg Landing (Shiloh) on the Tennessee River. General Halleck, in command of the western theater of the war, orders Buell to join Grant for an attack against Corinth. The Battle of Shiloh, or Pittsburg Landing, is fought, in which Grant and his Army of the Tennessee, including many new recruits, make a determined stand at "the Hornet's Nest." Shiloh causes more casualties than had been accumulated in all American wars before that date,

Union gunboats at Malvern Hill provided artillery support for attempts to move on Richmond. *(Library of Congress, Prints and Photographs Division, LC-USZC4–5820)*

Prior to the Battle of Antietam, Union scouts in the foreground observe Confederates crossing the Potomac. *(Library of Congress, Prints and Photographs Division, LC-USZC2–3813)*

with 13,047 Union killed, wounded, and missing, and 10,699 Confederate killed, wounded, and missing. The slaughter represents a new level and shocks observers and leaders in both North and South.

May 5: The Battle of Williamsburg is fought in which McClellan's forces take the city.

May 31–June 1: The battle of Seven Pines (or Fair Oaks) is fought, in which the Confederates take heavy casualties but prevent Union forces from moving into Richmond.

June 12–14: General J. E. B. Stuart takes a cavalry division for a reconnaissance in force, known as the "Ride around McClellan."

June 25–July 1: A series of battles known as the Seven Days includes engagements at Frayser's Farm and Malvern Hill. In these encounters, Union forces are held off from Richmond.

August 29–30: The Battle of Second Bull Run (or Second Manassas) is fought, in which General John Pope attempts to marshal his Union forces against Stonewall Jackson's dismounted cavalry in a position along an unfinished rail line, only to be attacked on the left about noon on August 30 by Confederate troops under General James Longstreet. The advance by some 28,000 Confederate troops, the largest single assault of the war, crushes Pope's forces, driving them back on Bull Run, and they retreat to Centreville.

September 17: The Battle of Antietam (or Sharpsburg) is fought. In the bloodiest single day of the war, the Army of the Potomac, under General George McClellan, drives off an attempt by the Army of Northern Virginia, under Robert E. Lee, to approach Washington through the mountains west and North of the city in Maryland. Although McClellan operates with some foreknowledge of Lee's disposition of troops because of an accidental discovery of a lost order, Union forces are slow to move, and Lee is reinforced at the last moment by the arrival of Stonewall Jackson and his forces. Nevertheless, Lee is driven back and abandons his advance into Maryland.

December 13: Burnside leads a futile attack against Confederate forces well positioned on the high ground beyond the town of Fredericksburg, Virginia, with Union forces suffering about 12,000 casualties.

1863

May 3: The Chancellorsville battle is fought, in which Confederate forces drive Union troops under General Joseph Hooker back across the Rappahannock River; Stonewall Jackson is mortally wounded while returning from a reconnaissance and will die from the wound and pneumonia on May 10.

July 1–3: Gettysburg battle. In this battle, Union forces under General Meade hold the ground just south of the town of Gettysburg; the Confederacy reaches its high-water mark with a charge led by General George Pickett on Cemetery Ridge, repulsed by Union defenders.

July 4: Vicksburg falls to the Union. In this battle, Grant leads the capture of the river city with the surrender of over 30,000 Confederate troops

September 19–20: The Battle of Chickamauga is fought in which Confederates under Braxton Bragg halt the advance of Union forces under General William Rosecrans attempting to march from Chattanooga, Tennessee, into northern Georgia.

October–November: Union forces under Rosecrans and Hooker are besieged in Chattanooga, with Confederates cutting rail connections and holding the high ground of Lookout Mountain, Raccoon Mountain, and Missionary Ridge.

October 26–November 1: A small fleet of steamers and barges brings supplies to Chattanooga, opening the so-called Cracker Line that allows Union forces to withstand the siege.

November 23–27: The Battle of Chattanooga is fought, in which Confederate troops are finally driven from the high ground around Chattanooga. The overall battle is fought in several separate engagements over the five-day period. General U.S. Grant receives credit for the Union victory.

November 23: The Battle of Chattanooga commences with skirmishes at Orchard Knob and Bushy Knob. Fresh troops under Sherman appear as if marching on parade before their surprise attack on Orchard Knob.

November 24: The Battle of Lookout Mountain is fought, with a Union victory. Much of the advance, led by General Hooker, is obscured by fog and mist until late in the day, when Union troops are finally seen advancing on the crest; the engagement will become known as the Battle Above the Clouds.

November 25: The Battle of Missionary Ridge is fought, with Union forces taking the high ground and turning Confederate artillery on the retreating Confederates.

November 26: Skirmishes are fought at Chickamauga Station, Pea Vine Valley, and Pigeon Hills, Tennessee, and at Graysville, Georgia.

November 27: An engagement is fought at Ringgold Gap, Taylor's Ridge, Georgia. Over the five days of fighting, the Union estimates its own losses in killed, wounded, and missing as about 4,000 out of about 37,000 engaged. The victories in Tennessee lead the Union generals to believe they can win the war in the following year.

December: In Virginia, Union general George Meade withdraws after encountering a strong Confederate position at Mine Run and Locust Grove in late November. Harsh winter weather and the Confederate field fortifications bring a halt to Union military action in Virginia for the winter.

Eyewitness Testimony

Laus Deo! [Praise God!] The best day we have seen since war began. The Norfolk papers announce Burnside's occupation of Roanoke Island, the whole rebel force prisoners, the gunboats captured, and Elizabeth City abandoned and burned; alleged severe loss on our side, but that is doubtless magnified by rebel report. Burnside is pushing on, up Albemarle Sound, it would seem. Hurray for Burnside! Even better than this is the news from the West. Our gunboats have made their way up the Tennessee River and into northern Alabama as far as Florence on an unopposed reconnaissance, and found strong Union feeling manifested at many points on the river. This seems reliable and is most important. I did not expect it.

> *George Templeton Strong, Northern philanthropist, commenting on Union advances in his diary entry of February 12, 1862, in Allan Nevins, ed., A Civil War Diary, p. 206.*

Yesterday I received pressing messages from Smith and others begging me to go to the front. I started with half a dozen aides and some fifteen orderlies, and found things in a bad state. Hancock was engaged with a vastly inferior force some two miles from any support. Hooker fought nearly all day without assistance, and the mass of the troops were crowded together where they were useless. I found everybody discouraged, officers and men; our troops in wrong positions, on the wrong side of the woods; no system, no co-operation, no orders given, roads blocked up.

As soon as I came upon the field the men cheered like fiends, and I saw at once that I could save the day. I immediately reinforced Hancock and arranged to support Hooker, advanced the whole line across the woods, filled up the gaps, and got everything in hand for whatever might occur. The result was that the enemy saw that he was gone if he remained in his position, and scampered during the night. His works were very strong, but his loss was very heavy. The roads are in such condition that it is impossible to pursue except with a few cavalry.

It is with the utmost difficulty that I can feed the men, many of whom have had nothing to eat for twenty-four hours and more. I had no dinner yesterday, no supper; a cracker for breakfast, and no dinner yet. I have no baggage; I was out in the rain all day and until late at night; slept in my clothes and boots, and could not even wash my face and hands. I, however, expect my ambulance up pretty soon, when I hope for better things. I have been through the hospitals, where are many of our own men and of the rebels. One Virginian sent for me this morning and told me that I was the only general from whom they expected any humanity. I corrected this mistake.

[Williamsburg] is a beautiful little town; several very old houses and churches, pretty gardens. I have taken possession of a very fine house which Joe Johnston occupied as his headquarters. It has a lovely flower-garden and conservatory. If you were here I should be much inclined to spend some weeks here.

> *General George McClellan, in a letter to his wife, commenting on his satisfaction after the Battle of Williamsburg, May 6, 1862, from McClellan's Own Story, as reproduced in Henry Steele Commager, ed., The Blue and the Gray: The Story of the Civil War as Told by Participants, p. 120.*

The firing was then violent at Seven Pines, and within a half hour the three Federal divisions were broken and driven from their position in confusion. It was then evident, however, from the obstinancy of our adversaries at Fair Oaks, that the battle would not be decided that day. I said so to the staff-officers near me, and told them that each regiment must sleep where it might be standing when the firing ceased for the night, to be ready to renew it at dawn next morning.

General Ambrose Burnside and staff officers pose for a camp photo at Warrenton, Virginia, November 1862. *(Library of Congress, Prints and Photographs Division, LC-DIG-cwpb-01705)*

About half-past 7 o'clock I received a musket-shot in the shoulder, and was unhorsed soon after by a heavy fragment of shell which struck my breast. I was borne from the field—first to a house on the roadside, thence to Richmond. The firing ceased before I had been carried a mile from it. The conflict at Fair Oaks was terminated by darkness only. . . . The only thing [Jefferson Davis] ought to have done, or had time to do, was postponed almost twenty hours—the putting General Lee, who was near, in command of the army.

The operations of the Confederate troops in this battle were very much retarded by the broad ponds of rain-water,—in many places more than knee-deep,—by the deep mud, and by the dense woods and thickets that covered the ground.

Confederate general Joseph E. Johnston, recalling the Battle of Seven Pines/Fair Oaks, May 31–June 1, 1862, in his memoir of the battle published in Robert U. Johnson and Clarence C. Buel, Battles and Leaders of the Civil War, *Vol. II, p. 215.*

Here the Williamsburg "old stage" road is intersected by the Nine-mile road, at a point seven miles east of Richmond, was fought the first great contest between the Confederate Army of Northern Virginia and the Federal Army of the Potomac. The junction of these two roads is called Seven Pines. About one mile from Seven Pines, where the Nine-mile road crosses the Richmond and the York River Railroad, there is a station called Fair Oaks. Before the action ended there was a good deal of fighting near the latter place. The Federals called the action of May 31st and June 1st the battle of Fair Oaks. . . .

In the wood the opposing lines were close to each other, in some places not more than twenty five or thirty yards apart. The contest continued until dark without material variation in the position of either line on that part of the field after I reached the extreme front, until the firing had ceased at dark, when I ordered the line to fall back to the edge of the field and reform. In the meantime Whiting's brigade and the right of Pettigrew's had been forced back to the clump of trees just north of Fair Oaks Station, where the contest was kept up until night.

On reaching the open field in rear of the line where Hampton's and Hatton's brigades had been engaged, I heard for the first time that General Johnston had been very seriously wounded and taken from the field an hour or more before. I was second in rank in his army,

therefore the command, for the time being devolved upon me.

Confederate general Gustavus W. Smith, describing the exact location of the Battle of Seven Pines, May 31–June 1, 1862, in his memoir of the battle published in Robert U. Johnson and Clarence C. Buel, Battles and Leaders of the Civil War, *Vol. II, pp. 220, 247.*

We were now twenty five miles from Richmond on the "James River Road." Had the enemy been aware of our position, it would have been easy for him to throw a force between us and Richmond, and so cut us off. But the Federal general was not well served by his scouts nor did his cavalry furnish him with accurate information of our movements. Relying upon the mistakes of the enemy, [General J. E. B.] Stuart resolved to march straight on into Richmond by the River road on which we now lay. To accomplish this with the greater safety, it was necessary for him to march at once. Accordingly, I was ordered to take the advance guard and move out. As soon as the cravings of hunger were appeased, sleep took possession of us. Although in the saddle and in motion, and aware that the safety of the expedition depended on great vigilance in case the enemy should be encountered, it was hard to keep awake. I was constantly falling asleep, and awaking with a start when almost off my horse. This was the condition of every man in the column. Not one had closed his eyes in sleep for forty-eight hours.

The full moon lighted us on our way as we passed along the River road, and frequently the windings of the road brought us near to and in sight of the James River, where lay the enemy's fleet. In the gray twilight of the dawn of Sunday, we passed the "Double Gates," "Strawberry Plains," and "Tighlman's gate" in succession. At "Tighlman's" we could see the masts of the fleet, not far off. Happily for us, the banks were high, and I imagine they had no lookout in the rigging, and we passed by unobserved. The sight of the enemy's fleet had aroused us somewhat, when "Who goes there?" rang out in the stillness of the early morning. The challenger proved to be a vidette of the 10th Virginia Cavalry, commanded by Colonel J. Lucius Davis, who was picketing that road. Soon I was shaking hands with Colonel Davis and receiving his congratulations. Then we crossed the stream by the jug factory, up toward "New Market" heights, by the drill house, and about a mile beyond we called halt for a little rest and food. From this point the several regiments were dismissed to their respective camps. . . .

The most important result was the confidence the men had gained in themselves and in their leaders. The country rang out with praises of the men who had raided entirely around General McClellan's powerful army, bringing prisoners and plunder from under his very nose. The Southern papers were filled with accounts of the expedition, none accurate, and most of them marvelous.

Confederate colonel W. T. Robins, describing the conclusion of J. E. B. Stuart's "Ride around McClellan" on the morning of June 14, 1862, in his memoir published in Robert U. Johnson and Clarence C. Buel, Battles and Leaders of the Civil War, *Vol. II, p. 275.*

The Seven Days' Fighting, although a decided Confederate victory, was a succession of mishaps. If Jackson had arrived on the 26th [of June],—the day of his own selection,—the Federals would have been driven back from Mechanicsville without a battle. His delay there, caused by obstructions placed in his road by the enemy, was the first mishap. He was too late in entering the fight at Gaines's Mill, and the destruction of Grapevine Bridge kept him from reaching Frayser's farm until the day after that battle. If he had been there, we might have destroyed or captured McClellan's army. Huger was in position for the battle of Frayser's farm, and after his batteries had misled me into opening the fight he subsided. Holmes and Magruder, who were on the New Market road to attack the Federals as they passed that way, failed to do so.

General McClellan's retreat was successfully managed; therefore, we must give it credit for being well managed. He had 100,000 men, and insisted to the authorities at Washington that Lee had 200,000. In fact, Lee had only 90,000. General McClellan's plan to take Richmond by a siege was wise enough, and it would have been a success if the Confederates had consented to such a programme. In spite of McClellan's excellent plans, General Lee, with a force inferior in numbers, completely routed him, and while suffering less than McClellan, captured over six thousand of his men. General Lee's plans in the Seven Days Fight were excellent, but were poorly executed. General McClellan was a very accomplished soldier and a very able engineer, but hardly equal to the position of field-marshal as a military chieftain. He organized the Army of the Potomac cleverly, but did not handle it skilfully when in actual battle. Still I doubt if his retreat could have been better handled, though the rear of his army should have been more positively either in his own hands or in the hands of Sumner.

Confederate general James Longstreet, commenting in his memoir regarding the retreat of Union general George McClellan during and after the battle of Frayser's Farm during the Seven Days Battle retreating from Richmond, June 21–28, in his memoir of the battle published in Robert U. Johnson and Clarence C. Buel, Battles and Leaders of the Civil War, *Vol. II, pp. 404–405.*

John Chesnut gives us a spirited account of their ride around McClellan. I sent the letter to his grandfather. He says the women ran out, screaming with

General James Longstreet was credited with several outstanding Confederate victories, including the rout of Federal troops at Chickamauga. However, his disagreements with Lee, including his objections to the disastrous charge against Cemetery Ridge during the Battle of Gettysburg, made him the subject of continuing debate. *(Library of Congress, Prints and Photographs Division, LC-DIG-cwpb-06084)*

joyful welcome, as soon as they caught sight of the grey uniform. They brought handfulls and armfulls of food for them. One grey-headed man, after preparing a hasty meal for them, knelt and prayed for them as they snatched it. They were in the saddle from Friday until Sunday. They were used up, and so were their horses. He writes for clothes and more horses.

Miss S. C. says: "No need to send any more of his fine horses, to be killed or captured by the Yankees." She will wait and see how the siege of Richmond ends, for though in patriotism she is bent, she bears a frugal mind. The horses will go, all the same, as Johnny wants them.

Mary Chesnut, planter-class diarist, in her entry for June 24, 1862, recording her reaction to news of the "Ride around McClellan" received from her husband in Richmond, in A Diary From Dixie, *p. 257.*

The fight was opened this morning at day brake & an awful canonading continued on boath sides until about 10 A.M. when it partially ceased & small arms took the place for a short time. The fight continued unceasingly & most furiously lasting the entire day & until 9 O'clk at night when all things quieted down except the rumbling of the ambulances, which were going all night. Great many wounded on our side but not many killed. Enemys loss not known as boath parties held about the same position as when the fight commenced.

Diary entry of John S. Tucker, commissary clerk of the Greensboro Guards, an Alabama unit, reporting his observations on the Battle of Antietam, September 17, 1862, as extracted and published in G. Ward Hubbs, ed., Voices from Company D: Diaries by the Greensboro Guards, Fifth Alabama Infantry Regiment, Army of Northern Virginia, *p. 110.*

I told you in the letter I wrote from Washington something about the battles of Bull Run and Chantilly and as I would much rather write of victories than defeats (Although you can hardly call Chantilly a defeat as the enemy were foiled in their attempt to cut off our baggage train, though the loss on our side was heavy and included Generals Kearney and Stephens) I will tell you of what we have done for the last two weeks. We left Washington by the road leading to Frederick Md, on Sunday Sept 7th and moved by easy marches, untill Thursday Sept 11th when our advance came up with part of the Artillery force of the enemy who were posted in a very commanding position on a range of high hills on the opposite side of a stream called the Monochey (Monacacy) River. As soon as our advance

came within range the enemy opened fire but our Artillery soon got to work throwing shot and shell so fast that the enemy were forced to leave without our Infantry being engaged at all. After the enemy fell back our forces advanced in three or four different Collumns, each takeing a different road. . . .

After resting a few hours in the morning we pushed on again our Division takeing the lead and late in the afternoon of the 16th we found the enemy had concluded to make another stand at a stream about 100 feet wide called Antietam Creek. The bank on their side of the creek was very high and very steep and was covered with heavy woods which gave them a great advantage over us. It was so late in the afternoon that it was decided not to make an attack that night so we filed off into a field and stoped for the night. The only place where we were, that our Artillery could cross was at a stone Bridge some 20 ft. wide, where the enemy had made temporary breastworks of fence rails and logs behind which they could lay almost concealed from us while we would have to advance to the bridge through open fields in plain sight of them. . . . After about half an hour the enemys fire began to slacken a little, and soon the order was given for our Brigade to charge. The 51st Pennsylvania had the right of our Brigade, and should have crossed first, but our boys could not wait, and with the cry of remember Reno, we started for the Bridge the 51st Penn and our Regt crossing together. As soon as the rebels saw us start on a charge they broke and run and the fight at the bridge was ended. . . .

At daylight on the morning of Sept 19th we found the enemy had left and we moved forward about 3 miles to the Potomac River where we are now and as near as I can find out the enemy are all out of Md.

George Washington Whitman, brother of the poet Walt Whitman, to their mother, dated September 21, 1862, describing his participation in the battles of South Mountain and Antietam, on September 11–17, in Jerome Loving, ed., Civil War Letters of G. W. Whitman, *pp. 65–66.*

The enemy were posted in an almost impregnable position on a range of hills which they have covered with breastworks for Artillery and Rifle pitts for Infantry while between them and the Town from which we had to advance is an open plain swept on all parts by their guns and at the foot of the hills is a narrow creek, with a steep muddy bank on each side, over which it would be impossible to charge and as *they* were almost entirely protected by their breastworks you can imagine what an advantage they had over us. . . . Our whole Brigade formed in line and advanced beautifuly over the plain and up to the bank of the creek, under a most terrible fire of Rifle balls, Cannister, and Shell, after getting to the edge of the creek we lay down and blazed away untill night Other Brigades and Divisions followed us in and lay down behind us but we could get no further, and after dark the fireing ceased and we all fell back to the Town except 3 Brigades who was left to hold the ground untill morning when we supposed the fight would be renewed but Sunday passed and no fighting. On Sunday night our Regt went out on Picket within 200 ft of the enemys breastworks but we were protected by a slight raise of the ground but we had to lay down flat all the time for as soon as we got up the Rebs cracked away at us, last night all the troops fell back on this side of the river takeing up the bridge and here we are now.

> *George Washington Whitman, brother of the poet Walt Whitman, to their mother, dated December 16, 1862, describing his participation in the Battle of Fredericksburg on December 13, in Jerome Loving, ed.,* Civil War Letters of G. W. Whitman, *pp. 75–76.*

I gathered my couriers about me and went forward to find General Jackson. The storm of battle had swept far on to the east and become more and more faint to the ear, until silence came with night over the fields and woods. As I rode along that old turnpike, passing scattered fragments of Confederates looking for their regiments, parties of prisoners concentrating under guards, wounded men by the roadside and under the trees at Talley's and Chancellor's, I had reached an open field on the right, a mile west of Chancellorsville, when, in the dusky twilight, I saw horsemen near an old cabin in the field. Toward them, I found Rodes and his staff engaged in gathering the broken and scattered troops that had swept the two miles of battle-field. "General Jackson is just ahead on the road, Captain," said Rodes; "tell him I will be here at this cabin if I am wanted." I had not gone a hundred yards before I heard firing, a shot or two, and then a company volley upon the right of the road, and another upon the left. A few moments farther on I met Captain Murray Taylor, an aide of A. P. Hill's, with tidings that Jackson and Hill were wounded, and some around them killed, by fire of their own men. Spurring my horse into a sweeping gallop, I soon passed the Confederate line of battle, and some three or four rods on its front, found the general's horse beside a pine sapling on the left,

and a rod beyond a little party of men caring for a wounded officer. The story of the sad event is briefly told, and, in essentials, very much as it came to me from the lips of the wounded general himself, and in everything confirmed and completed by those who were eye-witnesses and near companions.

When Jackson had reached the point where his line now crossed the turnpike, scarcely a mile west of Chancellorsville, and not half a mile from a line of Federal troops, he had found his front line unfit for the farther and vigorous advance he desired, by reason of the irregular character of the fighting, now right, now left, and because of the dense thickets, through which it was impossible to preserve alignment. . . . impatient and anxious, the general rode forward on the turnpike, followed by two or three of his staff and a number of couriers and signal sergeants. He passed the swampy depression and began the ascent of the hill toward Chancellorsville, when he came upon a line of the Federal infantry lying on their arms. Fired at by one or two muskets . . . he turned and came back toward his line, upon the side of the road to his left. As he rode near to the Confederate troops, just placed in position and ignorant that he was in front, the left company began firing to the front, and two of his party fell from their saddles dead—Captain Boswell, of the Engineers, and Sergeant Cunliffe, of the Signal Corps. Spurring his horse across the road to his right, he was met by a second volley from the right company of Pender's North Carolina brigade. Under this volley, when not two rods from the troops, the general received three balls at the same instant. One penetrated the palm of his right hand was cut out that night from the back of his hand. A second passed around the wrist of the left arm and out through the left hand. A third ball passed through the left arm half-way from shoulder to elbow. The large bone of the upper arm was splintered to the elbow-joint, and the wound bled freely.

> *Account by Reverend James Power Smith, captain of the Confederate army, describing how General Thomas (Stonewall) Jackson was wounded by his own troops, May 3, 1863, at the Battle of Chancellorsville, in his narrative in Robert U. Johnson and Clarence C. Buel,* Battles and Leaders of the Civil War, *Vol. II, pp. 209–211.*

Pickett said, "General, shall I advance?"

The effort to speak the order failed, and I could only indicate it by an affirmative bow. He accepted the duty, with seeming confidence of success, leaped on his horse, and rode gaily to his command. I mounted and spurred for Alexander's post. He reported that the batteries he had reserved for the charge with the infantry had been spirited away by General Lee's chief of artillery, that the ammunition of the batteries of position was so reduced that he could not use them in proper support of the infantry. He was ordered to stop the march at once and fill up his ammunition chests. But alas! There was no more ammunition to be had. . . .

Confederate batteries put their fire over the heads of the men as they moved down the slope, and continued to draw the fire of the enemy until the smoke lifted and drifted to the rear, when every gun was turned upon the infantry columns. The batteries that had been drawn off were replaced by others that were fresh. Soldiers and officers began to fall, some to rise no more, others to find their way to the hospital tents. Single files were cut here and there; then the gaps increased, and an occasional shot tore wider openings, but closing the gaps as quickly as made, the march moved on. . . .

Pickett's lines being nearer, the impact was heaviest upon them. Most of the field officers were killed or wounded. Colonel Whittle of Armistead's brigade, who had been shot through the right leg at Williamsburg and lost his left arm at Malvern Hill, was shot through the right arm, then brought down by a shot through his left leg.

General Armistead, of the second line, spread his steps to supply the places of fallen comrades. His colors cut down, with a volley against the bristling line of bayonets, he put his cap on his sword to guide the storm. The enemy's massing, enveloping numbers held the struggle until the noble Armistead fell beside the wheels of the enemy's battery. Pettigrew was wounded but held his command.

General Pickett, finding the battle broken while the enemy was still reinforcing, called the troops off. There was no indication of panic. The broken files marched back in steady step. The effort was nobly made and failed from blows that could not be fended.

Confederate general James Longstreet, describing Pickett's charge against the Union position on Cemetery Ridge during the Battle of Gettysburg, July 3, 1863, in his memoir, From Manassas to Appomattox: Memoirs of the Civil War in America *as reproduced in Henry Steele Commager, ed.,* The Blue and the Gray: The Story of the Civil War as Told by Participants, *pp. 629–630.*

The great, desperate, final charge came at 4. The Rebels seemed to have gathered up all their strength and desperation for one fierce, convulsive effort, that should sweep over and wash out our obstinate resistance. They swept up as before: the flower of their army to the front, victory staked upon the issue. In some places, they literally lifted up and pushed back our lines; but that terrible "position" of ours!—wherever they entered it, enfilading fires from half a score of crests swept away their columns like the merest chaff. Broken and hurled back, they easily fell into our hands and on the center and left, the last half-hour brought more prisoners than all the rest. . . .

As the tempest of fire approached its height [General Gibbon] walked along the line, and renewed his orders to the men to reserve their fire. The Rebels—three lines deep—came steadily up. They were in point–blank range.

At last the order came! From thrice six thousand guns, there came a sheet of smoky flame, a crash, a rush of leaden death. The line literally melted away; but there came the second, resistless still. It had been our supreme effort—on the instant we were not equal to another.

Up to the rifle-pits, across them, over the barricades—the momentum of their charge, the mere machine strength of their combined action—swept them on. Our thin line could fight, but it had not weight enough to oppose to this momentum. It was pushed behind the guns. Right on came the Rebels. They were upon the guns—were bayoneting the gunners—were waving their flags above our pieces.

But they had penetrated to the fatal point. A storm of grape and canister tore its way from man to man, and marked the track with corpses straight down their line! They had exposed themselves to the enfilading fire of the guns on the western slope of Cemetery hill; that exposure sealed their fate.

The line reeled back—disjointed already—in an instant in fragments. Our men were just behind the guns. They leaped forward upon the disordered mass; but there was little need for fighting now. A regiment threw down its arms, and with colors at its head, rushed over and surrendered. All along the field, smaller detachments did the same. Webb's brigade brought in 800: taken in as little time as it requires to write the simple sentence that tells it. Gibbon's old division took 15 stand of colors . . .

It was a fruitless sacrifice. They gathered up their broken fragments, formed their lines, and slowly

The view from Seminary Ridge toward Cemetery Ridge at Gettysburg is depicted as imagined in the battle. Visitors today can stand on the same ground and visualize the scene. *(Library of Congress, Prints and Photographs Division, LC-USZC4–1178)*

marched away. It was not a rout, it *was* a bitter, crushing defeat. For once, the Army of the Potomac had won a clean, honest, acknowledged victory.

Journalist Whitelaw Reid, writing under the pen-name Agate for the Cincinnati Gazette, *describing Pickett's Charge at Gettysburg, July 3, 1863, as quoted in Horace Greeley,* The American Conflict, *Vol. II, page 386.*

The jostling, swaying lines on either side boil, and roar, and dash their flamy spray, two hostile billows of a fiery ocean. Thick flashes stream from the wall, thick volleys answer from the crest. No threats or expostulation now, only example and encouragement. All depths of passion are stirred, and all combatives fire, down to their deep foundations. Individuality is drowned in a sea of clamor, and timid men, breathing the breath of the multitude, are brave. The frequent dead and wounded lie where they stagger and fall—there is no humanity for them now, and none can be spared to care for them. The men do not cheer or shout; they growl, and over that uneasy sea, heard with roar of musketry, sweeps the muttered thunder of a storm of growls. Webb, Hall, Devereux, Mallon, Abbot among the men where all are heroes, are doing deeds of note.

Now the loyal wave rolls up as if it would over-leap its barrier, the crest. Pistols flash with the muskets. My "Forward to the wall" is answered by the Rebel counter-command, "Steady, men!" and the wave swings back. Again it surges, and again it sinks. These men of Pennsylvania, on the soil of their own homesteads,

the first and only to flee the wall, must be the first to storm it . . . "Sergeant, forward with your color. Let the Rebels see it close to their eyes once before they die." The color sergeant of the 72nd Pa., grasping the stump of the severed lance in both his hands, waved the flag above his head and rushed towards the wall. "Will you see your color storm the wall alone?" One man only starts to follow. Almost halfway to the wall, down go color bearer and color to the ground—the gallant sergeant is dead. The line springs—the crest of the solid ground with a great roar, heaves forward its maddened load, men, arms, smoke, fire, a fighting mass. It rolls to the wall—flash meets flash, the wall is crossed—a moment ensues of thrusts, yells, blows, shots, and undistinguishable conflict, followed by a shout universal that makes the welkin ring again, and the last and bloodiest fight of the great battle of Gettysburg is ended and won.

Account by Union lieutenant colonel Frank Aretas Haskell, aide-de-camp to General John Gibbon, describing the repulse of Pickett's charge at Gettysburg on July 3, 1863, in his book-length letter to his brother, later published as The Battle of Gettysburg, *as quoted in Henry Steele Commager, ed.,* The Blue and the Gray: The Story of the Civil War as Told by Participants, *pp. 635–636.*

I rode into Vicksburg with the troops, and went to the river to exchange congratulations with the navy upon our joint victory. At that time I found that many of the citizens had been living under-ground. The ridges upon which Vicksburg is built, and those back to the Big Black, are composed of a deep yellow clay, of great tenacity. Where roads and streets are cut through, perpendicular banks are left, and stand as well as if composed of stone. The magazines of the enemy were made by running passage-ways into this clay at places where there were deep cuts. Many citizens secured places of safety for their families by carving out rooms in these embankments. A door-way in these cases would be cut in a high bank, starting from the level of the road or street, and after running in a few feet a room of the size required was carved out of the clay, the dirt being removed by the door-way. In some instances I saw where two rooms were cut out, for a single family, with a door-way in the clay wall separating them. Some of these were carpeted and furnished with considerable elaboration. In these the occupants were fully secure from the shells of the navy, which were dropped into the city, night and day, without intermission.

General Ulysses S. Grant, commenting on the surrender of Vicksburg, July 4, 1863, in Personal Memoirs of U. S. Grant, *selected as "The Vicksburg Campaign," in Robert U. Johnson and Clarence C. Buel,* Battles and Leaders of the Civil War, *Vol. III, p. 535.*

As soon as our troops took possession of [Vicksburg], guards were established along the whole line of parapet, from the river above to the river below. The prisoners were allowed to occupy their old camps behind the intrenchments. No restraint was put upon them, except by their own commanders. They were rationed about as our own men, and from our supplies. The men of the two armies fraternicized as if they had been fighting for the same cause. When they passed out of the works they had so long and so gallantly defended, between lines of their late antagonists, not a cheer went up, not a remark was made that would give pain. I believe there was a feeling of sadness among the Union soldiers at seeing the dejection of their late antagonists. . . .

At Vicksburg 31,600 prisoners were surrendered, together with 172 cannon, about 60,000 muskets and a large amount of ammunition. The small-arms of the enemy were far superior to the bulk of ours. Up to this time our troops at the west had been limited to the old United States flint-lock muskets changed into percussion, or the Belgian musket imported early in the war—almost as dangerous to the person firing it as to the one aimed at—and a few new and improved arms. These were of many different calibers, a fact that caused much trouble in distributing ammunition during an engagement. The enemy had generally new arms, which had run the blockade, and were of uniform caliber. After the surrender I authorized all colonels, whose regiments were armed with inferior muskets, to place them in the stack of captured arms, and replace them with the latter. A large number of arms, turned in to the ordnance department as captured, were these arms that had really been used by the Union army in the capture of Vicksburg.

General Ulysses S. Grant, commenting on the surrender of Vicksburg, July 4, 1863, in Personal Memoirs of U.S. Grant, *selected as "The Vicksburg Campaign," in Robert U. Johnson and Clarence C. Buel,* Battles and Leaders of the Civil War, *Vol. III, pp. 536–537.*

The enemy opens a terrific fire; but up the hill our men advance; now the enemy's bullets begin to tell upon the lines, and men fall to the right and left, dead and wounded; but the rest move on undismayed, firing rapidly as they advance; but the artillery and infantry fire is too hot for them, although they have fought most gallantly, and, halting under the crest where some protection is had, the lines are dressed, and General Preston, reassuring them by his presence, rides down the lines and coolly examines each man's cartridge-box, and says, "Men, we must use the bayonet,—the bayonet,—we will give them the bayonet!" The men, one and all cry out, "Go ahead, General! We are not whipped yet!" Confidence restored by the General's cool demeanor, and with the enthusiasm of the troops raised to the highest pitch, Preston rides to the front and centre of his line, and leads the way with splendid dash and bravery, waving his cap above his head, his gray hair floating in the breeze.

William Owen, who served with the Washington Artillery of Louisiana, from In Camp and Battle with the Washington Artillery, *describing the Battle of Chickamauga, September 20, 1863, as quoted in Henry Steele Commager, ed.,* The Blue and the Gray, *p. 888.*

The torn-up track to Ringgold had been relaid, so we went on to that place and arrived about dark. I found what had been the Bragg hospital filled with wounded men awaiting transportation. Oh, how sad and dreary all appeared! There was not a single light in the whole building, except that which came from a fire outside, around which stood several slightly wounded soldiers shivering from cold. The balconies were filled with wounded men, wrapped in their blankets, lying on the floors. I found one room full, where all were suffering for want of water. These men were waiting to be transported to the cars . . .

Diary entry for September 28, 1863, of Kate Cumming, a Scots-born nurse who served with the Confederate forces, describing care for the wounded after the Battle of Chickamauga, from Gleanings from Southland; Sketches of Life and Manners of the People of the South Before, During and After the War of Secession, *as selected in Henry Steele Commager,* The Blue and the Gray, *p. 782.*

The only soldier I could find who claimed any knowledge of the business of a river pilot was a man named Williams, who had steered on a steam-ferry running between Cincinnati and Covington. Him I put into the wheel-house, and as I had once owned a fourth interest in a steamboat, and fooled away considerable money and time with her, I had learned enough of the wheel to know which way to turn it, and of the bell-pulls to signal Stop, Back, and Go ahead. I went with Williams into the wheel-house and put [former lake boat mate] Davis on the bows, to keep a lookout. As the night grew dark, and finally black, Davis declared he could see nothing, and came back wringing his hands and saying we would "surely be wrecked if we did not land and tie up."

"There's a light ahead now, Davis, on the north shore."

"Yes, and another on the South, I think."

"One or both must be rebels' camp-fires."

We tried to keep the middle of the river, which is less than a musket-shot across in any part. After a long struggle against wind and tide we got abreast of the first camp-fire, and saw the sentry pacing back and forward before it, and hailed:

"Halloo! There. What troops are those?"

Back came the answer in unmistakable Southern patois: "Ninth Tennessee. Run your old tea-kittle ashore here, and give us some hot whisky."

The answer was not comforting. I knew of no Tennessee regiment in the Union service except one, or part of one, commanded by Colonel Stokes, and where that was I did not know. So we put the boat over to the other shore as fast as possible, and to gain time I called out:

"Who's in command?"

"Old Stokes, you bet."

"Never mind, Williams, keep her in the middle. We're all right. –How far to Kelley's Ferry?"

"Rite over thar whar you see that fire. They're sittin' up for ye, I reckon."

"Steady, Williams. Keep around the bend and steer for the light."

And in due time we tied the steamboat and barges safely to shore, with 40,000 rations and 39,000 pounds of forage, within five miles of General Hooker's men, who had half a breakfast ration left in haversacks; and within eight or ten miles of Chattanooga, where our cakes of hard bread and a quarter pound of pork made a three day's ration. In Chattanooga there were but four boxes of hard bread left in the commissary warehouses on the morning of the 30th [of October]. About midnight I started an orderly to report to General Hooker the safe arrival of the rations. The orderly returned about sunrise, and reported that the news went through the camps faster than his horse, and the soldiers were jubilant, and cheering "The Cracker line open. Full

rations, boys! Three cheers for the Cracker line," as if we had won another victory, and we had.

Assistant Quartermaster William G. Le Duc, U.S. Volunteers, recalling the passage of his barge up the Tennessee River to Chattanooga, opening the supply line to the besieged Union forces there on the night of October 31, 1863, in a letter composed November 1, 1863, in his memoir, entitled "The Little Steamboat that Opened the Cracker Line," in Robert U. Johnson and Clarence C. Buel, Battles and Leaders of the Civil War, *Vol. III, p. 678.*

I witnessed a painful sight this afternoon—the shooting of two federal soldiers. As it may be of interest I will give you a description of it. The two men belonged to Illinois regiments: one of the 44th and another to the 88th, both of our division, which as you know is commanded by General Sheridan. The men had been tried for desertion, found guilty and sentenced to be shot. One brigade of the division under arms, with colors flying and band playing formed about noon in nearly a hollow square with one side entirely open. Thousands of soldier spectators gathered about those who stood under arms. Bout one P.M. a solemn procession composed of two details of infantry, one in front of the prisoners and one in the rear, marched into the inclosure. Behind the first company and immediately in front of the prisoners their coffins were borne each upon the shoulders of four men. In the rear of the doomed men marched the second company with the rifles at the right shoulder shift and bayonets fixed. A band playing a solemn tune marched with slow and measured step in front of the little procession. General Sheridan and staff were present. All were mounted and in full uniform. The General had a broad yellow sash over his shoulder drawn across his breast and down under his sword belt. He sat motionless upon his big black horse which stood just a little in front of the other horsemen. When the procession arrived at the open side of the square it was halted, the coffins were placed upon the ground, when the prisoners knelt and the chaplain prayed. They then arose, apparently very calm, and sat erect each upon his coffin. A bandage was then bound over the eyes of each. A platoon of soldiers with loaded rifles stood a few paces in front. There was a strange silence for a moment and then the voice of command rang out. "Ready!" "Aim!" "Fire!" And each of the prisoners fell back over his coffin, dead.

It was hard to see men thus killed by their own comrades but you have no idea how many have deserted, encouraged by friends at home to do the disgraceful act. Sad as the scene this afternoon was, it will have a wholesome effect upon the whole division.

Washington Gardner, Union soldier, in a letter to a friend, November 14, 1863, reporting the execution of two soldiers for desertion under General Sheridan's command at the Battle of Chattanooga, reprinted in Henry Steele Commager, ed., The Blue and the Gray: The Story of the Civil War as Told by Participants, *p. 512.*

"I didn't order [the troops] up," said Sheridan; "but we are going to take the ridge!" He then asked Avery for his flask and waved it at a group of Confederate officers, standing just in front of Bragg's headquarters, with the salutation, "Here's at you!" At once two guns—the "Lady Breckinridge," and the "Lady Buckner"—in front of Bragg's headquarters were fired at Sheridan and the group of officers about him. One shell struck so near as to throw dirt over Sheridan and Avery. "Ah!" said the general, "that is ungenerous; I shall take those guns for that!"...

The men fighting and climbing up the steep hill, sought the roads, ravines, and less rugged parts. The ground was so broken that it was impossible to keep a regular line of battle. At times their movements were in shape like the flight of migratory birds—sometimes in line, sometimes in mass, mostly in V-shaped groups, with the points toward the enemy. At these points regimental flags were flying, sometimes drooping as the bearers were shot, but never reaching the ground, for other brave hands were there to seize them. Sixty flags were advancing up the hill. Bragg was hurrying large bodies of men from his right to the center. They could be seen hastening along the ridge. Cheatham's division was being withdrawn from Sherman's front. Bragg and Hardee were at the center urging their men to stand firm and drive back the advancing enemy now so near the summit—indeed so near that the guns, which could not be sufficiently depressed to reach them, became useless. Artillerymen were lighting the fuses of shells, and bowling them by hundreds down the hill. The critical moment arrived when the summit was just within reach. At six different points and almost simultaneously, Sheridan's and Wood's divisions broke over the crest,—Sheridan's first, near Bragg's headquarters; and in a few minutes Sheridan was beside the guns that had been fired at him, and claiming them as captures of his division. Baird's division took the works on Wood's left almost immediately afterward; and then Johnson came

upon Sheridan's right. The enemy's guns were turned upon those who still remained in the works and soon all were in flight down the eastern slope.

Brevet Brigadier General Joseph S. Fullerton, U.S. Volunteers, assistant adjutant-general, IV Army Corps, describing the attack of the Army of the Cumberland that captured Missionary Ridge, November 25, 1863, helping to lift the siege of Chattanooga, in his memoir, The Army of the Cumberland at Chattanooga, *in Robert U. Johnson and Clarence C. Buel,* Battles and Leaders of the Civil War, *Vol. III, p. 726.*

About half-past 3 P.M., the immense force in front of our left and center advanced in three lines, preceded by heavy skirmishers. Our batteries opened with fine effect, and much confusion was produced, before they reached musket range. In a short time, the roar of musketry became very heavy, and it was soon apparent that the enemy had been repulsed in my immediate front.

Whilst riding along the crest, congratulating the troops, intelligence reached me that our line was broken on my right, and that the enemy had crowned the ridge. Assistance was promptly dispatched to that point under Brig.-Gen. Bate, who so successfully maintained the ground in my front; and I proceeded to the rear of the broken line to rally our retiring troops, and return them to the crest to drive the enemy back. Gen. Bate found the disaster so great that his small force could not repair it. About this time, I learned that our extreme left had also given way, and that my position was almost surrounded. Bate was immediately directed to form a second line in the rear, where, by the efforts of my staff, a nucleus of stragglers had been formed, upon which to rally.... All to the left, however, except a portion of Bate's division, was entirely routed, and in rapid flight; nearly all the artillery having been shamefully abandoned by its infantry support. Every effort which could be made by myself and staff, and by many other mounted officers, availed but little. A panic, which I had never before witnessed, seemed to have seized upon officers and men, and each seemed to be struggling for his personal safety, regardless of his duty or his character.... Having secured much of our artillery, they soon availed themselves of our panic, and, turning our guns upon us, enfiladed our lines, both right and left, rendering them entirely untenable. Had all parts of the line been maintained with equal gallantry and persistence, no enemy could ever have dislodged us; and but one possible reason presents itself to my mind in explanation of this bad conduct in veteran troops, who had never before failed in any duty assigned them, however difficult and hazardous. They had for two days confronted the enemy, marshalling his immense forces in plain view, and exhibiting to their sight such a superiority in numbers, as may have intimidated weak minds and untried soldiers. But our veterans had so often encountered similar hosts, when the strength of position was against us, and with perfect success, that not a doubt crossed my mind.

Confederate general Braxton Bragg, in his official report of the Confederate defeat at the Battle of Missionary Ridge that contributed to the lifting of the Confederate siege of Chattanooga, on November 25, 1863, written on November 30, as reprinted in Horace Greeley, The American Conflict, *pp. 443–444.*

My regiment moved forward with the others of the brigade, assembling on the colors as far as it was possible to do on the way, until, in ascending the steepest part of the slope, where every man had to find or clear his own way through the entanglement, and in the face of a terrible fire of musketry and artillery, the men of the different regiments of the brigade became generally intermingled; and when the brigade finally crowned the enemy's works on the crest of the ridge, the regimental and even the company organizations had become completely merged in a crowd of gallant and enthusiastic men, who swarmed over the breastwork and charged the defenders with such promptness and vigor that the enemy broke and fled, leaving their artillery in battery, and barely getting away a portion of the caissons and limbers. Six 12-pounder Napoleon guns were thus captured by our brigade, two of them by men of my regiment. Hardly had a lodgment in the works been gained when the enemy's reserves made a furious counter-attack upon our men, yet in confusion. This attack was promptly met by a charge *en masse* by the crowd, which after a few minutes of desperate hand-to-hand fighting, cleared the ridge, leaving the place in our undisputed possession, with some 200 or 300 prisoners. The captured artillery was turned upon the retreating enemy and manned by volunteers from the different regiments, but darkness soon closed over the field and the firing ceased. The regiments were assembled, and, after collecting and caring for the dead and wounded, we bivouacked on the ridge for the night.

Report of Lieutenant Colonel Judson W. Bishop, 2nd Minnesota Infantry, describing the advance of Union troops to Missionary Ridge, on November 25, dated November 30, 1863, from Official Records of the War of the Rebellion, *Series I, Vol. 31, p. 535.*

6

Emancipation and the Mind of Lincoln
July 1862–March 1865

Although abolitionists and radical Republicans continually urged Lincoln to take stronger actions against slavery from the beginning of the war, Lincoln hesitated. His reasons were to some extent political, as the Union hold on the border states was tenuous. Furthermore, even in non-slaveholding regions of the loyal states, many Democrats criticized Lincoln for actions that seemed of dubious constitutionality, including the suspension of the writ of habeas corpus and the arrest of state legislators in Maryland. Throughout the states of Ohio, Indiana, and Illinois, Peace Democrats, sometimes in the majority in many districts, clearly favored the preservation of slavery and opposed any measures in the direction of emancipation. The Constitution and the laws of the United States recognized slavery and treated slaves as both persons and property. The Constitution expressly forbade the

Although the Emancipation Proclamation was widely criticized for not actually freeing any slaves, many saw it as a historic document. In this print, Lincoln is shown struggling with the wording of the draft. *(Library of Congress, Prints and Photographs Division, LC-USZC4–1425)*

seizure of property without due process of law. Thus, any measure attacking the status of slaves as property would only add further arguments for regarding Lincoln as scoffing at the very Constitution he had pledged to uphold. Lincoln constantly asserted that he believed all men should be free, but also insisted that his actions were designed to preserve the Union and the Constitution.

In May 1861, General Butler had found a way to liberate slaves by declaring those that had been used to support the rebellion as contraband of war, and that measure would have some limited application as a means of liberating slaves within existing law. Nevertheless, by the late spring and early summer of 1862, Union officers in areas conquered from the seceding states found themselves in very complex situations with regard to the African-American population.

In mid-July 1862, Lincoln took several steps that showed he had worked out a pathway through the dilemmas surrounding emancipation and the employment of African-American men as soldiers. Quietly, he confided to two of his trusted cabinet members, Gideon Welles and William Seward, that he planned to announce the emancipation of slaves in all the areas in rebellion as a war measure. Congress acted too, passing the 1862 Confiscation Act, which Lincoln signed on July 17. The act granted freedom to slaves belonging to disloyal owners, with any such slaves escaping to U.S. lines declared immediately free. The act, as well as Lincoln's still secret plan for more general emancipation, would not affect slaves in loyal border states. Furthermore, the Confiscation Act made it clear that slave owners, even in areas in rebellion, who declared or could prove they were loyal, would remain unaffected. The Confiscation Act included additional funding for the earlier colonization plans. On the same day that Lincoln signed the Confiscation Act, he also signed an act repealing the 1792 law that prohibited African Americans from serving in the federal army. The way was legally clear to enlist free northern African Americans and freed slaves in the Union army, although no immediate steps were taken in that direction.

By the end of July 1862, as a result of the various measures enacted up to that time, black people living in those areas of the Confederacy occupied by Union troops could be legally classified into six groups. A number were free men and women, those either born free or manumitted by individual action before the war. Population estimates put the number of free African Americans in the United States in 1860 at about 400,000, of whom more than 250,000 lived in the slave states. Another group were contrabands under wartime practice as suggested by Butler and endorsed by Secretary of War Cameron and then enacted into law in the Confiscation Act of 1861. Contrabands under this principle and law were those who had fled to Union lines, were presumed to have been used by the Confederate forces to support the war effort, and who lived in contraband camps. The Confiscation Act of 1861 declared such contrabands as free.

A third group consisted of slaves, still resident on plantations both behind Union lines and within the areas controlled by the Confederacy. However, since some of the planters in areas of the Confederacy taken over by Union troops declared themselves loyal to the Union and

Lincoln had few moments of repose after his election as president; this portrait of him with his son Tad captures one such interlude. *(Library of Congress, Prints and Photographs Division, LC-USZC4–2777)*

were willing to sign loyalty oaths, it appeared there were no legal grounds for forcing their emancipation under the Confiscation Act of 1862. Clearly slaves in loyal states, such as Maryland and Kentucky, had not been affected by the Confiscation Acts. Other slaves remained on plantations of clearly Confederate sympathizers and under the terms of the Confiscation Act of 1862, they were freed. In large Southern towns and cities, there were numerous black refugees who had simply walked away from their owners, some of whom were loyal Unionists, some of whom were pro-Confederate. In March 1862, Congress had prohibited the military from assisting in the return of any slaves to their owners without regard to the professed loyalty or disloyalty of those owners. The situation in the Sea Island area, where owners had abandoned both slaves and plantations, was unique, and the experiments tried there in 1861 and 1862 were directed at employing the black population without clarifying their status as free or slave. The slaves in the Sea Islands became free under the terms of the 1862 Confiscation Act, as their owners could be presumed to be disloyal. For military officers throughout the area of expanding Union control, the status of slaves was thus an extraordinarily complex question that varied from state to state, and even from county to county, and that changed from month to month; several officers wrote to headquarters requesting help in sorting out the situation.[1]

The public was confused as well. In response to an open letter by Horace Greeley in the New York *Tribune* asking his intentions regarding emancipation, Lincoln published an eloquent reply, August 22, 1862, stating that his intent was to save the Union. If freeing the slaves helped to save the Union, he would free them; if freeing some and leaving others alone would help save the Union he would do that. However, when he sent the letter, Lincoln had already decided how he would proceed. Over a month before, he had already developed his plans for the Emancipation Proclamation, and, on July 22, he had shared his plans with other members of the cabinet.

The proclamation came in two stages, a preliminary announcement on September 22, 1862, timed to come after the Union success at Antietam, and the proclamation itself on January 1, 1863. In the preliminary announcement, Lincoln stated that, as of the coming January 1, he would declare free all slaves held in areas then in rebellion. By this measure, he would *not* be declaring free any slaves in the loyal border states or in those counties in Virginia or parishes in Louisiana already under Union control. Constructed in this fashion, emancipation would clearly be a wartime measure directed only against slaveholders in the regions still in control of the Confederacy as of January 1, 1863; loyal slaveholders in the border states or in regions already conquered by the Union from the Confederacy would have no direct political grievance against Lincoln. Furthermore, by announcing the proclamation in September, Lincoln was giving states in the Confederacy a chance to withdraw from the rebellion, declare their loyalty, and preserve their slaves. Some abolitionists feared this would happen and the chance to free slaves as a war measure would be diminished or eliminated. Lincoln could and did justify the proclamation as strictly a war measure to help suppress the rebellion.

On January 1, 1863, with the issuance of the proclamation, there was widespread celebration among freedmen, contrabands, and most antislavery supporters, despite the fact that the proclamation specifically listed counties and parishes in the already-conquered areas of the seceding states that were exempted from its effect. Nearly all if not all of the African Americans celebrating had been free prior to the proclamation. More cynical observers in the Union, in the

Confederacy, and in Europe, observed that Lincoln's proclamation of January 1 applied only to areas where the Union had no power to enforce it. In effect, they observed, the proclamation did not free any slaves whatsoever. For such reasons, Lincoln critics at the time and later believed the proclamation was at best a halfway measure, and at worst, an attempt to divide the Confederacy with a promise of exclusion from the proclamation, an attempt that would have no visible success. On the other hand, Lincoln admirers saw the preliminary proclamation and the final proclamation as a stroke of genius, reflecting Lincoln's ability to find a logical pathway through a complex political problem that could achieve the contradictory goals of attacking slavery in the Confederacy while leaving it untouched in loyal states. The proclamation, such admirers believed,

The Emancipation Proclamation was printed in a decorated commemorative edition to memorialize its significance. *(Library of Congress, Prints and Photographs Division, LC-USZ62–9795)*

demonstrated the mind of Lincoln at its best, finding a way between the horns of a dilemma that was at once creative and dramatic.

Furthermore, such Lincoln advocates argued, as the Union lines advanced into the areas that had been in rebellion on January 1, 1863, the advancing army was now a liberating army. Without attacking the position of slavery in the border states, Lincoln had been able to make the war for the Union a war for ending slavery in most of the United States—without violating the Constitution and without requiring that Congress take a vote on the emancipation question that might further divide the Union.

Despite the criticism of skeptics and despite the complexity of the exclusion clauses of the Emancipation Proclamation, the simple fact was that, by 1863, Lincoln was already perceived in the North as a historic figure for his decision to link emancipation and the war and to make the liberation of slaves a war goal. The war for the Union had become a war for freedom. Observers immediately compared his action to the 1861 emancipation of serfs in Russia by the czar and viewed the two acts together as proof of the advance of civilization. He had helped cement the idea that the 19th century was one of progress. Abolitionists now confidently expected slavery to end in the rest of the United States, and also in Cuba, Santo Domingo, Brazil, and the Dutch colonies in the Western Hemisphere within a few years. Indeed, their expectations were realized over the next two decades.

The debate over whether Lincoln had indulged in a clever logical trap for rebel slaveholders or had implemented a weak halfway measure soon gave way to a simpler view, that he had brought the day of liberation, the jubilee, as the freedmen called it. His place in history as the Great Emancipator had been established.

GOVERNMENT LANDS AND LABOR CONTRACTS

Since the army was prohibited from returning slaves to owners, whether loyal or disloyal, commanders in the field in Louisiana and the rest of the Mississippi Valley had to make pragmatic decisions on the ground regarding conditions of the African-American population. In 1862 and 1863 some Union commanding officers in that area began to treat fugitive slaves, contrabands, runaways, slaves still on plantations, and even freedmen more or less equally. The patterns and practices that emerged there would survive into later years, as new areas fell under Union control and even after formal state actions of emancipation. The decisions and methods of the army commanders in regard to race relations in this brief period served as precedents and set standards that at once advanced the status of black Americans out from under slavery, but settled that status in a halfway state characterized by poverty, subservience to whites with power and money, and exposure to discrimination, prejudice, and a second-class citizenship. Some of the practical solutions that seemed to work in 1863 froze into patterns that lasted another century.

With the seizure of New Orleans in April 1862 and the advance of Union forces north through Louisiana and south and east through Tennessee under Grant, the number of African Americans released from the control of their owners began to escalate rapidly, from the tens of thousands in Virginia and the Sea Islands to hundreds of thousands in the west. In the Mississippi Valley, planters did not flee from their plantations as they had in the Sea Islands, but grudgingly acquiesced in Union administration. Rather quickly during 1862 in Louisiana,

General Benjamin Butler and his successor, General Nathaniel Banks, confronted the issue of what to do regarding the vast population of African Americans, some emancipated under contraband principles and the 1861 confiscation act and others who had simply walked away from their plantations but could not be returned by the army to disgruntled planters because of the congressional prohibition on military enforcement of the Fugitive Slave Act enacted in March 1862.

In addition to Southern discomfort with his slave policies General Butler enraged Southern sensibilities in another way when he issued an order in response to incidents in which women in New Orleans intentionally snubbed Union officers and men. He stated that any woman who insulted a Union soldier should be treated as a woman of the streets, plying her trade. In response, Jefferson Davis issued an order that Butler, if captured, was to be treated as a criminal, not as a prisoner of war. Henceforth, some in the Southern press referred to the general as "Beast Butler," not only for his emancipation methods, but for his insult to Southern ladies.

To keep the plantations running and the African-American population employed and fed, Butler and Banks instituted a system of regulated labor contracts between former planters and freed African-American laborers. Areas already conquered by Union troops were not subject to the forthcoming Emancipation Proclamation when the proclamation went into effect on January 1, 1863. The exclusion of certain Louisiana parishes from the effect of the proclamation left the generals with a further complication, that slavery was technically legal in areas that were under Union control as of the end of December 1862, but would be technically illegal in parishes conquered after that date. In this ambiguous and unsettled situation, military commanders worked out practical solutions and kept passing the legal complexities to the bureaucrats back in Washington. While the solutions resulted in what might be called in a later age disaster relief or refugee welfare, those solutions did little to improve the long-term prospects of the former slaves. Furthermore, since white army officers had stereotyped views of blacks, they rarely made any distinction between those who had been free before the war and those freed under the various recent actions. Free men of color, some of whom were property owners and a few who themselves had owned plantations and slaves, reacted indignantly when they had to provide proof of employment to Union troops enforcing the full-employment contract laws.

On December 17, 1862, General Ulysses S. Grant appointed army chaplain John Eaton as general superintendent of contrabands for the Department of the Tennessee. Eaton began to set up contraband camps and home farms and arranged a system of having the government occupy abandoned or "sequestrated" lands and then lease the lands to freedmen. Eaton's plans put freedmen in charge of their own leaseholds under army supervision. After a dispute between the Treasury Department and the army as to supervision of freedmen affairs in the Mississippi Valley region, the army emerged in control of the freedmen, but not of the lands; it adopted a system of army enforcement of labor contracts with white landowners that had developed under Butler and Banks in Louisiana, rather than the original Eaton plan of government appropriation of lands with leases to freedmen. The Eaton plan of temporary reallocation of lands directly to former slaves, which might have evolved into a plan of land reform, simply gave way to the concept of white property owners' employment of black labor under some degree of government regulation.

In Louisiana, Banks made it clear that, even though some 150,000 slaves had been exempted from the effect of the Emancipation Proclamation by their location in parishes that were in Union hands on January 1, 1863, they would be treated as equal to those who had been emancipated and that they would be expected to work either under contract with landowners or on government projects. The resolution worked out, like so many other decisions and policies regarding African Americans, was an ad hoc, clumsy arrangement. Somewhat influenced by the ideal that slavery was inappropriate (but only partially outlawed, depending on the exact location of a plantation on January 1, 1863), the arrangement was shaped by racial prejudices, respect for white owners' title to the land, and practical concerns about ensuring that displaced laborers, runaways, and refugees find employment and access to food, clothing, and medical care. No one, not even the most explicitly bigoted of Union generals, wanted his record to show that thousands of African-American refugees had starved to death under his jurisdiction. The status of slaves who had left plantations in the parishes under the control of the Union on January 1, 1863, was not legally changed to that of freedmen until a new constitution was adopted in Louisiana in September 1864, outlawing slavery in the state.

At first Butler and Banks provided rations and support to indigent former slaves in and around New Orleans by taking the proceeds from crops raised on sequestrated plantations of pro-Confederacy landowners, and using those funds to purchase food. However, by October 1863, when the management of seized plantations passed to the Treasury Department, those funds were no longer available to the army, and the army's own supply of rations was insufficient for both the military and the refugees. The solution was to force all ablebodied former slaves to accept employment, either with planters or with the army.

Banks and Eaton attempted to enforce the labor contracts between landowners and workers by investigating complaints of abuses. At the same time, they sought to ensure that all former slaves were employed by the enforcement of vagrancy laws. Unemployed, disabled, or aged blacks were rounded up and sent to government-managed home farms, where their labor at least partially offset the cost of their maintenance. Unfortunately, even when the terms of the labor contracts guaranteed a minimal income that was sufficient to live on, many landowners took advantage of the situation by delaying cash payments and by charging food, clothing, and medical care against the earned payment, and thus leaving the laborers with a negligible balance or even in debt at the end of the season. The usually strident *Liberator* at first found General Banks's report of his operations quite straightforward and acceptable. Without a revolution in land ownership, however, the pattern that emerged was in fact a form of peonage that left the African-American plantation worker very little better off than under slavery. A black worker was theoretically free to leave a plantation, but if he was not soon employed elsewhere, he could be arrested for vagrancy and forced to work on a government-run plantation or even assigned to a planter. Where workers found themselves in debt when charges for food and shelter exceeded their compensation, planters could claim that they were owed work and insist that the workers stay on the plantation to pay off the debt. Within months, radical Republican journalists and abolitionists recognized the similarity between the emerging system and that of peonage, and were quick to criticize it. But the system remained in place.

The conditions of peonage persisted long after the war in one form or another, including debt servitude and other arrangements, such as sharecropping and tenant farming, backed up by enforcement of vagrancy laws. Even after later legislation sought to ameliorate such conditions, the fact that wealth and power remained in the hands of a relatively small and elite class, much of it descended from the ante-bellum planters, meant that opportunities to achieve economic or social progress for African Americans remained very limited in the former Confederacy.[2]

LAND REFORMS THAT FAILED

On the Sea Islands surrounding Beaufort and Port Royal, South Carolina, some of the freed slaves did acquire land and held it after the war. However, white missionaries, teachers, and military officers believed that the plantations would best be operated by Northern whites, either farmers or plantation operators, using Northern methods. The obvious disrepair of the plantations, the fact that they had been planted very inefficiently, and the obvious opportunity for Northern enterprise led such observers to recommend the settlement and development of the region by white settlers from the North, and several of the plantation overseers employed by the army and the Department of the Interior stayed on to set up such plantations under organizations funded by capitalists during and after the war. The opportunity to use the Sea Island experiment as a land-reform system in which the plantations were transferred to the hands of the freedmen was largely forgotten.[3]

The plantations belonging to two of the most well-known Confederates, Robert E. Lee and Jefferson Davis, were confiscated for the purpose of providing lands for former slaves. In Mississippi, several plantations located at Davis Bend had represented the holdings of the Confederate president's family. Grant had the lands confiscated, and they were settled by former slaves, many of whom had belonged to the Davis family. A leader among the slaves was Isaiah Montgomery, who had been a steward on one of Davis's plantations. Outsiders remarked on how well the slaves fared at operating the plantations themselves, but the Davis family filed suit to reclaim the lands at the end of the war. Eventually, all the Davis plantations were restored to Davis heirs. The black refugees, under the leadership of Isaiah Montgomery established a new town nearby, Mound Bayou, and for decades it was widely recognized as a successful example of black self-government. Robert E. Lee's estate in Alexandria, acquired from the estate of his wife who was a descendant of Martha Washington, was set up as a freedmen's village, settled by several hundred freed slaves from northern Virginia and the District of Columbia. The freedmen's village persisted as a federal enclave for several decades, when, by Supreme Court decision, it was closed down and the land converted into a national cemetery for Union dead. The land is now the Arlington National Cemetery and includes the Tomb of the Unknown Soldier and the graves of many distinguished leaders, such as John F. Kennedy.[4]

A more extensive land reform was attempted by General W. T. Sherman in January 1865, when he proclaimed all the coastal lands of South Carolina and Georgia as available for settlement by freed slaves. Rather than provide a complex food distribution system or labor system, Sherman simply proposed that whites evacuate the area, and that small companies of black families settle the lands, to be supplied by army steamers and river boats. Thousands of families were settled on the lands, but, at the end of the war, former white owners were able to bring suit in land courts to reclaim the farms and plantations on the ground that no clear title had been transferred under Sherman's Field Order #15. The only area where substantial land distribution to the former slaves took place was on the Sea

Islands, where some lands had been confiscated for back taxes and then legally transferred to freedmen and where other lands were sold to freedmen by the land and plantation companies operated by northern capitalists. The Sea Islands had the highest proportion of black ownership of land of any region of the former Confederacy in the decades after the Civil War.

ARMY SERVICE

Although black soldiers had served in the American Revolution, they were barred from the U.S. Army by a law passed in 1792, although some state militias accepted black volunteers after that date. Aboard ships, blacks served as stewards, stokers for coal-fired steam engines, and in maintenance but not in combat roles. Although some free blacks sought to join in suppressing the Confederacy in the first months of the war, the Union War Department generally prevented any such service until Congress altered the law.

Under pressure from black leaders and from generals demanding more troops, the Union finally agreed in the late summer of 1862 to begin recruiting black soldiers. In July, Lincoln signed the act repealing the 1792 law. The process was regularized and approved by the War Department in August 1862, with units established first in Louisiana and South Carolina. In early 1863, recruiters began to enlist volunteers in more areas conquered from the Confederacy. In some cases the volunteers were found among freed prisoners from jails or recent refugees who had fled as contrabands to Union lines after serving as unarmed labor forces in the Confederate army. Many of the black volunteers, however, were already free black men, from both the North and South.

Army officers monitoring the recruitment of black volunteers in Missouri, Tennessee, and other states confronted a vexing legal situation. Recruiters tended to round up volunteers and forcibly recruit reluctant former slaves throughout the slave states under Union control. In the case of men already freed by the contraband ruling or by either of the confiscation acts, such freedmen clearly could volunteer if they chose to do so. However, recruiters also began to bring in slaves belonging to planters who claimed to be loyal and who claimed that their labor was needed to work the tobacco farms and other plantations. In some cases, the claims of loyalty were genuine enough. Such owners demanded compensation for the lost labor; disloyal owners pretended to be loyal in order to get similar compensation. Officers desperately requested clarification from headquarters as to which recruits should be accepted, whether to grant compensation to loyal slave owners, whether the slaves were free on admission to the service or only after dismissal from the army, and other related legal questions beyond the capacity of the local officers to sort out.

In November 1863, the problems began to be solved. In General Orders #135 from the Headquarters of the Department of Missouri, Assistant Adjutant General Green spelled out exact procedures. He stated that loyal owners were entitled to a just compensation of $300 for a slave who volunteered for service, but that the owners had to provide papers freeing the slave and an oath of allegiance to the government, as well as proof of title to the slave. Furthermore, no owner who had supported the rebellion at any time could make a claim of compensation. Cases under dispute would be settled by a board to be appointed by the president. White volunteers received a $300 bounty personally, while the bounty for slaves went to their owners.

By Christmas 1863, with the clarification of orders and vigorous recruiting, the adjutant general in Vicksburg could report a total of 20,000 black troops recruited to cavalry, infantry, and artillery regiments from the states of Mississippi, Louisiana, Tennessee, Arkansas, Missouri, Alabama, and Iowa. These figures did not include two regiments raised in eastern Tennessee, and some 15,000 recruited in the Department of the Gulf under Generals Butler and Banks. At the same time, the army officially refrained from recruiting any slaves in the loyal border states of Delaware, Maryland, West Virginia, Kentucky, and Missouri.

Altogether, 166 black regiments were eventually organized despite the difficulties. Fewer than 100 black men were promoted to the officer rank, and black units had white officers from the rank of lieutenant up through general. A total of some 178,000 African Americans served in the Union army, and another 30,000 served in the Union navy. About another 200,000 African Americans worked in non-combatant and logistical roles in the Union army.

General David Hunter first attempted to organize an African-American regiment, the 1st South Carolina Volunteer Infantry, in May 1862, among the freed slaves of the Sea Island area, forcibly recruiting at least some of them. However, since he had not received War Department authorization, the unit was disbanded. It was later reorganized by general Rufus Saxton and then led, after November 10, 1862, by Colonel Thomas Wentworth Higginson. Under his command the unit saw action in several engagements in the Georgia-Florida border area, including an assault on Jacksonville, Florida. Although the First South Carolina Volunteer Infantry could claim to be the first African-American regiment in the Civil War, the fact that it was organized, then disbanded and reorganized after other black army units had been established somewhat complicated that claim.

Jefferson Davis, Southern politicians, and Confederate army officers were outraged at the recruiting of black troops, whether freemen or freedmen, and at first regarded them as subject to laws against servile insurrection. When Davis ordered black prisoners of war shot, Lincoln responded that an equal number of Confederate prisoners would receive the same treatment. Davis officially relented, but battlefield executions of black prisoners remained common, reported with dreadful regularity in letters sent home and in diaries kept by Confederate soldiers. Furthermore, while captured white officers of African-American regiments were paroled and exchanged, black prisoners from the same units were simply held in camps, and many were sold as slaves. In all, black regiments in the Union army participated in over 400 battles and engagements and won a total of 16 Congressional Medals of Honor.

In the Confederacy, the idea of liberation in exchange for voluntary service by slaves received very strong support from some quarters. The Irish-born Confederate general Patrick Cleburne went so far as to develop a lengthy memorial outlining and justifying the concept of recruiting slaves into the Confederate army and offering them freedom as a reward. Cleburne's memorial, which he submitted through channels in January 1864, was suppressed within a month. Jefferson Davis and his close leadership continued to oppose the concept of recruiting slaves to serve as soldiers, finally accepting the concept only in March 1865. Davis proposed the idea to the Confederate congress, but its approval came too late to affect the course of the war. Only a few companies of Confederate black troops were put into the lines, and only a few scattered reports of engagements of such troops against Union forces survived the chaos at the end of the war. For those politicians most closely tied to the plantation class, sacrificing slavery to preserve the Confederacy made no sense, since in their view the purpose of the Confederacy had been to preserve slavery. If slavery was to be destroyed, the Southern states might as well remain in the United States, many believed.

DRAFT RIOTS

By mid–1863, the Union's war goals had gradually evolved from simply preserving the Union. With the Confiscation Act of 1862 and the Emancipation Proclamation, it was clear that, as the Union troops moved deeper into the Confederacy, Union victories would result in freeing slaves. Furthermore, as the first draft call was put in place in July 1863, the elements of the Northern white population most affected by the draft were those most threatened by the prospect of emancipation of slaves. The poorer, foreign-born population, most of whom voted for Democratic Party candidates, had been exposed to the idea in Democratic newspapers that every action of the Lincoln administration was either unconstitutional or oppressive, or both. Since any well-off man listed in the draft notice could hire a substitute for about $300 to replace him, it seemed the draft was aimed particularly at the poor. Day laborers began to feel competition from African-American freedmen available to take jobs vacated by whites who had volunteered for military service. In New York City, all these factors came together.

The draft lists were published in New York City on Sunday, July 12, 1863, and the reality of the draft sank in. On Monday mobs formed and attacked and set fire to the draft office on Third Avenue and 46th Street and to other buildings. Soon streetcars were abandoned by their operators, and crowds gathered to watch the fires. Groups of looters attacked and sometimes killed African Americans wherever they were found in the city, and a newly built Colored Orphan Asylum was burned down.

Despite the protests of men of influence, the city's mayor at first delayed calling for military assistance to put down the riot. Governor Seymour addressed the rioters with a speech promising to attempt to get the draft law suspended, for which he was roundly attacked by Horace Greeley and the New York *Tribune*. It seemed to Greeley that Seymour was suggesting that the rioters had been justified. Gradually, with troops sent into the city on Wednesday and with volunteer groups of wealthy civilians armed by city officials, the rioters were repressed. No official count of the number of rioters killed was ever assembled, as many were secretly buried, but estimates ran as high as 1,000. Republicans tended to blame Governor Seymour and the Democratic newspapers for playing into the hands of the Confederacy by inflaming the population. In retrospect, however, underlying racial prejudice, coupled with a draft that seemed calculated to place the burden on the poorest classes, had caused the worst Northern race riot of the war years.[5]

In New York, the prosperous attorney and investor, George Templeton Strong, one of the founders of the United States Sanitary Commission that provided aid and medical care to Union troops, was outraged at the draft riots, and his diary entries for July 1863 represent one of the best eyewitness accounts of the events. Even though concerned about the plight of African Americans, his disdain for Irish immigrants and his patronizing sympathy for innocent black victims of the mob showed that, even among supporters of Lincoln in the North, varieties of prejudice ran deep. Greeley, Strong, and other pro-Union New Yorkers believed that the spread of the news of the Union victories at Gettysburg and Vicksburg helped rally Northern morale and win support for the draft.[6]

Riots and outbreaks of violence spread to other cities, including the mining districts of Pennsylvania, cities such as Troy and Albany, and elsewhere. Provost marshals reported organized conspiracies of draft-resisters, some armed with weapons, including artillery, that were rumored to be ready to fight the draft. Some believed that the Democratic Party and organizations such as the Knights of the Golden Circle sponsored and encouraged resistance to the draft. Gradually, however, as the draft quotas were adjusted to meet the complaints of governors and to take into account the number of volunteers from different regions and as news of Union victories in the field set in, the riots and resistance died down.

BLACK LEADERSHIP

During the war, leaders and spokesmen among the free black population of the North reflected a wide variety of viewpoints. As events unfolded, the expressed opinions of black leaders evolved. Lincoln's endorsement of colonization and his explicit statements that the two races could not live compatibly together brought a storm of protest from white abolitionists and from black spokesmen throughout the North. Lincoln's refusal to endorse the emancipation actions of Generals Frémont and Hunter gave black leaders reason to remain suspicious of Lincoln's motives throughout early 1862. A black journalist, George E. Stephens, a correspondent to the *Anglo-African* who moved with General Joseph Hooker's troops in Maryland and Virginia, reported how contraband policy worked out in practice and was appalled at episodes of mistreatment of contrabands and slaves by white Union troops.

Despite the opposition to forced deportation, several prominent black spokesmen endorsed the idea of voluntary emigration to Haiti, including not only James Redpath and James T. Holly, but also Henry Highland Garnet, William Wells Brown, H. Ford Douglass, and George Lawrence, who edited the New York edition of Redpath's *Pine and Palm* and succeeded Redpath as leader of the Haitian immigration effort after Redpath's disillusionment. Frederick Douglass opposed the Haitian movement, and his views evolved from suspicion of Republicans and of Lincoln, to active support for Lincoln by 1863.

After the recruitment of black troops into the Union army in the summer and fall of 1862 and after the Emancipation Proclamation, a clearer pattern of support for the Union cause emerged among Northern freedmen. Several previously critical spokesmen like Douglass endorsed Lincoln's measures and urged support for the Union cause. Martin Delany, a freedman born in Virginia and raised in the North, had studied medicine at Harvard and had become a noted advocate of African emigration in the late 1850s and of Haitian emigration in the first years of the Civil War. Beginning in 1863, however, Delany worked as a recruiter for the army, then joined the service and was granted a commission as major.

In January 1863, the War Department approved the raising of a regiment of African-American troops

A commemorative lithograph print of Abraham Lincoln was published in 1865 by Kimmel and Forster, New York City. *(Library of Congress, Prints and Photographs Division, LC-USZC4–11368)*

by Governor John Andrew of Massachusetts. Since the black population in Massachusetts was too small to support a whole regiment, the governor appointed a wealthy white abolitionist, George L. Stearns, to form a committee to raise money for recruiting efforts. With the fund established, Stearns hired a group of prominent black spokesmen to help in the recruiting in other Northern states, including William Wells Brown, Frederick Douglass, Charles L. Remond, Henry Highland Garnet, and Martin Delany. The ease with which Brown, Garnet, and Delany shifted from support of the Haitian emigration plan to support for the establishment of the 54th Massachusetts Regiment suggests that both ideas held the attraction of what a later generation would call black power.

Several factors hindered the recruiting effort. Jobs were more plentiful for civilians with the drain on manpower by the war and with booming industrial production. As the war ground on through 1862 and 1863, reports of the frightful slaughter and conditions took much of the initial romance out of the attraction of war. Further reports of official and unofficial slaughter of black prisoners of war also filtered back to the home front. The recruiters had an uphill fight, made more difficult by the refusal of the War Department to pay black troops equally with white troops.

Black soldiers did not receive full pay. White privates earned $13 a month, while black soldiers were paid $7. The all-black 54th Massachusetts Regiment rejected the pay altogether, claiming that if Uncle Sam could not afford full pay for them, he probably could not afford even half-pay. Other units marched into battle with the battle cry, "for Uncle Sam and seven dollars a month." Abolitionists and free black organizations in the North took up the crusade and began to collect money to compensate the families of the half-pay black troops, especially of those who refused the pay. Late in the war, the protests succeeded, and the army agreed to equal pay. In June 1864, back pay for those still surviving was granted, but only if they had been free before April 1861, by this means granting equal pay to free black men, like those who made up most of the 54th Massachusetts Regiment, but still denying it to those who had been recruited from among contrabands and from slaves belonging to disloyal and loyal owners. In March 1865, back pay up to the same level as whites was granted to all surviving African-American soldiers.

CITIZENSHIP

Although the Emancipation Proclamation was widely remembered as the single stroke that broke the chains of the slave, the reality was much more piecemeal. Emancipation came in complex stages and in a variety of ways, affecting different regions at different dates. Among the last states to emancipate the slaves were the border states. Arkansas, a member of the Confederacy, under Union occupation approved a new constitution that abolished slavery on March 16, 1864. Maryland enacted a new constitution banning slavery that came into effect November 1, 1864; Missouri abolished slavery in that state by an act of a constitutional convention, January 11, 1865; Tennessee abolished slavery with an amendment to the state constitution on February 22, 1865.

Under the Thirteenth Amendment to the Constitution, ratified on December 6, 1865, slavery was abolished everywhere in the United States. The only significant areas in which slaves had not already been emancipated by other means and thus affected by this amendment were the state of Kentucky, a few counties and districts in Virginia, and scattered groups elsewhere. For example, West Virginia had incorporated a gradual emancipation provision in its constitution, requiring that slaves born before July 4, 1863, reach the age of 25 before being freed, so the Thirteenth Amendment clarified as free the children and young men and women between ages three and 25 in that state. In five states—Missouri, Tennessee, Maryland, Louisiana, and Arkansas—slaves had been freed by state constitutional action before the amendment passed; throughout the Gulf States, Texas, the Carolinas, and Virginia, the Emancipation Proclamation freed slaves as the Union army advanced. Some slaves had been freed by joining the Union army in border states; later, Congress emancipated the wives and children of any slaves who had joined. In much of the Confederacy, slaves walked off their plantations when Union troops arrived, and the army was prohibited from returning them by the amendment to the Articles of War, enacted March 13, 1862. Thus, regardless of the legal niceties, many tens of thousands of slaves simply freed themselves by the nonviolent but meaningful act of leaving their masters behind.

Some Union officers and black troops were glad to proclaim the Emancipation Proclamation as they advanced through the seceded states in the last two years of the war, although the news reached some slaves quite late. In fact, the word of emancipation did not reach many slaves in Texas until June 19, 1865. Celebrations by Texas's black population, into the 20th and 21st centuries, were traditionally called *Juneteenth,* commemorating the announcement of the proclamation in Galveston. Some loyal owners in the border states were compensated for the emancipation of slaves enlisted in the army, while others were not. Years later, the Fourteenth Amendment to the Constitution outlawed the payment of any remaining claims for compensation to former slaveowners.

As emancipation proceeded by all of these various means through 1864 and 1865, abolitionists and black leaders turned their attention to other rights of citizenship, most notably the question of the right to vote. Of the 24 Northern states, only six (Maine, Massachusetts, Rhode Island, New Hampshire, Vermont, and New York) allowed African-American men to vote before the Civil War. In New York, the black franchise was limited by a property qualification for blacks but not for whites. Other Northern states had held referenda on constitutional amendments to extend the vote to blacks but those measures had been soundly defeated by the enfranchised white male electorate. Where blacks could vote in the 1864 election, they almost unanimously voted Republican, contributing to the defeat of the pro-Southern Democratic governor of New York, Horatio Seymour.

Abolitionists, black and white, encouraged their Republican allies to extend the suffrage to blacks, both North and South, citing the potential practical political value of such suffrage extension, with the defeat of Seymour as proof of their point. Some abolitionists believed that suffrage should be extended to all freedmen who could read and write, little realizing that such a measure would be used in later decades to deny the vote to African Americans while extending it through grandfather exclusion clauses or through unequally administered tests to illiterate whites. Whether or not to extend the suffrage to include blacks and how to define and protect their status as citizens would become debate issues during the postwar years of Reconstruction.

CHRONICLE OF EVENTS

1862

July 13: Lincoln confides his plans for an emancipation proclamation to cabinet members Gideon Welles and William Seward.

July 17: Lincoln signs the Second Confiscation Act, granting freedom to slaves in rebellious states whose owners support the Confederacy. Slaves escaping to U.S. lines are declared free. The act does not affect slaves or slave owners in the loyal border states or in lands under federal control where the owners have declared their loyalty to the Union.

July 17: The president signs an act that repeals a 1792 law that barred African Americans from serving in the army; the new act specifically authorizes the recruitment of free blacks and freedmen into military service. This Militia Act of 1862 also provides for the emancipation of any slave who volunteers for military

Abraham Lincoln visited the battlefield at Antietam, meeting with Allan Pinkerton there. His advisers worried that he would be a target for Confederate sharpshooters. *(Library of Congress, Prints and Photographs Division, LC-B8171–7949)*

service and for their families, if they belong to disloyal owners.

July 22: Lincoln presents the draft of the preliminary emancipation proclamation to the cabinet.

August 25: The War Department authorizes the raising of five regiments of African-American troops in the South Carolina Sea Islands; General Rufus Saxton receives orders that the soldiers are to be paid and issued rations the same as other soldiers in the army.

September 22: Lincoln issues the preliminary Emancipation Proclamation. The emancipation is to take place on January 1, 1863, and is to affect only those slaves in areas then remaining under rebellion. The preliminary proclamation promises to extend the effect of the July 17 Confiscation Act to slave owners within areas of rebellion who do not necessarily support the rebellion by 1863.

September 27: In New Orleans, General Benjamin Butler establishes units of free blackmen; he later sets up black military units composed of freedmen as well. Butler appoints black officers, an action later reversed by his successor, General Banks.

October: Promoter Bernard Kock plans to start a cotton plantation in the Caribbean, with financing from New York and utilizing 1,000 freedmen. Lincoln has Kock investigated and turns down the proposal. Within two weeks, financiers Charles Tuckerman and Paul S. Forbes will propose the same arrangement, and Lincoln will agree but limit the number of freed African Americans to 500.

October 3: Virginia passes an Act of Public Defense, empowering the governor to requisition Virginia slaves to work as military laborers; eventually some 180,000 black Virginians will serve in logistical support of the Confederacy.

November: In Louisiana, General Butler recruits three regiments of African-American troops, known as the *Corps d'Afrique.*

November 7: In the Sea Islands the first African-American unit organized under War Department orders is formed as the First South Carolina Volunteers; meanwhile, recruiting for black regiments composed of freedmen in the West goes forward, while several Northeastern states begin to raise regiments of volunteer freemen.

December: Union general Rufus Saxton, commanding the Department of the South, orders contrabands in his jurisdiction settled on abandoned lands and grants them two acres and tools. In exchange they are to turn over a share of their crops to the government.

December 17: Union general U.S. Grant appoints chaplain John Eaton as general superintendent of contrabands for the Department of the Tennessee; Eaton sets up contraband camps and home farms in the Mississippi Valley.

December 24: Confederate president Jefferson Davis orders that all captured black soldiers be turned over to state authorities for having participated in servile insurrection, a crime punishable by death.

1863

January 1: The Emancipation Proclamation goes into effect, specifically excluding from its reach all areas within Union control within the seceded states, as well as the loyal border states. Thus it is criticized for having absolutely no effect, as it extends only to regions over which the Union cannot exercise any authority. Among the areas exempted are the Eastern Shore counties of Northampton and Accomac in Virginia, and other mainland Virginia counties and those Louisiana parishes occupied by Union forces where planters retain ownership and control of slaves.

January 29: Union general Nathaniel Banks, in command in Louisiana, establishes regulations for freedmen's labor contracts and conditions in the state.

March: Mitchelville is established as a freedmen community on Hilton Head.

April: Four hundred sixty-eight freedmen board the ship *Ocean Ranger* at Fortress Monroe, Virginia, and sail for Ile a Vache, Haiti.

May 1: The Confederate congress passes a law authorizing President Davis to order the execution of captured officers of black units at the discretion of military tribunals, with enlisted men to be turned over to state authorities.

May 22: The Union army establishes through General Orders 143 a Bureau of Colored Troops and begins recruitment.

May 27: The 1st and 3rd Louisiana Native Guards, African-American regiments, participate in an assault on Port Hudson in Louisiana and perform with extreme heroism. The conservative white press in the North praises the bravery of the troops.

June 4: The Union War Department announces that black troops will receive half the pay of white troops, overriding the order of August 25, 1862.

July: Lincoln hears that the financiers behind the Île-à-Vache colony have hired Bernard Kock. He has Kock fired, but word continues to come back that the settlers are starving.

Henry Louis Stephens published this lithograph card in 1863, which shows an African-American slave celebrating his freedom. *(Library of Congress, Prints and Photographs Division, LC-USZCN4–50)*

July 12–16: New York City is wracked by draft riots in which mobs of whites burn the draft office, the Colored Orphan Asylum, and some homes. The mobs also beat up and kill some free black men; an estimated 1,000 rioters are killed as troops restore order. Exact figures are never published.

July 18: The African-American 54th Massachusetts Regiment, under Colonel Robert G. Shaw, fights a desperate battle before Battery Wagner, near Charleston, losing 281 of 600 men, including Shaw.

July 30: Lincoln threatens retaliation if black troops are executed or enslaved when captured by the Confederacy; nevertheless, such practices continue.

October 3: The Union War Department orders recruitment of slaves in Maryland, Missouri, and Tennessee, with compensation to loyal owners.

December 4: A freedman's village, consisting of tents, later to be replaced by frame houses, is erected on the estate of Robert E. Lee in Arlington, Virginia; it will survive for 20 years, then be converted to Arlington National Cemetery under a Supreme Court decision.

1864

January 2: Confederate general Patrick Cleburne (along with a group of other officers) submits a proposal for the enlistment of slaves into the Confederate army, granting them their freedom as a condition of service.

January 31: The Cleburne memorial is suppressed by General Joseph E. Johnston.

March 11: The Confederate congress passes an act to employ slaves and up to 20,000 free African Americans in the army, in noncombat roles; in addition to construction work on fortifications and defense lines, the men will work as shoemakers, wheelwrights, cooks, teamsters, and in other noncombatant roles.

March 16: A new constitution is ratified in Arkansas, abolishing slavery in the state.

March 20: The surviving 368 settlers at Île-à-Vache are returned to the United States aboard the *Marcia C. Day.*

March 28: General Lorenzo Thomas sets aside property at Davis Bend, Mississippi, for the settlement of freedmen; the black community established there will later set up the black-governed town of Mound Bayou.

April 8: U.S. Senate approves a constitutional amendment abolishing slavery.

April 17: The Union suspends prisoner exchanges with the Confederacy because of the Confederacy's refusal to exchange black prisoners.

June 7: The Union army begins recruiting slaves in Kentucky with or without the consent of their owners, with compensation to loyal owners.

June 15: The U.S. House of Representatives votes down the constitutional amendment abolishing slavery.

June 15: Congress approves equal pay for black soldiers; the payment is retroactive for black soldiers who were free on the date of their enlistment if the date of their freedom was prior to April 19, 1861; it thus does not grant equal back pay to slaves freed during the war.

June 20: Congress votes a pay raise to all privates, black and white, in the army.

July 2: Congress rescinds all appropriations for overseas colonization of freedmen.

July 30: In the Battle of the Crater outside Petersburg, black troops caught in the exploded mine crater are slaughtered by Confederates.

September 5: Louisiana adopts a new constitution that formally abolishes slavery.

October: The governors of Alabama, Georgia, Mississippi, North Carolina, South Carolina, and Virginia meet in Georgia to call for increased military use of slaves.

November 1: A new constitution goes into effect in Maryland, having been approved by the voters in October, abolishing slavery in the state.

1865

January 11: The Missouri state constitutional convention abolishes slavery in that state.

January 16: General William T. Sherman issues Special Field Order #15, granting land from abandoned plantations to freedmen along the Atlantic coast from Charleston, South Carolina, to the St. James River in Florida. Sherman leaves the settlement details to General Rufus Saxton; nearly all this land is later taken back by former owners, as no formal title to the land is transferred under the field order.

January 31: The U.S. House of Representatives passes the Thirteenth Amendment to the Constitution, formally declaring slavery unconstitutional; the amendment is sent to state legislatures for ratification.

February 18: African-American troops are among the first to enter Charleston.

February 22: Tennessee enacts an amendment to the state constitution abolishing slavery in the state.

March 3: Congress passes a joint resolution freeing wives and children of all black soldiers; the law also grants equal back pay to all black soldiers, whether free or slave prior to their enlistment.

March 3: The Freedmen's Bureau is established.

March 3: Virginia's General Assembly repeals restrictions on African-American troops bearing arms upon recommendation of General Robert E. Lee.

March 13: The Confederate congress passes a plan to enlist 300,000 slaves in the Confederate army and to offer them freedom for service.

March 23: The Confederate war department issues orders governing enlistment of slaves.

EYEWITNESS TESTIMONY

As is ever the case when our troops fall back from the enemy's country, large numbers of contrabands or fugitive slaves follow in our wake. At the last battle of Bull Run, this whole region was depopulated of its slaves. None remain but the aged, infirm, young, and a few of that class of treacherous, pampered and petted slaves, known as house servants. Large numbers are flocking around us here, they come from Fauquier Co. Women and children are walking, as if for dear life, to reach Washington, which is considered by every negro within the boundaries of the Old Dominion, as his city of refuge. There is one case which may be worthy of notice. George and Kitty Washington, and four remaining children belonged, with seventy others, to a man named Joe Weaver, living near Warrenton Junction. Our forces evacuated that place yesterday morning. Weaver had carried off to Richmond two other children of Washington but our troops came on him before he could get the rest away. Kitty knew that as soon as the Union soldiers left that she and her children would be carried down South, so she took as many of her things as she and her husband could conveniently carry, and turned her steps Northward. Her little children walked so slowly that the rebel cavalry watching the movements of our troops came near capturing them; but they struck the woods, and reached here in the drenching rain about 12 o'clock. They say that they saw a great many others on the way. They also stated that all negroes caught attempting to escape are ordered to be shot.

> *George E. Stephens, African-American newspaper correspondent, to the editor of the* Weekly Anglo-African, *commenting on the plight of contrabands in northern Virginia, on November 20, 1862, as quoted in Donald Yacovone,* Voice of Thunder, *pp. 208–209.*

Will Uncle Abe Lincoln stand firm and issue his promised proclamation on the first of January, 1863? Nobody knows, but I think he will. . . . Jefferson Davis's precious proclamation!! Butler and all Butler's commissioned officers to be hanged, whenever caught. Ditto all armed Negroes, and all white officers commanding them. This is the first great blunder Jeff has committed since the war began. It's evidence not only of barbarism but of weakness, and will disgust his foreign admirers (if anything can) and strengthen the backbone of the North at the same time. If he attempts to carry it out, retaliation becomes a duty, and we can play at extermination quite as well as Jeff Davis.

> *George Templeton Strong, northern philanthropist, reporting his observations on Jefferson Davis's threat to execute General Butler and captured black troops, in his diary entry for December 27, 1862, in Allen Nevins, ed.,* Diary of the Civil War, 1860–1865, *pp. 282–283.*

The services began at half past eleven o'clock, with prayer by our chaplain, Mr. Fowler, who is always, on such occasions, simple, reverential, and impressive. Then the President's Proclamation was read by Dr. W. H. Brisbane, a thing infinitely appropriate; a South Carolinian addressing South Carolinians, for he was reared among these very islands, and here long since emancipated his own slaves. . . . All this was according to the programme. Then followed an incident so simple, so touching, so utterly unexpected and startling, that I can scarcely believe it on recalling, though it gave the key-note to the whole day. The very moment the speaker had ceased, and just as I took and waved the flag, which now for the first time meant anything to these poor people, there suddenly arose, close beside the platform, a strong male voice (but rather cracked and elderly), into which two women's voices instantly blended, singing, as if by an impulse that could no more be repressed than the morning note of the song sparrow.—

"My Country, 'tis of thee,
Sweet land of liberty,
Of thee I sing!"

People looked at each other, and then at us on the platform, to see whence came this interruption, not set down in the bills. Firmly and irrepressibly the quavering voices sang on, verse after verse; others of the colored people joined in; some whites on the platform began, but I motioned them to silence. I never saw anything so electric; it made all other words cheap; it seemed the choked voice of a race at last unloosed. Nothing could be more wonderfully unconscious; art could not have dreamed of a tribute to the day of jubilee that should be so affecting; history will not believe it; and when I came to speak of it, after it was ended, tears were everywhere. If you could have heard how quaint and innocent it was! Old Tiff and his children might have sung it; and close before me was a little slave-boy, almost white, who seemed to belong to the party, and even he must join in. Just think of it!—the first day they had ever had a country, the first flag they had ever seen which promised anything to their people, and here, while mere spectators stood in silence, waiting for my stupid words, these simple souls burst out in their lay, as if they were by their own hearths at home! When they stopped, there was nothing to do for it but to speak, and I went on; but the life of the whole day was in those unknown people's song.

Union general Thomas Wentworth Higginson, describing the New Year's Day festivities, January 1, 1863, following the reading of the Emancipation Proclamation at Camp Saxton, near Beaufort, South Carolina, in his diary, Army Life in a Black Regiment, *as quoted in Allen Nevins, ed.,* The Blue and the Grey, *p. 334.*

Indigo was formerly cultivated to some extent, but this Sea Island district has for many years been mainly devoted to the raising of the great staple, Cotton. By far the choicest article produced in the world grows upon these lands, where our loyal regiments are now encamped. New Orleans, Mobile, Upland, Midland or foreign qualities never secure so ready a sale or high a price. And it is to me striking evidence of the want of thrift and enterprise among the former planters here, that on these islands, where alone the best quality of Sea Island cotton could be grown, scarcely one fourth of the land was under cultivation, and that was cultivated to disadvantage. For the want of labor-saving machinery and agricultural implements, the education and freedom

In this fanciful depiction, the Emancipation Proclamation is read to a family of slaves by a black Union soldier. *(Library of Congress, Prints and Photographs Division, LC-USZ62–5334)*

of the workmen, the manuring and wise managing of the soil, they raised smaller crops at greater expense than was needful. This I learned by personally visiting some twenty different plantations and by careful inquiry.

Now these valuable lands are for sale, having been forfeited to the United States by reason of the non payment of the direct taxes charged thereon . . .

Here, then, is a splendid opportunity to purchase, at a low price, valuable real estate, by any one desiring a home in the sunny South. Besides, cotton, such as can be produced here, brings at present an enormous price. In view of the almost total loss of the crop for two years past, the exhaustion of the stock on hand, and the increased demand which must follow the renewal of business upon the return of peace, there can scarcely be any reduction of price for a number of years. Will not, then, the enterprising men of the free States secure and cultivate these forfeited and neglected acres? I know farmers in New England, who if they were here in person, with their sleek, fat teams and improved implements of husbandry, would soon turn out these limping, long-eared donkeys over which the crows caw so dolorously . . . They would raise this whole sluggish Southern country from its long sleep, shake off the lethargy which has so long impeded its progress, and work out the destiny which nature and nature's God intended it to acccomplish.

Eyewitness account by New Englander Reverend C. Nason, from Beaufort, South Carolina, detailing his reaction to conditions in the Sea Islands and encouraging Northern farmers to immigrate to the region, dated February 5, 1863, as published in Zion's Herald and Wesleyan Journal *34, no. 11 (March 18, 1863), p. 42.*

In February 1863, *Harper's Weekly* published this woodcut of freed slaves coming into Union lines. *(Library of Congress, Prints and Photographs Division, LC-USZ62–112158)*

I listened for two hours this morning to the stories of a toothless old slave with one blind eye who had come up the river from near Memphis. He told me a lot of stuff. He said his master sold his wife and children to a cotton planter in Alabama to pay his gambling debts, and when he told his master he couldn't stand it, he was tied to the whipping post stripped and given 40 lashes. The next night he ran to the swamps. The bloodhounds were put on his track and caught him and pulled him down. They bit him in the face and put out his eye and crushed one of his hands so he could not use it. He stripped down his pants and showed me a gash on one of his hips where one of the hounds hung unto him until he nearly bled to death. This happened in sight of Nashville, the capital of Tennessee.

Report of discussion with an escaped slave, by a young Union private, Chauncey Cooke, in a letter to his mother, dated March 21, 1863, from Letters of a Badger Boy in Blue, *as quoted in Allen Nevins, ed.,* The Blue and the Grey, *pp. 470–471.*

. . . I went to Wall street . . . but the rumors grew more and more unpleasant, so I left it at once and took a Third Avenue car for uptown. At the Park were groups and small crowds in more or less excitement (which found relief afterwards, I hear, in hunting down and maltreating sundry unoffending niggers), but there was nothing to indicate serious trouble. The crowded car went slowly on its way. . . . At Thirteenth Street the track was blocked by a long line of stationary cars that stretched indefinitely up the Avenue, and I took to the sidewalk. Above Twentieth Street all shops were closed, and many people standing and staring or strolling uptown, not riotously disposed but eager and curious. Here and there a rough could be heard damning the draft. No policemen to be seen anywhere. Reached the seat of war at last, Forty-sixth Street and Third Avenue [the address of the draft headquarters]. Three houses on the Avenue and two or three on the street were burned down: engines playing on the ruins—more energetically, I'm told, than they did when their efforts would have been useful.

The crowd seemed just what one commonly sees at any fire, but its nucleus of riot was concealed by an outside layer of ordinary peaceable lookers-on. Was told they had beat off a squad of police and another of "regulars" (probably the Twelfth Militia). At last, it opened and out streamed a posse of perhaps five hundred, certainly less than one thousand, of the lowest Irish day laborers. The rabble was perfectly homogeneous. Every brute in the drove was pure Celtic—hod-carrier or loafer. They were unarmed. A few carried pieces of fence-paling and the like. . . .

George Templeton Strong, northern philanthropist, reporting his observations on the draft riots in New York City, in his diary entry for July 13, 1863, in Allen Nevins, ed., Diary of the Civil War, 1860–1865, *pp. 335–337.*

About 7 o'clock . . . the crowd of boys began to be swelled by a different class of roughs, who appeared on the ground with clubs in their hands, and from their appearance, had evidently been engaged in the more bloody work up town. They immediately gathered around the Tribune office and commenced a series of the most unearthly groans and demoniac yells. In a few moments one of the more forward among them commenced an attack upon the door of the publication office, which was locked, but which soon gave way to the pressure of the mob, who amid the crashing of broken doors and windows, rushed in . . . In less than five minutes the office was completely gutted, and the desks and counters upset and broken. At length a platoon of the First Ward Police came rushing up Nassau-street, and on seeing them the mob, which numbered not less than four hundred men and boys, ran like so many sheep, leaving Printing-House-Square, in less than three minutes, almost as clear of people as it is of a Sunday morning. It was a striking illustration of the cowardice of a mob when confronted by a handful of determined officers of the law. Several shots were fired by the policemen at ringleaders of the mob—but, so far as is known, none of them took effect. One of the policemen was also shot at by a rioter, the ball taking effect in the back. The wound is serious, but it is thought not dangerous. Before leaving the office, the rioters set fire to the building, but it was extinguished by a policeman before much damage was done.

Outrages upon Colored Persons.

Among the most cowardly features of the riot, and one which indicated its political *animus* and the cunningly devised cue that had been given to the rioters by the instigators of the outbreak, was the causeless and inhuman treatment of the negroes of the City. It seemed to be an understood thing throughout the City that the negroes should be attacked wherever found, whether they offered any provocation or not. As soon as one of these unfortunate people was spied, whether on a cart, a railroad car, or in the street, he was imme-

diately set upon by a crowd of men and boys, and unless some man of pluck came to his rescue, or he was fortunate enough to escape into a building he was inhumanly beaten and perhaps killed. There were probably not less than a dozen negroes beaten to death in different parts of the City during the day.

Extract from a news story covering the draft riots of New York, entitled "The Mob in New-York. Resistance to the Draft—Rioting and Bloodshed. Conscription Offices sacked and Burned. Private Dwellings Pillaged and Fired," detailing the attack on the Tribune *building and attacks on African Americans,* New York Times, *July 14, 1863, p. 1.*

It is absurd and futile to attribute this outburst of ruffianism to anything else than sympathy with the Rebels. If as some pretend, it results from dissatisfaction with the $300 exemption, why are negroes indiscriminately assailed and beaten almost or quite to death? Did *they* prescribe this exemption? On the contrary, are they not almost uniformly poor men, themselves exposed to the draft, and unable to pay $300? What single thing have they done to expose them to this infernal, cowardly ruffianism? What can be alleged against them, unless it be that they are generally hostile to the Slaveholders' Rebellion? And how are the drafting officers responsible for the $300 clause?

We may just as well look the facts in the face? These riots are "a fire in the rear" on our defenders in the field. They are, in purpose and in essence, a diversion in favor of Jeff. Davis and Lee. Listen to the yells of the mob, and the harangues of its favorite orators, and you will find them surcharged with "nigger," "Abolition," "Black Republican," denunciation of prominent Republicans, *The Tribune,* &c., &c.—all very wide of the draft and the exemption. . . . It is the fear, stimulated by the recent and glorious triumphs of the Union arms, that Slavery and the Rebellion must suffer, which is at the bottom of all this arson, devastation, robbery, and murder. And this fact should arouse every devotee of Liberty and Law to oppose to the rioters the sternest resistance.

Editorial in the New York Tribune, *July 15, 1863, probably by Horace Greeley, cited in Horace Greeley,* The American Conflict, *Vol. II, pp. 504–505.*

Believing that the contaminating influence of the riot in the city of New York would doubtless cease with its suppression, which I thought would certainly occur by that day at farthest, I acceded to the suggestion [to temporarily suspend the draft]; but on the morning of the next day, although there was no drafting going on, the riot broke out and the mob indulged in a counterpart of the depradations which have been occurring in the city of New York, destroying the office of a certain newspaper, the Troy Times, sacking the building, as well as the house of a prominent citizen, tearing down a colored people's church, releasing prisoners from the jail, &c.

Under this state of things, and the militia being unreliable, and as the city of Albany was on the verge of a riot, I authorized Captain Hughes to give the notice that the draft had been suspended. This, however, did not seem to have the effect of immediately stopping the riot, as many of the depradations took place after the notice had been given, but doubtless before citizens could disseminate it sufficiently to bring it to the understanding of the rioters. To quiet the apprehensions in [Albany] I published also that the draft had been suspended in Troy, and that there was no draft occurring in Albany, as it had not yet been ordered. I resorted to this step, after a full realization of the situation and open conviction that it was the only course to pursue. The Provost-Marshal-General will remember that the government of this State is in the hands of individuals whose party has not manifested at all times a co-operative interest in the measures of the Administration, and the inflammatory editorials of its journals in this city and State, and the open and vituperative condemnation of such measures by respectable and influential citizens in the hearing of the illiterate, have under the stimulation of designing men given rise to organizations of a secret nature among the myriads of molders and other workingmen, not only in this city and in Troy, but I believe also in every city and village of this state. The draft, of course, has furnished to the leaders the pretext of a potent opposition to the General Government. It is sufficiently apparent throughout the whole of this division that this opposition is deeply seated among the great mass of the people, whose recklessness of consequences is wholly unaccountable excepting upon the suspicion that it rests upon the security of numbers. The Irish as a class are involved in this opposition, and form, as they always do, the sub-structure of the mob, and in neither of these cities are there any other military bodies left than those composed of the Irish, and they are thoroughly unreliable, as conceded by the authorities themselves. The military of this city were under orders from the Governor to proceed to New York on

Monday last, but they refused to go, for what reason it is apparent, when it was currently believed that the draft in Troy and Albany was very soon to occur, and that it would take place simultaneously in both cities.

Description of problems enforcing the draft in upstate New York prepared by acting assistant provost marshal general, Major Frederick Townsend, in a letter, July 16, 1863, to the office of the U.S. provost marshal general, Colonel James B. Fry, in Washington, in Official Records of the War of the Rebellion, *Series III, Vol. 3, pp. 515–516.*

The State of Missouri having adopted an ordinance of emancipation, the civil tribunals being in operation in the greater part of the State, the Federal courts never having suspended their functions, and the President's proclamation of freedom never having been extended in Missouri, some questions arise as to the powers and duties of the military authorities in this department so far as they affect the people of Missouri, and I would be pleased to have your views and instructions in regard to them, and particularly as to what authority, if any, the military may assume in respect to the slaves of loyal men, and also in respect to negroes made free by operation of the several acts of Congress. First. Are the military authorities to determine the question of freedom or slavery under the provisions of acts of August 6, 1861 and of July 17, 1862, and to give certificates of freedom to the slaves of disloyal persons? . . .

The question arises whether in a loyal State, or at least those parts of it where the civil tribunals perform their regular functions, the whole matter is to be left subject to their jurisdiction, or whether the military may interfere and undertake to execute the provisions of the acts of Congress in this respect . . . It is very clear to my mind that those persons declared free by the fourth section of the act of August 6, 1861, and by the ninth section of the act of July 17, 1862, are free by the operation of the law and the disloyal acts of their owners, and that no judicial decree is necessary to perfect their freedom. Is it any part of the duty of the military authorities to furnish evidence of such freedom, or must they be left to plead the acts either in suit for freedom or in defense against the person claiming their service or labor?

These questions, of course do not apply to the proclamation of the President of January 1, 1863. Under that proclamation the military and naval authorities are expressly required to enforce its provisions and to give protection to the persons liberated by it.

Major General J. M. Schofield, from the headquarters of the Department of the Missouri in St. Louis, writing to Secretary of War Edward Stanton, describing the complexities of the status of slaves in the state and asking for clarification of the responsibilities of the army, July 17, 1863, in Official Records of the War of the Rebellion, *Series II, Vol. 3, p. 525.*

To prevent vagrancy, demoralization, immoralities, and expense to the Government, all officers are forbidden to admit within their lines and harbor runaway negroes, unless their services are needed, or in cases where humanity demands it. In these cases lists of the persons admitted and the reasons for their admittance will be forwarded to the provost-marshal-general of this department without delay.

To insure protection and prompt payment to colored persons employed in the engineer department or as laborers, they will be organized and mustered into service by detachments or companies, as infantry, and then assigned to duty. . . .

In the absence of civil law commanders of troops will exert their authority to prevent injustice and disorders, whether coming from masters or their servants, requiring each to perform their legal duties, wherever intervention is practicable and demanded by justice and humanity.

Excerpt from General Orders #172, headquarters of the Department of the Cumberland, Winchester, Tennessee, issued July 23, 1863, by command of Major General Rosecrans, signed by J. Bates Dickson, assistant adjutant general, in Official Records of the War of the Rebellion, *Series III, Vol. 3, pp. 559–560.*

Ma, how do you like the idea of sending all the Negroes to some of the interior states and selling them and buying gold with the money? All but two or three of the most trusty ones, so there will be no danger of our losing all by the war. Sell horses, stock, and everything, only a few cows are living on the place. That part of the country is subject to be overrun by the enemy at anytime, and we may lose everything someday. Pole could take them to Alabama or Louisiana or some other state and sell them for a good price and not be gone from home very long. Negroes bring very good prices up here, and I reckon as good in those states. I think it must be the safe plan. But I will leave all to you, do as you are doing if you think it best.

Private Jerome Bonaparte Yates, of the 16th Mississippi Infantry, writing to his mother in Hinds County, Mississippi, August 21, 1863, from his camp at Orange Court House, Virginia, urging her to sell the family's slaves, in Robert G. Evans, ed., The 16th Mississippi Infantry: Civil War Letters and Reminiscences, *p. 197.*

From all I can see and hear at the North and from the hopeless state of the rebels I am fully convinced you will shortly be overwhelmed with the cry for "The Union as it was, and the Constitution as it is." Slavery will thus be fixed on us forever, and all our blood and treasure will have been expended in vain. Cannot this be prevented by a general arming of the negroes and a general destruction of all the property of the slaveholders, thus making it their interest to get rid of slavery?

Let me take the men you can spare from this city [St. Nicholas, New York], land at Brunswick, Ga., march through the heart of Georgia, Alabama, and Mississippi to New Orleans, arming all the negroes and burning the house and other property of every slaveholder. A passage of this kind would create such a commotion among the negroes that they themselves could be left to do the rest of the work. I am a firm believer in the maxim that "Slaveholders have no rights a negro is bound to respect." I have the honor to be, very respectfully, your most obedient servant, D. Hunter, Major-General.

Letter from General David Hunter to Secretary of War Stanton, August 31, 1863, requesting that African-American troops be employed to start a slave insurrection through the Gulf states, in Official Records of the War of the Rebellion, *Series III, Vol. 3, p. 740.*

Sir: I arrived at Headquarters Department of the Cumberland on Tuesday at 3 p.m. and immediately presented your letter to Major-General Rosecrans. He received me very kindly, and I remained with him until 1 o'clock a.m., in conversation during the intervals of business. He was very free in his expression of opinions, but explicit in his directions, sociable, and I think perfectly reliable; is heartily in favor of the employment of colored troops and will do all he can to forward the work. . . .

General Rosecrans directed me to ask:

First. Can slaves of loyal citizens of Tennessee be enlisted in the Army without the consent of their masters?

Second. Will all enlisted men become freemen at the expiration of their term of military service?

Third. Do non-commissioned officers receive higher pay than privates? If so, how much.

A reply to these questions by telegram to me at Nashville is desirable. I think this will prove the best department in the country in which to commence thorough work. Its organization is said to be good, and I find the officers pride themselves on the exact performance of their duties. The citizens are in a much better state of preparation for the change than I had expected.

The negroes are physically superior to any I have seen, and appear bright and intelligent.

General Rosecrans directed me to send North for colored men who could read and write a fair hand for non-commissioned officers, twenty to each regiment. I have already taken measures to obtain them.

Communication from Major George L. Stearns, commissioner for organization of colored troops, to Secretary of War Edwin Stanton, seeking instructions on the recruiting of African-American soldiers from Nashville, Tennessee, September 11, 1863, in Official Records of the War of the Rebellion, *Series II, Vol. 3, pp. 785–786.*

I have received your letter of the 21st instant requesting me to give facilities to recruiting officers for colored regiments in Missouri, &c.

I am still desirous, as I always have been, to do all in my power to promote this object, but I have recently met with difficulties and embarrassments which have rendered it necessary for me to stop recruiting for colored regiments in Missouri. The men who are clearly proper subjects for enlistments, as I understand the orders of the War Department, have nearly all left Missouri in one way or another. There are, doubtless, some left who are entitled to their freedom under the confiscation act, but much the larger number belong to men who have always been loyal, or who cannot be convicted of any disloyal act since the date of the confiscation act. I have heretofore taken it for granted that it was the desire of the War Department to enlist only such colored men as are legally entitled to their freedom, and it is now practically impossible for me or any other military officer to decide the nice legal questions involved in almost all cases which arise.

Moreover, it is found by experience that the recruiting officers do not even attempt to make any discrimination between the slaves of loyal and those of disloyal men, but go through the country picking up all they can induce to go with them, and in some cases forcing them away.

The President has, I believe, the legal authority to receive negroes into the service without regard to the loyalty of their masters. If it his wish to exercise this authority in Missouri, I will cheerfully carry out your instructions on the subject.

Practically, it must be done without regard to the claims of loyal men, and if this policy is to be adopted it should be so declared, in order that the people may understand that it is the act of the Government.

The execution of this policy at the present time would occasion much hardship to the loyal farmers, on account of the consequent loss of their tobacco and other crops. Yet they will submit to it without much complaint if the Government wants their slaves as troops. Two or three months hence it can be done without much injury to the State.

Please inform me of the wishes of the Government in regard to this matter and I will carry them out without delay.

Major General J. M. Schofield, from the headquarters of the department of the Missouri in St. Louis, writing to Brigadier General L. Thomas, adjutant general of the U.S. Army in Memphis, describing the complexities of the status of slaves in the state and asking for clarification of which African Americans could be recruited into the army, September 26, 1863, in Official Records of the War of the Rebellion, *Series II, Vol. 3, p. 849.*

This sum, $374,241.98, fed the destitute in this city alone, and has been reimbursed to the commissary department by your order from the proceeds of property sequestrated and sold by the commission of sequestration instituted prior to your arrival and command of the Department of the Gulf.

The cost of subsisting the colored population and destitute beyond the limits of the city has been borne by the Subsistence Department of the Army, without compensation, at an expense nearly if not equal to that of the subsistence of our entire army for an equal period prior to this rebellion.

These are unequaled and unheard-of charities in any age or country, by any army, and completely reverse the very general rule of subsisting armies upon the countries in which they operate—for here we actually support the poor of the country we occupy.

Under the system inaugurated by you in the early spring of employing the vagrant and freed colored population by the cultivation of the abandoned plantations of those in arms against us, they were not only in a fair way of providing for themselves, but for their children and own infirm people. The transfer, however, of all these plantations to another department of the Government deprives you entirely of this means of aid to the great number of old and young negroes whose labor is not available in making plantation crops, and who are not provided for by that department of the Government now cultivating these lands.

The fund arising from the sale of sequestrated property, referred to above, is exhausted. The inclement winter months now at hand will again enormously increase the number of destitute families. In ten days other means must be found to provide for these wants. Without further orders the commissaries of subsistence must discontinue the issue of supplies to the destitute in this city.

Humanity, common sense, and necessity all would seem to require that if the General Government is to continue to provide for these people it should be done from the proceeds of property coming into the hands of Treasury agents from seizures and plantation culture.

The burden of providing for the poor should go with the available means of those who have brought destitution upon them. If these are not sufficient, this city at least, by taxes or loans, should contribute the necessary balance. In the meantime, however, I have the honor to request your instructions and orders for my government and that of the department under my charge.

Colonel E. G. Beckwith, chief of the office of the commissary of subsistence of the U.S. Army in New Orleans, to General Nathaniel Banks, reporting on refugee assistance to African Americans in and around New Orleans and requesting the sale of confiscated properties to provide further funding for that purpose, October 24, 1863, in Official Records of the War of the Rebellion, *Series III, Vol. 3, p. 927.*

The authorities at Washington give transportation—without subsistence—to all teachers, and give them rations while teaching.

The government also sent early Rev. Mr. French, and then Mr. Pierce, to look after and in every possible way provide for these people, furnishing employ-ment, instruction, etc. Nobly and successfully did these gentlemen accomplish that work, then so difficult but important. Brigadier-General Rufus Saxton, now military governor of the Departmentof the South, embracing South Carolina, Georgia, and Florida, who appears to be not only a high-minded and successful military officer, but also a Christian gentleman, has only carried out the true purposes and wishes of the general goveernment in his steady and vigorous support of these patriotic and philanthropic measures. . . .

Notwithstanding the contrabands are now numerous on all the skirts of the rebellion, we were more anxious to see their condition at Port Royal and vicinity than elsewhere, because we knew more had been done for them in that region, and also that the slaves of South Carolina have been supposed more servile and degraded than in most other parts of the South. Then, also, we had once some acquaintance with the slave population of that state and desired to make some comparison. It has seemed to us, for the lst year especially, that on that territory more than any other the experiment is to be made, and the question settled, whether or not free labor, education, and religion will succeed with the recently and suddenly emancipated slaves. Success or failure there will be success or failure with the whole four millions.

When the war began to result in emancipation these questions came rushing upon us from all quarters: Will these colored men enlist and fight? Will they work? Can they be educated? Will they be provident? Can they be elevated in social position to respectable citizens? These are the questions now being settled in this momentous experiment. That these men will enlist and fight as freely and courageously as white men the "war news" has already settled. That they will work as cheerfully, as rapidly, and as successfully as when slaves, and far more so, all reports agree, and I am an eye-witness. An intelligent and observant superintendent of several plantations informs me that the cotton crop raised for the government by these laborers would be this year twice, if not three times as large as last year, before they were fully organized for labor, and had very little and irregular pay. And though now the average pay of the hands, good and poor, men, women, and children, would be scarcely more than twenty-five cents per day, yet out of this they would live with far more comfort and respectability than when they were slaves. This shows whether or not they can be provident. More, strange as it may seem, out of these small earnings, with what they are getting from their own little resources, such as a cotton patch of their own, or raising vegetables, which they sell to the army, etc., they are saving a little money with which they are intending to purchase lands confiscated and to be sold soon.

One fact to show this. While in Beaufort the other day, five colored men called on Brother French to consult him how they could secure some land when the sale comes off. He immediately sought to know their ability to pay for land; and he found that these five men, at the low current prices, could pay for two thousand acres! These, however, were not representative men; they were the sharp ones, more and more of whom are beginning to appear. Many of these have had their small sums hidden away, sometimes in the ground, before the rebellion. . . .

There are probably more than three thousand children already in schools, besides hundreds if not thousands either in extra classes or under private instruction. Most of these a year and a half since knew not one letter of the alphabet. Hundreds of them I saw early in this month in their schools, and heard many read in plain reading quite tolerably and spell quite sharply. I never saw white scholars who had made greater progress in the same length of time . . .

Article by Reverend L. D. Barrows, a Methodist clergyman and teacher from Massachusetts, entitled "The Freedmen of the South," reporting his observations on the conditions of the freed slaves at the Sea Islands for the Christian Advocate and Journal, *38, no. 46 (November 12, 1863), p. 362.*

They charged the blown up part of the works with two lines. They gained the works formally [sic-formerly] occupied by Elliot's Brigade which they held until two of our brigades of this division was sent for. Then they charged and recaptured the works and with them one thousand prisoners and twenty flags. Most of the Negroes were killed after they surrendered. The ground was covered with dead Negroes. Some was killed after they were taken to the rear. Only sixty or seventy was saved from the river. The Yankee loss is estimated at three thousand, ours at six or seven hundred. . . . The men in the fight say the Negroes fought better than the whites. So it is all stuff about them not making soldiers. . . . The enemy asked for permission to bury their dead, which was granted, then they put one hundred in one grave. They were all killed in one hole, the place where they blew our line up. Such blow ups do not pay. A few more such and Grant will have a corps less . . .

Private Jerome Bonaparte Yates, of the 16th Mississippi Infantry, writing to his sister Marie in Hinds County, Mississippi, August 3, 1864, from Petersburg, Virginia, describing the slaughter of African-American troops by the Confederates at the "Crater," in Robert G. Evans, ed., The 16th Mississippi Infantry: Civil War Letters and Reminiscences, *pp. 281–282.*

General Banks estimates the number of slaves in Louisiana exempted from emancipation by President Lincoln's Proclamation of January 1, 1863, at 150,000. Now, not one of these wears a chain, or is amenable to any slave master. In regard to their industrial employment, which has been so often denounced as mere serfdom, he declares that "It was established upon the basis of absolute and perfect freedom of the negro in all respects and all considerations, to make him as independent and to prepare him for as perfect an independence as that enjoyed by any other class of people on this continent." They were at liberty to select their own employer, and go where they pleased; only they were expected to labor in support of themselves and families somewhere, if not upon the plantations, then upon the government works. "Both parties," he avers, "accepted the proposition readily—those who were engaged in the cultivation of the soil, *because they had no alternative*—the negro, because he had no other desire," having his freedom and that of his wife and children secured, and getting for them clothing and rations from the government, besides educational privileges, in addition to a stipulated pecuniary remuneration. Nothing was done without the concurrence of the negroes; they brought to the government their own terms of labor, which were complied with; the planters yielded; and the result is good will, mutual satisfaction, and growing prosperity. So successful has been the experiment that General Banks says he does not believe there is required any change whatever in the state of labor that has been in operation in Louisiana for two years past. In view of their peculiar situation, he believes that the wages of the laboring men in that State have been as remunerative as those of Massachusetts, or any other part of the country. Why certain exactions were made of the planters and the laborers alike, he shows in a satisfactory manner.

As for the charge of serfdom, nothing of the kind exists. There is not a court in the State that does not recognize a negro, whether free or whether enslaved before the war, as a freeman entitled to all the rights and all the protection of a white man . . .

Extract from an editorial in The Liberator, *entitled "Major General Banks," summarizing and approving the report of General Nathaniel Banks on the system of contract labor for slaves and freedmen established in Louisiana under his administration, as presented in a talk to the Boston Young Men's Christian Association, Vol. 34, No. 36 (November 11, 1864), p. 182.*

Should [the slave] be retained in servitude or should his emancipation be held out to him as a reward for faithful service, or should it be granted at once on the promise of such service; and if emancipated, what action should be taken to secure for the freed man the permission of the State from which he was drawn to reside within its limits after the close of his public service. . . .

The subject is to be viewed by us, therefore, solely in the light of policy and our social economy. When so regarded, I must dissent from those who advise a general levy and arming of the slaves for the duty of soldiers. Until our white population shall prove insufficient for the armies we require and can afford to keep in the field, to employ as a soldier the negro who has merely been trained to labor, and as laborer the white man accustomed from his youth to the use of fire-arms, would scarcely be deemed wise or advantageous by any; and this is the question now before us. But should the alternative ever be presented of subjugation or of the employment of the slave as a soldier, there seems no reason to doubt what should then be our decision. . . . The appalling demoralization, suffering, disease and death which have been caused by partially substituting the invaders' system of police for the kind relation previously subsisting between the master and the slave, have been a sufficient demonstration that external interference with our institution of domestic slavery is productive of evil only.

Confederate president Jefferson Davis, commenting on the prospect of enlisting slaves in the Confederate army and offering them emancipation in exchange for their service, reported in an article entitled, "Jeff. Davis on the Arming of Slaves," The Liberator, *Vol. 34, No. 47 (November 18, 1864), p. 186.*

I venture [a suggestion] concerning suffrage—a subject you are now debating. *Give the ballot to all who can read, and deny it to all who can not!* It is strange that this proposition—approved, as it is, by every wise man's private conviction—is so generally omitted from the public law. Democratic government is grounded on the intelligence of the people. Every voter is a legislator for every other. The theory, therefore, is, that the voter must cast an intelligent vote. But what shall be the entitling measure of intelligence? Let it be the lowest measure consistent with the public safety. What is the lowest measure? If a man who could *not read* was once counted fit for an English king, let a man who *can* read be counted fit for an American voter. This is the simplest, easiest, and best of tests.

What is the practical value to your Convention? It affords a beautiful, just and equitable disposition of your disputed point of negro suffrage. I asked the radicals in St. Louis, "Will you permit black men, who fight for the Union, to vote for the Union?" "No!" said they; "the blacks are too ignorant." "You are not opposed then to negro suffrage because the negro is black, but because he is ignorant." They answered, "When the negro knows how to vote, we will give him the ballot." Now, this is well. The negro should not vote till he knows how. Nor should the white man. Deny the ballot to both, so long as they can not read; give it to both as soon as they learn. *To-day, in Missouri, more whites than blacks are unable to read.* To grant the ballot to these ignorant whites, and deny it to these ignorant blacks, is a mere caprice of prejudice. Grant it to neither till they earn it by alphabet and spelling-book. On the other hand, to deny negro suffrage entirely—to say, for instance, to a black man who is intelligent and thrifty, "you may pay taxes on twenty thousand dollars' earnings, but you shall not have a vote"—this violates the divinely-ordained democracy of mankind, and is an affront to Him who is no respecter of persons.

Is negro suffrage an untried novelty, that it should be feared? Not at all. Many years ago, Maryland and North Carolina sent their free negroes to the polls. A few days ago, Gratz Brown told you truly that except for the negro vote in New York State, the calamity called Horatio Seymour would have been repeated at the last election. I believe with Frederick Douglass, that "if a negro knows as much when sober as an Irishman when drunk, he knows enough to vote." There is no reason why your State should not now receive the noblest of political constitutions. Such a basis of suffrage would command the assent and admiration of the world. Rendering impartial justice to all classes, it would crown its makers with everlasting remembrance.

Now is the golden hour for Missouri. Let not her convention tarnish their opportunity by any stain of injustice and inequality.

Theodore Tilton, abolitionist and journalist, advising Missouri radicals to incorporate a literacy qualification for suffrage in the state's new constitution as a means of extending suffrage to literate African-American men, in a letter to the Missouri Democrat, *dated January 5, 1865, reprinted in* The Liberator, *under the title "Negro Suffrage—A letter from Theodore Tilton," Vol. 35, No. 3 (January 20, 1865), p. 10.*

Nothing more amazing marks the history of this war than its action upon slavery, by which the work of [the National Freedmen's Relief Association] is prepared.

Few at first thought of emancipation as one of the fruits of war; but the people soon saw its justice and wisdom, and after a time, that great act of emancipation was promulgated, which has made the name of Abraham Lincoln forever memorable.

Then necessarily arose the question, whether black men should be called to take part in the war for union, now become, also, a war for freedom. The intuitions of the people answered this question also in advance of the authorities; but the authorities followed, and now we have some two hundred thousand black men under arms, and no man longer doubts that they are soldiers.

And now comes another question. Shall the loyal blacks of rebel States be permitted to protect themselves, and protect white loyalists also by their votes, from new oppressions by amnestied but still vindictive rebels? I cannot doubt what a just and magnanimous people will determine. They will say, "Let ballots go with ballots; let freedom be defended by suffrage," and again legislation and administration will bow to the majesty of the people.

To prepare freedmen for the new duties and responsibilities which have already come upon them, and are yet to come, is the special work of this association. Immediate relief for immediate wants is indeed its first care; but its larger and higher duty and purpose is to enable them to provide for themselves, and make them useful and worthy citizens.

It is part of the vast work of amelioration and education by which our whole nation is to be advanced to higher and better national life, and prepared for the grand future which is to make all its glorious past dim by comparison. He who doubts its first success, must doubt the goodness of God toward man.

Chief Justice Salmon Chase, commenting on suffrage for African-American men, in "Remarks of Chief Justice Chase," when taking the chair of the annual meeting of the National Freedmen's Relief Association, held in the chamber of the House of Representatives in Washington, on February 26, 1865, reported in The Liberator *35, no. 10 (March 10, 1865), p. 39.*

7 Sea Dogs and Submarines
1863–1865

Naval forces, even more than land forces, depend on industry and technology in the form of ship construction, innovation, and weaponry. In the era of the Civil War this was especially true, as technology moved rapidly in the age of steam, as heavy ordnance and armor were developed and improved with new techniques of metal working, and as electrical devices began to proliferate. Considering the fact that the Northern states had a distinct advantage over the South because the industrial revolution had already taken hold there and because Northern factories and shops had begun to organize along efficient lines, it is surprising how well the Confederacy did with the limited means at its disposal. While the technical and industrial advantages of the Union had only minor effects on the battles fought on land, the discrepancy between the two sections definitely shaped the nature of the conflict at sea. As Confederate secretary of the navy Stephen Mallory attempted to meet the Confederacy's strategic objectives, he did so with intelligence, innovation, and with a small but accomplished cadre of officers.

Mallory was one of only two cabinet officers to serve throughout the war under Jefferson Davis, and Mallory set the naval strategies and chose the personnel to carry them out. Although breaking the blockade was an early objective, Mallory focused on preventing the Union navy from using its dominance of the sea lanes to attack major Southern seaports and to land troops. Another strategic goal was to disrupt and possibly destroy Union merchant shipping on the high seas. However, the South had entered the war without a navy and, for the most part, before the war had relied on Northern-owned and foreign shipping companies for its import and export trade.

With very few resources at their command, Secretary Mallory and his naval officers and crews came close to meeting their strategic objectives. Although the Union took New Orleans early in the war and partially closed access to most other ports with the blockade, the Confederate navy was able to prevent Union naval forces landing troops to take Mobile, Charleston, Wilmington, Galveston, and Richmond until the last months of the war. Relying on a handful of ships, most of them built in Britain, Confederate cruisers severely disrupted the American merchant fleet, sent war-risk insurance rates high, and contributed to the long-range decline of the American maritime flag as owners transferred ships to British and other registries.

Union secretary of the navy Gideon Welles also had clear strategic objectives. In addition to maintaining the blockade and supporting army operations with river gunboats and steamers, he sought to suppress the Confederate commerce raiders and to use the fleet to conduct combined operations with the army in taking the Southern cities that were ports or could be reached from the sea along river systems or estuaries, such as Wilmington, North Carolina. With the help of the State Department, Welles sought to prevent the Confederacy from purchasing ships in Europe and from using neutral ports for refitting the ocean cruisers or capitalizing on the cruisers' captures by condemning and selling them abroad. He only partially succeeded in these goals.

The innovations of the Confederacy in developing mines, known in the period as torpedoes, together with the general superiority of shore-based artillery in fortresses over water-borne ordnance, helped account for the failure of the Union to launch a major invasion of the South from the sea, with most of the early Union successes in attacking the Confederacy from the sea consisting of captured off-shore and barrier islands. New Orleans, captured by Union naval forces in April 1862, was the only major Confederate seaport taken by the Union before the last six months of the war.

As part of the strategy of defense with limited means, Mallory sponsored development of floating and emplaced torpedoes and of submarines and shallow-draft, semi-submersible torpedo boats. The innovative methods accounted for several spectacular successes and changed the course of maritime warfare forever. Between the sea dogs of the high-seas cruisers, and the mines and submarines in inland waters, the Confederate navy made a strong showing.

THE BLUE-WATER CRUISERS

Although the efforts of U.S. ambassadors and consuls abroad did limit the use of foreign ports by Confederate cruisers, six of the eight Confederate cruisers that attacked American merchant ships at sea were built in Britain. As the depredations of the cruisers became known and as the Confederacy began to lose crucial battles on land throughout 1863, British policy toward the Confederacy hardened. U.S. ambassador to Britain Charles Francis Adams was able to prevent the Confederacy from acquiring several ships in Britain including two powerful ironclad, steam-propelled ships, the Laird rams, in the last year of the war. Furthermore, British governors of colonies around the world became less welcoming of the Confederate navy cruisers, despite continued public sympathy for the cause of secession in some of those regions. Throughout the war, the Union press, politicians, and naval officers continued to regard the cruiser officers and crews as pirates. But when captured by Union forces, the sea-dog officers were treated as prisoners of war, not as criminals. The captured cruiser crews, especially those recruited in Britain or other neutral countries, were sometimes quietly allowed to escape or book passage out of the United States.

Confederate secretary of the navy Mallory sent agents to purchase ships overseas, primarily in England but also in France. The Confederate agent in Britain, James Bulloch, through the use of deceptions and misdirection as well as sophisticated business operations, succeeded in getting four cruisers built in Britain and outfitted at isolated anchorages in the Atlantic Ocean, in the Azores, Bahamas, and Madeira islands. As those ships became available, naval officers who

The British aid to the Confederacy in the form of ships sold or constructed for the Confederate navy was a cause for bitter resentment in the North. *(Library of Congress, Prints and Photographs Division, LC-USZ62–17728)*

had resigned their commissions in the U.S. Navy to fight for the Confederacy shipped out as passengers through the blockade, made their way to Europe or to the islands, where they took command of the ships to act as commerce raiders. Crewed largely by British sailors, the ships acquitted themselves well. While only eight commerce raiders were able to operate, their attacks on U.S. merchant ships and whalers had a disastrous effect.

Altogether some 215 ships were captured by eight Confederate cruisers. Two of the eight commerce-raiding ships were American-built and took 20 merchant ships between them, *Sumter* 18 and *Nashville* two. Two ships were nearly identical blockade runners built in Britain and converted into commerce raiders, and they captured 46 ships, *Tallahassee* 39 and *Chickamauga* seven. Four were built in Britain and outfitted outside of British waters as warships. These four accounted for 150 of the prizes, *Florida* 37, *Georgia* nine, *Alabama* 66, and *Shenandoah* 38. Another 21 ships were seized by a small crew who manned other ships seized at sea including, in sequence, the *Clarence* (itself captured by the *Florida*), and then the *Tacony,* and finally the *Archer.* The *Lapwing,* captured by the *Florida,* also took one ship. The total number of seizures of ships at sea, including those captured by crews put aboard captured ships, came to 237.[1]

The number of seizures of the eight cruisers and their captured auxiliaries does not reflect the immediate impact or the lasting effect of the Confederate high-seas fleet. Although only two or three of the eight cruisers operated at the same time, their attacks on shipping tied up Union naval ships in searching for them, ships that otherwise might have been employed in strengthening the blockade. Many of the captured or destroyed Union ships were small schooners, whalers, and fishing vessels, but they also included the Union navy's steamship *Hatteras,* the Union revenue cutters *Harriet Lane* and *Caleb Cushing,* six magnificent clipper ships, and two ocean-going steamers. Dozens of other neutral ships were stopped, examined, and released, spreading word of the cruisers' voyages throughout the world's merchant fleets. The cruisers operated not only off the Atlantic coast of the United States, but also in the Caribbean Sea and the Atlantic, Indian, Pacific, and Arctic oceans. Captured crews, officers, and passengers were released to temporarily detained neutral ships, or to American ships released at sea, or at ports around the world. Although the prisoners landed safely ashore by one means or another, many of them complained bitterly about the indignity, discomfort, danger, and financial losses they incurred, and their stories were widely circulated in the newspapers of the day. Such accounts only increased the impact of the cruiser campaign on Northern morale.

Many American shipowners permanently switched the ownership and registry of their vessels to Britain or other neutrals, with the consequence that the United States never fully recovered the position it had held before the Civil War as a great merchant marine power. It has been estimated that Confederate cruisers destroyed about 110,000 tons of Union merchant shipping, and that another 800,000 tons transferred ownership or flag to foreign countries. The total U.S. merchant fleet engaged in foreign commerce in 1860 was about 2.4 million tons. Considering that the tonnage lost by destruction and transfer represented well over a third of the merchant fleet and that America never again achieved its position of dominance in the maritime carrying trade, the impact of eight Confederate cruisers was of historic proportions.[2]

CRUISER METHODS

Confederate cruiser commanders employed the common *ruse de guerre* of showing a false flag, either the Union or British, while approaching a potential victim ship. If the ship still attempted to elude capture, the cruiser would chase it and fire a blank shot. If the pursued vessel did not stop, a calculated near miss by a solid shot would usually bring it to a halt. Then, revealing the true allegiance of the cruiser at the last moment, an officer and a few crew members would be sent to board the prize.

Since Confederate cruisers could not bring their prizes into Confederate ports because of the blockade and since neutral ports would not admit Confederate prizes, cruiser captains made their decisions as to the disposition of captured ships on the spot. After examining the ship's documents, the makeup of the officers and crew, and such factors as the build of the ship and correspondence found aboard and even the accents of the captured ship's officers to determine if they were Yankees, cruiser captains would decide whether the ship was indeed a Union merchant ship or carried Union cargo. Some neutral cargo was destroyed by mistake, while sometimes cleverly faked documents convinced the cruiser captains to release a ship. Some ships were released on a bond, with a promise to pay the Confederate government after a peace was signed between the Confederacy and the Union, and, of course, those bonds were never collected. Most often when a ship and cargo were determined to be Union, the Confederates would seize any cash, cargo, munitions, and supplies that might prove useful, transfer the crew and passengers to the cruiser, and then burn the captured ship. Most captured crews and passengers would be released ashore or to another ship as soon as possible, although sometimes a few members of the captured crew would volunteer to join the Confederate service. Five captured ships (*Lapwing, Clarence, Tacony, Archer,* and *Conrad*—rechristened *Tuscaloosa*) were commissioned into service as auxiliary cruisers or tenders. In one case, that of the bark *Sea Bride,* Confederate officers were able to arrange its sale in South Africa. Of the total of 237 captures at sea, 176 were destroyed, nearly all by burning.

The officers of the cruisers developed standard procedures for burning their prizes. An incendiary crew would board the vessel, ensure that all passengers and animals except rats had been removed, together with any documents, cash, and needed supplies or equipment, then proceed to chop up furniture and cupboards, stacking the kindling in well-ventilated cabins and on deck. The piles of wood would then be doused with kerosene, whale oil, or even butter or lard from the ship's galley. When all was in readiness, the incendiary crew would assemble in a launch or lifeboat, officers would ignite the kindling piles, and then jump aboard the launch that would pull away quickly. Within minutes, usually before the crew reached their own ship, sails, rigging, and the hull would be enveloped in flames, and the ship would then burn to the water line. The procedure was far safer than scuttling a wooden ship, which might float just beneath the surface, representing a danger to other shipping. A burning ship at night could be seen for many miles, announcing the raid to other ships in the vicinity. For this reason, some cruiser captains would collect several prizes and then simultaneously burn them all before moving on to a new raiding area.

Raphael Semmes became the most notorious of the Confederate commanders of high-seas commerce-raiding ships. *(Library of Congress, Prints and Photographs Division, LC-USZC4–2385)*

EARLY CAREERS OF THE CRUISERS

The blockade and the lack of suitable ships delayed the beginning of the cruiser strategy. However, as early as July 1861, Raphael Semmes, aboard the converted blockade-runner CSS *Sumter,* captured and released a series of Union brigs and barks in the Atlantic Ocean. By December, he was beginning the practice of either burning the ships or bonding them. The *Sumter,* however, was slow and inefficient as a cruiser. It had limited storage space for coal. After its six-month cruise, it had destroyed seven ships and either released or bonded another 10.

More effective cruising got off to a slow start. On August 17, 1862, the British-built *Oreto* was refitted and armed as CSS *Florida* at an uninhabited island in the Bahamas. However, the commander, John Newland Maffitt, and his crew came down with yellow fever as they installed the armaments and loaded supplies. At first, the undermanned ship took refuge in Cuban waters. Realizing the ship needed work and that a healthy, full crew had to be assembled, Maffitt made a daring run with the ship into Mobile Bay on September 4, 1862, past the Union blockade ships that steamed outside the Confederate-held Fort Morgan, which guarded the entrance there. In Mobile, Maffitt gradually recovered his health, gathered a crew, began training them, conducted repairs, and then prepared for another run out of the bay to engage in raiding. Meanwhile, late in 1862, Raphael Semmes took command of a new Confederate cruiser, the CSS *Alabama* in the Madeira Islands, and began burning and bonding whaling vessels and cargo ships in the Atlantic.

CSS *ALABAMA* AND CSS *FLORIDA*

In January 1863, Semmes entered American waters on the *Alabama* at about the same time that the *Florida* was ready to begin its cruise after slipping out past the blockading fleet at Mobile Bay on January 17. Thus, early in 1863, the Union suddenly faced the fact that two powerful and fast, British-built Confederate cruisers seriously menaced American shipping. The attack of the cruisers began in earnest. Both the *Alabama* and the *Florida* were equipped with sails as well as new steam engines, and both had ample storage for coal. Both could achieve speeds of about 15 knots, easily outrunning most merchant ships and often the steam gunboats sent to chase them. Both had propellers that could be raised to reduce drag when under sail.

After surviving a hurricane, Semmes took the *Alabama* into the Gulf of Mexico and headed for the port of Galveston. Union forces offshore appeared ready to launch an invasion of the port, and Semmes hoped to interdict a troop transport. On January 11, 1863, Semmes sighted a fleet of Union warships off the port and lurked in the distance. Eventually one of them, the auxiliary cruiser *Hatteras,* sailed away from the others to investigate.

Semmes ordered the *Alabama* to sail slowly out of view of the main body of ships. After dusk, the *Hatteras* hailed the *Alabama,* asking for identification. Semmes responded, claiming to be an English ship, and in turn asked for identification. Although he was almost certain that he was facing an American warship, he did not want to make a mistake. On hearing the indistinct reply that confirmed it was a United States ship, Semmes hauled up the Confederate flag and opened fire. After a brief exchange of fire, the Confederate cruiser disabled the engines of the *Hatteras.* In a few minutes, the captain of the *Hatteras* lowered his flag and fired a signal of surrender. *Alabama* rescued the crew of the sinking *Hatteras,* taking them as prisoners of war. The fight had lasted 13 minutes, and proved that Confederate cruisers were at least a match for some U.S. warships. The prisoners were landed in Jamaica, and the *Alabama* continued its cruise. Between January 1863 and January 1864, Semmes and his crew captured and burned or bonded another three dozen American ships, sailing off South America, around South Africa, and into the Indian Ocean.

Over the months January to August 1863, Maffitt cruised in the *Florida,* seizing another 24 merchant ships. As word of these captures on the high seas came back from released prisoners, politicians and the press demanded that Secretary Welles do something to stop the disaster. However, Maffitt and Semmes always managed to stay well ahead of the pursuit throughout this period.

LIEUTENANT CHARLES READ AND HIS CRUISE

One of the more remarkable episodes in Confederate commerce raiding occurred when Captain Maffitt of the CSS *Florida* decided on May 6, 1863, to release one of his captured ships, the sail-powered coffee-freighter *Clarence,* into the hands of a spirited young lieutenant, Charles Read, and a crew of 20. The ship was armed with one portable 6-pound howitzer, pistols, and muskets—not a very intimidating set of weapons.

Sailing off the east coast of the United States, Read had at first considered raiding into the Chesapeake to destroy shipping and to steal a steamer with a commando raid. However, learning from a stopped British ship that the entrance to those waters was too well guarded, he made his way into the shipping lanes between Bermuda and the Atlantic coast of the United States. With no powerful cannon aboard, Read had his crew saw off spare spars, paint them black, and then mount them to look like heavy 32-pounders. Operating as independent raiders, Read's crew captured and destroyed two merchant barks on June 5 and June 9, 1863, taking the crews aboard the small *Clarence.* Then, on June 12, the crew stopped the bark *Tacony* and transferred their arms, crew, and prisoners to that ship. They then burned the *Clarence* and proceeded to use the *Tacony* as a Confederate cruiser.

Over the next few days, the *Tacony* captured and destroyed shipping off New Jersey, New York, and Southern New England, including fishing schooners and larger ships. Read recognized that the prisoners could themselves create a psychological effect, and he planted rumors among them that his operation was part of a whole fleet of commerce raiders attacking Union shipping throughout the western Atlantic. Released aboard bonded ships, the captured crews carried the news of his depredations and his exaggerated tales to reporters ashore; the technique worked. The secretary of the U.S. Navy, Gideon Welles, dispatched at least 38 armed ships to search for the nonexistent mystery fleet. Hailed on two occasions by searching naval craft, Lieutenant Read said that he had sighted the *Tacony* chasing a large East India trading vessel, sending the pursuing ships off on fictional headings. He continued seizing schooners and brigs. He finally transferred his crew to the *Archer* on June 24 and burned the *Tacony.*

Using the *Archer,* Reade decided to raid the harbor of Portland, Maine, even though he was now out of ammunition for his single working cannon. His first goal there was to seize a large passenger steamer in port, the *Chesapeake.* However, his engineer doubted if he could start the steamer's engines all by himself. Read then realized that the fast revenue cutter, *Caleb Cushing,* could be an easier target. Powered by sails and therefore not dependent on a coal supply, it would make a good raider; furthermore, it was armed with cannon.

Stealing aboard under cover of darkness, his crew commandeered the cutter with pistols and cutlasses, then sought to get it out of the harbor before pursuit could be organized. After struggling with a fouled anchor line, and running against an adverse tide, the crew got the *Caleb Cushing* moving. The ship slowly pulled out of the harbor and sailed about 20 miles to sea before several steam vessels, manned with hastily assembled militias and local volunteers, caught up with the fleeing cutter. Read questioned the *Caleb Cushing's* captured officers and crew, but they refused to disclose the hiding places of ammunition. Read could get off only five shots from the cutter's guns before he faced the threat of being boarded. Loading prisoners and crew into the cutter's lifeboats, he set the ship afire, using the well-known methods. As he was captured, the fires reached the ship's powder magazine, and it exploded.

Counting the *Archer,* which was recaptured by the Union, Read and his crew had taken 22 ships in 21 days. The value of the destroyed fishing schooners and other vessels was not immense. Even so, Read had created panic, had embarrassed the Union navy, and had tied up more than three dozen naval ships looking for a succession of nearly unarmed, slow sailing vessels. Read and his crew were imprisoned in Boston's Fort Warren. Later, Read would be released and would fight again in one of the war's final maritime battles.

In a short-lived career, another British-built cruiser, the CSS *Georgia* under the command of William Maury, took nine captures between April and October 1863. The ship was not very successful, partly because it was a steamer with only auxiliary sails and had to depend on a steady coal supply. Since neutral ports generally limited the amount of coal sold to belligerent vessels, and sometimes completely refused to sell coal, Maury and his ship had a disappointing career. After being immobilized by the French in the port of Cherbourg, the ship was finally released, steamed into Liverpool, and was sold to the British in June 1864.

Even though the slow-steaming *Georgia* had a far less dramatic campaign than the other cruisers, it had contributed to the problems of the Union through 1863. Altogether, *Florida, Alabama, Georgia,* and the raiding party under Lieutenant Read netted over 90 ships in 1863.

As word came in of each capture and release or burning, U.S. ambassador Adams in Britain intensified his efforts to prevent the outfitting of several warships that promised to tip the high-seas maritime balance entirely in the direction of the Confederacy. He employed a network of spies and constantly pressured the British government about suspicious ship construction, Confederate agents, and potential violations of British neutrality.

ALEXANDRA, CANTON, AND THE LAIRD RAMS

In mid-1863, the Confederates had at least five major ironclads under construction in different shipyards in Europe. Two heavily armed gunboats, under way in France, had been ordered at the cost of $500,000 each. Despite Union efforts to divert them, one of them eventually ended up in Confederate hands as the *Stonewall,* but too late to affect the course of the war. The British seized a small ship launched in Liverpool, the *Alexandra,* built by the same firm that had turned out the *Florida*. Although the case for seizure was fought through the courts and the government's case was thrown out, the ship remained tied up in legal red tape and was never outfitted as a warship for the Confederacy.

Two ironclad cruisers were being built at the Laird works in Scotland, identified by their hull numbers, 294 and 295. Union spies were certain that the powerful Laird rams were being secretly built for the Confederacy, and they were right. Another ship, temporarily called the *Canton,* was a copy of the *Alabama*. It was under construction at another Scottish shipyard.

As Union agents uncovered information about these ships and Confederate agents attempted to obtain delivery, news of the outcome of land battles at Vicksburg and Gettysburg in July 1863 appeared to spell the end of Confederate hopes. Such defeats began to convince the British to take a stronger line in opposing the delivery of potential warships to the Confederacy. The two rams, outfitted with iron prongs on their bows, were intended to destroy the Union gunboats enforcing the blockade. They were finally purchased by the British government in October 1863. On the same day, Britain also seized the *Canton*.

The limited industrial capacity of the Confederacy began to tell on Mallory's shipbuilding program in the South in 1863. Even that limited capacity began to shrink under competition with the needs of the Confederate army and as Union armies gradually took over territory. Two ironclads under construction at Yazoo City in Mississippi were abandoned. Another was captured and burned in North Carolina. Construction began on others, never completed, on the Tombigbee River above Mobile. Even so, the Confederacy succeeded in putting several ironclads into service to protect the ports of North Carolina and Richmond, including the *Albemarle* and the *Raleigh,* both of which defeated and drove off more lightly-armored Union gunboats. Even with the supply of British-built ships in danger and with a struggle to find enough iron for domestic-built ironclad gunboats, Secretary Mallory had another hope, the ingenuity of Confederate inventors.

TORPEDOES

The development of torpedoes by Confederate officers and technicians took place on the inland waterways of the West and in the rivers and harbors of the Gulf and the Atlantic. The stories of some of the highly secret innovations were never fully revealed, while in other cases, memoirs and surviving reports gave quite explicit details. In the West, Captain Isaac Brown had destroyed the *Cairo* in 1862 and so intimidated the officers aboard other Union gunboats with improvised, river-emplaced torpedoes that he succeeded in defending the upper Yazoo River from attack by David Porter's fleet. In response, the Union developed a "torpedo rake," a primitive form of mine-sweeper. Constructed of logs with grappling hooks slung below, the bootjack-shaped rake was designed by Colonel Charles R. Ellet of the Union army. Even so, by the end of 1862, Admiral Porter admitted that the Yazoo was too full of torpedoes, backed up by shore emplacements of snipers, to be taken.

Confederate secretary of the navy Stephen Mallory was willing to try a wide variety of technological innovations, including ironclads, torpedo boats, mines, and submersibles. *(Library of Congress, Prints and Photographs Division, LC-DIG-cwpb-05609)*

Early in 1863, Captain Isaac Brown began to develop a new supply of torpedoes, with an improved design. Invented by two Texans, Dr. J. R. Fretwell and E. C. Singer, who was a relative of the Singer of sewing machine fame, the Fretwell-Singer torpedo was produced in numbers. It consisted of a floating cone of tin, partially filled with gunpowder. A rod made of iron, with a spring-activated plunger, ran through the heart of the device. When the torpedo came in contact with a passing ship, a saucer-shaped plate would fall from the neck of the cone, pulling out a safety pin. Then the spring-driven plunger would smash into a percussion cap inside the water-proof container of gunpowder, exploding the mine with enough force to sink a major river vessel. Although approved by a Confederate examining board, the approval came too late to provide a defense of Yazoo City in the spring of 1863. After helping the Confederate navy evacuate their yard at Yazoo City, Captain Brown went into hiding and placed several of the Fretwells to protect the city. On July 13, 1863, two of the mines ripped through the hull of the large Union *Baron de Kalb* gunboat sinking it as it approached the city.

In the East, Confederate general Gabriel Rains developed a type of land mine whose use was highly controversial. A veteran of the Seminole Indian wars earlier in the century, Rains had long experimented with explosives. He developed a type of booby-trap that Union officers decried as a barbarous murder weapon, rather than a legitimate weapon of war. Rains planted the devices along the sandy roadways leading to Richmond, disguising some in bags of flour or in wells where invading troops would set them off. When General Longstreet and others complained to the Confederate secretary of war that the mines were not the sort of device that a Southern gentleman could honorably employ, Rains was reassigned to work on river defenses. He was put in charge of the submarine defenses of the James and Appomattox rivers in June 1862. Rains soon came up with a device, known as a keg torpedo, that could be mass produced. Lager-beer barrels were confiscated throughout the Confederacy. Each was caulked and pitched, and then loaded with between 35 and 120 pounds of gunpowder, fixed with a friction fuse, and then moored in a harbor or river channel. The key to the device was a Rains invention, a highly sensitive friction fuse, whose design remained secret during the war, and consisted of a chemical mix of potassium chlorate, sulphuret of antimony, and powdered glass. The kegs were loaded so that the fused end floated upward. The chemical mixture was placed inside a thin copper shield, which, when slightly dented, activated the fuse and set off the main gunpowder charge. Cheap and easy to make, the Rains keg torpedoes became a major deterrent to Union fleets using the Virginia rivers.

John A. Dahlgren was a naval ordnance innovator and commander of the Southern Blockading Squadron for the Union navy. *(Library of Congress, Prints and Photographs Division, LC-B8172–1862)*

However, Rains's first success came from another invention of his, the frame torpedo. This consisted of a 15-inch artillery shell weighing almost 400 pounds and mounted on a log structure at the bottom of river and harbor channels. Rains constructed these barriers in the Ogeechee River, near Savannah, Georgia. In February 1863, when the captain of the Confederate cruiser *Nashville* attempted to break out to sea to join *Florida* and *Alabama,* he accidentally ran the ship aground. A group of Union monitors closed in to fire on the helpless raider, unknowingly advancing across a line of frame torpedoes emplanted by Rains. As the *Nashville* burned, the large, 844-ton monitor, USS *Montauk,* struck one of the mines, detonating it. The mine ripped a hole in the hull, and the *Montauk* captain, discovering that pumps could not keep ahead of the rising water, ran the monitor aground. Later, *Montauk* was patched and towed back to Port Royal, South Carolina, for repairs. Rains went on to provide torpedo defenses at Charleston and at Mobile.

In two major engagements, the Union navy attempted a frontal assault on the defenses of Charleston. The first such effort, led by Samuel Du Pont in April 1863, resulted in severe damage to the invading fleet, both from the ring of shore batteries and from Confederate vessels. Du Pont's successor, Admiral John

A. Dahlgren, also failed to reduce the harbor fortresses, although he was able to force the evacuation of Battery Wagner. Aided by the capture of a signals code book in the earlier battle, Confederates were able to predict the actions of the Union ships. The combination of shore fire, torpedo emplacement, and gunfire from several Confederate gunboats continued to keep Union forces from capturing Charleston from the sea.

DAVID TORPEDO BOATS

The Confederates developed the first torpedo boats, with the personal approval of Secretary Mallory. The Confederate navy's chief constructor, John Porter, assigned the work on one of the earliest ones to a shipyard in Charleston. Although hampered by the lack of iron for sheathing, the first torpedo boat was ready for launching in July 1863, although without armor. The small vessel sat so low in the water that it was almost submerged, and it burned high-quality anthracite coal that gave off little smoke. Named the *Torch,* the boat set out on an attack on August 21, 1863, against the Union ironclad *New Ironsides.* Even though the attack failed when the engine stalled and *Torch* could not be properly maneuvered, the sighting of the vessel spread panic in the Union navy. Not giving up on the idea, the Confederates further developed the idea of a small torpedo launch.

Built near Charleston, the *David* was 54 feet long and 5 feet 6 inches wide, shaped like a cigar. Fitted with buoyancy tanks, the boat could be partially submerged, with a torpedo on a 14-foot spar attached to the bow. The torpedo had four contact primers. The *David* was transported on a railroad flatcar to Charleston harbor and launched there. Painted gray, it was almost impossible to detect in the harbor waters. The commander was Lieutenant William Glassel, and the chief engineer was James H. Tombs.

Tombs left a detailed eyewitness account of the attack by the *David* on the *New Ironsides* on October 5, 1863. Spotted by the deck officer aboard the target ship, Glassel responded to the challenge with a shotgun blast. The *David* plunged ahead and the spar torpedo exploded beneath the *New Ironsides,* sending up a wave of water that put out the fire in the torpedo boat's small steam engine and threatened to sink the *New Ironsides.* Glassel jumped overboard and was captured, along with the engine stoker. However, Tombs swam back to the *David,* succeeded in getting the engine running, and pulled away, saving the *David* and another crew member. The damage to *New Ironsides* was considerable, but since the explosion had been along a dividing bulkhead, the ship did not sink. Even so, the ship had to be taken to drydock in Philadelphia to repair leaks, split beams, and cracks in the engine room framing. Repairs took over a year, although that fact was kept secret.[3]

The *David* made several more attacks, one against the USS *Memphis* in May 1864, and later against the U.S. steam frigate *Wabash.* The failure of the torpedoes to properly explode against the *Memphis* may have been due to sabotage by Union agents. Nevertheless, Mallory and General Beauregard recognized that the torpedo boat was a formidable weapon and rushed the completion of more of them. One was launched in Savannah, while another, the *Squib,* successfully damaged the USS *Minnesota,* a large steam frigate, near Newport News in Virginia on April 9, 1864. The Union commander of the South Atlantic blockading squadron, John A. Dahlgren, feared further attacks from the *David* class of torpedo boats; after the war he reported that he had found nine of them in the waters around Charleston. The total of those built in secrecy has never been determined.[4]

HUNLEY SINKS HOUSATONIC

The concept of a submarine had been attempted as early as the American Revolution, when David Bushnell built a one-man device, *Turtle,* with which he had attempted to blow up a British warship in New York harbor. In the first decades of the 19th century, there were at least 20 efforts at experimental submarine designs. The Union developed one, the *Alligator,* designed to attack the *Virginia,* but it was lost at sea in a storm in June 1862. One problem confronting submarine designers was the issue of propulsion. Steam engines simply would not work on a submerged vessel, where oxygen for the coal-fired engines was unavailable. The solution on most of the early designs was some form of hand-cranked propeller, operated by a small crew. The French developed another idea, the 146-foot-long *Plongeur,* driven by a compressed-air engine. It operated experimentally in 1863.

For the Confederacy, the concept of a submarine was highly attractive. Like the torpedo gunboat, the advantages were obvious, even though the technical barriers to success were intimidating. If solutions to the problems of negative buoyancy and propulsion could be found, submarines offered a means of attacking the powerful warships of the blockade, steaming slowly or anchored in waters just offshore of the major ports of the South.

Since so many records of the Confederacy were lost, and its naval archives destroyed at the end of the war, little is known of some of these experiments. In New Orleans, a group of private financiers constructed the *Pioneer* in 1862. Years after the Civil War, a hull was found near New Orleans and hauled ashore. Presumed to be the *Pioneer,* the cigar-shaped hull was not quite 20 feet long and may have once mounted an explosive on a spar rigged in front, although one set of documents suggested that the explosive would be towed.[5]

One of the participants in the design of the *Pioneer* was Horace L. Hunley, who moved from New Orleans to Mobile to experiment with the construction of a new design. The *Hunley* measured about 40 feet in length and carried its explosive on a spar mounted on the bow of the boat. The vessel had two hatches on short conning towers, with thick glass portholes. The crew consisted of nine men, including two officers. Eight men would work the cranks that turned the propeller, getting the boat up to five knots at full exertion. Hunley completed work on his device in Mobile, and it was then shipped to Charleston by rail on two flatcars. At Charleston, further experiments and tryouts were conducted. Known first as the *American Diver,* the vessel sported many innovations, including rubber gaskets to seal the hatches, a detachable keel to provide instant buoyancy, and pumps for the ballast tanks. The spar torpedo was in a copper vessel, with a double ignition system, consisting of contact percussion caps as well as a line that could be pulled to ignite the explosive.

Despite several such intelligent aspects of the design, the boat was difficult to handle, and, when air became scarce, crews could easily panic. On several trial runs, the craft sank, taking all or part of four crews to their deaths. By January 1863 one crew had died in Mobile and two in Charleston. On October 15, 1863, the little boat sank again, this time taking the life of Hunley himself. After his death, a more careful and measured training program began under Lieutenant George Dixon of the Alabama Infantry.

After training, and impatient to act, Dixon took the boat out at dusk on February 17, 1864, during a flat calm in the harbor. It was a moonlit night, and the officer of the deck aboard the Union blockade ship *Housatonic* spotted a strange object in the water at 8:45. He called general quarters, and the anchors were raised. The ship got under way, but an explosion ripped through the stern of the ship, sinking it in minutes. Damaged either by the explosion or by a lucky shot from the *Housatonic, Hunley* sank with all hands. *Housatonic* settled into the mud, and the crew climbed into the rigging to await rescue. Although justly famous for its mark in history as the first submarine ever to sink an enemy ship, the *Hunley* sank the *Housatonic* while operating on the surface.

No sooner had the submarine been invented and used, than Admiral Dahlgren of the South Atlantic blockading squadron, ordered immediate countermeasures. Assuming the attack on the *Housatonic* to have been made by a *David* torpedo boat, he ordered that Union ships be kept on the move, or, while anchored, that they be protected by log booms and chain-nets. Furthermore, Dahlgren spurred the development of torpedo boats by the Union that could attack Confederate ships with spar torpedoes. The first successful submarine had initiated an arms race among maritime powers that continued in various forms for the next century and more.[6]

KEARSARGE AND ALABAMA

The cruise of the *Alabama* came to an end in June 1864. After a stay in the port of Cherbourg, France, Captain Raphael Semmes decided to sail out of the harbor and take on the USS *Kearsarge,* under the command of John A. Winslow, just beyond the territorial waters of France. There were several reasons for his decision. If he had stayed longer, he ran the risk that the French would confiscate the ship. Furthermore, a more powerful Union warship, the steam frigate *Niagara,* at over 4,000 tons and carrying 36 guns, could easily blow *Alabama* out of the water and Semmes feared it would soon arrive. Semmes announced to his adversary that he was coming out to do battle, so that no one could claim that the cruiser was attacked while fleeing. Furthermore, he may have assumed that the two ships were an even match. After all, the crews were about the same size, with 149 on the *Alabama* and 163 on the *Kearsarge.* However, Semmes and his first officer, John M. Kell, both later claimed that they did not know that *Kearsarge* was protected by chain armor hung over the sides and then covered with planking. Their accounts convey a tone of disappointment that their final battle as naval ship against naval ship was not a fair and even match of wooden hull and gunfire. The protection of the chain armor on *Kearsarge,* combined with dampened gunpowder aboard *Alabama,* made the engagement far from an equal duel.

On Sunday, June 19, 1864, *Alabama* slowly moved out of the Cherbourg harbor, closely followed by a French warship *Couroune,* keeping close watch to ensure that Semmes left French waters before engaging in battle. As soon as *Alabama* sighted *Kearsarge,* the two ships steered for each other at full speed. At 1,800 yards, *Alabama* fired a long-range gun. Knowing the superiority of his guns at close range, Winslow steamed closer, and the two ships circled each other, exchanging broadsides. *Kearsarge* gunners were better practiced and their ammunition was in better condition. Even so, one shot from *Alabama* lodged

Union ships carried heavy weapons, such as these 11-inch Dahlgrens aboard the USS *Pawnee*. (*Library of Congress, Prints and Photographs Division, LC-USZ62–94892*)

in the sternpost of *Kearsarge,* but failed to detonate on impact. After about an hour, the superior gunnery of *Kearsarge* punched holes at the waterline of the Confederate cruiser. Semmes lowered his flag as a signal of surrender and sent a boat to *Kearsarge* to ask for help in off-loading the wounded and survivors as his ship sank. Winslow hesitated, however, apparently suspecting Semmes of some trickery. A nearby British yacht, observing the battle, sailed in and rescued Semmes and some of his officers, taking them to neutral England, where they were safe from capture. Altogether, 26 seamen aboard the *Alabama* died, most from drowning.

As word of the battle reached the Confederacy, the loss of the most successful of the Confederate cruisers was a blow to morale. Some, like Mary Chesnut, thought Semmes had acted rashly, out of a misguided sense that he had to match guns with a Union ship. However, the naval war was far from over.

DAMN THE TORPEDOES

Both Ulysses S. Grant and Admiral Farragut had developed plans for attacking the major port of Mobile, Alabama, but the assault was delayed until the summer of 1864. During the delay, the Confederate navy commissioned a large ironclad for defense of the city from any sea-borne attack, the CSS *Tennessee*. When Farragut planned an attack without army support, he had heard through intelligence channels of the development of the huge ironclad and sought similar ships to accompany his fleet. The Confederacy's meager resources were being turned to even more ironclad defenses, while the Union navy had few ironclads to spare. Finally the Union moved several ironclad monitors to the area to supplement Farragut's forces, including *Manhattan* and *Tecumseh* and two light-draft ironclads from the Mississippi squadron, the *Winnebago* and *Chickasaw.* The *Manhattan* and *Tecumseh* were huge by the standards of the day, at 2,100 tons and 225 feet long, incorporating lessons from the earlier *Monitor-Virginia* clash. Each carried 15-inch cannon, firing projectiles that weighed 430 pounds. The *Manhattan* and the *Chickasaw,* although smaller at 1,300 tons, were quite efficient. With a shallow draft of six feet, each ship mounted two turrets with four 11-inch Dahlgren cannons. Altogether, Farragut's four monitors represented a formidable force.

The Confederates supplemented *Tennessee* with two very slow floating batteries, *Huntsville* and *Tuscaloosa.* Furthermore, the Confederates commanded several land forts of strategic importance, including forts Gaines and Morgan at the entrance to Mobile Bay, and set out channel obstructions and contact-torpedoes that would force any incoming fleet under the guns of Fort Morgan.

In the attack on Mobile Bay on August 5, USS *Tecumseh* was damaged by the guns at Fort Morgan and drifted into the torpedo field, where the heavy ship plowed into a torpedo, detonated, and sank by the bow. The captain and 92 others went down with the ship.

As the wooden *Brooklyn* hesitated and then backed from the minefield, Farragut, strapped in the rigging of his flagship *Hartford,* shouted to his deck officer to damn the torpedoes and move ahead. USS *Hartford* then engaged CSS *Tennessee.* The large Confederate ironclad at first appeared to be repeating the battle at Hampton Roads, where *Virginia* had destroyed one wooden ship after another. But Farragut maneuvered his monitors and gunboats to attack the smaller Confederate ships. The next morning, the three small Union monitors—*Manhattan, Winnebago,* and *Chickasaw*—concentrated their fire on CSS *Tennessee,* and other gunboats joined in to bring down the Confederates' large ironclad. By 10 in the morning, the battle was over. Even though Farragut won a victory in this clash of ironclads, the Union had lost *Tecumseh,* had sustained damage to several of the wooden ships, and had suffered casualties of 145 officers and men killed and another 180 wounded. Farragut, with his shouted command from the rigging, went down in history as one of the naval heroes of the war.

With control of the bay, Union forces reduced Fort Morgan over the next two weeks, finally taking it on August 23. Even so, the city of Mobile remained in Confederate hands, and it would take a later advance by ground troops to reduce it. The Confederate navy had lost the battle of Mobile Bay and had lost the massive CSS *Tennessee* because it did not have the industrial capacity to match the Union's production of ironclad ships and heavy ordnance.

The South was rife with rumors of continuing submarine experiments, some of which may have been true but were never revealed because of the secrecy surrounding the design and construction of the boats. One such boat, the *St. Patrick,* known as a Trout Boat, was built at Selma, Alabama, and intended for the defense of Mobile. It was propelled on the surface by a small steam engine, and, when submerged, the propeller was hand-cranked. Designed by John Halligan, the ingenious device went through laborious and repeated trials and was not ready for the fateful battle at Mobile in August 1864. Finally, Confederate officers lost patience with Halligan, who sometimes removed crucial parts of the submarine so that his superiors would not take the boat into action without him. Over Halligan's objections, Confederate sailors finally outfitted it for action in

February 1865. Mounting a 40-pound charge on a spar, the boat was used in an unsuccessful attack on one of the Union ships in Mobile Bay. After the torpedo failed to detonate, the partially submerged sub pulled alongside the USS *Octorora,* where a Union sailor grabbed it by the hot smokestack. Unable to hold it for more than a moment, he released the small sub which was then driven off by a hail of gunfire from the target ship. That submarine was never used again.[7]

The North turned the torpedo-boat concept against the Confederacy. A young Union officer, Commander Wiliam B. Cushing, proposed to destroy the ironclad CSS *Albemarle,* moored near Plymouth, North Carolina, where it helped to keep open some of the last Confederate ports for blockade runners. On the night of October 27, 1864, he slipped *Picket Boat No. 1* past withering gunfire, over slippery floating barricade logs, and set off a torpedo near the huge ironclad. Cushing and one of his men swam to safety, and *Albemarle* sank in eight feet of water. The Union was then able to retake Plymouth and the Roanoke River.

LAST CRUISES OF THE SEA DOGS

With the loss of the *Alabama* in June 1864, the Confederacy's cruiser strategy suffered a serious blow. However, in August 1864, the former blockade-runner *Tallahassee* ventured out into the North Atlantic on a 10-day cruise that netted 33 ships. Operating off New York, *Tallahassee* burned pilot boats, immigrant ships, and others, taking care to incur no casualties. However, when *Tallahassee's* Captain John Taylor Wood brought the ship into a neutral Canadian port, he found an inhospitable reception. With the decline in Confederate fortunes by late 1864, and with the hardening of British policy, Confederate cruisers were no longer welcome, even for short refueling stays. On the return to North Carolina, the ship faced a controversy.

Some believed the raid had only hardened Union policy and drawn attention to North Carolina ports. The name of the ship was changed to the *Olustee,* and on a separate cruise, it bagged six more ships. At the same time *Chickamauga* conducted raids. *Chickamauga* was a sister ship that resembled *Tallahassee/Olustee* and was sometimes mistaken for it by Union merchant vessels and pursuing Union naval ships. However, the glory days of cruising were over, and the short 1864 campaign of these blockade-runners converted to cruisers was probably a bad strategy. The two cruisers took ships of little value, they deprived the blockade runner fleet of needed ships, and they drew attention to North Carolina's Fort Fisher and the last open ports of the Confederacy. The *Olustee* converted once again, appropriately, to the *Chameleon,* and returned to its career as a blockade-runner before finally escaping to England.

In that same 1864 summer, *Florida* continued its cruise, under the command of Charles M. Morris, capturing 10 more Union ships between July and September. The cruiser anchored in Bahia, Brazil, in the fall for repairs, and, while there, the ship was seized on October 7, 1864, by the USS *Wachusett,* under Commander Napoleon Collins. Since both ships were in the harbor, Collins's act was a direct and gross violation of Brazilian neutrality, loudly protested both by the Confederacy and Brazil. Under Collins, the USS *Wachusett* towed the *Florida* to the Chesapeake, where it sank after collision with an army transport. Although Collins was later convicted by a court-martial for his violation of international law, Secretary of the Navy Welles set aside the sentence. The illegal act under the rules of the sea had severely reduced the Confederate threat. With

Nashville destroyed, with *Georgia* confiscated in Britain, with *Alabama* sunk off France, with *Florida* captured by the Union and then sunk, and with *Tallahassee/Olustee* and *Chickamauga* retired by November 1864, it seemed the Confederate cruiser strategy was finished.

In Europe, however, Confederate agents Bulloch in Britain and Slidell in France continued to struggle to get warships out to sea despite the growing efficiency of Union spies and resistance by the European powers. The Confederacy's only European-built ironclad, completed in France, equipped and commissioned as *Stonewall,* was tracked by Union ships off Spain and Portugal. However, that potential raider relied on coal and never saw action. The captain eluded Union pursuit and steamed into Cuban waters, where the ship was impounded early in 1865.

However, one other ship, the British-built *Sea King,* was acquired by the Confederacy and slipped quietly out of British waters late in 1864. It rendezvoused off the Madeira Islands with another ship, *Laurel,* carrying coal and arms. *Sea King* was armed there and commissioned as the *Shenandoah* on October 23, 1864, beginning a remarkable cruise under Lieutenant James I. Waddell. Under orders to destroy the Union whaling fleet, Waddell took his ship halfway around the world, reaching the North Pacific in the summer of 1865. Out of touch with any source of news, Waddell kept sinking whalers and transferring their crews to ships that he bonded for several months after Appomattox. By the time he finally got a reliable news account from a British ship out of San Francisco in June 1865, he had captured 38 ships and destroyed vessels and cargoes estimated at over $1 million. Fearing that he and his crew might be tried as pirates, he sailed from the North Pacific around Cape Horn to England, where he surrendered his ship to British authorities in November 1865. *Shenandoah* was the only Confederate ship to have circumnavigated the Earth, and Waddell was the last Confederate naval officer to stop fighting.

Lincoln's secretary of the navy, Gideon Welles, brought organizational skills to his post. *(Library of Congress, Prints and Photographs Division, LC-B813–1375)*

PRECEDENTS AND PARALLELS

The Confederacy's use of maritime commando tactics, commerce raiding, and advances in technology to devise mines that could be detonated remotely or automatically, all represented the tactics of asymmetric warfare in which the weaker side employs methods that do not rely on pitting equivalent forces against each other. The Confederacy suffered from blockade and relied on weapons of stealth such as submarines, torpedoes, and mines, and upon commerce-raiding on the high seas to offset the strength of the Union, a much more powerful maritime power. A few large ironclads, scraped together from salvaged railroad iron, helped hold off the Union navy in crucial engagements. Even with these strategies, the lack of ship-building and iron-foundry facilities prevented the Confederate navy from matching the Union in sheer numbers, tonnage, and firepower of warships.

Despite the handicaps faced by the Confederacy, the cruiser campaign so damaged the Union merchant fleet that the United States never again challenged Britain as a competitor for the carrying trade of the world. In contrast to the lasting positive consequences of the war, such as the ending of slavery and the formation of a stronger central government capable of playing a major role in world affairs, the destruction of America's promise as a maritime power was a major and enduring negative outcome. However, the battles that would decide the outcome of the war were fought on land, and the last two years of the Civil War saw a level of slaughter in the clash of armies ashore that shocked the world.

CHRONICLE OF EVENTS

1863

January 1: Confederate forces drive off the blockading squadron at Galveston, Texas, and capture the Union revenue cutter *Harriet Lane;* USS *Westfield* is abandoned and blown up.

January 11: CSS *Alabama* under Raphael Semmes sinks the USS *Hatteras* off Galveston, Texas.

January 11–July 25: Alabama captures and burns 20 ships, then sails, via Jamaica, to Bahia, Brazil, thence to Capetown.

January 16: CSS *Florida,* after repairs and outfitting in Mobile, breaks out past the Union blockade. *Florida* eventually takes or destroys 38 prizes.

January 17: Confederate ships *Josiah Bell* and *Uncle Ben* engage the Union fleet off Sabine Pass, Texas, and disrupt the blockade. Confederates capture the USS *Morning Light* and USS *Velocity.*

January 31: Confederate ironclads CSS *Palmetto State* and CSS *Chicora* attempt to break the blockade at Charleston; they damage Union ships *Mercedita* and *Keystone State,* but the blockade remains in force.

February 28: USS monitor *Montauk,* under command of John L. Worden, former commander of the USS *Monitor,* steams up the Ogeechee River in Georgia, where it destroys the Confederate privateer *Rattlesnake* (the former *Nashville*). However, *Montauk* is severely damaged by a Rains frame torpedo and has to be towed to Port Royal for repair.

April 5: U.S. minister to Britain Charles Francis Adams protests the construction and outfitting in England of *Alexandra,* a commerce raider for the Confederate navy.

April 7: USS *New Ironsides* and eight other ironclads under Rear Admiral Du Pont attack the Confederate defenses in Charleston harbor. The eight ships with Du Pont are *Weehawken, Passaic, Montauk, Patapsco, Catskill, Nantucket, Nahant,* and the partially-armored *Keokuk.* Five Union ships are disabled by fire from shore batteries (*Keokuk,* which later sank, *Nantucket, Weehawken, Passaic,* and *Patapsco*), and the attack is halted. Despite the use of 15-inch guns and extensive damage to Fort Sumter, the fighting efficiency of the fort is not affected very seriously. Secretary Welles loses confidence in Du Pont as a consequence of this failed attack.

April 9: Off the French coast, English-built *Virginia* is rechristened CSS *Georgia.* Under Commander William L. Maury, the commerce raider will take nine prizes by the end of October.

May 6: CSS *Florida* captures the brig *Clarence;* the captured brig is placed in Confederate service under Lieutenant Charles Read.

June 12: The *Clarence* captures the bark *Tacony;* Lieutenant Read transfers his crew and weapons to the *Tacony* and burns the *Clarence.*

June 17: In a clash of ironclads, the Union *Weehawken* and the *Nahant* defeat and capture CSS *Atlanta* (formerly *Fingal*) early in the morning at the mouth of the Wilmington River in Wassaw Sound, Georgia. The ship is later commissioned in the U.S. Navy, February 2, 1864, and serves in the blockade and in the James River.

Frank Leslie's Illustrated Newspaper published this sketch of the Union gunboat *Commodore Barney* being blown up by an underwater mine on August 4, 1863. *(Library of Congress, Prints and Photographs Division, LC-USZ62–132414)*

June 20: CSS *Alabama* captures the bark *Conrad* and commissions it as an auxiliary cruiser, or tender, *Tuscaloosa*.

June 24: The *Tacony* captures the *Archer;* then the Confederate crew transfers to the *Archer* and burns the *Tacony*.

June 27: Confederate crew from the *Archer* captures the U.S. revenue cutter *Caleb Cushing,* at Portland, Maine; 20 miles off coast, the crew burns the cutter, which explodes, and they are taken prisoner. The *Archer* is recaptured by Union forces.

July 4: John A. Dahlgren, recently promoted to admiral, relieves Admiral Samuel F. Du Pont of command of the South Atlantic blockading squadron; the recently deceased admiral Andrew Hull Foote had been slated to replace Du Pont.

July 13: The 512-ton Union gunboat *Baron de Kalb* is destroyed by a Fretwell-Singer torpedo implanted in the Yazoo River by a Confederate team headed by Captain Isaac Brown.

July 25: CSS *Alabama* arrives off South Africa.

August 5: CSS *Alabama* captures the American bark *Sea Bride* off South Africa; the ship is disguised and sold, the only capture by Confederates ever sold.

August 5: USS *Commodore Barney* is damaged by a Confederate electric-detonated torpedo in the James River.

August 23: Admiral Dahlgren renews attempts to reduce the forts at Charleston by gunfire from ships.

August 29: Five crew members are lost during a test run of the CSS *H. L. Hunley* when it is swamped by wake of a passing ship and sinks.

September 6: Confederates evacuate Battery Wagner on Morris Island at the entrance to Charleston Harbor after bombardment from Union ships.

September 7: USS *Weehawken* runs aground during attacks at Charleston.

September 8: Union gunboats *Clifton* and *Sachem* surrender to Confederate forces at Sabine Pass, Texas.

September 9: Confederate forces repel an attack by U.S. Marines and sailors on Fort Sumter, partly due to the ability of the Confederates to decode signals between Union ships after recovering a codebook from the wreck of USS *Keokuk*.

September 24: CSS *Alabama* departs South Africa to sail the Indian Ocean and the Straits of Malacca.

October 5: The Confederate semi-submersible gunboat *David*, mounting a spar torpedo, attacks the USS *New Ironsides* in the Charleston blockade, inflicting serious damage and causing leaks that are repaired over a period of months.

October 9: In Britain, two twin-turret oceangoing ironclads are seized by the British government at the Laird shipyards. They are the *North Carolina* and the *Mississippi,* under secret contract to the Confederate government; both Laird rams later serve with the Royal Navy.

October 15: *Hunley* sinks during a practice dive, and the inventor, H. L. Hunley, and seven crew members drown.

December 6: USS *Weehawken* sinks off Charleston with the loss of 30 members of the crew, presumably because of an accident.

1864

January–March: Captain Raphael Semmes, aboard *Alabama,* cruises in the Indian Ocean and back to Capetown.

January: The British rule that *Tuscaloosa* (armed tender of the *Alabama*) is an uncondemned prize and seize the ship in Capetown for return to its owners. Title to the ship is disputed until the end of the war.

February 17: Confederate submarine *Hunley* sinks the 1,240-ton USS *Housatonic* with a spar torpedo and then is lost with all hands. This is the first engagement in which a submarine sinks an enemy warship. Union officers at first assume the attack is by a *David*-class torpedo boat.

April: The first of the Union's single-turret Canonicus-class monitors is launched. This class of monitors carries two 15-inch smoothbore guns and a crew of 85. These monitors primarily serve in blockading operations.

Ironclad gunboat, USS *Weehawken,* battles a storm on January 20, 1863. *(Library of Congress, Prints and Photographs Division, LC-USZ62–126951)*

April 9: Confederate torpedo boat *Squib* severely damages Union steam frigate *Minnesota* near Newport News, Virginia.

April 19: Operating out of North Carolina, the CSS *Albemarle,* a newly launched ironclad casemate ram, sinks the USS *Southfield* at Plymouth and succeeds in capturing the naval base there.

May 5: CSS *Albemarle* severely damages USS *Sassacus* and USS *Wyalusing,* then retreats up the Roanoke River; the Union captures CSS *Bombshell* in the same battle near Plymouth, North Carolina.

May 6: Confederates sink the 542-ton U.S. gunboat *Commodore Jones* with an electrical torpedo on the James River in Virginia.

June 11: CSS *Alabama* enters Cherbourg harbor in France for repairs.

June 19: USS *Kearsarge* sinks the Confederate commerce raider CSS *Alabama* off Cherbourg, France; under Raphael Semmes, the *Alabama* had captured or destroyed some 66 ships, with a value estimated at $6.5 million.

July 10: CSS *Florida* captures and scuttles the mail steamer *Electric Spark,* one of two Union steam merchant ships lost to Confederate raiders.

July 20: The Confederate raider CSS *Tallahassee* is commissioned. The raider eventually captures and bonds or burns 38 ships.

August 5: Battle of Mobile Bay. Admiral Farragut leads a fleet of 18 ships past the forts at the entrance to Mobile Bay, "damns" the torpedoes, and defeats the Confederate warships defending the city. The Union loses the 1,034-ton monitor USS *Tecumseh* to a torpedo. Union forces surround and capture one of the best Confederate ironclads, the casemate ram *Tennessee,* which the Union uses in the bombardment of Fort Morgan later in the month.

August 9–23: U.S. naval ships bombard Fort Morgan, Alabama.

October: The first of four Monadnock monitors is commissioned; the USS *Monadnock* serves in the North Atlantic blockading squadron, and will later participate in an attack on Fort Fisher, North Carolina, December 1864 and January 1865. The ship will later cross the Atlantic to Britain.

October 7: USS *Wachusett,* under Commander Napoleon Collins, seizes the commerce raider CSS *Florida* while both are in harbor at the Brazilian port of Bahia. Collins's act is a gross violation of Brazilian neutrality. Under Collins, *Wachusett* tows the *Florida* to the Chesapeake, where it is sunk after collision with an

Admiral Farragut had himself lashed to a mast to better view the attack on Mobile Bay. His command, "Damn the torpedoes," captured the imagination of the Union public and entered naval lore. *(Library of Congress, Prints and Photographs Division, LC-USZC4–1887)*

army transport. After two later court-martials, Collins is convicted of violating neutrality, but the penalty is waived by Secretary Welles.

October 19: The last British-built Confederate cruiser to enter service, the CSS *Shenandoah,* formerly disguised as the merchant ship *Sea King,* is commissioned as a commerce raider off the Madeira Islands under Lieutenant James Iredell Waddell, who is under orders to destroy the Union whaling fleet.

October 27: Union officer William B. Cushing, in *Picket Boat No. 1,* detonates a spar torpedo, sinking the CSS *Albemarle;* with this victory, the Union gains control of the Roanoke River and Plymouth, North Carolina.

December 9–10: Two Union ships, *Oswego* and the tug *Bazely,* are sunk by torpedoes in the Roanoke River.

December 24–25: A Union fleet attempts to take Fort Fisher at the mouth of the Cape Fear River in

North Carolina. USS *Monadnock,* the only one of this large class of monitors to see service in the war, participates in the battle.

1865

January 13–15: USS *New Ironsides,* now under Rear Admiral David Porter, leads a successful attack by ironclads against Fort Fisher at the entrance to the Cape Fear River in North Carolina. *Monadnock* participates in this battle as well.

January 15: The Union's 1,875-ton ironclad *Patapsco* strikes a torpedo off Charleston and sinks in less than a minute, taking 62 members of the crew to their deaths.

January 23: French-built ironclad cruiser CSS *Stonewall* (under the cover name *Olinda*) is delivered to Confederate captain Thomas Jefferson Page off Brittany, and sails for El Ferrol, Spain.

January 30–March 24: *Stonewall* undergoes repairs at El Ferrol, then departs for Lisbon, Portugal. Union captain Thomas Craven, with *Niagara* and *Sacramento,* does not engage *Stonewall* off Portugal and will later be charged with dereliction of duty.

February 17–18: During the evacuation of Charleston, Confederate sailors scuttle three of their ships with explosions: *Palmetto State, Chicora,* and *Charleston.*

February 25: The Confederate submarine *St. Patrick,* mounting a spar torpedo, is driven off from an attack on the USS *Octorara* in Mobile Bay.

March 1: The flagship of the South Atlantic Blockading Squadron, USS *Harvest Moon,* is sunk by a torpedo on a voyage from Georgetown to Charleston.

March 4: Union transport ship *Thorn* is sunk in the Cape Fear River by a torpedo.

March 12–April 14: Confederate torpedoes destroy eight Union vessels of various sizes in the Blakely River and in Mobile Bay, Alabama.

April 9: Despite the surrender of Robert E. Lee at Appomattox, Confederate naval forces continue military action until news of the collapse of the Confederate government reaches them.

April 24: During an effort by Lieutenant Charles Read to take the ram CSS *Webb* down the Mississippi and out to sea to continue commerce raiding, the ship is stopped at New Orleans and then destroyed by its crew.

May 8: Confederate commodore Ebenezer Farrand surrenders the Mobile squadron that had taken refuge in the Tombigbee River.

May 11: CSS *Stonewall* enters the port of Havana, Cuba, where it is sold for $16,000 to pay the crew.

June 3: Commander Jonathan Carter of the CSS ironclad *Missouri* surrenders the ship in Louisiana.

June 23: Lieutenant Waddell, commander of CSS *Shenandoah,* captures a ship containing a San Francisco newspaper reporting Lee's surrender and Jefferson Davis's proclamation that the war should continue.

June 28: Fully two months after the Confederate defeat, CSS *Shenandoah* captures 11 Union whaling ships in the Bering Sea.

August 2: CSS *Shenandoah* commander Waddell learns of the Confederate defeat from a British ship.

November 6: Seven months after the surrender of Lee, Lt. James I. Waddell turns over the cruiser CSS *Shenandoah* to British authorities in Liverpool. Waddell had circumnavigated the globe and had taken or destroyed 39 prizes during a year in Confederate service. Altogether eight Confederate navy commerce raiders (and ships they capture and commission) capture or sink 237 prizes.

Eyewitness Testimony

Upon the afternoon of the 11th inst., at half-past two o'clock, while at anchor in company with the fleet under Commodore Bell, off Galveston, Texas, I was ordered by signal from the United States flagship *Brooklyn* to chase a sail to the Southward and eastward. I got under way immediately and steamed with all speed in the direction indicated. After some time the strange sail could be seen from the *Hatteras,* and was ascertained to be a steamer, which fact I communicated to the flagship by signal. I continued the chase and rapidly gained upon the suspicious vessel. Knowing the slow rate of speed of the *Hatteras,* I at once suspected that deception was being practiced and hence ordered the ship to be cleared for action, with everything in readiness for a determined attack and a vigorous defence. . . .

I came within easy speaking range—about seventy-five yards—and upon asking, "What steamship is that?" received the answer, "Her Britannic Majesty's ship Vixen." I replied that I would send a boat aboard, and immediately gave the order. In the meantime, the vessels were changing positions, the stranger endeavoring to gain a desirable position for a raking fire. Almost simultaneously with the piping away of the boat, the strange craft again replied, "We are the Confederate steamer *Alabama*" which was accompanied with a broadside. I, at the same moment, returned the fire. Being well aware of the many vulnerable points of the *Hatteras,* I hoped, by closing with the *Alabama* to be able to board her and thus rid the seas of the piratical craft. I steamed directly for the *Alabama,* but she was enabled by her great speed (and the foulness of the bottom of the *Hatteras,* and, consequently, her diminished speed) to thwart my attempt when I had gained a distance of but thirty yards from her. At this range, musket and pistol shots were exchanged. The firing continued with great vigor on both sides. At length a shell entered amidships in the hold, setting fire to it, and at the same instant—as I can hardly divide the time—a shell passed through the sick bay, exploding in an adjoining compartment, also producing fire. Another entered the cylinder, filling the engine room and deck with steam, and depriving me of my power to manoeuvre the vessel or to work the pumps upon which the reduction of the fire depended . . .

It was soon reported to me that the shells had entered the *Hatteras* at the waterline, tearing off entire sheets of iron, and that the water was rushing in, utterly defying every attempt to remedy the evil, and that she was rapidly sinking. . . . To prevent the blowing up of the *Hatteras* from the fire which was making much progress, I ordered the magazine to be flooded, and afterward a lee gun was fired. The *Alabama* then asked if assistance was desired, to which an affirmative answer was given.

Union captain H. C. Blake, describing the destruction of USS Hatteras *by* CSS Alabama *off the coast of Texas on January 11, 1863, as quoted in Raphael Semmes,* The Confederate Raider Alabama, *pp. 167–169.*

Very soon one of the steamers was seen to be getting up steam, and in about an hour and a half afterwards she was reported to be underway, standing out for us. I lowered the propeller and directed steam to be got in readiness, and awaited the approach of the stranger, who overhauled us very slowly and seemed to reconnoiter us as he approached with great caution. I was standing all this time under topsails, away from the bar, and the stranger was approaching me stern on. . . . He came on quite boldly, and when within hailing distance of us hailed us and enquired, "What ship is that?" To which we responded, "Her Majesty's steamer *Petrel,*" and in turn enquired who he was. We could not make out his reply, although we repeated our enquiry several times. During this colloquy, I endeavored to place myself in a raking position astern of him, which he as carefully avoided by keeping his port broadside to me. From this maneuver I knew him pretty certainly to be an enemy, and having approached within about 200 yards, I directed my first lieutenant to ask again what ship it was, being loth to fire upon him without a reply, fearing that I might by possibility make a mistake. This time we heard his reply very distinctly—that he was a United States something or other; the name we could not make out. I then directed the first lieutenant to tell him that this was the Confederate States steamer *Alabama,* and to open fire upon him immediately, which we did from our starboard battery. . . . Both of us kept up a rapid fire of both artillery and rifles, when after the lapse of thirteen minutes, the enemy fired two guns from his off or starboard side and showed a light above his deck in token of his being whipped. . . . The prize proved to be the U.S. gunboat *Hatteras.* . . .

Extract from the journal of Commander Raphael Semmes of CSS Alabama, *describing the engagement with USS* Hatteras *off Galveston on January 11, 1863, in* Official Records of the Union and Confederate Navies in the War of the Rebellion, *Series 1, Vol. 2:* Operations of the Cruisers, January 1, 1863– March 31, 1864, *pp. 721–722.*

My first duty after the usual morning's muster at quarters was to hold a court of general sessions for the discharge of my vagabonds, many of who were still in irons and a beautiful-looking set of fellows they were when their irons were removed, and they were brought on deck for this purpose. They were now all sober, but the effects of the late debauches were visible upon the persons of all of them. Soiled clothing, blackened eyes, and broken noses, frowsy, uncombed hair, and matted and disordered beard, with reddened eyes that looked as if sleep had long been a stranger to them—these were the principal features. Poor Jack! How much he is to be pitied! Cut loose early from the gentle restraints of home and brought into contact with every descripiton of social vice at an age when it is so difficult to resist temptation, what wonder is it that we find him a grownup child of nature subject to no other restraint than such as the discipline of his ship imposes on him?

Confederate captain Raphael Semmes, of CSS Alabama, *regarding the holding of disciplinary actions aboard ship on January 26, 1863, against members of his crew who had become too rowdy during shore leave in Kingston, Jamaica, from his memoir,* The Confederate Raider Alabama, *p. 186.*

On the 2d of June, being in latitude 15°01 and longitude 34°56 at half-past three A.M., or just before daylight, we passed a large ship on the opposite tack. We were under topsails only, standing leisurely across the great highway. We immediately wore ship and gave chase, crowding all sail. When day dawned, the fugitive was some six or seven miles ahead of us, and as the chase was likely to be long, I fired a gun and hoisted the Confederate colors to intimate to the stranger that I would like him to be polite and save me the trouble of catching him by heaving to. Pretty soon, I fired a second gun—blank cartridge—with the same intent. But the stranger had faith in his heels, and instead of heaving to, threw out a few more kites to the balmy morning breeze. But it was of no use. Both ships were on a wind, and the *Alabama* could in consequence use her monster trysails. My large double glasses—themselves captured from a Yankee ship, the captain of which had probably bought them to look out for the "pirate"—soon told the tale. We were gaining, but not very rapidly. Still anxious to save time, when we had approached within about four miles of the stranger, we cleared away our pivot rifle and let him have a bolt. We did not quite reach him, but these rifle bolts make such an ugly whizzing and hissing and humming as they pass along that their commands are not often disobeyed. The stranger clewed up and backed his main yard and hoisted the Federal colors. We were alongside of him about half-past eleven A.M.—the chase having lasted eight hours. . . . The prisoners and such "plunder" as we desired, being brought on board the Alabama, the ship was consigned to the flames.

Confederate captain Raphael Semmes, describing the capture of the Amazonian, *a merchant ship, off Brazil on June 2, 1863, in his memoir,* The Confederate Raider Alabama, *pp. 244–245.*

On the 20th of June, we observed in latitude 25°48 and found the weather so cool as to compel us to put on our thick coats. On that day we made another capture. It was the *Conrad* of Philadelphia from Buenos Ayres for New York with part of a cargo of wool. There were certificates found on board claiming the property as British, but as there were abundant circumstances in the *res gestae* pointing to American ownership, I disregarded the certificates and condemned both ship and cargo as good prize. The *Conrad* being a tidy little bark of about three hundred and fifty tons with good sailing qualities, I resolved to commission her as a cruiser. Three or four officers and ten or a dozen men would be sufficient crew for her, and this small number I could spare from the *Alabama* without putting myself to material inconvenience. Never, perhaps, was a ship of war fitted out so promptly before. The *Conrad* was a commissioned ship with armament, crew, and provisions on board, flying her pennant, and with sailing orders signed, sealed, and delivered before sunset on the day of her capture. I sent Acting-Lieutenant Low on board to command her and gave him Midshipman George T. Sinclair as his first lieutenant; and promoted a couple of active and intelligent young seamen as masters' mates to serve with Mr. Sinclair as watch officers. Her armament consisted of the two 12-pounder brass rifled guns which we had captured from the Yankee mandarin who was going out on board the Talisman to join the Taepings; twenty rifles, and a half a dozen revolvers. I called the new cruiser the *Tuscaloosa,* after the pretty little town of that name on the Black Warrior River in the state of Alabama. It was meet that a child of the *Alabama* should be named after one of the towns of the state. The baptismal ceremony was not very elaborate. When all was ready—it being now about five P.M.—at a concerted signal the *Tuscaloosa* ran up the Confederate colors, and the crew of the *Alabama* leaped into the rigging, and taking off their hats, gave three hearty cheers! The cheers were answered by the small crew of the newly commissioned ship, and the ceremony was over. Captain Low had now only to fill away and make sail on his cruise. Our first meeting was to be at the Cape of Good Hope. My bantling was thus born upon the high seas in the South Atlantic Ocean, and no power could gainsay the legitimacy of its birth. . . . England was afterward compelled to acknowledge it . . .

> *Captain Raphael Semmes of the* Alabama, *describing the commissioning of the captured bark* Conrad *as the cruiser* Tuscaloosa, *June 20, 1863, in his memoir,* The Confederate Raider Alabama, *pp. 249–250.*

On the morning of the 26th of June we made Portland light. Off Portland I picked up two fishermen, who, taking us for a pleasure party, willingly consented to pilot us into Portland. From the fishermen I learned that the revenue cutter *Caleb Cushing* was in the harbor of Portland, and the passenger steamer to New York—a stanch, swift propeller—would remain in Portland during the night. I at once determined to enter the harbor, and at night to quietly seize the cutter and steamer.

At sunset we entered the harbor and anchored in full view of the shipping. I explained to my officers what I expected to do after dark. My engineer, Mr. Brown, expressed his doubts as to his ability to start the engines of the steamer proposed to be captured without the assistance of another engineer. I felt confident that Mr. Brown would do his utmost to perform the duty required of him, but as the nights were very short it was evident that if we failed to get the steamer underway, after waiting to get up steam, we could not get clear of the forts before we were discovered. As the wind was blowing moderately out of the harbor, I then decided to capture the cutter, and after getting from under the forts to return and fire the shipping.

At 1:30 a.m. we boarded the cutter *Caleb Cushing* and captured her, without noise or resistance. As the cable could not be slipped, it was 2 o'clock before we got underway. The wind was now very light, the tide was running in, and before we could get from under the guns of the forts day dawned.

At 10:00 a.m., when about 20 miles off the harbor, two large steamers and three tugs were discovered coming out of Portland. The cutter was cleared for action, and as soon as the leading steamer was in range, we opened fire upon her. After firing five rounds from the pivot gun, I was mortified to find that all projectiles for that gun were expended. From the movements of the enemy's steamers it was evident that they intended to attack us simultaneously on each side and endeavor to clear our deck with their sharpshooters. It was plain that we could offer but an ineffectual resistance, and therefore I directed the cutter to be set on fire and the crew to take to the boats. At 11:30 I surrendered myself and crew to the steamer *Forest City.* At 12 o'clock the cutter blew up.

> *Lieutenant C. W. Read, of the Confederate navy, reporting to Secretary of the Navy Stephen Mallory on the seizure of the revenue cutter,* Caleb Cushing, *on June 27, 1863, in a report sent October 19, 1864,* Official Records of the Union and Confederate Navies in the War of the Rebellion, *Series 1, Vol. 2: Operations of the Cruisers, January 1, 1863–March 31, 1864, p. 657.*

Rebel pirates are playing the deuce with our commerce. They are now engaged in the chivalric work of burning fishing smakes off Cape Sable. But their sending boats into Portland Harbor and capturing the revenue cutter *Caleb Cushing* does them credit. She was pursued and blown up and her crew brought back in irons, however.

> *George T. Strong northern philanthropist, in his diary entry for June 27, 1863, commenting on Confederate cruiser actions and the attack on the* Caleb Cushing, *in Allen Nevins, ed.,* The Diary of George Templeton Strong, *p. 326.*

July 13, 1863

So poor in resources were we, that in order to make a beginning I borrowed a five gallon glass demijohn, and procuring from the army the powder to fill it and an artillery friction tube to explode it, I set these two enterprising men to work with a coil of small iron wire which they stretched from bank to bank, the demijohn filled with inflammable material being suspended from the middle, some feet below the surface of the water, and so connected with the friction tube inside as to ignite when a vessel should come in contact with the wire. Soon after it was put in position, the iron-clad *Cairo* came up the river, and keeping the middle of the stream, hit the demijohn, and within twelve minutes went to the bottom in thirty feet of water.

In this way a belligerent vessel was "neutralized" by an enemy's torpedo. The moral strength thus added to our defenses may be inferred from an anecdote reported to me soon after. One of our Confederate people went on board a Union gun-boat off the mouth of the Yazoo, under flag of truce, and met there an old messmate and friend, and said banteringly to him, "Tom, why don't you go up and clean out the Yazoo?" "I would as soon think of going to [hell] at once," was the answer, "for Brown has got the river chock-full of torpedoes."

I also made a contract with Dr. Fretwell and Mr. Norman, then at Yazoo City, for fifty or more of these destructives on Dr. Fretwell's plan—automatic action on being brought in contact with a vessel or boat. But the difficulty of procuring materials prevented the completion of the contract for the whole number in time.

On the morning of the Union advance upon Yazoo City [July 13, 1863], I had myself placed two of these "Fretwells" half a mile below our land-battery of one rifled 6-inch gun—handled by the same men—the same gun, in fact, that had aided in the defense of Fort Pemberton. The *De Kalb,* had there felt this gun, and it came twice within its range on this day,—retiring both times without unreasonable delay,—but when our sailor crew found themselves uncovered by our land force, and a whole division of Union men within rifle-range, they withdrew under order, and the *De Kalb,* seeing our gun silent advanced for the third time, getting as far as the torpedoes, and there suddenly disappearing beneath the waters of the Yazoo.

Captain Isaac Brown, CSN, recalling the emplacement of torpedoes in the Yazoo River, July 13, 1863, as published in Robert Underwood Johnson and Clarence Clough Buel, Battles and Leaders of the Civil War, *Vol. III, p. 580.*

The *David* struck the *Ironsides* about 15 feet on the starboard quarter, and the torpedo some 6 ½ feet below the surface. The *David* was going full speed when she struck, but the engine had just been reversed. The concussion was severe; so much so that along with the volume of water thrown up and into the *David* the engine was disabled, and would not work. I reported this to Lieutenant Glassell, who then gave orders for us all to abandon the *David* as she was apparently sinking. The *Ironsides* kept up a severe fire with small arms, for at the time we were so close to her quarter, she could not use her large guns. While hanging on to the *David,*

and trying to keep away from the bullets, I noticed that a great many struck a large iron buoy, that was a great distance off the bow of the *Ironsides.* Sullivan, the fireman, did not leave the boat until I told him to, and then Lieutenant Glassell and he, each having a life preserver, swam away in the direction of the Yankee transports. As the flood of water had taken the rest of the preservers, I also went overboard, but without a life preserver, and started to swim in the direction of Morris Island; but looking back and seeing that the *David* was still afloat, concluded to swim back and make another effort to save her. On reaching her, I found that Pilot Cannon was hanging to the life lines, as he could not swim a stroke.

After getting aboard the *David* and righting the engine, (the trouble was caused by a piece of the iron ballast being thrown between parts of the machinery), I hauled Cannon aboard, started up fires, and, when ready, started the engine ahead, made the turn up stream between the *Ironsides* and a monitor just east of her, and as we turned came almost near enough to the monitor's quarter to touch her. As we headed toward the harbor and through the fleet and guard boats, they all fired wild, for they were about as badly rattled as we were. We passed right between the two guard boats, but for some reason neither fired a shot at us.

Account by Confederate engineer James H. Tomb, describing the attack of the David *on the* New Ironsides, *October 5, 1863, in R. Thomas Campbell, ed.,* Engineer in Gray, Memoirs of Chief Engineer James H. Tomb, CSN, *pp. 68–71.*

The effect of submarine torpedoes exploded in contact with the bottoms of vessels is generally understood; for though experiments have been very limited, their results, and particularly the results of the attempt upon the *Ironsides* at Charleston and upon a gunboat on the James River, have been instructive and satisfactory.

As to the best means of thus using submarine torpedoes in offensive war much speculation and many interesting devices have been called forth. But as yet no practicable plan that I am aware of has been devised for the construction of such a vessel as this mode of warfare demands, and as General Beauregard evidently refers to. That they may be carried beneath the water at the end of a spar attached to the stem of a vessel and exploded by impact against an opposing ship with terrible effect upon it, and without serious injury to the torpedo vessel, is well understood. . . .

It is proper to say, however, that it will always be in the power of the enemy to anchor his ship and protect her against torpedo boats by means familiar to seamen and readily attainable, and similar to those now employed to protect the *Ironsides*. And it is believed that the Federal ironclads anchored at Charleston Harbor can protect themselves against such attacks with more certainty than against those made by heavy guns or heavy rams.

Extract from a letter sent by the Confederate secretary of the navy, S. R. Mallory, to General P. G. T. Beauregard, responding to suggestions regarding the construction of boats especially designed to carry torpedo weapons, December 19, 1863, in Official Records of the Union and Confederate Navies in the War of the Rebellion, *Series I, Vol. 15,* Operations: South Atlantic Blockading Squadron, October 1, 1863–September 30, 1864, *pp. 699–700.*

About 8:45 P.M. the officer of the deck, Acting Master J. K. Crosby, discovered something in the water about 100 yards from and moving towards the ship. It had the appearance of a plank moving in the water. It came directly towards the ship, the time from when it was first seen till it was close alongside being about two minutes.

During this time the chain was slipped, engine backed, and all hands called to quarters.

The torpedo struck the ship forward of the mizzenmast, on the starboard side, in a line with the magazine. Having the after pivot gun pivoted to port we were unable to bring a gun to bear upon her. About one minute after she was close alongside the explosion took place, the ship sinking stern first and heeling to port as she sank.

Most of the crew saved themselves by going into the rigging, while a boat was dispatched to the *Canandaigua*. This vessel came gallantly to our assistance and succeeded in rescuing all but [six] ... officers and men missing and supposed to have been drowned.

Account by Lieutenant F. J. Higginson of the Housatonic *after that ship had been sunk by the placement of a spar torpedo by CSS Hunley, in the first successful use of a submarine in warfare, February 17, 1864, in* Official Records of the Union and Confederate Navies in the War of the Rebellion, *Series I, Vol. 15,* Operations: South Atlantic Blockading Squadron, October 1, 1863–September 30, 1864, *p. 328.*

The *Paul Jones* is just in, with the unpleasant news of the disaster to the *Housatonic*. ... The success of this attempt will no doubt cause a resort to the torpedoes along the whole line of blockade, and it behooves the commanding officer to resort to every precaution to avert a series of disasters.

As the torpedo boat passed by the ironclads within the bar, I think the inference is fair that the means used to protect them have been tried by the "Davids," perhaps, unknown to us, and found sufficient.

All vessels at anchor, inside or outside, are therefore to use outriggers and hawsers with netting, or if outside, are to keep underway.

You will take any further measures that you may deem necessary to keep off these torpedoes.

You will at once clear the inner harbor of all vessels not required for the blockading vessels. Some can leave for [Port Royal, South Carolina] or Stono, and those which remain inside must anchor in the least water, with outriggers, etc.

The *Wabash* may leave for this port, as she is not capable of much movement, and is too valuable a mark for the torpedoes.

Admiral John Dahlgren, in an order dated February 19, 1864, to Captain S. C. Rowan of the Union navy, requiring precautions to be taken after the successful attack on the Housatonic *on February 17, in* Official Records of the Union and Confederate Navies in the War of the Rebellion, *Series I, Vol. 15,* Operations: South Atlantic Blockading Squadron, October 1, 1863–September 30, 1864, *p. 338.*

The Department will readily perceive the consequences likely to result from this event; the whole line of blockade will be infested with these cheap, convenient, and formidable defenses, and we must guard every point. The measures for prevention may not be so obvious.

I am inclined to the belief that in addition to the various devices for keeping the torpedoes from the vessels, an effectual preventive may be found in the use of similar contrivances.

I would therefore request that a number of torpedo boats be made and sent here with dispatch. ...

I have attached more importance to the use of torpedoes than others have done, and believe them to constitute the most formidable of the difficulties in the way to Charleston. Their effect on the *Ironsides*, in October, and now on the *Housatonic*, sustains me in this idea.

The Department will perceive from the printed injunctions issued that I have been solicitous for some time in regard to these mischievous devices, though it may not be aware of the personal attention which I have also given to the security of the ironclads; I naturally feel disappointed that the rebels should have been able to achieve a single success, mingled with no little concern, lest, in spite of every precaution, they may occasionally give us trouble. . . .

I desire to suggest to the Department the policy of offering a large reward of prize money for the capture or destruction of a "David;" I should say not less than $20,000 or $30,000 for each. They are worth more than that to us.

Extract from a report by Admiral John Dahlgren to Secretary of the Navy Gideon Welles, commenting on his expectation that the Confederacy will employ more torpedoes, in the aftermath of the attack on the Housatonic, *February 19, 1864, in* Official Records of the Union and Confederate Navies in the War of the Rebellion, *Series I, Vol. 15,* Operations: South Atlantic Blockading Squadron, October 1, 1863–September 30, 1864, *pp. 329–330.*

I have now to explain that this decision was not founded on any general principle respecting the treatment of prizes captured by the cruisers of either belligerent, but on the peculiar circumstances of the case. The *Tuscaloosa* was allowed to enter the port of Cape Town, and to depart, the instructions of the 4th of November not having arrived at the cape before her departure. The captain of the *Alabama* was thus entitled to assume that he might equally bring her a second time into the same harbor, and it becomes unnecessary to discuss whether, on her return to the cape, the *Tuscaloosa* still retained the character of a prize, or whether she had lost that character and had assumed that of an armed tender to the *Alabama,* and whether that new character, if properly established and admitted would have entitled her to the same privilege of admission which might be accorded to her captor, the *Alabama.*

Her Majesty's Government have, therefore, come to the opinion, founded on the special circumstances of this particular case, that the *Tuscaloosa* ought to be released, with a warning, however, to the captain of the *Alabama* that the ships of war of the belligerents are not to be allowed to bring prizes into British ports,

and that it rests with her to decide to what vessels that character belongs.

Further instructions from the duke of Newcastle to the governor of the Cape of Good Hope, requiring that CSS Tuscaloosa *(former* Conrad*) be restored to its Confederate officers and crew, March 10, 1864, in* Official Records of the Union and Confederate Navies in the War of the Rebellion, *Series 1, Vol. 3:* Operations of the Cruisers, April 1, 1864– December 30, 1865, *p. 715.*

Between 9 and 10 o'clock, June 19th, everything being in readiness, we got under way and proceeded to sea. We took the western entrance of the harbor. The *Couronne,* accompanied us, also some French pilot-boats and an English steam yacht, the *Deerhound,* owned by a rich Englishman. . . . The walls and fortifications of the harbor, the heights above the town, the buildings, everything that looked seaward, was crowded with people. About seven miles from the land the *Kearsarge* was quietly awaiting our arrival.

Officers in uniforms, men at their best, Captain Semmes ordered them sent aft, and mounting a gun-carriage made them a brief address:

"Officers and seamen of the *Alabama*: You have at length another opportunity to meet the enemy, the first that has presented to you since you sank the *Hatteras.* In the meantime you have been all over the world, and it is not too much to say that you have destroyed and driven for protection under neutral flags one-half of the enemy's commerce, which at the beginning of the war covered every sea. This is an achievement of which you may well be proud, and a grateful country will not be unmindful of it. The name of your ship has become a household word wherever civilization extends. Shall that name be tarnished by defeat? [An outburst of Never! Never!] The thing is impossible. Remember that you are in the English Channel, the theatre of so much of the naval glory of our race. The eyes of all Europe are at this moment upon you! The flag that floats over you is that of a young Republic that bids defiance to her enemies, whenever and wherever found! Show the world that you know how to uphold it. Go to your quarters!"

We now prepared our guns to engage the enemy on our starboard side. When within a mile and a-quarter he wheeled, presenting his starboard battery to us. We opened on him with solid shot, to which he soon replied, and the action became active. To keep our respective broadsides bearing we were obliged to fight in a circle around a common center, preserving a distance of three quarters of a mile. When within distance of shell range, we opened on him with shell. The spanker gaff was shot away and our ensign came down. We replaced it immediately at the mizzen masthead.

The firing now became very hot and heavy. Captain Semmes, who was watching the battle from the horse block, called out to me, "Mr. Kell, our shell strike the enemy's side, doing little damage, and fall off in the water; try solid shot." From this time we alternated shot and shell.

The battle lasted an hour and ten minutes. . . . The chief engineer now came on deck and reported "the furnace fires put out," whereupon Captain Semmes ordered me to go below and "see how long the ship could float."

I did so, and returning said, "Perhaps ten minutes."

"Then, sir," said Captain Semmes, "cease firing, shorten sail, and haul down the colors. It will never do in this nineteenth century for us to go down and the decks covered with our gallant wounded."

This order was promptly executed, after which the *Kearsarge* deliberately fired into us five shots.

> *John MacIntosh Kell, executive officer aboard the* Alabama, *recounting the battle with the* Kearsarge *off the coast of France, June 19, 1864, in his memoir,* Recollections of a Naval Life, including the Cruises of the Confederate States Steamers "Sumter" and "Alabama," *as reproduced in Henry Steele Commager,* The Blue and the Gray, *pp. 875–876.*

The firing now became very hot, and the enemy's shot and shell soon began to tell upon our hull, knocking down, killing, and disabling a number of men in different parts of the ship. Perceiving that our shell, though apparently exploding against the enemy's sides, were doing but little damage, I returned to solid shot firing, and from this time onward alternated with shot and shell. After the lapse of about one hour and ten minutes our ship was ascertained to be in a sinking condition, the enemy's shell having exploded in our sides and between decks, opening large apertures, through which the water rushed with great rapidity. . . . I now hauled down my colors to prevent the further destruction of life, and dispatched a boat to inform the enemy of our condition. Although we were now but 400 yards from each other, the enemy fired upon me five times after my colors had been struck, dangerously wounding several of my men. It is charitable to suppose that a ship of war of a Christian nation could not have done this intentionally. . . .

At the end of the engagement it was discovered by those of our officers who went alongside the enemy's ship with the wounded that her midship section on both sides was thoroughly iron-coated, this having been done with chains constructed for the purpose, placed perpendicularly from the rail to the water's edge, the whole covered over by a thin outer planking, which gave no indication of the armor beneath. This planking had been ripped off in every direction by our shot and shell, the chain broken and indented in many places, and forced partly into the ship's side. She was most effectually guarded, however, in this section from penetration. . . . The enemy was heavier than myself, both in ship, battery, and crew; but I did not know until the action was over that she was also ironclad.

> *Selection from the official report of Captain Raphael Semmes on the battle between the* Alabama *and the* Kearsarge, *on June 19, 1864, dated June 21, 1864, and prepared in Southampton, England, in* Official Records of the Union and Confederate Navies in the War of the Rebellion, *Series 1, Vol. 3:* Operations of the Cruisers, *April 1, 1864–December 30, 1865, p. 650.*

Admiral Semmes, of whom we have been so proud, is a fool after all. He risked the *Alabama* in a sort of duel of ships, and now he has lowered the flag of the famous *Alabama* to the *Kearsarge*. Forgive who may, I cannot!

> *Planter-class diarist Mary Chesnut in her diary entry for July 25, 1864, in Ben Ames Williams, ed.,* A Diary from Dixie, *p. 421.*

Sir it is with feelings of indescribable pain, indignation, and horror, caused by the treacherous and cowardly behavior of the commander of the U.S.S. *Wachusett,* aided by the U.S. consul, who was on board the steamer at the time and escaped in her, that I now present myself before you to report the circumstances that have taken place, and most solemnly and firmly to protest against the outrage committed in the harbor of a neutral nation against a vessel belong to a country considered and recognized as a belligerent by the Government of Brazil . . .

At 3:15 a.m. on the 7th instant, that the U.S.S. *Wachusett,* disrespecting and dishonoring the Brazilian flag, and taking advantage of the absence of half of the crew of my vessel, moved from her anchorage, without the least effective resistance being made by the Brazilian fort or men-of-war, and cowardly and treacherously boarded the *Florida,* which, after a short but determined resistance, was compelled to surrender to superior force. The *Florida* was then taken in tow of the

Wachusett and towed to sea without the Brazilian forts or men of war being able to prevent it, although the United States steamer passed by them twice.

Lieutenant C. M. Morris, commander of CSS Florida, *protesting to the president of the province of Bahia in Brazil the violation of Brazilian neutrality that took place when the USS* Wachusett *seized the Confederate ship in the Brazilian harbor and towed it away, in a letter written the next day, October 8, 1864, from* Official Records of the Union and Confederate Navies in the War of the Rebellion, *Series 1, Vol. 3:* Operations of the Cruisers, *April 1, 1864– December 30, 1865, p. 634.*

Ordering all steam, went at the dark mountain of iron in front of us. A heavy fire was at once opened upon us, not only from the ship, but from men stationed on the shore. This did not disable us, and we neared them rapidly. A large fire now blazed upon the bank, and by its light I discovered that there was a circle of logs around the *Albemarle,* boomed well out from her side, with the very intention of preventing the action of torpedoes. To examine them more closely, I ran alongside until amidships, received the enemy's fire and sheered off for the purpose of turning a hundred yards away and going to the booms squarely.... This was my only chance of success, but once over the obstruction, my boat would never get out again. As I turned, the whole back of my coat was torn by buckshot, and the sole of my shoe was carried away ...

My clothing was perforated with bullets as I stood in the bow, the heel-jigger in my right hand and the exploding line in the left. We were near enough then, and I ordered the boom lowered until the forward motion of the launch carried the torpedo under the ram's overhang. A strong pull of the detaching line, a moment's wait for the torpedo to rise under the hull, and I hauled in the left hand.... The explosion took place at the same instant that 100 pounds of grape at 10 feet range crashed among us, and the dense mass of water thrown out by the torpedo came down with choking weight upon us.

Union officer William B. Cushing, describing the destruction of the CSS Albemarle *by a spar torpedo mounted aboard a steam launch, early on the morning of October 28, 1864, as quoted in Philip Van Doren Stern,* The Confederate Navy, *pp. 220–221.*

You must not think it strange that you did not hear from me while at Ferrol. On every day after my return there I expected to leave the port and consequently to encounter the two Yankee men-of-war. For many days the weather was evidently too unfavorable.... I remained off the harbors of Ferrol and Coruna (where lay the Yankee men-of-war, the *Niagara* and *Sacramento,* with steam up, in full view) until 8:30 p. m., but neither of them made a move from their anchors. This will doubtless seem as inexplicable to you as it is to myself and all of us. To suppose that these two heavily armed men-of-war were afraid of the *Stonewall* is to me incredible; and yet the fact of their conduct was such as I state it to you.... no man could have supposed that two such Yankee men-of-war would have declined to meet the *Stonewall* on such a day. I suppose their object will be to encounter us somewhere at sea, where we may have such weather as to weaken the power of the *Stonewall.* But how Captain Craven can excuse himself for not meeting her yesterday is a thing I can not conceive. Unless he has a reason beyond his control his commission would not be worth much in most navies.

Confederate captain Thomas J. Page, commander of the steam-ram, Stonewall, *commenting in a letter to Commander Bulloch on the failure of Union ships* Niagara *and* Sacramento *to engage in a gun battle off the Spanish coast, March 25, 1865, in* Official Records of the Union and Confederate Navies in the War of the Rebellion, *Series 1, Vol. 3:* Operations of the Cruisers, *April 1, 1864– December 30, 1865, pp. 741–742.*

On the morning of the 24th, a dead calm prevailing, with a smooth, glassy sea, [*Stonewall*] again made her appearance outside and to the northward of Coruna, accompanied, as on the two former occasions, by the Spanish steam frigate *Conception.* At this time the odds in her favor were too great and too certain, in my humble judgment, to admit of the slightest hope of being able to inflict upon her even the most trifling injury, whereas, if we had gone out, the *Niagara* would most undoubtedly have been easily and promptly destroyed. So thoroughly a one-sided combat I did not consider myself called upon to engage in. As she had left her boats behind her, my impression was that she would return again to Ferrol, but on Saturday morning she was reported as being still outside and lying under a point of land to the northward of Ferrol. In the afternoon, however, I learned that she was last seen early in the morning steaming rapidly to the westward, when immediately after paying our bills on shore for coal, etc., we got underway and made the best of our way to [Lisbon], our progress being considerably retarded by the inability of the *Sacramento* to keep up with us.... I have been compelled to lose sight of one of the most formidable ironclad vessels now afloat.

The captured Confederate ship *Stonewall* was photographed on the Potomac. The Capitol building is visible in the background. *(Library of Congress, Prints and Photographs Division, LC-B8171–7912)*

It may appear to some that I ought to have run the hazard of a battle, but according to my judgment I shall ever feel that I have done all that could properly be attempted toward retarding the operations and progress of that vessel.

> *Union commodore Craven, in a letter of March 29, 1865, to Secretary of the Navy Gideon Welles (later introduced in Craven's court-martial for dereliction of duty), justifying his decision not to engage in battle with the Confederate ram* Stonewall *on March 24, off Ferrol, Spain, in* Official Records of the Union and Confederate Navies in the War of the Rebellion, *Series 1, Vol. 3:* Operations of the Cruisers, April 1, 1864–December 30, 1865, *p. 461.*

At 9:30 a.m. made Ascension Island bearing W.N.W. At 10:30 commenced steaming. Discovered four vessels at anchor close in under the land. At 11:30 took a pilot; steamed inside the reef; came to with both anchors in 15 fathoms. From meridian to 4 p.m.: Fitted out four boats and boarded each vessel; they proved to be the American whalers *Edward Cary* of San Francisco; the *Hector,* of New Bedford; the *Pearl,* of New London, and the *Harvest,* of Honolulu nominally, but really an American under false colors, having no bill of sale on board, bearing American name, and in the same trade as before; consequently condemned her as prize in connection with the other three. From 4: to 6: Engage transferring stores, etc., from prizes to our ship; took the captains and mates of each ship on board of us and confined them in irons. From 6 to 8: Confined one of the captains in double irons and gagged him for disrespect; enlisted one man in the Marine corps.

> *Abstract from the log of Lieutenant James I. Waddell, commander of the Confederate cruiser* Shenandoah, *describing the capture of four Union whaling vessels at Ascension Island on April 1, 1865, from* Official Records of the Union and Confederate Navies in the War of the Rebellion, *Series 1, Vol. 3:* Operations of the Cruisers, April 1, 1864–December 30, 1865, *p. 788.*

My orders directed me to visit certain seas in preference to others. In obedience thereto I found myself in May, June, and July of this year in the Okhotsk Sea and Arctic Ocean. Both places, if not quite isolated, are still so far removed from the ordinary channels of commerce that months would elapse before any news could reach there as to the progress or termination of the American war. In consequence of this awkward circumstance I was engaged in the Arctic Ocean in acts of war as late as the 28th day of June, in ignorance of the serious reverses sustained by our arms in the field and the obliteration of the Government under whose authority I have been acting.

This intelligence I received for the first time on communicating at sea, on the 2d of August, with the British bark *Barracouta,* of Liverpool, fourteen days from San Francisco. Your lordship can imagine my surprise at the receipt of such intelligence, and I would have given to it little consideration if an Englishman's opinion did not confirm the war news, though from an enemy's port. I desisted instantly from further acts of war, and determined to suspend further action until I had communicated with a European port, where I would learn if that intelligence were true. . . . I was in an embarrassing position; I diligently examined all the law writers at my command, searching a precedent for my guidance in the future control, management, and final disposal of the vessel. I could find none. History is, I believe, without a parallel.

Comments regarding the dilemma faced by hearing of the end of the Civil War nearly four months after Appomattox, in a letter from Lieutenant James I. Waddell, commander of the Confederate cruiser Shenandoah, *to earl Russell, British secretary of state for foreign affairs, on surrendering the ship to the British government on November 6, 1865, from* Official Records of the Union and Confederate Navies in the War of the Rebellion, *Series 1, Vol. 3:* Operations of the Cruisers, April 1, 1864–December 30, 1865, *p. 784.*

8
The Turning of the Tide
January 1864–December 1864

The year 1864 saw the Civil War turn even uglier than it had in the previous two and a half years. Early in 1864, General Grant ended the prisoner-exchange system. Both sides attacked civilian facilities in daring raids that took Union troops to the edge of Richmond and Confederate troops to the northern outskirts of Washington, D.C. The war came to civilians in ways that had not been anticipated at the opening of the conflict. Union troops shelled and burned the Virginia Military Institute and other civilian properties; in response, Confederates burned the city of Chambersburg, Maryland. The reprisals continued when Union troops swept through the Shenandoah Valley intentionally destroying farms and livestock. Later, General William Tecumseh Sherman turned his troops loose to forage their way across Georgia, destroying homes, farms, tanneries, orchards, and whole towns. In Virginia, as the war around Richmond and Petersburg settled into a long-term engagement between trenches facing each other, the battles extended into a war of attrition. Sharpshooters and bushwhackers increasingly targeted individuals, acts that resembled murder more than warfare. The Union planting of a huge mine under Confederate lines outside Petersburg led to a debacle in which Union troops were slaughtered. The Confederate planting of torpedoes, or land mines, on roads in front of Union troops also demonstrated the desperation that had led both sides to abandon some of the traditional rules of war.

Throughout 1864, two different war-fighting strategies were employed by the Confederacy. In Virginia, Lee continued to defend the capital at Richmond by a combination of strong defenses and attacks on Union forces, although as his forces dwindled, he shifted from his aggressive style to a more defensive mode. As commander of the Union armies, Grant moved to the Virginia theater where he directly supervised the army operating under Meade. Near Richmond, the battle lines settled into trench warfare by midyear, with the facing earthworks circling from east of Richmond south around Petersburg. Grant patiently wore down the Confederate resistance, accepting heavy losses while gradually depleting the Confederacy's manpower and will to fight, and by striking at the Confederate's supply lines and resources. Lee's defensive methods and Grant's offensive strategy resembled those of the combatants on the Western Front 50 years later, in World War I. Grant and later French, British, and German generals of the Great War explicitly adopted the brutal concept of war by attrition.

In the Tennessee-Georgia theater, in the heartland of the South, the war took a different shape. During the first half of the year Confederate general Joseph E. Johnston adopted a strategy of fighting defensive battles, falling back and yielding territory in order to preserve his army. As Johnston's forces retreated through northwestern Georgia, Sherman's armies attempted to flank the defenders, constantly pushing them back. By contrast with the armies under Lee in Virginia, Johnston's army suffered a far lower percentage of casualties. Johnston's willingness to sacrifice territory to preserve his soldiers anticipated the tactics of national liberation forces in the late 20th century, as in China or Vietnam. Such methods may have been more suited to the status of the Confederacy as a militarily weaker combatant with fewer troops, with a popular base of support, and a wide territory through which to operate.

LEADERSHIP AND STRATEGY DECISIONS

Early in 1864, both Lincoln and Davis made decisions about leadership that would affect the outcome of the war. These command changes were generally more successful on the Union side. On February 23 Jefferson Davis appointed General Braxton Bragg to command all the Confederate armies. Braxton Bragg had lost battles and had failed to follow up on some victories, and his role in supervising the generals of the Confederate armies was that of figurehead, not operational commander. On February 24, the U.S. Congress reinstated the rank of lieutenant general and, on March 9, Lincoln formally appointed Grant to that rank. Three days later, Grant assumed command of all Union armies, relieving General in Chief Henry Halleck. Grant moved his command to Virginia, where he set up camp next to Meade, transmitting orders through Meade. The appointment of Grant horrified many in the North, who despised his disheveled appearance, reputation for drinking and cigar-smoking, and willingness to order thousands of his men into desperate battles in which both sides suffered enormous casualties. In several ways, he did not live up to the stereotype of the handsome, courageous, and gallant officer in a resplendent uniform that appealed to the public of the era. Nevertheless, Lincoln responded to Grant's critics by saying, "He fights." Grant, with his insistence on taking leadership in the field and making tough decisions that his subordinates were unwilling or constitutionally incapable of making, went far to account for the eventual Union victory.

In both North and South, drastic measures were considered and some adopted on both sides, in hopes of bringing the war to a conclusion. On January 2, Irish-born Confederate general Patrick Cleburne circulated at a command conference his memorandum proposing the arming of slaves, which was quickly suppressed. On February 13 the Confederate congress authorized the suspension of habeas corpus by the president to enforce the draft and to apprehend deserters, although the Confederacy had to deal with continued obstruction from state governors, particularly Joseph Brown of Georgia. The Confederates planned daring raids and behind-the-lines sabotage, including a plan to free prisoners of war in Chicago and an attempt to burn New York City. Combined with the increasing tempo of retaliations and destruction of civilian properties, the war clearly had moved to a new level of intensity.[1]

One of the Union's most drastic policy changes, reflecting the changed tone of the war, came when Grant ordered the ending of prisoner exchanges. He ended the exchanges on the grounds that Confederates were not paroling black prisoners, but employing or leasing them as slaves. However, probably more important to his decision, Grant had found that the honor system of paroles that had been used early in the war was not working. Troops that he had paroled at the conquest of Memphis in the summer of 1863, on the promise they would return to their homes and not fight until they were released from their parole by the freeing of an equivalent number of Union troops, had simply not waited for their official release. Hundreds of those same troops were recaptured in the 1863 campaigns around Chickamauga and Chattanooga. Grant recognized that, if he were to defeat the Confederacy by attrition and annihilation, the Union would have to keep prisoners so that they would be permanently out of action until the end of the war. Although negotiations over possible prisoner exchange systems continued off and on through 1864, the earlier widespread system of exchanged paroles was never reinstated. One unintended consequence of Grant's decision to end the traditional honor system was severe overcrowding at the Confederate prison camp, Fort Sumter, near Andersonville, Georgia. Eventually 13,000 of the 45,000 prisoners at Anderson would die in captivity. With superior manpower numbers and a policy of attrition, Grant's policy made sense in military, if not humanitarian terms.

Irish-born Confederate general Patrick Cleburne circulated a proposal to allow slaves to join the Confederate army and earn their freedom. He was one of several Confederate generals to perish at the Battle of Franklin, Tennessee. *(Library of Congress, Prints and Photographs Division, LC-USZ62–107446)*

Throughout 1864, the battles fell into two main theaters. In the heartland region stretching from Tennessee through Alabama and Georgia, Sherman led his forces, with supply lines down from Ohio through Kentucky and central Tennessee, southeastward toward Atlanta and eventually pushed them to the southeast Atlantic coast. In the northeastern theater in Virginia, Union troops attempted to drive off the defenders of Richmond and take the Confederate capital. Both efforts proceeded simultaneously.

GRANT'S ORDERS—RESOURCES OR ARMIES

Grant gave similar instructions to Sherman in the heartland and to Meade in Virginia. He ordered them both to destroy the enemy army and the resources that supported the army. That is, Meade was directed to destroy Lee's Army of Northern Virginia, while Sherman was ordered to destroy Johnston's Army of Tennessee. Meade and Sherman each interpreted the order in his own fashion.

Meade emphasized the destruction of the army and the severance of the rail lines that brought resources from the rest of the South into Richmond, a process that continued after Grant came to Virginia to personally supervise the operations there. Sherman, in the heartland, fought to get into the interior of the enemy's country and inflict damage on war resources. Sherman emphasized this aspect of his orders over the destruction of troops. As he attacked toward Atlanta he repeatedly allowed much of Johnston's army to slip away. Sherman's policy represented a good decision on his part, as Atlanta was important as the major junction point of a rail network connecting the arms center at Selma and iron and coal supplies of Alabama to Richmond. With Atlanta's factories and rail hub in Union control, the supply problems of the Confederacy would become immense.

Sherman brought three armies, totaling some 100,000 soldiers, from Chattanooga to march through northwestern Georgia toward Atlanta. His three armies represented a formidable force, capable of constantly threatening to outflank and turn the opponents. The three Union armies were the Army of the Cumberland, the Army of the Ohio, and the Army of the Tennessee. The latter term was a bit confusing, as Johnston's opposing 62,000 Confederate forces were known as the Army of Tennessee. Johnston, on his side, hoped to erode Union forces and morale, and, if possible, to entrap one of Sherman's armies and destroy it. He was elusive, avoiding decisive battle and preserving his forces, and fought only when he had the best positions.

Sherman followed the Confederate Army of Tennessee deep into Georgia, with battles at Snake Creek Gap (May 7–12), then, in sequence, Resaca, Rome Crossroads, Adairsville, and Cassville. Most of the entrapment attempts failed, but Sherman's Army of the Tennessee did get badly mauled at Kennesaw Mountain on June 27, 1864, resulting in the last major Confederate victory in that region. Frustrated at his failed attempts to outflank Johnston, Sherman ordered a frontal attack on a well-entrenched position, in 100-degree heat. In that engagement, Union casualties were 2,051 to about 432 on the Confederate side. Even though Johnston prevailed at Kennesaw Mountain, he once again retired from the field, fearing entrapment, to fall back farther. Again, Sherman pursued. As Johnston retreated, Sherman's supply lines stretched out, eventually elongating to some 475 miles through generally hostile territory, from Louisville, Kentucky, through Nashville, Tennessee, and finally to the vicinity of Atlanta, Georgia.[2]

Confederate cavalry kept slashing at these extended lines. However, the Union army monopolized the rail line, built well-engineered block houses near bridges and other vulnerable points, and set up repair yards that were highly organized in business-like Northern-style. Union troops built new bridges and laid new track any time a Confederate force damaged or destroyed part of the system. The Union maintenance of locomotives, rolling stock, bridges, and rail lines was crucial to the defense of the supply line.

Johnston hoped that Nathan Bedford Forrest and his strong and elusive cavalry would destroy the constantly extending Union line of communication. However, Jefferson Davis and later General Bragg sent Forrest on missions to attack other Union forces scattered through Tennessee, repeatedly avoiding defeat at the hands of Union cavalry sent out to get him. Johnston complained that Forrest's cavalry was never properly employed to concentrate on Sherman's lines of communication. Even without the attack on Sherman's rear that he pleaded for, Johnston's delaying defensive tactic worked fairly well, forcing Sherman to take 74 days to advance 100 miles. After the battle at Kennesaw Mountain, Johnston kept pulling back, arriving near Atlanta at Peachtree Creek in mid-July 1864.

Johnston later justified his strategy, arguing that he could have worn down the Union army eventually by preserving his forces and attacking or defending only when he had ideal positions. He continued to believe that by drawing Sherman farther into the hostile interior of the deep South, he would eventually be able to isolate him from his line of supply and communication and destroy both the invading Union army and the Union's patience with the war.

By July, however, President Jefferson Davis regarded Johnston's mobile tactic as defeatist. Johnston's plans to place weak Georgia militia in the defense line around Atlanta and to keep his troops mobile to find the best positions for engagements with Sherman appeared to tip the balance for Jefferson Davis. Facing complaints from politicians and from the public, and after getting a report on the situation from Braxton Bragg, Davis replaced Johnston on July 17 with John Bell Hood. Hood, who had a reputation as an aggressive soldier, if not a highly sophisticated strategist or planner, tried to adopt methods similar to those Lee had used earlier in the war, aggressively taking the battle to the enemy. Furthermore, even though it was well understood at the time that a frontal attack on a well-defended position had little chance of success, Hood urged his commanders to use precisely that desperate method. Some officers and enlisted men in his army believed Hood was rash, egotistical, and possibly unbalanced. Immediately after Hood took over the Army of Tennessee, the army fought four engagements that failed to destroy Sherman's forces, and only depleted Hood's forces further.

FROM JOHNSTON TO HOOD

Hood, although severely wounded, with one leg amputated and one arm paralyzed, clearly was eager to adopt a far more aggressive style of warfare than Johnston. Sherman, who had been frustrated at not being able to pin down major units of Johnston's force, now had the opportunity.

Hood's aggressive style was a failure for several reasons. Hood often ignored good advice recommending flanking and cavalry attacks that might have helped his efforts, constantly urging courageous but costly infantry charges straight into defended positions. Hood's relations with his subordinate officers were terrible by contrast to those that Lee maintaned with his officers. Hood apparently took both laudanum and alcohol for the pain from his wounds, which may have clouded his judgment; he changed his battle plans repeatedly, intrigued against other officers, blamed subordinates for his own mistakes, and blamed the troops more generally for cowardice in not attacking defended positions. He was adept at political intrigues and had the support of Davis, if not his own subordinate officers and soldiers. Historians of the war have debated whether Hood's erratic command derived from his condition and his reliance on drugs, his personality, or from the desperate position in which he found himself. A few even have expressed admiration for his willingness to fight in contrast to Johnston's evasive methods, somewhat reflecting the view held by Jefferson Davis. In any case, in a period of less than five months, his leadership resulted in the end of Confederate hopes for victory in the heartland theater of the war.[3]

Sherman and his generals were actually glad to see Hood take over from Johnston, because Hood's tactics tended to play into their hands. Sherman's generals were able to secure solid defensive positions around Atlanta; Hood's orders

General Joseph E. Johnston sacrificed territory to preserve his Army of Tennessee as he retreated toward Atlanta. Viewing Johnston's tactics as defeatist, Jefferson Davis replaced him with General John B. Hood. *(Library of Congress, Prints and Photographs Division, LC-USZ62–03202)*

to his subordinates were unclear or uncoordinated, and the first attacks all resulted in heavy Confederate losses. The four major Atlanta battles, fought from July 20 to September 1, were designated Peachtree Creek, Atlanta, Ezra Church, and Jonesboro. In each of these, Confederate losses were greater than Union losses, and Johnston's method of preserving his army to fight another day was abandoned. Although figures were poorly kept, especially on the Confederate side, it seems that in the first three battles under Hood's direction, the Confederates lost nearly 20,000 troops, while the Union lost less than 10,000. Together these battles culminated in Union forces cutting the last rail lines into Atlanta from the southwest. Hood ordered the evacuation of his troops from Atlanta, and they attempted to destroy stores of ammunition and locomotives left behind. To the surprise of Sherman, who did not realize that Hood had departed, his troops were able to move into the abandoned city early on September 2. The news of the fall of Atlanta greatly assisted Republican political chances in the North over the next two months. The news put an end to radical Republican efforts to hold a new nominating convention to select a candidate other than Lincoln and weakened the position of those Democrats who argued that the North should seek a negotiated peace with the South.

Jefferson Davis recognized that, although Hood was aggressive by contrast to Johnston, Hood had failed to stop Sherman. He appointed P. G. T. Beauregard to oversee Hood, but Beauregard simply consulted with him, leaving decisions, even bad ones, to Hood. With the disrupted state of communications throughout the Gulf states, Beauregard was often out of touch with Hood for weeks at a time. Confederates attempted but failed to entrap Union forces over the next few weeks, as Sherman refused to be lured into a decisive battle in an unfavorable position. Hood moved gradually toward Sherman's rear communication line and then toward central Tennessee. Sherman sent some forces toward Nashville under General Schofield and asked General George H. Thomas to prepare defenses there. Thomas gathered garrisons from around Tennessee, accumulating a large defensive army over the late summer and fall of 1864.

Hood's movements and his intentions remained unclear to Sherman and appeared to represent shifting plans. Hood's scheme, as it evolved, was to unite with Forrest's cavalry for an attack through central Tennessee and thence north toward Kentucky and the Ohio River. He apparently hoped with the conquest of Tennessee to win new recruits from the state, and then to be able to march to the east to support Lee at Richmond. But weather conditions and transport problems delayed the start of his plan for several weeks through the fall and early winter, turning what might have been a good idea into a forlorn dream of glory that increasingly had less and less chance of success.

Even before Johnston's removal from command, Union brigadier general Samuel D. Sturgis led 8,500 cavalry and infantrymen in June against 4,300 Confederate cavalry under Nathan Bedford Forrest in Tennessee. In a decisive victory at Brice's Crossroads, however, Forrest drove back the federal force and captured 18 guns and 1,600 prisoners. After Hood started maneuvering around to Sherman's rear to attack toward Tennessee, Forrest's cavalry raided directly into the center of Memphis on August 21 and forced Union major general C. C. Washburne to flee in his underwear. Forrest reported killing or capturing 400 Union troops and capturing 300 horses and mules, while losing only 20 killed and wounded in this Memphis raid. Forrest then turned east and attempted to link up with Hood for the planned attack on Nashville. After delays imposed by high water levels in the rivers, Forrest finally caught up with Hood in November, and together they hoped to be able to push northward through central Tennessee.

MEANWHILE IN VIRGINIA: BERMUDA HUNDRED, WILDERNESS, SPOTSYLVANIA, PETERSBURG

Between May 5 and May 16, 1864, the Battle of Bermuda Hundred was fought, in which Union general Benjamin Butler's forces were finally bottled up behind his own defenses. Butler's 39,000-man Army of the James planned to move up the neck of land to take Richmond from the southeast of the city, but Butler defended each position as he advanced, moving slowly. He cut a railroad track on May 7 at Walthall Junction, but then, on May 9, his forces were stopped at Swift Creek or Arrowfield Church. Butler engaged the Confederates at Drewry's Bluff on May 16, and then was forced to withdraw behind his own defensive line.

Grant received a report on the disposition of the troops, in which one of his staff officers pointed out that the neck of land between Richmond and the Bermuda Hundred Peninsula, where Butler was entrenched, resembled the neck of a bottle. Grant repeated the observation in a report to headquarters, which was released to the press. Newsmen delighted in the expression, "Bottled-up-Butler." Grant later regretted that it appeared he had offered the sarcastic observation himself. Nevertheless, Butler's methods and poor generalship, combined with his already notorious reputation for initiating the contraband policy and for insulting the Confederate ladies of New Orleans, appeared to discredit him in the eyes of many contemporaries and later analysts.

The battles that followed in mid-1864 in the Virginia theater, known by the names Wilderness, Spotsylvania, Cold Harbor, and Petersburg have been collectively called the "overland campaign." There were an estimated 65,000 Union casualties in all of these battles, which cost the Confederates about 35,000 casualties. From the Union point of view, the effort expended trying to take Richmond became extremely debilitating and depressing. Cumulatively, the Union losses over the summer may have had an effect in the 1864 political campaign, helping the Peace Democrats. Nevertheless, Grant believed the only way to win was to abandon the method of glorious individual battles and turn to a steady and relentless campaign of destruction of the enemy.

Lee's forces suffered severe casualties in the Battle of the Wilderness, May 5 and 6. Faced with the loss of troops, Lee had to curb his aggressive style and prepare for a more defensive battle at Spotsylvania. Building fieldworks and trenches that foreshadowed those of World War I, Lee put his troops into a defensive situation that became one of the classics of military history. Grant's assault after assault against the well-constructed earthworks hardened his own view of the war as one of attrition. The conflict turned into slaughter as Mississippi troops counterattacked to take a salient known as the Bloody Angle, where the earthworks became slippery with blood, and bodies piled several deep, under which the dying movements of the wounded could be seen in the mix of mud, blood, and brains. When the salient was finally abandoned by the Confederates, Union burial details tried to sort out the mangled bodies, using ammunition box sides as headstones, and simply burying the Confederate dead in common graves by covering the corpses in the abandoned trenches. On May 12 at Spotsylvania, the casualties were staggering as Grant lost 9,000 troops, while Lee lost 8,000.[4]

The Battle of the Wilderness led to huge losses on both sides, but Grant understood the concept of a war of attrition. The Union could replace lost soldiers, but the Confederacy could not. *(Library of Congress, Prints and Photographs Division, LC-USZC4–1748)*

The battles at the Wilderness and Spotsylvania were hardly decisive Union victories, and Grant's failure to overwhelm Lee's smaller numbers was roundly condemned in the North. In the short run, Spotsylvania was seen as a severe Union defeat, but Grant took a longer view, seeing both battles as just parts of the strategy of destruction. Critics pointed out that Grant was poor at planning details, at scheduling, and at collecting and distributing useful intelligence for his generals. But the battles, no matter how badly fought, did succeed in advancing Grant's goal of costs in the Confederate manpower.

By May 12, Grant's direct command had reduced the role of Meade to that of a glorified staff officer, and Meade resented the fact that his officers, troops, and journalists recognized the position he was in, even though Grant made the wise political decision of recommending Meade for promotion. Meade became increasingly frustrated at the arrangement, finally angrily blowing up and expelling a journalist from his camp who had dared to praise Grant. Meade had a more cautious style, and if he had been in complete charge, the great bloodbath of Spotsylvania might not have occurred. Yet it was precisely Grant's willingness to use the Union's overwhelming numbers to batter down Lee that began to spell the end of Confederate control of Virginia. At the time, Grant's critics worried that the slaughter of his own troops and the loss of his own officers in the bloody engagements would compromise his own army's ability to fight. It seemed, even to officers inured to the concept, that attrition might cost too much.

Grant planned a frontal attack against the worn-down Confederate forces defending the Richmond perimeter, and at dawn on June 3, he threw half of his army, some 60,000 men, against the well-defended Confederate lines at Cold Harbor, not far from the site of the Gaines Mill engagement during the Seven Days' battle of 1862. Looking at the Confederate defenses from their forward positions, Grant's seasoned troops knew the attack was hopeless, and many of them wrote their last letters home, pinned their names to their uniforms to be sure their bodies could be identified, and then marched into the hail of bullets.

In eight minutes, almost 8,000 Union soldiers fell dead or seriously wounded. The attack was a disaster.

From Cold Harbor, east of Richmond, Grant moved forces quickly to the south of Richmond, hoping to attack the city from a new angle and to sever the rail connections that ran down into southern Virginia and North Carolina. However, Grant's subordinate commanders, particularly Butler, failed to strike before Lee was able to send Beauregard to organize the defense along a line just south of Petersburg. Later critics complained that Grant's forces were too slow to move, since the door to Petersburg had stood ajar for four days. By June 15, 1864, 48,000 Union troops attacked 5,400 Confederate defenders under Beauregard. Lee sent more reinforcements, then both sides began to dig into more permanent trench lines. Thus, Richmond became somewhat more isolated, as Union forces on the east and south of the city sought to cut it off from possible aid from Confederate armies in southern Virginia and North Carolina.

On the Petersburg front, the Battle of the Crater took place on July 30, resulting in a devastating defeat for federals, with 3,793 federal casualties. A 4-ton powder charge planted in a tunnel secretly dug beneath the Confederate line was exploded at 4:45 in the morning, but the federal IX Corps put itself at a disadvantage by attacking directly through the resulting crater. Most of the deaths were African-American troops, many shot after being wounded.

Although the 10-month struggle that lasted from the summer of 1864 to the early spring of 1865 was often called a siege, Petersburg and Richmond continued to be in communication by rail with the rest of the Confederacy through to August. The trenches eventually reached a length of 26 miles. Grant kept trying to move westward to the south of Petersburg, to cut the rail lines that supplied Richmond and to prevent Lee from linking up with the Army of Tennessee, once again under the command of General Johnston, moving up through the Carolinas. Union troops severed the Welden rail line in August, but the Confederates simply transshipped goods by wagon around the severed line, keeping open a trickle of supplies into Richmond through the winter of 1864–65.

EARLY AND SHERIDAN

While battles raged around Richmond, Confederate cavalry under Jubal Early launched a raid toward Washington, D.C., by way of Hagerstown and Frederick, Maryland. The advance was held up for a day at the Monocacy River between Frederick and Rockville by a hastily assembled Union force under Major General Lew Wallace. Then, on July 10 and 11, Jubal Early's troops marched by way of Rockville, Maryland, to Silver Spring just to the north of Washington. Exhausted by the heat and the long march, the Confederate troops hoped to strike into the city, but met convalescent Union soldiers who were pressed into the defense of the capital. Grant also hastily shifted more troops from the Petersburg front to defend the capital, moving them by steamer up through the coastal waters, the Chesapeake, and the Potomac River. Encountering stiff resistance at Fort Stevens just inside the District of Columbia line, Early retreated to Strasburg in Virginia. During the retreat of Early's forces, he sent two brigades under General John McCausland, who raided up into Pennsylvania for the last time. Partially in response to the raid by General David Hunter in which he shelled and burned the Virginia Military Institute and destroyed private property in the town of Lexington, Virginia, in June, McCausland asked the town fathers of Chambersburg for either $100,000 in gold or $500,000 in greenbacks as indemnification for the prior destruction of Confederate private property. After waiting a few hours for a response, McCausland evacuated 3,000 residents of Chambersburg and then set the town on fire. Northern journalists responded with horror.

Grant reacted to Early's raid on the capital and McCausland's destruction of Chambersburg by organizing the Army of the Shenandoah under General Philip Sheridan to pursue Early. Sheridan's forces were subject to attack by bushwhackers and snipers, and they often responded with reprisals on civilians suspected of harboring the bushwhackers by the burning of their homes and occasional executions. In the Valley, as the Shenandoah Valley theater of war was called, the war turned very ugly. Although not as static as the conflict around Richmond, nor as spectacular as the fall of Atlanta, the destruction of civilian property and the bitter conflict in the Valley served as further proof that the war was no longer being fought by gentlemen who scrupulously tried to follow traditional rules.

SHERMAN'S MARCH

Sherman's troops were able to move into Atlanta on September 2, after Hood evacuated. The city fell without a battle. Within a few days, Sherman ordered the remaining civilians evacuated, causing an uproar as an inhumane act. His memo in reply to a request by the mayor and council to call off the evacuation was widely published, causing further shock. His rejection of the request, noting that war was not pleasant, seemed callous or even brutal to Southerners. Over the period of September and October, Sherman sent three corps under General John M. Schofield to help Thomas hold Nashville, and then Sherman shadowed Hood's movements in Georgia, trying to determine what the erratic Hood was up to. Sherman realized that, although Hood's Army of Tennessee had escaped his grasp, the political and industrial impact of taking Atlanta was immense.

He soon sought to politicize the war in other ways. Failing in an effort to obtain a separate peace with the state of Georgia, he then conceived the plan to abandon his communications back to Chattanooga and to emulate the Shenandoah method and destroy resources from Atlanta to the coast. He proposed the plan to Grant and eventually Grant agreed, allowing Sherman to adopt and expand on the Sheridan policy of attacking resources. Sherman took the Sheridan method further, abandoning his own supply lines leading back to Tennessee and requiring his troops to draw their supplies from local resources. In mid-November, Sherman began the March to the Sea, with two broad columns of troops living off the land and destroying resources. Sherman had a vision: destroy the will, cut the railroads, but don't chase the army. After sending stores back north via Nashville, Sherman even withdrew the

Union general William T. Sherman adopted a scorched-earth policy in his advance through Georgia; he also ordered his troops to live off the land. He became well-hated throughout the South for his actions. (Library of Congress, Prints and Photographs Division, LC-DIG-cwpb-07315)

railroad defense garrisons that had once protected the lines from Chattanooga to Atlanta to concentrate forces. He assembled four corps, totaling 55,000 infantry, 5,000 cavalry, 64 guns, and 2,000 artillery men. He ordered them to advance as four infantry corps along four parallel roads. Each regiment was allowed only one wagon. The troops were to subsist on what they could find for themselves. Only corps commanders had the authority to destroy mills and houses. As their own horses were exhausted and worn out, Sherman planned to seize horses and mules, particularly from the rich. Capturing pigs and cattle from local farms and plantations, then barbecuing the slaughtered animals over campfires, his troops soon became known as Sherman's bummers, as they bummed off the local resources.

Sherman expected Georgians to put up some defense, but the Georgia militia, consisting mostly of underage and overage troops, was outnumbered and ineffective against Sherman's battle-hardened veterans, and the March to the Sea was remembered as a pleasant foraging expedition by Union troops and as one of the great atrocities of the war by resident Georgians. The march took about five weeks, from mid-November to late December.

HOOD'S DEBACLE AT FRANKLIN

Federal forces under John Schofield stopped the advance of Hood in his planned invasion through Tennessee at the small town of Franklin, on November 30, 1864. It was in this conflict that six Confederate generals were killed, including the Irish-born Cleburne. In this decisive Battle of Franklin south of Nashville, much of Hood's Army of Tennessee was virtually destroyed, through a combination of poor leadership on the part of Hood and his officers, and an excellent defensive position of the Union forces. Schofield had organized defenses around the southern edge of the town, with field ordnance strategically placed, with an excellent trench system, and with clear fields of fire and tangles of thorny Osage orange to

Defending Union forces at Franklin, Tennessee, held off the Confederate Army of Tennessee under John Hood in a decisive battle. Hood and the Army of Tennessee never recovered from the slaughter. *(Library of Congress, Prints and Photographs Division, LC-USZC4–1732)*

slow the enemy approach. At Franklin, Hood's tactics of head-on collision against strongly defended trench lines resembled the disastrous attempts at frontal attack employed by the British at Gallipoli and along the Belgian front during World War I. Hood's army lost 1,750 killed, another 5,500 wounded or captured in the single five-hour engagement at Franklin. Hood did not allow Forrest to circle around behind Schofield's defenders to sever Schofield's Northward retreat line toward Nashville, even though the cavalry officer suggested that tactic.

At Franklin the Union defenders were entrenched on high ground, and they had protected their positions with abatis made of trees and Osage orange hedges, which had been widely employed as thorny thickets to confine livestock and were the direct predecessor of barbed wire. Although the defenders did not have machine guns, many of them had breech-loading and repeating rifles, allowing rapid fire that, in volume, approached that of machine-gunners in later wars. Cannon were used, not for long-range bombardment but for direct cannister shot into advancing troops. The inability of the Confederate command to recognize the futility of an advance against well-armed and well-prepared troops in trenches, was compounded by the fact that officers did not communicate with the rear to obtain changes in orders. Furthermore, as officers were killed, their troops became isolated, taking cover in the terrain, where they were simply slaughtered, much as troops were killed in fruitless advances on the western front through the barbed-wire tangles of no-man's land throughout 1914–17.[5]

Even though the Union defense held, after the battle Union general Schofield retreated with his army to Nashville, fearing that his path to the North would be cut off by a cavalry raid around to his rear. Hood pursued northward with his surviving troops. The remaining attackers were defeated south of Nashville by stronger forces under Thomas. Retreating to the south through ice-encrusted

Sharpened wooden stakes, or *chevaux-de-frise* were employed by both sides as defensive fortifications in the field. *(Library of Congress, Prints and Photographs Division, LC-DIG-cwpb-02602)*

roads, Hood's troops, many of them barefoot and hatless, represented only a fraction of the Army of Tennessee. With deaths, missing and captured men, and desertions, the 60,000 men that Johnston had once commanded were reduced to less than 15,000. Hood was defeated but not at all disillusioned in the correctness of his methods. He did recognize he had failed in his goals, and he voluntarily resigned his command in January 1865.

A CHRISTMAS PRESENT FOR LINCOLN

Sherman's March to the Sea ended with the taking of Savannah on December 21. There he met up with Union naval forces and sent Lincoln a telegram announcing that he presented the city of Savannah as a Christmas present. Although the annihilation plan had not succeeded exactly as planned, due to Hood's desperate measures, the destruction of the Confederate armies and resources was well underway. The long deadlock through 1862 and 1863 appeared well broken, with the destruction of Atlanta, the capture of Savannah, and the end of the Army of Tennessee as an effective fighting force. With Sherman preparing to march north to destroy Columbia and Charleston, the South was effectively defeated.

However, the constitutional system of the Confederacy, which placed all foreign and military policy in the hands of the president, prevented negotiation of a peace settlement or outright surrender by the Confederate congress, which was so disposed. The vice president, governors, and senators all called for peace, but Jefferson Davis regarded surrender or peace negotiations as a failure to honor his oath of office. He reasoned that a defeat of some armies in the field or the loss of some territory did not bring the existence of his new nation to an end. To others, the destruction of the Army of Tennessee and the battered perimeter around Richmond that slowly consumed the Army of Northern Virginia, meant that the end was near.

CHRONICLE OF EVENTS

1864

January 2: General Patrick Cleburne circulates his memorandum proposing the arming of slaves at a command conference under General Joseph Johnston. The memo is suppressed.

February 13: The Confederate Congress authorizes the suspension of habeas corpus by the president to enforce the draft and to apprehend deserters.

February 22: Confederate cavalry under Major General Nathan Bedford Forrest engage Union cavalry under Brigadier General William Sooy Smith at Okolona, Mississippi, resulting in a substantial victory for Forrest, when Smith retreats into Memphis.

February 23: Jefferson Davis appoints General Braxton Bragg to command all the Confederate armies.

February 24: The U.S. Congress reinstates the rank of lieutenant general.

February 28–March 3: A Union cavalry raid on Richmond, led by Generals George Armstrong Custer and Hugh Judson Kilpatrick and Colonel Ulric Dahlgren (brother of Admiral John A. Dahlgren), fails. Dahlgren is killed in the action; he carried orders to kill Jefferson Davis.

March 9: Lincoln formally appoints Grant to the rank of lieutenant general.

Confederate general Stephen Dodson Ramseur was fatally wounded at the Battle of Cedar Creek. In this image, General George Custer of the U.S. Cavalry has his horse bow in salute of Ramseur, who was a former classmate and friend at West Point. *(Library of Congress, Prints and Photographs Division, LC-USZC4–1223)*

March 10: Lincoln orders Grant to take command of the Union armies.

March 12: Grant assumes command of all Union armies, relieving General in Chief Henry Halleck.

April 17: Grant orders the ending of prisoner exchanges on the grounds that Confederates are not exchanging black prisoners, but employing or leasing them as slaves. The decision leads to overcrowding at Confederate prison camp Fort Sumter, near Andersonville, Georgia. Eventually, 13,000 of the 45,000 prisoners at Andersonville will die in captivity.

May 2: Troops under Confederate general Nathan Bedford Forrest massacre surrendering African-American troops at Fort Pillow.

May 5–7: The Battle of the Wilderness is fought in which the Federals suffer some 17,000 casualties, and the Confederate casualties number about 7,000. Grant displays his dogged determination to wear down Lee's army by attrition. The 43 days from the Battle of the Wilderness through the Battle of Cold Harbor are known as the Overland Campaign.

May 5–16: The Battle of Bermuda Hundred is fought in which Butler's forces are bottled up behind his own defenses.

May 7: Major General William Sherman begins to move 100,000 men in three armies from Chattanooga toward Atlanta. The three armies are the Army of the Tennessee under James B. McPherson, the Army of the Ohio under John M. Schofield, and the Army of the Cumberland under George Thomas.

May 9: Union general Sedgwick is killed by a sharpshooter.

May 12: The Battle of Spotsylvania Court House is fought as a continuation of the Battle of the Wilderness. Federal forces again lose some 9,000 casualties, while Confederate casualties are about 8,000.

May 12: In the face of Sherman's advance, Confederate general Johnston pulls back from Dalton to Resaca, Georgia.

May 15: Johnston retreats from his good position at Resaca, fearing that Sherman's forces will move around to his flank and he will be trapped against the Oostenaula River.

May 29: The Confederate army issues an order prohibiting fraternization with Union pickets or skirmishers.

May 31–June 12: The Battle of Cold Harbor, near Richmond, is fought, in which Grant attempts to move around to his own left and south of Lee to attack Richmond. The battle is fought on and near the battle-

This facsimile print of a work by Thure De Thulstrup depicts the awful hand-to-hand combat in the Battle of Spotsylvania Court House, May 1864. *(Library of Congress, Prints and Photographs Division, LC-USZC4–1749)*

grounds of the Seven Days' battles of 1862. Assaulting strong Confederate positions, in 10 minutes on June 3 the Federals lose 7,000 men. On the 12th, Grant begins to secretly move the Union army toward the James River.

June 7: General Meade orders the expulsion from his camp of a journalist who had praised the arrival of General Grant.

June 10: Acting under orders from Sherman, Union brigadier general Samuel D. Sturgis leads 8,500 cavalry and infantrymen against 4,300 Confederate cavalry under Nathan Bedford Forrest. In a decisive victory at Brice's Crossroads, Forrest drives back the federal force and captures 18 guns and 1,600 prisoners.

June 12: On a raid, General David Hunter orders the shelling and burning of the Virginia Military Institute in Lexington, Virginia.

June 14: Grant's forces cross the James River to the southeast of Richmond.

June 15: The Petersburg campaign begins. After Butler botches an attack on Petersburg, Beauregard is able to bring in reinforcements and fortify a line outside and to the south of the city. Lasting 10 months, the subsequent battles will settle into a trench warfare that will foreshadow conditions in World War I, 50 years later. The trenches will eventually reach a length of 26 miles.

June 27: In the battle of Kennesaw Mountain, Johnston finally arrests the advance of Sherman toward Atlanta; despite Sherman's frontal assault on Johnston, the Federals are turned back.

July 3–9: Johnston continues his retreat toward Atlanta in the face of Sherman's advance.

July 9: A raid by Confederate cavalry under Jubal Early via Hagerstown and Frederick, Maryland, toward Washington, D.C., is stopped at the Monocacy River by a hastily-assembled Union force under Major General Lew Wallace.

July 11: Jubal Early's troops arrive in Silver Spring, Maryland, by way of Rockville to the North of Washington, and convalescent Union soldiers are pressed into the defense of the capital. Grant shifts troops from the Petersburg front to defend the Union capital. Encountering stiff resistance as well as excessive heat, Early retreats to Strasburg in Virginia. Grant responds to Early's raid on the capital by organizing the Army of the Shenandoah under Phil Sheridan to pursue Early. Sheridan's orders include devastation of the countryside, a forerunner of Sherman's tactic in Georgia.

July 14: In an engagement at Tupelo, Tennessee, 14,000 Federal troops under Major General A. J. Smith hold their ground against 10,000 under Nathan Bedford Forrest. However, after the defense, Smith will pull back to Memphis, and Forrest will continue to maraud and harass the extended supply lines to Sherman that run from Tennessee into Georgia.

July 17: Jefferson Davis replaces Johnston with John Bell Hood, displeased with Johnston's tactic of withdrawal. Hood is determined to destroy the armies under Sherman and attempts to emulate R. E. Lee's aggressive battle tactics.

July 20–September 1: Four major battles are fought around Atlanta, including Peachtree Creek, Atlanta, Ezra Church, and Jonesboro. Hood's tactics fail to carry the day. Together these battles will culminate in cutting the rail lines to Atlanta and in the occupation of Atlanta by Union troops on September 2.

July 20: The Battle of Peachtree Creek opens the approach to Atlanta by Sherman's forces after Hood attempts to defeat each of Sherman's armies separately. Hood's forces lose some 5,000 casualties to about 2,000 Federal casualties at Peachtree Creek. Hood's reckless style is compared unfavorably with Johnston's more measured tactic of studied retreats.

July 22: The Battle of Atlanta just southeast of Atlanta is fought after Hood sends a large force on a nighttime march to move behind federal lines, but the attack fails. Hood, who claims his resistance lifts morale, loses some 10,000 men to 4,000 Union losses.

July 28: The Battle of Ezra Church to the southwest of Atlanta is fought in which Hood sends two corps to stop Sherman's forces from cutting rail lines. The Federals hold off Confederate attacks all afternoon, resulting in Federal casualties of some 732 to about 4,300 Confederate casualties.

July 30: On the Petersburg front, the Battle of the Crater takes place resulting in devastating defeat for the Federals, with 3,793 Federal casualties. After a 4-ton powder charge in a tunnel secretly dug beneath Confederate lines is exploded at 4:45 in the morning, the Federal IX Corps advances directly through the resulting crater. Most of the deaths are African-American troops, many shot to death after being wounded.

July 30: Troops under Confederate general John McCausland burn the city of Chambersburg, Pennsylvania, after attempting to obtain a payment as indemnification for the destruction of the Virginia Military Institute.

August 7–March 2, 1865: Sheridan's Army of the Shenandoah begins a devastation campaign in the Shenandoah valley. Battles will include engagements through September and October as Sheridan pursues Early and rallies his troops after a counterattack by Early in October at Cedar Creek. Sheridan finally defeats the remnants of Early's army March 2, 1865, at Waynesboro, Virginia.

August 21: Nathan Bedford Forrest's cavalry raids directly into the center of Memphis and forces Union major general C. C. Washburne to flee in his underwear. Forrest reports killing or capturing 400 Union troops

After the fall of Charleston, Union troops found these Blakely guns in the courtyard of the arsenal. *(Library of Congress, Prints and Photographs Division, LC-B8171–3096)*

and capturing 300 horses and mules, while losing only 20 killed and wounded.

August 31–September 1: The Battle of Jonesboro to the South of Atlanta takes place after Hood hears that Union troops are tearing up rail lines into Atlanta; Confederate losses are 1,700 to only 170 for the Federal forces. Realizing that the rail lines into the city are now held by Union troops, Hood evacuates Atlanta after setting fire to his own ammunition train on the afternoon of September 1.

September 2: Sherman's troops enter Atlanta under Major General Henry Slocum, and Sherman receives word of the advance into the city on the morning of September 3.

September 7: Sherman orders the evacuation of Atlanta by all remaining civilians.

October 5: Confederate lieutenant general Hood attempts to destroy Sherman's supply lines from Chattanooga. Confederate troops under Major General Samuel G. French attack an ill-defended Union rail junction at Allatoona, Georgia, but fall back after hearing the false rumor that a major Union force is coming to rescue the federal outpost.

November 16: Sherman begins the March to the Sea with two broad columns of troops living off the land and destroying resources, and much of Atlanta is destroyed by fire.

November 25: A team of four Confederate officers attempt to start a major fire in New York City by igniting fires in 19 different hotels, two theaters, and Barnum's Museum. The fires are all contained, and the Confederate saboteurs escape to Canada by train.

November 29–November 30: Confederate general Hood orders a campaign into Tennessee, with disastrous battle casualties at Franklin, Tennessee, south of Nashville in which his army loses 1,750 killed, another 5,500 wounded or captured. Among the dead are six Confederate generals, including Cleburne; the battle and a follow-up attack toward Nashville virtually destroy the remnants of the Confederate Army of Tennessee.

December 8: Approaching Savannah, Union troops under Sherman encounter land mines and employ Confederate prisoners in mine-clearing.

December 21: Sherman's March to the Sea ends with the taking of Savannah, Confederate forces slip away to the north.

EYEWITNESS TESTIMONY

This scarcity of food made it necessary to send almost half of the artillery-horses and all the mules not required for camp-service to the valley of the Etowah, where long forage could be found, and the sources of supply of grain were nearer. . . . In the course of the inspection made as soon as practicable, I found the condition of the army much less satisfactory than it had appeared to the President on the 23rd of December [1863]. There was a great deficiency of blankets; and it was painful to see the number of bare feet in every regiment. . . . The President was informed that two of the four brigades inspected by me that day were not in condition to march, for want of shoes. There was a deficiency, in the infantry, of six thousand small-arms. The artillery horses were generally still so feeble from long, hard service and scarcity of forage, that it would have been impossible to manoeuver our batteries in action, or to march with them at any ordinary rate on ordinary roads. It was long before they could draw the guns through fields.

Confederate general Joseph Johnston, recalling his report to President Jefferson Davis of January 15, 1864, on the condition of the Army of Tennessee, in his memoir, Narrative of Military Operations, *pp. 278–279.*

The home guard of the country turned out against the raiders, and after being joined by a detachment from the Forty-second Battalion of Virginia Cavalry and some furloughed cavalry-men of Lee's army, surprised and attacked the retreating column of Dahlgren, killed the leader, and captured nearly one hundred prisoners, with negroes, horses, etc.

On the body of Dahlgren was found an address to his officers and men, another paper giving special orders and instructions, and one giving his itinerary, the whole disclosing the un-soldierly means and purposes of the raid, such as disguising the men in our uniform, carrying supplies of oakum and turpentine to burn Richmond, and, after releasing their prisoners on Belle Isle, to exhort them to destroy the hateful city, while on all was impressed the special injunction that the city must be burned, and "Jeff Davis and Cabinet killed."[6]

The prisoners, having been captured in disguise, were under the usages of war, liable to be hanged as spies, but their protestations that their service was not voluntary, and the fact that as enlisted men they were subject to orders, and could not be held responsible for the infamous instructions under which they were acting, saved them from the death-penalty they had fully

incurred. Photographic copies of the papers found on Dahlgren's body were taken and sent to General Lee, with instructions to communicate them to General Meade, commanding the enemy's forces in his front, with an inquiry as to whether such practices were authorized by his Government, and also to say that, if any question was raised as to the copies, the original paper would be submitted. No such question was then made, and the denial that Dahlgren's conduct had been authorized was accepted.

Jefferson Davis, recalling the death of Union cavalry colonel Ulric Dahlgren, after the defeat of the raid on Richmond on March 3, 1864, in his memoir, The Rise and Fall of the Confederate Government, *pp. 506–507.*

I gave the necessary order to move the troops to the right, and as they rose to execute the movement the enemy opened a sprinkling fire, partly from sharp-shooters. As the bullets whistled by, some of the men dodged. [General John Sedgwick] said laughingly. "What! what! men, dodging this way for single bullets! What will you do when they open fire along the whole line? I am ashamed of you. They couldn't hit an elephant at this distance." A few seconds after, a man who had been separated from his regiment passed directly in front of the general and at the same moment a sharp-shooter's bullet passed with a long shrill whistle very close, and the soldier, who was then just in front of the general, dodged to the ground. The general touched him gently with his foot, and said, "Why, my man, I am ashamed of you, dodging that way," and repeated the remark, "They couldn't hit an elephant at this distance." The man rose and saluted, and said good-naturedly, "General, I dodged a shell once, and if I hadn't, it would have taken my head off. I believe in dodging." The general laughed and replied, "All right, my man; go to your place."

For a third time the same shrill whistle, closing with a dull, heavy stroke, interrupted our talk, when, as I was about to resume, the general's face turned slowly to me, the blood spurting from his left cheek under the eye in a steady stream. He fell in my direction; I was so close to him that my effort to support him failed, and I fell with him.

Colonel Charles H. Tompkins, chief of the artillery, standing a few feet away, heard my exclamation as the general fell, and turning, shouted to his brigade-surgeon, Dr. Ohlenschlager. Major Charles A. Whittier, Major T. W. Hyde, and Lieutenant-Colonel

Kent, who had been grouped near by, surrounded the general as he lay. A smile remained upon his lips but he did not speak. The doctor poured water from a canteen over the general's face. The blood still poured upward in a little fountain. The men in the long line of rifle-pits, retaining their places from force of discipline, were all kneeling with heads raised and faces turned toward the scene; for the news had already passed along the line.

Union brevet major general Martin T. McMahon, describing the death of General John Sedgwick, May 9, 1864, near Spotsylvania Court House, Virginia, in Battles and Leaders of the Civil War, *Vol. 4, p. 175.*

Marching at day to Spotsylvania Court House. Halted on the roadside and began making protection against the numerous shells that were traversing the air. Got orders again very soon to face about and march to the left where musketry and artillery were rolling in beautiful sublimity. The enemy, under cover of a dense fog this morning, had found their masses over an angle of our works and captured a portion of Johnson's Division. To check these masses and recover the lost line was the duty assigned to our brigade. The enemy seems to have concentrated their whole urging of war at this point. Shell of every kind and shape from mortars and field·pieces raked the approaches of reinforcements, while a forest of muskets played with awful fury over the ground itself. We advanced by the flank till at a close distance, then fired at right angles to the right, the brigade's length fronted and charged. All the lost line which our brigade covered was captured, but still a portion of the angle on our right remained in the enemy's hands, from which all day they passed on our flank a most galling fire. The fighting was terribly severe and against tremendous odds, but we maintained the position all day. . . . The timber in our rear was almost devoid of limbs and bark, and one oak at our works nearly two feet in diameter was cut down by Minie balls. The day was showery, and our persons and faces became badly begrimed. We retired in the morning at three a.m. under a severe fire of musketry, which was kept up unremittingly . . .

James Johnston Kirkpatrick, enlisted man in the Confederate Company C of the 16th Mississippi Infantry Regiment, in his diary entry for May 12, 1864, describing the exchange of fire at the Battle of Spotsylvania Court House, Virginia, in Robert G. Evans, ed., The 16th Mississippi Infantry: Civil War Letters and Reminiscences, *pp. 254–255.*

We are now behind our works at Dallas [Georgia]. The boys say there is a town in our Front that Uncle Billy [the United States Army] wants to visit. He ought to if he wants to, thats sure, but the Johnnys [Confederates] are auful saucy and we shall have to fight for it. When we made our first assault we pushed our skirmish line up pretty close and I crawled up a little way till I could see a fort and heavy earth works in our Front. I came pretty near getting shot by a sharp shooter. He cut the button off the side of my cap. I told Co. [Albert] Heath what I had seen and now we have built a heavy line of works. We cut trees and lay the trunks on top of one another in line till we have built it up like a solid straight fence 3 feet high, then dig a ditch about 4 feet wide and two deep, throwing the dirt on the out side; then if we have time, dig another on the outside and fill up the dirt thicker. Then we cut poles—with a notch in the end on both sides—and lay the notched ends on top of the logs. Then lay other logs called head logs in the notches. Then we can fire under the head logs and not expose ourselfs much.

Theodore Upson, an enlisted man in the 100th Indiana Volunteer Regiment, describing the advance through Georgia toward Atlanta and the battle outside Dallas, Georgia, in his journal entry for May 29, 1864, in Oscar Winther, ed., With Sherman to the Sea, *pp. 108–109.*

It having been reported to these headquarters that our pickets and skirmishers have allowed those of the enemy to advance to within very short distance of our lines, and that the pickets of the two lines are becoming too familiar, it is hereby ordered that no communication whatever should be had between our pickets and those of the enemy. The latter must be fired upon whenever they are seen within range of our guns; due precaution, however, being taken to prevent a waste of ammunition. No exchange of papers will be permitted, and no communication of any kind allowed, except under flag of truce sent by a division commander by direction of these headquarters. Division commanders will see that this order, like all other general and special orders relating to their commands is read to the troops. This order is dictated by a stern military necessity, as the forbidden practice affords positive advantages to the enemy in procuring information and directing his force; but even if this necessity did not exist, the commanding general still deeply deplores the moral disgrace incurred by his troops in anything like voluntary or unnecessary association with the savage foes who are not only warring against us, but persecuting our women and children, and destroying private property. The hands of such a foe are unworthy the friendly or courteous touch of a Confederate soldier.

Special Orders No. 15 by Jonathan M. Otey, assistant adjutant-general, to General Beauregard, Headquarters, Department of North Carolina and Southern Virginia, May 29, 1864, prohibiting fraternization with Union troops, in Official Records of the Union and Confederate Armies, *Series I, Vol. 36, (Part III), p. 849.*

Edward Crapsey, a correspondent of the Philadelphia Inquirer, having published in that journal of the 2d instant a libelous statement on the commanding general of this army calculated to impair the confidence of the army in their commanding officer, and which statement the said Crapsey has acknowledged to have been false, and to have been based on some idle camp rumor, it is hereby ordered that he be arrested and paraded through the lines of the army with a placard marked "libeler of the press," and that he then be put without the lines and not permitted to return.

The provost-marshal-general will see that this order is promptly executed.

The commanding general trusts that this example will deter others from committing like offenses, and he takes this occasion to notify the representatives of the public press that, whilst he is ready at all times to extend to them every facility for acquiring facts and giving circulation to the truth, he will not hesitate to punish with the utmost rigor all instances like the above where individuals take advantage of the privileges accorded to them to circulate falsehood and thus impair the confidence which the public and army should have in their generals and other officers.

By command of Major-General Meade.

Order issued on June 7, 1864, by Assistant Adjutant-General S. Williams, on staff of General Meade, detailing the punishment to be meted out to journalist Edward Crapsey, who had asserted in a news item published on June 2 that credit for saving the day should go to Grant, rather than to Meade, in Official Records of the Union and Confederate Armies *Series I, Vol. 36, (Part III) p. 670.*

Just when we had concluded our examination, and the abandonment of the hill had been decided upon, a party of soldiers, that had gathered behind us from mere curiosity, apparently tempted an artillery offi-

cer whose battery was in front, six or seven hundred yards from us, to open his fire upon them; at first firing shot very slowly. Lieutenant-General [Leonidas] Polk, unconsciously exposed by his characteristic insensibility to danger, fell by the third shot, which passed from left to right through the middle of his chest. The death of this eminent Christian and soldier, who had been distinguished in every battle in which the Army of Tennessee had been engaged, produced deep sorrow in our troops. Major-General [William Wing] Loring, the officer next in rank in the corps, succeeded temporarily to its command.

Confederate general Joseph Johnston, commenting on the death of General (and Episcopal Bishop) Leonidas Polk, on June 14, 1864, at Pine Mountain, near Marietta, Georgia, in his memoir, Narrative of Military Operations, *p. 337.*

When the troops of the Army of Northern Virginia had been fighting every day for twenty days, during a part of which time they had received only one-quarter pound of meat when other troops were getting one-third, on the recommendation of the chief commissary the meat ration was increased to one-half pound. On the 1st of June, the twenty-sixth day of the fighting, application was made for whisky to be issued to them, on the ground that they were broken down and needed the stimulant. It being impossible to issue the whisky, coffee and sugar were given in lieu of it as an extra issue. On the 11th June, when the army had enjoyed a little rest and had to some extent recovered from the effect of continuous marching and fighting, the meat ration was reduced to one-third pound. The extra issue of coffee and sugar was and is continued on the ground that it is absolutely necessary, not on account of what the men are doing, but what they have gone through. As recommended by the Secretary of War an order has been given for the extra issue of coffee and sugar to be made to the local troops now serving in the field. How long it will be possible to continue to issue the present ration will depend on the success in running the blockade, and the amount of money gotten from the Treasury. The funds now received are hardly more than enough to pay hospital expenses, and entirely inadequate to purchase a sufficiency of food for the army.

Commissary-General of Subsistence of the Confederacy, L. B. Northrup, June 16, 1864, commenting on problems of supply, in Official Records of the Union and Confederate Armies, *Series I, Vol. 36 (Part III), p. 899.*

Took up line of march at 4 A.M., marched very rapid all day, had an awful hard time today, driving cattle in the dust. Passed through Rockville, found a good many sympathizers of ours. Citizens along the road assured us of capturing the city. Our troops passed by the residence of Frank P. Blair, found any quantity of things, which he was bound to leave in hasty departure from home. Our boys made use of everything portable. The Yankees commenced shelling us pretty severe which lasted all the evening. We camped in 6 miles of the city, our boys skirmishing all the evening.

Henry Beck, a soldier in the Greensboro Guards of the 5th Alabama Infantry, noting in his diary the attack toward Washington, D.C., through Rockville, Maryland, on July 11, 1864, in G. Ward Hubbs, ed., Voices from Company D, *p. 299.*

We moved at daylight on the 11th, [General John] McCausland on the Georgetown pike, while the infantry, preceded by [General John Daniel] Imboden's cavalry under Colonel Smith, turned to the left at Rockville, so as to reach the 7th street pike which runs by Silver Springs into Washington. Jackson's cavalry moved on the left flank. The previous day had been very warm, and the roads were exceedingly dusty, as there had been no rain for several weeks. The heat during the night had been very oppressive, and but little rest had been obtained. This day was an exceedingly hot one, and there was no air stirring. While marching, the men were enveloped in a suffocating cloud of dust, and many of them fell by the way from exhaustion. Our progress was therefore very much impeded, but I pushed on as rapidly as possible, hoping to get into the fortifications around Washington before they could be manned. Smith drove a small body of cavalry before him into the works on the 7th street pike, and dismounted his men and deployed them as skirmishers. I rode ahead of the infantry and arrived in sight of Fort Stevens on this road a short time after noon, when I discovered that the works were but feebly manned.

Rodes, whose division was in front, was immediately ordered to bring it into line as rapidly as possible, throw out skirmishers, and move into the works if he could. My whole column was then moving by flank, which was the only practicable mode of marching on the road we were on, and before Rodes's division could be brought up we saw a cloud of dust in the rear of the works toward Washington, and soon a column of the enemy filed into them on the right and left, and skirmishers were thrown out in front, while an artillery

fire was opened on us from a number of batteries. This defeated our hopes of getting possession of the works by surprise, and it became necessary to reconnoiter. . . . This reconnoissance consumed the balance of the day.

The rapid marching and the losses at Harper's Ferry, Maryland Heights, and Monacacy had reduced my infantry to about 8000 muskets. Of these a very large number were greatly exhausted by the last two days' marching, some having fallen by sunstroke, and not more than one-third of my force could have been carried into action.

Confederate general Jubal Early, recalling his raid through Rockville and Silver Spring, Maryland, in an attempt to occupy Washington, D.C., July 11, 1864, in Battles and Leaders of the Civil War, *Vol. 4, pp. 497–498.*

Thus, from Dalton to Resaca, from Resaca to Adairsville, from Adairsville to Alatoona, from Alatoona to Kennesaw, from Kennesaw to the Chattahoochee, and then to Atlanta, retreat followed retreat, during seventy-four days of anxious hope and bitter disappointment, until at last the Army of Tennessee fell back within the fortifications of Atlanta. The Federal army soon occupied the arc of a circle extending from the railroad between Atlanta and the Chattahoochee River to some miles south of the Georgia Railroad (from Atlanta to Augusta) in a direction north and northeast of Atlanta. We had suffered a disastrous loss of territory. . . .

When it became known that the Army of Tennessee had been successively driven from one strong position to

This postwar print depicts the Battle of Kennesaw Mountain, June 27, 1864, as Confederate troops under Joseph E. Johnston sought to delay Sherman's advance on Atlanta. *(Library of Congress, Prints and Photographs Division, LC-USZ62–7928)*

another, until finally it had reached the earthworks constructed for the exterior defense of Atlanta, the popular disappointment was extreme. The possible fall of the "Gate City," with its important railroad communication, vast stores, factories for the manufacture of all sorts of military supplies, rolling-mill and foundries, was now contemplated for the first time at its full value, and produced intense anxiety far and wide. From many quarters, including such as had most urged his assignment, came delegations, petitions, and letters, urging me to remove General Johnston from the command of the army, and assign that important trust to some officer who would resolutely hold and defend Atlanta. While sharing in the keen sense of disappointment at the failure of the campaign which pervaded the whole country, I was perhaps more apprehensive than others of the disasters likely to result from it, because I was in a position to estimate more accurately their probable extent. . . . Still I resisted the steadily increasing pressure which was brought to bear to induce me to revoke his assignment, and only issued the order relieving him from command when I became satisfied that his declared purpose to occupy the works at Atlanta with militia levies and withdraw his army into the open country for freer operations, would inevitably result in the loss of that important point, and where the retreat would cease could not be foretold.

President Jefferson Davis, describing his decision on July 17, 1864, to dismiss General Joseph Johnston and replace him with General John Bell Hood, in his memoir, The Rise and Fall of the Confederate Government, *pp. 555–557.*

On the 17th, Major-General Wheeler reported that the whole Federal army had crossed the Chattahoochee, and was near it, between Roswell and Powers's Ferry. At ten o'clock P.M., while Colonel Prestman was with me receiving instructions in relation to his work of the next day on the intrenchments of Atlanta, the following telegram was received from General Cooper, dated July 17th:". . . I am directed by the Secretary of War to inform you that, as you have failed to arrest the advance of the enemy to the vicinity of Atlanta, far in the interior of Georgia, and express no confidence that you can defeat or repel him, you are hereby relieved from the command of the Army and Department of Tennessee, which you will immediately turn over to General Hood.". . .

Next morning I replied to the Hon Secretary's telegram: "Your dispatch of yesterday received and obeyed . . . As to the alleged cause of my removal,

I assert that Sherman's army is much stronger compared with that of Tennessee, than Grant's compared with that of Northern Virginia. Yet the enemy has been compelled to advance much more slowly to the vicinity of Atlanta, than to that of Richmond and Petersburg; and penetrated much deeper into Virginia than into Georgia. Confident language by a military commander is not usually regarded as evidence of competence."

General Joseph Johnston, recalling his reaction on July 17, 1864, to the order dismissing him from command of the Confederate Army of Tennessee, in his memoir, Narrative of Military Operations, *pp. 348–349.*

We were all very much interested in the Mine, and a great many expected that the explosion of it would be the signal for the fall of Petersburg. On the eve of the 30th, every preparation was made to take advantage of the confusion that the explosion of the Mine would create among the rebels.

Half past three A.M. July 30th was the time set for the springing of the Mine. Three o'clock found Gen'l. Willcox & staff at Roemer's Battery, anxiously waiting to see the Rebel Fort go up—staff officers roaming about looking at watches—in a mad hurry for the time to come, but growing hot and uncomfortable as the hour drew near—four o'clock and no sings of the young earthquake.

Fifteen minutes of five, a rumbling sound and a cry, "There it goes."

And what a grand sight it was—like a fountain of earth with jets high up in the air—down near the ground it would fall over like a pond lily—clouds of dust would roll out from the Crater—Soon, very soon, the earth settled—The four (4) tons of powder had done its work—It had hurled about four hundred men and a number of guns—As soon as the earth had settled, our troops moved forward to the Crater—The enemy had opened from all their guns and we were under a heavy fire.

Union captain L. C. Brackett, in a letter of August 4, 1864, to Marie Willcox, describing the Battle of the Crater on July 30, 1864, in Robert Garth Scott, ed., Forgotten Valor: The Memoirs, Journals and Civil War Letters of Orlando B. Willcox, *p. 558.*

Gentlemen: I have your letter of the 11th, in the nature of a petition to revoke my orders removing all the inhabitants from Atlanta. I have read it carefully, and give full credit to your statements of the distress that will be occasioned, and yet shall not revoke my orders, because they were not designed to meet the humanities of the case, but to prepare for the future struggles in which millions of good people outside of Atlanta have a deep interest. We must have peace, not only at Atlanta, but in all America. To secure this, we must stop the war that now desolates our once happy and favored country. To stop war, we must defeat the rebel armies which are arrayed against the laws and Constitution that all must respect and obey. To defeat those armies, we must prepare the way to reach them in their recesses, provided with the arms and instruments which enable us to accomplish our purpose. Now I know the vindictive nature of our enemy, that we may have many years of military operations from this quarter; and therefore, deem it wise and prudent to prepare in time. The use of Atlanta for warlike purposes is inconsistent with its character as a home for families. There will be no manufactures, commerce, or agriculture here, for the maintenance of families, and sooner or later want will compel the inhabitants to go. Why not go now, when all the arrangements are completed for the transfer, instead of waiting till the plunging shot of contenting armies will renew the scenes of the past month. Of course, I do not apprehend any such thing at this moment, but you do not suppose this army will be here until the war is over. I cannot discuss this subject with you fairly, because I cannot impart to you what we propose to do, but I assert that our military plans make it necessary for the inhabitants to go away, and I can only renew my offer of services to make their exodus in any direction as easy and comfortable as possible.

You cannot qualify war in harsher terms than I will. War is cruelty, and you cannot refine it; and those who brought war into our country deserve all the curses and maledictions a people can pour out. I know I had no hand in making his war, and I know I will make more sacrifices today than any of you to secure peace. But you cannot have peace and a division of our country. If the United States submits to a division now, it will not stop, but will go on until we reap the fate of Mexico, which is eternal war. The United States does and must assert its authority, wherever it once had power; for if it relaxes one bit to pressure, it is gone, and I believe that such is the national feeling. This feeling assumes various shapes, but always comes back to that of Union. Once admit the Union, once more acknowledge the authority of the national Government, and, instead of devoting your houses and streets and roads to the dread uses of war, I and this army become at once your protectors and supporters, shielding you from danger, let it

come from what quarter it may. . . . You might as well appeal against the thunder-storm as against the terrible hardships of war. They are inevitable, and the only way the people of Atlanta can hope once more to live in peace and quiet at home, is to stop the war, which can only be done by admitting that it began in error and is perpetuated in pride.

> *General William T. Sherman, in his reply to the petition of the mayor and council of Atlanta to rescind his order of civilian evacuation, September 12, 1864, in* Personal Memoirs of General W. T. Sherman, *Vol. 2, p. 125.*

While lying at the Opequon about 12 [noon on September 19, 1864] I received orders to leave my smallest brigade to guard the trains and move the balance of my command rapidly to the front on the Winchester pike, where the Sixth and Nineteenth Corps had been for some time warmly engaged with the enemy. I left the Second Brigade and started at once with the First and Third. The pike was filled with wagons, artillery, ambulances, and stragglers running back from the scene of action, very seriously impeding my progress. After proceeding about two miles, I reported in person to General Crook, and under his supervision, formed my command in two lines on the right of the pike and in the rear of a heavy wood, in front of which the Nineteenth Corps was posted and was at the time fighting the enemy. . . . When these dispositions were made General Sheridan arrived upon the ground and directed me, as soon as Colonel Duval's division arrived . . . to move forward and charge the enemy and drive him from the woods in which he was posted about 600 yards to my front. General [William] Emory informed me that his [Nineteenth] corps had charged the enemy in this wood about an hour previous to my arrival and had been repulsed and driven back. A rousing cheer from the opposite side of Red Bud Run announced Colonel Duval's approach, and the order was at once given to move forward, which was done with alacrity. After moving about 300 yards through the open field the enemy's artillery and musketry opened very briskly upon my lines, but its effect was to increase the impetuosity of the command, and with deafening yells and cheers the men rushed forward and reached the wood to find the enemy breaking and running in confusion. A rapid pursuit was made, firing as briskly as possible and cheering most lustily. Deep ravines and entangling brushwood prevented the preservation of lines, and as the command emerged into the open country beyond, all technical order was gone, the two brigades were merged into a victorious throng, each idividual of which was bent on pursuing and punishing the enemy, and all eagerly running and loading and firing and cheering. The enemy's left was entirely broken and we had passed beyond the left of his line that still remained intact, and receiving from it a fire into our left flank and rear . . . After facing to the left a succession of stone walls gave excellent cover to the enemy and from behind them we received a very severe musketry fire, and at time suffered heavily from artillery, but we steadily advanced and beat back the enemy. The more advanced would take shelter behind a stone wall or such other protection as the irregularity of the surface of the land would afford; others would rush forward and take position beside these; soon a strong line would be formed and another advance made to the next stone wall or protection. After proceeding upward of a mile the Nineteenth Corps came up in our rear, and from that time forward assisted in driving the enemy. . . . The conduct of officers and men was as a general thing deserving of the highest praise. I have never witnessed more zeal and daring than was here displayed. It is true our lines were broken and gone, but had we moved in such a manner as to preserve our lines, the enemy would have escaped unhurt or else driven us back.

Report of Colonel Joseph Thoburn of the Union's First Infantry Division of West Virginia, on the Battle of Winchester (or Opequon), September 19, 1864, commenting on the success of the unconventional tactic of advancing by squads and taking cover rather than marching in brigade order, in Official Records of the Union and Confederate Armies During the War of the Rebellion, *Series I, Vol. 43 (Part I), pp. 368–369.*

In moving back to this point the whole country from the Blue Ridge to the North Mountains has been made untenable for a rebel army. I have destroyed over 2,000 barns filled with wheat, hay, and farming implements; over seventy mills filled with flour and wheat; have driven in front of the army over 4[,000] head of stock, and have killed and issued to the troops not less than 3,000 sheep. This destruction embraces the Luray Valley and Little Fort Valley, as well as the main valley. A large number of horses have been obtained, a proper estimate of which I cannot now make. Lieut. John R. Meigs, my engineer officer, was murdered beyond Harrisonburg, near Dayton. For this atrocious act all the houses within an area of five miles were burned. Since I came into the Valley, from Harper's Ferry up to Harrisonburg, every train, every small party, and every straggler has been bushwacked by people, many of whom have protection papers from commanders who have been hitherto in this valley. From the vicinity of Harrisonburg over 400 wagon-loads of refugees have been sent back to Martinsburg; most of these people were Dunkers and had been conscripted. The people here are getting sick of the war; heretofore they have had no reason to complain, because they have been living in great abundance. I have not been followed by the enemy up to this point, with the exception of a small force of rebel cavalry that showed themselves some distance behind my rear guard today . . . McNeill was mortally wounded and fell into our hands. This was fortunate, as he was the most daring and dangerous of all the bushwhackers in this section of the country. . . .

I sent a party of cavalry through Thornton's Gap and Front Royal. Thornton's Gap I have given up, as of no value. With this disposition of forces, I will move infantry round the mountains, via Strasburg, as soon as possible. Tomorrow I will continue the destruction of wheat, forage, &c., down to Fisher's Hill. When this is completed the [Shenandoah] Valley, from Winchester up to Staunton, ninety-two miles, will have but little in it for man or beast.

General Philip Sheridan, in a report from Woodstock, Virginia, October 9, 1864, in Official Records of the Union and Confederate Armies, *Series I, Vol. 43 (Part I), p. 31.*

Toward 6 o'clock in the morning of [October 19, 1864], the officer on picket duty at Winchester came to my room, I being yet in bed, and reported artillery firing from the direction of Cedar Creek. I asked him if the firing was continuous or only desultory, to which he replied that it was not a sustained fire, but rather irregular and fitful. I remarked: "It's all right; Grover has gone out this morning to make a reconnoissance, and he is merely feeling the enemy." I tried to go to sleep again, but grew so restless that I could not, and soon got up and dressed myself. A little later the picket officer came back and reported that the firing, which could be distinctly heard from his line on the heights outside of Winchester, was still going on. I asked him if it sounded like a battle, and as he again said that it did not, I still inferred that the cannonading was caused by Grover's division banging away at the enemy simply to find out what he was up to. However, I went downstairs and requested that breakfast be hurried up, and at the same time ordered the horses to be saddled and in readiness, for I concluded to go to the front before any further examinations were made in regard to the defensive line.

We mounted our horses between half-past 8 and 9, and as we were proceeding up the street which leads directly through Winchester, from the Logan residence, where Edwards was quartered, to the Valley Pike, I noticed that there were many women at the windows and doors of the houses, who kept shaking their skirts at us and who were otherwise markedly insolent in their demeanor, but supposing this conduct to be instigated by their well-known and perhaps natural prejudices, I ascribed to it no unusual significance. On reaching the edge of the town I halted a moment, and there heard quite distinctly the sound of artillery firing in an unceasing roar. Concluding from this that a battle was in progress, I now felt confident that the women along the street had received intelligence from the battlefield by the "grape-vine telegraph," and were in raptures over some good news, while I as yet was utterly ignorant of the actual situation. Moving on, I put my head downward toward the pommel of my saddle and listened intently, trying to locate and interpret the sound, continuing in this position till we had crossed Mill Creek, about half a mile from Winchester. The result of my efforts in the interval was the conviction that the travel of the sound was increasing too rapidly to be accounted for by my own rate of motion, and that therefore my army must be falling back.

Union general Philip Sheridan rallied his troops, riding along their line of retreat at Winchester, Virginia. His charismatic leadership was captured in a widely printed poem by Thomas Buchanan Read, and in numerous dramatic paintings and cartoons. *(Library of Congress, Prints and Photographs Division, LC-USZ62–2350)*

Union general Philip Sheridan, recounting his discovery of Confederate general Jubal Early's troops at Cedar Creek in the Shenandoah Valley on October 19, 1864, which led to his rallying the Union forces and the defeat of Early's army, as recalled in Personal Memoirs of P. H. Sheridan, *pp. 68–75.*

Loaded up 250 bushels of Major Williams' wheat this morning. Started wagons and men off in various directions and in a few hours the wagons came back loaded, and the men with plenty of hogs, cattle and sheep. Mrs. Williams wanted to buy my pocket knife, and I gave it to her. Started for camp about 11 o'clock. [Captain] Moulton and I rode ahead rapidly, trusting to luck to escape guerillas, and reached camp safely a little after dark, leaving the foraging party to come on as fast as they could. Result of Expedition—about 1000 bushels wheat, 150 sheep, 50 hogs, 75 cattle and 30 bushel sweet potatoes, besides a large amount of poultry. The valleys of Northwestern Georgia, between Lookout Mountain and Taylor's ridge, are beautiful, well watered, well cultivated and productive.

Union major James A. Connolly, describing the results of a foraging expedition during Sherman's March to the Sea, in his diary entry for October 24, 1864, in Paul Angle, ed., Three Years in the Army of the Cumberland, *p. 284.*

The country through which I have passed and in which I have operated has been left in such a condition as to barely leave subsistence for the inhabitants. The property destroyed, viz, grain, forage, flouring mills, tanneries, blast furnaces, &c., and stock driven off, has inflicted a severe blow on the enemy. The money value of this property could not have been less than $3,000,000. There is still considerable forage and stock in the valley, east of the Blue Ridge, adjacent to the headwaters of the Rappahannock.... I have the honor to report that during the operations of my command, since under my immediate control, I have endeavored to execute all orders from headquarters promptly and to the letter, fearless and regardless of rebel consequences. On the 5th and 13th [of October 1864] it became my duty, though painful and repugnant to my own feelings, to order the execution of three Confederate bushwhackers, in retaliation for two Union soldiers murdered by guerillas, believing it to be the only means of protection to our soldiers against the operations of all such illegal and outlawed bands of horse-thieves and murderers, recognized and supported by rebel authorities, for which

I have been threatened by the Richmond press. But by this I cannot be intimidated in the discharge of my duties under orders. And I wish it distinctly understood by the rebel authorities that if two to one is not sufficient I will increase it to twenty-two to one, and leave the consequences in the hands of my Government.

Union general William Henry Powell, reporting on operations against bushwhackers in the Shenandoah Valley, October 27, 1864, in Official Records of the Union and Confederate Armies, *Series I, Vol. 43, (Part I), pp. 510–511.*

Presently another horseman appeared, then another and another, until at least twenty were in sight on the crest of the hill. They were evidently too strong for us, even if we had been well armed which we were not. . . . But look! The gray clad horsemen are starting forward and now they are waving a white handkerchief. It must be a deputation of citizens coming out to surrender the capital to us. So the General thought; so we all thought. The General [Absalom Baird], directed Colonel [Orlando Metcalfe] Poe to go forward and meet the party and see what they wanted and who they were. Forward dashed Poe, and there we sat watching the scene with intense anxiety. Can it be possible that we are to meet with such good fortune as to receive the formal surrender of Georgia's capital? Poe meets the horsemen, they halt a few moments, then Poe returns, and they all come on to where the General Captain [E.K.] Butrick and myself are waiting in the road. We ask each other what this means. Can there be treachery here? Do they mean to deceive us with a white flag and capture us all? They approach within 200 yards and we plainly see their rebel uniforms. Shall we run or stand? Moments are precious. They come steadily on. The General looks pale. I *feel* pale and nervous, but the General stands, and therefore I *must.* They reach us, rein up their horses and the gray clad officer riding at the head of the party salutes the General and announces himself and party as Kilpatrick's [Union] scouts just from Milledgeville; they say they rode through the city, and that there is not a rebel soldier there. Hurrah! Milledgeville is ours, and our sensations are now quite different from what they were ten minutes ago.

Union major James A. Connolly, noting in his diary the approach of Union troops to Milledgeville, Civil War capital of Georgia, and encountering Union scouts wearing Confederate uniforms as a ruse de guerre, *on November 22, 1864, in Paul Angle, ed.,* Three Years in the Army of the Cumberland, *pp. 316–317.*

We are going toward the Ogeechee, and citizens tell us we will find very poor country all the way from the Oconee to the Ogeechee. Our foragers came into camp tonight pretty well loaded, and I can't imagine where they found so much stuff through this country. I suppose the negroes assisted them. Where can all the rebels be? Here we are riding rough shod over Georgia and nobody dares to fire a shot at us. We burn their houses, barns, fences, cotton and everything else, yet none of the Southern braves show themselves to punish us for our vandalism. Perhaps they are preparing a trap to catch us all, but I don't think we will go into their trap, if we can find anyway to go around it. We don't care where we come out; would a little rather come out at Savannah, but if we can't do that we'll go somewhere else. Georgia is an excellent state for foraging. We are living finely, and the whole army would have no objection to marching around through the State for the next six months. Indeed, the whole trip thus far has been a holiday excursion, but a very expensive one to the rebels.

Union major James A. Connolly, noting in his diary the lack of Confederate resistance to Sherman's March to the Sea, on November 25, 1864, in Paul Angle, ed., Three Years in the Army of the Cumberland, *p. 322.*

On came the enemy, as steady and resistless as a tidal wave. A couple of guns, in the advance line, gave them a shot and galloped back to the works. A volley from a thin skirmish-line was sent into their ranks, but without causing any delay to the massive array. A moment more, and with that wild "rebel yell" which, once heard, is never forgotten, the great human wave swept along, and seemed to ingulf the little force that had so sturdily awaited it.

The first shock came, of course, upon the two misplaced brigades of Wagner's division, which, through some one's blunder, had remained in their false position until too late to retire without disaster. They had no tools to throw up works; and when struck by the resistless sweep of Cleburne's and Brown's divisions, they had only to make their way, as best they could, back to the works. In that wild rush, in which friend and foe were intermingled, and the piercing "rebel yell" rose high above the "Yankee cheer," nearly seven hundred were made prisoners. But, worst of all for the Union side, the men of Reilly's and Strickland's brigades dared not fire, lest they should shoot down their own comrades, and the guns, loaded with grape and canister, stood silent in the embrasures. With loud shouts of

"Let's go into the works with them," the triumphant Confederates, now more like a wild, howling mob than an organized army, swept on to the very works, with hardly a check from any quarter. So fierce was the rush that a number of the fleeing soldiers—officers and men—dropped exhausted into the ditch, and lay there while the terrific contest raged over their heads, till, under cover of darkness, they could crawl safely inside the intrenchments. . . .

Where there was nothing to hinder the Union fire, the muskets of Stiles and Casement's brigades made fearful havoc; while the batteries at the railroad cut plowed furrows through the ranks of the advancing foe. Time after time they came up to the very works, but they never crossed them except as prisoners. More than one color-bearer was shot down on the parapet. It is impossible to exaggerate the fierce energy with which the Confederate soldiers, that short November afternoon, threw themselves against the works, fighting with what seemed the very madness of despair. There was not a breath of wind, and the dense smoke settled down upon the field, so that, after the first assault, it was impossible to see at any distance.

Union colonel Henry Stone, member of the staff of General George Henry Thomas, describing the Battle of Franklin, November 29, 1864, in Battles and Leaders of the Civil War, *Vol. 4, pp. 451–453.*

On the 8th [of December], as I rode along, I found the column turned out of the main road, marching through the fields. Close by, in the corner of a fence, was a group of men standing around a handsome young officer, whose foot had been blown to pieces by a torpedo [mine] planted in the road. He was waiting for a surgeon to amputate his leg, and he told me that he was riding along with the rest of his brigade staff of the Seventeenth Corps, when a torpedo trodden on by his horse had exploded, killing the horse and literally blowing off all the flesh from one of his legs. I saw the terrible wound, and made full inquiry into the facts. There had been no resistance at that point, nothing to give warning of danger, and the rebels had planted eight-inch shells in the road, with friction-matches to explode them by being trodden on. This was not war, but murder, and it made me very angry. I immediately ordered a lot of rebel prisoners to be brought from the provost-guard, armed with picks and spades, and made them march in close order along the road, so as to explode their own torpedoes, or to discover and dig them up. They begged hard, but I reiterated the order and could hardly help laughing at their stepping so gingerly along the road, where it was supposed sunken torpedoes might explode at each step, but they found no other torpedoes till near Fort McAllister.

General William Tecumseh Sherman, encountering road-mines on December 8, 1864, on the approach to Savannah, and commenting on his response of forcing Confederate prisoners to clear a path through the mines, in Personal Memoirs of General W. T. Sherman, *Voll. II, p. 194.*

9

Partisan Politics
September 1861–November 1864

During the Civil War, Lincoln worked in the partisan atmosphere of a two-party system with both Republicans and Democrats, while Jefferson Davis had no clear party system. In the Confederacy, all congressmen and governors gave up party labels, although most were former Democrats. This remarkable difference between the political systems in the North and the South has struck some observers as so important that they believe it contributed to the victory of the Union and the defeat of the Confederacy. The argument runs that, since Lincoln had a party system, he could identify friends and opponents clearly and could more easily control opposition since it had political expression, was focused, and was defeated at the polls in 1864. That electoral defeat, in the American tradition, meant that the minority consented to the majority decision and somewhat put to rest organized Democratic resistance to Republican rule as a threat to the Union. However, the political reality of the Union was quite a lot more complicated than what might be thought possible of a simple two-party system.

Within Lincoln's own Republican Party, divisions between radicals, who wanted a more aggressive conduct of the war and a clear policy of using the war to emancipate the slaves, and moderates, who wanted a less aggressive attitude toward the South as well as a more moderate policy on emancipation, represented a severe split. Radicals and moderates struggled for influence in the cabinet, in Congress, and for political control of states. For the most part, Lincoln was identified more with the moderate or conservative wing, than with the radical wing of his party. He resisted the actions of individual generals like Frémont and Hunter to declare emancipation within their own jurisdictions. He argued for gradual, compensated emancipation, rather than immediate abolition of slavery, and he supported deportation and colonization abroad of freed slaves. In 1864, he proposed a plan for readmission of former Confederate states to the Union when 10 percent of the voting electorate signed a loyalty oath to the United States, while radicals thought such a plan far too lenient to the rebels.

Only after Congress had passed the Confiscation Act of 1862 did Lincoln adopt the Emancipation Proclamation. Even that measure was seen by radicals as a step backward, for it promised to have no effect in areas of the former Confederacy that declared their loyalty rather than exposing such loyal areas to emancipation by means of the Confiscation Act. Between the date of the announcement of the Emancipation Proclamation in September 1862 and its promulgation in January 1863, radicals feared that Lincoln would use presidential power to actually roll back the effect of the Confiscation Act of 1862 and limit emancipation only to those regions that had not given up or been defeated by January 1, 1863. For all these reasons, radical Republicans in Congress, who saw the war as a means to destroy slavery and, at the same time, to punish the seceding states, found Lincoln, with his insistence that the war was simply to preserve the Union, with or without slavery, extremely soft on the Confederacy and on slavery itself.

Of course, individual Republican congressmen and senators differed in their motives and opinions. The radical faction in the Senate was led by Benjamin Wade of Ohio, Zachariah Chandler of Michigan, and Lyman Trumbull of Illinois. Chandler and Wade made much of their background as self-made men. Trumbull harbored jealousy of Lincoln's success, and, although he had never been an advocate of the rights of African Americans, he argued for punishing the South. Other radicals included Charles Sumner of Massachusetts and John P. Hale, a former Free-Soil Party member from New Hampshire. In the House of Representatives, Thaddeus Stevens of Pennsylvania emerged during the war as witty, sarcastic, determined, and probably the most influential radical in the lower chamber of Congress. Some other Republicans were less hot-headed, and several were effective, pragmatic politicians who hoped to aid Lincoln in finding solutions. In the Senate, William P. Fessenden of Maine supported the president with just such a stand.

Twentieth-century artist Douglas Volk painted this portrait of a pensive Lincoln in 1922. *(Library of Congress, Prints and Photographs Division, LC-USZ62–130959)*

As far as the Democrats were concerned, they too were divided. Copperheads flirted with treason in supporting the Confederate cause, while more moderate Democrats argued that the war was a failure. However, sincere Copperheads, like Congressman Clement Vallandigham of Ohio, opposed Lincoln and the war not out of direct sympathy for the Confederacy or for the institution of slavery, but from a mix of motives that included opposition to Lincoln's violation of civil liberties, opposition to the draft, fear that radical measures would raise the status of blacks, and concern that blacks would migrate en masse to the Northern states. Thus Copperheadism was not, as the Republicans claimed, simply pro-Confederacy treason or sympathy with rebellion, but was based on a set of values that included defense of civil liberties and belief in local self-government, combined with deeply-held and often vicious racial prejudice. In the North, racist attitudes and racial hostility were strongest in the Northern "border states," that is, Illinois, Ohio, Indiana, and Pennsylvania, and in New York City.

Opposed to the Copperheads were many Democrats who saw Vallandigham's position as close to treason and who supported the war. These War Democrats tended to support Lincoln's administration, but some believed that under Democratic leadership, the war could be conducted more effectively.

With such a complex mix of political crosscurrents, Lincoln did not have a stable two-party system that allowed him to identify friends and enemies, but, faced at least four active and identifiable factions: two or more factions within his own Republican Party and two factions in the Democratic Party. Furthermore, the situation was fluid, with shifting alignments on specific issues. Lincoln came to endorse the attempt to fuse the moderate faction of his own party with the War faction of the Democratic Party to create a Union Party, which succeeded in crucial states and was relatively ignored in other states. The organization and effectiveness of the Union Party varied from state to state, but it was a good device for bringing together War Democrats and Republicans into a single political organization in the elections from 1861 through 1864. In this period, there were state and local elections every year, with congressional elections in 1862 and 1864 and of course the presidential election in 1864.

Lincoln recognized that to win reelection in 1864 he would need support in the core Northern border states that lay in a line from Pennsylvania to Illinois. To win those states he had to attract War Democrats. Furthermore, he hoped to bring the Confederate states back into the Union and to win their adherence to his program. Both his plan for readmission of the Confederate states and his plans regarding slavery were calculated to appeal, not to the radicals within his own Republican Party, but to the emerging coalition of moderate Republicans and War Democrats, especially those in the states from New York and Pennsylvania through Illinois.

Lincoln's concept regarding the former Confederate states was to establish some means by which they would be readily accepted back into the Union, be represented in Congress, and count in the presidential elections. The radicals wanted to treat the former Confederate states as territories or as conquered lands. Lincoln's 10-percent plan for reconstruction and for readmission of the former Confederate states was far more moderate than the plan of the radicals. In July 1864 Congress passed the Wade-Davis bill, requiring that before representatives from Confederate states would be readmitted to Congress, a majority of voters would have to sign a loyalty oath.

Lincoln's concept regarding slaves was to ensure their emancipation, probably in some form of graduated, compensated emancipation (which some Unionist slaveholders in the Confederacy and slaveholding border states appeared ready to accept), while the radicals supported immediate and uncompensated emancipation. The slaves themselves, by voting with their feet, simply made it clear that they regarded the war as the opportunity to end slavery. Looking ahead in 1864, Lincoln wanted to implement a plan of gradual and compensated emancipation and work to admit the Confederate states, both ideas strongly opposed by the radical Republicans.

Political realignment during the war reflected the crosscurrents. Ohio held a state election in the fall of 1861. Neither party could be sure of winning on a regular partisan platform, and the Republican state executive committee decided to give up its regular party organization and call for a Union convention, to be held in Columbus on September 5. War Democrats joined with Republicans to nominate a War Democrat, David Tod, for governor, and the Union ticket went on to win. Senator Benjamin Wade, who was up for reelection by the legislature, cooperated with the coalition, despite his misgivings as a radical. Republican leadership in other states where the party was weak—Connecticut, Delaware, New Jersey, Pennsylvania—followed the example of Ohio over the next few years. However, where the Republicans dominated and had no need for War Democrat support, as in some states of New England and the upper

Midwest, the Republicans took on the new party label as Unionists, but kept their old Republican organization without incorporating War Democrats. For their part, War Democrats were glad to throw their candidates and support in with Republicans in some Union Party coalitions, as many of them believed that the Peace Democrats flirted with treason.

After Ohio developed a Union Party in the fall of 1861 to harness War Democrats with Republicans and as other Northern border states followed suit, Lincoln adopted and supported that strategy. The Union Party label and organization temporarily replaced the Republican Party over the next few elections. Furthermore, Lincoln encouraged Union Party development with other patronage appointments. In the 1863 elections, Republicans and War Democrats ran as Union Party members, winning the crucial Ohio governorship and Pennsylvania governorship, where Andrew Curtin was reelected.

Because of such complications, rather than facing a clear set of supporters and opponents, Lincoln faced a constantly changing set of political challenges. When radicals in the House under the leadership of Henry Dawes of Massachusetts investigated Secretary of War Cameron's corrupt practice of awarding contracts to

Lincoln's secretary of war, Edwin Stanton, changed his allegiance from the Democratic Party to become a Republican and firm supporter of Lincoln. *(Library of Congress, Prints and Photographs Division, LC-USZ62–101375)*

friends, in December 1861 Cameron tried to win their support by authorizing the freeing of slaves and arming them, without first getting Lincoln's approval. Lincoln replaced Cameron with Edwin Stanton. Lincoln's appointment of former Democrat Stanton as secretary of war reflected the Union Party approach. Even so, Stanton personally turned in a radical direction.

The struggle within the Union/Republican Party for control of policies toward the Confederates and slavery continued before and after the Emancipation Proclamation. Thaddeus Stevens urged immediate emancipation but was willing to support a clause for compensation to loyal slaveholders. In 1861 and 1862, Congress could support neither colonization nor immediate emancipation. However, in 1862 Congress began to move on the issues—amending the articles of war to prohibit officers from returning slaves to owners, whether loyal or disloyal. Lincoln did not communicate this order directly to officers. Congress responded with compensated emancipation in the District of Columbia, prohibiting slavery in the territories, and repealing the Fugitive Slave Law in the period March through June of 1862. Avid radicals outside of Congress, like Horace Greeley of the New York *Tribune,* and renowned abolitionists and literary figures such as Wendell Phillips, Orestes Brownson, and Gerritt Smith kept up a barrage of criticism of Lincoln for adopting halfway measures that compromised with slavery or that allowed weak generals to remain in command.

Through 1863 and 1864 opposition to Lincoln in the North took several forms besides pressure from the radicals for more definitive measures regarding the ending of slavery. For Copperheads, Lincoln's infringement of civil liberties provided one focus. Some Peace Democrats, like Congressman George Pendleton of Ohio, continued to argue that the Confederate states had every right to secede and that Lincoln's measures to suppress the right of secession represented violations of the Constitution. War Democrats, like McClellan, urged, without specifics, a more vigorous prosecution of the war. Moderate Republicans tended to support Lincoln, although some of them worried he went too far with his emancipation measures. For radicals, candidates like Salmon Chase and General John C. Frémont, with more aggressive antislavery and anti-Confederate policies, seemed attractive. However, both of these more radical Republicans had "baggage" that weakened their chances for winning support even among the radicals. Frémont had lost the election of 1856 and had a record as an incompetent general, while Salmon Chase displayed an eagerness to run for the office, regarded in that age as a disqualification. Voters believed that anyone who actively sought office showed a degree of personal ambition inappropriate in a public servant.

THE SOUTH

Jefferson Davis had no party system, but only supporters and opponents. His most notable opponents were Zebulon Vance, governor of North Carolina, who had been a declared Unionist before secession; Vice President Alexander Stephens, who had been a Cooperationist during the secession crisis; and Georgia's Governor Joseph Brown who actively subverted the Confederate draft in his state. All three stood for greater states' rights. To varying extents and with varying effectiveness, they each obstructed the tendency of Jefferson Davis to establish a centralized nation out of the Confederacy. The issue in the South focused on the question of whether or not the core doctrine of states' sovereignty that had provided the justification for secession could be sustained as the new confederated nation went to war to preserve its independence. Abraham Lincoln had predicted in his 1861 inaugural speech that the principle of the minority's sovereign right to secede would inevitably lead to dissolution of the Confederacy. By 1863 and 1864, his prediction seemed very apt.

On the other hand, Davis appeared to be able to get what he wanted from his Congress, and the opposition, such as it was, was strongest in Georgia and North Carolina. It should be remembered that Lincoln had similar difficulty with local governments (especially Horatio Seymour in New York State and Mayor Thurlow Weed in New York City), as well as with other Peace Democrats holding positions as legislators, mayors, and governors in Ohio and elsewhere. So, to depict the South as so severely weakened by states' rights in contrast to a politically united North ignores the complexity of Lincoln's political situation and may exaggerate the weakness of Davis. The fact that Davis had been elected to a six-year term and, under the Confederate constitution, would not face an election during the war, also strengthened his hand.

Despite the one-party structure and a longer term of office than Lincoln had, Davis clearly faced prob-

Vice President of the Confederacy Alexander Stephens was dissatisfied with the leadership of Jefferson Davis and tended to stay away from Richmond. *(Library of Congress, Prints and Photographs Division, LC-B8172–1430)*

lems. The elections to the Confederate Congress were held in the fall of 1863, after a series of Confederate military defeats and with Southern morale sinking. Individual candidates ran without party organization, on such issues as the draft, management of Confederate finances, operation of blockade runners, and the issue of tax in kind or goods. Without parties, some factions seemed to emerge, with supporters of Joseph E. Johnston representing one group who opposed Jefferson Davis. Louis Wigfall, who had served under Johnston, was elected to the Confederate senate from Texas in 1862, and Wigfall spoke out in 1863 against Davis. Price inflation, food shortages, and bitterness over Davis's management of the war coalesced. The Confederate congress, before the 1863 election, had 26 out of 106 members openly opposed to Davis. After the election, the number of anti-Davis members climbed to 41, and 12 out of 26 senators were also anti-Davis. Although party designations had vanished, former Whigs and Constitutional Union candidates took several governorships, including Mississippi and Alabama. The Confederate congress included representatives of areas not really part of the Confederacy, such as Kentucky and Missouri, as well as occupied sections of Mississippi, Tennessee, Louisiana, and Arkansas. Since elections could not be held for the Confederate congress in areas under control of Union troops, representatives from these states and areas tended to be reelected by handfuls of refugees from the regions, and they remained pretty staunch Davis supporters for the most part. Since, if the war was settled by negotiation, these occupied districts would apparently fall to the Union, the congressmen from the shadow districts had every reason to demand a fight to the bitter end, and some of them represented the strongest supporters of Davis. In the 1863 election, both Georgia and North Carolina had no Union occupiers, and it was noteworthy that of the new congressmen elected in those states, 16 out of 19 were Davis opponents. Thus, where Confederate control was strongest, Davis was most opposed; where Confederate control was weak or nonexistent, Davis partisans predominated. The Confederate politicians advocating a negotiated peace were called conservatives, tories, or reconstructionists, although no real parties coalesced around these labels.

The three leaders of politics in Georgia were Vice President Alexander Stephens, Governor Joseph Brown, and former general Robert Toombs. Brown appointed several thousand Georgians to state office so they would be exempted from the Confederate draft. Georgia's senators both voted against suspension of habeas corpus in February 1864. When the measure passed over their opposition, Stephens was outraged. He had his brother introduce a measure in the Georgia legislature condemning the suspension of the writ of habeas corpus as an attack on basic rights. Both Governor Brown and Vice President Stephens urged a negotiated settlement of the war on the basis of a Northern recognition of Southern independence. The measure may have been intended, not to bring about an actual settlement, but to strengthen the hand of Copperhead advocates of peace in the North. However, the Stephens-Brown initiative for a peace settlement outraged Southern editorialists and Davis himself.

Pockets of outright opposition to the war continued in the Appalachian Mountains, from eastern Tennessee and western North Carolina south into a few mountain counties of Alabama and Georgia. As Confederate deserters fled to these regions, the combination of Unionists, tories, and reconstructionists meant that for all practical purposes, the mountain region was outside of Confederate control. In North Carolina, Zebulon Vance and many reconstructionists made it clear, however, that they supported the war. William Holden, publisher of the *North*

Carolina Standard from Raleigh, claimed to represent the Conservative Party and threw his support to Vance, stressing state independence within the Confederacy. By late 1863 and 1864, Holden began organizing peace meetings that Davis supporters regarded as treasonous. A solid block of North Carolina congressmen opposed Davis. However, as Holden became more outspoken in his anti-war campaign, Vance broke with the Conservatives and Holden, with Holden deciding to run for the governorship on his own in 1864. In the North, Lincoln supporter Horace Greeley believed that it would be wise to open negotiations toward peace to strengthen Holden's hand. However, by alleging that Holden was flirting with treason, Vance won reelection with a strong showing among North Carolina troops. Despite Vance's independence from Davis, he had kept the state in the Confederate camp.

Thus, even in the South, with a no-party or one-party system, politics remained lively and tended to serve as a channel for arguments over crucial issues of war and peace, state-central government relations, and personal loyalty to the leadership. While there was no clear two-party system in the Confederacy, politics there still served as a means by which such disputes were peaceably expressed and to an extent resolved.[1]

Zebulon Vance, governor of North Carolina, remained critical of Jefferson Davis, one example of several severe political divisions within the Confederacy. *(Library of Congress, Prints and Photographs Division, LC-DIG-cwpbh-04049)*

THE VALLANDIGHAM EXILE

Through 1863 and 1864, a previously obscure Ohio congressman, Clement Vallandigham, rose to national and international notoriety. Although he was defeated for reelection to the U.S. Congress in the elections held in October 1862, his term did not expire until the end of the 37th Congress, in March 1863. A committed Copperhead, Vallandigham introduced a resolution in Congress in December 1862 condemning Lincoln for usurpation of power and trying to establish a dictatorship, the very position held by Jefferson Davis. The resolution was easily defeated, but Vallandigham persisted, giving another speech in Congress in January 1863 condemning the whole Republican Party for supporting the Northern dictatorship.

In Ohio, General Burnside was in charge of maintaining order, as commandant of the district and of the Army of the Ohio (before being replaced by General Schofield). Burnside rashly issued General Order No. 39 in April 1863 prohibiting speeches or publications critical of the administration, declaring such material as treason. Widely criticized for this infringement of civil liberties, Burnside stuck with his decision. Outraged, Vallandigham, now a former congressman, decided to challenge the law, and gave a heated speech in Mount Vernon, Ohio, on May 1, attacking the Republican administration and being specifically critical of Burnside's attempted suppression of free speech. Burnside ordered Vallandigham's arrest by army troops, who conducted a dramatic nighttime arrest at his home. Vallandigham fired a gun out the window in a vain attempt to attract local police or other supporters, but he was taken from his home and brought before a military commission for trial. Although newspapers carried the story, Burnside made no official report to the War Department. When Lincoln heard that the military court had condemned Vallandigham to a term in prison, he issued an order to Burnside to have Vallandigham transferred to Confederate lines.

The exile of Vallandigham satisfied no one, particularly Vallandigham himself, who did not find a warm welcome in the Confederacy. Transferred to the care of General Braxton Bragg on May 25, he quickly traveled across the Confederacy to Richmond, where he briefly met with officials, before arranging transportation by way of a blockade runner to Bermuda. In defiance of Burnside and Lincoln, Ohio Democrats nominated Vallandigham for governor of the state while he was still in the Confederacy. After shipping to Bermuda and thence to Canada, Vallandigham set up political headquarters in Windsor, Ontario, in effect conducting his campaign for governor while out of the country. In the October 1863 elections in Ohio, Vallandigham was defeated for the post of governor by the War Democrat, John Brough, running on the Union Party platform.

However, the nation had not heard the last of former congressman Vallandigham. He returned to the United States, where Lincoln decided not to rearrest him but to ignore him. With his celebrity from the exile and campaign, Vallandigham was highly regarded among Copperhead or Peace Democrats, and, accordingly, his voice would be important in the nominating convention for the Democratic Party held in 1864 in Chicago.[2]

1864 POLITICS

The greatest political challenge to Lincoln's control came in the election of 1864. In 1864, the Democrats believed they had a good chance at taking the presidency. Early in the summer, they were encouraged by a stagnant Union war effort, with no end in sight. The misery of death, mounting debts, infringement of civil liberties, suspension of habeas corpus, and destruction of the battlefield areas could only redound to their political benefit, they believed. Furthermore, despite his moderation and resistance to the radicals, Lincoln had adopted several key policies that were extremely unpopular because they were perceived by Democrats as too radical and too pro-African American. He had endorsed emancipation in the proclamation, which horrified the racial ideas of most Northern whites, especially those in the border North. The fact that his party contained more advanced radicals who urged the granting of civil rights to blacks and the fact that he had come to endorse emancipation allowed his Democratic opponents to evoke explicit racial hostility.

Democratic campaigners and newspapers asserted that Lincoln had mixed ancestry, that he advocated interracial sexual relations, and that he sought to grant blacks equal status with whites. The military draft had generated not only opposition, but also riots that had then turned on blacks, as in the summer of 1863 in New York. The use of black troops appeared to be a radical concept, and, indeed, was heartily supported by most radical Republicans but horrified Democrats, whose racism went unconcealed. Even for Democrats who did not evoke racial issues, the violation of civil liberties by the administration and the suggestion that Lincoln sought to establish a dictatorship raised other fears. Despite the defection of War Democrats to the Union Party, Democrats still sought to call on party loyalty. After all, Democrats were the oldest party, tracing their ancestry back to Jefferson and Jackson; before Lincoln, the Democrats had lost the Presidency only twice since 1800—to Whig William Henry Harrison in 1840 and to Whig Zachary Taylor in 1848. Although weakened by internal dissension, the Democrats were numerous, had thousands of local clubs supporting them, and a long tradition of running political campaigns and winning them. In New Jersey, New York, Pennsylvania, and the states along the Ohio River, they had strong organizations, many office holders, and hundreds of thousands of voters. With so much hostility to Lincoln and with the popular dismay at the casualties from the war, their chances seemed good.

When Lincoln issued a "To Whom It May Concern" letter on July 18, 1864, defining the conditions for Confederate readmission to the Union, he included a requirement that the Confederate states abolish slavery. That measure further diminished his support among War Democrats and some conservative Republicans. Coupled with the Emancipation Proclamation, the recruitment of black troops, and battlefield emancipation, Lincoln's desire to impose the condition of abolition for readmission fed the Democrats' claim that Lincoln endorsed "miscegenation." The word itself first appeared in public discourse during this campaign, introduced in an anonymous pamphlet published by the *New York World*. The pamphlet, purporting to be a secret Republican publication, pretended to promote interracial marriage as a solution to the race problem. Soon, the word *miscegenation* showed up widely in cartoons used in other Democratic newspapers, and in name-calling. The Democratic press labeled the Emancipation Proclamation the Miscegenation Proclamation.

When the Democratic national convention met in Chicago in August 1864, the Union had suffered several military defeats, and that gave further encouragement to the Democrats. At the convention, the hostility to Lincoln, to the failing war, and to the specter of altered race relations, all emboldened and empowered the Peace wing of the Democratic Party. Vallandigham emerged as the most prominent leader of that wing, and, together with Fernando Wood, the former mayor of New York City, he advanced a platform plank asking for a cease-fire and a negotiated settlement with the Confederacy. The convention ratified the plank. However, as part of a compromise between Peace and War Democrats, the convention then nominated General George B. McClellan, a War Democrat, as the party's presidential nominee. The two peace candidates for the nomination, Governor Horatio Seymour of New York and former governor Thomas Seymour of Connecticut, supported by Wood and Vallandigham, were defeated. So the result was a War Democrat running on a Peace Democrat platform, a compromise that made no one in the party entirely happy. As a further attempt to appeal to the Peace Democrat wing, Congressman George Pendleton of Ohio, a Peace Democrat, was chosen as the nominee for the vice presidency. Campaign posters suggested that Vallandigham, the most notorious of the Peace Democrats, would be selected as secretary of war.

McClellan, known as the "Young Napoleon" for his short stature, dark good looks, and self-assurance, was a weak choice despite several qualifications, including the fact that he was nationally known. Although he was popular with his troops, he had been widely criticized for the slow campaign on the Peninsula and for failing to pursue Lee after the Battle of Antietam. His hesitancy probably sprang from a concern that he not expose the troops to unnecessary casualties, but his critics personified his tactics as based on cowardice. Although still on the army rolls as an officer, he had had no military assignment for months. In accepting the nomination, McClellan repudiated the peace plank in his own platform by insisting that the negotiated readmission of the Confederate states to the Union would come only after they surrendered in the field. Peace Democrats were disgruntled by his backing away from the platform, but believed that with control of his cabinet, and if they controlled Congress, reconciliation with the Confederacy would be possible.

Even though McClellan was handicapped by divided support and by a mixed reputation, Lincoln was not at all sure of his own chances for reelection. After all, no president since Andrew Jackson had been reelected for a second term, and Lincoln was well aware that the Republican Party was a tenuous regional organization, only recently created out of an amalgam of Free-Soilers, anti Kansas-Nebraska Democrats, American Know-Nothings, and former Whigs. The patchwork quilt of factions did not compare well to the strong and long-standing Democratic Party organization. The cobbled-together quality of the party was even more apparent when it was restructured as the Union Party to incorporate War Democrats.

Furthermore, opposition to Lincoln's candidacy flourished, even among Republicans. Radicals continued to agitate for a more genuinely antislavery candidate and for one committed to punishing the seceding

General George McClellan won the Democratic nomination for Union president in 1864, yet disavowed the peace plank in his party's platform. *(Library of Congress, Prints and Photographs Division, LC-USZ62–100855)*

states, even after the Baltimore Union Party nominating convention. Radicals flirted with holding a second convention, with the possibility of nominating either Frémont or Chase. Lincoln made his cabinet members sign a pledge to cooperate with McClellan, if he were elected, between the November 1864 elections and the March 1865 inauguration, to help bring about a Confederate defeat. The goal would be to get the South to surrender before McClellan, as the next president, would have a chance to offer negotiation terms. The fact that Lincoln took this precaution demonstrated how unsure he was of his own chances in the election.

Despite Lincoln's concerns, only a few days after McClellan's nomination, the war began to turn in the Union's favor. When news reached the North of Sherman's occupation of Atlanta on September 2, Lincoln's chances for winning the election improved.[3]

THE 1864 CAMPAIGN

The election of 1864, in the midst of the war, was marked by a number of dirty tricks and vicious campaigning, as well as some simple appeals. Republicans reflected the homespun logic so much favored by Lincoln by urging, "Don't change horses in the middle of the stream." On a more sinister note, Republican supporters smeared the Democrats with the charge of disloyalty. Political cartoons by Thomas Nast and broadsides made the Democrats appear as traitors. One Republican pamphlet accused the Peace Democrats of working out a secret collaboration with the Confederates. Joseph Holt, the judge advocate general of the army, prepared a report on the Northern secret societies of Confederate sympathizers, including the Sons of Liberty. Just before the election, Republican Party officials distributed thousands of copies of the report, with the implication that the secret societies were associated with the Democrats. Indeed, it was true that many Peace Democrats did associate with the Sons of Liberty, that Vallandigham himself supported the organization, and that there was an abortive plan to rally armed Democrats to free Confederate prisoners held in prison camps in Illinois during the Democratic National convention in Chicago.

The Democrats resorted to dirty tricks and vicious campaigning, planting fears of racial amalgamation. In Indiana, white girls dressed in white dresses marched with signs urging Democratic Party voters to save them from having to marry black husbands. Democratic columnists suggested that the number of interracial births had vastly increased among white New England schoolteachers serving in the South, in the District of Columbia, and in New Orleans under the rule of Benjamin Butler.

The Union soldiers were a crucial part of Lincoln's voting support. In the 1863 off-year elections, they had tended to vote Republican. In 1864, Secretary of War Edwin Stanton made sure that soldiers received absentee ballots from those states that had such arrangements, and also insisted that soldiers be furloughed to return to vote, especially in New Jersey and Pennsylvania. Lincoln personally wrote to Generals Sherman, Meade, Sheridan, and Rosecrans to allow men from Indiana, Pennsylvania, and Missouri to be furloughed to be able to vote in their home districts. He also asked Secretary of the Navy Gideon Welles to release sailors for voting in New York. Democrats spread the news that the Republicans had encouraged Massachusetts soldiers stationed in Indiana to vote there, where the elections were held in October. However, irregularities on the other side were also common, as usual in American elections, and fraud on both sides tended to balance out.

Salmon Chase, while serving as Lincoln's secretary of the treasury, actively criticized Lincoln, sought the presidency for himself, and then resigned his post. *(Library of Congress, Prints and Photographs Division, LC-DIG-cwpbh-00710)*

THE CHASE AND FRÉMONT CANDIDACIES

Lincoln's own secretary of the treasury, Salmon Chase of Ohio, represented a threat to Lincoln's candidacy from the radical end of the spectrum. In December 1863, when Lincoln announced his 10-percent plan for reconstructing the Confederate states, dissatisfaction with Lincoln among abolitionists and radicals reached a new pitch. Chase had a long-standing commitment to racial justice, and, by contrast to Lincoln, seemed to have a clear-cut position. Chase was supported by several influential leaders, including Senator John Sherman and Representatives James Garfield and James Ashley (all from Ohio), as well as the journalist Whitelaw Reid, who reported on Washington news for the *Cincinnnati Gazette*. Senator Samuel Pomeroy of Kansas also backed Chase, partly out of pique that his suggestions for patronage in Kansas had been ignored. Chase worked for his own campaign by helping in the preparation of a biography and using appointments in the Treasury Department to favor his supporters.

Early in 1864, Chase supporters circulated a pamphlet, known as the Pomeroy Circular, which was leaked to the press, calling for a new president and suggesting Chase was the appropriate candidate. A minor scandal developed through February at the idea of a member of the cabinet displaying this sort of disloyalty to the president in time of war, and radicals backed off from their support of Chase. Even some of the Ohio Republicans dropped their support. Shortly after the Pomeroy Circular scandal, Chase withdrew his candidacy. When he offered to resign in June, Lincoln accepted the resignation. Chief Justice Taney died on October 12; Lincoln, who knew that Chase wanted the position, hesitated to appoint him immediately. Perhaps out of an effort to reestablish his loyalty to the president, Chase went on the campaign trail, and soon Lincoln appointed him to the Court. Lincoln said that he would rather have swallowed a chair.

The other serious challenge to Lincoln's renomination by the Union/Republican Party was mounted by supporters of General John C. Frémont. Lincoln had overruled Frémont's Missouri emancipation order in 1861 and had also removed him from command. Disgruntled radical Republicans held a rump convention in Cleveland a week before the regular convention in Baltimore, calling themselves The Radical Democracy. Among those attending were representatives of German-American antislavery voters in Missouri, together with a few notable abolitionists and radicals, including Frederick Douglass, Elizabeth Cady Stanton, and Wendell Phillips. Lincoln sent representatives to report on this convention. The delegates to the Cleveland convention insisted on a war without compromise, a constitutional amendment to outlaw slavery, and the extension of equal civil rights to African Americans. They also included a plank that served as a slap at Lincoln's policy of limiting civil liberties, by insisting on free speech and a free press, as well as maintaining the right of habeas corpus. The delegates also endorsed a plank calling for a one-term limitation on the president. They selected Frémont for president and former Democratic congressman from New York, John Cochrane, as their vice-presidential candidate.

Lincoln and Union Party regulars simply ignored Frémont and his Radical Democracy group. Frémont was particularly upset that Postmaster General Montgomery Blair had ignored Frémont's suggestions for patronage in Missouri and instead had taken nominees suggested by his brother, Francis P. Blair, Jr., who was a power in Missouri politics. Radical senator Zachariah Chandler negotiated with Frémont, finally getting statements from Frémont and Cochrane officially withdrawing from the race. Athough there was no explicit bargain, Lincoln later accepted the resignation of Blair, which many thought served as compensation for Frémont's withdrawal.

THE 1864 ELECTION RESULTS

Despite Lincoln's concern and the Democrats' hopes that McClellan would win, the victory in Mobile Bay in August and the fall of Atlanta in September and the generally weakened position of the Confederacy helped Lincoln. Early voting on state issues and candidates showed Union Party gains. In September, Maine and Vermont voted Union Party. In October, elections in Ohio, Indiana, and Pennsylvania registered Union Party gains. In the November presidential election, some 78 percent of the eligible Union electorate cast ballots. Lincoln received an Electoral College landslide, with 212 electors to McClellan's 21. His popular vote for the presidency of 55 percent was one of the largest in terms of percentage in the 19th century, outdone only by Jackson's 1828 election and Grant's reelection in 1872. Of course, it should be remembered that Lincoln's majority of 55 percent was based only on those states in the Union in 1864.

As Horace Greeley and other observers had predicted, the War Department policy of encouraging furloughs and absentee voting paid off for the Republicans. Twelve states that had absentee ballot systems also allowed a separate count of soldier ballots. Of these votes, Lincoln received almost 120,000, and McClellan received just over 34,000. Indiana did not permit absentee ballots, but Sherman released several thousand Indiana soldiers to return to the state, while recuperating Indiana soldiers in military hospitals were sent home if they were able to travel. In New York and Connecticut, the soldier vote was not distinguished from civilian votes, and the soldier vote may have carried those states for Lincoln. In Maryland, the soldier vote contributed to a constitutional amendment in the state abolishing slavery.

The Democrat McClellan won electors only in New Jersey, Delaware, and Kentucky. Congress refused to count Electoral College votes cast in occupied Confederate states, including Virginia, Tennessee, and Louisiana. The ethnic and cultural lines appeared to hold, with Republicans gaining support from native-born farmers, skilled and professional workers, those of New England descent, younger voters, and especially military personnel. Democrats tended to win in the cities, even including some wards in Boston, and among Irish- and German-Americans.

The Union Party and Republicans also gained seats in Congress, getting 149 to 42 in the House and 42 to 10 in the Senate. Republicans also won majorities in several state legislatures. The only governorship they lost in 1864 was in McClellan's home state of New Jersey. When the final vote was cast on November 8, Lincoln had 2,330,552 popular votes to McClellan's 1,835,985 votes. Despite Lincoln's apparent sweep of the Electoral College, the Democratic party was not destroyed, but only damaged by the defection of some War Democrats to the Union Party and by the Republican attacks of disloyalty. McClellan won some 48 percent of the vote in the crucial Northern border states from New York to Illinois. Furthermore, Democrats actually made some numerical gains over the 1860 vote in Indiana, Pennsylvania, and New York.[4]

The election had demonstrated several important facts. Even though a war was being fought and the president had been challenged on numerous aspects of his war policy, his policy toward African Americans, and his attitude toward readmission of the seceding states, he had won a resounding victory. The traditional electoral process went forward much as it had in the past, and Northern Democrats appeared resigned to the loss, looking forward to building on strength to try again in later elections. The American democratic process, despite its usual name-calling, voter fraud, charges of irregularity, and back-room political deals, seemed to be working in the traditional way. In that sense, the vibrant and living two-party or multiparty system in the North did serve as a way of strengthening the Union and strengthening Lincoln's hand. With Confederate armies in shambles, with Sherman in control in Georgia and moving into the Carolinas, and with Grant pressing Lee on the lines around Richmond and Petersburg, it was apparent that the Confederacy could not count on a politically weakened Union administration for a last chance at salvaging the Southern effort. When the election returns came in, and Lincoln faced a second inauguration, it was clear that a Confederate defeat was only a matter of months. Contemporary observers saw the election as a vindication of Lincoln's policy of continuing the war until the Confederate armies surrendered, rather than adopting some form of negotiated peace.[5]

Even with Lincoln and the Republicans firmly in control and the North on the path to victory, Lee held on to a stubborn resistance in Richmond, while the battered remnants of the Army of Tennessee tried to work their way past Sherman to come to the relief of Lee. Clearly, a determined push by Union forces would be required to bring the war to a conclusion.

CHRONICLE OF EVENTS

1861

September 5: Ohio Republicans reorganize as the Union Party, issuing a call on this date for a state convention. This is the first known Union Party organization. The Union Party nominates War Democrat David Tod for governor.

1862

Winter: The Committee on the Conduct of the War is dominated by radicals, who accuse losing generals of pro-Southern sympathies.

January: Republicans expel Indiana Democrat Jesse Bright from the Senate.

January 8: Connecticut Union Democrats join with Republicans in organizing a Union Party convention.

January 15: Lincoln replaces Secretary of War Simon Cameron (a radical Pennsylvanian) with War Democrat Edwin M. Stanton.

July 17: The 1862 Confiscation Act is passed, to go into effect in September.

August 19: The Union Party of Delaware holds a convention.

September 1: Governor Joseph Brown of Georgia denounces the establishment of martial law in Georgia by the Confederate government.

September 22: Lincoln, issues the Emancipation Proclamation but postpones emancipation until after the congressional mid-term elections, offending the radicals.

October elections: Largely because of the Emancipation Proclamation, Illinois, Indiana, and Pennsylvania go for the Democrats; the Union Party loses three senators; the Democrats gain 33 seats in the House. However, the Union/Republican coalition continues to hold a majority, and some moderate Unionists are among those defeated, thus strengthening the hands of the radical Republicans in the Union Party caucus in the Congress.

October 14: Peace Democrat Clement L. Vallandigham, member of Congress from Ohio, is voted out in state election.

November: Democrats win the governorships of New Jersey and New York.

December 6: Vallandigham introduces a resolution in Congress condemning Lincoln for trying to establish a dictatorship.

1863

January: The Republican caucus in the House of Representatives determines not to seat any representative elected from occupied Confederate states.

January 14: Vallandigham gives a speech in Congress condemning Republican dictatorship.

April 13: General Burnside issues General Order No. 38 in Ohio, defining criticism of the administration as treason.

March: The Union Party carries New Hampshire.

May 1: Ex-congressman Clement Vallandigham delivers a blistering speech in Mount Vernon, Ohio, attacking military rule and suppression of free speech

Clement Vallandigham emerged as the leader and spokesman of the Copperhead branch of the Northern Democratic Party, advocating a negotiated peace with the Confederacy. After being arrested for a speech challenging Union policies, he was briefly "exiled" to the Confederacy. He shipped out to Canada and returned overland to participate in the 1864 Democratic nominating convention. *(Library of Congress, Prints and Photographs Division, LC-DIG-cwpbh-01194)*

by the Lincoln administration, in explicit defiance of Burnside's General Order No. 38.

May 5: Burnside has Vallandigham arrested for the speech he gave on May 1

May 19: Lincoln has Secretary of War Stanton override Burnside's summary court decision to imprison Vallandigham and orders him sent over Confederate lines by General Rosecrans.

May 25: Vallandigham is transferred across Confederate lines to General Braxton Bragg.

June: Draft riots in New York City and elsewhere; the reaction of Governor Horatio Seymour clearly identifies him with the Peace Democrats.

June 1: Burnside orders the *Chicago Times* suppressed; Lincoln immediately countermands the order.

June 11: Ohio Democrats nominate Vallandigham for governor, to campaign from exile.

June 17: Vallandigham gets aboard a blockade runner in Wilmington, N.C., to go to Canada, by way of Bermuda.

July 2: Vallandigham departs Bermuda for Canada.

July 4: Union victories at Gettysburg and Vicksburg help dispel Union Party defeatism.

July 11: Vallandigham arrives in Quebec, then settles in Niagara, and finally in Windsor, Ontario, on August 24.

October: Vallandigham is defeated in the election for Ohio governor by John Brough, a War Democrat on the Union ticket.

November: The 1863 elections in Ohio and Pennsylvania, in which Unionists take War Democrat votes away from the Democratic Party, represent a watershed in U.S. history, in which the Democratic Party is tarred with the treason label, and a large section of formerly Democratic votes shift to the Union Party, many of them held as part of the Republican Party thereafter.

December: In his annual message, Lincoln announces the 10-percent plan, opposed by Congress. His idea is to get the seceding states, on a piecemeal basis, admitted to the Union and thereby weaken the resistance of remaining seceded states. (Arkansas, Tennessee, and Louisiana are so organized. Radicals dislike the plan, as they tend to want the Confederate states to be administered as occupied or conquered territories.)

1864

June 7–8: At the Union Party national convention in Baltimore, party leaders substitute Andrew Johnson for Hannibal Hamlin as Republican nominee for vice president in order to get a Southerner and a War Democrat on the Union ticket. Johnson is a former Unionist Democratic senator from Tennessee who did not resign his seat; Lincoln had appointed him as governor in occupied Tennessee.

June 16: Vallandigham returns from exile, and Union commanders hesitate to re-arrest him. Lincoln refuses to order his arrest; his supporters are Peace Democrats who try to prevent the nomination of War Democrat George McClellan for the presidency.

July: Congress passes the Wade-Davis bill, but Lincoln kills it with a pocket veto. The Wade-Davis bill would require loyal majorities before any organization of state governments in states of the former Confederacy.

August 5: The Battle of Mobile Bay encourages Union Party supporters.

August 29–31: At the Democratic Party national convention at Chicago, Vallandigham claims that the Sons of Liberty were organized just to offset the Union League and were not a treasonous group; Peace Democrats support Horatio Seymour of New York and Thomas Seymour of Connecticut; Vallandigham and Fernando Wood get their peace plank written into the platform. The peace platform plank is later repudiated by McClellan in his letter accepting the nomination.

September 2: Atlanta is occupied by Union forces. Union victories in Atlanta and Mobile Bay put an end to radical Republican challenges to Lincoln's renomination.

October 11: The Pennsylvania election returns three more Republicans to Congress, thus gaining 15 of the 24 congressional seats from that state; 15,000 of the 20,000 Union popular majority are represented by furloughed soldiers. Republicans also gain in October voting in Ohio and Indiana.

October 13: Maryland votes on a new constitution, which includes emancipation, and the constitution narrowly passes, supported by soldier votes.

November 8: In the presidential election, Lincoln gets 2,330,552 popular votes while McClellan gets 1,835,985. The Electoral College vote is 231 to 21.

EYEWITNESS TESTIMONY

The October Elections. Tickets in Nomination in Ohio, Indiana, Iowa, and Minnesota. On Monday, Oct. 8, Iowa and Minnesota, and on Tuesday, Oct. 9., Pennsylvania, Ohio and Indiana hold their annual State elections. These contests have little significance the present year, except in those States where the sympathizers with the rebels have succeeded in finding candidates who are willing to sacrifice their political future for the sake of attaining an altogether unenviable notoriety in the present. . . . Minnesota also elects State officers, county officers and members of the Legislature. There are three tickets in the field—the Republicans, which bears the names of the present incumbents; Union, composed of Republicans and Democrats upon a war platform, and a straight Democratic ticket on a peace platform . . . Ohio elects a full state ticket. The union between the Republicans and War Democrats is complete, and there is every prospect that Mr. Vallandigham and his friends will find themselves in a minority which will be positively alarming to themselves.

The two tickets are as follows:

	Union Ticket	**Peace Ticket**
Governor	David Tod	Hugh J. Jewett
Lt. Gov.	Benj. Stanton	John G. Marshall
Sec of State	Benj. R. Cowen	WW Armstrong
Treasurer	G.V. Dorsey	Geo. W. Holmes

> *Extract from news report entitled, "The October Elections," describing the first appearance of Union Party tickets in Minnesota and Ohio, in the fall elections of 1861, from the* New York Times, *October 6, 1861, p. 5.*

The Mass Union Convention assembled at 10 o'clock this morning. The attendance was much smaller than was expected. Hon. Jas. T. Pratt presided. The doings were participated in by Union Democrats and Republicans, representing each county in the state. The forenoon was principally occupied in arranging preliminaries and discussing resolutions.

The policy of nominating a State ticket by this Convention was fully discussed, and it was decided to nominate a ticket at the afternoon session. A committee of four from [each] county was appointed, to report a ticket for State officers. They reported:

For Governor—Wm. A. Buckingham, of Norwich.
For Lieutenant-Governor—Roger Averill, of Danbury.

For Secretary of State—J. Hammond Trumbull, of Hartford.
For Treasurer—Gabriel W. Coit, of Middletown.
For Comptroller—Leman W. Cutler, of Watertown.

The Governor, Secretary and Comptroller are Republicans, and now in office. The Lieutenant-Governor and Treasurer are Union Democrats. The ticket was adopted unanimously, and it is expected that the Republican Convention, which meets on the 16th [of January 1862] will adopt the same ticket.

The resolutions were for sinking all party lines, and uniting with one heart and voice in the one great object of aiding and sustaining the Government of the United States in its present mighty struggle for National existence. That all who refuse at this crisis to give the Government a hearty support, are liable to the imputation of being her secret foes. A conditional Union man is an unconditional traitor. For the support of the Government in the vigorous prosecution of the war, we pledge our lives, our fortunes, and our sacred honor.

A State Central Committee was appointed, who were authorized to proceed to the organization of the Union Party of Connecticut.

The Convention was disappointed in the non-appearance of Hon. Andy Johnson, of Tennessee. Arriving in New-York, on his way to Hartford, he was suddenly called to Kentucky to take part in a forward movement of our troops there.

The convention adjourned.

> *Newspaper account of the formation of the Union party in Connecticut on January 8, 1862, as published in "The Connecticut Mass Union Convention,"* New York Times, *January 9, 1862, p. 8.*

The delegates of the Union Party of this State met yesterday at Dover—150 in Number—and nominated William Cannon, Esq. for Governor. Hon. George P. Fisher, the present incumbent of the solitary seat allotted to Delaware in the House of Representatives, was nominated by acclamation.

The telegraph has anticipated this intelligence, but I recur to it to draw attention for a moment to the politics of this State, which, although the smallest in the Union, occupies a central and not unconspicuous position among the other States. It is one of the few States in which there exists the necessity of a Union Party—the only State represented in the Senate of the United States by Secessionists. I say Secessionists, for Mr. Bayard's opinions are no secret; and while Saulsbury might desire to pass for a Union man in some quarters, there are others in which he follows Bayard as closely as one rat follows another in a cellar. Thus represented, and conscious of a wide-spread, half-silent, insidious, cowardly, yet active, feeling of disaffection at the war among the baser sort of citizens in the two lower Counties of the State, the Unionists have gone to the length of organizing a party that shall trample out and quench the half-lighted, smouldering, ineffectual fires of disunion, which in this State are as malignant as they are futile.

This party will carry the election this Fall, without doubt. It will place a loyal Senator next March in the seat now occupied by Bayard, and this will be the last of the ridiculous and contemptible longing after secession which has crept into Lower Delaware. . . .

The Union party comprises all the Republicans, Old Line Whigs, Douglas Democrats, and Bell-Everett men; the latter a very large class, having cast, in 1860, 49 votes more than the Republicans. There is a probability that one half the Breckinridge Democrats will vote with the Union party also; certainly one-third will; this is conceded by well-informed politicians with whom I have conversed since the Union Convention. The Chairman of this Convention, Charles I. DuPont, was a Breckinridge Democrat, the only brother of Commodore DuPont; the nominee for Governor was also a Breckinridge Democrat; both these gentlemen have great influence—Cannon in the lower, and DuPont in the upper portion of the State.

In spite of the fact that Bayard and Saulsbury misrepresent Delaware in the United States Senate, and draw with them a crowd of perverts, the contributions of this State to the [Union] army have been large.

Report by "Blackbridge," a correspondent to the New York Times, *entitled "Political Affairs in Delaware. Action of the Union State Convention—The Nominations—The Military Movement," noting the rise of Union sentiment in the state, datelined August 20, 1862, as published in the* New York Times, *August 27, 1862, p. 2.*

The skies are brightening. The reactionaries are losing strength every hour, and henceforth they will be without power over the people. There is no place where one can discover a change of sentiment among the people so quickly as in Congress, especially in the House of Representatives. The Congressman does not always heed the popular will with sufficient readiness, but the observer can easily see by his conduct that he is conscious that he is disobeying it. The change for the better in Congress, in this respect, within a fortnight, is marked. The "Copperheads" (excuse the slang word for its expressiveness) are by no means so defiant as they were a short time ago. Upon the opening of Congress, Voorhees, Vallandigham, Cox, Powell, Saulsbury, Bayard, and others whom I will not mention, were bold and joyous in their demeanor. They had lost the sneering, malignant manners of previous sessions, and were good-natured even, so certain were they that this war and the Administration were about to be arrested and overthrown. Vallandigham spoke too quickly in favor of stopping the war, and Fernando Wood was not shrewd in showing his hand so openly in his tactics displayed at Albany. I find now that even the acknowledged "Copperheads" in Congress are shy, silent, and begin to grow ugly, which is the surest sign of all that they are discouraged. . . . Even Wadsworth, in the House, the worst of the Kentuckians in Congress upon the slavery question, made a solemn declaration that in spite of the acts of the Administration, which the people of Kentucky disliked, they would stand by the old flag, and would never dishonor it. These are small facts when taken singly, but together they form an important mass of evidence, going to show that the Government will really lose nothing from disaffection in any quarter by the strong anti-slavery position which it takes. All loyal men will stand by it through every emergency,

This *Harper's Weekly* cartoon shows three pro-Confederate Copperhead politicians advancing on Columbia, symbol of the Union. *(Library of Congress, Prints and Photographs Division, LC-USZ62–132749)*

and the disloyal may as well take their stand with the enemy first as last.

Report to the editors of the Republican journal, the Independent, *entitled "Our Washington Correspondence," commenting on the weakness of the Copperhead position in early 1863, authored by "D. W. B.," dated February 9, 1863, published February 12, 1863, Vol. 15, no. 741, p. 1.*

Today I saw the memorandum of Mr. Ould, of the conversation held with Mr. Vallandigham [while briefly in exile in Richmond, Virginia], for file in the archives. He says if we *can only hold out* this year that the peace party of the North would sweep the Lincoln dynasty out of political existence. He seems to have thought that our cause was sinking, and feared we would submit, which would, of course, be ruinous to his party! But he advises strongly against any invasion of Pennsylvania, for that would unite all parties at the north, and so strengthen Lincoln's hands that he would be able to crush all opposition, and trample upon the constitutional rights of the people.

Mr. V. said nothing to indicate that either he or the party had any other idea than that the Union would be reconstructed under Democratic rule. The President [of the Confederacy, Jefferson Davis] indorsed, with his own pen, on this document, that, in regard to invasion of the North, experience proved the contrary of what Mr. V. asserted. But Mr. V. is for restoring the Union, amicably of course, and if it cannot be so done, then possibly he is in favor of recognizing our independence. He says any reconstruction which is not voluntary on our part, would soon be followed by another separation, and a worse war than the present one.

Confederate government official John B. Jones, commenting on the viewpoint of former Ohio congressman Clement Vallandigham, during his temporary exile in the Confederacy, in a diary entry for June 2, 1863, in Earl Schenck Miers, ed., A Rebel War Clerk's Diary, *pp. 227–228.*

Hon. Preston King, of N.Y., from the Committee on Credentials, reported in favor of admitting all the delegates claiming seats, but those from South Carolina and the "Conservative" Unionists from Missouri: the delegations from the Territories, from the District of Columbia, and from the States of Virginia, Tennessee, Louisiana, Florida, and Arkansas, not to be entitled to vote. Upon consideration, this report was over-ruled so far as to authorize—by a vote of 310 to 151—the

Jefferson Davis, Confederate president, was fixed in his views, and in practice, acted as his own secretary of War. *(Library of Congress, Prints and Photographs Division, LC-USZ62–15993)*

delegates from Tennessee to vote; those from Louisiana and Arkansas were likewise authorized to vote, by 307 to 167. The delegates from Nebraska, Colorado, and Nevada, were then allowed also to vote; but not those from Virginia, Florida and the remaining territories.

Horace Greeley, recalling the seating of delegates at the Republican national convention in Baltimore, June 7, 1864, in his memoir, The American Conflict, *p. 658.*

I understand the meeting, whose resolutions I am considering, to be in favor of suppressing the rebellion by military force—by armies. Long experience has shown that armies can not be maintained unless desertion shall be punished by the severe penalty of death. The case requires, and the law and the constitution, sanction this punishment. Must I shoot the simple-minded soldier boy who deserts, while I must not touch a hair of a wiley agitator who induces him to desert? This is none the less injurious when effected by getting a father, or brother, or friend, into a public meeting, and there working upon his feelings, till he is persuaded to write the soldier boy, that he is fighting in a bad cause, for a wicked administration of a contemptable government, too weak to arrest and punish him if he shall desert. I think that in such a case, to silence the agitator, and save the boy, is not only constitutional, but, withal, a great mercy.

> *Extract from a letter by Abraham Lincoln to prominent New York Democratic politician Erastus Corning, responding to a petition from a Democratic protest meeting in Albany, New York, held May 16, 1863, and chaired by Corning, regarding the arrest of Clement Vallandigham, sent about June 12, as collected in Roy P. Basler, ed.,* The Collected Works of Abraham Lincoln, *Vol. VI, p. 269.*

Messrs. [Clement C.] Clay and [John P.] Holcombe made the most of [Lincoln's To Whom It May Concern note of July 18] in a public manifesto, intended to "fire the Southern heart," and to disaffect those in the loyal States who were anxious for honorable peace at the earliest moment. And there was a very widespread impression that the overture of the Confederates had not been met in the manner best calculated to strengthen the National cause and invigorate the arm of its supporters. In other words, it was felt that—since the overture originated with them—they should have been allowed to make their own proposition, and not required in effect to make one dictated to them from our side, however inherently reasonable.

> *Comment by Horace Greeley on the failure of the negotiations with Confederate representatives that he had attempted to arrange with Lincoln in early July 1864, in his memoir,* The American Conflict, *p. 655.*

To Whom It May Concern:
Any proposition which embraces the restoration of peace, the integrity of the whole Union, and the abandonment of Slavery, and which comes by and with an authority that can control the areas now at war against the United States, will be received and considered by the Executive Government of the United States, and will be met by liberal terms on substantial and collateral points; and the bearer or bearers thereof shall have safe conduct both ways.

> *Statement issued by President Abraham Lincoln, July 18, 1864, setting forth terms that would be required for peace negotiations with the Confederacy, as quoted by Horace Greeley in his memoir,* The American Conflict, *p. 665.*

Here let me repeat the statement, which you are aware I have more than once made, that I have not taken a single step nor said one word for the purpose of influencing the action of any political Convention, & that I am not an aspirant for nomination for the Presidency. It is my firm conviction that no man should seek that high office, and that no true man should refuse it, if it is spontaneously conferred upon him, & he is satisfied that he can do good to his country by accepting it. Whoever is nominated for the Presidency in opposition to the present incumbent, it will be upon principles differing widely from those which have controlled his course. Should the result of the election be in his favor—no harm will have inured to him from the contest. Should a majority of the loyal voters of the country decide in favor of his opponent it will be upon a struggle of principles not of men. Now situated as your country is, its fate trembling in the balance, anyone who pledges himself not to oppose the reelection of the actual incumbent as a condition of obtaining office or employment places himself upon the horns of a dilemma.

If he does not conscientiously approve the policy of the incumbent, he simply sells his self respect honor & truth—as well as his country for a price.

Or he says by implication at least, that he does fully approve of all the measures of the incumbent, & that he regards the question of merely a choice of men, & not of principles or measures.

No one who knows me will suppose that I could accept the first alternative. The second is inadmissible for the reason that I do not approve of the policy and measures of the present President.

> *General George B. McClellan, in a letter to Francis P. Blair, rejecting a suggestion from Blair that he refuse the Democratic nomination for president in exchange for an appointment to active command, sent about July 22, 1864, in Stephen Sears, ed.,* The Civil War Papers of George B. McClellan, *pp. 583–584.*

Saturday night and Sunday night, till past midnight, the leaders of the Peace Democracy, as they call themselves were making speeches to the crowds assembled round the various hotels and in Court-House yard. I heard many of their speeches, and have read them all, as far as they were reported by the Chicago organ of that party, *The Times.*

Yesterday, the 29th, the Convention met in a building holding some thousand, at noon, and in due time chose Horatio Seymour, of New York, President. Today, they have been at work on the platform, drawn up by Vallandigham, and on the candidate. The McClellan party had imported about one thousand of the Roughs of New York city, headed by Isaia Rynders, to clamor for McClellan. Some five hundred of the same class were imported from Philadelphia, headed by the same Rynders, to aid in compelling the Convention to nominate McClellan. Many leaders of guerilla bands in Missouri and other Slave States are here, brought on to see to it that the Convention is true to the Southern rebels, and also to see what can be done to relieve the rebels now held as prisoner in Camp Douglas.

I have just come from the Convention. I have witnessed many pubic gatherings in various cities in Europe and America, but never before have I witnessed a gathering of so large a number of brutal, drunken, ferocious men as I have seen gathered from all parts of the nation in this city the past four days. Multitudes of them are armed with revolvers and bowie knives, and they make no secret of the fact. It is computed that there are fifteen thousand here from abroad. The watchwords that have been put forth in speeches made in and out of the Convention, and which have been endorsed by silence and otherwise, are such as the following—"Down with Lincoln by ballots or bullets!" "Subjugation of the North to slaveholders and their allies by ballots or by bullets!" "Burn, desolate and devastate, wherever a partisan of Lincoln dare show his head!" "Cut the throat of every d—d Lincolnite!" This was repeated over and over in speeches made in front of the Tremont House, and the question was put to the multitude, "Will you help us?" "Yes, yes, yes, we will!" was the response made by many in the crowd.

Report by abolitionist correspondent Henry C. Wright, in a letter to William Lloyd Garrison, datelined August 20, 1864, and published as an article, "The Chicago Convention," in the Liberator *Vol. 34, No. 37 (September 9, 1864), p. 147.*

Several delegations having cast their votes for Horatio Seymour when the call of the States had been gone through with, Gov. Seymour remarked that some gentlemen had done him the honor to name him for the nomination. It would be affectation to say that their expressions of preference did not give him pleasure, but he owed it to himself to say that many months ago he advised his friends in New-York that, for various reasons, private and public, he could not be a candidate for the Chicago nomination. Having made that announcement, he would lack the honor of a man, he would do great injustice to those friends to permit his name to be used now. As a member of the New-York delegation, he personally thought it advisable to support an eminent jurist of that State for the nomination, but he was not actuated in this by any doubt of the ability or patriotism of the distinguished gentleman who has been placed in nomination. He knew that Gen. McClellan did not seek the nomination. He knew that that able officer had declared that it would be more agreeable to him to resume his position in the army, but he will not honor any the less the high position assigned him by the great majority of the country, because he has not sought it. He desired to add a few words in reference to Maryland and her honored delegates here. . . . He would pledge his life that when Gen. McClellan is placed in the Presidential Chair, he will devote all his energies to the best interests of his country, and to securing, never again to be invaded, all the rights and privileges of the people under the laws and the Constitution.

The President then announced the vote, which was received with deafening cheers, the delegates and the vast audience rising, the band playing, and the cheering lasting for several minutes. . . .

Mr. Vallandigham said that from the first moment he had been animated by but one sentiment in this convention—peace, to the end that there might be peace in the land. He then moved that the nomination of Gen. George B. McClellan be the unanimous sense of the convention.

Report of the Democratic nominating convention, August 31, 1864, entitled: "Chicago Convention. McClellan Nominated for President. Pendleton, of Ohio, for Vice President. Vallandigham Moves to make the Nomination Unanimous. A Peace Horse and a War Horse. Adjournment of the Convention," published in the New York Times, *September 1, 1864, p. 1.*

We had a hundred guns for the nomination of Gen. Geo. B. McClellan. I fear there will not be as many for him at the time of the election. His nomination and election to the Presidency, are, to the people of Rhode Island, two different events entirely. If Vallandigham, Wood, Cox & Co., can swallow the "little Napoleon," Rhode Island can't. If the Gen. reckons these traitors among his friends and supporters, Rhode Island asks to be counted out. Rhode Island has been guilty, in her elections in the past, of many very wicked things; but I cannot believe that she is so far lost to all morality, justice, humanity and reason, as to throw herself into the arms of these supporters and defenders of Jeff Davis.

> *Comment by a correspondent with the pen name "Pokanoket," on the reaction of Rhode Island to the nomination of General McClellan for the presidency by the Democratic convention in Chicago, published in the column, "Rhode Island-Political," in* Zion's Herald and Wesleyan Journal *Journal 35, no. 36 (September 7, 1864), p. 142.*

The existence of more than one Government over the region which once owned our flag is incompatible with the peace, the power and the happiness of the people.

The preservation of our Union was the sole avowed object for which the war was commenced.

It should have been conducted for that object only, and in accordance with those principles which I took occasion to declare when in active service.

Thus conducted, the work of reconciliation would have been easy, and we might have reaped the benefits of our many victories on land and sea.

The Union was originally formed by the exercise of a spirit of conciliation and compromise. To restore and preserve it, the same spirit must prevail in our councils and in the hearts of the people.

The reestablishment of the Union in all its integrity, is, and must continue to be the indispensable condition in any settlement. So soon as it is clear or even probable, that our present adversaries are ready for peace, upon the basis of the Union, we should exhaust all the resource of statesmanship practised by civilized nations, and taught by the traditions of the American people, consistent with the honor and interests of the country to secure such peace, re-establish the Union and guarantee for the future the constitutional rights of every State. The Union is the one condition of peace—we ask no more.

> *Extract from the final draft of the statement of George B. McClellan, written in Orange, New Jersey, September 8, 1864, accepting the Democratic nomination, but rejecting the terms of the peace plank in the platform by insisting on acceptance of restoration of the Union by the Confederacy as a pre-condition to a peace settlement, as published in Stephen Sears, ed.,* The Civil War Papers of George B. McClellan, *p. 595.*

Mr. Burt (late member of [the Confederate] Congress), writes from Abbeville that Vice-President A. H. Stephens crossed the Savannah River where Sherman's raiders were galloping through the country, in great alarm. To the people near him he spoke freely on public affairs, and criticised the President's policy severely, and the conduct of the war generally. He said the enemy might now go where he pleased, our strength and resources were exhausted, and that we ought to make *peace.* That we could have elected any one we might choose President of the United States, and intimated that this would enable us to secure terms, etc., which was understood to mean reconstruction of the Union.

> *Confederate government official John B. Jones, commenting on the political position of Confederate vice president Alexander Stephens, in a diary entry for September 15, 1864, in Earl Schenck Miers, ed.,* A Rebel War Clerk's Diary, *p. 420.*

Yankee politics have simplified themselves very much. From such indications as reach me Lincoln will walk over the course. McClellan stepped off his platform in his letter of acceptance, and is as strong a war man as Lincoln. He would be a much more formidable one to us because he would constantly offer peace and reconstruction on the basis of the Constitution, which would rapidly develop a reconstruction party in the South. Such a party is now beginning to form under the stress of disaster. Men begin, too, to talk calmly about emancipation, some as a cheap price for peace; others as good absolutely because we cannot afford to be under the ban of all the world, though right in the abstract.

> *Comment by Confederate head of the Bureau of War, Robert Kean, in his diary entry for September 25, 1864, in Edward Younger, ed.,* Inside the Confederate Government—The Diary of Robert Garlick Hill Kean, *p. 174.*

It is as much an art to make a popular meeting as to make a clock; and both these arts flourish in Yankeeland. Of course, great popular meetings are based on great popular enthusiasm. Without this enthusiasm, no meetings however well arranged, can be successful. . . . We are led to these remarks after having witnessed a stupendous spectacle (surprising to everyone who saw it, both managers and guests) at Woodstock, Conn., on Wednesday of last week—where in a quiet village of 700 voters, and five miles distant from a railroad station, a Union meeting was held numbering fifteen thousand people! Never have we seen, in any rural district, so magnificent an assemblage—whose picturesque effect was still further heightened by the gilding it caught from a beautiful mid-October day. The village green, from the church at one end to the academy at the other, was a dense mass of people, encamped like an army with banner. Fifteen towns and villages, near and far, sent processions of delegates, each with music, flags, evergreens, symbolic devices, mottoes, and a variety of fantastic oddities, interesting and indescribable. These paraphernalia of the festival were all noticeably in good taste, commendable both in design and execution; and the wonder is, how many dexterous fingers—young men's and maiden's—must have been at work upon them for weeks beforehand. Eight full brass-bands and thirty-five bands of drum and fife made spirit-stirring music enough for Gen. Grant's army; in addition to which, moreover several glee-clubs and choirs added human voices to the noise of the instruments—all swelling the battle-cry of Freedom! The entrance to the Common was under a green arch, inscribed with the words "Freedom or Slavery"—a sentiment which the author of Thurlow Weed's late letter would have thought inappropriate, but which the plain country-people of Connecticut knew to be the pith of the whole question.

Correspondent, commenting on a Union Party rally in Woodstock, Connecticut, held October 12, 1864, extracted from "How to Make a Great Campaign Meeting," The Independent *Vol. 16, no. 829 (October 20, 1864), p. 4.*

The meetings at Tammany Hall were of particular interest in the closing week of the Presidential campaign. We heard all the celebrities of the Wigwam deliver addresses. But the climax was reached when a monster torchlight procession was formed to march the full length of Broadway, which was reviewed by General George B. McClellan from the balcony of the Fifth Avenue Hotel. [Confederate Army Colonel Robert M.] Martin and I were on hand early and circulated through the surging politicians who thronged the corridors and upper hall of the hotel. McClellan was the idol of the great assemblages in New York, though the Republican demonstrations in favor of Mr. Lincoln were equally enthusiastic.

After we had surveyed the scene inside of the Fifth Avenue Hotel, Martin and I went into the great crowd which filled Madison Square. Rostrums had been erected for outdoor speakers. Among these James T. Brady had been announced, and we watched for his appearance, when we pushed our way to a position near his stand and listened to his address. He was regarded

as the foremost public man in New York who openly criticised the conduct of the war. He used strong language on this occasion.

The procession began to pass about 8.30 o'clock, coming up Broadway, and continued until 1 o'clock in the morning. It was not uncommon to hear hisses and groans for Lincoln from the ranks, and the President was caricatured in many ludicrous and ungainly pictures. Indeed, there was a vicious sentiment voiced all along the line of the procession against the draft and every one connected with the management of the war. The spirit of revolt was manifest and it only needed a start and a leadership.

John W. Headley, Confederate undercover officer, remembering his attendance at a McClellan torchlight parade, November 6, 1864, in New York City, in his memoir, Confederation Operations in Canada and New York, *p. 268.*

Despatches kept coming in all the evening showing a splendid triumph in Indiana, showing steady, small gains all over Pennsylvania, enough to give a fair majority this time on the home vote. Guess from New York and Albany which boiled down to about the estimated majority against us in the city, 35,000, and left the result in the State still doubtful.

A despatch from Butler was picked up & sent by Sanford, saying that the City had gone 35,000 McC. & the State 40,000. This looked impossible. The State had been carefully canvassed & such a result was impossible except in view of some monstrous and undreamed of frauds. After a while another came from Sanford correcting former one & giving us the 40,000 in the State.

Sanford's despatches all the evening continued most jubilant: especially when he announced that most startling majority of 80,000 in Massachusetts.

General Eaton came in and waited for news with us. I had not before known that he was with us. His denunciations of Seymour were especially hearty and vigorous.

John Hay, assistant personal secretary to Abraham Lincoln, commenting on the reception of election results at the White House as received by telegraph, in his diary entry for November 8, 1864, from Tyler Dennett, ed., Lincoln and the Civil War in the Diaries and Letters of John Hay, *as cited in Henry Steele Commager,* The Blue and the Gray, *p. 1,095.*

10

To Appomattox Court House and Beyond

November 1864–July 1865

In the weeks that followed the reelection of Lincoln, leaders and the public in both North and South realized that the end of the war was near. In the Confederacy, Vice President Alexander Stephens and others had hoped that the election of Democratic nominee George McClellan on a peace platform, despite McClellan's repudiation of that platform, would open the door for some negotiated peace. With Lincoln's victory and the apparent endorsement of his policies by the Northern electorate, hopes for a quick peace settlement faded. Yet Stephens and others in the Confederate government continued to search for some means to negotiate an end to the war, with or without the support of President Davis.

In the North, with the old Congress still holding its seats, but recognizing that the electorate had spoken, and in response to the request of Lincoln in his annual address to Congress of December 4, 1864, the House of Representatives took up reconsideration of the Thirteenth Amendment to the Constitution that would abolish slavery everywhere in the United States. Although the amendment had been passed by the Senate, the House of Representatives had failed to yield the necessary two-thirds majority in the vote taken in April 1864. However, Lincoln had insisted that passage of the amendment be included as a provision of the Republican platform in the election of 1864, and the House passed the amendment with a vote of 119 to 56 on January 31, 1865. Meanwhile, the areas held by Confederate troops dwindled to a protective line around Richmond held by the Army of Northern Virginia under Lee and to a fluid front in South Carolina. After reaching Savannah in December 1864, Sherman began moving north, forcing the evacuation of Charleston and then Columbia, South Carolina, in early 1865.

With railroad lines severed, civilian populations facing starvation, and with most of the factories that provided arms and ammunition either in Union hands or destroyed, Confederate resources were stretched to the breaking point. During the winter months of 1864–65, Lee found his army holding lines around Richmond and Petersburg that were slowly eroding, as troops daily surrendered in small numbers to Union forces or simply walked off to go home. Despite all the heroic battles of the prior four years, whose names were already becoming legendary, it appeared by January 1865 that the end of the war might come by erosion, rather than in any clear military defeat. So it seemed to journalists, military officers, political leaders, and diarists.

At the core of the Confederacy, Jefferson Davis had surrounded himself with a cabinet that tended to reflect his own views. Although not troubled by elections, Davis had dealt with opposition in his administration by frequent dismissals and shifts of key personnel. By January 1865, Davis had had four secretaries of state, six secretaries of war, and six attorneys general and had arranged many minor shake-ups at lower levels. Judah P. Benjamin had served in all three of the major secretaryship positions and was Davis's secretary of state at the end of the war.

Benjamin, a brilliant lawyer of Jewish ancestry, was a bit of an anomaly in the Davis cabinet. Since Davis knew that the Confederacy would never select a Jew to replace him, he may have seen Benjamin as someone whose well-known competence would never become a threat to his own position. With his cabinet jobs, Benjamin attained the highest rank of any Jew in any U.S. government in the 19th century. He was a loyal Davis supporter, but many of the other cabinet members, especially those who disagreed with Davis, were shunted from position to position or out of the government entirely to limit their power or reduce their potential for becoming a center of an oppositional viewpoint.

By early 1865, those surrounding Davis, even if they disagreed with him, understood that it would be nearly impossible to get Davis to accept advice he did not want to hear. General Joseph Johnston, whom Davis had dismissed and replaced earlier with Hood, made it clear that he thought Davis was stubborn and unrealistic and would volunteer to tell Davis bad news. Few others had the intestinal fortitude to stand up to Davis in open disagreement.[1]

Jefferson Davis made it clear to those who surrounded him, including his congress, that he firmly believed that the Confederate states had every right to secede from the Union and to form their own government. In the view of Davis, it was Lincoln who acted unconstitutionally. Davis believed and frequently said that Lincoln had usurped power by sending United States troops into the Confederate nation. With bitter rhetoric, he repeatedly detailed a long litany of crimes perpetrated by Union officers and political leaders. Despite Davis's inflexibility, as the situation of the Confederacy became desperate in the winter of 1864–65, he was willing to try a couple of expedients that had been urged by others. One was the principle of limited recruitment of slaves into the Confederate army with a promise of emancipation for service, as long as the owners of the slaves and the states concurred. Originally suggested by Irish-born Confederate general Patrick Cleburne in a memorandum circulated and then suppressed early in January 1864, an almost identical measure was enacted by the Confederate congress and signed into law by Davis on March 13, 1865. No appropriations were made to implement the measure, and the evacuation and collapse of the Confederate government followed so soon after the decision, that it appeared to have no practical effect whatsoever, beyond the rumored organization of a couple of African-American companies of troops.

Another effort that Davis undertook was to explore the possibility of peace negotiations with the Union. Although Lincoln had made it clear that the only acceptable terms of settlement were the complete surrender of Confederate troops in the field and the restoration of United States government authority in the seceded states, Davis persisted in the view that the war could be settled as one between two nations, with some sort of treaty or convention. An opportunity to explore such a settlement came with the visit of Francis P. Blair, Sr., to Richmond, early in January 1865.

FRANCIS P. BLAIR AND HAMPTON ROADS

Francis P. Blair regarded himself as a leading member of the Republican Party. Born in Kentucky and a slave owner, he had settled in Silver Spring, Maryland, just beyond the District of Columbia line. He was the founder of the *Washington Globe* and had been its editor from 1830 to 1845. His son, Montgomery Blair, was Lincoln's postmaster general until late in 1864, and, incidentally, the owner of Blair House on Lafayette Square across from the White House, later a presidential guest house. Another son, Francis P. Blair, Jr., was a Union general and influential in Missouri. The Blairs had political clout in both Maryland and Missouri politics, and Blair's control of patronage through the postmastership had made the family a core part of the Republican administration. Father Blair, as Lincoln called Francis Sr., was quick to give unsolicited advice. Several times during the war he had visited Lincoln to provide such advice, to which Lincoln listened politely before proceeding to ignore it.

When Jubal Early led his raid on Washington by way of Rockville and Silver Spring in the summer of 1864, his troops had made a point of stopping by Blair's Silver Spring home to wreak some vengeance on "Old Blair" for his pro-Union sentiments, targeting him particularly, because he was one of only a few prominent slaveholders who had become Lincoln loyalists. In December, Blair asked Lincoln for a pass to enable him to travel into the Confederacy to make inquiries about papers taken from his home during the Early raid.

Although this personal reason was the ostensible justification for a pass, Blair made it clear that he hoped to feel out Confederate leaders as to possible surrender. His departure was delayed a bit, but on January 12, 1865, Blair succeeded in arranging a meeting with Jefferson Davis in Richmond. Davis heard Blair out as he read his statement out loud, with apologies for its editorial style. Blair's proposals seemed to Davis a little far-fetched. Blair suggested that in defense of the Monroe Doctrine, the Confederacy and the Union should sign a truce, and then, together, send an expedition of troops into Mexico to expel the French forces there. Davis listened to the idea without comment, and then asked if Blair's views represented his own or those of the Union administration. Blair made it clear that he had no instructions or authority from Lincoln, but that he could easily deliver a message or communication. Realizing that Blair was acting on his own, and represented his own ideas and not those of anyone else, Davis asked him to convey to Lincoln his willingness to appoint commissioners who would meet with duly appointed commissioners from the Union government to discuss a way to bring the bloodshed to an end between the two countries. He drafted a short note to that effect, which he asked Blair to deliver to Lincoln. Within a week, Blair returned with a note from Lincoln that suggested he was open to receiving commissioners who could speak for those forces resisting the authority of the United States. Lincoln's reply, received on January 21, pointedly avoided any implication that Davis or anyone else on the Confederate side in the conflict represented a government. The fact that Lincoln completely ignored Davis's comment about peace between two countries was very obvious.

Once again, Lincoln had displayed his ability to create a strategic dilemma for his opponents. If Davis rejected the opportunity for a meeting, it would be clear that Lincoln had offered to negotiate and Davis had turned him down. If Davis accepted the negotiation, it would mean that his commissioners were not being received as representatives of a separate government, as Davis had stated in his letter sent by way of Blair, but only as individuals with some authority to speak for those troops acting against the United States, in effect, for those in rebellion. While Richmond rumbled with rumors of congressional initiative to open negotiations regardless of the Confederate president's position, Davis fumed. He was angry at the insult implicit in Lincoln's response, but, regardless of the logical trap, he decided to appoint commissioners to meet with those of the Union. He chose Confederate senator Robert M. T. Hunter (who had served as his secretary of state July 1861–February 1862), Vice President Alexander Stephens, and Assistant Secretary of War John A. Campbell. Both Hunter and Stephens were noted for their earlier attempts to oppose secession, and Stephens in particular had dropped out of active participation in the Confederate government over his insistence that peace should be negotiated. Campbell was a pragmatic administrator, quite loyal to Davis and his viewpoint, who had survived several cabinet reshuffles in his assistant secretary position.

The delegation was delayed in crossing the lines, with Campbell and the others convinced that the delay was intentional. On January 31, the Union House of Representatives passed the Thirteenth Amendment abolishing slavery by a clear two-thirds majority. Celebrations in Washington and a confident mood swept the Union. Campbell believed that Seward wanted this vote in hand to indicate the strength from which he entered negotiations. The Confederate delegates were then allowed to cross the lines, taken in hand by a Union representative, and arrived aboard the Union's *River Queen* for the conference on February 3 at Hampton Roads. There they were met first by Secretary of State William Seward, and then, in full session, with Lincoln. The brief meeting became known as the Hampton Roads Peace Conference.

When Stephens explored the Monroe Doctrine idea put forward by Blair, Lincoln grew impatient and explained that the only terms that would be open for discussion would be the surrender of troops and the restoration of Union control. When Hunter and Stephens protested that such a discussion reflected only submission, Lincoln and Seward pointed out that they had never used that term. Stephens argued that a convention between parties could speak to peace on other terms than complete surrender, without implying any mutual recognition of the status of the parties negotiating. He began to cite examples from history to illustrate his point, but Lincoln brushed off the reference to history by suggesting that the commissioners would have to take up any historical points with Seward. He could not enter into a convention with any entity whose existence the United States did not recognize, but he was willing to consider a cease-fire, surrender of troops, and the ready application of presidential pardons for any offenses that might be considered by the civil or military courts. When Campbell suggested that he had never considered that his actions put his neck at risk, Lincoln replied, apparently with some pique, that there were plenty of oak trees about from which one might conveniently be hanged.

When Stephens, Hunter, and Campbell returned to Richmond and submitted their report, the Confederate congress was indignant. Like Davis, they found Lincoln's position insulting, and Davis and others made several speeches denouncing the Union for unconstitutional behavior, refusal to recognize the diplomatic law of nations, and for perpetuating the bloody war. Davis was not alone in rejecting the concept that the actions of the Confederate armies were those of rebels against a legally-established government and in insisting that they were a sovereign nation fighting an international war to preserve their independence after an invasion by a foreign power. However, it was also clear by February that Lincoln was not about to accept a settlement that recognized the claims of the Confederacy to be an independent nation. Even so, Lincoln had offered to accept surrender, and the onus of rejecting the terms and prolonging the conflict was clearly on the representatives of the Confederacy.

FREEDMEN'S BUREAU AND INAUGURATION

In the press of events, Lincoln had little time to anticipate exactly how the South would be reconstructed and rejoined with the Union, once the defeat was completed. On March 3, Congress established the Freedmen's Bureau, an organization devoted to taking out of military hands the growing problem of providing relief and protection to the former slaves. With emancipation apparently permanent, some system of providing a transition for the freedmen was required. The bureau began its work with little clear mandate except a sense that basic concerns of humanity had to be met, in the form of housing, food, clothing, and medical care. Social engineering of the sort developed in the 20th century was unknown, and the managers of the Freedmen's Bureau would face problems far beyond the experience of the era to readily resolve.

Lincoln was inaugurated for his second term on March 4 and delivered a warm and well-thought-out inaugural address. He visualized the end that was coming and urged his supporters to face the future "with malice towards none and charity for all." The sentiment seemed to reflect Lincoln's own set of values and set a tone and a goal to which others could aspire. The essential humanity of Lincoln's approach, captured in that phrase, would be remembered long after as suggesting the kind of reconstruction he would implement if he could. Even African-American spokesman and leader Frederick Douglass, who thought Lincoln moved too slowly for the sake of social justice, had to admit that the inaugural speech had been fine. Douglass pressed his way past the White House guards to offer his congratulations, believing himself to be the first African American to have been invited to attend a presidential inauguration.

However, events moved rapidly through the next few weeks, leaving little time for the implementation of the hopeful promise of either the Freedmen's Bureau legislation or of Lincoln's sentiments. Before social or political reconstruction could be considered, the guns had to fall silent.

FROM RICHMOND TO APPOMATTOX COURT HOUSE

After taking Savannah in December 1864 and presenting it as a Christmas present to Lincoln, Sherman and his bummers began moving through South Carolina. The scavenging and foraging for supplies reached new heights in South Carolina, as many of the troops under Sherman believed that state deserved special punishment. Columbia, South Carolina, was occupied February 17, and, while Sherman's troops encamped there, the city burned to the ground. The Confederate mayor blamed Sherman's troops for setting and spreading the fires, while Sherman and his officers protested that his men had attempted to put them out. At least half of the city burned to the ground. Then Union troops moved into Wilmington, North Carolina. With the closure of that port, the last major blockade-running avenue for the Confederacy was cut off. On Lee's insistence, Joseph Johnston took over the remnants of the Army of Tennessee on February 23, after Hood's resignation, and attempted to maneuver through North Carolina, hoping to effect a link-up with Lee's forces or at least stall any attempt by Sherman to cross through North Carolina and combine with Grant's forces to overwhelm Lee.

By the end of March, however, Grant was able to finally sever the tenuous overland routes into Petersburg and Richmond from the south with an expedition under Philip Sheridan that took Dinwiddie Court House. Lee recognized that he would have to evacuate Richmond. On April 2 Union troops found the fortresses around Petersburg lightly manned as Confederate troops pulled out; in a series of desperate, hand-to-hand clashes, Union forces cleared the forts and advanced on Petersburg. Lee withdrew his troops and headed west, hoping to pick up a trainload of supplies at Amelia Court House. The Confederate government agencies withdrew to Danville, carrying wagon loads of records and supplies. A rear guard of Confederate troops burned the bridges into Richmond and set fire to the warehouses full of supplies and armaments. In a spectacular fire, the warehouse district of Richmond was destroyed, with multiple explosions. Police and rear-guard troops tried to stop the looting and to destroy stores of whisky, but the city dissolved in chaos just as federal troops moved in on April 3. Lincoln immediately visited Richmond, where he was welcomed by throngs of African Americans. He visited the statehouse, sat briefly in Jefferson Davis's chair, and held discussions with several state legislators. Rumors spread that Lincoln was willing to accept some sort of state-by-state surrender. While no official contemporary statements back up the concept, memoirists later suggested that Lincoln was reaching for some sort of peace terms that would allow Southern state governments to remain in place.[2]

Lee's retreat was marred by confusion as expected supplies never caught up with his marching columns, and his troops went several days without food. Deserters and stragglers continued to walk away, or to sit by the side of the road to await capture.

The fall of Richmond on April 2, 1865, meant the end of the Confederacy was near. *(Library of Congress, Prints and Photographs Division, LC-USZC2–2298)*

The Army of Northern Virginia kept shrinking, with about 30,000 remaining under Lee's command as they encamped near Appomattox Court House. There, Lee received a message from Grant on April 7 suggesting a negotiated surrender, and the two generals met at the home of Wilmer McLean. Ironically enough, McLean had moved to Appomattox in order to avoid the war, when his property farther to the north was overrun during the First Battle of Bull Run. In a solemn and dignified session on April 9, Lee and Grant agreed to the terms of surrender. Grant conceded the right not only of officers to take their personal weapons, baggage, and horses, but also the right of enlisted men to remove horses they personally owned as they returned home. Lee made it clear to his officers that continuing the war as irregular troops or guerrillas, while feasible, would not result in a victory, but only in further death and destruction of the country, and that he agreed that the Army of Northern Virginia should simply surrender and disband. Both Lee and Grant departed, Lee toward his home and Grant to his headquarters at City Point near Richmond. On April 12, the flags and weapons were surrendered formally. Union troops shared their rations of bacon and hardtack with the starving remnants of the Army of Northern Virginia.

Clearly, with the fall of Richmond, the war had come to an end. The surrender at Appomattox Court House a week later represented the end of the military operation in a more formal sense. Nevertheless, Jefferson Davis refused to accept the inevitable. When General Joseph Johnston met with Davis at the temporary quarters of the Confederate government in Danville, he found Davis still claiming that vast numbers of troops could be raised, especially if

Robert E. Lee and Ulysses S. Grant sign the articles of capitulation in the parlor of Wilmer McLean's home at Appomattox Court House on April 9, 1865, almost four years exactly after the first shot at Fort Sumter. (Library of Congress, Prints and Photographs Division, LC-USZ62–2480)

Robert E. Lee's quiet dignity and devotion to Virginia made him a lasting symbol of the Lost Cause. *(Library of Congress, Prints and Photographs Division, LC-USZ62– 103217)*

deserters and draft-evaders were rounded up. Johnston explained that he had at his command some 13,500 effective troops, and that they were opposed by an estimated 350,000 troops in several Union armies. The only reasonable option was some sort of planned surrender, or the unattractive alternative of piece-meal surrender at the discretion of individual officers. The only legitimate function left to the Confederate government, Johnston told Davis, was to arrange an honorable peace. Davis gave no support for a nego-tiated surrender, explaining that he had tried that with Lincoln already and had been rejected, and that Lincoln would not give any recognition to the official position of Davis. He remained angry at that personal point of privilege the rest of his life. The remnants of the Davis government continued to move on, at first guarded by some 2,000 cavalry, and then by smaller and smaller units as they headed southwestward. It was clear to Johnston that he would have to work out his own surrender, and he and Sherman maneuvered through North Carolina, jockeying for position.[3]

FORD'S THEATER

Before Johnston's troops could be cornered by Sherman, events in Washington changed the final days of the war. John Wilkes Booth, a handsome, egotistical actor with decided pro-Confederate views, finally brought his plans for an assassination to a conclusion. For months, Booth had worked with a small following of associates, at first on a plan to kidnap Lincoln and release him in exchange for the release of Confederate prisoners. When Union forces began releasing prisoners early in 1865, Booth changed his plan to one of simultaneously assassinating President Lincoln, Vice President Andrew Johnson, and Secretary of State William Seward. His associates were an odd lot of individuals who were swayed by Booth, including Lewis Powell (alias Lewis Paine), George Atzerodt, and David Herold. They met at a boarding house operated by Mary Surratt, whose son, John Surratt, was in touch with Confederate agents in Canada.

On the night of April 14, 1865, Lincoln agreed to attend a performance of a comedy, *Our American Cousin,* at Ford's Theater in Washington. Although he had invited General and Mrs. Grant to attend, Grant had given his apolo-gies and embarked on a train for a well-earned leave of absence at his home in Bordentown, New Jersey. Booth, who was personally known at the theater, walked up to the private box overlooking the stage where Lincoln, his wife Mary, and a military officer were watching the play. At about 10:15 P.M. Booth fired a single shot into the back of Lincoln's head, then, wielding his knife, jumped to the stage a few feet below. A spur on one of his boots caught on a flag draped over the edge of the box, and he fell awkwardly onto the stage, breaking a bone in his left leg. The people in the audience were stunned and confused, not sure whether Booth's arrival was part of the play. Raising the knife and, according to some reports, shouting the motto of the state of Virginia, "Sic Semper Tyrannis" (thus always to tyrants), Booth pushed past the actors and out the rear of the theater to the alley behind, where he had left a horse. He urged the horse to a gallop and was soon heading out of town.

Lincoln's wound was clearly mortal. He was taken across the street to a boarding house where doctors attempted to make him comfortable. He died early the next day, April 15, at 7:22 A.M. Later that morning, Andrew Johnson was sworn in as president. Ironically, Booth had killed the one leader of the Union most disposed to a generous peace with minimal punishment of the members of the Confederacy.

One of Booth's associates, George Atzerodt, got cold feet; instead of assassinating Vice President Johnson, he lurked near Johnson's hotel, getting progressively more drunk through the evening. Another conspirator, Lewis Paine, attacked Seward at his home. Pretending to be bringing a prescription to the bedridden Seward, Paine broke his pistol attacking members of the household. Confronting Seward, who was covered in a tough body cast to recover from a fall, Paine slashed at him with a dagger, severely wounding the secretary of state. Despite their serious wounds, all the members of the household survived. Paine ran off and went into hiding for several days. The next Monday, he walked into the Surratt boarding house just as federal agents were questioning occupants of the building, and he was arrested. His identity was confirmed by members of the Seward household who had struggled with him the night of the assassination.

Booth met up with Herold, and together they rode through southern Maryland, stopping at the home of Dr. Samuel Mudd, a Confederate sympathizer who provided a temporary splint for Booth's broken leg. Departing Mudd's house, Herold and Booth hid out in southern Maryland for several days, while a major search for them developed. They were finally surrounded in a barn where they had taken refuge near Port Royal, Virginia, southeast of Fredericksburg. At the barn, Booth was shot to death on April 27 and Herold was captured.

The death of Lincoln was a shock to the nation and the world. Lincoln was the first American president to be assassinated. Furthermore, his assassination came just as the nation was beginning to celebrate the end of the war and beginning to accept the multiple and complex consequences of the war: emancipation, some sort of reconstruction with reconciliation, and a policy of pardon and parole of those who had led the Confederacy.

As president, Andrew Johnson immediately announced that the conspiracy to kill Lincoln, Seward, and himself was a broad one, and that it was inspired by Jefferson Davis. In addition to posting rewards for the capture of Booth and Herold, Johnson announced rewards for the capture of Jefferson Davis, Vice President Stephens, and other members of the Confederate government.

The funeral proceedings for Lincoln became a mass event, as his body was first placed in the Capitol rotunda, and then put aboard a special black-draped railroad train for transport to Springfield, Illinois, for burial. The week-long procession was viewed by millions, as the casket

John Wilkes Booth recruited several others to join his assassination plot, including the reputedly slow-witted George Atzerodt, pictured here. *(Library of Congress, Prints and Photographs Division, LC-USZ62–22995)*

was removed from the train in several cities along the way and carried in a funeral cortege through the city streets. In New York City alone, an estimated one million mourners attended the funeral procession. The heartfelt outpouring of grief was genuine, reflecting the fact that, despite his opponents and his political difficulties, Lincoln had won the support of the Union with his patience, his willingness to face difficult choices, and his often brilliant leadership through crisis after crisis. Some observers believed that Lincoln's death would put an end to any sentiment to treat the Confederacy with leniency, and that those who argued for a punitive Reconstruction would find their position strengthened by the tragedy.

FURTHER SURRENDERS

While the nation struggled with grief, the remnants of the Confederate government and army were rounded up. At Durham Station, North Carolina, Sherman offered Johnston surrender terms that went beyond those offered to Lee, in an effort at shaping a broader treaty of peace. Under the Johnston surrender terms, the Confederate state governments would be allowed to retain power and administration and would take possession of military stores. When President Andrew Johnson heard these terms, he immediately ordered that Sherman withdraw the offer and renew hostilities if Johnston did not accept surrender terms identical to those that Grant had offered to Lee. Grant was sent to Sherman to insist on the change, and, on April 26, Johnston accepted the revised terms. Johnston and some newspaper editorialists were convinced that Sherman's original plan, giving recognition to Confederate state governments, had the tacit or explicit approval of Lincoln, and that it was rescinded by Andrew Johnson only in the heat of anger over Lincoln's assassination.[4]

On May 4, Confederate general Richard Thomas surrendered the troops under his command, representing the district of Alabama, Mississippi, and East Louisiana at Citronelle, Alabama. Although the terms were similar to those provided to Lee, Thomas also secured assurances that his troops would be provided with rations and transportation to their homes.

Meanwhile, Jefferson Davis's entourage continued to shrink. Secretary of the Navy Stephen Mallory left the group, resigning officially on May 3, near Washington, Georgia. With his former postmaster John H. Reagan now serving as secretary of the treasury, and reputedly in charge of disbursing the last gold of the Confederate treasury to accompanying troops, the small group moved from private home to home, sometimes camping out overnight. Finally, on May 10, 1865, near Irwinsville, Georgia, Union troops surrounded the Davis refugees at a wooded campsite. According to rumors, Mrs. Davis had provided her husband with a lady's dress as a disguise, and the president of the Confederacy was given away by the cavalry boots protruding from beneath the skirt. Such an ignominious end of the regime was gleefully heralded and taken as straight fact in the Northern press, with radical newspapers demanding the execution of Davis for his crimes, including, it was assumed, his complicity in the assassination of Lincoln.

Other Confederate military units surrendered one by one, more or less on the same terms offered to Lee, with sometimes a provision for transportation and rations to assist the disbanded troops to return to their homes, with terms similar to those obtained by General Thomas in Alabama. A troop of Union guerrillas tracked down and shot the outlawed Confederate guerrilla William Quantrill on May 10, 1865, near Taylorsville, Kentucky; Quantrill died of his wound on June

6. A skirmish between Union and Texas troops on the Rio Grande on May 11 was the last recorded engagement of the Civil War between regular forces on both sides. General E. Kirby Smith, whose trans-Mississippi section of the Confederacy had operated almost as a separate nation, continued to hold out, and rumors circulated of surrender negotiations over a period of weeks. Finally, on May 26, 1865, Kirby Smith accepted terms similar to those accepted by Thomas in Alabama. A Confederate brigade of Native Americans serving under Cherokee brigadier general Stand Watie was the last group to officially surrender, on June 23. The war, rather than coming to a clear-cut end at Appomattox, had gradually petered out. Even the last engagements of the war seemed anti-climactic to the readers of Northern newspapers, who turned their attention to the sensational news coming out of the military tribunal set up in Washington, D.C., to try the assassination conspirators.

TRIAL AND EXECUTION

Although President Andrew Johnson had originally assumed that Davis and other Confederate officials were implicated in the assassination conspiracy, and that hundreds of plotters would be rounded up, the affair was much smaller in scale. Davis, along with several other Confederate officials, was imprisoned, with Davis held in a specially-converted casemate at Fortress Monroe in Virginia. He was kept in confinement for two years without trial and finally released, while the other Confederate officials were released within months from various prisons.

Altogether eight individuals accused of participating in the assassination were brought before a military tribunal convened in Washington: David Herold, George Atzerodt, Lewis Paine, Mary Surratt, Edwin Spangler, Michael O'Laughlin, Samuel Arnold, and Dr. Samuel Mudd. Although the defendants had legal counsel, the proceedings were marred by outrageous claims, dubious evidence, and irregular proceedings. After testifying for the government, several witnesses simply vanished, and so were not available for cross-examination. Herold, Atzerodt, Paine, and Surratt were sentenced to be hanged; O'Laughlin, Arnold, Mudd, and Spangler were given prison terms. The evidence against Mary Surratt was quite circumstantial, and a broad movement to obtain presidential clemency in her case resulted in petitions to Andrew Johnson, including one signed by the judges who had decided the case. Johnson claimed he never saw the petitions, and she and the other three were duly executed on July 7, 1865. She was the first woman ever to be executed by the United States government. The bodies were quickly interred in plain pine coffins near the scaffold at Washington's Old Penitentiary. Dr. Mudd,

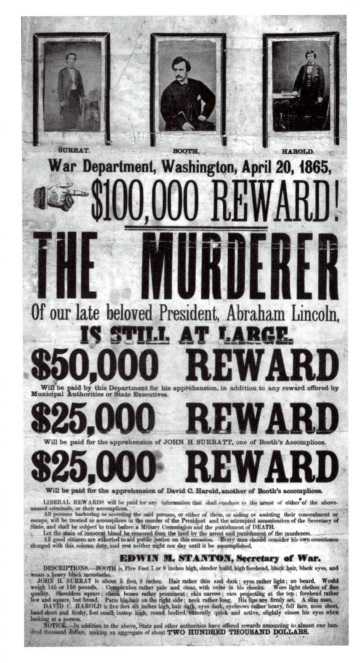

Andrew Johnson immediately offered rewards for the capture of Booth and the other assassins. He believed Jefferson Davis had sanctioned the plot. *(Library of Congress, Prints and Photographs Division, LC-USZC4–5341)*

After the war, Confederate president Jefferson Davis was held in this prison cell made out of an artillery casemate emplacement at Fortress Monroe in Virginia. He was never brought to trial and was eventually released on bail provided by contributions, including some from former notorious opponents of secession. *(Library of Congress, Prints and Photographs Division, LC-USZCN4–273)*

who had treated Booth's broken leg and then had delayed notifying authorities, was incarcerated at a remote prison fortress on the Dry Tortugas Islands off Florida. After an epidemic of yellow fever there, in which he served as a doctor helping the staff, he was finally pardoned by President Johnson on February 8, 1869, a few weeks before the end of Johnson's term of office.[5]

Jefferson Davis and the other Confederate officials were never brought to trial for complicity in the assassination, and that spurious charge simply faded away. More significantly, they were never brought to trial for treason. Thus, Davis never had the satisfaction of arguing in his own defense in a court of law that the act of secession was legal under the Constitution, although he devoted the rest of his life to making that argument in speeches and in print, long after others had decided that he was arguing for a lost cause.

The collapse of the Confederacy, the piecemeal surrender of Confederate armies, and the occupation of the seceded states by Union troops, together with the sudden and tragic assassination of Lincoln, shaped the unfolding drama of Reconstruction. Lincoln had succeeded in establishing his view that the secession statutes were illegal acts of rebellion, but that had been demonstrated only by military power, not by legal procedure. The Thirteenth Amendment, if ratified by sufficient states, would put to an end any effort to reestablish slavery. Yet few leaders had given very serious thought to the exact process by which former slaves were to be incorporated into the economy, society, and polity of the nation. The Freedmen's Bureau was structured only as a relief organization, not as an agency for social change. The assassination had ended the war on a bitter tone, hardening hearts against any move toward easy reconciliation between the sections. After Booth, it was hard to expunge malice and adopt a tone of charity for all. Without any trials that settled guilt on the leaders of the Confederacy or any official requirement that they admit their error, the adherents to the lost cause would continue to resist any changed power arrangements. The fighting phase of the war was over, but a final settlement of the other aspects of the conflict would take decades.

CHRONICLE OF EVENTS

1864

November 8: Lincoln wins the presidential election by a 411,000 vote majority, with electoral college results of 212 to 21.

December 4: Lincoln urges Congress to pass the Thirteenth Amendment.

December 19: The Electoral College vote is taken in Congress; Congress refuses to accept the Lincoln-Johnson electors from Tennessee; the 212–21 electoral vote does not include any votes from seceded states.

December 28: In response to a request from Francis Blair, Sr., that he be allowed to visit Richmond on a personal matter, Lincoln gives Blair a pass to cross into the Confederacy.

December 30: Jefferson Davis approves receiving Blair.

1865

January 12: Blair visits Jefferson Davis with a peace proposal involving a truce and a joint war against Mexico in defense of the Monroe Doctrine. He is sent back with a note suggesting that approved commissioners from both countries should meet to discuss terms.

January 18: Lincoln writes a letter for Blair to take to Davis, rejecting the concept of two countries, but suggesting that commissioners representing those in command of forces in rebellion would be received.

January 21: Blair has his second meeting with Davis and returns to Washington.

January 23: Following the disasters to Confederate forces at Franklin and Nashville, General Hood is relieved of command at his own request.

January 31: The United States House of Representatives passes the Thirteenth Amendment ending slavery in the United States. Some of the votes cast against the amendment reflect a concern that the vote will disturb the rumored peace negotiations. (The necessary two-thirds of state legislatures will ratify the amendment by December 18, 1865.)

February 3: The Hampton Roads Peace Conference meets. President Lincoln and Secretary of State William Seward meet Confederate vice president Alexander Stephens, Senator R. M. T. Hunter, and Assistant Secretary of War John A. Campbell on board the USS *River Queen*. The Confederate delegates reject the Union terms of unconditional surrender. Lincoln explains that the United States cannot negotiate with an entity whose existence it denies.

February 6: At a meeting welcoming back the Hampton Roads commissioners, Davis exhorts them never to yield on the issue of separate sovereignty. The Confederate congress treats the Lincoln reaction as insulting.

February 16: Confederate general Hardee evacuates Charleston; Confederate general Beauregard evacuates Columbia, South Carolina, which is burned; the source of the fires, whether looters or Union troops, is disputed.

February 22: Union troops occupy Wilmington, North Carolina, cutting off the last blockade-running entry to the Confederacy.

March 3: The U.S. Congress passes a law establishing the Freedmen's Bureau.

March 4: Lincoln is inaugurated and delivers his second inaugural address, asking for "malice towards none, charity for all."

March 13: Jefferson Davis signs the Negro Soldier Act allowing owners to volunteer slaves for duty, who may be freed with permission of owner and state. There is no record that any African-American Confederate units participated in the war.

March 31: Union General Philip Sheridan leads troops to Dinwiddie Court House, to the southwest of Petersburg, cutting off Lee from regions farther south and forcing Lee to abandon Richmond and attempt to link with Johnston in North Carolina.

April 2: The siege of Petersburg ends; the Confederate government evacuates by rail to Danville.

April 2–3: Richmond is evacuated; stores and bridges are burned; Confederate naval forces destroy their ships and serve as infantry.

April 3: Celebrations in New York and Washington herald the fall of Richmond as the end of the Confederacy.

April 4: Lincoln visits Richmond and sits in Davis's chair. He is warmly received by the African-American population of the city.

April 5: Davis urges continued resistance in a proclamation from Danville.

April 7: Grant asks Lee to consider surrender.

April 9: At Appomattox Court House, Lee agrees to surrender to Grant in a meeting at the home of Wilmer McLean. Lee signs the terms of formal surrender. The Army of Northern Virginia is to be disbanded; at the suggestion of Lee and as an afterthought, Grant allows departing troops to retain their horses and officers to retain their sidearms. Union troops share rations with the starving Confederates.

April 10: Lincoln delivers an impromptu speech to a celebrating crowd at the White House, humorously suggesting that the Union army has "captured as a prize" the song *Dixie* and orders it played.

April 11: The last forts held by the Confederates in Mobile, Alabama, are abandoned.

April 11: Lincoln delivers a speech suggesting suffrage for educated African Americans and supporting the readmission of Louisiana to the Union. John Wilkes Booth and Lewis Paine are in the crowd.

April 12: The Army of Northern Virginia surrenders its weapons and battleflags and is dispersed.

April 14: At about 10:15 P.M., during a performance of *Our American Cousin,* Lincoln is shot by Booth at Ford's Theater in Washington. Lewis Paine attacks Secretary of State William Seward in his bed at about the same time, wounding him, but not fatally. George Atzerodt, who had intended to kill Vice President Johnson, instead gets drunk. At 10:45, Lincoln is moved to a bed at 453 10th Street, across from the theater.

April 15: Booth and accomplice David Herold flee through southern Maryland, arriving at the home of Dr. Samuel Mudd at about 4 A.M. Mudd treats Booth's broken left leg.

April 15: Lincoln is pronounced dead at 7:22 A.M. Andrew Johnson is inaugurated president. Johnson announces a reward for the capture of the assassins and for Jefferson Davis and fellow Confederate officials, presumed to be co-conspirators in the assassination.

When John Wilkes Booth shot President Lincoln at Ford's Theater, most in the audience witnessed the crime but were too shocked to react. *(Library of Congress, Prints and Photographs Division, LC-USZ62–12426)*

April 16: The nation goes into mourning over Lincoln's death; eulogies and prayers are offered at Sunday sermons.

April 17: Sherman accepts Johnston's offer to surrender all Confederate forces and recognizing the Confederate state governments.

April 17: Lewis Powell (using the alias Lewis Paine), who attempted an assassination of William Seward while disguised as a laborer, is arrested at the Surratt house.

April 18: Sherman's terms to Johnston are announced publicly.

April 18: Lincoln's body is laid in state in the White House, then moved to the Capitol Rotunda.

April 20: Jefferson Davis and his entourage move by wagon and horseback to Charlotte, North Carolina.

April 20: George Atzerodt, a Booth associate, is arrested; after five days of hiding in swamps in Charles County, Maryland, Booth and David Herold attempt to cross the Potomac to Virginia, but get lost in the fog and land on the Maryland side.

April 21: A special train carrying Lincoln's body departs Washington bound for Springfield, Illinois, by way of Philadelphia, New York, Buffalo, Cleveland, and Chicago. It will arrive May 4 after the cortege is seen by an estimated seven million people. At several cities along the way, the body will be transported by carriage in a funeral procession.

April 22: Booth and Herold succeed in getting to the Virginia side of the Potomac.

April 23: Booth and Herold hitch a ride to the Rappahanock River farther south in Virginia.

April 24: President Andrew Johnson orders Sherman to resume hostilities within 24 hours unless Johnston accepts the terms offered earlier to Lee.

April 24: Authorities arrest Dr. Samuel Mudd, who had treated Booth's broken leg but had delayed reporting Booth's presence.

April 25: Grant transmits instructions to Sherman regarding surrender; Sherman immediately indicates to Johnston that the only terms acceptable are those offered to Lee.

April 25: In transit to Springfield, Lincoln's body is escorted through New York City by 11,000 troops and a parade estimated at 75,000 civilians, and is viewed by 1 million.

April 26: Johnston accepts the revised terms of surrender at Durham Station, North Carolina.

April 26: Booth is surrounded and shot in a barn near Port Royal in northern Virginia. Herold is taken prisoner. Booth dies the next morning from the gunshot.

General Joseph Johnston, shown here as he surrendered to General Sherman, commanded the Confederate Army of Tennessee during a brilliant withdrawal to Atlanta, but Jefferson Davis replaced him with John Hood, who was far more reckless. *(Library of Congress, Prints and Photographs Division, LC-USZ62–105593)*

April 27: The ship *Sultana,* carrying released prisoners from Andersonville and other prisons, explodes in the Mississippi River north of Memphis, killing over 1,000 recently-released prisoners of war.

April 27: David Herold is transported to the Washington Navy Yard and incarcerated aboard the monitor *Montauk* with other arrested conspirators.

April 29: President Johnson removes restrictions on trade with states in the former Confederacy.

May 3: With the Confederate government on the run, Davis accepts the resignation of Secretary of the Navy Stephen Mallory near Washington, Georgia. The fugitive Confederate government has moved from Charlotte, North Carolina, via Yorkville and Abbeville, South Carolina. The only remaining cabinet member is John H. Reagan, former postmaster general, now serving as secretary of the treasury.

May 4: Confederate lieutenant general Richard Taylor surrenders the Confederate forces of the Department of Alabama, Mississippi, and East Louisiana at Citronelle, Alabama, on terms similar to those offered to Lee (including transportation and subsistence).

May 4: Lincoln's body is interred at Oak Ridge Cemetery in Springfield, Illinois.

May 6: The U.S. adjutant general orders all Confederate prisoners of war released. The number released after the end of hostilities is about 63,000.

May 9: The military trial of eight accused assassination conspirators begins at the Old Penitentiary in Washington, D.C.

May 10: Jefferson Davis is captured near Irwinville, Georgia. To the delight of Northern cartoonists, he is wearing his wife's shawl, reported by rumor to be a woman's dress as disguise. Union troops fire at each other mistakenly, inflicting friendly-fire casualties.

May 11: In a clash between Union and Confederate troops at Palmito Ranch on the Rio Grande in Texas, Confederates drive back Union attackers. This is the last pitched battle of the war.

May 22: Jefferson Davis is imprisoned at Fortress Monroe, Virginia. He is held without trial until May 1867. Reagan and Vice President Stephens are held briefly at Fort Warren in Boston and released.

May 26: Confederate general E. Kirby-Smith surrenders the Trans-Mississippi Department to Union general E. R. S. Canby, under the same terms accepted by Lee and Johnston. Texas troops had already taken supplies and headed for home in large numbers.

June 19: The Emancipation Proclamation is announced in Galveston, Texas, a date later celebrated as Juneteenth in the state.

June 23: Confederate Cherokee brigadier general Stand Watie surrenders the First Indian Brigade to Union forces at Doaksville, near Fort Towson, in the Choctaw Nation (Indian Territory), the last surrender of a Confederate general in command of troops.

July 7: After a trial before a military tribunal (May 9–June 29), noted for many procedural flaws, four of the convicted conspirators in the Lincoln assassination are executed in Washington, D.C.: Mary Surratt, Lewis Paine, David Herold, and George Atzerodt. Others (Dr. Samuel Mudd, Samuel Arnold, Edmund Spangler, Michael O'Laughlin) are given prison sentences.

Eyewitness Testimony

[Francis P. Blair] stated, in explanation of his position, that he, being a man of Southern blood, felt very desirous to see the war between the States terminated, and hoped by an interview with me to be able to effect something to that end; that after receiving the pass which had been sent to him by my direction, he sought before returning to have a conversation with Mr. Lincoln; had two appointments for that purpose, but on each occasion was disappointed, and from the circumstances, concluded that Mr. Lincoln avoided the interview, and therefore came not only without credentials but without such instructions from Mr. Lincoln as enabled him to speak for him. His views, therefore, were to be regarded merely as his own, and said they were perhaps merely the dreams of an old man, etc. He said, despairing of being able to see me, he had determined to write to me, and had the rough draft of a letter which he had prepared, and asked permission to read it. Soon after commencing to do so, he said (pleasantly) that he found his style was marked by his old pursuit, and that the paper appeared too much like an editorial. He omitted therefore, portions of it, reading what he considered the main points of his proposition. He had a response from me to the arguments and suggestions which he desired to offer. I therefore allowed him to read without comment on my part. When he had finished, I inquired as to his main proposition, the cessation of hostilities and the union of the military forces for the common purpose of maintaining the "Monroe Doctrine"—how that object was to be reached. He said that both the political parties of the United States asserted the Monroe doctrine as a cardinal point of their creed; that there was a general desire to apply it to the case of Mexico. For that purpose a secret treaty might be made, etc. I called his attention to my past efforts for negotiation, and my inability to see—unless Mr. Lincoln's course in that regard should be changed—how we were to take the first step. He expressed the belief that Mr. Lincoln would now receive commissioners, but subsequently said he could not give any assurance on that point, and proposed to return to Washington to explain his project to Mr. Lincoln, and notify me, if his hope proved well founded, that Mr. Lincoln would now agree to a conference for the purpose of entering into negotiations.

Jefferson Davis, commenting in a memo for the record dated January 12, 1865, on his conversations with Francis Blair over a possible peace negotiation, cited in his memoir, The Rise and Fall of the Confederate Government, *pp. 612–613.*

Old Blair came after all, on the 11th. He had interviews with the Secretary of War and especially with the President. The result of which, as far as I have heard, is that the President addressed a letter in which he stated that he would receive any minister, envoy, commissioner or agent who might be sent by the United States, or he would send one there. Blair expressed himself hopeful that something would be effected on this, and said he hoped to accomplish the sending or receiving of a commissioned agent to negotiate. I am told that he declared that all idea of confiscations and punishments would be laid aside. It is said that great pressure was brought to bear on the President in connection with Blair's visit. I also hear that the House of Representatives have been debating in secret on a proposition for the appointment of commissioners. Some represent that this is proposed to be done independently of the President; others deny this and say it is recommendatory to the President. Upon a vote it is said the proposition was lost by three votes and was then reconsidered, and will pass. A majority of Congress is represented to me to be in favor of treating for peace. Whether all these propositions imply independence as a *sine qua non* is not stated. The number is certainly increasing of those who do not insist on that, but would make peace with reconstruction on old grounds of property and right, and not a few would agree to gradual emancipation.

Robert Garlick Hill Kean, head of the Confederate Bureau of War, describing in his diary rumors surrounding the meeting between Francis Blair and Jefferson Davis on January 12, 1865, in Edward Younger, ed., Inside the Confederate Government, *pp. 187–188.*

. . . delay was produced by which they were kept at City Point until Thursday morning from Monday night. Judge [John A.] Campbell thinks this was in order to give time for the announcement of the vote in the Yankee House of Representatives on the emancipation amendment to the Constitution and the action of the Eastern states legislatures on it—all of which Seward, who was all the while at Old Point, was waiting for, and brought out in the conference. . . . [Confederate Vice President Alexander] Stephens reminded Lincoln of their intimacy in the time when they served on the secret committee together, which engineered the election of General Taylor. . . . Lincoln appeared to have become impatient and interrupted with the remark that there was but one ground on which propositions could be made or received, and that was the restoration of the national authority over all places in the states. This diverted the discussion, but Mr. Seward said he desired to hear Mr. Stephens out; his view was one in which he was interested.

Mr. Stephens cited historical instances of nations at war laying aside their quarrel to take up other matters of mutual interest to both. Mr. Lincoln replied that he knew nothing about history, "You must talk history to Seward." It having become distinctly understood that no terms short of reconstruction were to be considered, Judge Campbell took up the discussion and inquired searchingly into their ideas and of the manner of it. It was brought out distinctly that submission was contemplated pure and simple, though they called our envoys to witness that they never used the word "submission." Their phrase was "restoration of the national authority." The terms of Lincoln's message in December last were all they had to offer.

On the subject of their penal legislation, Lincoln said that we must accept all the consequences of the application of the law, that he would be disposed to use liberally the power confided to him for the remission of pains and penalties. In this connection Judge Campbell remarked that he had never regarded his neck as in danger. Lincoln replied that there were a good many oak trees about the place where he lived, the limbs of which afforded many convenient points from which he might have dangled. This was said with temper, and was the only exhibition of it at all. They said there could be no convention on this subject with us either as a national government or as states, as to make such a convention would be a recognition. Mr. Hunter replied that this did not follow; there were frequent instances of such conventions, as between Charles I and the parliament. Lincoln answered, "And Charles I lost his head; that's all I know about that; you must talk history to Seward." Judge Campbell stated the difference between the law of conquest and a pacification by convention. They left no opening for any convention. Everything was to be settled by the laws of Congress and the decisions of the courts.

> *Robert Garlick Hill Kean, head of the Confederate Bureau of War, describing in his diary reports of the meeting of the peace commissioners at the Hampton Roads conference, on their return to Richmond, February 5, 1865, in Edward Younger, ed.,* Inside the Confederate Government, *pp. 194–196.*

For the first time in my life, and I suppose the first time in any colored man's life, I attended the reception of President Lincoln on the evening of the inauguration. As I approached the door I was seized by two policemen and forbidden to enter. I said to them that they were mistaken entirely in what they were doing, that if Mr. Lincoln knew that I was at the door he would order my admission, and I bolted in by them. On the inside I was taken charge of by two other policemen, to be conducted as I supposed to the President, but instead of that they were conducting me out the window on a plank.

"Oh," said I, "This will not do, gentlemen," and as a gentleman was passing in I said to him, "Just say to Mr. Lincoln that Fred. Douglass is at the door."

He rushed in to President Lincoln, and almost in less than half a minute I was invited into the East Room of the White House. A perfect sea of beauty and elegance, too, it was. The ladies were in very fine attire, and Mrs. Lincoln was standing there. I could not have been more than ten feet from him when Mr. Lincoln saw me; his countenance lighted up, and he said in a voice which was heard all around: "Here comes my friend Douglass." As I approached him he reached out his hand, gave me a cordial shake, and said: "Douglass, I saw you in the crowd today listening to my inaugural address. There is no man's opinion that I value more than yours: what do you think of it?" I said, "Mr. Lincoln, I cannot stop here to talk with you, as there are thousands waiting to shake you by the hand;" but he said again: "What did you think of it?" I said, "Mr. Lincoln, it was a sacred effort," and then I walked off. "I am glad you liked it," he said.

> *Frederick Douglass, African-American leader and journalist, commenting on his attendance at the White House inaugural ball, March 4, 1865, from his article in Allen Thorndike Rice, ed.,* Reminiscences of Abraham Lincoln by Distinguished Men of His Time, *pp. 191–193, as quoted in James M. McPherson, ed.,* The Negro's Civil War, *pp. 264–265.*

Our men deployed so as to cover every part of the walls of the fort and detailed twenty-five men to hold the gate in the rear. Now the solid-shot and bombshells found in the fort came into use. Our men hurled them on the heads of the enemy in the ditch. The fuses of bombshells were fired and rolled on them. This work did not stop until all, or nearly all of the solid cannon balls and shells were gone. Brick chimneys built to tents for artillerymen were thrown down and the bricks thrown at the enemy. Numbers of efforts to scale the walls were made, but the Federal soldiers would not act together, and consequently, the most daring ones were shot down on the walls and fell on their comrades below. A color-bearer fell on the fort with his flag falling over on our side.

Confederate private Buxton Connerly, describing the holding action at Fort Gregg, April 2, 1865, while Mississippi troops attempted to slow the advance of Grant's forces on the defenses of Petersburg and Lee withdrew the Army of Northern Virginia from Richmond to the west, in Robert G. Evans, ed., The 16th Mississippi Infantry-Civil War Letters and Reminiscences, *p. 392.*

I hurried to my command, and fifteen minutes later occupied Mayo's bridge, at the foot of 14th street [in Richmond], and made military dispositions to protect it to the last extremity. This done, I had nothing to do but listen for sounds and gaze on the terrible splendor of the scene. And such a scene probably the world has seldom witnessed. Either incendiaries, or (more probably) fragments of bombs from the arsenals, had fired various buildings, and the two cities, Richmond and Manchester, were like a blaze of day amid the surrounding darkness. Three high arched bridges were in flames; beneath them the waters sparkled and dashed and rushed on by the burning city. Every now and then, as a magazine exploded, a column of white smoke rose up as high as the eye could reach, instantaneously followed by a deafening sound. The earth seemed to rock and tremble as with the shock of an earthquake, and immediately afterward hundreds of shells would explode in air and send their iron spray down far below the bridge. As the immense magazines of cartridges ignited, the rattle as of thousands of musketry would follow, and then all was still for the moment, except the dull roar and crackle of the fast-spreading fires. At dawn we heard terrific explosions about "The Rocketts," from the unfinished iron-clads down the river.

By daylight, on the 3rd, a mob of men, women, and children, to the number of several thousands, had gathered at the corner of 14th and Cary streets and other outlets, in front of the bridge, attracted by the vast commissary depot at that point; for it must be remembered that in 1865 Richmond was a half-starved city, and the Confederate Government had that morning removed its guards and abandoned the removal of the provisions, which was impossible for the want of transportation. The depot doors were forced open and

The war left much of the infrastructure of the South in ruins, including much of its railroad rolling stock and track. This damaged locomotive was photographed in Richmond. *(Library of Congress, Prints and Photographs Division, LC-B8171–3155)*

a demoniacal struggle for the countless barrels of hams, bacon, whisky, flour, sugar, coffee, etc., etc., raged about the buildings among the hungry mob. The gutters ran whisky, and it was lapped as it flowed down the streets, while all fought for a share of the plunder. The flames came nearer and nearer, and at last caught in the commissariat itself.

Memoir of Confederate captain Clement Sullivan, describing the fall of Richmond, April 2 and April 3, 1865, in Robert Underwood Johnson and Clarence Buell, ed., Battles and Leaders of the Civil War, *Vol. 4, pp. 725–726.*

"I presume, General Grant, we have both carefully considered the proper steps to be taken, and I would suggest that you commit to writing the terms you have proposed, so that they may be formally acted upon."

"Very well," replied General Grant, "I will write them out." And calling for his manifold order-book, he opened it on the table before him and proceeded to write the terms. The leaves had been so prepared that three impressions of the writing were made. He wrote very rapidly, and did not pause until he had finished the sentence ending with "officers appointed by me to receive them." Then he looked toward Lee, and his eyes seemed to be resting on the handsome sword that hung at that officer's side. He said afterward that this set him to thinking that it would be an unnecessary humiliation to require the officers to surrender their swords, and a great hardship to deprive them of their personal baggage and horses, and after a short pause he wrote the sentence: "This will not embrace the side-arms of the officers, nor their private horses or baggage." When he had finished the letter he called Colonel (afterward General) Ely S. Parker, one of the military secretaries on the staff, to his side and looked it over with him and directed as they went along to interline six or seven words and to strike out the word "their," which had been repeated. When this had been done, he handed the book to General Lee and asked him to read over the letter. . . .

General Grant then said: "Unless you have some suggestions to make in regard to the form in which I have stated the terms, I will have a copy of the letter made in ink and sign it."

"There is one thing I would like to mention," Lee replied after a short pause. "The cavalrymen and artillerists own their own horses in our army. Its organization in this respect differs from that of the United States." This expression attracted the notice of our officers present, as showing how firmly the conviction was grounded in his mind that we were two distinct countries. He continued: "I would like to understand whether these men will be permitted to retain their horses?"

"You will find that the terms as written do not allow this," General Grant replied; "only the officers are permitted to take their private property."

Lee read over the second page of the letter again, and then said:

"No, I see the terms do not allow it; that is clear." His face showed plainly that he was quite anxious to have this concession made, and Grant said very promptly and without giving Lee time to make a direct request:

"Well, the subject is quite new to me. Of course I did not know that any private soldiers owned their animals, but I think this will be the last battle of the war—I sincerely hope so—and that the surrender of this army will be followed soon by that of all the others, and I take it that most of the men in the ranks are small farmers, and as the country has been so raided by the two armies it is doubtful whether they will be able to put in a crop to carry themselves and their families through the next winter without out the aid of the horses they are now riding, and I will arrange it in this way: I will not change the terms as now written, but I will instruct the officers I shall appoint to receive the paroles to let all the men who claim to own a horse or mule take the animals home with them to work their little farms." (This expression has been quoted in various forms and has been the subject of some dispute. I give the exact words used.)

Lee now looked greatly relieved, and though anything but a demonstrative man, he gave every evidence of his appreciation of this concession, and said, "This will have the best possible effect upon the men. It will be very gratifying and will do much toward conciliating our people."

A memoir of the signing at Appomattox Court House on April 9, 1865, by Union brevet brigadier general Horace Porter, in Robert Underwood Johnson and Clarence Buell, Battles and Leaders of the Civil War, *Vol. 4, pp. 738–739.*

This 1873 print of Lee surrendering to Grant is not precisely accurate with regard to the furnishings but may capture some of the solemnity of the event. *(Library of Congress, Prints and Photographs Division, LC-USZ62–132504)*

Col. Lee this afternoon surrendered his entire army to Lieut. Gen. Grant, officers and privates to retain private horses, arms & baggage. Officers & men to be permitted to return to their homes, but not be disturbed by the U.S. authorities as long as they observe the laws where they reside. All public property to be turned over to ordnance & quarter master depts. Remnant of Lee's army surrendered is about thirty thousand (30,000).

April 10th, surrender is completed this morning, munitions of war &c turned over to the U.S. and

Gen. Grant leaves for City Point at 11 o'clock this morning. The army of Northern Virginia is no more.

Telegram sent by Union adjutant general Schmechorn to General Orlando Willcox, April 10, 1865, announcing the surrender at Appomattox Court House, in Forgotton Valor: The Memoirs, Journals and Civil War Letters of Orlando B. Willcox, pp. 643–644.

For a week we remained [at Danville, Virginia] without news of Lee, which gave me great uneasiness as I feared Grant was pressing him back against the James River. I opened the [Confederate] War Office though the Secretary had not arrived, because I deemed it of great importance that the country should see that a government was in operation though Richmond was evacuated. On Monday, April [10] we heard of Lee's surrender at Appomattox Court House, having had no communication with him. The President and Cabinet made hasty preparations to leave Danville that night for Greensboro, North Carolina and did so without giving any orders to the bureau officers which caused great confusion. I got my cases off on a troop train the next day, and reached Greensboro on Thursday night. Found the President still there; also Generals Beauregard and Johnston, and General Breckinridge. Johnston was retreating by Raleigh and Hillsboro, on Greensboro and Salisbury, Sherman actively pressing. On Saturday the Presidential party again took wing with as little observation as might be with a wagon train. Stoneman's cavalry destroyed the railroad bridge between Greensboro and Salisbury over Deep river, and much of the tracks at Salisbury.

I followed in wagons on Sunday, but camped three days at High Point, being ordered to wait and move with Johnston's army.

Robert Garlick Hill Kean, head of the Confederate Bureau of War, describing in his diary the evacuation of the Confederate government through Virginia and North Carolina, April 11–14, 1865, in Edward Younger, ed., Inside the Confederate Government, p. 206.

I was determined not to give an opinion till Breckinridge came up, and I understood he was expected next day so said nothing. We had heard of Gen. Lee's surrender, but Breckinridge brought the first official news. I represented to Breckinridge that Mr. Davis ought to use his position to treat for terms and surrender us all—that it was the only function of Gov't he could now exercise—and it was much better than to let us be forced to surrender at discretion—and I proposed to him as

I knew there was no one about Mr. Davis who could be got to tell him so, that he should arrange so that I could tell him. He agreed with me and said there would be a Cabinet meeting that day and he would get me called before it. I was then staying with Beauregard in a [railroad] car about 100 yards from the house where Mr. Davis was, and I saw the Cabinet assemble. After between one and two hours I was sent for.

I represented to Mr. Davis that Grant had 150,000 men, Sherman 100,000, Canby 60,000, Thomas 40,000 and the only organized force to oppose all these large armies was my 13,500 men—that all our depots where we had been collecting muskets & all our places for making ammunition were in the hands of the Yankees, that we had reached a point in weakness, where our army could do no damage to the enemy—that he could not exercise any of the functions of government over the territory we were in and could not enforce the execution of any measures—that our army, therefore, could only devastate the country still more, besides drawing larger armies through it to destroy it—that the only function of Gov't he could now exercise would be to negotiate a surrender, which I advised him to do. In reply, he did not say anything more of raising large armies, but declared with considerable warmth that it was useless for him to attempt to negotiate—that he had already made overtures and they had refused to recognize or treat with him in his official capacity—&c. Finally, he agreed to my making an armistice with Sherman to see what terms of peace could be agreed upon.

When I met Sherman, we went beyond the armistice itself and set to work at the conditions of a treaty. Unfortunately Mr. Lincoln was shot and Mr. Johnson refused to agree to the terms. I believe Mr. Lincoln would have done so, because I was informed by officers on the other side that they had every reason to believe it—and because Sherman was just from him.

Comments by General Joseph Johnston on Jefferson Davis's refusal to negotiate a surrender in discussions at Danville, about April 13, 1865, as recorded by Confederate lieutenant Campbell Brown, an aide to General Ewell, in his diary, quoted in Terry L. Jones, ed., Campbell Brown's Civil War: With Ewell and the Army of Northern Virginia, pp. 309–310.

This gentleman learning that Gen. Grant was expected at the Theatre, took a seat in the dress circle opposite the President's and about ten o'clock was surprised to see Booth (whom he knew) making his way along the dress circle to the President's box. Booth stopped two steps from the door, took off his hat, and holding it in his left hand, leaned against the wall behind him. In this attitude he remained for half a minute; then, adds Mr. Ferguson, he stepped down one step, put his hand on the door of the little corridor leading to the box, bent his knee against it, the door opened, and Booth entered, and was for a time hidden from Mr. Ferguson's sight. Watching for his appearance inside to see who it was of the distinguished party he was apparently so intimate with, the shot and the smoke are the next things Mr. Ferguson remembers. Booth then sprang to the front of the box, laid his left hand on the railing front, but was checked an instant, evidently by his coat or pants being caught in something, or being held back by somebody. He had a knife in his right hand, which he also laid upon the railing where he already had his left, and vaulted out. As his legs passed between the folds of the flag decorating the box, his spur which he wore on the right heel, caught the drapery and brought it down, tearing a strip with it. When he let go the railing he still clutched the shining knife. He crouched as he fell, falling on one knee and putting forth both hands to help himself to recover an erect position, which he did with the rapidity and easy agility of an athlete.

Having recovered his equilibrium, Booth strode across the stage to the first entrance, passing behind the actor on the stage (Harry Hawk). When he reached the other side of the stage, just were he became invisible by passing into the rear entrance, he looked up, and Mr. Ferguson says he heard him say, "I have done it," and then lost sight of him. It does not appear from this statement that there was any flourishing of the dagger upon the stage, nor a repetition of the motto of Virginia. This latter, one writer has it, was yelled as he mounted his horse, held only sixty-five feet from the President's box.

Section of news item "Current Events," entitled "Statement of James P. Ferguson," from the New York Evangelist, *Vol. 36, No. 16, page 4, summarizing theatergoer and restaurant-owner Ferguson's eyewitness account of the assassination of Lincoln on April 14, 1865.*

Richmond.—The fires kindled in this city by the rebels were not extinguished until six hundred houses were destroyed. General Weitzel captured about 1000 rebel soldiers in the city, and 5000 wounded men were found in the hospitals. An immense amount of public property was left here by the rebels, including five hundred pieces of artillery, and 5000 stand of arms. The forts below Richmond were blown up and the iron-clads destroyed previous to the evacuation. Much suffering was found among the inhabitants, both rich and poor being alike destitute of food. Rations were issued to all who were willing to take the declaration of allegiance. Measures have been taken to remove the obstructions in James river, and it will soon be open again for navigation. The railroad connection with Washington is also about to be restored. The Richmond *Whig* states, that the city is very quiet and orderly, and provisions were again becoming plentiful at reasonable prices. No barrooms are allowed to be opened, and the whiskey that is found is seized and destroyed. R. M. T. Hunter and Judge Campbell, two of the late peace commissioners, still remain in Richmond. President Lincoln has spent several days there, and has admitted some of the leading Virginians to a personal conference.

"Summary of Events," April 15, 1865, published in a Philadelphia Quaker journal, The Friend, A Religious and Literary Journal *38, 33, p. 635.*

I meet you to-day, my friends and fellow countrymen, under circumstances of the greatest public grief and sorrow. I had risen early Saturday morning to complete the first of two sermons, having for my theme *Victory and its duties,* and expecting to have preached that sermon to you at this time. I waited for the morning paper, and when it came, it brought to me as it did to you, the intelligence of the most awful event in the history

At Petersburg, Virginia, Union troops remove captured artillery from Confederate fortifications. *(Library of Congress, Prints and Photographs Division, LC-B8171–3205)*

of this country. The carrier greeted me with a tearful and saddened countenance, exclaiming,—"Sad news this morning! The President is shot!" I could scarcely believe it true, yet I opened the paper and read the dispatches, and saw that it was so. Ere this news has spread through all parts of the land, kindling emotions in the heart of the nation which no words can describe. But yesterday we were joyous and hopeful, thanking God for his mercies, and congratulating each other upon the bright prospects of the future. Our recent victories gave promise of a speedy and lasting peace. We saw, as we supposed, the end of this terrible war. How suddenly and how awfully have our emotions been changed into those of the deepest sorrow! Who can refuse to weep? Who can withhold his tears or command his feelings at such a moment? And is it so? Has the President of these United States, the personal representative of the honor, glory and dignity of this nation, the man of the people's choice, the man who has guided the ship of State with consummate wisdom and unfaltering integrity during these stormy years, the man whom God seemed to have raised up and signally qualified for the duties of this great crisis—yes, has Abraham Lincoln, good in his greatness, and great in his goodness, fallen the victim of murderous assassination, just in the moment of our Triumph? And has his Honorable Secretary of State been assailed with the instrument of death for a like purpose? We pause in the profoundest astonishment. Our indignation in one direction, and our sorrow in the other, are past all utterance. The American people never felt as they do to-day. They never before had such an occasion for feeling. We all feel the dreadful blow. It has fallen upon us like a thunderbolt in the midst of our joys. To the deep and pungent thrill of the national hurt no human words can do any adequate justice.

From a sermon regarding the assassination of Lincoln, delivered by Reverend Samuel T. Spear, D.D., pastor of the South Presbyterian Church, Brooklyn, New York, on Sunday, April 16, 1865, published in The National Preacher and Village Pulpit, *May 1865, Vol. 39, No. 5, p. 131.*

Last night a mob of some 2,000 or more started for [Raleigh] saying they would destroy it. General Logan got in their front and ordered them back to their camps. They still went on. Then he told them that if they did not do so he would order the Artillery (which they could see) to fire into them with grape cainster [sic-cannister]. They gave it up and went back to camp. General Logan saved the City and it owes him a debt it

never can pay. We are pushing [Johnston's] Army hard and just now have learned that he has sent in a flag of truce. Negotiations are going on for a surrender. We have moved out to Morrisville about 15 miles East and North of [Raleigh]. We learn that Secretary Stanton at Washington is not satisfied with the terms General Sherman has offered General [Johnston] and his Johnnys, and we got some New York papers which say Sherman is a dangerous man and a worse traitor than Lee or any of the Southern Generals. They had better look a leedle out or they will have General Shermans Army to reckon with the first thing they know. We dont propose to have our General called such names. "Sherman a Traitor!" the Idea!

General Grant has been here and settled all the trouble.

Comment in his diary by Sergeant Theodore F. Upson, regarding the anger of troops at the news of Lincoln's assassination and their reaction to the official reprimand to Sherman over surrender terms offered to General Joseph Johnston, in the entry dated April 16, 1865, as published in Oscar Winther, ed., With Sherman to the Sea: Civil War Letters, Diaries, and Reminiscences of Theodore F. Upson, *p. 167.*

Late on Tuesday night [sic—Monday, April 17, 1865], a man disguised as a laborer and carrying a pick on his shoulder approached the house occupied by the family of Surratt in Washington. He was about to enter when arrested. Upon washing the dirt from his face, he was quite a different looking person from what his appearance indicated. He called himself Payne, and exhibited not a little embarrassment. He managed to ask in agitated tones, why he was arrested. The colored servant of Secretary Seward was sent for, when he immediately exclaimed, "That's the man! I know him by his general appearance and his mouth." The servant then said there could be no mistake. The man has been placed in safe custody, and is to be seen by Miss Fanny Seward for further identification.

News item in The Liberator, *April 21, 1865, Vol. 35, No. 16, p. 63, entitled "The Arrest of Secretary Seward's Assassin," describing the arrest of Seward's attempted assassin, Lewis Powell, alias Lewis Paine, on April 17.*

Only a few days since the fame of General Sherman stood upon the very pinnacle of greatness. He had astonished the world by the boldness, originality, and success of his generalship. The feeling and respect of nearly every soldier in his command towards him, had

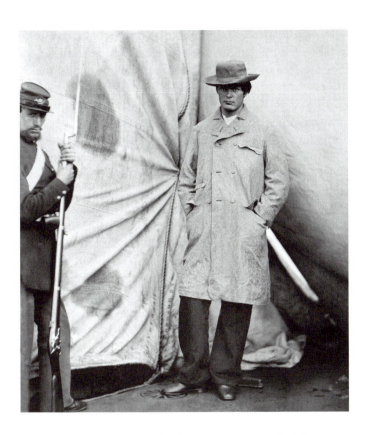

Lewis Payne, one of the assassination conspirators, attacked Secretary of State William Seward but failed to kill him. Payne had several aliases, including Lewis Powell and Lewis Paine. *(Library of Congress, Prints and Photographs Division, LC-B8171–7775)*

subject, but preserved a strange silence. Another spirit had come over that brave soldier. What was the cause? Was it a vaunting ambition that looked up to higher seats of power from the dizzy heights on which his bravery, his strategy and his success had placed him? Can it be possible that the offer of stolen Confederate gold had usurped in his heart the place of his former undoubted loyalty? Has a fit of insanity come over him, or has the wily politician outflanked his masterly generalship. Has the mysterious power of Catholicism paralyzed him? To something he has evidently fallen a victim, but precisely what we cannot now divine.

Editorial commenting on Sherman's offer of peace terms to Johnston, published in Zion's Herald and Wesleyan Journal, *May 3, 1865, Vol. 36, No. 18, p. 70.*

Jefferson Davis . . . was surprised in his camp near Irwinsville, Ga., on the morning of May 10, and attempted to escape in the disguise of an old woman. His wife arrayed him in her own dress, put on him her hood, and tied a scarf about his head so as to conceal his face completely. Thus disguised, Mrs. Davis took hold of one of his arms, and her sister of the other; and apparently supporting the tottering step of an old woman, they walked away from the camp toward a neighboring swamp. Four men of Colonel Richard's cavalry, however, stopped the trio, and began to ask questions. Mrs. Davis, who seems to have been devoted in her efforts to get her husband away safely, besought the soldiers to "allow her poor old mother to pass." The soldiers replied that it couldn't be done without an examination; "Jeff. Davis was around there somewhere, and they meant to have him!" And have him they did. One of them poked about the feet of the pseudo-grand-dame with his saber till he discovered a big pair of cavalry boots; and another pulled off the hood, when Jefferson Davis stood revealed in a choice and elegant costume of frock, pantaloons, boots, and beard. He was brought to terms when a Spencer rifle was pointed at him. It is related that one of our soldiers, when remonstrated with for "treating our President so," retorted by saying: "President! What's he President of?" Which was a very pertinent question.

Editorial describing the capture of Jefferson Davis on May 10, 1865, entitled "Miscellaneous—Jeff. Davis under Bolt and Bar," from The Independent, *17, no. 860, (May 25, 1865), p. 8.*

almost become adoration. He was sure to go into history, and take his place among the greatest military heroes. His name could not be mentioned in any audience composed of loyal people, without eliciting the most enthusiastic cheers. People were beginning to think that General Grant would hardly be able to stand above him in the hearts of the people.

What a change has suddenly come over that once proud name! His proposed conditions of peace to General Johnston have nearly, perhaps quite, ruined his reputation. We do not know what explanations he may be able to make to clear up his character before the loyal people. We will not hastily pass a final sentence upon him, but allow him time to speak for himself. But from the known circumstances of that incipient treaty, his prospects are exceedingly dark. He knew the conditions of the surrender of General Lee, and had been instructed to offer Johnston the same. He knew also, two days before, that President Lincoln had been assassinated. It is said that he went off alone arm in arm with Johnston, and remained with him a long time; that he did not confer with his subordinate officers on the

I have the honor to report that at daylight yesterday [May 10, 1865], at Irwinsville, I surprised and captured

Jeff. Davis and family, together with his wife, sisters and brother, his Postmaster-General Reagan; his private Secretary, Col. Harrison; Col. Johnson, Aid-de-Camp on Davis' staff; Col. Morris Lubbick, and Lieut. Hathaway; also, several important names, and a train of five wagons and three ambulances, making a most perfect success.

Had not a most painful mistake occurred, by which the Fourth Michigan and First Wisconsin came in conflict, we should have done better. This mistake cost us two killed, and Lieut. Boutle wounded through the arm, in the Fourth Michigan, and four men wounded in the First Wisconsin. This occurred just at daylight, after we had captured the camp. By the advance of the First Wisconsin they were mistaken for the enemy.

I returned to this point last night, and shall move right on to Macon, without waiting orders from you, as directed, feeling that the whole object of the expedition is accomplished.

It will take us at least three days to reach Macon, as we are at least seventy–five miles out, and our stock much exhausted. I hope to reach Hawkinsville to-night.

Dispatch of Lieutenant Colonel B. D. Pritchard, Fourth Michigan Cavalry, to Captain T. W. Scott, Adjutant General, Second Division, Headquarters 4th Michigan Cavalry, Cumberlandville, Georgia, May 11, in news item, New York Times, *entitled "Details of the Capture," May 15, 1865, p. 1.*

GEN. HALLECK has issued an order for the suppression of guerillas in Virginia and North Carolina. All persons found in arms against the Government in those states are declared robbers and outlaws. He has also instructed his officers to use their influence to reconcile all differences between freedmen and their former masters, and assures freedmen that they will be required to labor for the support of themselves and families, but they are free to select their own employment and make their own bargains.

GEN. SHERMAN'S TERMS—As the facts and circumstances which operated upon the mind of Gen. Sherman, in his recent treaty with Gen. Johnston become known, there is less disposition to censure him for the latitude taken. He had just had a long interview with President Lincoln, wherein the contingency of Johnston's surrender was thoroughly canvassed, and the paramount impression made by the President was that every possible magnanimity and kindness was to be shown the foe, just so soon as he should offer to lay down his arms. The President particularly desired that every cause of irritation, consistent with justice and national honor, should be obviated, with a view of winning back the affections of the Southern people to the old flag, rather than securing a forced and unwilling obedience to Federal rule. Gen. Sherman insists that his action was based upon this desire of the President.

FINIS—The only remaining forces of the rebellion are those of Kirby Smith on the Red river, and Dick Taylor's in Alabama. Kirby Smith made overtures the latter part of April to surrender his force on the same terms granted to Lee, and the surrender has doubtless ere this been accomplished. The absolute surrender of Dick Taylor is announced by a telegram from Gen. Wilson, at Macon, to the War Department.

All that is left of the rebellion, therefore, is its guerilla feature. The head and the body are both defunct, and guerillaism, which is the last of the rebel serpent, is all that exhibits signs of vitality.

Items from "Current Events," describing recent military actions in the Confederacy in the May 11, 1865 issue of the New York Evangelist, *Vol. 36, No. 19, p. 4.*

11
Reconstruction
March 1865–April 1877

There were two views of how to deal with the political status of the defeated Confederate states, one view held by the executive and one by the Congress. Lincoln and Andrew Johnson believed strongly that the problem of Reconstruction was the responsibility of the executive department. Their view was that there had been an insurrection; the executive had called out troops to suppress it. It was up to the military to determine when the insurrection had been suppressed; it was up to the executive to exercise the power of pardon and amnesty. And it was up to the executive to determine what conditions had to be met to qualify for amnesty.

Some members of Congress held the view that the states had indeed seceded or at least destroyed their old relationship with the Union and that they had been defeated as conquered provinces. Another view held that, by removing their representatives from Congress and by dissolving their governments and replacing them with new ones, the seceding states had reverted to the status of territories. In either case, whether the seceding states became conquered provinces or territories, it was the constitutional job of Congress to guarantee a republican form of government in those states. Further, it was in the power of Congress whether or not to admit elected legislators to the House and Senate from those states.

The Constitution had no specific provisions for this situation, and there was little guidance as to what constituted the correct constitutional procedure. The executive department relied on those clauses of the Constitution concerning rebellion and treason; the legislative department relied on those clauses that spoke to the republican form of government of the states and the admission of representatives to Congress. Since president and Congress had such differing constitutional bases and such separate agendas, the two views led to inevitable conflict.

LINCOLN'S RECONSTRUCTION GOALS

Lincoln, as a Republican politician, wanted reconstruction to progress in such a fashion that there would be a Republican Party in the South. Remembering his own Whig origins, he wanted a national party such as the Whigs had been, not a

At the end of the war, many of Charleston's buildings were damaged or destroyed from Union artillery fire. Children played among the ruins of the Circular Church, 150 Meeting Street. *(Library of Congress, Prints and Photographs Division, LC-B8171–3448)*

sectional party, such as the Republicans had been on the eve of the war. At least part of his mild reconstruction planning was based on a hope that the Union or Republican Party would be able to capture the support of the former Southern Whigs and create a truly national political base. Before Lincoln's death he made progress toward establishing loyal governments in Virginia, Tennessee, Louisiana, and Arkansas, all based on a combination of Whig-Unionists and those willing to take loyalty oaths to the Union. He attempted to get core Unionist governments set up in Louisiana and Tennessee to serve as a nucleus around which the new governments in those states could emerge. On December 8, 1863, he issued his proclamation of amnesty and reconstruction—the so-called 10 percent plan that would allow the establishment of governments once ten percent of the eligible voters signed a loyalty oath. In 1864, Congress passed the Wade-Davis plan, which required a majority (not 10%) to vote for state organizing conventions. However, to serve as a delegate to a state constitutional convention or to hold office in the newly established governments, under the congressional plan, individuals would also have to sign an "iron-clad" oath that they had never participated voluntarily in secession. This is the bill that Lincoln let go unsigned, or pocket-vetoed, but for which he also wrote a veto message in the summer of 1864.

Although the Confiscation Act of 1862 originally included a provision for the confiscation of the estates of Confederates, that provision was never enforced; Lincoln had not wanted to dispossess the planters of their land and believed that it was unconstitutional to deprive heirs of their property for the crimes of an individual ancestor. Lincoln hinted that the Emancipation Proclamation, as a war measure, only applied so far as it went during the war; he appeared to be suggesting that, if the South surrendered, emancipation would not be applied to areas under Confederate jurisdiction on the date of surrender. He urged the passage and ratification of the Thirteenth Amendment to the Constitution, partly because he believed that, without such an amendment, the wartime measures of emancipation might not be permanent.

From this evidence, it seems that Lincoln probably intended some sort of Reconstruction policy that would build on the old Whig and Unionist elements in the South to create a possibility of a Republican Party (or Union Party of some sort) with congressional delegations from the South. As to social policy, Lincoln was not nearly as egalitarian as the radicals in the Republican Party, and he probably would have endorsed only a program of gradual enfranchisement (perhaps with a literacy test). However, he was a superb politician and strategist and he might have understood that to achieve his goals he would have to yield in the radical direction of more rights and status for the former slaves, and he was certainly quite capable of matching wits with the radical strategists in Congress.

ANDREW JOHNSON AND RECONSTRUCTION

With Lincoln's death and his replacement by Johnson, who was politically incompetent, the chances of reconciling the natural divergence of viewpoints between the executive branch and the legislative branch were greatly diminished. Although many in Congress did not endorse a socially radical plan of Reconstruction, most Congressmen did believe that the question of how and under what terms the Southern states should be restored to political equivalency with the other states was in the jurisdiction of Congress.

Johnson talked tough in early 1865, and radicals thought he was with them. As a Tennessee-born, self-made man in the Jacksonian tradition, Johnson had always resented the power and arrogance of the wealthy planter class in the South. From his remarks and his acquiescence to the comments of others, Johnson appeared to support trials for leading Confederates and confiscation of their estates. He insisted that the states organized under his plan in 1865 had to exclude from positions of leadership former unpardoned Confederates. To be constituted as state governments with local jurisdiction, the defeated Confederate states had to endorse the Thirteenth Amendment abolishing slavery, and they had to repudiate the Confederate war debt. On their surface, these requirements imposed an implied transition that would bring the states into conformity with the Union, and, if rigorously enforced, would go far toward meeting the radical agenda. If he had coupled enforcement of his stated requirements for readmission with his indicated intention of confiscating planter estates of leading Confederates, radicals would have had little to complain about.

The reasons for his fall from grace with the radicals were several. Over the period 1865–66 he modified his views, accepting the fact that the former Confederate states did not actually abide by his own conditions. Secondly, he was a very poor politician and unsure of himself, often remaining silent when he should have given his opinion, and, at other times, making intemperate speeches off the cuff that insulted his supporters as well as his opponents. Furthermore, the radicals really never understood that Johnson was not a supporter of the emerging business culture in the North, and that he was willing to give the planter class power as long as they personally appealed to him for clemency. Nor did the radicals understand the degree to which Johnson shared the prevailing white view in the South that the African American was completely incapable of citizenship. As a Jacksonian, self-made man, as well as a racial bigot, he did support some socially democratic ideas such as public schools and the Homestead Act, but his social democracy was intended for whites only.

Johnson hoped to achieve Reconstruction between May and December 1865. The governments elected under his plan, however, were mostly dominated by ex-Confederates. Johnson may have expected the white underclass of the South to elect their own leadership, men like himself. However, the politically adept and experienced politicians were for the most part former Confederates. Many of those elected were in the very classes he had excepted from the effect of the amnesty, and they were elected in clear defiance of his explicit statement that they were not included in his blanket amnesty. But instead of refusing to allow them to hold office, he yielded and issued wholesale pardons. He issued 13,500 pardons, then pardoned all but a few hundred individuals on September 7, 1867. The pardons of ex-Confederate politicians and military officers pushed the Union men in the South to minority positions in the legislatures and in the state administrations. Furthermore, Johnson gave up on confiscation of estates, which he appeared to support at first, and was ready to recognize and accept the new governments even when they failed to meet his preconditions.

There are several explanations for why Johnson gave up on his attempt to exclude the former planter class from power and why he accepted the elections of those he had specifically excluded from the effect of his amnesty. His views on race were much closer to those of the Confederates than to those of the radicals in Congress. Perhaps he lacked the courage to enforce his restrictions on office holding, which would have required that he fly in the face of the electoral will of those who had voted. Such an action would have contradicted his proclaimed Jacksonian faith in the wisdom of the people expressed through the ballot. Perhaps he became converted to generous Reconstruction. It also seemed that he liked the personal power that came from making wealthy and formerly powerful aristocrats apply to him for pardon. It certainly seemed that planters and Confederates soon understood and exploited this personal weakness. In effect, the former Confederates were more adept at politics than he, and he found himself outflanked. By fall 1865, Johnson was in the position of having to defend the governments he had established, even though they were dominated by secessionists and even though they began to enact laws designed to keep African Americans in a status close to slavery. Stuck with his commitment, he had to stand by the governments he had encouraged and had to support them against attacks from Congress.

The governments established by the former Confederates under the Johnson rules in 1865 quite clearly set about establishing a caste system. Reports to the Joint Committee on Reconstruction described the failure of Reconstruction under Johnson to protect the freedmen; the Carl Schurz report was less critical of the social policies put in place under the Johnson governments, but still showed that the governments in the South were dominated by Confederate thinking. Schurz gave a candid report, indicating that token submission by the former planters was adopted as a necessity to get rid of federal troops. However, both the Joint Committee and Schurz noted that freedmen were being mistreated—any evidence of attempting to exercise rights was treated as "insolence" and often met with whipping, caning, or murder.

Furthermore, the reports showed, even Johnson's mild terms were not quite met. Some states repealed, but did not repudiate, the ordinances of secession; most appointed Confederates, rather than Southern Unionists or new Northern residents, to appointed positions. There were many other notable aspects of the resistance of the Johnson-sanctioned governments to the intent of the Johnson Reconstruction. Mississippi did not ratify the Thirteenth Amendment abolishing slavery; South Carolina did not repudiate Confederate debt, claiming it was so miniscule and so mixed with other debts that it could not be identified; Arkansas voted pensions for Confederate veterans. All the states rejected black suffrage; none of the Johnson governments established schools for blacks. Furthermore, the Johnson governments passed the Black Codes, intended to keep the slaves as propertyless workers. In short, the states disfranchised blacks, kept them in conditions resembling slavery, enacted segregation and legal discrimination, and empowered Confederate politicians and military officers to rule the states. About the only change from prewar conditions these states appeared to accept was the formal ending of the status of chattel slavery.[1]

In the Southern states where Johnson had allowed the establishment of governments, former secessionists, the most irresponsible class of leadership and the least willing to compromise, believed they had a free hand to establish a caste system to replace slavery. The social goal of these governments was to keep the freedmen as a subservient labor pool while denying them legal, political, and social advancement. That is, they did not expect blacks to be able to freely make their own contracts, to move about, to be able to use the courts to protect their

Northern congressmen and journalists were appalled to learn that recently freed African Americans were still treated much as slaves had been. In this print, a freedman's labor is being auctioned off in a scene very close to a slave auction of the prewar days. *(Library of Congress, Prints and Photographs Division, LC-USZ62–117139)*

rights, to vote, or to get an education. Radical goals on such topics seemed to them wrongheaded and liable only to raise the expectations of the former slaves, making them less tractable. In short, the secessionist-planter class leadership was willing to accept emancipation, but expected to replace it with a system that continued to make the freedmen available as laborers paid only at the subsistence level. They believed that removing slavery had worsened the position of African Americans, but that African Americans had no reason to expect, and no ability to utilize, the benefits of citizenship. Some were even reluctant to grant the former slaves the right to marry, but most may have been willing to yield on this point. The political leadership did not think it was appropriate to allow blacks to testify against whites in court, clearly assuming that blacks would be incapable of telling the truth. Johnson's program, if it had any intention of changing the social-political power structure in the seceded states, had failed.

CONGRESSIONAL REACTION TO JOHNSON'S PLAN

When Johnson took over the administration of Reconstruction during the summer and fall of 1865, Congress felt he had usurped their prerogatives. After all, he could have called them into session before their regular meeting in December, or he could have consulted extensively with leading members of Congress. Furthermore, it was his generous application of the amnesty and pardon power that allowed former Confederates to assume power. As the investigations of the progress of Reconstruction under Johnson's terms were completed, Northern journalists and congressional leadership grew outraged, fully convinced that the president had abandoned some of the most important Republican goals. Some suspected that he hoped for a Democratic nomination for the presidency in 1868. For all of these reasons, by early 1866 Johnson had lost the support of Congress, and Republican newspapers and journals throughout the North rumbled with angry editorials.

Congress assembled in December for the 1865–66 session with four factions. One was the small group of Northern Democrats, who were disorganized. They tended to throw their support to Johnson when they saw the pattern of radical opposition to him emerging. Second was a group of conservative Republicans who tended to be partisan but not radical. Radicals, the third group, included among others Charles Sumner of Massachusetts, Benjamin Wade of Ohio, Zachariah Chandler of Michigan, Thaddeus Stevens of Pennsylvania, and William Ashley of Ohio. Finally, there were some moderate Republicans, leaning toward Johnson, but wavering between radicals and conservatives. Although the Republicans were divided by factions, the radicals had the clearest vision of what the reconstructed South should be like. They believed that blacks should not only be freed from slavery, but also transformed into citizens, with access to education, some financial start on the path to prosperity, and guaranteed basic rights of equality in public and private matters. This egalitarian view, based on abolitionist views of the race issue, was far in advance of the views of the majority of both Southern and Northern whites. Nevertheless, it suggested a coherent agenda of what needed to be done; clearly, Johnson had done nothing to implement anything like such an agenda.

Because Johnson was stubborn and the Southern governments showed no sign of yielding over the course of the session from December 1865 to the summer of 1866, the moderates were driven into the camp of the radicals. Thus the egalitarian measures supported by radicals became attractive even to more moderate Republicans, if only as a way of punishing the recalcitrant rebels who had gained power under Johnson, and as a way of showing their opposition to Johnson himself.

The next two years saw a deep conflict between Congress and the president over three very fundamental issues. One was the relative power of the executive and Congress. A second was the relationship between state and federal responsibilities and powers. And third, underlying the other two, was a debate over exactly what terms should be imposed on the former Confederacy. Through these debates, the radicals continued to strive for measures that would protect the freedmen and elevate their status to that of full citizenship.

During debates on these intertwined issues, the radicals, led by Thaddeus Stevens in the House of Representatives and Sumner and Chandler in the Senate, held that the states had seceded and were now conquered provinces. In the Senate, Sumner argued that the Confederate states had reverted to territories, and Congress could set the rules. Even though the somewhat theoretical issue of whether the states had become conquered provinces or territories was hotly debated, it was clear that Congress expected to control the practical question of readmission of the seceded states to representation in the Congress.

Charles Sumner remained one of the most outspoken Radical advocates of civil rights for African Americans in the Senate during Johnson's administration. *(Library of Congress, Prints and Photographs Division, LC-DIG-cwpbh-02793)*

The central issue that divided Northern conservatives and radicals was the place of freed slaves in the society. Johnson held that the United States was still a white man's country. Johnson and his supporters viewed those whites who advocated black rights as hypocritical, crazy, vindictive, or venal. There may indeed have been some unconscious hypocrisy among the radicals, as well as some political hyperbole, but the radicals were also idealists. Radicals had achieved the transformation of the Civil War from one for union to one for freedom, and they did not intend to see this idealistic goal destroyed by former slaveholders or by Northern racists.

In December 1865, the radicals and moderates, constituting a clear majority of Congress, agreed not to seat any senators and representatives from the former Confederacy. In February 1866, both houses agreed not to seat any congressmen from a former Confederate state until both houses were satisfied that the state was entitled to representation. With these tools in hand, Congress was in a position to establish policy along lines dictated by the Republican majority representing the 19 Northern states. Another measure supported in December 1865 was the establishment of the Joint Committee on Reconstruction, consisting of six senators and nine representatives; even though moderates controlled it, its findings backed up the radical claims that the Johnson state governments had set out to establish racial oppression in the South.

In addition to the reports coming from the South, one precipitating event drove a clear wedge between Congress and Johnson. On February 22, 1866, Johnson delivered a speech in which he almost casually charged members of

Congress with treason. He claimed that Thaddeus Stevens, Wendell Phillips, and Charles Sumner were traitors, when in fact they were the most influential leaders of the Congress. Even though he had first made the remark in an off-hand manner, he repeated the charge several times, making it clear he believed it. Furthermore, he suggested that Congress had no jurisdiction since it did not include representatives of all the states. Johnson's vetoes of congressional Reconstruction bills passed in early 1866 finalized the break between Congress and president, confirmed when they easily overrode the vetoes with more than two-thirds of the required votes.

The election campaign of fall 1866 was bitter, and radicals won, not only taking more than two-thirds of both houses, but also gaining Republican margins in all Northern legislatures and taking all governor's races of that year. The fall elections were a clear repudiation of Johnson by Northern voters and an endorsement of the intent of Congress to proceed with its plan for Reconstruction. With radical control of Congress, and as the Northern population came to recognize that Johnson had yielded control to the former Confederates, it was clear that the power over Reconstruction policy would readily pass to Congress. Johnson's claims that Congress (which admitted representatives from Tennessee, but not from the other 10 states of the former Confederacy) was a rump organization with no legal standing, and his repeated charges of treason, inspired fears that he intended to impose a coup d'etat by arresting those congressmen and senators most opposed to him.

His behavior and ineptness spurred Congress to look into ways to remove him from office and to consider impeachment. In 1867, Congress took full charge of Reconstruction, passing further numerous bills over the president's veto. Before the Johnson administration, no Congress had overturned a presidential veto on any significant bill. There had been two minor cases of overturning vetoes before the Civil War, but they had not involved nationally important legislation.

CONGRESSIONAL RECONSTRUCTION AND IMPEACHMENT

The central aspect of the congressional Reconstruction plan consisted of establishing military governments in the South, empowered to hold constitutional conventions that would guarantee rights to blacks. The Fourteenth Amendment had to be passed by these states prior to considering the admission of their representatives to Congress. Although the Fourteenth Amendment left the question of suffrage to the states, it did make clear that the other rights of citizenship could not be denied on grounds of race or previous condition of servitude.

If a state approved the Thirteenth and Fourteenth amendments, the process of Reconstruction could proceed. The state constitutional conventions established under federal military control would produce provisional governments, elect congressmen and senators; if they met the conditions, Congress would accept the representatives, restoring the states to the Union. This plan could be readily hampered by Johnson if he appointed generals in the South who were not vigorous in carrying through the intent of the law. Nevertheless, even with moderate (rather than radical) generals, the system set up by Congress did yield radical governments across the remaining 10 states of the South.

After attempting in March 1868 to impeach Johnson on grounds that his attempt to dismiss Secretary of War Edwin Stanton was a violation of the Tenure

Radical congressman from Pennsylvania, Thaddeus Stevens, was a leader in the attempt to impeach Andrew Johnson. *(Library of Congress, Prints and Photographs Division, LC-USZ62–106848)*

of Office Act, Congress turned its attention to readmitting the states. Of the 10 still not represented, six were readmitted in June 1868, all with Republican administrations: Arkansas, Florida, North and South Carolina, Louisiana, and Alabama. Not yet admitted were Virginia, Texas, Mississippi, and Georgia. In these four states, political chaos, boycotted elections, and legislatures that refused to seat duly elected black members prohibited admission. Congress made the ratification of the Fifteenth Amendment, which explicitly guaranteed the right to vote to all men without regard to race or previous slavery, a condition for readmission of these remaining four states.

GRANT AND THE BOURBON DEMOCRATS

In the fall election of 1868, U. S. Grant was elected president. Although not a radical, Grant was willing to implement the radical program. Never too interested in the minute details of administration, Grant was also a poor judge of character in his appointments. Many of these appointees saw their jobs as a chance for graft, which, during the eight years of his two administrations, reached levels never before seen in the United States. After further military control and monitored elections supervised by uniformed troops, the remaining four states were admitted to the Union in 1870. Thus in 1870, briefly, radical Reconstruction was at work through 10 states of the South. However, some of the Republican governments in the South had gained power because Democrats had boycotted elections during the military occupation, suggesting that an easy way to regain power for the Democrats would be through the simple exercise of the ballot once the state had gained its seats in Congress.

Democrats began working to regain power, succeeding first in Tennessee in 1869, by elections in that year. The Democrats retaking power were known as Bourbons, recalling the effort of the Bourbon house in France to restore the ancien régime after the French Revolution. When Bourbons achieved power in the South, they claimed they had redeemed the state government, and thus, once in power, they were known as redeemers. State by state, Democratic Party redeemers gained control, usually charging the Republican governments with incompetence, over-spending, and graft. Most of these charges were false but were easily believed, simply because most white Southerners assumed that blacks in state government would be incapable of efficient administration. Democrats charged whites who worked in these governments with hypocrisy, venality, and disloyalty to the South and to the white race. Southern-born Unionists and former Whigs who worked with the governments were labeled scalawags; Northerners who had immigrated to the South with the army or with the Freedmen's Bureau were called carpetbaggers, suggesting that they carried their whole estate in a suitcase. Even facing such hostility, and in states with large black populations or with Republican governors willing to use state militias to protect the rights of blacks, radicals retained control for a few years. The period of radical Reconstruction, with mixed support from scalawags, carpetbaggers, black voters, and committed Republican governors, varied from a few months to several years, depending on the state. For the most part, such governments were dominated by their white members, with some 16 African Americans serving in Congress, two in the Senate, and several in state administrative positions below the rank of governor. In Louisiana, P. B. S. Pinchback, a black lieutenant governor, served as acting governor for just over a month.

After his dramatic adventures in seizing the Confederate ship *Planter,* Robert Smalls became one of several African-American members of Congress, serving 1875–85 from his home state, South Carolina. *(Library of Congress, Prints and Photographs Division, LC-DIG-cwpbh-03683)*

The process by which the Bourbon Democrats took power away from the Republicans varied from peaceful electoral means to illegal processes, such as forced resignations of governors, to violent means incorporating terror and bloodshed. In Virginia, as soon as the state was readmitted to the Union, the governor changed his party affiliation from Republican to Democrat, in 1870. In the 1870 election in North Carolina, Democrats took control of the legislature and in 1871 impeached the Republican governor. In the 1870 elections, Democrats took control of both the legislature and executive in Georgia. In 1873, the gubernatorial election in Texas was contested, and the Republican governor insisted on staying in power. Nevertheless, he was forced to resign before the end of his term, early in 1874. In Mississippi, in 1875, Democrats used their party organizations or local clubs, including such organizations as the Ku Klux Klan and the Knights of the White Camilia, to form terror groups that broke up Republican meetings, threatened and murdered black politicians and voters, prevented Republican ballots from being distributed, and forced Republican sheriffs to go into hiding. This system of organized violence and subversion of the political process became known as the Mississippi Plan, although similar practices had been used as early as 1868 in elections in New Orleans and in scattered locations in other states. It was later emulated in South Carolina to depose the Republican regime there.[2]

By 1876, Mississippi was "redeemed" and in Democratic Party hands, although the irony of using that term to define a process that had worked by explicit and open violence was not lost on many commentators, or on Congressional investigators. Nevertheless, the Republican organization in Mississippi was dead, and blacks were terrorized into not voting there. Later, the exclusion of blacks from the franchise in Mississippi and other Southern states would be achieved by a combination of less bloody methods, including poll taxes, intimidation at registration places, literacy tests, and refusal to allow blacks to participate in the primary elections of the Democratic Party. Even with these disabilities, a handful of African-American congressmen from former Confederate states continued to be elected after Reconstruction, into the 1880s and 1890s. By 1876, Republican regimes still held state power in Louisiana, Florida, and South Carolina, but in those states, federal troops had to be stationed in and around the state-houses to prevent assassination or forcible removal of the governments.[3]

RADICAL RECONSTRUCTION GOVERNMENTS' ACHIEVEMENTS AND FAILURES

The Bourbon Democrats leveled a wide range of arguments against the Republican regimes that they sought to overthrow in the period 1870–76. Charging these regimes with malfeasance and incompetence, they sought to win votes by the implied and explicit racism of their charges. Further, very few blacks in the South before the Civil War had achieved any education, and the vast majority of African Americans that Southern whites had encountered had been slaves. Whether forced into docility and obedience by the system of slavery or choosing to play a role of simplicity and compliance, slaves had rarely challenged the stereotypes that whites imposed on them. When black individuals showed a willingness to speak out against mistreatment, they were regarded as insolent or saucy. While similar prejudices also prevailed in the North, whites there had opportunities to see African Americans as free men and women, in some states exercising their vote, and in all states quietly pursuing their lives as laborers, tradesmen and craftsmen, mineworkers and millworkers, educators, clergymen, churchgoers, and journalists. So Northern whites, despite their prejudices, could conceive of some blacks playing perfectly competent roles in state government, although none had been elected to state office in any Northern state. However, when blacks appeared in state constitutional conventions and state legislatures in the South, whites in that region explicitly treated the event as a spectacle, a combination of amusing impossibility and a tragic mistake.[4]

When legal, semi-legal, and completely illegal and violent means were employed to bring down those governments, respectable and law-abiding Southern whites comforted themselves in the belief that a proper order of things was being restored. The legend of incompetence not only was politically useful, it also penetrated the historical treatments of the period, only to be revised and corrected in recent decades by careful historical research. The state debts of the Republican governments climbed due not to incompetence, but to the need to physically rebuild the Southern states, to issue bonds to support the construction of railroads, and the expenses associated with the establishment of public schools for both blacks and whites in states that had never funded public schools in the past. The few cases of bribery and embezzlement that developed in the

Republican governments were less severe than similar cases under Democratic governments and faded into insignificance by contrast to the great scandals taking place in Washington during the period.

Perhaps the greatest failure of the Republican regimes in the South was the reluctance to use available military force to retain power. In states like South Carolina and Mississippi, where state militia units made up of black troops might have been able to prevent wholesale election fraud and the use of terror by organized gangs of whites, governors were reluctant to employ such militias out of fear that their use would create an even worse backlash and further bloodshed. In many communities, the appearance of a company of black militia would have been met by an immense armed mob, and governors hesitated to provoke any such incidents.

Republican governments, whether administered by loyal pro-Union whites or by resettled whites from the North, tended to rely for support on the federal government. However, that support was never too reliable, as military officers varied in their commitment to radical social programs calling for equal rights for blacks, as Johnson removed from office some of the most outspoken generals, and as Congress turned its attention from issues of social justice to other concerns by the early 1870s.

REPUBLICANS ABANDON RADICALISM AND THE SOLID SOUTH

By the second administration of Grant, radicals in Congress began to abandon a concern with racial equality in the South for other issues, some closer to home. The Republican Party began to divide between those who adopted a strictly partisan view that holding office was the crucial issue, and those interested in reform. Those in the party who focused on retention of power were known as Stalwarts. The Stalwarts hoped to build the Republican Party into a lasting organization by careful distribution of patronage and by supporting the emerging business interests in mining, railroads, and industry. Reform-minded Republicans came to be known as Liberals, taking up issues such as reform of government job distribution and contracting, the establishment of a civil service, and the elimination of graft. While Stalwarts and Liberals contended for power within the Republican Party, the older radical goals of Reconstruction faded into the past. Those hoping to compromise between Stalwart and Reform wings were known as Mugwumps, reputedly from the concept that they kept their mug on one side of the fence and their wump on the other.

The reason for the change of focus from issues of racial justice to one of government and party management was partly due to the death of several key radical leaders, like Thaddeus Stevens, Horace Greeley, and Charles Sumner. Others, like Henry Ward Beecher, were discredited by personal scandal, in his case, an extended controversy over adultery charges. With its fuel diminished, the radical engine slowed down and lost steam pressure. By 1876, Southern radical leaders were more or less on their own, sustained by a few reluctant federal troops stationed at the statehouses in Florida, South Carolina, and Louisiana. In much of the rest of the South, Republicans, Unionists, and black spokesmen worried that gangs of white thugs would burn their houses or kill them if they dared to speak out for the racial causes that had been the core of the radical agenda.

What emerged in the South was a peculiar new political arrangement. In the Appalachian counties that had formed the core of Union support in the South, many former Whigs and Unionists remained attached to the Republican Party, supported by scatterings of black voters in the other counties where they retained the franchise. Thus in eastern Kentucky and Tennessee, northern Alabama and Georgia, and in western North Carolina and some counties of western Virginia, Republican strongholds continued into the 20th century. However, in the downstate counties in all of these states, former Whigs tended to join with Democrats in a new conservative alliance that established the "solid South." Democrats also dominated in Mississippi, Louisiana, Texas, and Arkansas. For the period from the 1870s through the mid-1950s, the former states of the Confederacy voted Democratic in presidential elections and returned largely Democratic delegations to the U.S. Senate and House of Representatives. With the Republican Party dominated by the Stalwart wing, and the Southern Democrats dominated by a conservative agenda that favored the preservation of the status quo, the Republicans and Dixiecrats tended to collaborate through the following decades. In one sense, the political collaboration between conservative Democrats in the South and conservative Republicans in the North, had its beginning in the election of 1876, whose outcome marked the end of Reconstruction.

THE ELECTION OF 1876 AND THE COMPROMISE OF 1877

In 1876, the Republicans nominated Congressman Rutherford B. Hayes, a moderate with a concern for civil service reform, for president, while the Democrats nominated Samuel Tilden. Tilden was a corporate lawyer in New York who rose to prominence with the support of the corrupt Tweed ring in the Democratic Party there, but who, as New York governor, joined the forces of reform in the Democratic Party. Thus both Hayes and Tilden had reputations as political reformers, but neither shared the earlier radical commitment to racial equality in the South. With all the former Confederate states now readmitted to Congress and therefore entitled to cast their electoral votes, the election was quite close. Tilden took a majority of the popular votes cast, by more than 200,000 votes. However, the Electoral College vote was in dispute. In the three Southern states with Republican governments still in power, Florida, South Carolina, and Louisiana, both Democrats and Republicans claimed to have won the election, with a total of 19 Electoral College votes between them. In addition, the Democratic governor of Oregon irregularly removed one Republican elector from that state, replacing him with a pro-Tilden elector. Thus the Electoral College vote after the election was 184 for Tilden, 165 for Hayes, with 20 in dispute. The majority necessary for victory was 185. While at first Hayes believed that Tilden had won, as the dispute over the Electoral College votes became well-known, Hayes began to believe he might have a chance at victory. Republican headquarters refused to concede the election.

The Constitution did not offer a pathway through this dilemma. The votes of the electors were to be received and counted by Congress, but which votes would be counted clearly mattered. If all the Hayes votes from the contested states were counted, he would be the winner. If any of the disputed votes were counted for Tilden, he would be the winner. Between the election in November

Samuel Tilden was declared the loser in the close election of 1876 only after considerable manipulation of the electoral returns in several states. *(Library of Congress, Prints and Photographs Division, LC-USZ62–14981)*

and the inauguration date in March, the country and the candidates nervously considered the impasse. Early in January, a Democrat, George Drew, was inaugurated as governor of Florida, but that did not change the fact that Florida had still submitted two slates of electors. To resolve the question, Congress established a 15-member electoral commission, carefully constructed to contain seven Democrats, seven Republicans, and one independent. Further, the agreed balance consisted of five senators, five congressmen, and five members of the Supreme Court. One of the Supreme Court justices, David Davis, was well known as an independent. However, before the commission could meet, Davis was appointed by the Illinois state legislature as a U.S. senator. Since it would not do to have six senators on the commission, he was replaced by another Supreme Court justice, Joseph Bradley, who was a Republican.

During February, in a series of four meetings held on February 9, 16, 23, and 28, the electoral commission met and, voting strictly on party lines of eight to seven in each case, decided to allocate all of the disputed Electoral College votes to Hayes. Although the Democrats had already pledged to abide by the decision and not to throw the country into further turmoil by refusing to accept the results, a further agreement was struck. Held behind closed doors at the Wormley Hotel in Washington, some sort of settlement was reached, although it may have simply served to confirm already-established agreements. Rumors of the Wormley Bargain spread. Republicans agreed to support a plan to establish a railroad route across the southern tier of states and agreed to support the removal of the remaining federal troops that were stationed at the statehouses in Louisiana and South Carolina, where federal troops helped prevent Democratic claimants from taking office. Further, Republicans agreed that the president would appoint a prominent Southerner to the cabinet. The date of the so-called Wormley Bargain or Compromise of 1877 was February 26, two days before the final award of Electoral College votes, and a week before the date of the presidential inauguration.

Congress met, accepted the recommendations of the electoral commission, awarded all the disputed electors to Hayes, and declared him elected president on March 2. Since March 4, the regular date of inauguration, fell on a Sunday, Hayes was privately inaugurated on March 3, and then publicly inaugurated on March 5, 1877. A week later, in announcing his cabinet appointments, Hayes selected former Democratic senator David Key of Tennessee as postmaster general. The position was important because it allowed the distribution of patronage positions; throughout the South over the next months, Democratic postmasters would replace Republican postmasters, removing one last leg of support for the Republican organizations in those states. On April 10, federal troops were recalled from the statehouse in South Carolina and returned to their barracks. Democrat Wade Hampton, whose election had been based on the application of the Mississippi Plan in South Carolina, began his term as governor. Two weeks later, federal troops quietly withdrew from the statehouse in Louisiana, and Democrat Francis Nicholls was inaugurated as governor of that state.

Whether or not the appointment of David Key and the removal of troops supporting the Republican regimes in South Carolina and Louisiana were the direct result of the Wormley Bargain or not, it was clear that Republicans had abandoned the effort to impose a new racial order on the South. As Bourbon Democrats strengthened their hold on the states of the former Confederacy, Republicans turned their attention to issues of industrial development, efficient government, and control of corruption and the excesses of patronage. Control of social policy returned to the states, where it remained for decades to come.

RECONSTRUCTION: SUCCESS OR FAILURE

Southern Democrats perpetuated the legend that the radical governments of the Reconstruction era had represented the imposition by force of incompetent and corrupt regimes, creating a tragic period of failed government. Supporters of civil rights for African Americans regarded Reconstruction as a tragic era as well, one that offered great opportunities for racial justice, but opportunities that had not been realized, either through land reform or through protection of equal rights. However, a longer view recognized that with the passage of the Thirteenth, Fourteenth, and Fifteenth amendments to the Constitution, the groundwork had been established for future progress.[5] Denial of civil rights and suffrage continued, but by subterfuge and extralegal means. Clearly the Constitution now called for equal treatment without regard to race and equal voting rights without regard to race, and those who fought for these goals in future decades had the Constitution on their side. So in one sense, the Reconstruction era had achieved great progress by incorporating into the law of the land an idealistic vision that had been shared only by a few black leaders, abolitionists, and Republican radicals. That vision would not be fully implemented for more than a century, but because the leaders of the 1860s generation had embedded their goals in the Constitution, the vision remained on the nation's agenda.

CHRONICLE OF EVENTS

1865

March 4: Lincoln is inaugurated for his second term.

April 9: Lee agrees to surrender to Grant at Appomattox Court House.

April 14: Lincoln is shot at Ford's Theater in Washington.

April 15: Lincoln dies at 7:22 A.M. Andrew Johnson is inaugurated president later in the day.

May 29: President Andrew Johnson issues two proclamations defining his Reconstruction policy: He will grant amnesty to Confederates who take an oath of allegiance, with a system of granting pardons to exempted classes; the amnesty frees the grantee from confiscation of estates under the Confiscation Act; exempted classes who had to apply for individual pardons comprise 14 groups, including all with taxable property over $20,000. The other proclamation organizes provisional governments, with an appointed governor for North Carolina (later extended to six other states), to convene conventions and amend their constitutions to abolish slavery and repudiate state war debt. The states have to proclaim the illegality of ordinances of secession, repudiate Confederate debts, and ratify the Thirteenth Amendment. The four states not covered are Louisiana, Virginia, Arkansas, and Tennessee, all of which have governments previously organized under Union control.

July–October: State conventions are held and temporary governments are replaced by newly elected legislatures and governors. The governments prohibit black migration. Unionists are elected in the upper South, secessionists in the Lower South. The governments and elected members to Congress include many leading Confederates.

November 24: Mississippi enacts the first of the Black Codes, setting up vagrancy provisions.

December 4: Johnson affirms the process of Reconstruction completed. A joint committee of 15 members of the House and Senate refuses to endorse the presidential actions.

December 18: The Thirteenth Amendment is formally adopted as part of the Constitution, after ratification by 27 states.

1866

February 19: Johnson vetoes a bill extending the Freedmen's Bureau on the grounds that Congress can not act with 11 states not represented.

February 22: In an intemperate speech, Johnson calls Thaddeus Stevens, Charles Sumner, and Wendell Phillips "Northern traitors."

March 27: Johnson vetoes the civil rights bill.

April: The Ku Klux Klan holds its first national convention.

April 9: Congress passes the civil rights bill over Johnson's veto. This is the first significant override of a presidential veto in American history.

April 28: The congressional joint committee reports on its investigations.

May 1–2: A severe race riot wracks Memphis; 46 African Americans are killed, and the African-American district is burned.

June 13: Congress approves the Fourteenth Amendment and submits it to the states for ratification on June 16; the amendment abrogates the 3/5 clause. Johnson denounces it and urges the states not to ratify it.

June 20: The Committee of Fifteen reports that Congress has power over the process of Reconstruction.

July 16: Congress overrides Johnson's veto of the bill extending the Freedmen's Bureau.

July 19: Tennessee ratifies the Fourteenth Amendment. (Ten other former Confederate states, with Johnson governments, vote it down.)

July 24: Congress accepts representatives of Tennessee, restoring it to the Union.

July 30: A race riot erupts in New Orleans as mobs and police break up a convention called to rewrite the state constitution. In the riot, 35 African Americans are killed and some 100 wounded.

August–September: Johnson goes on a speaking tour and reiterates treason charge against Thaddeus Stevens and Wendell Phillips; Johnson engages in insults with hecklers, the incident regarded as demeaning the office of the president.

August 20: Johnson proclaims that the insurrection is over and Reconstruction is fully accomplished.

October–November: Elections return a large majority of Republicans, in excess of two-thirds in each house of Congress. Republicans also win control of every Northern state legislature and win every contested governor's race.

December 3: In an address to Congress, Johnson again claims Reconstruction is complete.

1867

January 7: Congress begins an investigation of President Johnson for possible impeachment by

This symbolic drawing depicts a member of the Freedmen's Bureau standing between enraged whites and newly liberated African Americans. *(Library of Congress, Prints and Photographs Division, LC-USZ62–105555)*

empowering the Judiciary Committee to investigate whether Johnson is guilty of high crimes and misdemeanors.

January 8: Congress approves suffrage for African-American men in Washington, D.C.

January 10: The Senate approves a bill admitting Nebraska to the Union, on condition the state establish universal male suffrage. Johnson vetoes the act.

January 22: Congress passes an act giving Congress the power to call itself into special session and empowers the 40th Congress to come into session on March 4, 1867.

January 31: Congress guarantees the right to vote to all males over the age of 21 without regard to race in the federal territories.

February 8: The Senate overrides Johnson's veto regarding the admission of Nebraska.

February 9: The House of Representatives overrides Johnson's veto regarding the admission of Nebraska.

March 1: Johnson proclaims the admission of Nebraska to the Union with the requirement that it recognize suffrage without regard to race.

March 2: Johnson vetoes, and Congress overrides and passes on the same day, a Reconstruction Bill, dividing the 10 remaining, former Confederate states into five military districts, each district to be administered by a major general. For states' congressional representatives to be readmitted, the states must call new constitutional conventions elected by universal suffrage, guarantee African-American suffrage, and ratify the Fourteenth Amendment; ex-Confederates are disqualified from voting; the military will enforce these arrangements. Congress also passes the Tenure of Office Act. Under this act, the president cannot remove from office a Senate-approved official until the Senate has approved a replacement. Congress also passes the Command of the Army Act, requiring that all orders for the military must go through the general of the army, rather than directly from the president. By these actions of Congress, presidential Reconstruction ends and Congressional Reconstruction begins.

March 23: The Congressional Reconstruction Act becomes law, over Johnson's veto. The law requires military commanders to enroll voters.

March 30: The United States purchases Alaska from Russia.

June 3: The Judiciary Committee, investigating grounds for impeachment, decides, five to four, that there are no grounds.

June 20: Johnson issues orders limiting the powers of the military district governors.

July 19: The third Reconstruction Act, passed over Johnson's veto, becomes law. The act is passed in response to Johnson attempting to limit the powers of the military district governors.

August 12: To test the Tenure of Office Act, Johnson suspends Secretary of War Edwin Stanton.

September 7: Johnson pardons all but a few hundred ex-Confederates.

December 2: In his annual message to Congress, Johnson threatens to proceed in his own fashion on Reconstruction.

December 7: The House of Representatives votes on impeachment, rejecting it on grounds there are no indictable crimes, by vote of 57–108.

1868

February 21: Johnson removes Edwin Stanton as secretary of war in violation of the Tenure of Office Act, appointing U. S. Grant, and when Grant resigns Lorenzo Thomas as ad interim secretary. Stanton barricades himself in his office.

February 24: The House of Representatives passes impeachment charges against Johnson by a vote of 126 to 47. The charges are known as the Covode Resolutions.

March 4: In the Senate, the impeachment trial of Johnson begins.

March 11: The fourth Reconstruction Act becomes law, over Johnson's veto. This act allows new constitutions in the reconstructed states to be approved by a majority of those voting, rather than those registered or previously voting. This measure renders any boycott of an election ineffective.

March 31: The Iowa General Assembly approves a state constitutional amendment extending the suffrage to African-American men, the first state outside New England to do so on its own; universal suffrage had been established in the District of Columbia, the federal territories, and in Nebraska by congressional action.

May 16: Johnson is acquitted of the omnibus impeachment charge in a vote in the Senate, failing the required two-thirds by a single vote. The tally is 35 in favor, 19 opposed.

May 20–21: The Republican Party nominates Grant and Schuyler Colfax for president and vice president.

May 26: The Senate votes on two other articles of impeachment, with the same vote as cast on May 16.

June 22: Arkansas is readmitted to the Union.

June 25: In the Omnibus Act Congress readmits the following states to the Union: Alabama, Florida, Louisiana, and North and South Carolina (leaving out Texas, Virginia, Georgia, and Mississippi). The law prohibits the states from subsequently disenfranchising blacks. At this point, the six readmitted states have Republican administrations, generally imposed

This 1880 photo of Ulysses S. Grant gives no hint of the cancer of the throat from which he died in 1885. *(Library of Congress, Prints and Photographs Division, LC-USZ62–110720)*

by elections held under military enforcement of the election procedures.

July 4: Johnson pardons all but a few remaining Confederates.

July 9: Democrats nominate Horatio Seymour of New York and Francis Blair of Missouri for president and vice president.

July 9: The Fourteenth Amendment formally becomes part of the U.S. Constitution.

July 25: Congress admits representatives from Georgia.

September 3: African-American members of the Georgia legislature are expelled by white Republicans and Democrats.

November: Grant is elected president. (No votes are taken in three Southern states: Texas, Virginia, and Mississippi); Georgia and other readmitted Southern states cast their votes for Grant.

November: Minnesota voters approve a state constitutional amendment granting votes to African-American men. There are less than 300 black voters added by this action.

1869

January 13: Johnson reinstates Stanton

February 26: Congress passes the Fifteenth Amendment.

March: Georgia's representatives are expelled from Congress..

March 4: Grant is inaugurated.

October 4: Conservative (Redeemer) Democrats win control of the state of Tennessee.

November: Republican Edmund Davis is elected governor of Texas after the military closes many polling places and prevents many Democrats and former Confederates from voting.

December 29: Congress passes a bill requiring Georgia to ratify the Fifteenth Amendment and to restore African-American members of the legislature before being readmitted to the Union.

1870

January 26: Virginia is readmitted to the Union.

February 23: Mississippi is readmitted to the Union.

February 25: Hiram Revels is the first African American to be selected for the U.S. Senate; he represents Mississippi in the same seat once held by Jefferson Davis, serving until March 3, 1871.

March 30: The Fifteenth Amendment to the Constitution becomes law.

March 30: Texas is readmitted to the Union.

May 31: Congress passes the first Force Act; the intent is to enforce the Fifteenth Amendment.

July 15: Georgia is readmitted to the Union.

August 4: Conservative (Redeemer) Democrats take over North Carolina's government; the state legislature impeaches the Republican governor the next year.

November: In New Orleans, fear of violence from armed Democratic club squads prevents Republicans from voting; at some polling places, no Republican ballots are provided because no one can be found willing to distribute them.

December 5: Congress meets with all states represented, the first such meeting since 1860.

December 12: Congress seats Joseph H. Rainey, the first African-American member of the House of Representatives, representing South Carolina.

1871

February 28: Congress passes a second Force Act to enforce the Fifteenth Amendment

April 20: Congress passes another act to enforce the Fifteenth Amendment, known as the Ku Klux Klan act.

November 1: The state legislature in Georgia convenes, dominated by Redeemer Democrats; the next year, facing threat of impeachment, the governor, Rufus Bullock, resigns.

December: By the end of 1871, the following states have removed the Reconstruction-imposed Republican governments: Virginia, Tennessee, North Carolina, and Georgia; Congressional Reconstruction-established Republican regimes still hold power in the other seven former Confederate states.

1872

May 22: Congress passes the Amnesty Act, removing disqualifications for office from all but about 500 Confederates.

June 5–6: Republicans nominate Ulysses S. Grant for president in convention in Philadelphia.

July 9: Democrats nominate Horace Greeley for president in convention at Baltimore.

November 5: Grant is reelected president; Horace Greeley, the Democratic nominee, dies on November 29, and his Electoral College votes are distributed to four others.

Publisher of the New York *Tribune,* Horace Greeley remained an influence in the Republican Party and ran for president in 1872 on a Liberal Republican ticket, opposing Ulysses S. Grant. His radical reputation and his eccentricities contributed to his defeat, and he died before the electoral votes were counted. *(Library of Congress, Prints and Photographs Division, LC-USZC2–2598)*

December 11: Pinkney B. S. Pinchback, an African American who was elected lieutenant governor in 1871, becomes acting governor of Louisiana on the impeachment of the governor, Henry Warmouth. Pinchback serves just over a month, until January 13, 1873. Pinchback is the only African American to serve as governor of a state until 1989.

1874

January 14: Republican governor of Texas, Edmund Davis, resigns under pressure and yields his office to Democrat Richard Coke. The inauguration of Coke marks the end of Reconstruction in Texas.

November 3: Conservative Democrats take power in Alabama. Democrats win a majority in Congress, the first since 1860.

November 12: Conservative Democrat Augustus Garland is inaugurated governor of Arkansas. By this date, Bourbon or Conservative Democrat regimes are in power in Virginia, Tennessee, North Carolina, Alabama, Texas, Arkansas, and Georgia. Only Mississippi, Louisiana, Florida, and South Carolina of the former 11 Confederate states are in Republican control.

1875

March 1: Grant signs the second Civil Rights Act, guaranteeing equal access to public accommodation and to juries.

March 4: Blanche K. Bruce, a former slave, is appointed senator from Mississippi. He will serve the full six-year term until March 3, 1881.

July 31: After serving in the Senate representing Tennessee, Andrew Johnson dies of a stroke.

November: In Mississippi, Democrats use terror tactics and "counting out" to prevent blacks from voting. The method becomes known as the Mississippi plan.

November 16: Alabama enacts a new constitution, proposed by the Bourbon/Conservative Democrats.

1876

November 7: National election results are disputed, as are state elections in Florida, South Carolina, and Louisiana. Federal troops help maintain Republican regimes in the remaining three Southern states that have not been taken over by Bourbons: Florida, South Carolina, and Louisiana.

1877

January 2: Democrat George Drew is inaugurated as governor of Florida.

January 29: Congress sets up an electoral commission to allocate disputed Electoral College votes.

February 9: The electoral commission awards electors of Florida to Hayes. The commission acts on the remaining cases in meetings February 16, 23, and 28, all in favor of Hayes.

February 26: The Wormley Bargain, known as the Compromise of 1877, is rumored to have been made at a closed-door meeting of political leaders. Under this agreement, Republicans agree to support a Southern railroad route to the West Coast, to remove federal troops supporting governments in Louisiana and South Carolina, and to appoint a Southerner to the Cabinet in exchange for Democratic acquiescence in the outcome of the electoral commission vote for Hayes.

March 2: Rutherford Hayes is declared president.

March 3: In a private ceremony, Hayes is inaugurated.

March 5: Hayes is publicly inaugurated.

March 12: Hayes appoints former Confederate colonel and former Democratic senator David Key of Tennessee as postmaster general.

April 10: Federal troops are removed from the South Carolina statehouse, and return to their barracks; Democrat Wade Hampton begins a term as governor of South Carolina.

April 24: Federal troops are removed from the Louisiana statehouse to return to their barracks, and Francis Nicholls in Louisiana begins his term as governor. The era of Reconstruction ends with the establishment of Conservative Democratic regimes in all former Confederate states.

EYEWITNESS TESTIMONY

We are glad to know that, previously, Mr. Johnson had not been known as an intemperate man. Persons intimately associated with him had never known of his being the worse for liquor. Being ill for some time, his physician had prescribed for him brandy as a medicine, and by following that prescription, and by yielding to the urgency of friends, he imbibed too freely and became intoxicated. He has since keenly felt the disgrace, and deeply deplored it; and to prevent the recurrence of such a condition in the future, he has, we are credibly informed, solemnly pledged himself to the principle of total abstinence. We hope and trust that he will wholly refrain hereafter from intoxicating drinks. From what we have learned of him, through his acquaintances and friends, we believe his hand will not become unsteady again while he is called upon to guide the ship of state.

Comment by the editors of Zion's Herald and Wesleyan Journal, *on reports that newly sworn in president Andrew Johnson had become inebriated March 4, 1865, in an article entitled "President Johnson," Vol. 36, No. 17 (April 26, 1865), p. 66.*

Of one trait in the character of our President the country may be perfectly assured, and that is, of his uncompromising loyalty and his unalterable determination to maintain the Union and to enforce the laws. Nor are his opinions of a recent date. A personal friend and a great admirer of Andrew Jackson, he is of that old school of democratic politicians who believe in the Constitution and the Union and in the use of all necessary means to protect and preserve them. In the last days of Mr. Buchanan's wretched administration he took a firm and manly stand for the right, and in the memorable debate of March 2, 1861, on the report of the peace conference, Mr. Johnson denounced with remarkable energy and marked ability the projected treason, for which he was set upon by the whole crew of disloyal men, led on by the senator from Oregon.

Comment from the Boston Daily Advertiser *on the new president, Andrew Johnson, as published in* Littell's Living Age, *Vol. 29, No. 1,091 (April 29, 1865), p. 192.*

Hon. W. H. Seward: Your telegram of the 20th instant was not received in due time, owing to my absence from Columbia. The Convention having been dis-

solved, it is impracticable to enact any organic law in regard to the war debt. That debt is very small, as the expenditures of South Carolina were reimbursed by the confederate government. The debt is so mixed up with the ordinary expenses of the State that it cannot be separated. In South Carolina all were guilty of aiding the rebellion, and no one can complain of being taxed to pay the trifling debt incurred by his own assent in perfect good faith. The Convention did all that the President advised to be done, and I thought it wrong to keep a revolutionary body in existence and advised their immediate dissolution, which was done. There is now no power in the Legislature to repudiate the debt if it were possible to separate it from the other debts of the State. Even then it would fall on widows and orphans whose estates were invested in it for safety. B. F. Perry, Provisional Governor.

Letter from Provisional Governor B. F. Perry to Secretary of State William Seward, explaining why South Carolina did not comply with the requirement to repudiate the Confederate debt as established by President Johnson as a pre-condition for readmission to the Union, dated November 27, 1865, as collected in Edward McPherson, ed., The Political History of the United States of America During the Period of Reconstruction, *April 15, 1865–July 15, 1870, p. 23.*

Question. Did you hear anything said in Alabama about any design on the part of the negroes to seize upon the lands at Christmas?

Answer. No, sir; there was only this idea through all the southern States, that the negroes would not engage—would not make a contract to work beyond Christmas; that they expected something favorable was to turn up by Christmas. That was all, and the impression was universal.

Question. What was it that was expected to turn up?

Answer. They thought that the lands of the leading rebels were to be confiscated and given to them. That was the idea. I noticed another thing, that not a single loyal newspaper was circulating through those States; but I could find the New York News, the Chicago Times, and papers of that class, being sold by the boys.

Question. What is the character of those two papers?

Answer. Those two papers, if I understand it, have been very decidedly in the interest of the copperheads, in opposition to the government in its efforts to put down the rebellion, and in sympathy with the south. That is well understood—better by you, I suppose, than by me. I never found a loyal paper until I reached

Vicksburg, on my way back, and that was the Chicago Tribune. The people will not let them circulate.

Question. Did you hear anything said about circulating loyal papers at the south.

Answer. No sir.

Testimony recorded January 27, 1866; given by Mordecai Mobley, an official of the Interior Department, General Land Office, concerning a trip he had taken in October and November 1865 to Alabama, in response to questions from Senator John Howard of Michigan, as recorded in the Report of the Joint Committee on Reconstruction, *Part III, pp. 19–20.*

Question. What do [Southern whites] say generally about the emancipation of their slaves, either by President Lincoln's proclamation, by the amendment to the Constitution, or by any other means?

Answer. They have never liked it. They hoped that great trouble would arise from it. They delight in all the obstacles we find to the improvement of the freedman. So it seems to me. I say this of the majority. There are very many exceptions. There are a class of men at the south, in very small numbers, who have, at heart, probably always been with us, and who are now favorable to the improvement of the negro.

Question. In reference to these obstacles to the improvement of the negro, do you think from your observation that the southern people generally are endeavoring to increase these obstacles rather than to diminish them?

Answer. I think that is a very general disposition. They oppose negro schools generally. There is a great hate apparently towards northern teachers. Whatever we do for colored schools has to be done without any consultation with the southerners.

Question. What is the great ground of objection on their part toward the education of the blacks; why do they wish to see them remain in ignorance?

Answer. From their old habits they seem to feel that the negro must not become an equal. They understand that education and property and political privileges will make the negro so, and hence they oppose everything of the kind.

Question. You think this feeling arises rather from their old prejudices to the race?

Answer. Very much so. I heard gentlemen say in the legislature at Montgomery that they were determined that the blacks should not rise to be equals with white men, and that all their legislation would be based on that determination; that they must not have titles to land; that if they obtained possession of property, the next thing would be to claim the right of suffrage and all other political privileges. They perceive that these things come along logically from each other.

Question. Did that declaration on the part of members seem to find favor with the other members of the legislature or with the audience?

Answer. A member expressed this opinion to me privately in the lobby, but it was the same in substance as I had listened to in the debate in the house, the debate being on the constitutional amendment.

Question. Did you ever find a disloyal negro in the course of your travels?

Answer. I saw one during the war, who came into our army lines and said he was with the rebels; that is the only instance that I remember. It may be said that they are universally loyal.

Question. State what is the degree of attachment which they exhibit towards the Government of the United States?

Answer. Well, sir; it is unbounded. It was in Mr. Lincoln; it is now in the government, and in what they expect the government will do for them.

Question. You mean to say that universally they are the strong friends of the government?

Answer. I do. When, on the sea islands, a proposition was made to restore the lands to their original owners, there was a most distressing breaking in upon that confidence in the government which they had been cherishing. It would be impossible for any one to describe the feeling they manifested on that occasion. . . .

Question. Suppose all protection on part of the United States towards the freedmen should be withdrawn, including the Freedmen's Bureau and the presence of the military forces, thus leaving the freedmen to be dealt with by the authorities of the States solely, what would be the result?

Answer. They would suffer in all their interests as laborers; and as to attempting any education or improvement, the whole would be arrested, and, I think, turned backward.

Extract from the testimony of J. W. Alvord, an officer of the Freedmen's Bureau, in response to questions from Senator Jacob M. Howard of Michigan, before the Joint Committee on Reconstruction on February 3, 1866, describing conditions he had observed in several Southern states during 1865, from Report of the Joint Committee on Reconstruction to the Thirty-Ninth Congress, *Part II, pp. 235–236.*

Question. What did you discover in relation to the colored people?

Answer. I discovered that they were in a state of ignorance, generally, at that time of their own condition as freedmen. Some of them knew it. They all, of course, mistrusted it. They had all heard it from one another. A few knew it from their masters, and only a few; and what they did hear they had very little confidence to believe. Hearing that a party of Yankees, and especially a Yankee lady, was there, they commenced to gather around me for the facts, asking me their little questions in their own way, which was to the effect, if they were free, and if Abraham Lincoln was really dead. They had been told that he was dead; that he had been killed; but at the same time they had been informed that, now that he was dead, they were no longer free, but would be all slaves again; and with that had come the suspicion, on their part, that he was not dead, but that it was a hoax to hold them in slavery. They would travel twenty miles in the night, after their day's work was done, and I would find them standing in front of my tent in the morning to hear me say whether it was true that Abraham Lincoln was dead, and that they were free. I told them Abraham Lincoln was dead; that I saw him dead; that I was near him when he died; and that they were free as I was. The next question was, what they should do. There were questions between the negro and his master in regard to labor and in regard to pay. I saw or discovered that the masters were inclined to get their labor without pay. Of course I had no way of proving that, but I inferred it. They were at work. Most of them offered to work until Christmas time, and to take a part of the profits. General Saxton, I should think, made some regulation specifying just what portion of each crop the negroes should have. They were all very anxious to hear the rules read. The commandant of each post had issued certain rules and regulations. These they had never heard read, and they came to me to know what the paper said. The rules were published daily in the Macon papers. They said they had been told that General Wilson's orders said that they should work six days in the week hard, and half a day on Sunday. They wanted to know if it was so. My course with them was to read General Wilson's paper, as they called it. I have read it through sometimes forty times a day. They stood around my tent in great numbers on a Sunday; more than a hundred, men, women, and children, and every day more or less. Perhaps there were very few hours that I was not engaged in advising them, and attempting to decide some cause for them.

Extract from the testimony of Clara Barton, founder of the American Red Cross, in response to questions from Senator Jacob M. Howard of Michigan, before the Joint Committee on Reconstruction on February 21, 1866, describing conditions she had observed near Andersonville, Georgia, in the summer of 1865, from Report of the Joint Committee on Reconstruction to the Thirty-Ninth Congress, *Part III, p. 103.*

Question. Do I understand you to say that no instance has come under your observation where a South Carolina secessionist has renounced the doctrine of the rightfulness of secession?

Answer. Not one.

Question. How much willingness did you observe, upon the part of the whites of South Carolina, to allow civil rights to the blacks; that is, the domestic rights of father and child, husband and wife, &c., the right to acquire property by regular, legal title, and the right to sue in the courts, and obtain redress for their wrongs in that way?

Answer. The domestic relations, I think, they are willing to respect. They profess a willingness to have the negro testify in the courts, but it seems to me they generally take the ground that his testimony against a white man is of little worth. I think there is a decided opposition to the negro's holding real estate, by lease or in fee. The intense opposition that exists to the negro's settling on the sea-island lands is, I think, that it will establish a precedent; that the negro will thereby hold estate, the government acknowledging his right to hold it. They attach less weight to their theories than to the practical result of them; they are afraid if the negroes hold their lands by lease it will be difficult to get possession of them again. A reverend gentleman from the upper part of the State said, in reply to questions addressed to him on the subject, that the South Carolinians would never permit the negro to hold real estate—never! That was his individual sentiment. Some southern men profess to feel differently.

Extract from the testimony of Captain Alexander P. Ketchum, in response to questions from Senator Jacob M. Howard of Michigan, before the Joint Committee on Reconstruction on February 28, 1866, describing conditions he had observed in and around Charleston, South Carolina, during 1865, from Report of the Joint Committee on Reconstruction to the Thirty-Ninth Congress, *pp. 235–236.*

A case occurred in this place, a week ago today. A colored woman went to a Mrs. Vaughn's (I believe is the name) and remarked that she had come after her little girl. Mrs. V. Refused to give her up. There had been no contract for her hire. The woman insisted that she would have her child. Mrs. V. abused and threatened her; the negro after many provoking words replied "I am as free as you madam." Mrs. V. Thereupon became enraged and struck her, after this the woman left and in going out of the gate met the wife's husband. He was told that the negro "sauced" his wife, and he immediately "horsewhipped" her, and after that clubbed his whip and struck her severely over the head. She came to me bleeding and looking very badly, while her little girls were in tears, and seemed half frightened to death. I at once addressed a note to Mr. Williams, local superintendent, urging immediate action in the matter. He proceeded I thought reluctantly, carelessly and slowly. Today I sent him instructions referred to. My impression is that he will turn the case over to the civil authorities, if referred I do not believe a solitary thing will be done. I feel certain that a jury from this town would never convict the man, even for *an assault with a whip upon a woman,* because that woman is a negro & "sauced" the other woman, who is white. Can the colored people expect protection from such authorities yet a while? I shall watch this case with interest should it be referred.

> *Report on an incident in Arkansas, by the Honorable E. W. Gantt, an ex-Confederate turned Union supporter, employed by the Freedmen's Bureau as general superintendent, on May 27, 1866, describing the treatment of the African-American population in the southwestern part of the state, as reproduced in LaWanda Cox and John H. Cox, ed.,* Reconstruction, the Negro and the New South, *pp. 4–5.*

The evidence of an intense hostility to the Federal Union, and an equally intense love of the late Confederacy, nurtured by the war, is decisive. While it appears that nearly all are willing to submit, at least for the time being, to the federal authority, it is equally clear that the ruling motive is a desire to obtain the advantages which will be derived from a representation in Congress. Officers of the Union army on duty, and northern men who go South to engage in business, are generally detested and proscribed. Southern men who adhered to the Union are bitterly hated and relentlessly persecuted. In some localities prosecutions have been instituted in State courts against Union officers

for acts done in the line of official duty, and similar prosecutions are threatened elsewhere as soon as the United States troops are removed. All such demonstrations show a state of feeling which it is unmistakably necessary to guard.

The testimony is conclusive that after the collapse of the Confederacy the feeling of the people of the rebellious States was that of abject submission. Having appealed to the tribunal of arms, they had no hope except that by the magnanimity of their conquerors their lives, and possibly their property, might be preserved. Unfortunately, the general issue of pardons to persons who had been prominent in the rebellion, and the feeling of kindness and conciliation manifested by the Executive, and very generally indicated through the northern press, had the effect to render whole communities forgetful of the crimes they had committed, defiant towards the Federal Government, and regardless of their duties as citizens. The conciliatory measures of the Government do not seem to have been met even half way. The bitterness and defiance exhibited toward the United States under such circumstances is without a parallel in the history of the world. In return for our kind desire for the resumption of fraternal relations we receive only an insolent assumption of rights and privileges long since forfeited. The crime we have punished is paraded as a virtue, and the principles of republican government which we have vindicated at so terrible cost are denounced as unjust and oppressive.

> *Majority Report of the Joint Committee on Reconstruction, delivered by Senator William Fessenden and Congressman Thaddeus Stevens, June 18, 1866, detailing the resistance to reconstruction in the states of the former Confederacy, from Edward McPherson, ed.,* The Political History of the United States of America During the Period of Reconstruction, April 15, 1865–July 15, 1870, *p. 91. [or pp. 17–18 in* Report of the Joint Committee on Reconstruction *of the First Session, Thirty-Ninth Congress]*

I reckon I have pardoned more men, turned more men loose, and set them at liberty that were imprisoned, I imagine, than any other living man on God's habitable globe [Voice, "Bully for you!" cheers.] I turned forty-seven thousand of our men loose engaged in this struggle, with the arms we captured with them, and who were then in prison. I turned them loose. [Voice, "Bully for you!" and laughter.] Large numbers have applied for pardon, and I have granted them pardon; yet there are some who condemn, and hold me responsible for doing wrong. Yes, there are some who staid at home, who did not go into the field, that can talk about others being traitorous and being treacherous. There are some who can talk about blood and vengeance and crime and everything to make treason odious, and all that, who never smelt gunpowder on either side. [Cheers.] Yes, they can condemn others, and recommend hanging and torture, and all that. If I have erred, I have erred on the side of mercy. Some of these croakers have dared to assume they are better than was the Saviour of men himself—a kind of over-righteous—better than anybody else; and, although wanting to do Deity's work, thinking He cannot do it as well as they can. [Laughter and cheers.]

Yes, the Saviour of men came on earth and found the human race condemned and sentenced under the law; but when they repented and believed, He said Let them live. Instead of executing and putting the whole world to death, He went upon the cross, and there was nailed by unbelievers, there shed his blood that you might live. [Cheers.] Think of it; to execute and hang and put to death eight millions of people. Never! It is an absurdity. Such a thing is impracticable, even if it were right; but it is the violation of all law, human and divine. [Voice, "Hang Jeff Davis. You call on Judge Chase to hang Jeff Davis, will you?" Great cheering.] I am not the court, I am not the jury, nor the judge.

Before the case comes to me, and all other cases, it would have to come on application as a case for pardon. That is the only way the case can get to me. Why don't Judge Chase, the Chief Justice of the United States, in whose district he is—why don't he try him?[Loud cheers.] But perhaps I could answer the question, as sometimes persons want to be facetious and indulge in repartee. I might ask you a question, Why don't you hang Thad Stevens and Wendell Phillips? [Great cheering.] A traitor at one end of the line is as bad as a traitor at the other. I know that there are some that have got up their little pieces and sayings to repeat on public occasions—talking parrots that have been placed in their mouths by their superiors—who have not had the courage and the manhood to come forward and tell them themselves, but have understrappers to do their work for them. [Cheers.] I know there are some that talk about this universal elective franchise, upon which they wanted to upturn the Government of Louisiana and institute another, who contended that we must send men there to control, govern, and manage their slave population because they are incompetent to do it themselves. And yet then they turn around, when they get there, and say they are competent to go to Congress and manage all the affairs of State. [Cheers.]

Extract from a speech by Andrew Johnson, given at St. Louis, September 8, 1866, from Edward McPherson, ed., The Political History of the United States of America During the Period of Reconstruction, April 15, 1865–July 15, 1870, *pp. 139–140.*

The Elections of September, October and November last (1866), in all embracing nineteen of the loyal States, have settled the question as to the ascendency of the Republican party in the Fortieth Congress. To a large extent the Republican members of the Thirty-ninth Congress have been re-elected. In both Houses of the next Congress, the Republicans will have more than a two-thirds majority, and can therefore carry out their purposes of legislation in defiance of the Presidential veto. This is unquestionably a victory of Congress over

Andrew Johnson regarded himself as a Jacksonian Democrat, but his support in the Republican Party evaporated after he opposed the Radical Republican plans for Reconstruction. *(Library of Congress, Prints and Photographs Division, LC-USZC2–6419)*

the President. Both parties made an appeal to the popular judgment, and the result proves the appeal of the President to be a total failure, while that of Congress is a complete success.

The question which the people have determined by the late elections, is the great Problem of Reconstruction, submitted to the public judgment in a specific shape. The form of the question grew out of the conflict between the President and Congress, each having a specific plan for the reconstruction of the Rebel States, and neither being able to decide the point for the other. . . .

Probably no public man was ever more completely deserted or severely condemned by those whose votes placed him in power. Congress, on the other hand, presented a plan of reconstruction which to the majority of the people seemed better suited to the exigence of the times and the future safety of the nation. As we doubt not, one of the serious obstacles greatly harming the cause of the President consisted in the *man himself.* The disgraceful and mortifying circumstances connected with his inauguration as Vice-President; his speech in Washington on the 22nd of February, 1866; his singular tour through the country from Washington to Chicago and back again to Washington; the fact that he had abandoned the party that had chosen him to the Vice-Presidency, and was, moreover, wielding the patronage of the Government in favor of the Democratic party; the system of pardons by the wholesale granted to prominent Rebels—these, and the like circumstances were well calculated to bring the President into discredit with a large portion of the American people. They distrusted the man; and yet the chief cause of the President's failure must be sought in his policy of Reconstruction as compared with that of Congress. Here, mainly, the issue was joined; and here the verdict was rendered.

> *Comment by Reverend Samuel Spear, of Brooklyn, on the results of the fall elections of 1866, in an article entitled "The President and Congress," published in the January 1867 issue of* The American Presbyterian and Theological Review *Review 5, no. 17, pp. 28–29.*

Q. When did the work of registration commence in this city?

A. Somewhere about the 24th of September [1868].

Q. What was the condition of the city up to that time, as to peace and order?

A. Its condition was that of ordinary peace and quiet.

Q. What was the condition of the city of New Orleans between that time and up to the time of election.

A. About one week after the work of registration had commenced in New Orleans—that is to say, from about the 1st of October—up to the time of election, there was any amount of excitement, personal assaults, bloodshed, and violence growing out of political causes, so that in several of the wards the registers, from threats and violence, from fear of their own personal safety, closed their offices of registration. This fact was notorious and well known, because a committee of the legislature was appointed on the subject.

Q. When did the registration close?

A. On 24th October, as provided by the registry law; nine days before the day of election.

Q. Between the 24th October and the day of election state the condition of the city as to peace and order.

A. The condition of the city during that interval was of such a turbulent and excited character that the police force was utterly unable to perform its duties, and was withdrawn from the public streets. Bands of armed men, self-constituted guardians of the peace, paraded the streets for three or four days.

Q. State whether policemen were driven from their beats or position in the streets.

A. To my personal knowledge one man, a colored man, was chased and driven from his beat on Lafayette street, and took refuge in the station-house.

Q. State whether you saw any mobs in this city during that period.

A. I saw them repeatedly.

Q. State the number of men engaged in these mobs.

A. They varied in number from five, ten, and twenty, to as many as a hundred.

Q. Did you see any larger bodies than a hundred?

A. On Wednesday or Thursday night previous to the day of the election I saw a very large body of men on Canal street and on St. Charles street. That night a collision occurred between two processions. A large body of these men were armed and carried their arms openly—I mean the men in the democratic procession. Gunsmiths' stores, where arms were sold, were crowded by men purchasing or seeking to purchase arms during that period. Persons whom we knew to be republicans were refused the opportunity of purchasing arms. One day, included within the time between the closing of the registration and the election, and while the excitement was intense, Mr. Siskron, who was at that time acting as assistant secretary of state, or as clerk in the state department, went into a gunsmith's store next to the Republican office to purchase a pistol. I was there and they declined to sell him a pistol, because he was a republican. While there a colored man came in, whose name I do not know, and made application to purchase a pistol, which was also refused. Others, whom I knew to be democrats, were in the store and found no difficulty in purchasing. Many of them purchased without money, on a piece of paper, the contents of which I don't know, but which was passed over to the proprietor and the bearer was immediately supplied with arms and went away.

> *Testimony taken by Congressman Lionel Sheldon (of Louisiana) from William Baker, registrar of voters in Louisiana in the fall of 1868, before the congressional sub-committee of elections in Louisiana, held on May 8, 1869, as printed in* U.S. Congress, Serial Set Volume no 1435, Session No. 5, 41st Congress, Second Session, House Miscellaneous Document 154, *pp. 3–4.*

The most fashionable restaurant in Louisville is kept by two colored men, who call themselves George and Dan. Frederick Douglass, one of the most honored colored men in the United States, had just addressed a crowd of several thousand people, white and colored in the Exposition Hall. They were charmed with his eloquence and his philosophy. A few of his friends sought to honor him with a dinner at this fashionable restaurant. Their application was rejected. One hundred dollars would not purchase a dinner for him and a half dozen of his friends. Not because they did not admire the orator—they were proud of him; not that they did not feel disgusted at the course they felt compelled to take, but their business was at stake. If they fed Douglass, they must other colored men, and their business would be ruined.

> *Recollection of President E. H. Fairchild, of Berea College, commenting on an incident of racial discrimination in Louisville, Kentucky, on April 21, 1873, as printed in an article entitled "Equal Rights," in the* Independent, *Vol. 27, No. 1,363 (January 14, 1875), p. 27.*

The worst thing will be the Civil Rights Bill—Sumner's Supplementary—I know the maxim *De mortus nihil* &c but I have no use for those who prescribe for diseases without knowing their nature—Sumner knew no more of the actual condition of the colored man here than he realized his conditions on the Gold Coast—The bill with all respects to its author, is just like a blister-plaster put on a dozing man whom it is desirable to soothe to sleep—The most important thing in the world is to let the South forget the negro for a bit:—let him acquire property, stability and self respect; let as many as possible be educated; in short let the race itself get used to freedom self-dependence and proper self assertion; and then let this bill come little by little if necessary.—Of course, if it becomes law, it will be constantly avoided—No man can frame a statute which some other cannot avoid. For all its beneficent purposes it will be a dead letter—For its evil influences it will be vivid and active—It will be like the firebrands between the tails of Samson's foxes. It is just pure folly and results from what I have so long claimed, that the people of the North and our Legislators, will not study the people of the South—reasonably. They will not remember that a prejudice 250 years old (at least) should only be legislated against when *positively harmful.* And should always be let alone when it only conflicts with good doctrine—fine theory. It will utterly destroy the bulk of our common schools at the South. These States will throw them aside at once and the people, except in those where there is a colored majority,—will approve—They are not over fond of education here at the best. Our poor white people have to be fed a heap of soft corn to get them to take much stock in it, and the old slave owners *et cet.* do not see any great need in general education—A tax for free schools is as unwelcome as a vapor bath in dog days—If we get this fools' notion imposed on us, good bye schools in the South. It simply delays—puts back the thorough and complete rehabilitation of the South ten or twenty years—It is the idea of a visionary quack who prescribes for the disease without having made a diagnosis—

But pardon me. I did not mean to write all this—

> *Excerpt from a letter by Albion W. Tourgee, a Northern "carpetbagger" resident in North Carolina, who generally supported the guarantee of civil rights to African Americans, opposing the establishment of integrated schools, May 11, 1874, as published in LaWanda Cox and John H. Cox, eds.,* Reconstruction, the Negro and the New South, *pp. 125–126.*

That campaign in Yazoo has been called "the coronation of the Mississippi plan." So it was, for in twenty-six other counties of the State that year the enemy were less humane. In some of that number Republicans resisted by violence the aggressions of the enemy, and were massacred in crowds of ten, twenty, fifty, and in one county, it was said quite one hundred were killed. But in Yazoo, instead of summoning the unarmed colored men against the disciplined and fully equipped ranks of the white league, the Republican leaders made their fight upon the picket-line, trusting to the reserves at the North to fill their places when they should be all killed, many of them as was necessary to convince the Republicans that their opponents would kill if necessary, that they had the power to kill, and that there were none to forbid it, or to punish them for it afterward. Therefore the mass of the Republicans remained silent and passive. Ohio and Massachusetts had gone Democratic. Had I summoned a posse of colored men and resisted, of course there would have been a general massacre in Yazoo, too. That I would not do . . .

By such means as I have here but faintly detailed Yazoo and Mississippi were "redeemed."

Account by Albert Morgan, a "carpetbagger" from Wisconsin who settled in Mississippi and served as sheriff of Yazoo County before being driven from his position by armed force, describing the use of violence in the elections of November 1875 in Mississippi, in his memoir, Yazoo; or On the Picket Line of Freedom in the South, *as reproduced in Glenn M. Linden, ed.,* Voices from the Reconstruction Years, 1865–1877, p. 240.

In this print, published circa 1883, life on the plantation is romanticized, feeding the myth of an idyllic way of life that never really existed. *(Library of Congress, Prints and Photographs Division, LC-USZC4–2851)*

There are over 13,000 blacks to less than 6,000 whites in Madison County. Early in the campaign the Democrats organized their military clubs and began to breathe out threats and slaughter. Levi Hunt, a member of the Livingston Republican club, was shot and mortally wounded. The reign of terror began. The county was invaded by armed Democratic companies from Yazoo which had already been the scenes of outrages so gross that only seven Republican votes were cast in a county with a sure Republican majority of over 2,500. In order to prevent bloodshed, the Republican leaders made an agreement with the Democratic leaders which was called "a compromise." This word recalls the bad old times when slavery cracked its whip over a crouching Congress and demanded new concessions to "sanctify" its crimes. Then, as now, the surrender was styled a "compromise measure." The Madison County compromise consisted in giving the Democrats two members of the legislature, two members of the board of supervisors, and a justice of the peace in each of the supervisors' districts. At a free election the Democrats could not have elected a single officer. In publishing the terms of this surrender, the chairman of the Republican executive committee thus stated what the Democrats agreed to on their part:

"The Democrats expressly pledge themselves that all members of their party that may be named by the sheriff shall on election day attend the polls during the whole day and act as deputy sheriffs, . . . and that every person shall be allowed to vote as he sees fit, without any molestation or interference on the part of any person."

There was a public admission, never controverted by the Democrats, that without this surrender of the political right of the majority no freedom of election could have been secured. But in this "address to the Republicans of Madison County" the chairman (Henry R. Smith) also added, as his reason for consenting to the surrender, this much-revealing statement, which no Democrat has ever challenged, excepting at the safe distance of a thousand miles, in the halls of Congress:

"This arrangement was entered into by us solely in the interests of peace, to prevent scenes of riot and bloodshed, which are taking place in other counties of this state, to allay the prevailing excitement, and to restore peace, harmony, and good feeling among all classes of citizens of our community."

This was the compromise, and these the reasons for it. It only remains to say that the Republicans kept their faith. The Democrats got their offices.

James Redpath, African-American journalist, in an article entitled "The Mississippi Plan," detailing some of the acts of violence in the 1875 election in Mississippi, published in The Independent, *Vol. 28, No. 1,452 (September 28, 1876), page 1.*

The Presidential question is still undecided. For more than two weeks it has seemed almost certain that the three doubtful States would be carried by the Republicans. South Carolina is surely Republican. Florida is in nearly the same condition—both States being for the Republicans on the face of the returns, with the probability of increased majorities by corrections. Louisiana is the State which will decide. There is no doubt that a very large majority of the lawful voters are Republicans. But the Democrats have endeavored to defeat the will of the lawful voters by the perpetration of crimes whose magnitude and atrocity has no parallel in our history. By murder, and hellish cruelties, they at many polls drove the colored people away, or forced them to vote the Democratic ticket. It now seems probably that the Returning Board will have before them evidence which will justify the throwing out of enough to secure the State to those who are lawfully entitled to it.

Rutherford B. Hayes, Republican candidate for the presidency, commenting on the extended controversy over the Electoral College vote in the election of 1876, in his diary entry on Thanksgiving, November 30, 1876, T. Harry Williams, ed., Hayes, The Diary of a President, 1875–1881: Covering the Disputed Election, The End of Reconstruction, and the Beginning of Civil Service, *pp. 51–52.*

At this present time the result of the Presidential election is still unknown. The vote of a few obscure precincts in a single Southern State is to determine who is to be the next President of the United States, and which of the two great national parties is to be in power for the next four years. It is a momentous question, and it is to be decided by the action that is taken in regard to a few negro votes. Yet when the decision is once made by those whose legal duty it is to make it, we believe that the great body of our people will quietly acquiesce in it. It is unfortunate that the votes on which the issue depends have been cast in places around which suspicions of fraud have been gathering for a series of years. It is too much to expect that any decision likely to be arrived at will dissipate all these suspicions. Our hope is that the returning boards will court the fullest scruniny, and after a careful investigation, in every doubtful case, will act strictly according to the law and the evidence, and without any regard to its effect on the final summing up, so that their action in each case may bear the light of a severely impartial judicial inquiry . . .

What the decision may be, or ought to be, is a matter which lies entirely beyond our knowledge and our powers of conjecture. When on the day after the election, it was supposed that Mr. Tilden was chosen, we accepted what seemed to be the verdict of the people submissively and hopefully, and we shall continue in the same frame of mind if that verdict should be confirmed by the final returns. But if those whose duty is to count the votes make returns which change the apparent verdict and place Mr. Hayes at the head of our government, we trust that all loyal citizens will acquiesce in the result. There will of course be dishonest partisans who will cry out against such a decision as having been brought about by fraud. But these outcries, unless supported by decisive evidence, can have no weight with the great body of right-minded men, who belong to both political parties.

> Comment from "The Editor's Note Book," in
> The Unitarian Review and Religious Magazine,
> Vol. 6, No. 6 (December 1876), p. 671.

Prominent Republicans here and elsewhere have within the last month conceded that the Southern policy of the Administration during the last four years has been a wretched failure. Why this talk of letting the South govern itself locally hereafter? It is a concession that the attempt to set up and uphold carpet-bag governments in the South by the army is a failure. Even if it were a conceded fact that in South Carolina and Florida, the voting blacks are in a majority, still it is true that they are totally unfit to govern, that they cannot do it, and in a conflict with the sold minority of whites, representing the property and intelligence of the state, they are sure to go to the wall. If Gen. Grant four years ago had adopted the policy now urged by so many Republicans upon Gov. Hayes, he would have been renominated and re-elected by an overwhelming majority . . .

> Comment by editorialist "D. W. B." dated February 23, 1877, on the apparent Republican compromise to allow Democrats to rule in the South, part of the so-called compromise of 1877, from the Independent 29, no. 1,474 (March 1, 1877), p. 18.

APPENDIX A
Documents

1. The Wilmot Proviso, August 8, 1846
2. Clay's proposals for the Compromise of 1850, January 29, 1850
3. Calhoun's speech on the Compromise of 1850, March 4, 1850
4. Fugitive Slave Act, September 18, 1850
5. Kansas-Nebraska Act [excerpts], May 30, 1854
6. Lincoln's "House Divided" speech on accepting the Republican nomination for Illinois senator, June 1858
7. Freeport Doctrine, Stephen Douglas, August 27, 1858
8. John Brown's statement on his sentencing, November 2, 1859
9. South Carolina declaration of the causes of secession, December 24, 1860
10. Alabama ordinance of secession, January 11, 1861
11. Georgia declaration of secession, January 29, 1861
12. Jefferson Davis's first inaugural address (provisional president), February 18, 1861
13. Lincoln's first inaugural address, March 4, 1861
14. Confiscation Act of 1861, August 6, 1861
15. Grant-Buckner correspondence, February 16, 1862
16. Jefferson Davis's second inaugural address, February 22, 1862
17. McClellan to Lincoln, July 7, 1862
18. Lincoln: appeal to the border state representatives to favor compensated emancipation, July 12, 1862
19. Confiscation Act of 1862, July 17, 1862
20. Lincoln to Horace Greeley, August 22, 1862
21. Robert E. Lee to Jefferson Davis, September 3, 1862
22. Robert E. Lee's Special Field Order 191, September 9, 1862
23. Emancipation Proclamation, January 1, 1863
24. Lincoln to Grant, July 13, 1863
25. Lee to Davis, July 31, 1863
26. Gettysburg Address, November 19, 1863
27. Cleburne Memorial, January 2, 1864
28. Johnston to Hardee on the Cleburne Memorial, January 31, 1864
29. Wade Davis Bill [extracts] and veto message, July 18, 1864
30. Sherman to Mayor James Calhoun, September 12, 1864
31. Sherman order re march to the sea, November 9, 1864 [extracts]
32. Sherman to Halleck, December 24, 1864 [extracts]
33. Sherman's Special Field Order No. 15, January 16, 1865
34. Lincoln's second inaugural address, March 4, 1865
35. Lee's farewell statement, April 10, 1865

1. THE WILMOT PROVISO, AUGUST 8, 1846

Provided, That, as an express and fundamental condition to the acquisition of any territory from the Republic of Mexico by the United States, by virtue of any treaty which may be negotiated between them, and to the use by the Executive of the moneys herein appropriated, neither slavery nor involuntary servitude shall ever exist in any part of said territory, except for crime, whereof the party shall first be duly convicted

2. CLAY'S PROPOSALS FOR THE COMPROMISE OF 1850, JANUARY 29, 1850

It being desirable, for the peace, concord, and harmony of the Union of these States, to settle and adjust amicably all existing questions of controversy between them arising out of the institution of slavery upon a fair, equitable and just basis: therefore,

1. Resolved, That California, with suitable boundaries, ought, upon her application, to be admitted as one of the States of this Union, without the imposition by Congress of any restriction in respect to the exclusion or introduction of slavery within those boundaries.

2. Resolved, That as slavery does not exist by law, and is not likely to be introduced into any of the territory acquired by the United States from the republic of Mexico, it is inexpedient for Congress to provide by law either for its introduction into, or exclusion from, any part of the said territory; and that appropriate territorial governments ought to be established by Congress in all of the said territory, not assigned as the boundaries of the proposed State of California, without the adoption of any restriction or condition on the subject of slavery.

3. Resolved, That the western boundary of the State of Texas ought to be fixed on the Rio del Norte, commencing one marine league from its mouth, and running up that river to the southern line of New Mexico; thence with that line eastwardly, and so continuing in the same direction to the line as established between the United States and Spain, excluding any portion of New Mexico, whether lying on the east or west of that river.

4. Resolved, That it be proposed to the State of Texas, that the United States will provide for the payment of all that portion of the legitimate and bona fide public debt of that State contracted prior to its annexation to the United States, and for which the duties on foreign imports were pledged by the said State to its creditors, not exceeding the sum of dollars, in consideration of the said duties so pledged having been no longer applicable to that object after the said annexation, but having thenceforward become payable to the United States; and upon the condition, also, that the said State of Texas shall, by some solemn and authentic act of her legislature or of a convention, relinquish to the United States any claim which it has to any part of New Mexico.

5. Resolved, That it is inexpedient to abolish slavery in the District of Columbia whilst that institution continues to exist in the State of Maryland, without the consent of that State, without the consent of the people of the District, and without just compensation to the owners of slaves within the District.

6. But, resolved, That it is expedient to prohibit, within the District, the slave trade in slaves brought into it from States or places beyond the limits of the District, either to be sold therein as merchandise, or to be transported to other markets without the District of Columbia.

7. Resolved, That more effectual provision ought to be made by law, according to the requirement of the constitution, for the restitution and delivery of persons bound to service or labor in any State, who may escape into any other State or Territory in the Union. And,

8. Resolved, That Congress has no power to promote or obstruct the trade in slaves between the slaveholding States; but that the admission or exclusion of slaves brought from one into another of them, depends exclusively upon their own particular laws.

3. CALHOUN'S SPEECH ON THE COMPROMISE OF 1850, MARCH 4, 1850

"The Clay Compromise Measures"
by John C. Calhoun (read for him by Senator James M. Mason)

I have, senators, believed from the first that the agitation of the subject of slavery would, if not prevented by some timely and effective measure, end in disunion. Entertaining this opinion, I have, on all proper occasions, endeavored to call the attention of both the two great parties which divided the country to adopt some measure to prevent so great a disaster, but without success. The agitation has been permitted to proceed with almost no attempt to resist it, until it has reached a point when it can no longer be disguised or denied that the Union is in danger. You have thus had forced upon you the greatest and gravest question that can ever come under your consideration: How can the Union be preserved?

To give a satisfactory answer to this mighty question, it is indispensable to have an accurate and thorough knowledge of the nature and the character of the cause by which the Union is endangered. Without such knowledge it is impossible to pronounce with any certainty, by what measure it can be saved; just as it would be impossible for a physician to pronounce in the case of some dangerous disease, with any certainty, by what remedy the patient could be saved, without similar knowledge of the nature and character of the cause which produce it. The first question, then, presented for consideration in the investigation I propose to make in order to obtain such knowledge is: What is it that has endangered the Union?

To this question there can be but one answer,—that the immediate cause is the almost universal discontent which pervades all the States composing the Southern section of the Union. This widely extended discontent is not of recent origin. It commenced with the agitation of the slavery question and has been increasing ever since. The next question, going one step further back, is: What has caused this widely diffused and almost universal discontent?

It is a great mistake to suppose, as is by some, that it originated with demagogs who excited the discontent with the intention of aiding their personal advancement, or with the disappointed ambition of certain politicians who resorted to it as the means of retrieving their fortunes. On the contrary, all the great political influences of the section were arrayed against excitement, and exerted to the utmost to keep the people quiet. The great mass of the people of the South were divided, as in the other section, into Whigs and Democrats. The leaders and the presses of both parties in the South were very solicitous to prevent excitement and to preserve quiet; because it was seen that the effects of the former would necessarily tend to weaken, if not destroy, the political ties which united them with their respective parties in the other section.

Those who know the strength of party ties will readily appreciate the immense force which this cause exerted against agitation and in favor of preserving quiet. But, great as it was, it was not sufficient to prevent the widespread discontent which now pervades the section.

No; some cause far deeper and more powerful than the one supposed must exist, to account for discontent so wide and deep. The question then recurs: What is the cause of this discontent? It will be found in the belief of the people of the Southern States, as prevalent as the discontent itself, that they can not remain, as things now are, consistently with honor and safety, in the Union. The next question to be considered is: What has caused this belief?

One of the causes is, undoubtedly, to be traced to the long-continued agitation of the slave question on the part of the North, and the many aggressions which they have made on the rights of the South during the time. I will not enumerate them at present, as it will be done hereafter in its proper place.

There is another lying back of it—with which this is intimately connected—that may be regarded as the great and primary cause. This is to be found in the fact that the equilibrium between the two sections in the government as it stood when the Constitution was ratified and the government put in action has been destroyed. At that time there was nearly a perfect equilibrium between the two, which afforded ample means to each to protect itself against the aggression of the other; but, as it now stands, one section has the exclusive power of controlling the government, which leaves the other without any adequate means of protecting itself against its encroachment and oppression.

The result of the whole is to give the Northern section a predominance in every department of the government, and thereby concentrate in it the two elements which constitute the federal government: a majority of States, and a majority of their population, estimated in federal numbers. Whatever section concentrates the two in itself possesses the control of the entire government.

But we are just at the close of the sixth decade and the commencement of the seventh. The census is to be taken this year, which must add greatly to the decided preponderance of the North in the House of Representatives and in the Electoral College. The prospect is, also, that a great increase will be added to its present preponderance in the Senate, during the period of the decade, by the addition of new States. Two Territories, Oregon and Minnesota, are already in progress, and strenuous efforts are making to bring in three additional States from the Territory recently conquered from Mexico; which, if successful, will add three other States in a short time to the Northern section, making five States, and increasing the present number of its States from fifteen to twenty, and of its senators from thirty to forty.

On the contrary, there is not a single Territory in progress in the Southern section, and no certainty that any additional State will be added to it during the decade. The prospect then is, that the two sections in the Senate, should the efforts now made to exclude the South from the newly acquired Territories succeed, will stand, before the end of the decade, twenty Northern States to fourteen Southern (considering Delaware as neutral), and forty Northern senators to twenty-eight Southern. This great increase of senators, added to the great increase of members of the House of Representatives and the Electoral College on the part of the North, which must take place under the next decade, will effectually and irretrievably destroy the equilibrium which existed when the government commenced.

Had this destruction been the operation of time without the interference of government, the South would have had no reason to complain; but such was not the fact. It was caused by the legislation of this government, which was appointed as the common agent of all and charged with the protection of the interests and security of all.

The legislation by which it has been effected may be classed under three heads: The first is that series of acts by which the South has been excluded from the common territory belonging to all the States as members of the federal Union—which have had the effect of extending vastly the portion allotted to the Northern section, and restricting within narrow limits the portion left the South. The next consists in adopting a system of revenue and disbursements by which an undue proportion of the burden of taxation has been imposed upon the South, and an undue proportion of its proceeds appropriated to the North. And the last is a system of political measures by which the original character of the government has been radically changed. I propose to bestow upon each of these, in the order they stand, a few remarks, with the view of showing that it is owing to the action of this government that the equilibrium between the two sections has been destroyed, and the whole powers of the system centered in a sectional majority.

I have not included the territory recently acquired by the treaty with Mexico. The North is making the most strenuous efforts to appropriate the whole to herself, by excluding the South from every foot of it. If she should succeed, it will add to that from which the South has already been excluded 526,078 square miles, and would increase the whole which the North has appropriated to herself to 1,764,023, not including the portion that she may succeed in excluding us

from in Texas. To sum up the whole, the United States, since they declared their independence, have acquired 2,373,046 square miles of territory, from which the North will have excluded the South, if she should succeed in monopolizing the newly-acquired Territories, about three-fourths of the whole, leaving to the South but about one-fourth. Such is the first and great cause that has destroyed the equilibrium between the two sections in the government.

The next is the system of revenue and disbursements which has been adopted by the government. It is well known that the government has derived its revenue mainly from duties on imports. I shall not undertake to show that such duties must necessarily fall mainly on the exporting States, and that the South, as the great exporting portion of the Union, has in reality paid vastly more than her due proportion of the revenue; because I deem it unnecessary, as the subject has on so many occasions been fully discussed. Nor shall I, for the same reason, undertake to show that a far greater portion of the revenue has been disbursed in the North, than its due share; and that the joint effect of these causes has been to transfer a vast amount from South to North, which, under an equal system of revenue and disbursements, would not have been lost to her. If to this be added that many of the duties were imposed, not for revenue but for protection—that is, intended to put money, not in the Treasury, but directly into the pocket of the manufacturers—some conception may be formed of the immense amount which in the long course of sixty years has been transferred from South to North. There are no data by which it can be estimated with any certainty; but it is safe to say that it amounts to hundreds of millions of dollars. Under the most moderate estimate it would be sufficient to add greatly to the wealth of the North, and thus greatly increase her population by attracting immigration from all quarters to that section.

This, combined with the great primary cause, amply explains why the North has acquired a preponderance in every department of the government by its disproportionate increase of population and States. The former, as has been shown, has increased, in fifty years, 2,400,000 over that of the South. This increase of population during so long a period is satisfactorily accounted for by the number of immigrants, and the increase of their descendants, which have been attracted to the Northern section from Europe and the South, in consequence of the advantages derived from the causes assigned. If they had not existed—if the South had retained all the capital which has been extracted from her by the fiscal action of the government; and if it had not been excluded by the Ordinance of 1787 and the Missouri Compromise, from the region lying between the Ohio and the Mississippi Rivers, and between the Mississippi and the Rocky Mountains north of 36° 30 —it scarcely admits of a doubt that it would have divided the immigration with the North, and by retaining her own people would have at least equaled the North in population under the census of 1840, and probably under that about to be taken. She would also, if she had retained her equal rights in those territories, have maintained an equality in the number of States with the North, and have preserved the equilibrium between the two sections that existed at the commencement of the government. The loss, then, of the equilibrium is to be attributed to the action of this government.

There is a question of vital importance to the Southern section, in reference to which the views and feelings of the two sections are as opposite and hostile as they can possibly be. I refer to the relation between the two races in the Southern section, which constitutes a vital portion of her social organization. Every portion of the North entertains views and feelings more or less hostile to it. Those most opposed and hostile regard it as a sin, and consider themselves under the most sacred obligation to use every effort to destroy it.

Indeed, to the extent that they conceive that they have power, they regard themselves as implicated in the sin, and responsible for not suppressing it by the use of all and every means. Those less opposed and hostile regard it as a crime—an offense against humanity, as they call it and, altho not so fanatical, feel themselves bound to use all efforts to effect the same object; while those who are least opposed and hostile regard it as a blot and a stain on the character of what they call the "nation," and feel themselves accordingly bound to give it no countenance or support. On the contrary, the Southern section regards the relation as one which can not be destroyed without subjecting the two races to the greatest calamity, and the section to poverty, desolation, and wretchedness; and accordingly they feel bound by every consideration of interest and safety to defend it.

Unless something decisive is done, I again ask, What is to stop this agitation before the great and final object at which it aims—the abolition of slavery in the States—is consummated? Is it, then, not certain that if something is not done to arrest it, the South will be forced to choose between abolition and secession? Indeed, as events are now moving, it will not require the South to secede in order to dissolve the Union. Agitation will of itself effect it, of which its past history furnishes abundant proof—as I shall next proceed to show.

It is a great mistake to suppose that disunion can be effected by a single blow. The cords which bind these States together in one common Union are far too numerous and powerful for that. Disunion must be the work of time. It is only through a long process, and successively, that the cords can be snapped until the whole fabric falls asunder. Already the agitation of the slavery question has snapped some of the most important, and has greatly weakened all the others.

If the agitation goes on, the same force, acting with increased intensity, as has been shown, will finally snap every cord, when nothing will be left to hold the States together except force. But surely that can with no propriety of language be called a Union when the only means by which the weaker is held connected with the stronger portion is force. It may, indeed, keep them connected; but the connection will partake much more of the character of subjugation on the part of the weaker to the stronger than the union of free, independent, and sovereign States in one confederation, as they stood in the early stages of the government, and which only is worthy of the sacred name of Union.

Having now, senators, explained what it is that endangers the Union, and traced it to its cause, and explained its nature and character, the question again recurs, How can the Union be saved? To this I answer, there is but one way by which it can be, and that is by adopting such measures as will satisfy the States belonging to the Southern section that they can remain in the Union consistently with their honor and their safety. There is, again, only one way by which this can be effected, and that is by removing the causes by which this belief has been produced. Do this, and discontent will cease, harmony and kind feelings between the sections be restored, and every apprehension of danger to the Union removed. The question, then, is, How can this be done? There is but one way by which it can with any certainty; and that is by a full and final settlement, on the principle of justice, of all the questions at issue between the two sections. The South asks for justice, simple justice, and less she ought not to take. She has no compromise to offer but the Constitution, and no concession or surrender to make. She has already surrendered so much that she has little left to surrender. Such a settlement would go to the root of the evil, and remove all cause of discontent, by satisfying the South that she could remain honorably and safely in the Union, and thereby restore the harmony and fraternal feelings between the sections which existed anterior to the Missouri agitation. Nothing else can, with any certainty, finally and for ever settle the question at issue, terminate agitation, and save the Union.

But can this be done? Yes, easily; not by the weaker party, for it can of itself do nothing—not even protect itself—but by the stronger. The North has only to will it to accomplish it—to do justice by conceding to the South an equal right in the acquired territory, and to do her duty by causing the stipulations relative to fugitive slaves to be faithfully fulfilled—to cease the agitation of the slave question, and to provide for the insertion of a provision in the Constitution, by an amendment, which will restore to the South, in substance, the power she possessed of protecting herself before the equilibrium between the sections was destroyed by the action of this government. There will be no difficulty in devising such a provision—one that will protect the South, and which at the same time will improve and strengthen the government instead of impairing and weakening it.

But will the North agree to this? It is for her to answer the question. But, I will say, she can not refuse if she has half the love of the Union which she professes to have, or without justly exposing herself to the charge that her love of power and aggrandizement is far greater than her love of the Union. At all events, the responsibility of saving the Union rests on the North, and not on the South. The South can not save it by any act of hers, and the North may save it without any sacrifice whatever, unless to do justice and to perform her duties under the Constitution should be regarded by her as a sacrifice.

It is time, senators, that there should be an open and manly avowal on all sides as to what is intended to be done. If the question is not now settled, it is uncertain whether it ever can hereafter be; and we, as the representatives of the States of this Union regarded as governments, should come to a distinct understanding as to our respective views, in order to ascertain whether the great questions at issue can be settled or not. If you who represent the stronger portion, can not agree to settle them on the broad principle of justice and duty, say so; and let the States we both represent agree to separate and part in peace.

If you are unwilling we should part in peace, tell us so; and we shall know what to do when you reduce the question to submission or resistance. If you remain silent, you will compel us to infer by your acts what you intend. In that case California will become the test question. If you admit her under all the difficulties that oppose her admission, you compel us to infer that you intend to exclude us from the whole of the acquired Territories, with the intention of destroying irretrievably the equilibrium between the two sections. We should be blind not to perceive in that case that your real objects are power and aggrandizement, and infatuated, not to act accordingly.

I have now, senators, done my duty in expressing my opinions fully, freely, and candidly on this solemn occasion. In doing so I have been governed by the motives which have governed me in all the stages of the agitation of the slavery question since its commencement. I have exerted myself during the whole period to arrest it, with the intention of saving the Union if it could be done; and if it could not, to save the section where it has pleased providence to cast my lot, and which I sincerely believe has justice and the Constitution on its side. Having faithfully done my duty to the best of my ability, both to the Union and my section, throughout this agitation, I shall have the consolation, let what will come, that I am free from all responsibility.

4. Fugitive Slave Act, September 18, 1850

An Act to amend, and supplementary to, the Act entitled "An Act respecting Fugitives from Justice, and Persons escaping from the Service of their Masters," approved February twelfth, one thousand seven hundred and ninety-three.

Be it enacted by the Senate and House of Representatives of the United States of America in congress assembled, That the persons who have been, or may hereafter be, appointed commissioners, in virtue of any act of Congress, by the Circuit Courts of the United States and who, in consequence of such appointment, are authorized to exercise the powers that any justice of the peace, or other magistrate of any of the United States, may exercise in respect to offenders for any crime or offence against the United States, by arresting, imprisoning, or bailing the same under and by virtue of the thirty-third section of the act of the twenty-fourth of September seventeen hundred and eighty-nine, entitled "An Act to establish the Judicial courts of the United States," shall be, and are hereby, authorized and required to exercise and discharge all the powers and duties conferred by this act.

SEC. 2. And be it further enacted, That the Superior Court of each organized Territory of the United States shall have the same power to appoint commissioners to take acknowledgements of bail and affidavits and to take depositions of witnesses in civil causes, which is now possessed by the Circuit Court of the United States; and all commissioners who shall hereafter be appointed for such purposes by the Superior Court of any organized Territory of the United States, shall possess all the powers, and exercise all the duties, conferred by law upon the commissioners appointed by the Circuit Courts of the United States for similar purposes, and shall moreover exercise and discharge all the powers and duties conferred by this act.

SEC. 3. And be it further enacted, That the Circuit Courts of the United States, and the Superior Courts of each organized Territory of the United States, shall from time to time enlarge the number of commissioners, with a view to afford reasonable facilities to reclaim fugitives from labor, and to the prompt discharge of the duties imposed by this act.

SEC. 4. And be it further enacted, That the commissioners above named shall have concurrent jurisdiction with the judges of the Circuit and District Courts of the United States, in their respective circuits and districts within the several States, and the judges of the Superior Courts of the Territories, severally and collectively, in term-time and vacation; and shall grant certificates to such claimants, upon satisfactory proof being made, with authority to take and remove such fugitives from service or labor, under the restrictions herein contained, to the State or Territory from which such persons may have escaped or fled.

SEC. 5. And be it further enacted, That it shall be the duty of all marshals and deputy marshals to obey and execute all warrants and precepts issued under the provisions of this act, when to them directed; and should any marshal or deputy marshal refuse to receive such warrant, or other process, when tendered, or to use all proper means diligently to execute the same, he shall, on conviction thereof, be fined in the sum of one thousand dollars, to the use of such claimant, on the motion of such claimant, by the Circuit or District Court for the district of such marshal; and after arrest of such fugitive, by such marshal or his deputy, or whilst at any time in his custody under the provisions of this act,

should such fugitive escape, whether with or without the assent of such marshal or his deputy, such marshal shall be liable, on his official bond, to be prosecuted for the benefit of such claimant, for the full value of the service or labor of said fugitive in the State, Territory, or District whence he escaped: and the better to enable the said commissioners, when thus appointed, to execute their duties faithfully and efficiently, in conformity with the requirements of the Constitution of the United States and of this act, they are hereby authorized and empowered, within their counties respectively, to appoint, in writing under their hands, anyone or more suitable persons, from time to time, to execute all such warrants and other process as may be issued by them in the lawful performance of their respective duties; with authority to such commissioners, or the persons to be appointed by them, to execute process as aforesaid, to summon and call to their aid the bystanders, or posse comitatus of the proper county, when necessary to ensure a faithful observance of the clause of the Constitution referred to, in conformity with the provisions of this act; and all good citizens are hereby commanded to aid and assist in the prompt and efficient execution of this law, whenever their services may he required, as aforesad, for that purpose; and said warrants shall run, and be executed by said officers, any where in the State within which they are issued.

SEC. 6. And be it further enacted, That when a person held to service or labor in any State or Territory of the United States, has heretofore or shall hereafter escape into another State or Territory of the United States, the person or persons to whom such service or labor may be due, or his, her, or their agent or attorney, duly authorized, by power of attorney, in writing, acknowledged and certified under the seal of some legal officer or court of the State or Territory in which the same may be executed, may pursue and reclaim such fugitive person, either by procuring a warrant from some one of the courts, judges, or commissioners aforesaid, of the proper circuit, district, or county, for the apprehension of such fugitive from service or labor, or by seizing and arresting such fugitive, where the same can be done without process, and by taking, or causing such person to be taken, forthwith before such court, judge, or commissioner, whose duty it shall be to hear and determine the case of such claimant in a summary manner; and upon satisfactory proof being made, by deposition or affidavit, in writing, to be taken and certified by such court, judge, or commissioner, or by other satisfactory testimony, duly taken and certified by some court, magistrate, justice of the peace, or other legal officer authorized to administer an oath and take depositions under the laws of the State or Territory from which such person owing service or labor may have escaped, with a certificate of such magistracy or other authority, as aforesaid, with the seal of the proper court or officer thereto attached, which seal shall be sufficient to establish the competency of the proof, and with proof, also by affidavit, of the identity of the person whose service or labor is claimed to be due as aforesaid, that the person so arrested does in fact owe service or labor to the person or persons claiming him or her, in the State or Territory from which such fugitive may have escaped as aforesaid, and that said person escaped, to make out and deliver to such claimant, his or her agent or attorney, a certificate setting forth the substantial facts as to the service or labor due from such fugitive to the claimant, and of his or her escape from the State or Territory in which such service or labor was due, to the State or Territory in which he or she was arrested, with authority to such claimant, or his or her agent or attorney, to use such reasonable force and restraint as may be necessary, under the circumstances of the case, to take and remove such fugitive person back to the State or Territory whence he or she may have escaped as aforesaid. In no trial or hearing under this act shall the testimony of such alleged fugitive be admitted in evidence; and the certificates in this and the first [fourth] section mentioned, shall be conclusive of the right of the person or persons in whose favor granted, to remove such fugitive to the State or Territory from which he escaped, and shall prevent all molestation of such person or persons by any process issued by any court judge, magistrate, or other person whomsoever.

SEC. 7. And be it further enacted, That any person who shall knowingly and willingly obstruct, hinder, or prevent such claimant, his agent or attorney, or any person or persons lawfully assisting him, her, or them, from arresting such a fugitive from service or labor, either with or without process as aforesaid, or shall rescue, or attempt to rescue such fugitive from service or labor, from the custody of such claimant, his or her agent or attorney, or other person or persons lawfully assisting as aforesaid, when so arrested, pursuant to the authority herein given and declared; or shall aid, abet, or assist such person so owing service or labor as aforesaid, directly or indirectly, to escape from such claimant, his agent or attorney, or other person or persons legally authorized as aforesaid; or shall harbor or conceal such fugitive, so as to prevent the discovery and arrest of such person, after notice or knowledge of the fact that such person was a fugitive from service or labor as aforesaid, shall, for either of said offences, be subject to a fine not exceeding one thousand dollars, and imprisonment not exceeding six months, by indictment and conviction before the District Court of the United States for the district in which such offence may have been committed, or before the proper court of criminal jurisdiction, if committed within anyone of the organized Territories of the United States; and shall moreover forfeit and pay, by way of civil damages to the party injured by such illegal conduct, the sum of one thousand dollars, for each fugitive so lost as aforesaid, to be recovered by action of debt, in any of the District or Territorial Courts aforesaid, within whose jurisdiction the said offence may have been committed.

SEC. 8. And be it further enacted, That the marshals, their deputies, and the clerks of the said District and Territorial Courts, shall be paid, for their services, the like fees as may be allowed to them for similar services in other cases; and where such services are rendered exclusively in the arrest, custody, and delivery of the fugitive to the claimant, his or her agent or attorney, or where such supposed fugitive may be discharged out of custody for the want of sufficient proof as aforesaid, then such fees are to be paid in the whole by such claimant, his agent or attorney; and in all cases where the proceedings are before a commissioner, he shall be entitled to a fee of ten dollars in full for his services in each case, upon the delivery of the said certificate to the claimant, his or her agent or attorney; or a fee of five dollars in cases where the proof shall not, in the opinion of such commissioner, warrant such certificate and delivery, inclusive of all services incident to such arrest and examination, to be paid, in either case, by the claimant, his or her agent or attorney. The person or persons authorized to execute the process to be issued by such commissioners for the arrest and detention of fugitives from service or labor as aforesaid, shall also be entitled to a fee of five dollars each for each person he or they may arrest and take before any such commissioner as aforesaid, at the instance and request of such claimant, with such other fees as may be deemed reasonable by such commissioner for such other additional services as may be necessarily performed by him or them; such as attending at the examination, keeping the fugitive in custody, and providing him with food and lodging during his detention, and until the final determination of such commissioner; and, in general, for performing such other duties as may be required by such claimant, his or her attorney or agent, or commissioner in the premises, such fees to be made up in conformity with the fees usually charged by the officers of the courts of justice within the proper district or county, as near as may be practicable, and paid by such claimants, their agents or attorneys, whether such supposed fugitives from service or labor be ordered to be delivered to such claimants by the final determination of such commissioners or not.

SEC. 9. And be it further enacted, That, upon affidavit made by the claimant of such fugitive, his agent or attorney, after such certificate has been issued, that he has reason to apprehend that such fugitive will be rescued by force from his or their possession before he can be taken beyond the limits of the State in which the arrest is made, it shall be the duty of the officer making the arrest to retain such fugitive in his custody, and to remove him to the State whence he fled, and there to deliver him to said claimant, his agent, or attorney. And to this end, the officer aforesaid is hereby authorized and required to employ so many persons as he may deem necessary to overcome such force, and to retain them in his service so long as circumstances may require. The said officer and his assistants, while so employed, to receive the same compensation, and to be allowed the same expenses, as are now allowed by law for transportation of criminals, to be certified by the judge of the district within which the arrest is made, and paid out of the treasury of the United States.

SEC. 10. And be it further enacted, That when any person held to service or labor in any State or Territory, or in the District of Columbia, shall escape therefrom, the party to whom such service or labor shall be due, his, her, or their agent or attorney, may apply to any court of record therein, or judge thereof in vacation, and make satisfactory proof to such court, or judge in vacation, of the escape aforesaid, and that the person escaping owed service or labor to such party. Whereupon the court shall cause a record to be made of the matters so proved, and also a general description of the person so escaping, with such convenient certainty as may be; and a transcript of such record, authenticated by the attestation of the clerk and of the seal of the said court, being produced in any other State, Territory, or district in which the person so escaping may be found, and being exhibited to any judge, commissioner, or other officer authorized by the law of the United States to cause persons escaping from service or labor to be

delivered up, shall be held and taken to be full and conclusive evidence of the fact of escape, and that the service or labor of the person escaping is due to the party in such record mentioned. And upon the production by the said party of other and further evidence if necessary, either oral or by affidavit, in addition to what is contained in the said record of the identity of the person escaping, he or she shall be delivered up to the claimant. And the said court, commissioner, judge, or other person authorized by this act to grant certificates to claimants of fugitives, shall, upon the production of the record and other evidences aforesaid, grant to such claimant a certificate of his right to take any such person identified and proved to be owing service or labor as aforesaid, which certificate shall authorize such claimant to seize or arrest and transport such person to the State or Territory from which he escaped: Provided, That nothing herein contained shall be construed as requiring he production of a transcript of such record as evidence as aforesaid. But in its absence the claim shall be heard and determined upon other satisfactory proofs, competent in law.

5. KANSAS–NEBRASKA ACT [EXCERPTS] MAY 30, 1854

An Act to Organize the Territories of Nebraska and Kansas.

Be it enacted by the Senate and House of Representatives of the United States of America in Congress assembled, That all that part of the territory of the United States included within the following limits, except such portions thereof as are hereinafter expressly exempted from the operations of this act, to wit: beginning at a point in the Missouri River where the fortieth parallel of north latitude crosses the same; then west on said parallel to the east boundary of the Territory of Utah, the summit of the Rocky Mountains; thence on said summit northwest to the forty-ninth parallel of north latitude; thence east on said parallel to the western boundary of the territory of Minnesota; thence southward on said boundary to the Missouri River; thence down the main channel of said river to the place of beginning, be, and the same is hereby, created into a temporary government by the name of the Territory Nebraska; and when admitted as a State or States, the said Territory or any portion of the same, shall be received into the Union with [or] without slavery, as their constitution may prescribe at the time of the admission. . . .

SEC. 9. And be it further enacted . . . Writs of error, and appeals from the final decisions of said Supreme Court, shall be allowed, and may be taken to the Supreme Court of the United States, in the same manner and under the same regulations as from the circuit courts of the United States, where the value of the property, or the amount in controversy, to be ascertained by the oath or affirmation of either party, or other competent witness, shall exceed one thousand dollars; except only that in all cases involving title to slaves, the said writs of error, or appeals shall be allowed and decided by the said Supreme Court, without regard to the value of the matter, property, or title in controversy; and except also that a writ of error or appeal shall also be allowed to the Supreme Court of the United States, from the decision of the said Supreme Court created by this act, or of any judge thereof, or of the district courts created by this act, or of any judge thereof, upon any writ of habeas corpus, involving the question of personal freedom: Provided, that nothing herein contained shall be construed to apply to or affect the provisions to the "act respecting fugitives from justice, and persons escaping from the service of their masters," approved February twelfth, seventeen hundred and ninety-three, and the "act to amend and supplementary to the aforesaid act," approved September eighteen, eighteen hundred and fifty. . . .

SEC. 10. And Be it further enacted, That the provisions of an act entitled "An act respecting fugitives from justice, and persons escaping from the service of their masters," approved February twelve, seventeen hundred and ninety-three, and the provisions of the act entitled "An act to amend, and supplementary to, the aforesaid act," approved September eighteen, eighteen hundred and fifty, be, and the same are hereby, declared to extend to and be in full force within the limits of said Territory of Nebraska.

. . . . .

SEC. 14. And be it further enacted. . . . That the Constitution, and all Laws of the United States which are not locally inapplicable, shall have the same force and effect within the said Territory of Nebraska as elsewhere within the United States, except the eighth section of the act preparatory to the admission of Missouri into the Union approved March sixth, eighteen hundred and twenty, which, being inconsistent with the principle of non-intervention by Congress with slaves in the States and Territories, as recognized by the legislation of eighteen hundred and fifty, commonly called the Compromise Measures, is hereby declared inoperative and void; it being the true intent and meaning of this act not to legislate slavery into any Territory or State, nor to exclude it therefrom, but to leave the people thereof perfectly free to form and regulate their domestic institutions in their own way, subject only to the Constitution of the United States: Provided, That nothing herein contained shall be construed to revive or put in force any law or regulation which may have existed prior to the act of sixth March, eighteen hundred and twenty, either protecting, establishing, prohibiting, or abolishing slavery.

. . . . .

SEC. 19. And be it further enacted, That all that part of the Territory of the United States included within the following limits, except such portions thereof as are hereinafter expressly exempted from the operations of this act, to wit, beginning at a point on the western boundary of the State of Missouri, where the thirty-seventh parallel of north latitude crosses the same; thence west on said parallel to the eastern boundary of New Mexico; thence north on said boundary to latitude thirty-eight; thence following said boundary westward to the east boundary of the Territory of Utah, on the summit of the Rocky Mountains; thence northward on said summit to the fortieth parallel of latitude, thence east on said parallel to the western boundary of the State of Missouri; thence south with the western boundary of said State to the place of beginning, be, and the same is hereby, created into a temporary government by the name of the Territory of Kansas; and when admitted as a State or States, the said Territory, or any portion of the same, shall be received into the Union with or without slavery, as their Constitution may prescribe at the time of their admission: Provided, That nothing in this act contained shall be construed to inhibit the government of the United States from dividing said Territory into two or more Territories, in such manner and at such times as Congress shall deem convenient and proper, or from attaching any portion of said Territory to any other State or Territory of the United States. . . .

. . . . .

SEC. 28. And be it further enacted, That the provisions of the act entitled "An act respecting fugitives from justice, and persons escaping from, the service of their masters," approved February twelfth, seventeen hundred and ninety-three, and the provisions of the act entitled "An act to amend, and supplementary to, the aforesaid act," approved September eighteenth, eighteen hundred and fifty, be, and the same are hereby, declared to extend to and be in full force within the limits of the said Territory of Kansas.

. . . . .

SEC. 32. And be it further enacted. . . . That the Constitution, and all laws of the United States which are not locally inapplicable, shall have the same force and effect within the said Territory of Kansas as elsewhere within the United States, except the eighth section of the act preparatory to the admission of Missouri into the Union, approved March sixth, eighteen hundred and twenty, which, being inconsistent with the principle of non-intervention by Congress with slavery in the States and Territories, as recognized by the legislation of eighteen hundred and fifty, commonly called the Compromise Measures, is hereby declared inoperative and void; it being the true intent and meaning of this act not to legislate slavery into any Territory or State, nor to exclude it therefrom, but to leave the people thereof perfectly free to form and regulate their domestic institutions in their own way, subject only to the Constitution of the United States: Provided, That nothing herein contained shall be construed to revive or put in force any law or regulation which may have existed prior to the act of sixth of March, eighteen hundred and twenty, either protecting, establishing, prohibiting, or abolishing slavery.

6. Lincoln's "House Divided" Speech on Accepting the Republican Nomination for Illinois Senator, June 1858

MR. PRESIDENT AND GENTLEMEN OF THE CONVENTION: If we could first know where we are, and whither we are tending, we could better judge what to do, and how to do it. We are now far into the fifth year since a policy was initiated with the avowed object and confident promise of putting an end to slavery agitation. Under the operation of that policy, that agitation has not only not ceased, but has constantly augmented. In my opinion, it will not cease until a crises shall have been reached and passed. "A house

divided against itself cannot stand." I believe this government cannot endure permanently half slave and half free. I do not expect the Union to be dissolved—I do not expect the house to fall—but I do expect it will cease to be divided. It will become all one thing, or all the other. Either the opponents of slavery will arrest the further spread of it, and place it where the public mind shall rest in the belief that it is in the course of ultimate extinction; or its advocates will push it forward till it shall become alike lawful in all the States, old as well as new, North as well as South.

Have we no tendency to the latter condition?

Let any one who doubts carefully contemplate that now almost complete legal combination—piece of machinery, so to speak—compounded of the Nebraska doctrine and the Dred Scott decision. Let him consider not only what work the machinery is adapted to do, and how well adapted; but also let him study the history of its construction, and trace, if he can, or rather fail, if he can, to trace the evidences of design and concert of action among its chief architects, from the beginning.

The new year of 1854 found slavery excluded from more than half the States by State constitutions, and from most of the national territory by congressional prohibition. Four days later commenced the struggle which ended in repealing that congressional prohibition. This opened all the national territory to slavery, and was the first point gained.

But, so far, Congress only had acted; and an indorsement by the people, real or apparent, was indispensable to save the point already gained and give chance for more. This necessity had not been overlooked, but had been provided for, as well as might be, in the notable argument of "squatter sovereignty," otherwise called "sacred right of self-government," which latter phrase, though expressive of the only rightful basis of any government, was so perverted in this attempted use of it as to amount to just this: That if any one man choose to enslave another, no third man shall be allowed to object . . . Then opened the roar of loose declamation in favor of "squatter sovereignty" and "sacred right of self-government." "But," said opposition members, "let us amend the bill so as to expressly declare that the people of the Territory may exclude slavery." "Not we," said the friends of the measure; and down they voted the amendment.

While the Nebraska Bill was passing through Congress, a law case involving the question of a negro's freedom, by reason of his owner having voluntarily taken him first into a free State and then into a territory covered by the congressional prohibition, and held him as a slave for a long time in each, was passing through the United States Circuit Court for the District of Missouri; and both Nebraska Bill and lawsuit were brought to a decision in the same month of May, 1854. The negro's name was Dred Scott, which name now designates the decision finally made in the case. Before the then next Presidential election, the law case came to and was argued in the Supreme Court of the United States . . .

The election came. Mr. Buchanan was elected, and the indorsement, such as it was, secured. That was the second point gained . . . The Supreme Court met again; did not announce their decision, but ordered a reargument. The Presidential inauguration came, and still no decision of the Court; but the incoming President in his inaugural address fervently exhorted the people to abide by the forthcoming decision, whatever it might be. Then, in a few days, came the decision.

The reputed author of the Nebraska Bill finds an early occasion to make a speech at this capital indorsing the Dred Scott Decision, and vehemently denouncing all opposition to it. The new President, too, seizes the early occasion of the Silliman letter to indorse and strongly construe that decision, and to express his astonishment that any different view had ever been entertained!

At length a squabble springs up between the President and the author of the Nebraska Bill, on the mere question of fact, whether the Lecompton constitution was or was not, in any just sense, made by the people of Kansas; and in that quarrel the latter declares that all he wants is a fair vote for the people, and that he cares not whether slavery be voted down or voted up. I do not understand his declaration that he cares not whether slavery be voted down or voted up to be intended by him other than as an apt definition of the policy he would impress upon the public mind—the principle for which he declares he has suffered so much, and is ready to suffer to the end. And well may he cling to that principle. If he has any parental feeling, well may he cling to it. That principle is the only shred left of his original Nebraska doctrine. Under the Dred Scott Decision "squatter sovereignty" squatted out of existence, tumbled down like temporary scaffolding,—like the mold at the foundry, served through one blast and fell back into loose sand,—helped to carry an election, and then was kicked to the winds . . .

We cannot absolutely know that all these exact adaptations are the result of preconcert. But when we see a lot of framed timbers, different portions of which we know have been gotten out at different times and places and by different workmen,—Stephen, Franklin, Roger and James, for instance,—and we see these timbers joined together, and see they exactly make the frame of a house or a mill, all the tenons and mortises exactly fitting, and all the lengths and proportions of the different pieces exactly adapted to their respective places, and not a piece too many or too few, not omitting even scaffolding—or, if a single piece be lacking, we see the place in the frame exactly fitted and prepared yet to bring such piece in—in such a case we find it impossible not to believe that Stephen and Franklin and Roger and James all understood one another from the beginning, and all worked upon a common plan or draft drawn up before the first blow was struck . . .

Our cause, then, must be intrusted to, and conducted by, its own undoubted friends—those whose hands are free, whose hearts are in the work, who do care for the result. Two years ago the Republicans of the nation mustered over thirteen hundred thousand strong. We did this under the single impulse of resistance to a common danger, with every external circumstance against us. Of strange, discordant, and even hostile elements, we gathered from the four winds, and formed and fought the battle through, under the constant hot fire of a disciplined, proud, and pampered enemy. Did we brave all then to falter now?—now when that same enemy is wavering, dissevered, and belligerent? The result is not doubtful. We shall not fail—if we stand firm, we shall not fail. Wise counsels may accelerate or mistakes delay it, but, sooner or later, the victory is sure to come.

7. FREEPORT DOCTRINE, STEPHEN DOUGLAS, AUGUST 27, 1858

The next question propounded to me by Mr. Lincoln is, Can the people of a Territory in any lawful way, against the wishes of any citizen of the United States, exclude slavery from their limits prior to the formation of a State constitution? I answer emphatically, as Mr. Lincoln has heard me answer a hundred times from every stump in Illinois, that in my opinion the people of a Territory can, by lawful means, exclude slavery from their limits prior to the formation of a State constitution. Mr. Lincoln knew that I had answered that question over and over again. He heard me argue the Nebraska bill on that principle all over the State in 1854, in 1855, and in 1856, and he has no excuse for pretending to be in doubt as to my position on that question. It matters not what way the Supreme Court may hereafter decide as to the abstract question whether slavery may or may not go into a Territory under the Constitution, the people have the lawful means to introduce it or exclude it as they please, for the reason that slavery cannot exist a day or an hour anywhere, unless it is supported by local police regulations. Those police regulations can only be established by the local legislature; and if the people are opposed to slavery, they will elect representatives to that body who will by unfriendly legislation effectually prevent the introduction of it into their midst. If, on the contrary, they are for it, their legislation will favor its extension. Hence, no matter what the decision of the Supreme Court may be on that abstract question, still the right of the people to make a Slave Territory or a Free Territory is perfect and complete under the Nebraska bill. I hope Mr. Lincoln deems my answer satisfactory on that point.

8. John Brown's Statement on His Sentencing, November 2, 1859

I have, may it please the court, a few words to say.

In the first place, I deny everything but what I have all along admitted,—the design on my part to free slaves. I intended certainly to have made a clean thing of that matter, as I did last winter, when I went into Missouri and took slaves without the snapping of a gun on either side, moved them through the country, and finally left them in Canada. I designed to do the same thing again, on a larger scale. That was all I intended. I never did intend murder, or treason, or the destruction of property, or to excite or incite slaves to rebellion, or to make insurrection.

I have another objection; and that is, it is unjust that I should suffer such a penalty. Had I interfered in the manner which I admit, and which I admit has been fairly proved (for I admire the truthfulness and candor of the greater portion of the witnesses who have testified in this case),—had I so interfered in behalf of the rich, the powerful, the intelligent, the so-called great, or in behalf of any of their friends—either father, mother, sister, wife, or children, or any of that class—and suffered and sacrificed what I have in this interference, it would have been all right; and every man in this court would have deemed it an act worthy of reward rather than punishment.

The court acknowledges, as I suppose, the validity of the law of God. I see a book kissed here which I suppose to be the Bible, or at least the New Testament. That teaches me that all things whatsoever I would that men should do to me, I should do even so to them. It teaches me further to "remember them that are in bonds, as bound with them." I endeavored to act up to that instruction. I say, I am too young to understand that God is any respecter of persons. I believe that to have interfered as I have done—as I have always freely admitted I have done—in behalf of His despised poor, was not wrong, but right. Now if it is deemed necessary that I should forfeit my life for the furtherance of the ends of justice, and mingle my blood further with the blood of my children and with the blood of millions in this slave country whose rights are disregarded by wicked, cruel, and unjust enactments.—I submit; so let it be done!

Let me say one word further.

I feel entirely satisfied with the treatment I have received on my trial. Considering all the circumstances, it has been more generous than I expected. I feel no consciousness of my guilt. I have stated from the first what was my intention, and what was not. I never had any design against the life of any person, nor any disposition to commit treason, or excite slaves to rebel, or make any general insurrection. I never encouraged any man to do so, but always discouraged any idea of any kind.

Let me say also, a word in regard to the statements made by some to those connected with me. I hear it has been said by some of them that I have induced them to join me. But the contrary is true. I do not say this to injure them, but as regretting their weakness. There is not one of them but joined me of his own accord, and the greater part of them at their own expense. A number of them I never saw, and never had a word of conversation with, till the day they came to me; and that was for the purpose I have stated.

Now I have done.

9. South Carolina Declaration of the Causes of Secession, December 24, 1860

Declaration of the Immediate Causes Which Induce and Justify the Secession of South Carolina from the Federal Union

The people of the State of South Carolina, in Convention assembled, on the 26th day of April, A.D., 1852, declared that the frequent violations of the Constitution of the United States, by the Federal Government, and its encroachments upon the reserved rights of the

States, fully justified this State in then withdrawing from the Federal Union; but in deference to the opinions and wishes of the other slaveholding States, she forbore at that time to exercise this right. Since that time, these encroachments have continued to increase, and further forbearance ceases to be a virtue.

And now the State of South Carolina having resumed her separate and equal place among nations, deems it due to herself, to the remaining United States of America, and to the nations of the world, that she should declare the immediate causes which have led to this act.

In the year 1765, that portion of the British Empire embracing Great Britain, undertook to make laws for the government of that portion composed of the thirteen American Colonies. A struggle for the right of self-government ensued, which resulted, on the 4th of July, 1776, in a Declaration, by the Colonies, "that they are, and of right ought to be, FREE AND INDEPENDENT STATES; and that, as free and independent States, they have full power to levy war, conclude peace, contract alliances, establish commerce, and to do all other acts and things which independent States may of right do."

They further solemnly declared that whenever any "form of government becomes destructive of the ends for which it was established, it is the right of the people to alter or abolish it, and to institute a new government." Deeming the Government of Great Britain to have become destructive of these ends, they declared that the Colonies "are absolved from all allegiance to the British Crown, and that all political connection between them and the State of Great Britain is, and ought to be, totally dissolved."

In pursuance of this Declaration of Independence, each of the thirteen States proceeded to exercise its separate sovereignty; adopted for itself a Constitution, and appointed officers for the administration of government in all its departments—Legislative, Executive and Judicial. For purposes of defense, they united their arms and their counsels; and, in 1778, they entered into a League known as the Articles of Confederation, whereby they agreed to entrust the administration of their external relations to a common agent, known as the Congress of the United States, expressly declaring, in the first Article "that each State retains its sovereignty, freedom and independence, and every power, jurisdiction and right which is not, by this Confederation, expressly delegated to the United States in Congress assembled."

Under this Confederation the war of the Revolution was carried on, and on the 3rd of September, 1783, the contest ended, and a definite Treaty was signed by Great Britain, in which she acknowledged the independence of the Colonies in the following terms: "ARTICLE 1—His Britannic Majesty acknowledges the said United States, viz: New Hampshire, Massachusetts Bay, Rhode Island and Providence Plantations, Connecticut, New York, New Jersey, Pennsylvania, Delaware, Maryland, Virginia, North Carolina, South Carolina and Georgia, to be FREE, SOVEREIGN AND INDEPENDENT STATES; that he treats with them as such; and for himself, his heirs and successors, relinquishes all claims to the government, propriety and territorial rights of the same and every part thereof."

Thus were established the two great principles asserted by the Colonies, namely: the right of a State to govern itself; and the right of a people to abolish a Government when it becomes destructive of the ends for which it was instituted. And concurrent with the establishment of these principles, was the fact, that each Colony became and was recognized by the mother Country a FREE, SOVEREIGN AND INDEPENDENT STATE.

In 1787, Deputies were appointed by the States to revise the Articles of Confederation, and on 17th September, 1787, these Deputies recommended for the adoption of the States, the Articles of Union, known as the Constitution of the United States.

The parties to whom this Constitution was submitted, were the several sovereign States; they were to agree or disagree, and when nine of them agreed the compact was to take effect among those concurring; and the General Government, as the common agent, was then invested with their authority.

If only nine of the thirteen States had concurred, the other four would have remained as they then were—separate, sovereign States, independent of any of the provisions of the Constitution. In fact, two of the States did not accede to the Constitution until long after it had gone into operation among the other eleven; and during that interval, they each exercised the functions of an independent nation.

By this Constitution, certain duties were imposed upon the several States, and the exercise of certain of their powers was restrained, which necessarily implied their continued existence as sovereign States. But to remove all doubt, an amendment was added, which declared that the powers not delegated to the United States by the Constitution, nor prohibited by it to the

States, are reserved to the States, respectively, or to the people. On the 23d May, 1788, South Carolina, by a Convention of her People, passed an Ordinance assenting to this Constitution, and afterwards altered her own Constitution, to conform herself to the obligations she had undertaken.

Thus was established, by compact between the States, a Government with definite objects and powers, limited to the express words of the grant. This limitation left the whole remaining mass of power subject to the clause reserving it to the States or to the people, and rendered unnecessary any specification of reserved rights.

We hold that the Government thus established is subject to the two great principles asserted in the Declaration of Independence; and we hold further, that the mode of its formation subjects it to a third fundamental principle, namely: the law of compact. We maintain that in every compact between two or more parties, the obligation is mutual; that the failure of one of the contracting parties to perform a material part of the agreement, entirely releases the obligation of the other; and that where no arbiter is provided, each party is remitted to his own judgment to determine the fact of failure, with all its consequences.

In the present case, that fact is established with certainty. We assert that fourteen of the States have deliberately refused, for years past, to fulfill their constitutional obligations, and we refer to their own Statutes for the proof.

The Constitution of the United States, in its fourth Article, provides as follows: "No person held to service or labor in one State, under the laws thereof, escaping into another, shall, in consequence of any law or regulation therein, be discharged from such service or labor, but shall be delivered up, on claim of the party to whom such service or labor may be due."

This stipulation was so material to the compact, that without it that compact would not have been made. The greater number of the contracting parties held slaves, and they had previously evinced their estimate of the value of such a stipulation by making it a condition in the Ordinance for the government of the territory ceded by Virginia, which now composes the States north of the Ohio River.

The same article of the Constitution stipulates also for rendition by the several States of fugitives from justice from the other States.

The General Government, as the common agent, passed laws to carry into effect these stipulations of the States. For many years these laws were executed. But an increasing hostility on the part of the non-slaveholding States to the institution of slavery, has led to a disregard of their obligations, and the laws of the General Government have ceased to effect the objects of the Constitution. The States of Maine, New Hampshire, Vermont, Massachusetts, Connecticut, Rhode Island, New York, Pennsylvania, Illinois, Indiana, Michigan, Wisconsin and Iowa, have enacted laws which either nullify the Acts of Congress or render useless any attempt to execute them. In many of these States the fugitive is discharged from service or labor claimed, and in none of them has the State Government complied with the stipulation made in the Constitution. The State of New Jersey, at an early day, passed a law in conformity with her constitutional obligation; but the current of antislavery feeling has led her more recently to enact laws which render inoperative the remedies provided by her own law and by the laws of Congress. In the State of New York even the right of transit for a slave has been denied by her tribunals; and the States of Ohio and Iowa have refused to surrender to justice fugitives charged with murder, and with inciting servile insurrection in the State of Virginia. Thus the constituted compact has been deliberately broken and disregarded by the non-slaveholding States, and the consequence follows that South Carolina is released from her obligation.

The ends for which the Constitution was framed are declared by itself to be "to form a more perfect union, establish justice, insure domestic tranquility, provide for the common defence, promote the general welfare, and secure the blessings of liberty to ourselves and our posterity."

These ends it endeavored to accomplish by a Federal Government, in which each State was recognized as an equal, and had separate control over its own institutions. The right of property in slaves was recognized by giving to free persons distinct political rights, by giving them the right to represent, and burthening them with direct taxes for three-fifths of their slaves; by authorizing the importation of slaves for twenty years; and by stipulating for the rendition of fugitives from labor.

We affirm that these ends for which this Government was instituted have been defeated, and the Government itself has been made destructive of them by the action of the non-slaveholding States. Those States have assume the right of deciding upon the propriety of our domestic institutions; and have denied the rights of property established in fifteen of the States and recognized by the Constitution; they have denounced as sinful the institution of slavery; they have permitted open establishment among them of societies, whose avowed object is to disturb the peace and to eloign the property of the citizens of other States. They have encouraged and assisted thousands of our slaves to leave their homes; and those who remain, have been incited by emissaries, books and pictures to servile insurrection.

For twenty-five years this agitation has been steadily increasing, until it has now secured to its aid the power of the common Government. Observing the *forms* of the Constitution, a sectional party has found within that Article establishing the Executive Department, the means of subverting the Constitution itself. A geographical line has been drawn across the Union, and all the States north of that line have united in the election of a man to the high office of President of the United States, whose opinions and purposes are hostile to slavery. He is to be entrusted with the administration of the common Government, because he has declared that that "Government cannot endure permanently half slave, half free," and that the public mind must rest in the belief that slavery is in the course of ultimate extinction.

This sectional combination for the submersion of the Constitution, has been aided in some of the States by elevating to citizenship, persons who, by the supreme law of the land, are incapable of becoming citizens; and their votes have been used to inaugurate a new policy, hostile to the South, and destructive of its beliefs and safety.

On the 4th day of March next, this party will take possession of the Government. It has announced that the South shall be excluded from the common territory, that the judicial tribunals shall be made sectional, and that a war must be waged against slavery until it shall cease throughout the United States.

The guaranties of the Constitution will then no longer exist; the equal rights of the States will be lost. The slaveholding States will no longer have the power of self-government, or self-protection, and the Federal Government will have become their enemy.

Sectional interest and animosity will deepen the irritation, and all hope of remedy is rendered vain, by the fact that public opinion at the North has invested a great political error with the sanction of more erroneous religious belief.

We, therefore, the People of South Carolina, by our delegates in Convention assembled, appealing to the Supreme Judge of the world for the rectitude of our intentions, have solemnly declared that the Union heretofore existing between this State and the other States of North America, is dissolved, and that the State of South Carolina has resumed her position among the nations of the world, as a separate and independent State; with full power to levy war, conclude peace, contract alliances, establish commerce, and to do all other acts and things which independent States may of right do.

10. ALABAMA ORDINANCE OF SECESSION, JANUARY 11, 1861

An ordinance to dissolve the Union between the State of Alabama and other States united under the compact and style of the United States of America.

Whereas, The election of Abraham Lincoln and Hannibal Hamlin to the offices of President and Vice-President of the United States of America by a sectional party, avowedly hostile to the domestic institutions and peace and security of the people of the State of Alabama, following upon the heels of many and dangerous infractions of the Constitution of the United States, by many of the States and people of the Northern section, is a political wrong of so insulting and menacing a character as to justify the people of the State of Alabama in the adoption of prompt and decided measures for their future peace and security.

Therefore, be it declared and ordained, by the people of the State of Alabama, in Convention assembled, that the State of Alabama now withdraws from the Union, known as the United States of America, and henceforth ceases to be one of the said United States, and is and of right ought to be a sovereign independent State.

Sec. 2. And be it further declared and ordained by the people of the State of Alabama in Convention assembled, that all powers over the territories of said State, and over the people thereof, heretofore delegated to the Government of the United States of America, be, and they are hereby, withdrawn from the said Government and are hereby resumed and vested in the people of the State of Alabama.

And as it is the desire and purpose of the people of Alabama to meet the slaveholding States of the South who may approve of such a purpose, in order to frame a revisional as a permanent Government, upon the principles of the Government of the United States, be it also resolved by the people of Alabama, in convention assembled, that the people of the States of

Delaware, Maryland, Virginia, North Carolina, South Carolina, Florida, Georgia, Mississippi, Louisiana, Texas, Arkansas, Tennessee, Kentucky and Missouri, be and they are hereby invited to meet the people of the State of Alabama, by their delegates in Convention, on the 4th day of February next in Montgomery, in the State of Alabama, for the purpose of consultation with each other as to the most effectual mode of securing concerted, harmonious action in whatever measures may be deemed most desirable for the common peace and security.

And be it further resolved, That the President of this Convention be and is hereby instructed to transmit forthwith a copy of the foregoing preamble, ordinance and resolutions to the Governors of the several States named in the said resolutions.

Done by the people of Alabama, in Convention assembled, at Montgomery, this 11th day of January, 1861.

11. GEORGIA DECLARATION OF SECESSION, JANUARY 29, 1861

The people of Georgia having dissolved their political connection with the Government of the United States of America, present to their confederates and the world the causes which have led to the separation. For the last ten years we have had numerous and serious causes of complaint against our non-slave-holding confederate States with reference to the subject of African slavery. They have endeavored to weaken our security, to disturb our domestic peace and tranquility, and persistently refused to comply with their express constitutional obligations to us in reference to that property, and by the use of their power in the Federal Government have striven to deprive us of an equal enjoyment of the common Territories of the Republic. This hostile policy of our confederates has been pursued with every circumstance of aggravation which could arouse the passions and excite the hatred of our people, and has placed the two sections of the Union for many years past in the condition of virtual civil war. Our people, still attached to the Union from habit and national traditions, and averse to change, hoped that time, reason, and argument would bring, if not redress, at least exemption from further insults, injuries, and dangers. Recent events have fully dissipated all such hopes and demonstrated the necessity of separation. Our Northern confederates, after a full and calm hearing of all the facts, after a fair warning of our purpose not to submit to the rule of the authors of all these wrongs and injuries, have by a large majority committed the Government of the United States into their hands. The people of Georgia, after an equally full and fair and deliberate hearing of the case, have declared with equal firmness that they shall not rule over them. A brief history of the rise, progress, and policy of antislavery and the political organization into whose hands the administration of the Federal Government has been committed will fully justify the pronounced verdict of the people of Georgia. The party of Lincoln, called the Republican party, under its present name and organization, is of recent origin. It is admitted to be an antislavery party. While it attracts to itself by its creed the scattered advocates of exploded political heresies, of condemned theories in political economy, the advocates of commercial restrictions, of protection, of special privileges, of waste and corruption in the administration of Government, antislavery is its mission and its purpose. By antislavery it is made a power in the state. The question of slavery was the great difficulty in the way of the formation of the Constitution. While the subordination and the political and social inequality of the African race was fully conceded by all, it was plainly apparent that slavery would soon disappear from what are now the non-slave-holding States of the original thirteen. The opposition to slavery was then, as now, general in those States and the Constitution was made with direct reference to that fact. But a distinct abolition party was not formed in the United States for more than half a century after the Government went into operation. The main reason was that the North, even if united, could not control both branches of the Legislature during any portion of that time. Therefore such an organization must have resulted either in utter failure or in the total overthrow of the Government. The material prosperity of the North was greatly dependent on the Federal Government; that of the South not at all. In the first years of the Republic the navigating, commercial, and manufacturing interests of the North began to seek profit and aggrandizement at the expense of the agricultural interests. Even the owners of fishing smacks sought and obtained bounties for pursuing their own business (which yet continue), and $500,000 is now paid them annually out of the Treasury. The navigating interests begged for protection against foreign shipbuilders and against competition in the coasting trade. Congress granted both requests, and by prohibitory acts gave an absolute monopoly of this business to each of their interests, which they enjoy without diminution to this day. Not content with these great and unjust advantages, they have sought to throw the legitimate burden of their business as much as possible upon the public; they have succeeded in throwing the cost of light-houses, buoys, and the maintenance of their seamen upon the Treasury, and the Government now pays above $2,000,000 annually for the support of these objects. These interests, in connection with the commercial and manufacturing classes, have also succeeded, by means of subventions to mail steamers and the reduction in postage, in relieving their business from the payment of about $7,000,000 annually, throwing it upon the public Treasury under the name of postal deficiency. The manufacturing interests entered into the same struggle early, and has clamored steadily for Government bounties and special favors. This interest was confined mainly to the Eastern and Middle non-slave-holding States. Wielding these great States it held great power and influence, and its demands were in full proportion to its power. The manufacturers and miners wisely based their demands upon special facts and reasons rather than upon general principles, and thereby mollified much of the opposition of the opposing interest. They pleaded in their favor the infancy of their business in this country, the scarcity of labor and capital, the hostile legislation of other countries toward them, the great necessity of their fabrics in the time of war, and the necessity of high duties to pay the debt incurred in our war for independence. These reasons prevailed, and they received for many years enormous bounties by the general acquiescence of the whole country.

But when these reasons ceased they were no less clamorous for Government protection, but their clamors were less heeded—the country had put the principle of protection upon trial and condemned it. After having enjoyed protection to the extent of from 15 to 200 per cent upon their entire business for above thirty years, the act of 1846 was passed. It avoided sudden change, but the principle was settled, and free trade, low duties, and economy in public expenditures was the verdict of the American people. The South and the Northwestern States sustained this policy. There was but small hope of its reversal; upon the direct issue, none at all.

All these classes saw this and felt it and cast about for new allies. The antislavery sentiment of the North offered the best chance for success. An antislavery party must necessarily look to the North alone for support, but a united North was now strong enough to control the Government in all of its departments, and a sec-

tional party was therefore determined upon. Time and issues upon slavery were necessary to its completion and final triumph. The feeling of antislavery, which it was well known was very general among the people of the North, had been long dormant or passive; it needed only a question to arouse it into aggressive activity. This question was before us. We had acquired a large territory by successful war with Mexico; Congress had to govern it; how, in relation to slavery, was the question then demanding solution. This state of facts gave form and shape to the antislavery sentiment throughout the North and the conflict began. Northern antislavery men of all parties asserted the right to exclude slavery from the territory by Congressional legislation and demanded the prompt and efficient exercise of this power to that end. This insulting and unconstitutional demand was met with great moderation and firmness by the South. We had shed our blood and paid our money for its acquisition; we demanded a division of it on the line of the Missouri restriction or an equal participation in the whole of it. These propositions were refused, the agitation became general, and the public danger was great. The case of the South was impregnable. The price of the acquisition was the blood and treasure of both sections—of all, and, therefore, it belonged to all upon the principles of equity and justice.

The Constitution delegated no power to Congress to excluded either party from its free enjoyment; therefore our right was good under the Constitution. Our rights were further fortified by the practice of the Government from the beginning. Slavery was forbidden in the country northwest of the Ohio River by what is called the ordinance of 1787. That ordinance was adopted under the old confederation and by the assent of Virginia, who owned and ceded the country, and therefore this case must stand on its own special circumstances. The Government of the United States claimed territory by virtue of the treaty of 1783 with Great Britain, acquired territory by cession from Georgia and North Carolina, by treaty from France, and by treaty from Spain. These acquisitions largely exceeded the original limits of the Republic. In all of these acquisitions the policy of the Government was uniform. It opened them to the settlement of all the citizens of all the States of the Union. They emigrated thither with their property of every kind (including slaves). All were equally protected by public authority in their persons and property until the inhabitants became sufficiently numerous and otherwise capable of bearing the burdens and performing the duties of self-government, when they were admitted into the Union upon equal terms with the other States, with whatever republican constitution they might adopt for themselves.

Under this equally just and beneficent policy law and order, stability and progress, peace and prosperity marked every step of the progress of these new communities until they entered as great and prosperous commonwealths into the sisterhood of American States. In 1820 the North endeavored to overturn this wise and successful policy and demanded that the State of Missouri should not be admitted into the Union unless she first prohibited slavery within her limits by her constitution. After a bitter and protracted struggle the North was defeated in her special object, but her policy and position led to the adoption of a section in the law for the admission of Missouri, prohibiting slavery in all that portion of the territory acquired from France lying North of 36 [degrees] 30 [minutes] north latitude and outside of Missouri. The venerable Madison at the time of its adoption declared it unconstitutional. Mr. Jefferson condemned the restriction and foresaw its consequences and predicted that it would result in the dissolution of the Union. His prediction is now history. The North demanded the application of the principle of prohibition of slavery to all of the territory acquired from Mexico and all other parts of the public domain then and in all future time. It was the announcement of her purpose to appropriate to herself all the public domain then owned and thereafter to be acquired by the United States. The claim itself was less arrogant and insulting than the reason with which she supported it. That reason was her fixed purpose to limit, restrain, and finally abolish slavery in the States where it exists. The South with great unanimity declared her purpose to resist the principle of prohibition to the last extremity. This particular question, in connection with a series of questions affecting the same subject, was finally disposed of by the defeat of prohibitory legislation.

The Presidential election of 1852 resulted in the total overthrow of the advocates of restriction and their party friends. Immediately after this result the antislavery portion of the defeated party resolved to unite all the elements in the North opposed to slavery and to stake their future political fortunes upon their hostility to slavery everywhere. This is the party to whom the people of the North have committed the Government. They raised their standard in 1856 and were barely defeated. They entered the Presidential contest again in 1860 and succeeded.

The prohibition of slavery in the Territories, hostility to it everywhere, the equality of the black and white races, disregard of all constitutional guarantees in its favor, were boldly proclaimed by its leaders and applauded by its followers.

With these principles on their banners and these utterances on their lips the majority of the people of the North demand that we shall receive them as our rulers.

The prohibition of slavery in the Territories is the cardinal principle of this organization.

For forty years this question has been considered and debated in the halls of Congress, before the people, by the press, and before the tribunals of justice. The majority of the people of the North in 1860 decided it in their own favor. We refuse to submit to that judgment, and in vindication of our refusal we offer the Constitution of our country and point to the total absence of any express power to exclude us. We offer the practice of our Government for the first thirty years of its existence in complete refutation of the position that any such power is either necessary or proper to the execution of any other power in relation to the Territories. We offer the judgment of a large minority of the people of the North, amounting to more than one-third, who united with the unanimous voice of the South against this usurpation; and, finally, we offer the judgment of the Supreme Court of the United States, the highest judicial tribunal of our country, in our favor. This evidence ought to be conclusive that we have never surrendered this right. The conduct of our adversaries admonishes us that if we had surrendered it, it is time to resume it.

The faithless conduct of our adversaries is not confined to such acts as might aggrandize themselves or their section of the Union. They are content if they can only injure us. The Constitution declares that persons charged with crimes in one State and fleeing to another shall be delivered up on the demand of the executive authority of the State from which they may flee, to be tried in the jurisdiction where the crime was committed. It would appear difficult to employ language freer from ambiguity, yet for above twenty years the non-slave-holding States generally have wholly refused to deliver up to us persons charged with crimes affecting slave property. Our confederates, with punic faith, shield and give sanctuary to all criminals who seek to deprive us of this property or who use it to destroy us. This clause of the Constitution has no other sanction than their good faith; that is withheld from us; we are remediless in the Union; out of it we are remitted to the laws of nations.

A similar provision of the Constitution requires them to surrender fugitives from labor. This provision and the one last referred to were our main inducements for confederating with the Northern States. Without them it is historically true that we would have rejected the Constitution. In the fourth year of the Republic Congress passed a law to give full vigor and efficiency to this important provision. This act depended to a considerable degree upon the local magistrates in the several States for its efficiency. The non-slave-holding States generally repealed all laws intended to aid the execution of that act, and imposed penalties upon those citizens whose loyalty to the Constitution and their oaths might induce them to discharge their duty. Congress then passed the act of 1850, providing for the complete execution of this duty by Federal officers. This law, which their own bad faith rendered absolutely indispensible for the protection of constitutional rights, was instantly met with ferocious revilings and all conceivable modes of hostility. The Supreme Court unanimously, and their own local courts with equal unanimity (with the single and temporary exception of the supreme court of Wisconsin), sustained its constitutionality in all of its provisions. Yet it stands to-day a dead letter for all practicable purposes in every non-slave-holding State in the Union. We have their convenants, we have their oaths to keep and observe it, but the unfortunate claimant, even accompanied by a Federal officer with the mandate of the highest judicial authority in his hands, is everywhere met with fraud, with force, and with legislative enactments to elude, to resist, and defeat him. Claimants are murdered with impunity; officers of the law are beaten by frantic mobs instigated by inflammatory appeals from persons holding the highest public employment in these States, and supported by legislation in conflict with the clearest provisions of the Constitution, and even the ordinary principles of humanity. In several of our confederate States a citizen cannot travel the highway with his servant who may voluntarily accompany him, without being declared by law a felon and being subjected to infamous punishments. It is difficult to perceive how we could suffer more by the hostility than by the fraternity of such brethren.

The public law of civilized nations requires every State to restrain its citizens or subjects from committing acts injurious to the peace and security of any other State and from attempting to excite insurrection, or to lessen the security, or to disturb the tranquillity of their neighbors, and our Constitution wisely gives Congress the power to punish all offenses against the laws of nations.

These are sound and just principles which have received the approbation of just men in all countries and all centuries; but they are wholly disregarded by the people of the Northern States, and the Federal Government is impotent to maintain them. For twenty years past the abolitionists and their allies in the Northern States have been engaged in constant efforts to subvert our institutions and to excite insurrection and servile war among us. They have sent emissaries among us for the accomplishment of these purposes. Some of these efforts have received the public sanction of a majority of the leading men of the Republican party in the national councils, the same men who are now proposed as our rulers. These efforts have in one instance led to the actual invasion of one of the slave-holding States, and those of the murderers and incendiaries who escaped public justice by flight have found fraternal protection among our Northern confederates.

These are the same men who say the Union shall be preserved.

Such are the opinions and such are the practices of the Republican party, who have been called by their own votes to administer the Federal Government under the Constitution of the United States. We know their treachery; we know the shallow pretenses under which they daily disregard its plainest obligations. If we submit to them it will be our fault and not theirs. The people of Georgia have ever been willing to stand by this bargain, this contract; they have never sought to evade any of its obligations; they have never hitherto sought to establish any new government; they have struggled to maintain the ancient right of themselves and the human race through and by that Constitution. But they know the value of parchment rights in treacherous hands, and therefore they refuse to commit their own to the rulers whom the North offers us. Why? Because by their declared principles and policy they have outlawed $3,000,000,000 of our property in the common territories of the Union; put it under the ban of the Republic in the States where it exists and out of the protection of Federal law everywhere; because they give sanctuary to thieves and incendiaries who assail it to the whole extent of their power, in spite of their most solemn obligations and covenants; because their avowed purpose is to subvert our society and subject us not only to the loss of our property but the destruction of ourselves, our wives, and our children, and the desolation of our homes, our altars, and our firesides. To avoid these evils we resume the powers which our fathers delegated to the Government of the United States, and henceforth will seek new safeguards for our liberty, equality, security, and tranquillity.

12. JEFFERSON DAVIS'S FIRST INAUGURAL ADDRESS (PROVISIONAL PRESIDENT) FEBRUARY 18, 1861

GENTLEMEN OF THE CONGRESS OF THE CONFEDERATE STATES OF AMERICA, FRIENDS AND FELLOW-CITIZENS:

Called to the difficult and responsible station of Chief Executive of the Provisional Government which you have instituted, I approach the discharge of the duties assigned to me with an humble distrust of my abilities, but with a sustaining confidence in the wisdom of those who are to guide and to aid me in the administration of public affairs, and an abiding faith in the virtue and patriotism of the people.

Looking forward to the speedy establishment of a permanent government to take the place of this, and which by its greater moral and physical power will be better able to combat with the many difficulties which arise from the conflicting interests of separate nations, I enter upon the duties of the office to which I have been chosen with the hope that the beginning of our career as a Confederacy may not be obstructed by hostile opposition to our enjoyment of the separate existence and independence which we have asserted, and, with the blessing of Providence, intend to maintain. Our present condition, achieved in a manner unprecedented in the history of nations, illustrates the American idea that governments rest upon the consent of the governed, and that it is the right of the people to alter or abolish governments whenever they become destructive of the ends for which they were established.

The declared purpose of the compact of Union from which we have withdrawn was "to establish justice, insure domestic tranquillity, provide for the common defense, promote the general welfare, and secure the blessings of liberty to ourselves and our posterity;" and when, in the judgment of the sovereign States now composing this Confederacy, it had been perverted from the purposes for which it was ordained, and had ceased to answer the ends for which it was established, a peaceful appeal to the bal-lot-box declared that so far as they were concerned, the government created by that compact should cease to exist. In this they merely asserted a right which the Declaration of Independence of 1776 had defined to be inalienable; of the time and occasion for its exercise, they, as sovereigns, were the final judges, each for itself. The impartial and enlightened verdict of mankind will vindicate the rectitude of our conduct, and He who knows the hearts of men will judge of the sincerity with which we labored to preserve the Government of our fathers in its spirit. The right solemnly proclaimed at the birth of the States, and which has been affirmed and reaffirmed in the bills of rights of States subsequently admitted into the Union of 1789, undeniably recognize in the people the power to resume the authority delegated for the purposes of government. Thus the sovereign States here represented proceeded to form this Confederacy, and it is by abuse of language that their act has been denominated a revolution. They formed a new alliance, but within each State its government has remained, the rights of person and property have not been disturbed. The agent through whom they communicated with foreign nations is changed, but this does not necessarily interrupt their international relations.

Sustained by the consciousness that the transition from the former Union to the present Confederacy has not proceeded from a disregard on our part of just obligations, or any failure to perform every constitutional duty, moved by no interest or passion to invade the rights of others, anxious to cultivate peace and commerce with all nations, if we may not hope to avoid war, we may at least expect that posterity will acquit us of having needlessly engaged in it. Doubly justified by the absence of wrong on our part, and by wanton aggression on the part of others, there can be no cause to doubt that the courage and patriotism of the people of the Confederate States will be found equal to any measures of defense which honor and security may require.

An agricultural people, whose chief interest is the export of a commodity required in every manufacturing country, our true policy is peace, and the freest trade which our necessities will permit. It is alike our interest, and that of all those to whom we would sell and from whom we would buy, that there should be the fewest practicable restrictions upon the interchange of commodities. There can be but little rivalry between ours and any manufacturing or navigating community, such as the Northeastern States of the American

Union. It must follow, therefore, that a mutual interest would invite good will and kind offices. If, however, passion or the lust of dominion should cloud the judgment or inflame the ambition of those States, we must prepare to meet the emergency and to maintain, by the final arbitrament of the sword, the position which we have assumed among the nations of the earth. We have entered upon the career of independence, and it must be inflexibly pursued. Through many years of controversy with our late associates, the Northern States, we have vainly endeavored to secure tranquillity, and to obtain respect for the rights to which we were entitled. As a necessity, not a choice, we have resorted to the remedy of separation; and henceforth our energies must be directed to the conduct of our own affairs, and the perpetuity of the Confederacy which we have formed. If a just perception of mutual interest shall permit us peaceably to pursue our separate political career, my most earnest desire will have been fulfilled. But, if this be denied to us, and the integrity of our territory and jurisdiction be assailed, it will but remain for us, with firm resolve, to appeal to arms and invoke the blessings of Providence on a just cause.

As a consequence of our new condition and with a view to meet anticipated wants, it will be necessary to provide for the speedy and efficient organization of branches of the executive department, having special charge of foreign intercourse, finance, military affairs, and the postal service.

For purposes of defense, the Confederate States may, under ordinary circumstances, rely mainly upon their militia, but it is deemed advisable, in the present condition of affairs, that there should be a well-instructed and disciplined army, more numerous than would usually be required on a peace establishment. I also suggest that for the protection of our harbors and commerce on the high seas a navy adapted to those objects will be required. These necessities have doubtless engaged the attention of Congress.

With a Constitution differing only from that of our fathers in so far as it is explanatory of their well-known intent, freed from the sectional conflicts which have interfered with the pursuit of the general welfare it is not unreasonable to expect that States from which we have recently parted may seek to unite their fortunes with ours under the government which we have instituted. For this your Constitution makes adequate provision; but beyond this, if I mistake not the judgment and will of the people, a reunion with the States from which we have separated is neither practicable nor desirable. To

increase the power, develop the resources, and promote the happiness of a confederacy, it is requisite that there should be so much of homogeneity that the welfare of every portion shall be the aim of the whole. Where this does not exist, antagonisms are engendered which must and should result in separation.

Actuated solely by the desire to preserve our own rights and promote our own welfare, the separation of the Confederate States has been marked by no aggression upon others and followed by no domestic convulsion. Our industrial pursuits have received no check. The cultivation of our fields has progressed as heretofore, and even should we be involved in war there would be no considerable diminution in the production of the staples which have constituted our exports and in which the commercial world has an interest scarcely less than our own. This common interest of the producer and consumer can only be interrupted by an exterior force which should obstruct its transmission to foreign markets—a course of conduct which would be as unjust toward us as it would be detrimental to manufacturing and commercial interests abroad. Should reason guide the action of the Government from which we have separated, a policy so detrimental to the civilized world, the Northern States included, could not be dictated by even the strongest desire to inflict injury upon us; but otherwise a terrible responsibility will rest upon it, and the suffering of millions will bear testimony to the folly and wickedness of our aggressors. In the meantime there will remain to us, besides the ordinary means before suggested, the well-known resources for retaliation upon the commerce of an enemy.

Experience in public stations, of subordinate grade to this which your kindness has conferred, has taught me that care and toil and disappointment are the price of official elevation. You will see many errors to forgive, many deficiencies to tolerate, but you shall not find in me either a want of zeal or fidelity to the cause that is to me highest in hope and of most enduring affection. Your generosity has bestowed upon me an undeserved distinction, one which I neither sought nor desired. Upon the continuance of that sentiment and upon your wisdom and patriotism I rely to direct and support me in the performance of the duty required at my hands.

We have changed the constituent parts, but not the system of our Government. The Constitution formed by our fathers is that of these Confederate States, in their exposition of it, and in the judicial construction it has received, we have a light which reveals its true meaning.

Thus instructed as to the just interpretation of the instrument, and ever remembering that all offices are but trusts held for the people, and that delegated powers are to be strictly construed, I will hope, by due diligence in the performance of my duties, though I may disappoint your expectations, yet to retain, when retiring, something of the good will and confidence which welcome my entrance into office.

It is joyous, in the midst of perilous times, to look around upon a people united in heart, where one purpose of high resolve animates and actuates the whole—where the sacrifices to be made are not weighed in the balance against honor and right and liberty and equality. Obstacles may retard, they cannot long prevent the progress of a movement sanctified by its justice, and sustained by a virtuous people. Reverently let us invoke the God of our fathers to guide and protect us in our efforts to perpetuate the principles which, by his blessing, they were able to vindicate, establish and transmit to their posterity, and with a continuance of His favor, ever gratefully acknowledged, we may hopefully look forward to success, to peace, and to prosperity.

13. LINCOLN'S FIRST INAUGURAL ADDRESS, MARCH 4, 1861

Fellow-Citizens of the United States:

In compliance with a custom as old as the Government itself, I appear before you to address you briefly and to take in your presence the oath prescribed by the Constitution of the United States to be taken by the President "before he enters on the execution of this office."

I do not consider it necessary at present for me to discuss those matters of administration about which there is no special anxiety or excitement.

Apprehension seems to exist among the people of the Southern States that by the accession of a Republican Administration their property and their peace and personal security are to be endangered. There has never been any reasonable cause for such apprehension. Indeed, the most ample evidence to the contrary has all the while existed and been open to their inspection. It is found in nearly all the published speeches of him who now addresses you. I do but quote from one of those speeches when I declare that—I have no purpose, directly or indirectly, to interfere with the institution of slavery in the States where it exists. I believe I have no lawful right to do so, and I have no inclination to do so.

Those who nominated and elected me did so with full knowledge that I had made this and many similar declarations and had never recanted them; and more than this, they placed in the platform for my acceptance, and as a law to themselves and to me, the clear and emphatic resolution which I now read:

Resolved, That the maintenance inviolate of the rights of the States, and especially the right of each State to order and control its own domestic institutions according to its own judgment exclusively, is essential to that balance of power on which the perfection and endurance of our political fabric depend; and we denounce the lawless invasion by armed force of the soil of any State or Territory, no matter what pretext, as among the gravest of crimes.

I now reiterate these sentiments, and in doing so I only press upon the public attention the most conclusive evidence of which the case is susceptible that the property, peace, and security of no section are to be in any wise endangered by the now incoming Administration. I add, too, that all the protection which, consistently with the Constitution and the laws, can be given will be cheerfully given to all the States when lawfully demanded, for whatever cause—as cheerfully to one section as to another.

There is much controversy about the delivering up of fugitives from service or labor. The clause I now read is as plainly written in the Constitution as any other of its provisions:

"No person held to service or labor in one State, under the laws thereof, escaping into another, shall in consequence of any law or regulation therein be discharged from such service or labor, but shall be delivered up on claim of the party to whom such service or labor may be due."

It is scarcely questioned that this provision was intended by those who made it for the reclaiming of what we call fugitive slaves; and the intention of the lawgiver is the law. All members of Congress swear their support to the whole Constitution—to this provision as much as to any other. To the proposition, then, that slaves whose cases come within the terms of this clause "shall be delivered up" their oaths are unanimous. Now, if they would make the effort in good temper, could they not with nearly equal unanimity frame and pass a law by means of which to keep good that unanimous oath?

There is some difference of opinion whether this clause should be enforced by national or by State authority, but surely that difference is not a very material one. If the slave is to be surrendered, it can be of but little consequence to him or to others by which authority it is done. And should anyone in any case be content that his oath shall go unkept on a merely unsubstantial controversy as to how it shall be kept?

Again: In any law upon this subject ought not all the safeguards of liberty known in civilized and humane jurisprudence to be introduced, so that a free man be not in any case surrendered as a slave? And might it not be well at the same time to provide by law for the enforcement of that clause in the Constitution which guarantees that "the citizens of each State shall be entitled to all privileges and immunities of citizens in the several States"?

I take the official oath to-day with no mental reservations and with no purpose to construe the Constitution or laws by any hypercritical rules; and while I do not choose now to specify particular acts of Congress as proper to be enforced, I do suggest that it will be much safer for all, both in official and private stations, to conform to and abide by all those acts which stand unrepealed than to violate any of them trusting to find impunity in having them held to be unconstitutional.

It is seventy-two years since the first inauguration of a President under our National Constitution. During that period fifteen different and greatly distinguished citizens have in succession administered the executive branch of the Government. They have conducted it through many perils, and generally with great success. Yet, with all this scope of precedent, I now enter upon the same task for the brief constitutional term of four years under great and peculiar difficulty. A disruption of the Federal Union, heretofore only menaced, is now formidably attempted.

I hold that in contemplation of universal law and of the Constitution the Union of these States is perpetual. Perpetuity is implied, if not expressed, in the fundamental law of all national governments. It is safe to assert that no government proper ever had a provision in its organic law for its own termination. Continue to execute all the express provisions of our National Constitution, and the Union will endure forever, it being impossible to destroy it except by some action not provided for in the instrument itself.

Again: If the United States be not a government proper, but an association of States in the nature of contract merely, can it, as a contract, be peaceably unmade by less than all the parties who made it? One party to a contract may violate it—break it, so to speak—but does it not require all to lawfully rescind it?

Descending from these general principles, we find the proposition that in legal contemplation the Union is perpetual confirmed by the history of the Union itself. The Union is much older than the Constitution. It was formed, in fact, by the Articles of Association in 1774. It was matured and continued by the Declaration of Independence in 1776. It was further matured, and the faith of all the then thirteen States expressly plighted and engaged that it should be perpetual, by the Articles of Confederation in 1778. And finally, in 1787, one of the declared objects for ordaining and establishing the Constitution was "to form a more perfect Union."

But if destruction of the Union by one or by a part only of the States be lawfully possible, the Union is less perfect than before the Constitution, having lost the vital element of perpetuity.

It follows from these views that no State upon its own mere motion can lawfully get out of the Union; that resolves and ordinances to that effect are legally void, and that acts of violence within any State or States against the authority of the United States are insurrectionary or revolutionary, according to circumstances.

I therefore consider that in view of the Constitution and the laws the Union is unbroken, and to the extent of my ability, I shall take care, as the Constitution itself expressly enjoins upon me, that the laws of the Union be faithfully executed in all the States. Doing this I deem to be only a simple duty on my part, and I shall perform it so far as practicable unless my rightful masters, the American people, shall withhold the requisite means or in some authoritative manner direct the contrary. I trust this will not be regarded as a menace, but only as the declared purpose of the Union that it will constitutionally defend and maintain itself.

In doing this there needs to be no bloodshed or violence, and there shall be none unless it be forced upon the national authority. The power confided to me will be used to hold, occupy, and possess the property and places belonging to the Government and to collect the duties and imposts; but beyond what may be necessary for these objects, there will be no invasion, no using of force against or among the people anywhere. Where hostility to the United States in any interior locality shall be so great and universal as to prevent competent resident citizens from holding the Federal offices, there will be no attempt to force obnoxious strangers among the people for that object. While the strict legal right may exist in the Government to enforce the exercise of these offices, the attempt to do so would be so irritating and so nearly impracticable withal that I deem it better to forego for the time the uses of such offices.

The mails, unless repelled, will continue to be furnished in all parts of the Union. So far as possible the people everywhere shall have that sense of perfect security which is most favorable to calm thought and reflection. The course here indicated will be followed unless current events and experience shall show a modification or change to be proper, and in every case and exigency my best discretion will be exercised, according to circumstances actually existing and with a view and a hope of a peaceful solution of the national troubles and the restoration of fraternal sympathies and affections.

That there are persons in one section or another who seek to destroy the Union at all events and are glad of any pretext to do it I will neither affirm nor deny; but if there be such, I need address no word to them. To those, however, who really love the Union may I not speak?

Before entering upon so grave a matter as the destruction of our national fabric, with all its benefits, its memories, and its hopes, would it not be wise to ascertain precisely why we do it? Will you hazard so desperate a step while there is any possibility that any portion of the ills you fly from have no real existence? Will you, while the certain ills you fly to are greater than all the real ones you fly from, will you risk the commission of so fearful a mistake?

All profess to be content in the Union if all constitutional rights can be maintained. Is it true, then, that any right plainly written in the Constitution has been denied? I think not. Happily, the human mind is so constituted that no party can reach to the audacity of doing this. Think, if you can, of a single instance in which a plainly written provision of the Constitution has ever been denied. If by the mere force of numbers a majority should deprive a minority of any clearly written constitutional right, it might in a moral point of view justify revolution; certainly would if such right were a vital one. But such is not our case. All the vital rights of minorities and of individuals are so plainly assured to them by affirmations and negations, guaranties and prohibitions, in the Constitution that controversies never arise concerning them. But no organic law can ever be framed with a provision specifically applicable to every question which may occur in prac-

tical administration. No foresight can anticipate nor any document of reasonable length contain express provisions for all possible questions. Shall fugitives from labor be surrendered by national or by State authority? The Constitution does not expressly say. May Congress prohibit slavery in the Territories? The Constitution does not expressly say. Must Congress protect slavery in the Territories? The Constitution does not expressly say.

From questions of this class spring all our constitutional controversies, and we divide upon them into majorities and minorities. If the minority will not acquiesce, the majority must, or the Government must cease. There is no other alternative, for continuing the Government is acquiescence on one side or the other. If a minority in such case will secede rather than acquiesce, they make a precedent which in turn will divide and ruin them, for a minority of their own will secede from them whenever a majority refuses to be controlled by such minority. For instance, why may not any portion of a new confederacy a year or two hence arbitrarily secede again, precisely as portions of the present Union now claim to secede from it? All who cherish disunion sentiments are now being educated to the exact temper of doing this.

Is there such perfect identity of interests among the States to compose a new union as to produce harmony only and prevent renewed secession?

Plainly the central idea of secession is the essence of anarchy. A majority held in restraint by constitutional checks and limitations, and always changing easily with deliberate changes of popular opinions and sentiments, is the only true sovereign of a free people. Whoever rejects it does of necessity fly to anarchy or to despotism. Unanimity is impossible. The rule of a minority, as a permanent arrangement, is wholly inadmissible; so that, rejecting the majority principle, anarchy or despotism in some form is all that is left.

I do not forget the position assumed by some that constitutional questions are to be decided by the Supreme Court, nor do I deny that such decisions must be binding in any case upon the parties to a suit as to the object of that suit, while they are also entitled to very high respect and consideration in all parallel cases by all other departments of the Government. And while it is obviously possible that such decision may be erroneous in any given case, still the evil effect following it, being limited to that particular case, with the chance that it may be overruled and never become a precedent for other cases, can better be borne than could the evils of a different practice. At the same time, the candid citizen must confess that if the policy of the Government upon vital questions affecting the whole people is to be irrevocably fixed by decisions of the Supreme Court, the instant they are made in ordinary litigation between parties in personal actions the people will have ceased to be their own rulers, having to that extent practically resigned their Government into the hands of that eminent tribunal. Nor is there in this view any assault upon the court or the judges. It is a duty from which they may not shrink to decide cases properly brought before them, and it is no fault of theirs if others seek to turn their decisions to political purposes.

One section of our country believes slavery is right and ought to be extended, while the other believes it is wrong and ought not to be extended. This is the only substantial dispute. The fugitive-slave clause of the Constitution and the law for the suppression of the foreign slave trade are each as well enforced, perhaps, as any law can ever be in a community where the moral sense of the people imperfectly supports the law itself. The great body of the people abide by the dry legal obligation in both cases, and a few break over in each. This, I think, can not be perfectly cured, and it would be worse in both cases after the separation of the sections than before. The foreign slave trade, now imperfectly suppressed, would be ultimately revived without restriction in one section, while fugitive slaves, now only partially surrendered, would not be surrendered at all by the other.

Physically speaking, we can not separate. We can not remove our respective sections from each other nor build an impassable wall between them. A husband and wife may be divorced and go out of the presence and beyond the reach of each other, but the different parts of our country can not do this. They can not but remain face to face, and intercourse, either amicable or hostile, must continue between them. Is it possible, then, to make that intercourse more advantageous or more satisfactory after separation than before? Can aliens make treaties easier than friends can make laws? Can treaties be more faithfully enforced between aliens than laws can among friends? Suppose you go to war, you can not fight always; and when, after much loss on both sides and no gain on either, you cease fighting, the identical old questions, as to terms of intercourse, are again upon you.

This country, with its institutions, belongs to the people who inhabit it. Whenever they shall grow weary of the existing Government, they can exercise their constitutional right of amending it or their revolutionary right to dismember or overthrow it. I can not be ignorant of the fact that many worthy and patriotic citizens are desirous of having the National Constitution amended. While I make no recommendation of amendments, I fully recognize the rightful authority of the people over the whole subject, to be exercised in either of the modes prescribed in the instrument itself; and I should, under existing circumstances, favor rather than oppose a fair opportunity being afforded the people to act upon it. I will venture to add that to me the convention mode seems preferable, in that it allows amendments to originate with the people themselves, instead of only permitting them to take or reject propositions originated by others, not especially chosen for the purpose, and which might not be precisely such as they would wish to either accept or refuse. I understand a proposed amendment to the Constitution—which amendment, however, I have not seen—has passed Congress, to the effect that the Federal Government shall never interfere with the domestic institutions of the States, including that of persons held to service. To avoid misconstruction of what I have said, I depart from my purpose not to speak of particular amendments so far as to say that, holding such a provision to now be implied constitutional law, I have no objection to its being made express and irrevocable.

The Chief Magistrate derives all his authority from the people, and they have referred none upon him to fix terms for the separation of the States. The people themselves can do this if also they choose, but the Executive as such has nothing to do with it. His duty is to administer the present Government as it came to his hands and to transmit it unimpaired by him to his successor.

Why should there not be a patient confidence in the ultimate justice of the people? Is there any better or equal hope in the world? In our present differences, is either party without faith of being in the right? If the Almighty Ruler of Nations, with His eternal truth and justice, be on your side of the North, or on yours of the South, that truth and that justice will surely prevail by the judgment of this great tribunal of the American people.

By the frame of the Government under which we live this same people have wisely given their public servants but little power for mischief, and have with equal wisdom provided for the return of that little to their own hands at very short intervals. While the people retain their virtue and vigilance no Administration by any extreme of wickedness or folly can very seriously injure the Government in the short space of four years.

My countrymen, one and all, think calmly and well upon this whole subject. Nothing valuable can be lost by taking time. If there be an object to hurry any of you in hot haste to a step which you would never take deliberately, that object will be frustrated by taking time; but no good object can be frustrated by it. Such of you as are now dissatisfied still have the old Constitution unimpaired, and, on the sensitive point, the laws of your own framing under it; while the new Administration will have no immediate power, if it would, to change either. If it were admitted that you who are dissatisfied hold the right side in the dispute, there still is no single good reason for precipitate action. Intelligence, patriotism, Christianity, and a firm reliance on Him who has never yet forsaken this favored land are still competent to adjust in the best way all our present difficulty.

In your hands, my dissatisfied fellow-countrymen, and not in mine, is the momentous issue of civil war. The Government will not assail you. You can have no conflict without being yourselves the aggressors. You have no oath registered in heaven to destroy the Government, while I shall have the most solemn one to "preserve, protect, and defend it."

I am loath to close. We are not enemies, but friends. We must not be enemies. Though passion may have strained it must not break our bonds of affection. The mystic chords of memory, stretching from every battle-field and patriot grave to every living heart and hearth-stone all over this broad land, will yet swell the chorus of the Union, when again touched, as surely they will be, by the better angels of our nature.

14. CONFISCATION ACT OF 1861, AUGUST 6, 1861

An Act to confiscate Property used for Insurrectionary Purposes.

Be it enacted by the Senate and House of Representatives of the United States of America in Congress assembled, That if, during the present or any future insurrection against the Government of the United States, after the President of the United States shall have declared, by proclamation, that the laws of the United States are opposed, and the execution thereof obstructed, by combinations too powerful to be suppressed by the ordinary course of judicial proceedings, or by the power vested in the marshals by law, any person or persons, his, her, or their agent, attorney, or employee, shall purchase or acquire, sell or give, any property of whatsoever kind or description, with intent to use or employ the same, or suffer the same to be used or employed, in aiding, abetting, or promoting such insurrection or resistance to the laws, or any person or persons engaged therein; or if any person or persons, being the owner or owners of any such property, shall knowingly use or employ, or consent to the use or employment of the same as aforesaid, all such property is hereby declared to be lawful subject of prize and capture wherever found; and it shall be the duty of the President of the United States to cause the same to be seized, confiscated, and condemned.

SEC. 2. And be it further enacted, That such prizes and capture shall be condemned in the district or circuit court of the United States having jurisdiction of the amount, or in admiralty in any district in which the same may be seized, or into which they may be taken and proceedings first instituted.

SEC. 3. And be it further enacted, That the Attorney-General, or any district attorney of the United States in which said property may at the time be, may institute the proceedings of condemnation, and in such case they shall be wholly for the benefit of the United States; or any person may file an information with such attorney, in which case the proceedings shall be for the use of such informer and the United States in equal parts.

SEC. 4. And be it further enacted, That whenever hereafter, during the present insurrection against the Government of the United States, any person claimed to be held to labor or service under the law of any State, shall be required or permitted by the person to whom such labor or service is claimed to be due, or by the lawful agent of such person, to take up arms against the United States, or shall be required or permitted by the person to whom such labor or service is claimed to be due, or his lawful agent, to work or to be employed in or upon any fort, navy yard, dock, armory, ship, entrenchment, or in any military or naval service whatsoever, against the Government and lawful authority of the United States, then, and in every such case, the person to whom such labor or service is claimed to be due shall forfeit his claim to such labor, any law of the State or of the United States to the contrary notwithstanding. And whenever thereafter the person claiming such labor or service shall seek to enforce his claim, it shall be a full and sufficient answer to such claim that the person whose service or labor is claimed had been employed in hostile service against the Government of the United States, contrary to the provisions of this act.

15. Grant-Buckner Correspondence, February 16, 1862

HEADQUARTERS ARMY IN THE FIELD

Camp near Fort Donelson
February 16, 1862.

General S. B. BUCKNER,
Confederate Army.

SIR: Yours of this date, proposing armistice and appointment of commissioners to settle terms of capitulation, is just received. No terms except unconditional and immediate surrender can be accepted. I propose to move immediately upon your works.

I am, sir, very respectfully, your obedient servant,
U.S. GRANT,
Brigadier-General, Commanding.

HEADQUARTERS,
Dover, Tenn.
February 16, 1862.

Brig. Gen. U.S. GRANT,
U.S.A.

SIR: The distribution of the forces under my command incident to an unexpected change of commanders and the overwhelming force under your command compel me, notwithstanding the brilliant success of the Confederate arms yesterday, to accept the ungenerous and unchivalrous terms which you propose.

I am, sir, your very obedient servant,
S. B. BUCKNER,
Brigadier-General, C. S. Army.

16. Jefferson Davis's Second Inaugural Address, February 22, 1862

Fellow-Citizens: On this the birthday of the man most identified with the establishment of American independence, and beneath the monument erected to commemorate his heroic virtues and those of his compatriots, we have assembled to usher into existence the Permanent Government of the Confederate States. Through this instrumentality, under the favor of Divine Providence, we hope to perpetuate the principles of our revolutionary fathers. The day, the memory, and the purpose fitly associated.

It is with mingled feelings of humility and pride that I appear to take, in the presence of the people and before high Heaven, the oath prescribed as a qualification for the exalted station to which the unanimous voice of the people has called me. Deeply sensible of all that is implied by this manifestation of the people's confidence, I am yet more profoundly impressed by the vast responsibility of the office, and humbly feel my own unworthiness.

In return for their kindness I can offer assurances of the gratitude with which it is received; and can but pledge a zealous devotion of every faculty to the service of those who have chosen me as their Chief Magistrate.

When a long course of class legislation, directed not to the general welfare, but to the aggrandizement of the Northern section of the Union, culminated in a warfare on the domestic institutions of the Southern States—when the dogmas of a sectional party, substituted for the provisions of the constitutional compact, threatened to destroy the sovereign rights of the States, six of those States, withdrawing from the Union, confederated together to exercise the right and perform the duty of instituting a Government which would better secure the liberties for the preservation of which that Union was established.

Whatever of hope some may have entertained that a returning sense of justice would remove the danger with which our rights were threatened, and render it possible to preserve the Union of the Constitution, must have been dispelled by the malignity and barbarity of the Northern States in the prosecution of the existing war. The confidence of the most hopeful among us must have been destroyed by the disregard they have recently exhibited for the all time-honored bulwarks of civil and religious liberty. Bastiles filled with prisoners, arrested without civil process or indictment duly found; the writ of habeas corpus suspended by Executive mandate; a State Legislature controlled by the imprisonment of members whose avowed principles suggested to the Federal Executive that there might be another added to the list of seceded States; elections held under threats of a military power; civil officers, peaceful citizens, and gentlewomen incarcerated for opinion's sake—proclaimed the incapacity of our late associates to administer a Government as free, liberal, and human as that established for our common use.

For proof of the sincerity of our purpose to maintain our ancient institutions, we may point to the Constitution of the Confederacy and the laws enacted under it, as well as to the fact that through all the necessities of an unequal struggle there has been no act on our part to impair personal liberty or the freedom of speech, of thought, or of the press. The courts have been open, the judicial functions fully executed, and every right of the peaceful citizen maintained as securely as if a war of invasion had not disturbed the land.

The people of the States now confederated became convinced that the Government of the United States had fallen into the hands of a sectional majority, who would pervert that most sacred of all trusts to the destruction of the rights which it was pledged to protect. They believed that to remain longer in the Union would subject them to a continuance of a disparaging discrimination, submission to which would be inconsistent with their welfare, and intolerable to a proud people. They therefore determined to sever its bonds and establish a new Confederacy for themselves.

The experiment instituted by our revolutionary fathers, of a voluntary Union of sovereign States for the purposes specified in a solemn compact, and been perverted by those who, feeling power and forgetting right, were determined to respect no law but their own will. The Government had ceased to answer the ends for which it was ordained and established. To save ourselves from a revolution which, in its silent but rapid progress, was about to place us under the despotism of numbers, and to preserve in spirit, as well as in form, a system of government we believed to be peculiarly fitted to our condition, and full of promise for mankind, we determined to make a new association, composed of States homogenous in interest, in policy, and in feeling.

True to our traditions of peace and our love of justice, we sent commissioners to the United States to propose a fair and amicable settlement of all questions of public debt or property which might be in dispute. But the Government at Washington, denying our right to self-government, refused even to listen to any proposals for a peaceful separation. Nothing was then left to do but to prepare for war.

The first year in our history has been the most eventful in the annals of this continent. A new Government has been established, and its machinery put in operation over an area exceeding seven hundred thousand square miles. The great principles upon which we have been willing to hazard everything that is dear to man have made conquests for us which could never have been achieved by the sword. Our Confederacy has grown from six to thirteen States; and Maryland, already united to us by hallowed memories and material interests, will, I believe, when able to speak with unstifled voice, connect her destiny with the South. Our people have rallied with unexampled unanimity to the support of the great principles of constitutional government, with firm resolve to perpetuate by arms the right which they could not peacefully secure. A million of men, it is estimated, are now standing in hostile array, and waging war along a frontier of thousands of miles. Battles have been fought, sieges have been conducted, and, although the contest is not ended, and the tide for the moment is against us, the final result in our favor is not doubtful.

The period is near at hand when our foes must sink under the immense load of debt which they have incurred, a debt which in their effort to subjugate us has already attained such fearful dimensions as will subject them to burdens which must continue to oppress them for generations to come.

We too have had our trials and difficulties. That we are to escape them in the future is not to be hoped. It was to be expected when we entered upon this war that it would expose our people to sacrifices and cost them much, both of money and blood. But we knew the value of the object for which we struggle, and understood the nature of the war in which we were engaged. Nothing could be so bad as failure, and any sacrifice would be cheap as the price of success in such a contest.

But the picture has its lights as well as its shadows. This great strife has awakened in the people the highest emotions and qualities of the human soul. It is cultivating feelings of patriotism, virtue, and courage. Instances of self-sacrifice and of generous devotion to the noble cause for which we are contending are rife throughout the land. Never has a people evinced a more determined spirit than that now animating men, women, and children in every part of our country. Upon the first call the men flew to arms, and wives and mothers sent their husbands and sons to battle without a murmur of regret.

It was, perhaps, in the ordination of Providence that we were to be taught the value of our liberties by the price which we pay for them.

The recollections of this great contest, with all its common traditions of glory, of sacrifice and blood, will be the bond of harmony and enduring affection amongst the people, producing unity in policy, fraternity in sentiment, and just effort in war.

Nor have the material sacrifices of the past year been made without some corresponding benefits. If the acquiescence of foreign nations in a pretended blockade has deprived us of our commerce with them, it is fast making us a self-supporting and an independent people. The blockade, if effectual and permanent, could only serve to divert our industry from the production of articles for export and employ it in supplying commodities for domestic use.

It is a satisfaction that we have maintained the war by our unaided exertions. We have neither asked nor received assistance from any quarter. Yet the interest involved is not wholly our own. The world at large is concerned in opening our markets to its commerce. When the independence of the Confederate States is recognized by the nations of the earth, and we are free to follow our interests and inclinations by cultivating foreign trade, the Southern States will offer to manufacturing nations the most favorable markets which ever invited their commerce. Cotton, sugar, rice, tobacco, provisions, timber, and naval stores will furnish attractive exchanges. Nor would the constancy of these supplies be likely to be distributed by war. Our confederate strength will be too great to tempt aggression; and never was there a people whose interests and principles committed them so fully to a peaceful policy as those of the Confederate States. By the character of their productions they are too deeply interested in foreign commerce wantonly to disturb it. War of conquest they cannot wage, because the Constitution of their Confederacy admits of no coerced association. Civil war there cannot be between States held together by their volition only. The rule of voluntary association, which cannot fail to be conservative, by securing just and impartial government at home, does not diminish the security of the obligations by which the Confederate States may be bound to foreign nations. In proof of this, it is to be remembered that, at the first moment of asserting their right to secession, these States proposed a settlement on the basis of the common liability for the obligations of the General Government.

Fellow-citizens, after the struggle of ages had consecrated the right of the Englishman to constitutional representative government, our colonial ancestors were forced to vindicate that birthright by an appeal to arms. Success crowned their efforts, and they provided for their posterity a peaceful remedy against future aggression.

The tyranny of an unbridled majority, the most odious and least responsible form of despotism, has denied us both the right and the remedy. Therefore we are in arms to renew such sacrifices as our fathers made to the holy cause of constitutional liberty. At the darkest hour of our struggle the Provisional gives place to the Permanent Government. After a series of successes and victories, which covered our arms with glory, we have recently met with serious disasters. But in the heart of a people resolved to be free these disasters tend but to stimulate to increased resistance.

To show ourselves worthy of the inheritance bequeathed to us by the patriots of the Revolution, we must emulate that heroic devotion which made reverse to them but the crucible in which their patriotism was refined.

With confidence in the wisdom and virtue of those who will share with me the responsibility and aid me in the conduct of public affairs; securely relying on the patriotism and courage of the people, of which the present war has furnished so many examples, I deeply feel the weight of the responsibilities I now, with unaffected diffidence, am about to assume; and, fully realizing the inequality of human power to guide and to sustain, my hope is reverently fixed on Him whose favor is ever vouchsafed to the cause which is just. With humble gratitude and adoration, acknowledging the Providence which has so visibly protected the Confederacy during its brief but eventful career, to thee, O God, I trustingly commit myself, and prayerfully invoke thy blessing on my country and its cause.

17. McClellan to Lincoln, July 7, 1862
Head Quarters,
Army of the Potomac Camp
near Harrison's Landing, Va.
July 7th 1862

(Confidential)
Mr. President
You have been fully informed, that the Rebel army is in our front, with the purpose of overwhelming us by attacking our positions or reducing us by blocking our river communications. I can not but regard our condition as critical and I earnestly desire, in view of possible contingencies, to lay before your Excellency, for your private consideration, my general views concerning the state of the rebellion; although they do not strictly relate to the situation of this Army or strictly come within the scope of my official duties. These views amount to convictions and are deeply impressed upon my mind and heart.

Our cause must never be abandoned; it is the cause of free institutions and self government. The Constitution and the Union must be preserved, whatever may be the cost in time, treasure and blood. If secession is successful, other dissolutions are clearly to be seen in the future. Let neither military disaster, political faction or foreign war shake your settled purpose to enforce the equal operation of the laws of the United States upon the people of every state.

The time has come when the Government must determine upon a civil and military policy, covering the whole ground of our national trouble. The responsibility of determining, declaring and supporting such civil and military policy and of directing the whole course of national affairs in regard to the rebellion, must now be assumed and exercised by you or our cause will be lost. The Constitution gives you power sufficient even for the present terrible exigency.

This rebellion has assumed the character of a War: as such it should be regarded; and it should be conducted upon the highest principles known to Christian Civilization. It should not be a War looking to the subjugation of the people of any state, in any event. It should not be, at all, a War upon population; but against armed forces and political organizations. Neither confiscation of property, political executions of persons, territorial organization of states or forcible abolition of slavery should be contemplated for a moment. In prosecuting the War, all private property and unarmed persons should be strictly protected; subject only to the necessities of military operations. All private property taken for military use should be paid for or receipted for; pillage and waste should be treated as high crimes; all unnecessary trespass sternly prohibited; and offensive demeanor by the military towards citizens promptly rebuked. Military arrests should not be tolerated, except in places where active hostilities exist; and oaths not required by enactments—Constitutionally made—should be neither demanded nor received. Military government should be confined to the preservation of public order and the protection of political rights.

Military power should not be allowed to interfere with the relations of servitude, either by supporting or impairing the authority of the master; except for repressing disorder as in other cases. Slaves contraband under the Act of Congress, seeking military protection, should receive it. The right of the Government to appropriate permanently to its own service claims to slave labor should be asserted and the right of the owner to compensation therefore should be recognized. This principle might be extended upon grounds of military necessity and security to all the slaves within a particular state; thus working manumission in such state—and in Missouri, perhaps in Western Virginia also and possibly even in Maryland the expediency of such a military measure is only a question of time. A system of policy thus constitutional and conservative, and pervaded by the influences of Christianity and freedom, would receive the support of almost all truly loyal men, would deeply impress the rebel masses and all foreign nations, and it might be humbly hoped that it would commend itself to the favor of the Almighty. Unless the principles governing the further conduct of our struggle shall be made known and approved, the effort to obtain requisite forces will be almost hopeless. A declaration of radical views, especially upon slavery, will rapidly disintegrate our present Armies.

The policy of the Government must be supported by concentrations of military power. The national forces should not be dispersed in expeditions, posts of occupation and numerous Armies; but should be mainly collected into masses and brought to bear upon the Armies of the Confederate States; those Armies thoroughly defeated, the political structure which they support would soon cease to exist.

In carrying out any system of policy which you may form, you will require a Commander in Chief of the Army; one who possesses your confidence, understands your views and who is competent to execute your orders by directing the military forces of the Nation to the accomplishment of the objects by you proposed. I do not ask that place for myself. I am willing to serve you in such position as you may assign me and I will do so as faithfully as ever subordinate served superior.

I may be on the brink of eternity and as I hope forgiveness from my maker I have written this letter with sincerity towards you and from love of my country. Very respectfully your obdt svt

Geo B McClellan
Maj Genl Comdg

18. LINCOLN: APPEAL TO THE BORDER STATE REPRESENTATIVES TO FAVOR COMPENSATED EMANCIPATION, JULY 12, 1862

Gentlemen. After the adjournment of Congress, now very near, I shall have no opportunity of seeing you for several months. Believing that you of the border-states hold more power for good than any other equal number of members, I feel it a duty which I can not justifiably waive, to make this appeal to you. I intend no reproach or complaint when I assure you that in my opinion, if you all had voted for the resolution in the gradual emancipation message of last March, the war would now be substantially ended. And the plan therein proposed is yet one of the most potent, and swift means of ending it. Let the states which are in rebellion see, definitely and certainly, that, in no event, will the states you represent ever join their proposed Confederacy, and they can not, much longer maintain the contest. But you can not divest them of their hope to ultimately have you with them so long as you show a determination to perpetuate the institution within your own states. Beat them at elections, as you have overwhelmingly done, and, nothing daunted, they still claim you as their own. You and I know what the lever of their power is. Break that lever before their faces, and they can shake you no more forever.

Most of you have treated me with kindness and consideration; and I trust you will not now think I improperly touch what is exclusively your own, when, for the sake of the whole country I ask "Can you, for your states, do better than to take the course I urge?" Discarding punctillio, and maxims adapted to more manageable times, and looking only to the unprecedentedly stern facts of our case, can you do better in any possible event? You prefer that the constitutional relation of the states to the nation shall be practically restored, without disturbance of the institution; and if this were done, my whole duty, in this respect, under the constitution, and my oath of office, would be performed. But it is not done, and we are trying to accomplish it by war. The incidents of the war can not be avoided. If the war continue long, as it must, if the object be not sooner attained, the institution in your states will be extinguished by mere friction and abrasion—by the mere incidents of the war. It will be gone, and you will have nothing valuable in lieu of it. Much of its value is gone already. How much better for you, and for your people, to take the step which, at once, shortens the war, and secures substantial compensation for that which is sure to be wholly lost in any other event. How much better to thus save the money which else we sink forever in the war. How much better to do it while we can, lest the war ere long render us pecuniarily unable to do it. How much better for you, as seller, and the nation as buyer, to sell out, and buy out, that

without which the war could never have been, than to sink both the thing to be sold, and the price of it, in cutting one another's throats.

I do not speak of emancipation at once, but of a decision at once to emancipate gradually. Room in South America for colonization, can be obtained cheaply, and in abundance; and when numbers shall be large enough to be company and encouragement for one another, the freed people will not be so reluctant to go.

I am pressed with a difficulty not yet mentioned—one which threatens division among those who, united are none too strong. An instance of it is known to you. Gen. Hunter is an honest man. He was, and I hope, still is, my friend. I valued him none the less for his agreeing with me in the general wish that all men everywhere, could be free. He proclaimed all men free within certain states, and I repudiated the proclamation. He expected more good, and less harm from the measure, than I could believe would follow. Yet in repudiating it, I gave dissatisfaction, if not offence, to many whose support the country can not afford to lose. And this is not the end of it. The pressure, in this direction, is still upon me, and is increasing. By conceding what I now ask, you can relieve me, and much more, can relieve the country, in this important point. Upon these considerations I have again begged your attention to the message of March last. Before leaving the Capital, consider and discuss it among yourselves. You are patriots and statesmen; and, as such, I pray you, consider this proposition; and, at the least, commend it to the consideration of your states and people. As you would perpetuate popular government for the best people in the world, I beseech you that you do in no wise omit this. Our common country is in great peril, demanding the loftiest views, and boldest action to bring it speedy relief. Once relieved, its form of government is saved to the world; its beloved history, and cherished memories, are vindicated; and its happy future fully assured, and rendered inconceivably grand. To you, more than to any others, the privilege is given, to assure that happiness, and swell that grandeur, and to link your own names therewith forever.

19. Confiscation Act of 1862, July 17, 1862

An Act to suppress Insurrection, to punish Treason and Rebellion, to seize and confiscate the Property of Rebels, and for other Purposes.

Be it enacted by the Senate and House of Representatives of the United States of America in Congress assembled, That every person who shall hereafter commit the crime of treason against the United States, and shall be adjudged guilty thereof, shall suffer death, and all his slaves, if any, shall be declared and made free; or, at the discretion of the court, he shall be imprisoned for not less than five years and fined not less than ten thousand dollars, and all his slaves, if any, shall be declared and made free; said fine shall be levied and collected on any or all of the property, real and personal, excluding slaves, of which the said person so convicted was the owner at the time of committing the said crime, any sale or conveyance to the contrary notwithstanding.

SEC. 2. And be it further enacted, That if any person shall hereafter incite, set on foot, assist, or engage in any rebellion or insurrection against the authority of the United States, or the laws thereof, or shall give aid or comfort thereto, or shall engage in, or give aid and comfort to, any such existing rebellion or insurrection, and be convicted thereof, such person shall be punished by imprisonment for a period not exceeding ten years, or by a fine not exceeding ten thousand dollars, and by the liberation of all his slaves, if any he have; or by both of said punishments, at the discretion of the court.

SEC. 3. And be it further enacted, That every person guilty of either of the offences described in this act shall be forever incapable and disqualified to hold any office under the United States.

SEC. 4. And be it further enacted, That this act shall not be construed in any way to affect or alter the prosecution, conviction, or punishment of any person or persons guilty of treason against the United States before the passage of this act, unless such person is convicted under this act.

SEC. 5. And be it further enacted, That, to insure the speedy termination of the present rebellion, it shall be the duty of the President of the United States to cause the seizure of all the estate and property, money, stocks, credits, and effects of the persons hereinafter named in this section, and to apply and use the same and the proceeds thereof for the support of the army of the United States, that is to say:

First. Of any person hereafter acting as an officer of the army or navy of the rebels in arms against the government of the United States.

Secondly. Of any person hereafter acting as President, Vice-President, member of Congress, judge of any court, cabinet officer, foreign minister, commissioner or consul of the so-called confederate states of America.

Thirdly. Of any person acting as governor of a state, member of a convention or legislature, or judge of any court of any of the so-called confederate states of America.

Fourthly. Of any person who, having held an office of honor, trust, or profit in the United States, shall hereafter hold an office in the so-called confederate states of America.

Fifthly. Of any person hereafter holding any office or agency under the government of the so-called confederate states of America, or under any of the several states of the said confederacy, or the laws thereof, whether such office or agency be national, state, or municipal in its name or character: Provided, That the persons, thirdly, fourthly, and fifthly above described shall have accepted their appointment or election since the date of the pretended ordinance of secession of the state, or shall have taken an oath of allegiance to, or to support the constitution of the so-called confederate states.

Sixthly. Of any person who, owning property in any loyal State or Territory of the United States, or in the District of Columbia, shall here-after assist and give aid and comfort to such rebellion; and all sales, transfers, or conveyances of any such property shall be null and void; and it shall be a sufficient bar to any suit brought by such person for the possession or the use of such property, or any of it, to allege and prove that he is one of the persons described in this section.

SEC. 6. And be it further enacted, That if any person within any State or Territory of the United States, other than those named as afore-said, after the passage of this act, being engaged in armed rebellion against the government of the United States, or aiding or abetting such rebellion shall not, within sixty days after public warning and proclamation duly given and made by the President of the United States, cease to aid, countenance, and abet such rebellion, and return to his allegiance to the United States, all the estate and property, moneys, stocks, and credits of such person shall be liable to seizure as aforesaid, and it shall be the duty of the President to seize and use them as aforesaid or the proceeds thereof. And all sales, transfers, or conveyances, of any such property after the expiration of the said sixty days from the date of such warning and proclamation shall be null and void; and it shall be a sufficient bar to any suit brought by such person for the possession or the use of such property, or any of it, to allege and prove that he is one of the persons described in this section.

SEC. 7. And be it further enacted, That to secure the condemnation and sale of any of such property, after the same shall have been seized, so that it may be made available for the purpose aforesaid, proceedings in rem shall be instituted in the name of the United States in any district court thereof, or in any territorial court, or in the United States district court for the District of Columbia, within which the property above described, or any part thereof, may be found, or into which the same, if movable, may first be brought, which proceedings shall conform as nearly as may be to proceedings in admiralty or revenue cases, and if said property, whether real or personal, shall be found to have belonged to a person engaged in rebellion, or who has given aid or comfort thereto, the same shall be condemned as enemies' property and become the property of the United States, and may be disposed of as the court shall decree and the proceeds thereof paid into the treasury of the United States for the purposes aforesaid.

SEC. 8. And be it further enacted, That the several courts aforesaid shall have power to make such orders, establish such forms of decree and sale, and direct such deeds and conveyances to be executed and delivered by the marshals thereof where real estate shall be the subject of sale, as shall fitly and efficiently effect the purposes of this act, and vest in the purchasers of such property good and valid titles thereto. And the said courts shall have power to allow such fees and charges of their officers as shall be reasonable and proper in the premises.

SEC. 9. And be it further enacted, That all slaves of persons who shall hereafter be engaged in rebellion against the government of the United States, or who shall in any way give aid or comfort thereto, escaping from such persons and taking refuge within the lines of the army; and all slaves captured from such persons or deserted by them and coming under the control of the government of the United States; and all slaves of such persons found on [or] being within any place occupied by rebel forces and afterwards occupied by the forces of the United States, shall be deemed captives of war, and shall be forever free of their servitude, and not again held as slaves.

SEC. 10. And be it further enacted, That no slave escaping into any State, Territory, or the District of Columbia, from any other State, shall be delivered up, or in any way impeded or hindered of his liberty, except for crime, or some offence against the laws, unless the person claiming said fugitive shall first make oath that the person to whom the labor or service of such fugitive is alleged to be due is his lawful owner, and has not borne arms against the United States in the present rebellion, nor in any way given aid and comfort thereto; and no person engaged in the military or naval service of the United States shall, under any pretence whatever, assume to decide on the validity of the claim of any person to the service or labor of any other person, or surrender up any such person to the claimant, on pain of being dismissed from the service.

SEC. 11. And be it further enacted, That the President of the United States is authorized to employ as many persons of African descent as be may deem necessary and proper for the suppression of this rebellion, and for this purpose he may organize and use them in such manner as he may judge best for the public welfare.

SEC. 12. And be it further enacted, That the President of the United States is hereby authorized to make provision for the transportation, colonization, and settlement, in some tropical country beyond the limits of the United States, of such persons of the African race, made free by the provisions of this act, as may be willing to emigrate, having first obtained the consent of the government of said country to their protection and settlement within the same, with all the rights and privileges of freemen.

SEC. 13. And be it further enacted, That the President is hereby authorized, at any time hereafter, by proclamation, to extend to persons who may have participated in the existing rebellion in any State or part thereof, pardon and amnesty, with such exceptions and at such time and on such conditions as he may deem expedient for the public welfare.

SEC. 14. And be it further enacted, That the courts of the United States shall have full power to institute proceedings, make orders and decrees, issue process, and do all other things necessary to carry this act into effect.

20. LINCOLN TO HORACE GREELEY, AUGUST 22, 1862

Hon. Horace Greeley:

Dear Sir.

I have just read yours of the 19th. addressed to myself through the New-York Tribune. If there be in it any statements, or assumptions of fact, which I may know to be erroneous, I do not, now and here, controvert them. If there be in it any inferences which I may believe to be falsely drawn, I do not now and here, argue against them. If there be perceptable [sic] in it an impatient and dictatorial tone, I waive it in deference to an old friend, whose heart I have always supposed to be right.

As to the policy I "seem to be pursuing" as you say, I have not meant to leave any one in doubt.

I would save the Union. I would save it the shortest way under the Constitution. The sooner the national authority can be restored; the nearer the Union will be "the Union as it was." If there be those who would not save the Union, unless they could at the same time save slavery, I do not agree with them. If there be those who would not save the Union unless they could at the same time destroy slavery, I do not agree with them. My paramount object in this struggle is to save the Union, and is not either to save or to destroy slavery. If I could save the Union without freeing any slave I would do it, and if I could save it by freeing all the slaves I would do it; and if I could save it by freeing some and leaving others alone I would also do that. What I do about slavery, and the colored race, I do because I believe it helps to save the Union; and what I forbear, I forbear because I do not believe it would help to save the Union. I shall do less whenever I shall believe what I am doing hurts the cause, and I shall do more whenever I shall believe doing more will help the cause. I shall try to correct errors when shown to be errors; and I shall adopt new views so fast as they shall appear to be true views.

I have here stated my purpose according to my view of official duty; and I intend no modification of my oft-expressed personal wish that all men everywhere could be free.
Yours,
A. Lincoln.

21. ROBERT E. LEE TO JEFFERSON DAVIS, SEPTEMBER 3, 1862

Head Qurs Alex: & Leesburg Road near
Drainsville [Va.] 3d September 1862
Mr. President—

The present seems to be the most propitious time, since the commencement of the war, for the Confederate Army to enter Maryland. The two grand armies of the U.S. that have been operating in Virginia, though now united, are much weakened and demoralized. Their new levees, of which, I understand, sixty thousand men have already been posted in Washington, are not yet organized, and will take some time to prepare for the field. If it is ever desired to give material aid to Maryland, and afford her an opportunity of throwing off the oppression to which she is now subject, this would seem the most favorable. After the enemy had disappeared from the vicinity of Fairfax C. H. and taken the road to Alexandri[a] & Washington, I did not think it would be advantageous to follow him further. I had no intention of attacking him in his fortifications, and am not prepared to invest them. If I possessed the necessary munitions, I should be unable to supply provisions for the troops. I therefore determined while threatening the approaches to Washington to draw the troops into Loudon, where forage and some provisions can be obtained, menace their possession of the Shenandoah Valley, and if found practicable, to cross into Maryland.

The purpose, if discovered, will have the effect of carrying the enemy north of the Potomac, and if prevented, will not result in much evil. The army is not properly equipped for an invasion of an enemy's territory. It lacks much of the material of war, is feeble in transportation, the animals being much reduced, and the men poorly provided with clothes, and in thousands of instances, are destitute of shoes. Still we cannot afford to be idle, and though weaker than our opponents in men and military equipments, must endeavor to harass, if we cannot destroy them. I am aware that the movement is attended with much risk, yet I do not consider success impossible, and shall endeavor to guard it from loss. As long as the army of the enemy are employed on this frontier, I have no fears for the safety of Richmond, yet I earnestly recommend that advantage be taken of this period of comparative safety, to place its defence, both by land and water, in the most perfect condition. A respectable force can be collected to defend its approaches by land, and the steamer *Richmond* I hope is now ready to clear the river of hostile vessels. Should Genl Bragg find it impracticable to operate to advantage on his present frontier, his army, after leaving sufficient garrisons, could be advantageously employed in opposing the overwhelming numbers which it seems to be the intention of the enemy now to concentrate in Virginia. I have already been told [by] prisoners that some of [Don Carlos] Buell's Cavalry have been joined to Gen'l. [John] Pope's Army, and have reason to believe that the whole of [George B.] McClellan's, the larger portions of [Ambrose E.] Burnside's & [Jacob D.] Coxe's, and a portion of [David] Hunter's, are united to it, what occasions me most concern is the fear of getting out of ammunition. I beg you will instruct the Ordnance Dept: to spare no pains in manufacturing a sufficient amount of the best kind, & to be particular in preparing that for the Artillery, to provide three times as much of the long range ammunition, as of that for smooth bore or short range guns.

The points to which I desire the ammunition to be forwarded, will be made known to the Department in time. If the Qur. Master's Department can furnish any shoes, it would be the greatest relief.

We have entered upon September, and the nights are becoming cool. I have the honor to be with high respect Your Ob't Servant,

R. E. Lee. Gen'l.

22. ROBERT E. LEE'S SPECIAL FIELD ORDER 191, SEPTEMBER 9, 1862 (THE "LOST" ORDERS, FOUND BY UNION TROOPS)

HEADQUARTERS, ARMY OF NORTHERN VIRGINIA

September 9th, 1862

Special Orders, No. 191

III. The Army will resume its march to-morrow, taking the Hagerstown road. General Jackson's command will form the advance, and after passing Middletown, with such portions as he may select, take the route toward Sharpsburg, cross the Potomac at the most convenient point, and by Friday night take possession of the Baltimore and Ohio Railroad, capture such of the enemy as may be at Martinsburg, and intercept such as may attempt to escape from Harper's Ferry.

IV. General Longstreet's command will pursue the same road as far as Boonsboro', where it will halt with the reserve, supply, and baggage trains of the army.

V. General McLaws with his own division and that of General R. H. Anderson, will follow General Longstreet; on reaching Middletown he will take the route to Harper's Ferry, and by Friday morning possess himself of the Maryland Heights and endeavor to capture the enemy at Harper's Ferry and vicinity.

VI. General Walker, with his division after accomplishing the object in which he is now engaged, will cross the Potomac at Check's ford, ascend its right bank to Lovettsville, take possession of Loudoun Heights, if practicable, by Friday morning, Keyes's ford on his left, and the road between the end of the mountain and the Potomac on his right. He will, as far as practicable,

cooperate with General McLaws and General Jackson in intercepting the retreat of the enemy.

VII. General D. H. Hill's division will form the rear guard of the army, pursuing the road taken by the main body. The reserve artillery, ordnance, and supply trains, etc., will precede General Hill.

VIII. General Stuart will detach a squadron of cavalry to accompany the commands of Generals Longstreet, Jackson, and McLaws, and, with the main body of the cavalry, will cover the route of the army and bring up all stragglers that may have been left behind.

IX. The commands of Generals Jackson, McLaws, and Walker, after accomplishing the objects for which they have been detached, will join the main body of the army at Boonsboro' or Hagerstown.

X. Each regiment of the march will habitually carry its axes in the regimental ordinance-wagons, for use of the men at their encampments, to procure wood, etc.

By command of General R. E. Lee.

R. H. Chilton, Assistant Adjutant-General.

Major-General D. H. Hill, Command Division.

23. EMANCIPATION PROCLAMATION, JANUARY 1, 1863

By the President of the United States of America:

A Proclamation.

Whereas, on the twenty-second day of September, in the year of our Lord one thousand eight hundred and sixty-two, a proclamation was issued by the President of the United States, containing, among other things, the following, to wit:

"That on the first day of January, in the year of our Lord one thousand eight hundred and sixty-three, all persons held as slaves within any State or designated part of a State, the people whereof shall then be in rebellion against the United States, shall be then, thenceforward, and forever free; and the Executive Government of the United States, including the military and naval authority thereof, will recognize and maintain the freedom of such persons, and will do no act or acts to repress such persons, or any of them, in any efforts they may make for their actual freedom."

"That the Executive will, on the first day of January aforesaid, by proclamation, designate the States and parts of States, if any, in which the people thereof, respectively, shall then be in rebellion against the United States; and the fact that any State, or the people thereof, shall on that day be, in good faith, represented in the Congress of the United States by members chosen thereto at elections wherein a majority of the qualified voters of such State shall have participated, shall, in the absence of strong countervailing testimony, be deemed conclusive evidence that such State, and the people thereof, are not then in rebellion against the United States."

Now, therefore I, Abraham Lincoln, President of the United States, by virtue of the power in me vested as Commander-in-Chief, of the Army and Navy of the United States in time of actual armed rebellion against the authority and government of the United States, and as a fit and necessary war measure for suppressing said rebellion, do, on this first day of January, in the year of our Lord one thousand eight hundred and sixty-three, and in accordance with my purpose so to do publicly proclaimed for the full period of one hundred days, from the day first above mentioned, order and designate as the States and parts of States wherein the people thereof respectively, are this day in rebellion against the United States, the following, to wit:

Arkansas, Texas, Louisiana, (except the Parishes of St. Bernard, Plaquemines, Jefferson, St. John, St. Charles, St. James Ascension, Assumption, Terrebonne, Lafourche, St. Mary, St. Martin, and Orleans, including the City of New Orleans) Mississippi, Alabama, Florida, Georgia, South Carolina, North Carolina, and Virginia, (except the forty-eight counties designated as West Virginia, and also the counties of Berkley, Accomac, Northampton, Elizabeth City, York, Princess Ann, and Norfolk, including the cities of Norfolk and Portsmouth[)], and which excepted parts, are for the present, left precisely as if this proclamation were not issued.

And by virtue of the power, and for the purpose aforesaid, I do order and declare that all persons held as slaves within said designated States, and parts of States, are, and henceforward shall be free; and that the Executive government of the United States, including the military and naval authorities thereof, will recognize and maintain the freedom of said persons.

And I hereby enjoin upon the people so declared to be free to abstain from all violence, unless in necessary self-defence; and I recommend to them that, in all cases when allowed, they labor faithfully for reasonable wages.

And I further declare and make known, that such persons of suitable condition, will be received into the armed service of the United States to garrison forts, positions, stations, and other places, and to man vessels of all sorts in said service.

And upon this act, sincerely believed to be an act of justice, warranted by the Constitution, upon military necessity, I invoke the considerate judgment of mankind, and the gracious favor of Almighty God.

In witness whereof, I have hereunto set my hand and caused the seal of the United States to be affixed.

Done at the City of Washington, this first day of January, in the year of our Lord one thousand eight hundred and sixty three, and of the Independence of the United States of America the eighty-seventh.
By the President: ABRAHAM LINCOLN
WILLIAM H. SEWARD, Secretary of State.

24. LINCOLN TO GRANT, JULY 13, 1863

Executive Mansion,
Washington, July 13, 1863.
Major General Grant
My dear General:

I do not remember that you and I ever met personally. I write this now as a grateful acknowledgment for the almost inestimable service you have done the country. I wish to say a word further. When you first reached the vicinity of Vicksburg, I thought you should do, what you finally did—march the troops across the neck, run the batteries with the transports, and thus go below; and I never had any faith, except a general hope that you knew better than I, that the Yazoo Pass expedition, and the like, could succeed. When you got below, and took Port-Gibson, Grand Gulf, and vicinity, I thought you should go down the river and join Gen. Banks; and when you turned Northward East of the Big Black, I feared it was a mistake. I now wish to make the personal acknowledgment that you were right, and I was wrong.

Yours very truly
A. Lincoln

25. LEE TO DAVIS, JULY 31, 1863

Camp Culpeper [Virginia]
July 31, 1863
Mr. President

Your note of the 27 [sic] enclosing a slip from the Charleston *Mercury* relative to the battle of Gettysburg is received. I much regret its general censure upon the operations of the army, as it is calculated to do us no good either at home or abroad. But I am prepared for similar criticism & as far as I am concerned the remarks fall harmless. I am particularly sorry however that from partial information & mere assumption of facts that injustice should be done any officer, & that occasion should be taken to asperse your conduct, who of all others are most free of blame. I do not fear that your position in the confidence of the people, can be injured by such attacks, & I hope the official reports will protect the reputation of every officer. These cannot be made at once, & in the meantime as you state much falsehood may be promulgated. But truth is mighty & will eventually prevail. As regards the article in question I think it contains its own contradiction. Although charging Heth with the failure of the battle, it expressly states he was absent wounded. The object of the writer & publisher is evidently to cast discredit upon the operations of the Government & those connected with it & thus gratify feelings more to be pitied than to be envied. To take notice of such attacks would I think do more harm than good, & would be just what is desired. The delay that will necessarily occur in receiving official reports has induced me to make for the information of the Department a brief outline of operations of the army, in which however I have been unable to state the conduct of troops or officers. It is sufficient to show what was done & what was not done. No blame can be attached to the army for its failure to accomplish what was projected by me, nor should it be censured for the unreasonable expectations of the public. I am alone to blame, in perhaps expecting too much of its prowess & valour. It however in my opinion achieved under the guidance of the Most High a general success, though it did not win a victory. I thought at the time that the latter was practicable. I still think if all things could have worked together it would have been accomplished. But with the knowledge I then had, & in the circumstances I was then placed, I do not know what better course I could have pursued. With my present knowledge, & could I have foreseen that the attack on the last day would have failed to drive the enemy from his position, I should certainly have tried some other course. What the ultimate result would have been is not so clear to me. Our loss has been heavy, that of the enemy's proportionally so. His crippled condition enabled us to retire from the country comparatively unmolested. The unexpected state of the Potomac was our only embarrassment. I will not trespass upon Your Excellency's time more. With prayers for your health & happiness, & the recognition by your grateful country of your great services.

I remain truly & sincerely yours,
R. E. Lee

26. GETTYSBURG ADDRESS, NOVEMBER 19, 1863

Four score and seven years ago our fathers brought forth on this continent, a new nation, conceived in Liberty, and dedicated to the proposition that all men are created equal.

Now we are engaged in a great civil war, testing whether that nation, or any nation so conceived and so dedicated, can long endure. We are met on a great battle-field of that war. We have come to dedicate a portion of that field, as a final resting place for those who here gave their lives that that nation might live. It is altogether fitting and proper that we should do this.

But, in a larger sense, we can not dedicate—we can not consecrate—we can not hallow—this ground. The brave men, living and dead, who struggled here, have consecrated it, far above our poor power to add or detract. The world will little note, nor long remember what we say here, but it can never forget what they did here. It is for us the living, rather, to be dedicated here to the unfinished work which they who fought here have thus far so nobly advanced. It is rather for us to be here dedicated to the great task remaining before us—that from these honored dead we take increased devotion to that cause for which they gave the last full measure of devotion—that we here highly resolve that these dead shall not have died in vain—that this nation, under God, shall have a new birth of freedom—and that government of the people, by the people, for the people, shall not perish from the earth.

27. CLEBURNE MEMORIAL, JANUARY 2, 1864

Commanding General, The Corps, Division, Brigade and Regimental Commanders, of the Army of Tennessee.

General: Moved by the exigency in which our country is now placed, we take the liberty of laying before you, unofficially, our views of the present state of affairs. The subject is so grave, and our views so new, we feel it a duty both to you and the cause that before going further we should submit them for your judgment and receive your suggestions in regard to them. We therefore respectfully ask you to give us an expression of your views in the premises. We have now been fighting for nearly three years, have spilled much of our best blood, and lost, consumed or thrown to the flames an amount of property equal in value to the specie currency of the world. Through some lack in our system the fruits of our struggles and sacrifices have invariably slipped away from us and left us nothing but long lists of dead and mangled. Instead of standing defiantly in the borders of our territory or harassing those of the enemy, we are hemmed in today into less than two-thirds of it, and still the enemy menacingly confronts us at every point with superior forces. Our soldiers see no end to this state of affairs except in our own exhaustion; hence, instead of rising to the occasion, they are sinking into a fatal apathy, growing weary of hardships and slaughter which promises no results. In this state of things it is easy to understand why there is a growing belief that some black catastrophe is not far ahead of us, and that unless some extraordinary change is soon made in our condition we must overtake it. The consequences of this condition are showing themselves more plainly every day; restlessness of morals spreading everywhere, manifesting itself in the army in a growing disregard for private rights; desertion spreading to a class of soldiers it never dared to tamper with before; military commissions sinking in the estimation of the soldier; our supplies failing; our firesides in ruins. If this state continues much longer we must be subjugated. Every man ought to endeavor to understand the meaning of subjugation before it is too late. We can give but a faint idea when we say it means the loss of all we now hold most sacred—slaves and all other personal property, lands, homesteads, liberty, justice, safety, pride, manhood. It means that the history of this heroic struggle will be written by the enemy; that our youth will be taught by Northern school teachers; will learn from Northern school books their version of the war; will be impressed by all the influences of history and education to regard our gallant dead as traitors, or maimed veterans as fit objects for derision. It means the crushing of Southern manhood, the hatred of our former slaves, who will, on a spy system, be our secret police. The conqueror's policy is to divide the conquered into factions and stir up animosity among them, and in training an army of Negroes the North no doubt holds this thought in perspective. We can see three great causes operating to destroy us: First, the inferiority of our armies to those of the enemy in point of numbers; Second, the poverty of our single source of supply in comparison with his several sources; Third, the fact that slavery, from being one of our chief sources of strength at the commencement of the war, has now become, in a military view, one of our chief sources of weakness.

The enemy already opposes us at every point with superior numbers, and is endeavoring to make the preponderance irresistible. President Davis, in his recent message, says the enemy "has recently ordered a large conscription and made a subsequent call for volunteers, to be followed, if ineffectual, by a still further draft." In addition, the President of the United States announces that "he has already in training an army of 100,000 Negroes as good as any troops," and every fresh raid he makes and new slice of territory he wrests from us will add to this force. Every soldier in our army already knows and feels our numerical inferiority to the enemy. Want of men in the field has prevented him from reaping the fruits of his victories, and has prevented him from having the furlough he expected after the last reorganization; and when he turns from the wasting armies in the field to look at the source of supply, he finds nothing in the prospect to encourage him, our single source of supply is that portion of our white men fit for duty and not now in the ranks. The enemy has three chief sources of supply: First, his own motley population; Secondly, our slaves; and Thirdly, Europeans whose hearts are fired into a crusade against us by fictitious pictures of the atrocities of slavery, and who meet no hindrance from their governments in such enterprise, because these governments are equally antagonistic to the institution. In touching the third cause, the fact that slavery has become a military weakness, we may rouse prejudice and passion, but the time has come when it would be madness not to look at our danger from every point of view, and to probe it to the bottom. Apart from the assistance that home and foreign prejudice against slavery has given the North, slavery is a source of great strength to the enemy in a purely military point of view, by supplying him with an army from our granaries; but it is our most vulnerable point, a continued embarrassment, and in some respects an insidious weakness. Wherever slavery is disturbed, whether by actual presence of the approach of the enemy, or even by a cavalry raid, the whites can no longer with safety to their property openly sympathize with our cause. The fear of their slaves is continually haunting them, and from silence and apprehension many of these soon learn to wish the war stopped on any terms. The next stage is to take the oath to save the property, and they become dead to us, if not open to our enemies. To prevent raids we are forced to scatter our forces, and war not free to move and strike like the enemy; his vulnerable points are carefully selected and fortified depots. Ours are found in every point where there is a slave to set free. All along the lines slavery is comparatively valueless to us for labor, but of great and increasing worth to the enemy for information. It is an omnipresent spy system, pointing out our valuable men to the enemy, revealing our positions, purposes, and resources, and yet acting so safely and secretly that there is no means to guard against it. Even in the heart of our country, where our hold upon this secret espionage is firmest, it waits but the opening fire of the enemy's battle line to wake it, like a torpid serpent, into venomous activity.

In view of the state of affairs what does our country propose to do? In the words of President Davis, "no effort must be spared to add largely to our effective forces as promptly as possible. The sources of supply are to be found in restoring to the army all who are improperly absent, putting an end to substitution, modifying the exemption law, restricting details, and placing in the ranks such of the able-bodied men now employed as wagoners, nurses, cooks, and other employees, as are doing service for which the Negroes may be found competent." Most of the men improperly absent, together with many of the exempts and men having substitutes, are now without the Confederate lines and cannot be calculated on. If all the exempts capable of bearing arms were enrolled, it will give us the boys below eighteen, the men above forty-five, and those persons who are left at home to meet the wants of the country and the army; but this modification of the exemption law will remove from the fields and manufactories most of the skill that directs agriculture and mechanical labor, and, as stated by the President, "details will have to be made to meet the wants of the country," thus sending many of the men to be derived from this source back to their homes again. Independently of this, experience proves that striplings, and men above conscript age, break down and swell the sick lists more than they do the ranks. The portion now in our lines of the class who have substitutes is not on the whole a hopeful element, for the motives that created it must have been stronger than patriotism, and these motives, added to what many of them will call a breach of faith, will cause some to be not forthcoming, and others to be unwilling and discontented soldiers. The remaining sources mentioned by the President have been so closely pruned in the Army of Tennessee that they will be found not to yield largely. The supply from all these sources, together with what we now have in the field, will exhaust the white race, and though it should greatly exceed expectations and put us on an equality with the enemy, or even give us temporary advantages, still we have no reserve to meet unexpected disaster or to supply a protracted struggle.

Like past years, 1864 will diminish our ranks by the casualties of war, and what source of repairs is there left to us? We therefore see in the recommendation of the President only a temporary expedient, which at best will leave us twelve months hence in the same predicament we are in now. The President attempts to meet only one of the depressing causes mentioned; for the other two he has proposed no remedy. They remain to generate lack of confidence in our final success, and to keep us moving down hill as heretofore. Adequately to meet the causes which are now threatening ruin to our country, we propose, in addition to a modification of the President's that we retain for the service for the war all troops now in service, and that we immediately commence training a large reserve of the most courageous of our slaves, and further that we guarantee freedom within a reasonable amount of time to every slave in the South who shall remain true to the Confederacy in the war. As between the loss of independence and the loss of slavery, we assume that every patriot will freely give up the latter—give up the Negro slaves rather than be a slave himself. If we are correct in this assumption it only remains to show how this great national sacrifice is, in all human probabilities, to change the current of success and sweep the invaders from our country.

Our country has already some friends in England and France, and there are strong motives to induce these nations to recognize and assist us, but they cannot assist us without helping slavery, and to do this would be in conflict with their policy for the last quarter of a century. England has paid hundreds of millions to emancipate her West Indies slaves and break up the slave trade. Could she now consistently spend her treasure to reinstate slavery in this country? But this barrier once removed, the sympathy and the interests of these and other nations will accord with our own, and we may expect from them both moral support and financial aid. One thing is certain, as soon as the great sacrifice to independence is made and known in foreign countries there will be a complete change of front in our favor of the sympathies of the world. This measure will deprive the North of the moral and material aid which it now derives from the bitter prejudices with which foreigners view the institution, and its war, if continued, will henceforth be so despicable in their eyes that the source of recruiting will be dried up. It will leave the enemy's

Negro army no motive to fight for, and will exhaust the source from which it has been recruited. The idea that it is their special mission to war against slavery has held growing sway over Northern people for many years, and has at length ripened into an armed and bloody crusade against it. This baleful superstition has so far supplied them with a courage and constancy not their own. It is the most powerful and honestly entertained plank in their war platform. Knock this away and what is left? A bloody ambition for more territory, a pretended veneration for the Union, which one of their own most distinguished orators (Doctor Beecher in his Liverpool speech) openly avowed was only used as a stimulus to stir up the antislavery crusade, and lastly the poisonous and selfish interests which are the fungus growth of war itself. Mankind may fancy it a great duty to destroy slavery, but what interest can mankind have in upholding this remainder of the Northern War Platform? Their interests and feelings will be diametrically opposed to it. The measure we propose will strike dead all John Brown fanaticism, and will compel the enemy to draw off altogether, or in the eyes of the world to swallow the Declaration of Independence without the sauce and disguise of philanthropy. This delusion of fanaticism at an end, thousands of Northern people will have leisure to look at home and to see the gulf of despotism into which they themselves are rushing.

The measure will at one blow strip the enemy of foreign sympathy and assistance, and transfer them to the South; it will dry up two of his three sources of recruiting; it will take from his Negro army the only motive it could have to fight against the South, and will probably cause much of it to desert over to us; it will deprive his cause of the powerful stimulus of fanaticism, and will enable him to see the rock on which his so-called friends are now piloting him. The immediate effect of the emancipation and enrollment of Negroes on the military strength of the South would be: To enable us to have armies numerically superior to those of the North, and a reserve of any size we might think necessary; to take the offensive, move forward, and forage on the enemy. It would open to us in prospective another and almost untouched source of supply, and furnish us with the means of preventing temporary disaster, and carrying on a protracted struggle. It would instantly remove all the vulnerability, embarrassments, and inherent weakness which no longer find every household surrounded by spies; the fear that sealed the master's lips and the avarice that has, in many cases, tempted practically to desert us would alike

be removed. There would be no recruits awaiting the enemy with open arms, no complete history of every neighborhood with ready guides, no fear of insurrection in the rear, or anxieties for the fate of loved ones when our armies moved forward. The chronic irritation of hope deferred would be joyfully ended with the Negro, and the sympathies of his whole race would be due in his native South. It would restore confidence in an early termination of the war with all its inspiring consequences, and even if contrary to all expectations the enemy should succeed in overrunning the South, instead of finding a cheap ready-made means of holding it down, he would find a common hatred and thirst for vengeance, which would break into acts at every favorable opportunity, would prevent him from settling on our lands, and render the South a very unprofitable conquest. It would remove forever all selfish taint from our sauce and place independence above every question of property. The very magnitude of the sacrifice itself, such as no nation has ever voluntarily made before, would appall our enemies, destroy his spirit and finances, and fill our hearts with a pride and singleness of purpose which would clothe us with new strength in battle. Apart from all other aspects of the question, the necessity for more fighting men is upon us. We can only get a sufficiency by making the Negro share the danger and hardships of the war. If we arm and train him and make him fight for the country in her hour of dire distress, every consideration of principle and policy demand that we should set him and his whole race who side with us free.

It is a first principle with mankind that he who offers his life in defense of the State should receive from her in return his freedom and happiness, and we believe in the acknowledgment of this principle. The Constitution of the Southern States has reserved to their respective governments the power to free slaves for meritorious service to the State. It is politic besides. For many years, ever since the agitation of the subject of slavery commenced, the Negro has been dreaming of freedom, and his vivid imagination has surrounded that condition with so many gratifications that it has become the paradise of his hopes. To attain it he will tempt dangers and difficulties not exceeded by the bravest soldiers in the field. The hope of freedom is perhaps the only moral incentive that can be applied to him in his present condition. It would be preposterous then to expect him to fight against it with any degree of enthusiasm, therefore we must bind him to our cause by no doubtful bonds; we must leave no possible loophole for treachery to creep in. The slaves are dangerous now, but armed, trained, and collected in an army they would be a thousand fold more dangerous; therefore, when we make soldiers of them we make free men of them beyond all question, and thus enlist their sympathies also. We can do this more effectually than the North can now do, for we can give the Negro not only his own freedom, but that of his wife and child, and can secure it to him in his old home. To do this we must immediately make his marriage and parental relations sacred in the eyes of the law and forbid their sale. The past legislation of the South concedes that a large free middle class of Negro blood, between master and slave, must sooner or later destroy the institution. If, then, we touch the institutional all, we would do best to make the most of it, and by emancipating the whole race upon reasonable terms and within such reasonable time as will prepare both races for the change, secure to ourselves all the advantages, and to our enemies all the disadvantages that can arise, both at home and abroad, from such a sacrifice. Satisfy the Negro that if he faithfully adheres to our standard during the war he shall receive his freedom and that of his race. Give him as an earnest of our intentions such immediate immunities as will impress him with our sincerity and be in keeping with his new condition, enroll a portion of his class as soldiers of the Confederacy, and we change the race from a dreaded weakness to a position of strength.

Will the slaves fight? The helots of Sparta stood their master good stead in battle. In the great sea fight of Lepanto where the Christians checked forever the spread of Mohammedanism over Europe, the galley slaves of portions of the fleet were promised freedom, and called on to fight at a critical moment of the battle. They fought well, and civilization owes much to those brave galley slaves. The Negro slaves of Saint Domingo, fighting for freedom, defeated their white masters and the French troops sent against them. The Negro slaves of Jamaica revolted, and under the name of the Maroons held the mountains against their masters for 150 years, and the experience of this war has been so far that half-trained Negroes have fought as bravely as many other half-trained Yankees. If, contrary to the training of a lifetime, they can be made to face and fight bravely against their former masters, how much more probable is it that with the allurement of a higher reward, and led by those masters, they would submit to discipline and face dangers.

We will briefly notice a few arguments against this course. It is said republicanism cannot exist without the institution. Even were this true, we prefer any form of government of which Southern people may have the moulding, to one forced upon us by a conqueror. It is said the white man cannot perform agricultural labor in the South. The experience of this army during the heat of summer from Bowling Green, Kentucky to Tupelo, Mississippi, is that the white man is healthier when doing reasonable work in the open field than at any other time. It is said an army of Negroes cannot be spared from the fields. A sufficient number of slaves is now administering to luxury alone to supply the place of all we need, and we believe it would be better to half the able-bodied men off a plantation than to take the one master mind that economically regulates its operations. Leave some of the skill at home and take some of the muscle to fight with. It is said slaves will not work after they are freed. We think necessity and a wise legislation will compel them to labor for a living. It is said it will cause terrible excitement and some disaffection from our cause. Excitement is far preferable to the apathy which now exists, and disaffection will not be among the fighting men. It is said slavery is all we are fighting for, and if to give it up we give up all. Even if this were true, which we deny, slavery is not all our enemies are fighting for. It is merely the pretense to establish sectional superiority and a more centralized form of government, and to deprive us of our rights and liberties. We have now briefly proposed a plan which we believe will save our country. It may be imperfect, but in all human probability it would give us our independence. No objection ought to outweigh it which is not weightier than independence. If it is worthy of being put in practice it ought to be mooted quickly before the people and urged earnestly by every man who believes in its efficiency. Negroes will require much training; training will require time, and there is danger that this concession to common sense may come too late.

P. R. Cleburne, Major-General Commanding Division
[*et al.*—13 other officers]

28. JOHNSTON TO HARDEE ON THE CLEBURNE MEMORIAL, JANUARY 31, 1864

Dalton
January 31, 1864

Lieutenant General Hardee, Major-Generals Cheatham, Hindman, Cleburne, Stewart, Walker. Brigadier Generals Bate and P. Anderson.

General: I have received a letter from the Secretary of War in reference to Major-General Cleburne's memoir read in my quarter about the 2d instant. In this letter the honorable Secretary expresses the earnest conviction of the President "That the dissemination or even promulgation of such opinion under the present circumstances of the Confederacy, whither in the army or among the people, can be productive only of discouragement, distraction, and desertion." The agitation and controversy which must spring from the presentation of such views of officers high in the public confidence are to be deeply deprecated, and while no doubt or mistrust is for a moment entertained of the patriotic intents of the gallant author of the memorial, and such of his brother officers as may have favored his opinions, it is requested that you communicate to them, as well as all others present on the occasion, the opinions, as herein expressed, of the President, and urge on them the suppression, not only of the memorial itself, but likewise of all discussion and controversy respecting or growing out of it. I would add that the measures advocated in the memorial are considered to be little appropriate for consideration in military circles, and indeed in their scope pass beyond the bounds of Confederate action, and could under our Constitutional systems neither be recommended by the Executive to Congress nor be entertained by that body. Such views can only jeopard among the States and people unity and harmony, when for successful cooperation and the achievement of independence both are essential.

Most respectfully, your obedient servant,
J. E. Johnston, General.

P.S. Major-General Cleburne: Be so good as to communicate the views of the President, expressed above, to the officers of your division who signed the memorial. J. E. Johnston.

29. Wade Davis Bill [extracts] and Veto Message, July 18, 1864

A Bill to guarantee to certain States whose Governments have been usurped or overthrown a Republican Form of Government.

Be it enacted by the Senate and House of Representatives of the United States of America in Congress assembled, That in the states declared in rebellion against the United States, the President shall, by and with the advice and consent of the Senate, appoint for each a provisional governor, whose pay and emoluments shall not exceed that of a brigadier-general of volunteers, who shall be charged with the civil administration of such state until a state government therein shall be recognized as hereinafter provided.

SEC. 2. And be it further enacted, That so soon as the military resistance to the United States shall have been suppressed in any such state, and the people thereof shall have sufficiently returned to their obedience to the constitution and the laws of the United States, the provisional governor shall direct the marshal of the United States, as speedily as may be, to name a sufficient number of deputies, and to enroll all white male citizens of the United States, resident in the state in their respective counties, and to request each one to take the oath to support the constitution of the United States, and in his enrollment to designate those who take and those who refuse to take that oath, which rolls shall be forthwith returned to the provisional governor; and if the persons taking that oath shall amount to a majority of the persons enrolled in the state, he shall, by proclamation, invite the loyal people of the state to elect delegates to a convention charged to declare the will of the people of the state relative to the reestablishment of a state government subject to, and in conformity with, the constitution of the United States.

SEC. 3. And be it further enacted, That the convention shall consist of as many members as both houses of the last constitutional state legislature, apportioned by the provisional governor among the counties, parishes, or districts of the state, in proportion to the white population, returned as electors, by the marshal, in compliance with the provisions of this act. The provisional governor shall, by proclamation, declare the number of delegates to be elected by each county, parish, or election district; name a day of election not less than thirty days thereafter; designate the places of voting in each county, parish, or district, conforming as nearly as may be convenient to the places used in the state elections next preceding the rebellion; appoint one or more commissioners to hold the election at each place of voting, and provide an adequate force to keep the peace during the election.

. . . . .

SEC. 5. And be it further enacted, That the said commissioners, or either of them, shall hold the election in conformity with this act, and, so far as may be consistent therewith, shall proceed in the manner used in the state prior to the rebellion. The oath of allegiance shall be taken and subscribed on the poll-book by every voter in the form above prescribed, but every person known by or proved to, the commissioners to have held or exercised any office, civil or military, state or confederate, under the rebel usurpation, or to have voluntarily borne arms against the United States, shall be excluded, though he offer to take the oath; and in case any person who shall have borne arms against the United States shall offer to vote he shall be deemed to have borne arms voluntarily unless he shall prove the contrary by the testimony of a qualified voter. The poll-book, showing the name and oath of each voter, shall be returned to the provisional governor by the commissioners of election or the one acting, and the provisional governor shall canvass such returns, and declare the person having the highest number of votes elected.

SEC. 6. And be it further enacted, That the provisional governor shall, by proclamation, convene the delegates elected as aforesaid, at the capital of the state, on a day not more than three months after the election, giving at least thirty days' notice of such day. In case the said capital shall in his judgment be unfit, he shall in his proclamation appoint another place. He shall preside over the deliberations of the convention, and administer to each delegate, before taking his seat in the convention, the oath of allegiance to the United States in the form above prescribed.

SEC. 7. And be it further enacted, That the convention shall declare, on behalf of the people of the state, their submission to the constitution and laws of the United States, and shall adopt the following provisions, hereby prescribed by the United States in the execution of the constitutional duty to guarantee a republican form of government to every state, and incorporate them in the constitution of the state, that is to say:

First. No person who has held or exercised any office, civil or military, except offices merely ministerial, and military offices below the grade of colonel, state or confederate, under the usurping power, shall vote for or be a member of the legislature, or governor.

Second. Involuntary servitude is forever prohibited, and the freedom of all persons is guaranteed in said state.

Third. No debt, state or confederate, created by or under the sanction of the usurping power, shall be recognized or paid by the state.

. . . . .

SEC. 10. And be it further enacted, That, until the United States shall have recognized a republican form of state government, the provisional governor in each

of said states shall see that this act, and the laws of the United States, and the laws of the state in force when the state government was overthrown by the rebellion, are faithfully executed within the state; but no law or usage whereby any person was heretofore held in involuntary servitude shall be recognized or enforced by any court or officer in such state, and the laws for the trial and punishment of white persons shall extend to all persons, and jurors shall have the qualifications of voters under this law for delegates to the convention. The President shall appoint such officers provided for by the laws of the state when its government was overthrown as he may find necessary to the civil administration of the state, all which officers shall be entitled to receive the fees and emoluments provided by the state laws for such officers.

SEC. 11. And be it further enacted, That until the recognition of a state government as aforesaid, the provisional governor shall, under such regulations as he may prescribe, cause to be assessed, levied, and collected, for the year eighteen hundred and sixty-four, and every year thereafter, the taxes provided by the laws of such state to be levied during the fiscal year preceding the overthrow of the state government thereof, in the manner prescribed by the laws of the state, as nearly as may be; and the officers appointed, as aforesaid, are vested with all powers of levying and collecting such taxes, by distress or sale, as were vested in any officers or tribunal of the state government aforesaid for those purposes. The proceeds of such taxes shall be accounted for to the provisional governor, and be by him applied to the expenses of the administration of the laws in such state, subject to the direction of the President, and the surplus shall be deposited in the treasury of the United States to the credit of such state, to be paid to the state upon an appropriation therefor, to be made when a republican form of government shall be recognized therein by the United States.

SEC. 12. And be it further enacted, that all persons held to involuntary servitude or labor in the states aforesaid are hereby emancipated and discharged therefrom, and they and their posterity shall be forever free. And if any such persons or their posterity shall be restrained of liberty, under pretence of any claim to such service or labor, the courts of the United States shall, on habeas corpus, discharge them.

SEC. 13. And be it further enacted, That if any person declared free by this act, or any law of the United States, or any proclamation of the President, be restrained of liberty, with intent to be held in or reduced to involuntary servitude or labor, the person convicted before a court of competent jurisdiction of such act shall be punished by fine of not less than fifteen hundred dollars, and be imprisoned not less than five nor more than twenty years.

SEC. 14. And be it further enacted, That every person who shall hereafter hold or exercise any office, civil or military, except offices merely ministerial, and military offices below the grade of colonel, in the rebel service, state or confederate, is hereby declared not to be a citizen of the United States.

BY THE PRESIDENT OF THE UNITED STATES:

A PROCLAMATION:

WHEREAS, at the late session, congress passed a bill to "guarantee to certain states, whose governments have been usurped or overthrown, a republican form of government," a copy of which is hereunto annexed;

And whereas the said bill was presented to the President of the United States for his approval less than one hour before the sine die adjournment of said session, and was not signed by him;

And whereas the said bill contains, among other things, a plan for restoring the states in rebellion to their proper practical relation in the Union, which plan expresses the sense of congress upon that subject, and which plan it is now thought fit to lay before the people for their consideration;

Now, therefore, I, ABRAHAM LINCOLN, President of the United States, do proclaim, declare, and make known, that, while I am (as I was in December last, when by proclamation I propounded a plan for restoration) unprepared by a formal approval of this bill, to be inflexibly committed to any single plan of restoration; and, while I am also unprepared to declare that the free state constitutions and governments already adopted and installed in Arkansas and Louisiana shall be set aside and held for nought, thereby repelling and discouraging the loyal citizens who have set up the same as to further effort, or to declare a constitutional competency in congress to abolish slavery in states, but am at the same time sincerely hoping and expecting that a constitutional amendment abolishing slavery throughout the nation may be adopted, nevertheless I am truly satisfied with the system for restoration contained in the bill as one very proper plan for the loyal people of any state choosing to adopt it, and that I am, and at all times shall be, prepared to give the executive aid and assistance to any such people, so soon as the military resistance to the United States shall have been suppressed in any such state, and the people thereof shall have sufficiently returned to their obedience to the constitution and the laws of the United States, in which cases military governors will be appointed, with directions to proceed according to the bill.

In testimony whereof; I have hereunto set my hand, and caused the seal of the United States to be affixed. Done at the city of Washington this eighth day of July, in the year of our [L S.] Lord one thousand eight hundred and sixty-four, and of the Independence of the United States the eighty-ninth.

ABRAHAM LINCOLN.

By the President:

WILLIAM H. SEWARD, Secretary of State.

30. SHERMAN TO MAYOR JAMES CALHOUN, SEPTEMBER 12, 1864

HEADQUARTERS MILITARY DIVISION of the MISSISSIPPI in the FIELD

Atlanta, Georgia,

James M. Calhoun, Mayor,

E. E. Rawson and S. C. Wells, representing City Council of Atlanta.

Gentleman: I have your letter of the 11th, in the nature of a petition to revoke my orders removing all the inhabitants from Atlanta. I have read it carefully, and give full credit to your statements of distress that will be occasioned, and yet shall not revoke my orders, because they were not designed to meet the humanities of the cause, but to prepare for the future struggles in which millions of good people outside of Atlanta have a deep interest. We must have peace, not only at Atlanta, but in all America. To secure this, we must stop the war that now desolates our once happy and favored country. To stop war, we must defeat the rebel armies which are arrayed against the laws and Constitution that all must respect and obey. To defeat those armies, we must prepare the way to reach them in their recesses, provided with the arms and instruments which enable us to accomplish our purpose. Now, I know the vindictive nature of our enemy, that we may have many years of military operations from this quarter; and, therefore, deem it wise and prudent to prepare in time. The use of Atlanta for warlike purposes is inconsistent with its character as a home for families. There will be no manufacturers, commerce, or agriculture here, for the maintenance of families, and sooner or later want will compel the inhabitants to go. Why not go now, when all the arrangements are completed for the transfer, instead of waiting till the plunging shot of contending armies will renew the scenes of the past month? Of course, I do not apprehend any such things at this moment, but you do not suppose this army will be here until the war is over. I cannot discuss this subject with you fairly, because I cannot impart to you what we propose to do, but I assert that our military plans make it necessary for the inhabitants to go away, and I can only renew my offer of services to make their exodus in any direction as easy and comfortable as possible.

You cannot qualify war in harsher terms than I will. War is cruelty, and you cannot refine it; and those who brought war into our country deserve all the curses and maledictions a people can pour out. I know I had no hand in making this war, and I know I will make more sacrifices to-day than any of you to secure peace. But you cannot have peace and a division of our country. If the United States submits to a division now, it will not stop, but will go on until we reap the fate of Mexico, which is eternal war. The United States does and must assert its authority, wherever it once had power; for, if it relaxes one bit to pressure, it is gone, and I believe that such is the national feeling. This feeling assumes various shapes, but always comes back to that of Union. Once admit the Union, once more acknowledge the authority of the national Government, and, instead of devoting your houses and streets and roads to the dread uses of war, I and this army become at once your protectors and supporters, shielding you from danger, let it come from what quarter it may. I know that a few individuals cannot resist a torrent of error and passion, such as swept the South into rebellion, but you can point out, so that we may know those who desire a government, and those who insist on war and its desolation.

You might as well appeal against the thunder-storm as against these terrible hardships of war. They are inevitable, and the only way the people of Atlanta can hope once more to live in peace and quiet at home, is to stop the war, which can only be done by admitting that it began in error and is perpetuated in pride.

We don't want your Negroes, or your horses, or your lands, or any thing you have, but we do want and will have a just obedience to the laws of the United States. That we will have, and if it involved the destruction of your improvements, we cannot help it.

You have heretofore read public sentiment in your newspapers, that live by falsehood and excitement; and the quicker you seek for truth in other quarters, the better. I repeat then that, but the original compact of government, the United States had certain rights in Georgia, which have never been relinquished and never will be; that the South began the war by seizing forts, arsenals, mints, custom-houses, etc., etc., long before Mr. Lincoln was installed, and before the South had one jot or tittle of provocation. I myself have seen in Missouri, Kentucky, Tennessee, and Mississippi, hundreds and thousands of women and children fleeing from your armies and desperadoes, hungry and with bleeding feet. In Memphis, Vicksburg, and Mississippi, we fed thousands and thousands of the families of rebel soldiers left on our hands, and whom we could not see starve. Now that war comes to you, you feel very different. You deprecate its horrors, but did not feel them when you sent car-loads of soldiers and ammunition, and moulded shells and shot, to carry war into Kentucky and Tennessee, to desolate the homes of hundreds and thousands of good people who only asked to live in peace at their old homes, and under the Government of their inheritance. But these comparisons are idle. I want peace, and believe it can only be reached through union and war, and I will ever conduct war with a view to perfect an early success.

But, my dear sirs, when peace does come, you may call on me for any thing. Then will I share with you the last cracker, and watch with you to shield your homes and families against danger from every quarter.

Now you must go, and take with you the old and feeble, feed and nurse them, and build for them, in more quiet places, proper habitations to shield them against the weather until the mad passions of men cool down, and allow the Union and peace once more to settle over your old homes in Atlanta. Yours in haste, W. T. Sherman, Major-General commanding

31. SHERMAN ORDER re MARCH TO THE SEA, NOVEMBER 9, 1864 [EXTRACTS]

Headquarters Military Division of the Mississippi
In the Field, Kingston, Georgia
November 9, 1864

1. For the purpose of military operations, this army is divided into two wings viz:
The right wing, Major-General O. O. Howard commanding, composed of the Fifteenth and Seventeenth Corps; the left wing, Major-General H. W. Slocum commanding, composed of the Fourteenth and Twentieth Corps.
2. The habitual order of march will be, wherever practicable, by four roads, as nearly parallel as possible,

and converging at points hereafter to be indicated in orders. The cavalry, Brigadier-General Kilpatrick commanding, will receive special orders from the commander in chief.

3. There will be no general train of supplies, but each corps will have its ammunition—train and provision-train, distributed habitually as follows . . .

4. The army will forage liberally on the country during the march. To this end, each brigade commander will organize a good and sufficient foraging party, under the command of one or more discreet officers, who will gather, near the route traveled, corn or forage of any kind, meat of any kind, vegetables, corn-meal, or whatever is needed by the command, aiming at all times to keep in the wagons at least ten days' provisions for his command, and three days' forage. Soldiers must not enter the dwellings of the inhabitants, or commit any trespass; but during a halt or camp, they may be permitted to gather turnips, potatoes, and other vegetables, and to drive in stock in sight of their camp. To regular foraging-parties must be intrusted the gathering of provisions and forage, at any distance from the road traveled.

5. To corps commanders alone is entrusted the power to destroy mills, houses, cotton-gins, etc.; and for them the general principle is laid down: In districts and neighborhoods where the army is unmolested, no destruction of such property should be permitted; but should guerrillas or bush-whackers molest our march, or should the inhabitants burn bridges, obstruct roads, or otherwise manifest local hostility, then army commanders should order and enforce a devastation more or less relentless, according to the measure of such hostility.

6. As for horses, mules, wagons, etc., belonging to the inhabitants, the cavalry and artillery may appropriate freely and without limit; discriminating, however, between the rich, who are usually hostile, and the poor and industrious, usually neutral or friendly. Foraging-parties may also take mules or horses, to replace the jaded animals of their trains, or to serve as pack-mules for the regiments or brigades. In all foraging, of whatever kind, the parties engaged will refrain from abusive or threatening language, and may, where the officer in command thinks proper, give written certificates of the facts, but no receipts; and they will endeavor to leave with each family a reasonable portion for their maintenance,

7. Negroes who are able-bodied and can be of service to the several columns may be taken along; but each

army commander will bear in mind that the question of supplies is a very important one, and that his first duty is to see to those who bear arms. . . .

By order of Major-General W. T. Sherman, L. M. Dayton, *Aide-de-Camp.*

32. Sherman to Halleck, December 24, 1864 [extract]

Headquarters Military Division of the Mississippi, In the Field, Savannah, December 24, 1864
Major-General H. W. Halleck,
Chief-of-Staff,
Washington, D.C.
General:

I had the pleasure of receiving your two letters of the 16th and 18th instant to-day, and feel more than usually flattered by the encomiums you have passed on our recent campaign, which is now complete by the occupation of Savannah. . . .

I attach more importance to these deep incisions into the enemy's country, because this war differs from European wars in this particular: we are not only fighting hostile armies, but a hostile people, and must make old and young, rich and poor, feel the hard hand of war, as well as their organized armies. I know that this recent movement of mine through Georgia has had a wonderful effect in this respect. Thousands who had been deceived by their lying newspapers to believe that we were being whipped all the time now realize the truth, and have no appetite for a repetition of the same experience. To be sure, Jeff. Davis has his people under pretty good discipline, but I think faith in him is much shaken in Georgia, and before we have done with her South Carolina will not be quite so tempestuous.

I will bear in mind your hint as to Charleston, and do not think "salt" will be necessary. When I move, the Fifteenth Corps will be on the right of the right wing, and their position will naturally bring them into Charleston first; and, if you have watched the history of that corps, you will have remarked that they generally do their work pretty well. The truth is, the whole army is burning with an insatiable desire to wreak vengeance upon South Carolina. I almost tremble at her fate, but feel that she deserves all that seems in store for her.

Many and many a person in Georgia asked me why we did not go to South Carolina; and, when I answered that we were en route for that State, the invariable reply was, "Well, if you will make those people feel the utmost severities of war, we will pardon you for your desolation of Georgia."

I look upon Columbia as quite as bad as Charleston, and I doubt if we will spare the public buildings there as we did at Milledgeville. . . .

33. SHERMAN'S SPECIAL FIELD ORDER NO. 15, JANUARY 16, 1865
Headquarters Military Division of the Mississippi,
In the Field, Savannah, Georgia, January 16, 1865

1. The islands from Charleston south, the abandoned rice-fields along the rivers for thirty miles back from the sea, and the country bordering the St. John's River, Florida, are reserved and set apart for the settlement of the negroes now made free by the acts of war and the proclamation of the President of the United States.

2. At Beaufort, Hilton Head, Savannah, Fernandina, St. Augustine, and Jacksonville, the blacks may remain in their chosen or accustomed vocations; but on the islands, and in the settlements hereafter to be established, no white person whatever, unless military officers and soldiers detailed for duty, will be permitted to reside; and the sole and exclusive management of affairs will be left to the freed people themselves, subject only to the United States military authority, and the acts of Congress. By the laws of war, and orders of the President of the United States, the negro is free, and must be dealt with as such. He cannot be subjected to conscription, or forced military service, save by the written orders of the highest military authority of the department, under such regulations as the President or Congress may prescribe. Domestic servants, blacksmiths, carpenters, and other mechanics, will be free to select their own work and residence, but the young and ablebodied negroes must be encouraged to enlist as soldiers in the service of the United States, to contribute their share toward maintaining their own freedom, and securing their rights as citizens of the United States.

Negroes so enlisted will be organized into companies, battalions, and regiments, under the orders of the United States military authorities, and will be paid, fed, and clothed, according to law. The bounties paid on enlistment may, with the consent of the recruit, go to assist his family and settlement in procuring agricultural implements, seed, tools, boots, clothing, and other articles necessary for their livelihood.

3. Whenever three respectable negroes, heads of families, shall desire to settle on land, and shall have selected for that purpose an island or a locality clearly defined within the limits above designated, the Inspector of Settlements and Plantations will himself, or by such subordinate officer as he may appoint, give them a license to settle such island or district and afford them such assistance as he can to enable them to establish a peaceable agricultural settlement. The three parties named will subdivide the land, under the supervision of the inspector, among themselves, and such others as may choose to settle near them, so that each family shall have a plot of not more than forty acres of tillable ground, and, when it borders on some water-channel, with not more than eight hundred feet water-front, in the possession of which land the military authorities will afford them protection until such time as they can protect themselves, or until Congress shall regulate their title. The quartermaster may, on the requisition of the Inspector of Settlements and Plantations, place at the disposal of the inspector one or more of the captured steamers to ply between the settlements and one or more of the commercial points heretofore named, in order to afford the settlers the opportunity to supply their necessary wants, and to sell the products of their land and labor.

4. Whenever a negro has enlisted in the military service of the United States, he may locate his family in any one of the settlements at pleasure, and acquire a homestead, and all other rights and privileges of a settler, as though present in person. In like manner, negroes may settle their families and engage on board the gunboats, or in fishing, or in the navigation of the inland waters, without losing any claim to land or other advantages derived from this system. But no one, unless an actual settler as above defined, or unless absent on Government service, will be entitled to claim any right to land or property in any settlement by virtue of these orders.

5. In order to carry out this system of settlement, a general officer will be detailed as Inspector of Settlements and plantations whose duty it shall be to visit the settlements, to regulate their police and general arrangement, and who will furnish

personally to each head of a family, subject to the approval of the President of the United States, a possessory title in writing, giving as near as possible the description of boundaries; and who shall adjust all claims or conflicts that may arise under the same, subject to the like approval, treating such titles altogether as possessory. The same general officer will also be charged with the enlistment and organization of the negro recruits, and protecting their interests while absent from their settlements; and will be governed by the rules and regulations prescribed by the War Department for such purposes.

6. Brigadier-General R. Saxton is hereby appointed Inspector of Settlements and Plantations, and will at once enter on the performance of his duties. No change is intended or desired in the settlement now on Beaufort Island, nor will any rights to property heretofore acquired be affected thereby.

By order of Major-General W. T. Sherman,
L. M. Dayton, Assistant Adjutant-General.

34. Lincoln's Second Inaugural Address, March 4, 1865

Fellow-Countrymen:

At this second appearing to take the oath of the Presidential office there is less occasion for an extended address than there was at the first. Then a statement somewhat in detail of a course to be pursued seemed fitting and proper. Now, at the expiration of four years, during which public declarations have been constantly called forth on every point and phase of the great contest which still absorbs the attention and engrosses the energies of the nation, little that is new could be presented. The progress of our arms, upon which all else chiefly depends, is as well known to the public as to myself, and it is, I trust, reasonably satisfactory and encouraging to all. With high hope for the future, no prediction in regard to it is ventured.

On the occasion corresponding to this four years ago all thoughts were anxiously directed to an impending civil war. All dreaded it, all sought to avert it. While the inaugural address was being delivered from this place, devoted altogether to saving the Union without war, urgent agents were in the city seeking to destroy it without war—seeking to dissolve the Union and divide effects by negotiation. Both parties deprecated

war, but one of them would make war rather than let the nation survive, and the other would accept war rather than let it perish, and the war came.

One-eighth of the whole population were colored slaves, not distributed generally over the Union, but localized in the southern part of it. These slaves constituted a peculiar and powerful interest. All knew that this interest was somehow the cause of the war. To strengthen, perpetuate, and extend this interest was the object for which the insurgents would rend the Union even by war, while the Government claimed no right to do more than to restrict the territorial enlargement of it. Neither party expected for the war the magnitude or the duration which it has already attained. Neither anticipated that the cause of the conflict might cease with or even before the conflict itself should cease. Each looked for an easier triumph, and a result less fundamental and astounding. Both read the same Bible and pray to the same God, and each invokes His aid against the other. It may seem strange that any men should dare to ask a just God's assistance in wringing their bread from the sweat of other men's faces, but let us judge not, that we be not judged. The prayers of both could not be answered. That of neither has been answered fully. The Almighty has His own purposes. "Woe unto the world because of offenses; for it must needs be that offenses come, but woe to that man by whom the offense cometh." If we shall suppose that American slavery is one of those offenses which, in the providence of God, must needs come, but which, having continued through His appointed time, He now wills to remove, and that He gives to both North and South this terrible war as the woe due to those by whom the offense came, shall we discern therein any departure from those divine attributes which the believers in a living God always ascribe to Him? Fondly do we hope, fervently do we pray, that this mighty scourge of war may speedily pass away. Yet, if God wills that it continue until all the wealth piled by the bondsman's two hundred and fifty years of unrequited toil shall be sunk, and until every drop of blood drawn with the lash shall be paid by another drawn with the sword, as was said three thousand years ago, so still it must be said "the judgments of the Lord are true and righteous altogether."

With malice toward none, with charity for all, with firmness in the right as God gives us to see the right, let us strive on to finish the work we are in, to bind up the nation's wounds, to care for him who shall have borne the battle and for his widow and his orphan, to do all which may achieve and cherish a just and lasting peace among ourselves and with all nations.

35. LEE'S FAREWELL STATEMENT, APRIL 10, 1865

After four years of arduous service marked by unsurpassed courage and fortitude, the Army of Northern Virginia has been compelled to yield to overwhelming numbers and resources.

I need not tell the brave survivors of so many hard fought battles who have remained steadfast to the last that I have consented to this result from no distrust of them.

But feeling that valor and devotion could accomplish nothing that could compensate for the loss that must have attended the continuance of the contest, I determined to avoid the useless sacrifice of those whose past services have endeared them to their countrymen.

By the terms of the agreement, officers and men can return to their homes and remain until exchanged. You will take with you the satisfaction that proceeds from a consciousness of duty faithfully performed; and I earnestly pray that a Merciful God will extend to you His blessings and protection.

With an unceasing admiration of your constancy and devotion to your Country, and a grateful remembrance of your kind and generous consideration for myself, I bid you all an affectionate farewell.

R. E. Lee
Genl.

36. LEE TO DAVIS, APRIL 20, 1865

Mr. President

The apprehensions I expressed during the winter, of the moral condition of the Army of Northern Virginia, have been realized. The operations which occurred while the troops were in the entrenchments in front of Richmond and Petersburg were not marked by the boldness and decision which formerly characterized them. Except in particular instances, they were feeble; and a want of confidence seemed to possess officers and men. This condition, I think, was produced by the state of feeling in the country, and the communications received by the men from their homes, urging their return and the abandonment of the field. The movement of the enemy on the 30th March to Dinwiddie Court House was consequently not as strongly met as similar ones had been. Advantages were gained

by him which discouraged the troops, so that on the morning of the 2d April, when our lines between the Appomattox and Hatcher's Run were assaulted, the resistance was not effectual: several points were penetrated and large captures made. At the commencement of the withdrawal of the army from the lines on the night of the 2d, it began to disintegrate, and straggling from the ranks increased up to the surrender on the 9th. On that day, as previously reported, there were only seven thousand eight hundred and ninety-two (7892) effective infantry. During the night, when the surrender became known, more than ten thousand men came in, as reported to me by the Chief Commissary of the Army. During the succeeding days stragglers continued to give themselves up, so that on the 12th April, according to the rolls of those paroled, twenty-six thousand and eighteen (26,018) officers and men had surrendered. Men who had left the ranks on the march, and crossed James River, returned and gave themselves up, and many have since come to Richmond and surrendered. I have given these details that Your Excellency might know the state of feeling which existed in the army, and judge of that in the country. From what I have seen and learned, I believe an army cannot be organized or supported in Virginia, and as far as I know the condition of affairs, the country east of the Mississippi is morally and physically unable to maintain the contest unaided with any hope of ultimate success. A partisan war may be continued, and hostilities protracted, causing individual suffering and the devastation of the country, but I see no prospect by that means of achieving a separate independence. It is for Your Excellency to decide, should you agree with me in opinion, what is proper to be done. To save useless effusion of blood, I would recommend measures be taken for suspension of hostilities and the restoration of peace.

I am with great respect, yr obdt svt

R. E. Lee
Genl

37. THIRTEENTH AMENDMENT TO THE U.S. CONSTITUTION, DECEMBER 6, 1865

Section 1. Neither slavery nor involuntary servitude, except as a punishment for crime whereof the party shall have been duly convicted, shall exist within the United States, or any place subject to their jurisdiction.

Section 2. Congress shall have power to enforce this article by appropriate legislation.

38. FOURTEENTH AMENDMENT TO THE U.S. CONSTITUTION, JULY 9, 1868

Section 1. All persons born or naturalized in the United States, and subject to the jurisdiction thereof, are citizens of the United States and of the State wherein they reside. No State shall make or enforce any law which shall abridge the privileges or immunities of citizens of the United States; nor shall any State deprive any person of life, liberty, or property, without due process of law; nor deny to any person within its jurisdiction the equal protection of the laws.

Section 2. Representatives shall be apportioned among the several States according to their respective numbers, counting the whole number of persons in each State, excluding Indians not taxed. But when the right to vote at any election for the choice of electors for President and Vice President of the United States, Representatives in Congress, the Executive and Judicial officers of a State, or the members of the Legislature thereof, is denied to any of the male inhabitants of such State, being twenty-one years of age (See Note 15) and citizens of the United States, or in any way abridged, except for participation in rebellion, or other crime, the basis of representation therein shall be reduced in the proportion which the number of such male citizens shall bear to the whole number of male citizens twenty-one years of age in such State.

Section 3. No person shall be a Senator or Representative in Congress, or elector of President and Vice President, or hold any office, civil or military, under the United States, or under any State, who, having previously taken an oath, as a member of Congress, or as an officer of the United States, or as a member of any State legislature, or as an executive or judicial officer of any State, to support the Constitution of the United States, shall have engaged in insurrection or rebellion against the same, or given aid or comfort to the enemies thereof. But Congress may by a vote of two-thirds of each House, remove such disability.

Section 4. The validity of the public debt of the United States, authorized by law, including debts incurred for payment of pensions and bounties for services in suppressing insurrection or rebellion, shall not be questioned. But neither the United States nor any State shall assume or pay any debt or obligation incurred in aid of insurrection or rebellion against the United States, or any claim for the loss or emancipation of any slave; but all such debts, obligations and claims shall be held illegal and void.

Section 5. The Congress shall have power to enforce, by appropriate legislation, the provisions of this article.

39. FIFTEENTH AMENDMENT TO THE U.S. CONSTITUTION, FEBRUARY 3, 1870

Section 1. The right of citizens of the United States to vote shall not be denied or abridged by the United States or by any State on account of race, color, or previous condition of servitude.

Section 2. The Congress shall have power to enforce this article by appropriate legislation.

APPENDIX B
Biographies of Major Personalities

Barton, Clarissa Harlowe (Clara Barton)
(1821–1912) *U.S. nurse in the Civil War, founder of American Red Cross*

Clara Barton was born in Oxford, Massachusetts, in a middle-class family. Her father was a local politician and instilled in his children a sense of patriotism and service. The youngest of five children, Clarissa was virtually raised and educated by her older brothers. At age 11, she helped nurse one of her brothers back to health. She was quite precocious, although painfully shy. As a teenager, she began teaching, apparently out of a commitment to overcome her shyness. She studied at the Liberal Institute in Clinton, New York, and then, as a young teacher, she moved to Bordentown, New Jersey, to work in a subscription (or private) school. She also founded a free public school there, one of the first in the state, but she was soon displaced by a male principal. She then moved to Washington, D.C., where she took a position as a clerk in the Patent Office, demanding and receiving equal pay for equal work.

In 1861, when the 6th Massachusetts Regiment arrived in Washington, she set up a relief and aid program for the soldiers. Learning of the condition of men wounded at the Battle of Bull Run, or First Manassas, she placed an advertisement in a newspaper in Worcester, Massachusetts, asking for donations of medical supplies. She set up a small organization to distribute the materials to surgeons in the field. In 1862, as her work received notice, the surgeon general of the U.S. Army, William A. Hammond, gave her a pass to travel to the battlefields with army ambulances. Over the next three years, she worked with soldiers in the Virginia, Maryland, and South Carolina areas, attracting national attention. In particular, she drew recognition for her work at Antietam, at Fredericksburg, and at Bermuda Hundred, directing wagon loads of medical supplies to the front and providing direct nursing care to the wounded and sick. General Benjamin Butler appointed her superintendent of nurses in his command.

Barton also began a system of correspondence to track missing soldiers and prisoners of war held in Southern prison camps. At the end of the war, her health broken, she was advised to take a vacation in Europe.

During her extended stay, she learned of nursing programs there, and, during the Franco-Prussian War, she observed the operations of the newly-formed International Red Cross, which had been established in 1864. Since the organization was founded on an international agreement that would recognize Red Cross workers as noncombatants during international wars, and since the United States did not visualize participating in any international conflicts, the American government did not join in the international agreement at first. Nevertheless, Barton returned to the United States, organized a National Society of the Red Cross (the American Red Cross) in 1881, and began lobbying for official American participation in the international convention.

She convinced the government to recognize the American Red Cross to respond to natural catastrophes in the early 1880s. The organization provided aid during floods of the Mississippi and Ohio Rivers in 1882 and 1884. The Red Cross also worked to relieve conditions during the Texas famine of 1886, a yellow fever epidemic in Florida in 1887, an Illinois earthquake in 1888, and during the 1889 Johnstown, Pennsylvania, flood. Other countries recognized the need for such disaster assistance and, in 1884, the International Red Cross in Geneva passed the American Amendment to reflect the principle of disaster relief. The American Red Cross had its first wartime experience during the 1898 Spanish-American War. American aid during Barton's administration was sent to victims of the Boer War and of a flood in Galveston, Texas, in 1900.

Although she was the first president of the American Red Cross, from 1883 to 1903, she was a poor administrator, and she was forced to resign. She was active in women's rights and suffrage groups during the last years of her life. Never married, she remained committed to reform and to expanding medical services through nursing.

Beauregard, Pierre Gustave Toutant (1818–1893) *Confederate general*

Pierre Gustave Toutant Beauregard was born in Louisiana and was appointed to West Point, where he graduated in 1838. At West Point he earned the nickname, the Little Napoleon, no doubt because of his Creole background, dapper appearance, and refined manner. As an artillery officer and later as an engineer, he saw service in the Mexican War under General Winfield Scott. He participated in the sieges of Vera Cruz, Cerro Gordo, Contreras, Chapultepec, and Mexico City. He was wounded twice in the battles at Mexico City on September 13 and 14, 1847.

After the U.S.-Mexican War, he served as an engineer, working in the coast defenses along the Gulf Coast. In 1853, he was appointed captain of engineers, and, in 1861, he was briefly appointed superintendent at West Point. However, he promptly resigned that position and his U.S. Army commission and accepted a position with the Confederate army. As a brigadier general, he was sent to Charleston, where he ordered the firing on Fort Sumter. In one of the many ironies of the war, Fort Sumter was then under the command of Major Robert Anderson, a former friend and former West Point instructor of Beauregard.

After the war started, Beauregard served as second in command to J. E. Johnston at the first Battle of Manassas, or Bull Run (July 16, 1861). After being promoted to full general he succeeded to the command of the Army of Tennessee upon the death of A. S. Johnston at the Battle of Shiloh. He criticized Jefferson Davis after Bull Run for not having provided sufficient supplies for an attack on Washington, and, as the dispute continued, he was removed from command. In 1863, he returned to Charleston and took charge of the defense of the South Carolina and Georgia coastlines. Then, in May 1864, Beauregard was sent to work with Lee in Virginia, where his forces defeated those of B. F. Butler at Drewry's Bluff. Beauregard received credit for holding Petersburg against Grant's forces. In September 1864 he was given overall nominal command in the West, over John B. Hood's Army of Tennessee and Richard Taylor's Department of Alabama, Mississippi, and East Louisiana. However, he had no forces under his direct command, and he was unable to put up any effective resistance to the March to the Sea ordered by Union general W. T. Sherman. At the end of the war Beauregard served under General J. E. Johnston in North Carolina.

During the war he wrote *Principles and Maxims of the Art of War* (Charleston, 1863) and *Report of the Defence of Charleston* (Richmond, 1864). Following the end of the war Beauregard returned to New Orleans. There he was offered positions of command in the Rumanian army in 1866 and the army of the khedive of Egypt in 1869, both of which he declined. He served as president of the New Orleans, Jackson, and Mississippi Railroad and also worked for the Louisiana Lottery as a board member and then as a salaried manager of the lottery. He served a term as Louisiana's adjutant general. In later years he wrote several memoirs, including *A Commentary on the Campaign and Battle of Manassas* (New York, 1891). A memoir of his experiences in Mexico was published posthumously, *With Beauregard in Mexico: The Mexican War Reminiscences of P. G. T. Beauregard* (T. Harry Williams, ed., Baton Rouge, 1956).

Benjamin, Judah Philip (1811–1884) *U.S. senator from Louisiana, Confederate cabinet officer*

Judah Benjamin was born to observant Jewish parents on St. Croix in the Virgin Islands and moved with his parents to Savannah, Georgia, and later to Wilmington, North Carolina. He was admitted to Yale at age 14 and left after three years. He settled in New Orleans, where he studied law and entered legal practice in 1832. He gained recognition in the profession for coediting a digest of Louisiana appeal cases.

He prospered as a lawyer, purchasing a sugar plantation and 140 slaves, and married a member of the New Orleans creole elite, Natalie S. Martin. Active in Whig politics, he served in both houses of the state legislature and also as a delegate to state constitutional conventions. In 1852 he was selected by the Louisiana legislature for the U.S. Senate as a Whig; as the Whig Party collapsed in the mid-1850s, he declared himself a Democrat. He was chosen again as a Democrat for the U.S. Senate in 1858. He gained a reputation in the Senate as an able defender of the Southern position. He resigned from the Senate in February 1861, on the secession of Louisiana. In the Senate, he had met Jefferson Davis and had even challenged him to a duel on one occasion. However, Davis apologized for the incident that had provoked the challenge, and the two became friends. On the formation of the Confederacy, Davis appointed Benjamin as attorney general during the provisional government. In August 1861, Davis named Benjamin secretary of war. He served in that position until February 1862.

At that time, when Benjamin was secretary, the Confederacy recognized that it could not send needed supplies and reinforcements to General Henry A. Wise at Roanoke. The forces there surrendered. Benjamin agreed to take the blame for the surrender, thereby concealing the weakness of the Confederacy. The resignation was understood by Davis to represent a cover story, and he immediately appointed Benjamin secretary of state. Benjamin worked in that position to try to gain international recognition for the Confederacy.

As a cabinet officer, Benjamin gained a reputation for offering wise advice on a wide range of issues, and for remaining level-headed and self-effacing throughout the many disputes. In the last months of the war, as Davis came to accept the concept that slaves should be freed if they agreed to serve in the Confederate army, Benjamin was chosen to publicly announce the plan and test reactions. He and the concept were immediately denounced, although in the last weeks of the war, the Confederacy did adopt a modified version of the scheme.

With the assassination of Lincoln, conspiracy theorists developed the notion that Booth had been working for a Confederate espionage ring out of Canada, supported and operated secretly by Jefferson Davis and Judah Benjamin. Once again, Benjamin became a scapegoat for a notorious scandal. He quietly went into exile, escaping to Britain by way of Florida and the West Indies.

In Britain, he started a new life and never returned to the United States. He studied British law at Lincoln's Inn, then began practicing in 1866. He published a treatise on sales (*Benjamin on Sales*), which became a classic. He argued numerous cases, including some before the House of Lords as queen's counsel after 1872.

Benjamin very thoroughly destroyed his personal papers and left no reminiscences or accounts of his career. Biographers have had to reconstruct his life story from the accounts of others and from surviving correspondence in scattered repositories. Davis may have selected Benjamin for cabinet positions partly because of his brilliance as an attorney and strategic thinker and also because he recognized that no one of Jewish ancestry could compete with Davis for leadership within the circle of the Confederate administration. The fact that Benjamin was targeted for extremely hostile criticism clearly could be traced to contemporary Christian-

American attitudes toward Jews. Benjamin reached the highest position in government held by any Jew in the United States in the 19th century.

Benjamin's wife and daughter moved to Paris, and he visited them several times while in London. He retired from practice in 1883 and relocated to Paris, where he died the next year.

Booth, John Wilkes (1838–1865) *stage actor, assassin of Abraham Lincoln*

John Wilkes Booth was born in Bel Air, Maryland, the Ninth of 10 children of the British-born actor Junius Booth. He was raised primarily by his older brother, Edwin, and older sister, Asia Booth. He attended St. Timothy's Hall, an Episcopal military school in Catonsville, Maryland. His family maintained a farm in Bel Air and a town residence in Baltimore. John Wilkes Booth began his acting career with a performance at age 17 in 1855 at the Charles Street Theater in Baltimore with a part in Shakespeare's *Richard III*.

He later took up a lead position in a stock company based in Philadelphia, where his early performances were not very successful. Nevertheless, he continued, moving to Richmond, where he performed at the Marshall Theater in 1859. He joined the Richmond Grays, a militia unit, and was one of those on guard at the execution of John Brown in November 1859. He resigned from that unit immediately after the execution. As a handsome teenager and youth, he attracted many women, including several actresses, as well as Lucy Lambert Hale, the daughter of the Republican former senator from New Hampshire, to whom he may have been secretly engaged.

In the period 1860–64, Booth became a very well known actor, touring and giving performances in cities throughout the country, and, after the war began, in the North. However, his sympathies remained with the Confederacy. In 1864, he left the theater to seek a fortune in the new oil fields of western Pennsylvania, but soon dropped out of that business. After a trip to Montreal, Canada, in October 1864, where he met with Confederate agents, he conceived the idea of kidnapping Lincoln and recruited at least six fellow conspirators to effect the plot. The group met at Gautier's Restaurant, about three blocks from Ford's Theater in Washington, or at a rooming house operated by Mary Surratt. Booth's idea was to seize Lincoln, take him to Richmond, and there arrange that Lincoln be exchanged for all the Confederate prisoners held in Northern prison camps, so that they could return to battle. That plan was foiled on March 17, 1865, when Lincoln changed his plans to attend a performance at a hospital on the outskirts of Washington and instead went to a military ceremony.

The fall of Richmond, and then the surrender of Lee, convinced Booth to alter his plan to one of assassination. He expected his fellow conspirators to kill Vice President Johnson and Secretary of State Seward on the night of April 14, 1865. Booth was able to gain access to Ford's Theater, knowing the passages and exits quite well. He shot Lincoln in the head from behind, but his fellow assassins generally failed in their missions. One, George Atzerodt, backed out at the last minute, while another, Lewis Paine, succeeded only in wounding Secretary of State William Seward, who was in bed with a body cast that partially protected him from Paine's knife attack.

Booth broke his leg when leaping from the theater box to the stage after shooting Lincoln, and his escape through southern Maryland was hampered not only by the injury, but also by close pursuit by mounted troops. After hiding out for several days at various sympathizers' farms and in the woods, he made his way across the Potomac and Rappahannock. He then was caught in a barn, where he was shot; the barn burned down and he was dragged outside, where he died later on the morning of April 26.

Boyd, Belle (ca. 1845–1900) *spy for the Confederacy, actress*

Belle Boyd was born in Martinsburg, Virginia (now West Virginia). Although she later claimed to come from one of the best families of Virginia, in fact her family had very modest means. Even so, the Boyds made sure that their daughter received a good education. They sent her at the age of 12 to the Mount Washington Female College in Baltimore, Maryland. Although the school was run by a minister, Belle Boyd remained a bit of a tomboy and difficult to control. She finished her schooling at age 16, and her family and cousins arranged a coming-out party in Washington. Early in 1861, she returned to Martinsburg, where her father had already enlisted in the Confederate army.

When Union troops took over Martinsburg, they knew very well that the town harbored many Confederates and Confederate sympathizers. When a rowdy and drunken group of Union soldiers raided the Boyd home, in search of Belle Boyd's collection of Confederate flags as souvenirs, the family hid the flags. However, when one soldier then threatened to raise a Union flag over the house, Belle calmly took a pistol and killed him. After an officer investigated the incident, he thought it best to drop the whole matter, recognizing that a murder trial of a teenage Confederate girl would arouse the local population and only worsen the situation. Nevertheless, word of her act spread, and she became a local heroine. Perhaps inspired by her apparent immunity from punishment because of her age and gender, she began her espionage career immediately, at age 16.

She began carrying messages and information gathered from Union troops to Confederate lines, including several valuable details to General Stonewall Jackson. At first she simply wrote notes in her own handwriting, with no attempt to use a cipher. When one such communication fell into Union hands, she was apprehended and told that she could be executed for her behavior. She laughed off the charge and continued her efforts. Although espionage was a capital offense, she was only imprisoned, apparently because other officers agreed that her execution would have been too scandalous.

Over a four-year period, Belle Boyd was imprisoned twice, reported almost 30 times, and arrested on at least six different occasions. She consciously modeled herself on other female spies.

She was notorious for her good looks and attractive figure, for horseback riding, direct conversation with men, visiting men alone, staying in their tents or quarters, being a flirt, and singing "Maryland, my Maryland" and other Confederate songs while in prison in clear defiance of the prison rules. She often befriended her captors and won them over with a combination of flirtation, open conversation, and charm. She fell in love with a fellow prisoner in Washington, and they became engaged. She was finally paroled, but her fiancé was not.

While being transported as a prisoner aboard ship when banished to Canada and Britain, she romanced her Union guard, Samuel Wylde Hardinge, getting him to desert, then marry her. The episode created a newspaper sensation in Britain and then the United States. Hardinge was later convicted of treason and imprisoned, but finally released after the war. He died soon after. Belle married again, first to a traveling salesman, then to a traveling actor, who became her stage manager. She went on tour, describing her adventures, while wearing a Confederate uniform, and became an international hit. Her romantic nature, her unconventional behavior, and her challenge to feminine stereotypes made her a notorious international celebrity, during the war and for the rest of her life.

Bragg, Braxton (1817–1876) *Confederate general, commander of the Army of Tennessee*

General Braxton Bragg was born on March 22, 1817, in Warren County, North Carolina. He graduated near the top of his class in 1837 from West Point, and served in the artillery. In the war with Mexico he was brevetted captain for conduct in defense of Fort Brown, major for valor at Monterrey, and lieutenant colonel for his services at Buena Vista. After the U.S.-Mexican War, he resigned January 3, 1856, and became a planter at Thibodeaux, Louisiana. He served briefly in the Louisiana militia.

During the Civil War, Bragg earned a reputation as one of the most controversial of all Confederate officers. As with other prominent officers, both Union and Confederate, the jealousy of his subordinates and the second-guessing of his battle strategies generated disputes. Bragg was apparently socially distant but always correct in his demeanor, perhaps contributing to some of the complaints against him. However, many of his subordinate officers testified that he was an excellent commander, and they agreed that his tactical mistakes in battle situations could be seen only in retrospect.

Bragg was appointed brigadier general by the Confederate States of America in 1861 and was promoted to full general shortly after the defeat of Confederate forces at the Battle of Shiloh. He relieved General P. G. T. Beauregard, who had developed an inability to get along with Jefferson Davis. In the autumn of 1862, Bragg led a vigorous advance from eastern Tennessee across Kentucky and almost to the Ohio River, which, along with Lee's advance into Pennsylvania, constituted the high-water mark of the Confederacy. However, Bragg suffered from organizational difficulties and a badly defined division of responsibility between his command and those of generals Kirby Smith, and Buell. After the Battle of Perryville, fought on October 9, 1862, Bragg withdrew his forces into east Tennessee.

Disputes with General Leonidas Polk reached the ears of Jefferson Davis, who, after investigation, decided to retain Bragg in his position. Between December 31, 1862, and January 2, 1863, Bragg, at the head of the Army of Tennessee, fought the Battle of Murfreesboro against Union general William Rosecrans. Over the spring and early summer of 1863, Bragg pulled his forces back to Chattanooga, and then into northern Georgia. At the decisive battle at Chickamauga on Sep-

tember 19–20, 1863, however, Bragg turned the tide and pushed the Union troops under Rosecrans back to Chattanooga. He was later criticized for merely laying siege to that city rather than defeating the Union forces there. After being driven from Lookout Mountain, Bragg asked to be relieved of his command.

Jefferson Davis, who continued to have faith in Bragg, made him his personal military adviser. In that capacity, he investigated the charges against General Joseph E. Johnston who had replaced him, and who had led the slow retreat of the Army of Tennessee through northwestern Georgia to Atlanta. After Bragg reported to Davis that it appeared that Johnston had no plans to take the offensive against the advancing forces led by General W. T. Sherman, Davis replaced Johnston with Hood. Hood notoriously lost the next four major battles and virtually destroyed the Army of Tennessee in battles late in 1864 at Franklin and Nashville, Tennessee.

In the last days of the Confederacy, Bragg returned to active command of a division at the Battle of Bentonville on March 19, 1865. Retreating with the remnants of the Confederate government, he was captured on May 9, 1865, as he fled with Jefferson Davis into Georgia. After the war, he took a position as a civil engineer in New Orleans, and he also superintended harbor work at Mobile, Alabama. He died in Galveston, Texas, September 27, 1876.

Brown, John (1800–1859) *abolitionist leader, slave revolt planner*

John Brown was born in Torrington, Connecticut, and grew up in Ohio. He married twice, fathering 20 children. In general, Brown was a failure at nearly every venture he entered, including operating tanneries, raising sheep, and running a wool brokerage. Although he espoused a strict morality, he was in frequent financial trouble, being sued more than 20 times for defaulting on obligations. As he grew older, he became more and more convinced that he would have a dramatic role in freeing slaves by force of arms.

In 1855, he moved to Kansas with five of his sons. After a raid by proslavery bushwhackers on Lawrence, Brown led a small militia unit from his colony at Osawatomie on a reprisal raid. On May 24, 1856, he and six followers dragged five unarmed proslavery men and boys from their homes on Pottawatomie Creek and murdered them. Although there had been numerous killings in Kansas before between armed pro- and antislavery gangs, this was the first incident in which the victims were unarmed, and it became known as the Pottawatomie Massacre.

Over the period January 1857 to July 1859, Brown spent his time either attempting to raise funds for further military actions against slavery or in planning a slave insurrection. In February 1858, he revealed his plans for a major slave uprising to Frederick Douglass, who advised him that it was not practical. He received similar advice from a British soldier of fortune, Hugh Forbes. Nevertheless, he continued his efforts to raise money, and met with noted abolitionist Gerrit Smith. In addition, he talked with Thomas Wentworth Higginson, Theodore Parker, and other noted opponents of slavery. Later, most of these contacts denied learning any specifics of Brown's plan. Brown himself appeared to remain ambiguous as to whether he intended to use violence only to defend slaves once they were freed, or to use violence to free them. But his genteel supporters in the abolitionist community did understand that he intended to raise a force of armed men and to violate the law, which they believed was philosophically justified.

In April 1858, Brown convened a meeting in Chatham, Ontario, that produced a very strange document, a form of constitution for a wide territory to be run by freed slaves. His little band of 20 men had available hundreds of guns and some 1,000 lances. By attacking the Harpers Ferry arsenal, they hoped to obtain more weapons and use them to arm slaves in the proposed uprising. However, Brown made no effort to spread word of his impending insurrection among slaves, or to establish any liaison with potential recruits beyond his small force. The plan was nearly stopped when Hugh Forbes revealed it to two U.S. senators, and in response, Brown's financial backers told him to stop the plan and return to Kansas.

Brown did return to Kansas in June of 1858 and led a small raid in which he and his group freed 11 slaves and took them to Ontario. In 1859, he rented a farm near Harpers Ferry and used it as a base to organize his attack on the armory. On October 16, he led a team of 18 others to cut telegraph wires and seized the armory and rifle works at Harpers Ferry. A detail was sent out, kidnapped two slaveholders, and brought their slaves to the armory. The next morning, Brown captured and held as hostages some 40 citizens of the town of Harpers Ferry. Soon word of the events spread, and several militia units converged on the town, together with a unit of U.S. Marines under Lieutenant Colonel Robert E. Lee and his lieutenant, J. E. B. Stuart. Lee offered

to let Brown surrender, and, after he refused, a quick assault on Brown's forces, who had fortified themselves inside an engine house, resulted in the killing of 10 of Brown's men and the wounding of seven others, including Brown himself. The hostages were released, and Lee reported that there was no indication that any of the slaves brought in from the neighboring plantations had any intention of joining with Brown. They all returned with their masters to their plantations.

The lack of planning, and the notion that the slaves would join in an uprising when all the forces of the government, army, and militia were available to repress them, reflected, at the least, an impractical and peculiar thought process. Many assumed that Brown was insane. However, at his trial, he asked to make a statement that impressed his listeners with its forcefulness and sobriety. Even though he contradicted himself regarding whether or not he planned a more general uprising, his stoic bearing and firm commitment were striking.

The trial began on October 20, 1859, and lasted about a month. Brown was executed for the crime of treason on December 2, 1859, in Charlestown, Virginia (now in West Virginia). The raid, although poorly planned and executed, did serve to confirm fears in the South that northern abolitionists planned slave insurrections and raised concerns that the next one might have more success. In the North, Brown's execution was met by the tolling of thousands of church bells and the preaching of literally thousands of sermons identifying him as a martyr for liberty. The event clearly widened the division in the nation and contributed to the hardening of opinions on both sides.

Brown, Joseph E. (1821–1894) *governor of Georgia during the Civil War, U.S. senator from Georgia*

Joseph Brown was born in north Georgia, and, after preparatory school, attended a year of law school at Yale. He entered legal practice in 1846 and was appointed a judge in 1855. He developed a fortune in mining and in railroad operations and set himself apart from the dominant wealthy planter class, both in his interests and in his politics. In 1855, he was elected governor as a Democrat and reelected, serving for two-year terms until 1865. During the secession crises in early 1861, he was a strong advocate of secession for Georgia. Before the state convention voted to secede, he sent state troops to occupy Fort Pulaski, and his executive action in this regard and his open support for secession may have helped tip the balance in the convention.

During the war, it soon became apparent that Brown was a staunch supporter of states' rights, to the extent of opposing many measures of the Confederate government. Most notably, he fought the Confederate draft by appointing hundreds of individuals to state government positions, including a new bureaucracy devoted to delivering relief to the wives and families of soldiers. He also suggested that the exemption from the draft for planters with large numbers of slaves was unfair. When pressured to allow state officials, constables, and deputy sheriffs to be drafted, he insisted that the state had every right to define who should be exempted from the Confederate draft, and refused to consent to their release. He also protested against the Confederate policy regarding blockade running. In the last months of the war, Brown opposed the decision to allow the emancipation of slaves and their enlistment in the Confederate army. Brown became known throughout the Confederacy as one of the strongest opponents of Jefferson Davis, and the resistance of Georgia to the growing central power of the Confederacy was regarded by Davis as one of the reasons for the loss of the war.

After the war, Brown was arrested by Union forces and briefly held in prison. On his release, he announced that he was a Republican and urged his fellow Georgians to cooperate with the new regime. His political opponents suggested that his release from prison was contingent on his agreeing to becoming a Republican, a charge he denied. He was appointed chief justice of the Georgia supreme court, serving 1865–70. In 1880 he was appointed to fill a U.S. senate seat vacated by resignation, and in 1885 he was selected by the state legislature to serve as U.S. senator to 1891. As a senator during these terms, he was a Democrat. He emerged as one of the most powerful political bosses of Georgia in the last decades of the 19th century and developed a massive fortune based on his operation of the Western and Atlantic Railroad, mining interests, and land holdings throughout the state.

Burnside, Ambrose Everett (1824–1881) *Union general in the Civil War, governor of Rhode Island*
Ambrose Burnside was born in Liberty, Indiana. With the help of his father's political connections, he received an appointment to West Point, graduating in 1847. He served in the U.S.-Mexican War and remained in the U.S. Army until 1853. He then resigned and went into business in Rhode Island, in the manufacture of a breech-loading rifle. However, he was unsuccessful, and

had to assign the patent to his weapon to his creditors. He was nominated by the Democrats for Congress and worked with the Illinois Central Railroad in a position under George B. McClellan.

In the Civil War, Burnside commanded a brigade at First Bull Run and achieved the rank of brigadier general of volunteers. In 1862, he led an expedition to the North Carolina coast that won for the Union Roanoke Island, New Bern, Beaufort, and Fort Macon. He was promoted to major general and his repute spread. Although this achievement at North Carolina was partially and perhaps almost entirely the result of naval support, it brought him to the attention of Lincoln and the War Department as a possibly competent leader. They were mistaken. In fact, Burnside's only lasting contribution was his unusual style of facial hair, in which his moustache continued into the long hair in front of his ears, a style soon to be known as sideburns after his name.

Burnside's further army career was marked by numerous mistakes, some near disasters, and his relative disgrace as an officer. Although he commanded under General George McClellan in the Antietam campaign, his slowness in bringing his men to cross the so-called Burnside's Bridge over Antietam Creek (which most of his men could have waded across) was widely noted. Nevertheless, shortly after Antietam, he succeeded McClellan in command of the Army of the Potomac. He promptly arranged for a frontal attack via Fredericksburg with Richmond as the objective. However, delays in the arrival of pontoon equipment for crossing the Rappahannock at Fredericksburg allowed Lee time to prepare excellent positions for defense at Marye's Heights. After that costly defeat at Fredericksburg in December 1862, Burnside asked President Lincoln either to dismiss Joseph Hooker and several other officers who opposed his plans or to remove Burnside himself. While awaiting that decision, he initiated another attempt to march west of Fredericksburg, but, in this case, his forces were so bogged down in muddy roads on the infamous "Mud March," that they had to retreat. Lincoln relieved him of command and replaced him with Hooker.

Burnside was then assigned as commander of the Department of the Ohio from March to December 1863. There he arranged the arrest of the Copperhead former congressman Clement Vallandigham and dealt with the raid by Confederates under Morgan deep into Ohio. Burnside occupied east Tennessee (which had been a Union goal for two years), took Knoxville, and then turned aside James Longstreet's attempt to recapture Knoxville. In 1864 he returned to the Virginia theater, where he served under Meade and Grant. He was held responsible for the disaster that followed when a Union-planted mine created a huge crater at Petersburg in which advancing Union troops, many of whom were African American, were slaughtered. As a consequence of this debacle, Burnside was finally relieved of all command, and he resigned from the army April 15, 1865.

After the war, Burnside was elected governor of Rhode Island in 1866 and re-elected for annual terms in 1867 and 1868. He was selected by the state legislature to serve in the U.S. Senate in 1874, and he served there until his death in 1881.

Butler, Benjamin Franklin (1818–1893)
Massachusetts politician, Union general, member of Congress

Butler was born in Deerfield, New Hampshire, and attended Waterville College, graduating in 1838. He was admitted to the bar in Massachusetts in 1840 and began practicing as a trial lawyer in Lowell, Massachusetts. He was elected as a state representative in 1853 and as a state senator in 1858 on the Democratic ticket. In 1859, he ran for governor, but lost. In 1860, he supported John Breckinridge, the Southern Democrat nominated for the presidency, and Butler also ran on the same ticket for governor again.

In 1861, Butler quickly volunteered to join the Union cause, and, as a brigadier general of Massachusetts militia, he was crucial in making Annapolis and Baltimore safe for the transit of Lincoln to Washington. Recognized for these services, he was promoted to major general and given command of Fort Monroe. There, in May 1861, he refused to return several slaves to their owners, claiming they were contraband of war. His use of the term is generally regarded as the precedent for the contraband principle in freeing slaves, later incorporated into the Confiscation Act of 1861.

In 1862, after naval forces secured New Orleans, Butler was put in charge as commander of the occupation troops there. This was Butler's most controversial and notorious assignment during the war. He had one man hanged for insulting the U.S. flag, and he established his own headquarters in a luxurious hotel. When some women of New Orleans continued to insult U.S. troops in the street, Butler issued an order requiring that such women be treated as "women of the streets, plying their avocation." For this and other behaviors insulting the traditions of Southern chivalry, he was

soon called Beast Butler. In fact, Jefferson Davis issued an order that if Butler were captured, he should not be treated as a prisoner of war, but as an outlaw, and should be summarily shot.

In December 1862, Butler was replaced. He was given command of the Department of Southern Virginia and North Carolina, but his inept handling of troops, and the fact that his troops were pinned down by a smaller force under Confederate general P. G. T. Beauregard, led Grant to remark that he was bottled up, and the nickname Bottled Up Butler soon spread. Lincoln considered having Butler nominated as vice president on the Union ticket, as a way of winning support from War Democrats, but Butler declined. In October 1864, he took command of troops in New York City, charged with the task of maintaining order and preventing riots during the fall elections. He retired from the army and returned to Massachusetts before the end of the war.

Butler reentered politics as a radical Republican, serving terms in Congress from 1867 to 1875 and from 1877 to 1879. He was one of the authors of the impeachment articles against Andrew Johnson, and he was a House of Representatives prosecutor in the trial held before the Senate. When Johnson was not found guilty of high crimes and misdemeanors, Butler was blamed for inept handling of the case. Butler continued his career in politics, running for governor several times while serving in Congress. He was elected governor of Massachusetts with support from both the Greenback Party and the Democrats in 1882. He sought the presidency in 1884, nominated by the National Greenback Labor Party, but won only 175,370 votes to Grover Cleveland's 4.9 million and James G. Blaine's 4.8 million.

Butler's career as a military officer was quite undistinguished, except for his ability to draw public attention to himself. His stand on contrabands and his notorious contempt for Southern standards of gentility earned him a notoriety that appeared to help his political career during and after the Reconstruction period.

Chase, Salmon P. (1808–1873) *U.S. senator, secretary of the treasury, chief justice of the Supreme Court*
Salmon Chase was born in Cornish, New Hampshire, one of 11 children. On the death of his father, when he was 12 years old, he was put under the care of an uncle, Philander Chase, Episcopal bishop in Ohio. After two years there, he returned to New Hampshire and attended Dartmouth College, graduating in 1826. He

moved to Washington, D.C., where he took a position teaching and studied law under William Wirt, the attorney general of the United States and the father of one of his students. In 1829, he returned to Ohio to open a law practice in Cincinnati. Although scraping along with few clients, he gathered and published a three-volume collection of the statutes of Ohio at age 22, earning him a solid reputation.

Salmon Chase soon began taking on a variety of cases, some with antislavery aspects, including the case of James Birney, who claimed that his servant, Matilda, was free by virtue of living in a free state. Soon Chase was defending fugitive slaves, and he became known as the Attorney General of the Fugitive Slaves. He helped organize the Liberty Party, and in 1848 he helped establish the Free-Soil Party in Ohio. In 1849, he was selected by Free-Soil and Democratic legislators as U.S. senator from Ohio. In the Senate, he gained prominence for his opposition to the 1850 Fugitive Slave Act and the Kansas-Nebraska Act of 1854. In 1854–55 he organized the Anti-Nebraska Party, which soon became part of the growing Republican Party. In 1855 and 1857 he was elected governor of Ohio as a Republican.

Although nominated in 1856 and 1860 as a candidate for the Republican presidential nomination, he failed to win the party endorsement. He was selected again by the Ohio legislature for the Senate in 1860, but as he started his term, he was named by Lincoln to be secretary of the treasury.

As Lincoln's first secretary of the treasury, Chase took on a difficult set of responsibilities, overseeing the first national issuance of greenback currency, the establishment of an income tax, and the erection of a national banking system. However, Chase constantly disagreed with Lincoln and offered unsolicited advice on numerous matters that had nothing to do with the Treasury Department. On four occasions, he offered to resign. Finally, when Lincoln realized that Chase would seek the Republican nomination for the presidency in 1864, Lincoln accepted Chase's fourth letter of resignation. However, he soon appointed him to the Supreme Court, on the death of Roger Taney. Lincoln considered suggesting to Chase that his appointment was conditional on a promise not to run for the presidency, but thought better of it on the advice of Charles Sumner.

During the impeachment proceedings against Andrew Johnson, as chief justice, Chase presided over the Senate as a court. His insistence that the proceedings be conducted in a dignified and non-political,

judicious fashion irritated many of the radical Republicans who sought Johnson's conviction. As chief justice in the Supreme Court, Chase presided over a severely divided court, and he was frequently in the minority dissent. However, in the case of *Texas v. White,* in 1869, he wrote the majority opinion, ruling that the secession of Texas was itself unconstitutional, reaffirming the right of Congress to guarantee a republican form of government and thus to be in charge of the process of Reconstruction. Ironically, as chief justice, he argued that the Legal Tender Act for which he had lobbied while secretary of treasury, was unconstitutional.

Because of his impartial stand during the impeachment proceedings, Democrats considered that he might be an appropriate candidate for the presidency. However, the fact that he had favored voting rights for the freed slaves prevented his endorsement by that party, which generally opposed civil rights for African Americans. Chase died in 1873 in New York City.

Cleburne, Patrick Ronayne (1828–1864) *Irish-born Confederate major general, advocate of liberation of slaves to assist the Confederate cause*

Patrick Cleburne was born in Cork County, Ireland. As a young man, he attempted to qualify as a druggist in Britain, but failed the exam, and joined the British army. He later resigned and immigrated to the United States, where he worked as a druggist and later as a property lawyer, first in Ohio, then in Arkansas. On the outbreak of the Civil War, he enlisted with an Arkansas regiment and soon rose to the rank of brigadier general, and later to major general. He served under Hardee at Shiloh, and later at the Battle of Tunnel Hill near Chattanooga. He was credited with holding off Sherman's advance there and earned the nickname Stonewall of the West. He fought under Johnston and Hood in the retreat toward Atlanta. He was one of only two foreign-born officers in the Confederate service to reach the rank of major general. The other was Camille Jules-Marie, a minor French prince. Cleburne was regarded as one of the best officers in the Confederate service.

In the winter of 1863–64, Cleburne developed a proposal that the Confederacy should offer freedom to slaves in exchange for military service and secured the support of other officers for the concept. However, the suggestion, in the form of a circulated letter, was suppressed, not to surface again until the last months of the war, when the Confederate Congress and Jefferson Davis accepted the concept. Like Nathan Bedford Forrest, Cleburne developed a reputation for fighting at the head of his troops, and he was at the forefront of his division when, along with five other generals, he was killed at the Battle of Franklin on November 30, 1864.

Davis, Jefferson (1808–1889) *U.S. senator from Mississippi, secretary of war of the United States, president of the Confederate States of America*

Jefferson Davis was born in Kentucky in what is now Todd County, on June 3, 1808. His ancestors and family contained several distinguished military and political leaders in Virginia, and his wealthy and prominent family saw to it that he received a good education. On completion of a secondary course at Transylvania University in Kentucky, he was admitted to West Point at the age of 17 and graduated in 1828. He served in the U.S. Army in the period 1828–35. He married the daughter of Zachary Taylor, but his bride died shortly after their marriage.

In 1845, he remarried, to Varina Howell, the daughter of a wealthy Mississippi planter. Davis ran for the U.S. House of Representatives from Mississippi in that year, but resigned to volunteer his services in 1846 in the Mexican-American war. He served in that war under Captain Braxton Bragg. Davis returned to serve as secretary of war under Franklin Pierce, and twice was selected for the U.S. Senate from Mississippi. On the secession of South Carolina, Davis at first cautioned against rash moves, but when word reached him in Washington that Mississippi had seceded, he resigned his seat in the Senate. When the Confederacy formed, he was chosen, after several other candidates were considered, as provisional president. He was elected to the position on February 22, 1862.

Jefferson Davis, as president of the Confederacy, was a highly controversial figure. His critics charged him with excessively centralizing authority and playing favorites with his officers. After criticism mounted against General Braxton Bragg for failing to defeat Union forces at Chattanooga, Davis stood by Bragg and promoted him to be his personal military adviser. He opposed advice from Generals James Longstreet and Leonidas Polk suggesting that Bragg was indecisive. Davis had running controversies with several state governors, including Zebulon Vance of North Carolina and Joseph Brown of Georgia. Davis constantly countermanded military orders, and, in a move that has created a lasting controversy, he removed General Joseph E. Johnston from command of the Army of Tennessee and replaced him with General John B. Hood. Although

Davis opposed freeing slaves to fight on the Confederate side, he finally approved such a measure in March of 1865, too late for it to have any effect on the outcome of the war.

However, Davis had many contemporary supporters, as well as support from later commentators and historians. It was clear that he was an eloquent speaker and that once he joined the Confederate cause he was extremely loyal to that cause and to what he saw as his duty. Yet his critics see in his unbending and uncompromising stand, not only the reasons behind many Confederate military defeats, but also the blame for extending the war long after defeat had become obvious. In his memoirs, Davis argued the logic of his position, claiming that the states had a right to secede from the Union, that they had a right to voluntarily form a new nation, and that the unconstitutional behavior was not that of the secessionists, but of the Union in using force to suppress constitutional and legal actions. Unionists argued that the states had no right to unilaterally decide to leave the Union, any more than one party to a mutually binding contract has the right to declare the contract ended, but Davis never accepted that reasoning. After the war, he admitted that force of arms had proven that unilateral secession could not occur, but he continued to believe that the lost cause was the cause of liberty against a tyrannical and centralizing power concentrated in the United States government.

With the withdrawal of Lee's forces from Petersburg and Richmond in April 1865, Davis fled with remnants of his government, first to Danville, Virginia, and then farther south. Union troops captured Davis and a small entourage in Georgia and he was imprisoned at Fort Monroe. At first President Andrew Johnson accused him of participating in the plot to assassinate Abraham Lincoln. However, that charge was dropped. Although Davis demanded a trial for treason, he was released on bail after two years in confinement. The bail bond was signed by, among others, noted abolitionist and journalist, Horace Greeley. The entire case against Davis was later dropped. In retirement from public office, Davis tended to restrict his public appearances, but now and then he would be honored at a large reception. He served as president of an insurance company and devoted several years to writing his memoirs. He died in New Orleans on December 5, 1889, at the age of 81. His last home in Biloxi, Mississippi, was destroyed by Hurricane Katrina in 2005.

Dix, Dorothea Lynde (1802–1887) *teacher, mental health reformer, nursing administrator during the Civil War* Dorothea Dix was born in Hampden, Maine, the daughter of a dealer in religious tracts and sometime itinerant Methodist preacher. Although her father had come from a wealthy Boston family, he had chosen to live in a remote village in near poverty. He was an abusive alcoholic and his wife suffered from depression making Dorothea's early childhood quite difficult. She was given the task of raising her two younger brothers and developed an interest in teaching as she took care of them. At age 12, she went to live with her wealthy grandmother in Boston, and then with a great-aunt in Worcester, Massachusetts. At age 15 she started a school for girls in Worcester, and, later, on her grandmother's property in Boston, she opened a school for girls, arranging free classes for the poor while charging fees for the more affluent. The school provided an income, and her grandmother, who was very strict, nevertheless supported her in the project.

In 1836, suffering from tuberculosis, Dorothea Dix went to Europe, and, while there, heard of the death of both her mother and grandmother. Her grandmother left her an endowment that provided a steady income for the rest of her life. On her return to the United States, she was asked to substitute as a Sunday school teacher in a jail in East Cambridge, Massachusetts. There she was shocked to see the conditions in which prisoners were held, especially in the cellar where insane women were chained naked in unheated cells.

She vowed to work for reform of such conditions and began a life-long commitment to that cause. She toured institutions in Massachusetts, and developed a report or "memorial" describing in detail the deplorable conditions she encountered. The memorial was presented to the state legislature and soon resulted in the establishment of a new mental institution in Worcester. Building on this success, Dix spent the next few years touring state after state, preparing reports on conditions, and then having the reports presented to state legislators by prominent political leaders. In this way, several institutions were established. According to some accounts, she was ultimately responsible for the creation of 32 mental hospitals, 15 schools for the feeble minded, and one school for the blind, as well as several nursing schools.

She toured Europe again in 1854, and her lectures there led to a similar movement for reform of mental institutions. On the outbreak of the Civil War, Dix volunteered her service to the Union army, and she was appointed, at age 59, superintendent of Union female nurses. In that capacity, she recruited some 3,000 nurses and convinced military authorities that women nurses could be competent and useful. She was concerned that her recruits might use their position to find husbands, so she set up a series of strict rules to attempt to prevent any behavior that would lead to such developments. All recruits had to be over age 30, had to be plain rather than pretty, and had to adhere to a dress code, wearing only brown or black outfits and no jewelry. Partly as a consequence of her strict code, she became known as Dragon Dix. Her administration was flawed, and she tended not to follow army regulations. However, she was able to use her fame and contacts to obtain contributions of medical supplies and needed equipment.

She returned to her campaign for mental health reform after the war. Over the years, she published several books for children, containing moral instruction or filled with information to answer questions about nature. With her health failing, in 1881 she entered Trenton State Hospital in New Jersey (the first hospital founded under her influence) and lived there for the remaining six years of her life, maintaining an active correspondence.

Douglass, Frederick (1817–1895) *escaped slave, abolition journalist, diplomat* Douglass was born a slave on the eastern shore of Maryland, where he was raised by grandparents. His mother had given him the name Frederick Augustus Washington Bailey and told him that his father was white. He never met his father, and his mother died when he was six. At about the age of eight he was sent to Baltimore to work as a houseboy in the home of Hugh and Sophia Auld. Mrs. Auld taught him the alphabet and began to teach him to read before being prohibited by her husband.

Frederick continued to learn, however, picking up scraps of printed material and picking out words with the help of other children. At about the age of 15, he was sent back to the eastern shore to live on the plantation of a notoriously harsh slaveowner by the name of Edward Covey. Covey found the rebellious young Douglass difficult to control, and he was sent back to Baltimore. He worked there on an arrangement in which he hired his own time as a shipyard worker, paying his master part of his earnings every week. There he planned his escape, at the age of 20, by borrowing the papers of a black sailor and purchasing ship passage and rail tickets to New York.

He adopted the name of Frederick Douglass and settled in New Bedford, Massachusetts. There he married and began attending abolitionist meetings. In October 1841, he attended an antislavery convention on Nantucket Island and was asked to speak. Although unprepared, he gave a moving account of his childhood in slavery and his escape, which drew the attention of prominent abolitionists at the convention. He was asked to become a lecturer for the Massachusetts Anti-Slavery Society and worked with William Lloyd Garrison.

His lectures were so eloquent that many doubted whether he had really been raised as a slave. In order to dispel such doubts and to make a contribution to the growing antislavery literature, he published *Narrative of the Life of Frederick Douglass* in 1845. That work gave specific details and names of his early owners and plantation life, providing proof that he was indeed a fugitive slave. In order to avoid being apprehended and returned to slavery based on the evidence that he had published, he moved to Great Britain and Ireland over the period 1845–47, where he continued lecturing on slavery and abolitionism. With funds raised in Britain, Douglass was able to purchase his freedom, and he then returned to the United States and established a newspaper in Rochester, New York, the *North Star.*

He eventually broke with Garrison. Douglass believed that the U.S. Constitution provided a basis for African Americans to claim citizenship and rights, while Garrison saw the document as a compact with slavery. Douglass became deeply involved in discussions with other African-American leaders over the question of whether to seek rights in the United States or whether to emigrate. He attended several conventions throughout the early 1850s, arguing for moral suasion to bring white Americans around to support for civil rights and criticizing those who advocated emigration to Canada, the West Indies, or newly-independent Liberia. Through his newspaper, his biography, and his speaking engagements, he emerged as a prominent spokesman of African Americans by the mid- and late 1850s.

John Brown approached Douglass in 1858 for support in his intended raid in western Virginia. Although Douglass disapproved the idea as impractical, he was implicated as an accessory as were other abolitionists. Douglass briefly fled to Canada and Britain after Brown was arrested at Harpers Ferry.

During the Civil War, Douglass advocated the recruitment of free blacks and former slaves into the army. After Lincoln approved the plan, he asked Dou-glass to assist in recruiting efforts. Lincoln met with Douglass twice during the war to discuss the treatment and conditions of black soldiers.

After the war, beginning in 1870, Douglass published a Washington-based newspaper, the *New National Era.* As a reward and recognition for his services and as a symbolic gesture of Republican support for African Americans, Douglass received a series of federal government appointments over the period 1877–93. He served as marshal of the District of Columbia, recorder of deeds for the district, and later as consul-general to Haiti and *chargé d' affaires* to Santo Domingo. He expanded his first biography and published it in 1855 under the title *My Bondage and My Freedom.* He rewrote the work as *Life and Times of Frederick Douglass,* in 1881 and again in 1892. He died in Washington in 1895.

Foote, Andrew Hull (1806–1863) *admiral in the U.S. Navy, flag officer of the Mississippi River Squadron*
Andrew Hull Foote was born in New Haven, Connecticut. His father was U.S. senator Samuel Augustus Foote. Foote was accepted by the U.S. Military Academy at West Point and entered the class of 1826. However, he resigned and chose a naval career, accepting an appointment as a midshipman in the U.S. Navy in 1822. Foote served in a number of naval positions over the next decades, earning a reputation as a reformer with his support of church services, his successful campaign to eliminate the dispensing of grog (a dosage of rum and water) to sailors aboard ships, and his work in the West African Squadron, where he was engaged in capturing slave trading ships. His service aboard the USS *Perry* in the antislave trade mission (1849–51) left him with a strong antislavery commitment. He wrote and published a narrative of his service there as *Africa and the American Flag.*

In the period 1851–56, Foote served ashore, including an appointment to the U.S. Navy Efficiency Board, established by Commodore Samuel F. DuPont. In 1856, Foote was promoted to the rank of commander and assigned the USS *Portsmouth,* in the East India Squadron. In this service he led a landing party that took forts at Canton, China, in reprisal for an attack on his ship. Although 40 U.S. sailors were lost in the operation, the suppression of the forts and the 400 casualties among the Chinese helped establish the repute of the U.S. Navy in the Far East. In 1858 he took command of the Brooklyn Navy Yard.

With the beginning of the Civil War, Foote commanded the Mississippi River Squadron, building up the fleet from purchased steamers and newly-constructed gunboats. He organized and led the gunboat flotilla that participated in the capture of Fort Henry, Fort Donelson, and Island No. 10. He was wounded in the foot on February 14, 1862, during the battle for Fort Donelson. Later, when the wound continued to require attention, he was removed from the command. For his leadership in these engagements, he was promoted to rear admiral, July 16, 1862, and received a vote of thanks from the U.S. Congress. He was then put in charge of the Bureau of Equipment and Recruiting in Washington, D.C. He was appointed on June 4, 1863, to take over the Atlantic Blockading Squadron that operated out of the Sea Islands and blockaded Charleston. However, before he could take up his position, he died in transit on June 26 in New York City.

Forrest, Nathan Bedford (1821–1877) *slave trader, planter, Confederate cavalry officer*
Nathan Bedford Forrest was born in Marshall County, Tennessee, to William Forrest, a blacksmith and his wife. Nathan's father died when he was 16, and he provided for his mother and five younger brothers by raising stock and crops until his mother remarried. Forrest had no formal education whatsoever, although he reputedly grew quite proficient in math. As a young man, Forrest went into business, first in Hernando, Tennessee, with an uncle. Later, in 1857, he was in business for himself in Memphis dealing in real estate and slaves. He earned a large fortune in a short time and invested in a cotton plantation.

In June 1861, he enlisted as a private in a mounted rifle company, which later became a unit in the 7th Tennessee cavalry regiment. However, in July 1861, Forrest was authorized by the governor of Tennessee to recruit his own battalion of cavalry, which he financed with his own resources. He was appointed lieutenant colonel, commanding a force of about 650 men.

Over the next four years, he earned a controversial reputation as the most brilliant cavalry officer on either side of the Civil War. He was promoted to colonel of the 3rd Tennessee Cavalry in March 1862; to brigadier general of the Confederate States army in July 1862; then to major general, December 1863; and to lieutenant general in February 1865. He led a breakout of his troops from Fort Donelson on February 13, 1862, while most of the rest of the Confederate garrison surrendered to Grant. At Shiloh his forces captured a federal battery. On July 13, 1862, he attacked Union forces at Murfreesboro, capturing the entire garrison, as well as four cannon.

Forrest had several disputes with his commanding officers, including General Joseph Wheeler. Forrest participated with Wheeler in an unsuccessful attack on Fort Donelson and vowed never to serve under Wheeler again. Later, when army commander Braxton Bragg ordered Forrest to work under Wheeler, he protested and succeeded in being given an independent command in west Tennessee.

In the fall of 1862 he organized a new brigade with local recruiting, and then led them to several victories, the first near Lexington, Tennessee. Successes at Chickamauga, September 18, 1863, and at Okolona in February 1864, among others, enhanced his reputation. The battle that brought his name to the attention of the United States Congress and to the Northern press took place at Fort Pillow, Tennessee, April 12, 1864.

During the engagement at Fort Pillow, there were about 350 casualties among the 700 defenders, with the remaining 350 taken prisoner. A large number of mostly African-American civilians who had taken refuge in the fort were also killed. Rumors spread that Forrest had ordered "no-quarter," that is, the taking of no prisoners, leading to the massacre of many of the African-American defenders. Other charges included the burying alive of wounded survivors and the shooting of fleeing defenders in the back. The casualty figures and the testimony of many suggested it was the worst incident of its kind during the war. A U.S. congressional committee investigated the atrocity and concluded that Forrest had allowed his troops to commit the slaughter.

Since Forrest had been a slave trader before the war, since his tactics were rapid and ruthless, and since he had a personal reputation for strict and even violent discipline, he became a symbol for the North of the barbarism of the Confederacy. However, his supporters argued that Forrest had always shown complete propriety in his dealing with prisoners. At Fort Pillow, they claimed, he had attempted to restrain his men. Forrest's troops had continued the attack, they claimed, because defenders at Fort Pillow had failed to lower their flag as a signal of surrender. Some captured Union officers testified later that Forrest showed them every consideration, even punishing those of his own command responsible for their ill treatment. Whether justly or not, Forrest's name was inexorably linked with the Fort Pillow Massacre.

Forrest's military victories were remarkable because he was not a literate man, and his efforts at writing reflected that fact. Forrest had no military training whatsoever, but the lack of formal training may have been an advantage, rather than a disadvantage. He intuitively understood the need to move rapidly. He perfected techniques of surprise raids, flanking and rear attacks, and escapes through unexpected routes. He appeared to be a natural military genius. He was wounded several times (at least once accidentally by his own men), and by one count, he had 29 horses shot from under him. It was claimed that he personally killed or seriously injured some 30 Union officers and men.

Following the war, Forrest found his prewar fortune destroyed. He returned to cotton planting, and later engaged in railway construction. He served as president of the Selma, Marion, and Memphis Railroad. In politics, he represented Tennessee at the Democratic national convention of 1868. In keeping with his racist reputation earned as a slave trader and from the Fort Pillow Massacre, Forrest was reputed to be one of the organizers and leaders of the early Ku Klux Klan. He was called before Congress to testify about the organization in 1870–71, where, however, he claimed to know nothing about it. However, he is generally regarded as one of the founders of the original KKK.

Garrison, William Lloyd (1805–1879) *abolitionist, journalist, advocate of women's rights and pacifism*
William Lloyd Garrison was born in Newburyport, Massachusetts, and due to the early death of his father, a merchant seaman, his childhood was spent in a series of difficult apprenticeships and odd jobs. However, among the jobs was a stint working on the *Newburyport Herald,* where he learned the fundamentals of the newspaper business. In 1829, Garrison moved to Baltimore where he worked for Benjamin Lundy, who published the first abolitionist newspaper, the *Genius of Universal Emancipation.* While working for the paper, Garrison briefly joined the American Colonization Society (ACS) and supported that movement as an adjunct to abolition. However, he learned that many members of the ACS, especially those in the South, supported the movement to colonize freed slaves in Liberia not in order to advance emancipation, but in order to remove from the United States freed slaves who might serve as examples to slaves as well as to agitate for their freedom. Furthermore, Garrison learned that very few free African Americans endorsed the ACS, and he soon collected resolutions and other documents from free black religious congregations and secular meetings opposing the ACS. He had a fall-

ing out with Lundy over the issue of whether or not emancipation should be gradual or immediate.

He decided to establish his own newspaper, and on January 1, 1831, he published the first issue of the *Liberator.* He continued to print the newspaper for 35 years, closing it down only on December 29, 1865, after the ratification of the Thirteenth Amendment to the Constitution abolishing slavery. During the 35 years of its publication, the *Liberator* never achieved very extensive circulation, but other papers and journals subscribed to it and liberally quoted from it, magnifying Garrison's influence. Garrison published the collected resolutions opposing the ACS in *Thoughts on African Colonization* in 1832.

He remained committed to immediate abolition of slavery, and believed that if slavery were ended, African Americans could readily move to full citizenship, and that most of the basis for prejudice against them among whites would evaporate. He urged the achievement of his goals by moral suasion, rather than by violence, direct action, or even political action. Indeed, he opposed the idea of working through the United States government, believing the U.S. Constitution was essentially a compact with hell in that it endorsed slavery.

In 1831, he helped organize the New England Anti-Slavery Society and, two years later, the American Anti-Slavery Society, both of which supported the approach he advocated. He was president of the American Anti-Slavery Society from 1843 until 1865. Through the *Liberator* and through his speeches and organizational work, Garrison also supported the movements for women's suffrage, pacifism, and prohibition of alcohol. Throughout his career as a spokesman for these causes, however, he often alienated potential supporters with his extreme positions. Partly because of his strident language and partly because of his difficult personality, he was a poor organizer. More effective organizations developed with the American and Foreign Anti-Slavery Society, founded by Lewis Tappan, the Liberty and Free Soil political parties, and finally with the formation of the Republican Party. Garrison never lent his support to any of these political groups.

Garrison "discovered" Frederick Douglass and sponsored his early speaking career. However, Garrison and Douglass soon had a falling out when Douglass began to argue that the Constitution and the Declaration of Independence demonstrated that the United States was founded on principles that, if implemented, would bring social justice to African Americans. Garrison and Douglass used their respective publications to attack the positions of each other and never were able to reconcile their differences.

However, during the Civil War, Garrison modified his pacifism and his anti-political stand to urge that Lincoln move more rapidly toward emancipation. Ironically, Garrison, unlike the political radicals in the Republican Party, believed that the work of social justice was complete with the passage of the Thirteenth Amendment. While radicals like Thaddeus Stevens sought to implement land reform and to guarantee protections against racial violence, Garrison closed the *Liberator* and devoted the rest of his life to other causes such as women's suffrage and temperance.

Grant, Ulysses S. (1822–1885) *Union army officer, general of the armies, president of the United States*
Hiram Ulysses Grant was born in Point Pleasant, Ohio. When admitted to West Point in 1839, the congressman who recommended his appointment entered his name as Ulysses Simpson Grant, as Simpson was his mother's maiden name, and the new name stuck. No doubt he preferred the initials U.S.G. to H.U.G. As a youth, Grant had worked on his father's farm where he acquired skills as a horseman, and at West Point he earned a reputation for being the best rider in his class. However, he graduated well down in class ranking, and since there were no openings in the cavalry, he was appointed as a second lieutenant in the infantry. During the U.S.-Mexican War, he served under both Zachary Taylor and Winfield Scott. Although he was discouraged about that war, believing its very premise unjust, he served with distinction, earning promotions for action at Molino del Rey and in Mexico City at Chapultepec.

After the U.S.-Mexican War he was posted to California and Oregon, and he resigned his army commission in 1854. Rumors spread that he had become an alcoholic, and over the next few years he drifted from one failed position to another, as farmer, real estate salesman, county engineer, and customhouse clerk. His younger brothers operated a leather store in Galena, Illinois, and they gave him a position there as clerk. Generally regarded as a failure in 1861, his career over the next 15 years was spectacular.

When the Civil War began, Grant offered his services to General George McClellan, but was rejected. Instead, he received an appointment as colonel and later brigadier general of Illinois volunteers, and he succeeded in whipping his unit into shape. His first engagement in the war was not a notable success. He led an ill-prepared attack in Missouri in November 1861. However, in February 1862, he successfully led the defeat of Confederate forces at Forts Henry and Donelson. At Donelson, he told Confederate general Buckner, "No terms except unconditional and immediate surrender can be accepted," which Buckner found rather unchivalrous. In the North, however, Grant's reputation immediately soared; he became known as Unconditional Surrender Grant, and he was appointed major general.

Victories at Shiloh (April 1862), Vicksburg (July 1863), and Chattanooga (November 1863) solidified his reputation with Lincoln. Although rumors of his drinking and his failure to file timely reports led to demands for his dismissal, Lincoln admired his fighting spirit and promoted him to supreme command of all Union forces. Grant was promoted to the revived rank of lieutenant general in March 1864. He dispatched Sherman to divide the South by way of Georgia, and he worked personally with General Meade and the Army of the Potomac in a bloody struggle against Confederate forces in Virginia from June 1864 through the spring of 1865. Forces under General Sheridan defeated Lee's army on April 1, 1865, and Grant accepted Lee's surrender at Appomattox Court House on April 9. Grant's terms to Lee were strictly military and served as a model for later surrenders.

In 1866, Grant was commissioned general of the army, a rank that had not existed since the time of Washington. He was appointed *ad interim* secretary of war April 1867–January 1868, but then resigned. By not displacing Stanton, he earned credit with radical Republicans who sought to impeach President Andrew Johnson for violation of the Tenure of Office Act in ordering Stanton's dismissal. As a consequence of his war record and his diplomatic pathway through the dilemma posed by the cabinet post, Grant was nominated for the presidency in 1868 by the Republican Party. He won that election by a narrow popular vote margin, although with a clear majority in the Electoral College. His administration was marked by numerous scandals, including the effort of his personal friends, Jay Gould and James Fisk, to corner the gold market in 1869. Grant's own brother-in-law, Abel Rathbone Corbin, tried to influence Grant to prevent the government from selling gold during the scheme, but Grant refused to cooperate and ordered sales that helped thwart the plans of Gould and Fisk. Nevertheless, the gold scandal damaged Grant's reputation.

Despite the fact that liberal Republicans who were outraged at the corruption charges defected from the party in 1872 to support Horace Greeley for the presidency, Grant won an easy reelection victory. During his second term, the corruption continued: Grant's vice president, Schuyler Colfax, and Congressman James A. Garfield had taken stock in Credit Mobilier, a railroad construction firm that received excess profits from building the Union Pacific Railroad; the secretary of the treasury, W. A. Richardson, resigned to escape a vote of censure by Congress; Grant's private secretary, O. E. Babcock, was implicated in a scandal involving the Whiskey Ring; Secretary of War W. W. Belknap had to resign to prevent being impeached for taking bribes.

After retiring from the presidency, Grant went on a world tour, and his name was entered in nomination at the Republican convention for a third (non-consecutive) term, in 1880. Supported by the Stalwart faction, representing the Republican patronage system, he lost to a compromise ticket of James Garfield, with Chester Arthur (head of the Republican patronage system in New York State) as vice president. Grant then lent his name to a brokerage firm, Grant and Ward, that went bankrupt. His fortunes sank to a low ebb, and he even had to give up personal swords and souvenirs from his war years that he had offered as security for a loan. His supporters succeeded in getting his name restored to the officers' retired list, and he received a pension in his last years. Suffering from throat cancer, probably brought on by a lifetime of smoking cigars, he wrote his memoirs, which Samuel Clemens assisted in getting published. Grant died as the manuscript was completed. When published, it earned his family a large fortune, reputedly in the range of $450,000. He died in Mount McGregor, New York, and his tomb in New York City on Riverside Drive has become a noted landmark.

Greeley, Horace (1811–1872) *antislavery journalist, politician*

Horace Greeley was born in Amherst, New Hampshire, the son of a poor farmer. He received inadequate schooling, and, at the age of 14, he became an apprentice to a Vermont newspaper editor. He worked as a printer in New York State and in Pennsylvania and, in 1831 moved to New York City. In 1834, he founded the weekly news and literary magazine, the *New Yorker*. However, that publication was barely successful, and Greeley earned money editing Whig publications.

Through contacts with Whig politicians, including William Seward, Greeley took on the editorship in 1840 of the Whig campaign weekly publication, *The Log Cabin*. With the victory of W. H. Harrison in the presidential election, Greeley's notoriety spread. He received credit not only for the successful Whig paper, but also for his active part in the campaign giving speeches and managing the state Whig campaign.

In 1841, Greeley started a new newspaper, the *New York Tribune*. Although nominally Whig, the paper reflected Greeley's own personal interest in a wide variety of social and intellectual movements. He grew interested in utopian socialism, supporting the communitarian ideals of Fourier. He personally supported a community in New Jersey and another in Colorado and hired several spokespeople of radical ideas, including Karl Marx. George Ripley, the founder of the Brook Farm commune, was a regular contributor to Greeley's *Tribune*. Among other causes, Greeley opposed capital punishment, advocated temperance and women's rights, and criticized monopolies. He followed the Whig line by favoring protective tariffs, the Bank of the United States, and federally-sponsored internal improvements. The *Tribune* merged with *The Log Cabin* and the *New Yorker*, and Greeley expanded the paper's circulation to more than 250,000. The weekly edition of the *Tribune* was widely read throughout rural areas, greatly spreading Greeley's influence.

During the 1850s, he favored the Wilmot Proviso that would have banned slavery in territories acquired from Mexico, and he opposed the Kansas-Nebraska Act of 1854. In 1856, he supported the new Republican Party. However, he split with Seward in 1860, throwing his support finally to Lincoln in that election. In a famous exchange during the war, he published an open letter to Lincoln, entitled "The Prayer of Twenty Millions," demanding that Lincoln commit himself to emancipation. Lincoln's response, on August 22, 1862, cogently explained that he would restore the Union with slavery, or without slavery, or with some slavery, but that he would restore the Union. Greeley reluctantly supported Lincoln in the election of 1864. He participated in an aborted effort to open peace negotiations in Canada with the Confederacy in the summer of 1864.

Although a radical in many respects, Greeley favored amnesty for Confederate officials. He earned hostility from some Republicans by joining with others in signing a bail bond for Jefferson Davis. A supporter of Grant, he fell out with him over corruption and bribery in the Republican Party and failure to implement civil service reform. Along with Gideon Welles, Carl Schurz, and others, he established the Liberal

Republican movement. He was nominated on a fusion ticket of liberal Republicans and Democrats in 1872 for the presidency. After a bitter campaign in which Greeley was caricatured as a crank and an eccentric, Grant took 286 electoral votes to only 66 for Greeley's ticket. Disturbed by the death of his wife and the loss of the election, Greeley died November 29, 1872, before his electoral votes were formally tallied. They were distributed among other candidates.

Greenhow, Rose O'Neal (1817–1864) *spy, diplomatic courier for the Confederacy*

Rose O'Neal Greenhow was born in Port Tobacco, Maryland, in 1817. At an early age she moved from Rockville, Maryland, to Washington, D.C., where her beauty earned her a number of suitors. She married Dr. Robert Greenhow and bore four children. Greenhow's husband held a position in the State Department, which gave her access to social circles in the city. During the years before the war, she met numerous politicians from all over the country and was particularly impressed by John C. Calhoun, who may have inspired in her a loyalty to the cause of states' rights and the South.

A prominent figure in Washington society, she was a widow with a small daughter when the war began. With her contacts in society, she learned details of military planning and forwarded a secret message to General P. G. T. Beauregard prior to the first Battle of Bull Run. Some accounts, including one by Jefferson Davis, credited her information with contributing to that early Confederate victory.

Her espionage was not particularly well concealed, and she was arrested, held first under house arrest, and then in the Old Capital prison. She was confined in prison with her daughter, and that fact soon made the Union counter-espionage effort seem cruel and inhumane. While in jail, she continued to smuggle out notes. At a hearing, she claimed that if she had learned secrets, it was only because those intimate with Lincoln chose to pour them into her ear. The observation was probably true, but not a very sound legal defense. Although espionage by a civilian was a capital offense, the Union chose to deport her, rather than suffer the negative propaganda effect of execution or further embarrassment at keeping her confined. She was welcomed in Richmond and celebrated throughout the South, as the Rebel Rose. Her efforts appeared to fulfill public desires for romance, espionage, and adventure. Jefferson Davis personally received her, and she was feted by the elite of Richmond.

Davis commissioned her to travel to Britain, to lecture there and to make contacts for the Confederate cause. While living in London, she published an account of her earlier adventures, *My Imprisonment and the First Year of Abolition Rule at Washington,* which only added to her notoriety and legend. In Britain, she met several notables and became engaged to a British earl. She went on to Paris, where she was received at the court of Napoleon III. In 1864, she returned to the Confederacy by way of a British blockade-runner, the *Condor.*

The ship ran aground near Wilmington, North Carolina. Fearing that she might be captured by nearby Union gunboats, she fled to shore in a lifeboat. The boat capsized and Rose O'Neal Greenhow was drowned. Legend has it that she had some $2,000 in gold, royalties from the publication of her memoirs, and that the weight of it caused her to drown. That story may very well have been the product of newspaper reporters' imaginations. Her body was recovered, and she was buried with full military honors.

Grimké, Charlotte Forten (1837–1914) *African-American educator, civil rights activist*

Charlotte Forten was born into a wealthy African-American family in Philadelphia. Her grandfather, James Forten, had established a fortune as a sailmaker, and his children and grandchildren represented the elite of the Philadelphia black community on the eve of the Civil War. Charlotte Forten was raised by an aunt and tutored at home. She then attended a teacher-preparatory school in Salem, Massachusetts, and taught briefly in Salem. She was one of the first African-American women to be paid as a teacher in the United States. She published several poems in the *Liberator* and in the *Anglo-African.* During the Civil War, she served as a teacher in the new schools established in the Sea Islands. She taught at a school on St. Helena Island, along with Laura Towne.

While there, she struggled to communicate with her students, most of whom spoke only Gullah, the local African-influenced dialect, and who had never been exposed to the sort of literate background in which she had been raised. Her experiences were a mix of idealism and disappointment, recorded both in her journals and in a two-part article published in May and June 1864 in the *Atlantic Monthly,* as "Life in the Sea Islands." To her own dismay she admitted that she felt closer to the white abolitionists working in the Sea Islands than she did to the local people.

After the war she obtained a position as clerk in the U.S. Treasury Department, living in Washington. At age 41, she married a Presbyterian minister, Francis Grimké, nephew of the Grimké sisters Sarah and Angelina, who had established a reputation as crusading abolitionists. Charlotte Forten Grimké remained an advocate of equal rights throughout her life. She died in Washington in 1914.

Grimké, Sarah (1792–1873) and Angelina Grimké Weld (1805–1879)
South Carolina-born abolitionists, feminists

The two Grimké sisters of South Carolina are so often written about and discussed together that a joint biography of the two is appropriate. Both were born into the family of John Faucheraud Grimké, a wealthy South Carolina planter who owned hundreds of slaves and who was a prominent judge, serving as chief justice of the state supreme court. Sarah, the older of the two sisters, saw a slave being whipped when she was a small child and that experience, among others, turned her against slavery. Sarah aspired to go to college and read the books owned by one of her brothers. When Judge Grimké discovered she was studying, he prohibited any further study. However, Sarah took over the education of her sister Angelina, 13 years her junior, and in that process, furthered her own education.

When she was 26, Sarah escorted her father to Philadelphia for medical treatment, and there learned of the Quaker religion. Sarah returned to South Carolina after her father's death, but moved in 1821 to Philadelphia. On a return visit to Charleston, Sarah converted Angelina to the Quaker faith, and then Angelina joined Sarah to live in Philadelphia in 1829.

In that year, Angelina wrote a letter to the *Liberator* decrying slavery. The publication of the letter immediately caused a sensation in the apolitical Quaker movement, and the Grimké sisters were faced with a choice of renouncing their new faith or renouncing abolitionism. They chose to give up Quakerism and joined the abolitionist movement. Having put South Carolina, their authoritarian masculine environment, and now the Quaker faith behind them, they both seemed liberated to venture into new grounds. After being trained as speakers by Theodore Dwight Weld, the two began giving talks to small groups of abolitionists, and then to larger audiences. As white women from a privileged background, with firsthand knowledge of slavery, they were much sought after as speakers in abolitionist meetings. Whatever their background, many outside the abolitionist movement found it shocking that women would speak publicly on any subject, and especially on such a controversial one.

In 1836, Angelina published a pamphlet, *Appeal to the Christian Women of the South.* That work, together with Sarah's *Epistle to the Clergy of the Southern States,* also published in 1836, and Angelina's *Appeal to the Women of the Nominally Free States* in 1837, made them notorious to an even wider public. Broadening their thinking, they began to attack not only slavery, but also race prejudice, and argued that white women had a natural bond with slave women, anticipating the sentiment that inspired Harriet Beecher Stowe. As they were attacked in religious circles and in the press for daring to speak out in such a shocking fashion, they became more vigorous in defending their own rights, and in developing a feminist position. Angelina wrote and later published a series of letters to Catherine Beecher defending her right to speak, and then Sarah published *Letters on the Equality of the Sexes,* defending freedom of speech for women.

In 1838, Angelina Grimké married the nationally-known abolitionist Theodore Dwight Weld, and as she took up family duties, she more or less retired from the abolitionist crusade and from public speaking. Sarah Grimké moved into the Weld home as well. However, in 1839, the two sisters published a collection of newspaper stories from the South, entitled *American Slavery as It Is: Testimony of a Thousand Witnesses.* After the Weld household fell on hard times, the family opened a boarding school. Notable abolitionists sent their children to the school, which evolved into a cooperative community, with the name Raritan Bay Union. The Grimké sisters took in two mulatto children of one of their brothers, and both of the nephews took the Grimké name. Francis, one of the nephews, married Charlotte Forten.

The Grimké sisters had established a linkage between feminism and abolition, and between women's rights and civil rights that long outlasted their own lives. Due to their personal efforts, hundreds and perhaps thousands of women participated in the abolitionist crusade in the 1840s and 1850s.

Hood, John Bell (1831–1879) *Confederate general*
John Bell Hood was born in Kentucky, the son of a doctor and farmer. He attended West Point, graduating in 1853. He served in the cavalry in Texas, but resigned his first lieutenant's commission three days after the fall of Fort Sumter. Serving first as lieutenant, he rapidly rose to colonel in the Texas forces, and then

to brigadier general in the Confederate army in March 1862. He developed a reputation for courage under fire and for conceiving and executing aggressive assaults on Union positions.

After the Battle of Antietam, Hood was promoted to major general, and he led troops at Fredericksburg. After further service in Virginia, he led his division of Texas cavalry at Gettysburg where he suffered a severe wound in his left arm. After recovering, he served under general James Longstreet at Chickamauga, commanding a corps. There he was wounded again in the right leg, which had to be amputated. Despite Hood's injuries, Longstreet recommended him for further promotion.

Hood was then assigned to the Army of Tennessee. Serving under Joseph Johnston, Hood's career took a turn for the worse. He seemed to have difficulty coordinating his plans with other corps commanders, and he blamed others for his own mistakes in judgment. However, just at this time, Jefferson Davis became troubled with Johnston's policy: to fall back through Georgia, avoiding major clashes with Sherman's advancing forces. After considering reports from various officers and from Braxton Bragg, Davis decided to replace Johnston with Hood. The decision was immediately controversial, as troops under Johnston were intensely loyal to him, and some officers in the field distrusted Hood. Hood was responsible for Confederate forces suffering four defeats around Atlanta.

After Hood evacuated Atlanta, he attempted to attack Sherman's supply lines, and then led an ill-fated expedition into Tennessee. At the battles of Franklin and Nashville, the Army of Tennessee was nearly destroyed, losing most of its troops and many officers. Discredited and discouraged, Hood tendered his resignation, which was finally accepted in late January 1865. Davis recalled Hood to Richmond, and then sent him on a mission to Texas to raise a large army there. On his way there, Hood learned of the surrender at Appomattox, and he personally surrendered at Natchez, Mississippi. He was immediately paroled, and he then moved to New Orleans.

The debate over Hood's tactics and behavior and the decision to replace Johnston with Hood survived the war and has continued among contemporaries and historians ever since. Hood's critics blamed the failures at Atlanta, Franklin, and Nashville on him directly, accusing him either of being naturally rash and a poor planner, or excusing his missteps on the grounds that he may have been taking laudanum (an opiate) and

alcohol to lessen the pain of his wounds, thus clouding his judgment. Others are less harsh, suggesting that the defeats sprang more from superior Union equipment and manpower, better and more defensible positions held by Union forces, and the accidents of war.

After the war, Hood entered business in New Orleans and married a local woman, Anna Marie Hennan. He and his wife had 11 children, including three sets of twins. During the yellow fever epidemics that wracked New Orleans in 1878 and 1879, he lost his fortune, and then he, his oldest child, and his wife died, leaving 10 of the children orphaned. They were adopted by a variety of families in different states. Hood's memoirs entitled *Advance and Retreat,* were published in 1880 to provide funds for the orphans; it was republished in 1985.

Jackson, Thomas Jonathan (Stonewall Jackson)
(1824–1863) *Confederate general*

Thomas J. Jackson was orphaned at an early age and grew up in relative poverty in what is now West Virginia. Despite his poor education, he entered West Point and graduated in the top third of his class in 1846. He immediately served in the artillery in the U.S.-Mexican War. After the war he resigned from the army and in 1851 he took a teaching position at the Virginia Military Institute in Lexington, Virginia, in science and artillery. With little grounding in science, his teaching style tended to be stilted and by-the-book, and he was regarded by the students as dour, strict, old-fashioned, and an overly religious Calvinist Presbyterian.

At the outset of the Civil War, Jackson entered service as a colonel in the Confederate army. During the First Battle of Bull Run, or Manassas, Jackson earned his nickname. As the battle raged, Brigadier General Barnard Bee (who later died from a wound in the battle) remarked, "There is Jackson standing like a stone wall." Bee may have been complaining that Jackson refused to move his troops to come to Bee's aid, but nevertheless, the term stuck as a compliment, not a complaint. Jackson's brigade became officially designated the Stonewall Brigade, and Jackson was thereafter affectionately known as Stonewall Jackson.

Jackson impressed fellow officers both with his leadership in battle and in his thinking during planning conferences. He was promoted to brigadier general June 17, 1861, to major general October 7, 1861, and to lieutenant general October 10, 1862. His dismounted cavalry operated through the Shenandoah Valley successfully in early 1862 and at the Battle of

Second Manassas in August 1862. He was engaged in a long and bitter personal dispute with General William Loring and submitted his resignation from the Confederate army before being talked out of it.

During Lee's invasion of Maryland, Jackson led a force that captured a large number of prisoners at Harpers Ferry, and his troops assisted at Antietam. Perhaps his most important victory was when he led his corps around the Union right flank at Chancellorsville, breaking up the Union XI Corps. On May 2, 1863, while reconnoitering by horseback at night, he was wounded by his own men as he returned to his own lines. The shot shattered his left arm, and it had to be amputated. Lee was said to have remarked, "he has lost his left arm, but I have lost my right arm." On May 10, Jackson died from pneumonia that developed after the amputation.

Although he was regarded as a brilliant tactician, his command was noted for several flaws. He tended to give precise and strict instructions to his subordinates, not allowing them much latitude, and hence little opportunity for training or advancement, which would have been more suited to Lee's loose method of administration. Jackson seemed less able to work in a subordinate position himself than when operating independently. In addition to his long-running feud with Loring, he had several other disputes and tended to promote officers without talent. Nevertheless, his striking successes in Shenandoah campaigns, and at First and Second Manassas, at Antietam, and finally at Chancellorsville, earned him permanent recognition as one of the outstanding leaders of the Confederate army.

Johnson, Andrew (1808–1875) *proslavery Democratic politician from Tennessee, Abraham Lincoln's second vice president, president of the United States (1865–1869)*

Andrew Johnson was born in North Carolina to a poverty-stricken family. His father died when he was 14 years old, and he was apprenticed to a local tailor in Raleigh, North Carolina, and learned some of the rudiments of reading and writing. However, he and his brother both ran away and evaded recapture as runaways for several years. Returning to Raleigh, he found the tailor shop closed, so he and his mother and siblings moved to Greeneville, Tennessee, where Andrew established his own tailor shop. At the age of 17, he married Eliza McCardle. She helped him learn to read and taught him arithmetic. He made it a practice to listen to the reading of speeches while he worked, and soon his tailor shop became a gathering place for political discussions. Encouraged by his wife, Johnson soon engaged in formal debates and began to run for local office. By 1834, he had already served as town alderman and mayor. His politics in the 1830s were those of a Jacksonian Democrat and he made much of the fact that he was, in the Jacksonian tradition, a man of the people who had risen by his own talents.

Continuing his career in politics, Johnson served in the state legislature, then in the United States Congress, followed by a term as governor of Tennessee. When South Carolina and the Gulf states seceded, Johnson was serving as a first-term U.S. senator from Tennessee, aligned with the states' rights and proslavery Southern branch of the Democratic Party. However, Johnson was also a Unionist, and he resented the political power of the wealthy planters. After the firing on Fort Sumter, when Tennessee joined the Confederacy, Johnson refused to give up his seat in the U.S. Senate, the only senator from a seceded state to remain. In that position, he was warmly supported by Unionists and vilified throughout the Confederacy as a traitor. Lincoln appointed Johnson military governor of Tennessee, and in that position he urged Lincoln to exempt Tennessee from emancipation. Later, he came around to supporting the emancipation proclamation as a war measure.

In order to balance the presidential ticket, the Republican Party, reconstituted as the Union Party, nominated Johnson, a Southern Jacksonian Democrat, to run as Lincoln's second vice president. The Lincoln–Johnson ticket soundly defeated the Democratic ticket of George McClellan and George Pendleton. After Lincoln died from the gunshot wound inflicted by John Wilkes Booth on April 14, Andrew Johnson was sworn in as president. With the end of the Civil War at hand, Johnson immediately issued a reward for the capture of Booth and for Jefferson Davis.

Congress was not in session until December 1865, so Johnson had the period from April 1865 until December to bring some order to the defeated South. He announced a plan of amnesty that would require wealthier landowners to personally apply for pardons before being granted the right to vote and hold office. However, he granted those pardons very generously, apparently gratified to see members of the former elite of the South come to him for personal forgiveness. He demanded that Southern states, in order to be readmitted to the Union, abolish slavery and repudiate the Confederate war debt. His hope was that the states would select a new generation of political leaders, perhaps drawn from the same Jacksonian

Democratic background as himself, and ready to challenge the leadership of the planter class. However, many of the Southern states elected former and unpardoned Confederates to political positions, and the new coalition that he hoped for between poor whites and Unionists in the South did not emerge. At the same time, the state governments in the former Confederacy began to pass a series of vagrancy laws and black codes that effectively replaced slavery with systems of peonage. Blacks were forbidden to migrate or to be found without employment under pain of imprisonment. They could then be released from prison in the custody of white employers who would hold them to a term of employment until they earned back their fines. As a firm believer in the right of self-government, Johnson felt he had to accept the verdict of the white voters, and he did not challenge these new, conservative Democratic governments.

Over the next several years, Congress and the president fought for control of the Reconstruction process. In order to ensure that Johnson did not subvert Reconstruction by replacing congressionally approved cabinet members, Congress passed the Tenure of Office Act. When Johnson tested that law by attempting to dismiss Secretary of War Edwin Stanton, Congress moved to impeach Johnson for high crimes and misdemeanors. Although the articles of impeachment passed the House of Representatives by a vote of 126 to 47 in February 1868, during the trial before the Senate, Johnson was acquitted by one vote on the most serious charge, and the others were not pressed.

Because of Johnson's failure to achieve a meaningful Reconstruction and because of his falling out with Congress, he has often been regarded as one of the least effective U.S. presidents. After serving out his term as president, Johnson returned to Tennessee and reentered state politics. He was an unsuccessful candidate before the state legislature for the U.S. Senate in 1869, and he also lost an election for a seat in Congress as an independent candidate in 1872. Johnson was selected by the Tennessee legislature to serve in the U.S. Senate in 1874 and served from March 1875 until his death on July 31, 1875. He died at the home of his daughter near Elizabethton, Tennessee.

Lee, Robert Edward (1807–1870) *Confederate general, commander of the Army of Northern Virginia, general in chief of the armies of the Confederate States*
Born on the estate of Stratford in Westmoreland County, Virginia, in 1807, Robert E. Lee was the fifth son of Revolutionary War hero "Light Horse Harry" Lee. As his father lost some of his estate in land speculation and the remainder passed to another son by an earlier marriage, Robert E. Lee was raised in the city of Alexandria, where he attended local schools. He attended West Point, graduating second in his class in 1829. On graduation, he entered the engineer corps and worked on projects in Georgia, Virginia, and New York. He married Mary Ann Randolph Custis, the great-granddaughter of Martha Washington. During the U.S.-Mexican War, Lee served on the staff of General Winfield Scott, and he earned recognition and promotion from captain to colonel for bravery. The Custis home in Arlington, Virginia, became Lee's home on the death of his father-in-law in 1857.

Lee was at home in Arlington in 1859, when John Brown launched his abortive raid at Harpers Ferry. Lee accepted an appointment to lead a detachment of marines to Harper's Ferry, where he took command of various militia units that had arrived to put down the attempted slave insurrection.

During the period immediately after the firing on Fort Sumter, General Scott asked Lee to take command of Union forces in suppressing the Confederate rebellion. When it became clear that Virginia would join in secession, Lee resigned his commission in the U.S. Army on April 20, 1861. He went to Richmond, where the governor appointed him commander in chief of both the state militia and state naval forces of Virginia. A few weeks later, on May 14, with the transfer of Virginia forces to the Confederacy, Lee was appointed brigadier general in the Confederate army.

Lee's career as a Confederate officer got off to a slow start with service in western Virginia. However, with the wounding of General Joseph E. Johnston at the Battle of Seven Pines, May 31, 1862, Lee was given command of the Army of Northern Virginia. Lee took the military initiative and engaged the forces of Union general McClellan in a series of battles near Richmond, known as the Seven Days battles, in the period June 26 to July 1, 1862. Although the battles might be regarded as tactical defeats for the Confederacy, Lee succeeded in holding off McClellan. The Peninsular Campaign to take the Confederate capital was called off. With these battles, Lee gained recognition throughout the South as the savior of Richmond.

Lee led two expeditions to take the war to the Union side of the line, with a major battle at Antietam Creek in Maryland in August 1862, and another at Gettysburg in July 1863. During these battles and others, Lee demonstrated both his brilliance as a general and some of his weaknesses. He was daring and willing to divide his forces to strike a quick blow at his adversary. But in several battles he seemed to be unaware that massed troops moving across open fields against defended positions could be nearly destroyed by rifle fire. His dispute with James Longstreet over the disastrous charge to Cemetery Ridge at Gettysburg outlasted the lives of both of them. Lee has also been both criticized and praised for his tendency to issue somewhat open-ended orders to his subordinates, leaving the details of execution to them. In some situations, especially when supported by strong officers, such a method could work very well.

Jefferson Davis appointed Lee general in chief of the armies of the Confederate States, effective January 23, 1865. However, despite his broadened responsibilities, most of his attention was given to the defense of Richmond.

Lee had been forced into what amounted to a siege at Richmond and Petersburg, where his forces held out for about 10 months from the summer of 1864 until March 1865. There the battle lines settled into a form of trench warfare, foreshadowing conditions of World War I on the Western Front. Lee was able to maintain open communications with the Shenandoah and with resources in North Carolina until his forces, suffering from attrition and demoralization, had to be pulled out of the defense in 1865.

After his surrender of the Army of Northern Virginia on April 9, 1865, to General Grant, Lee returned to Richmond under parole. He urged his fellow officers to accept surrender and to avoid further bloodshed in any guerrilla style warfare, and his advice appeared to be followed by most regular units.

Lee accepted the presidency of Washington College in Lexington, Virginia, and the school grew in repute due to his prestige. After his death in 1870, his body was interred at the chapel at the college, now Washington and Lee University. Other members of his family are also buried in the crypt below the chapel. The Custis estate in Arlington was confiscated and used as a settlement for freedmen, and, after his death, was converted into Arlington National Cemetery.

Lincoln, Abraham (1809–1865) *president of the United States (March 4, 1861–April 13, 1865)*

Abraham Lincoln was born February 12, 1809, near Hodgenville, Kentucky. He was the son of a farmer and carpenter, Thomas Lincoln, and his wife, Nancy Hanks Lincoln. Both the Lincolns belonged to the section of the Baptist Church that opposed slavery. In 1816, the family moved to Indiana, which at that time was a rough frontier. Lincoln's mother died when he was nine years old, and his father remarried. Lincoln learned to read at several brief sessions in school and became an avid reader. At age 17, he took a flatboat trip to New Orleans, then rejoined his family and moved with them in 1830 to Illinois.

In 1831, Lincoln took a second flatboat trip to New Orleans, and, on his return, he moved out on his own, settling in New Salem, Illinois. There he operated a store and later was appointed local surveyor and postmaster. He gained the respect of his neighbors, was elected to four terms in the Illinois legislature in the period 1834–40 on the Whig ticket, and moved to the new capital of the state at Springfield. During this period, he studied law and received his license to practice in 1836. He soon gained a reputation for winning cases. In 1842 he married Mary Todd, and in 1846 he was elected to the U.S. Congress and served one term. While there, he opposed the U.S.-Mexican War and became known as an opponent of the extension of slavery. After his term, he returned to Illinois, still practicing law.

With the passage of the Kansas-Nebraska Act in 1854, he reentered politics. Lincoln tried for the Senate in 1854 and received some support for the Republican vice presidential nomination in 1856. In 1858, he gained more national prominence by debating with Democrat Stephen Douglas in several locations around Illinois as they competed for selection by the legislature as U.S. senator. Lincoln gained further recognition for his antislavery position in a speech at the Cooper Institute in New York City.

Lincoln won the nomination for the presidency on the third ballot at the national Republican convention in 1860. On November 6, he won in the election against three other candidates: Stephen Douglas as a Northern Democrat, John C. Breckinridge as a Southern Democrat, and John Bell as a candidate of the Constitutional Union Party. Lincoln won with approximately 40 percent of the popular vote and a clear majority of the Electoral College. He gave several speeches en route to his inauguration, trying out various ideas about how to deal with the mounting national crisis. By the time of his inauguration on March 4, 1861, the seven seceded states had met to form a provisional Confederate government.

Over the next four years, Lincoln dealt with constitutional, political, and financial crises that were far more severe than those faced by any other U.S. president. The Constitution did not have provisions to deal with the secession of states. Although the Constitution did not expressly forbid secession, Lincoln and most Northerners believed that once a state had joined the Union it could not announce its withdrawal, especially on the grounds that it did not approve the outcome of a presidential election. Thus Lincoln and his supporters viewed the secession as an act of rebellion after Confederate troops opened fire on Fort Sumter. Lincoln then used his constitutional powers to suppress the rebellion.

However, since the Confederacy, which grew to include 11 states, was so powerful and mounted both an army and a navy, for many purposes, Lincoln's War Department treated the conflict as if it were a war between nations. Confederate naval ships were regarded as pirates by the Northern press, but the ships and their sailors were treated as though they belonged to an enemy nation. Captured soldiers and officers were never tried for treason, but were treated as prisoners of war. Politically, Lincoln faced a severely divided country, with several factions within his own party and strong opposition from Northern Democrats.

To deal with the financial crisis brought on by the war, and in recognition of the transition of the nation from an agricultural to a commercial and industrial basis, Lincoln approved the National Banking Act, establishing a national currency. The act also created a network of national banks. Furthermore, he approved higher tariffs that protected some American industries, and he approved a charter for the first transcontinental railroad.

Lincoln's imposition of martial law in Northern states, his suspension of the right of habeas corpus, the arrest of legislators and city officials in Maryland, and many other measures were seen by his opponents as evidence of usurpation of power. On the other hand, Lincoln insisted on humane practices, and when sections of the South were conquered by Union troops, he worked to quickly establish some form of local self-government.

Lincoln's attitude toward slavery evolved during the war. Unlike abolitionists and radicals in his own party, Lincoln did not believe that the Constitution gave Congress the power to emancipate slaves. At first, he hoped to combine compensated emancipation as might be established by the separate states with a plan for colonization of freed slaves overseas. However, he decided in 1862 that, as a war measure, he could declare free those slaves held in areas in rebellion. On that war-

powers basis, he announced the Emancipation Proclamation that went into effect on January 1, 1863. He later supported and urged approval of a constitutional amendment abolishing slavery throughout the United States, including those areas that had been loyal to the Union, such as Kentucky and Delaware.

As a brilliant lawyer, as a political candidate, and as president, Lincoln displayed an ability to think strategically unmatched by any of his opponents. In the Lincoln-Douglas debates, in dealing with European powers that toyed with recognizing the Confederacy, in working with his Northern political supporters and opponents, as well as in dealing with the Confederacy itself, Lincoln often posed a problem in such a way that boxed his opponents into postions that offered few difficult choices, any of which would be damaging to them.

Lincoln employed a similar strategy in other situations. For example, by announcing the Emancipation Proclamation, he presented the still-seceded areas with a choice: They could surrender, and thus avoid the impact of the proclamation, or they could fight, knowing that, if Union troops moved into their areas, slavery would be destroyed. By one choice, they surrendered and kept their slaves; by the other, they risked losing everything. When Lincoln accepted a suggestion from Jefferson Davis that commissioners meet to consider peace early in 1865, Lincoln structured the Hampton Roads meeting in such a way that he would consider only surrender of troops in the field, with no conditions. If the terms for the meeting were accepted, there would be no recognition that the Confederacy had ever existed; if the terms were rejected, the onus of continuing the war until the South's armies were defeated would be upon the leaders of the Confederacy.

Although Lincoln had at first been reluctant to embrace emancipation as a war goal, he personally took the lead in converting the Civil War from one whose central purpose was to preserve the Union to one of liberation and freedom. For this reason, although the Emancipation Proclamation had no immediate effect and was viewed by some of his contemporaries as an empty gesture, his leadership on the difficult issues surrounding slavery justify his enduring reputation as the Great Emancipator.

A week after the surrender of Lee's Army of Northern Virginia at Appomattox Court House, Lincoln attended a play at Ford's Theater in Washington. There he was shot by John Wilkes Booth on the evening of April 14, 1865, and died the next morning from the wound. The national mourning for his death was profound and heartfelt, as millions of citizens viewed his funeral cortege as it passed through several cities of the North to his final resting place in a cemetery in Springfield, Illinois. Lincoln's wit, eloquence, and brilliant leadership had won him a place in the hearts of the nation and a place in history.

McClellan, George Brinton (1826–1885) *Union general, Democratic Party candidate for president in 1864, governor of New Jersey*

Born in Philadelphia, George McClellan graduated from West Point in 1846, the second in his class. He took a position with the U.S. Army engineers and served in the U.S.-Mexican War under Winfield Scott. He joined the cavalry in 1855, and then received an appointment to study European armies. He filed a report on the Crimean War, including details on the siege of Sebastopol. He studied Prussian and Hungarian cavalry saddles, and, slightly modifying their design, developed the McClellan saddle that was adopted and used for decades by the U.S. Army.

McClellan resigned his commission in 1857 and took a position with the Illinois Central Railroad as chief engineer and vice president. There he met both Lincoln, who did legal work for the company, and the detective Allan Pinkerton, who helped solve several robberies of railroad express cars. During the Civil War, McClellan served first as a major general in the Ohio Militia. He led the army of occupation of western Virginia, and in July 1861 was made commander of the Military Division of the Potomac in the Union army. He was appointed commander in chief of the army November 5, 1861, and held that post until March 11, 1862.

McClellan had a very high opinion of himself, and he was certain that he could administer the army better than Winfield Scott. He thus maneuvered and used his contacts to arrange promotions. Called the Young Napoleon by some in the press, he assured friends and reporters he had no ambition to become a dictator. His engineering and organizational skills came into play as he planned the Peninsular Campaign against Richmond. However, that campaign also revealed his personal weaknesses. He tended to believe Pinkerton's overblown assessments of Confederate strength. He spent months preparing advances. He refused to describe his plans to the secretary of war or even to Lincoln. By the time he advanced, Joseph Johnston had pulled back the Confederate forces.

Due to McClellan's delays and missteps, Lincoln finally suspended him from his broader command of all the armies in March 1862 in order to allow him to concentrate on the Richmond campaign. However, after the Seven Days battles in June 1862, McClellan still hesitated to advance on the confederate capital and remained entrenched at Harrison's Landing. Peeved at everyone else for his own failures, he criticized the War Department as well as his subordinates. The press changed their assessment of him, ridiculing him in editorials and cartoons.

After the defeat of Union forces at the Second Battle of Bull Run, Lincoln restored McClellan to active command. He was in charge when Lee invaded Maryland, and, despite a slow and piecemeal resistance, he was able to turn Lee's invasion at Antietam. Despite the mixed results of that battle, the Union chose to regard it as a victory. Finally he gave up his command on November 9, 1862, and retired to his home in Trenton, New Jersey, where he awaited further orders. This time, Stanton and Lincoln agreed not to reinstate McClellan with any command of troops.

In 1864, McClellan was nominated by the Democratic Party as candidate for the presidency. As a general and a recognized War Democrat, he represented a compromise in the party between the peace wing represented by former Ohio congressman Clement Vallandigham on the one hand and former New York mayor Fernando Wood and pro-war Democrats on the other. Although Peace Democrats dictated the party platform, the party ran McClellan in hopes of balancing the ticket with a well-known warrior. McClellan accepted the nomination with a letter that spelled out his disagreements with the platform, leaving supporters unclear on whether he would require an unconditional Confederate surrender, as he proposed, or whether he would be open to a negotiated peace, as advocated by many in his party, including George Pendleton, his vice-presidential running mate, and Vallandigham, who was considered for secretary of war.

The Battles of Mobile and Atlanta in August and September 1864 helped solidify support for Lincoln. Rumors that Peace Democrats planned an uprising and release of Confederate prisoners damaged that party's reputation. Several other factors contributed to McClellan's defeat: a vigorous Republican campaign, the victories of the Union army in the field, generous furlough plans that allowed soldiers to return to their home states for voting, and widespread, genuine Lincoln support. McClellan did not resign his army commission until election day, which also served as a source of criticism by his opponents.

McClellan remained active in politics, and he later served as governor of New Jersey, 1878–81. He died in Orange, New Jersey, in 1885.

Meade, George (1815–1872) *Union army officer*

George Meade was born in Cadiz, Spain, where his father was a naval agent for the United States and a merchant. Meade attended the school briefly operated by Salmon Chase in Washington, D.C. He entered West Point, graduating in 1835. He served in Florida and at the Watertown Arsenal in Massachusetts, but resigned from the army in 1836 to work as a civil engineer. He rejoined the army in 1842, where he worked in border survey and lighthouse work before seeing action in the U.S.-Mexican War. He returned to work as an engineer in the army after the U.S.-Mexican War.

At the beginning of the Civil War, he became a brigadier general of volunteers, in charge of one of the Pennsylvania brigades. After training, he and his unit saw action in the Peninsular Campaign under General George McClellan, where he was wounded at the Battle of Glendale. He participated in other battles, including Second Manassas and Antietam. He was in charge of V Corps at Chancellorsville.

On June 28, 1863, he was given command of the Army of the Potomac. In the Gettysburg campaign, he commanded the Union forces that succeeded in holding off Confederate attacks on July 2 and 3, 1863. Although a victory, Meade was strongly criticized for allowing the Confederate forces to escape back across the Potomac River. Even so, his strong showing at Gettysburg won him promotion to brigadier general in the regular army, and he received a resolution of thanks from the U.S. Congress. In 1864, Grant was appointed general in chief of the army and made his headquarters with Meade in the Army of the Potomac. Although nominally in charge of the Army of the Potomac, Meade at the same time was subordinate to Grant.

Meade, always impatient with newspaper reporters, sufficiently offended them that they informally conspired to report only his failures and to attribute any successes either to Grant or to Meade's subordinates. Thus Meade's long command during the battles of the Wilderness, Spotsylvania, Cold Harbor, and Petersburg received little favorable comment. Philip Sheridan, his junior, was promoted to major general before him. The lack of recognition in his own time has continued to some extent in the historical record, despite Meade's

crucial service both at Gettysburg and in the final months of the war.

After the war, he continued in the regular army, serving in command of departments and divisions in the East and South. While serving as an officer, he also became commissioner of Fairmount Park in Philadelphia from 1866 until his death. He was in charge of the army's Division of the Atlantic, based in Philadelphia, when he died as a result of pneumonia and old war wounds in 1872.

Pinkerton, Allan (1819–1884) *Scottish-born detective, founder of short-lived U.S. Secret Service, detective story author*

Allan Pinkerton was born in Glasgow, Scotland, the son of a sergeant in the municipal police. Pinkerton immigrated to the United States in 1842, first to Chicago and then to Dundee in Kane County, Illinois, where he set up a barrel-making business. After tracing and identifying a band of counterfeiters, he was selected deputy sheriff of Kane County. Appointed as sheriff of Cook County, with his office in Chicago, he developed a force of detectives to track down thieves stealing from the railroad companies. In 1852, he established the Pinkerton National Detective Agency, which focused on tracking thieves who stole from the railroad express companies.

Just before the inauguration of Lincoln in 1861, Pinkerton was asked by the president of the Philadelphia, Wilmington, and Baltimore Railroad to investigate rumors of a plot to sabotage Lincoln's train on its way, into Washington. His operatives reported hearing of a plot to assassinate Lincoln in Baltimore. Whether or not the plotters were competent, or, as some reports indicate, merely pro-secession Marylanders led by a hotel barber in Baltimore with a fertile imagination, Lincoln took Pinkerton's advice and slipped through Baltimore without stopping there. In April 1861, at the request of General George McClellan, Pinkerton set up an espionage network that provided information about Confederate forces, primarily in Virginia. Pinkerton adopted the cover name of Major E. J. Allen.

Pinkerton had a flair for publicity, and McClellan had heard of his work with railroad companies and had used his private detective services prior to the war. Pinkerton's men worked behind Confederate lines, penetrating the office of Judah Benjamin, Confederate secretary of war, a Confederate counter-espionage outfit, and even a Confederate spy team that operated between Richmond and Baltimore. Although his network was extensive and elaborate, Pinkerton's force had a difficult time establishing the reliability of information. More than one historian has attributed McClellan's hesitancy in attacking Confederate forces during the Peninsular Campaign in Virginia to the inflated figures about Generals Joseph Johnston and Robert E. Lee's force levels that McClellan received from Pinkerton. Even though McClellan heavily outnumbered his opponents, Pinkerton had convinced McClellan that he faced vastly superior forces.

After the war, Pinkerton continued operating his private detective agency, which still exists, making a massive recovery of nearly $700,000 in stolen money in 1866. However, in 1869, Pinkerton suffered a partial stroke and retired from the agency, leaving it to his sons to operate. They took the agency into anti-radical activity, breaking up the Molly Maguires, a radical organization that had advocated and used sabotage against coal mining companies. Later, the detective agency provided private armed forces to break up other union activities. Pinkerton began writing detective fiction, as well as his memoirs. Among his works are *The Molly Maguires and the Detectives* (1877), *Criminal Reminiscences and Detective Sketches* (1879), *The Spy of the Rebellion* (1883), and *Thirty Years a Detective* (1884). His novels include *The Expressman and the Detective* (1874), *The Detective and the Somnambulust* (1875), *Bucholz and the Detectives* (1878), and *The Burglar's Fate and the Detectives* (1884), in addition to collections of short stories.

Quantrill, William Clarke (1837–1865)
Confederate guerrilla leader

William C. Quantrill was born in Canal Dover, Ohio, and attended school there, becoming an assistant teacher at age 16. At age 18, he left home to move west into Illinois, and, a year later, moved to Kansas. He arrived in Kansas during the later phases of the local war there, then drifted west to Utah and Colorado. For a brief period late in 1859, he worked as a teacher in the town of Stanton, Kansas. However, he was soon unemployed and took up a variety of criminal activities in Lawrence, Kansas, in early 1860, including kidnapping slaves and selling them back to their owners. During this period he went under the name of Charley Hart, switching his allegiance between Kansas antislavery Jayhawkers and proslavery Missouri Border Ruffians, as the rival informal armies were known. Operating out of Blue Springs, Missouri, and nearby proslavery communities, Quantrill emerged as the leader of an informal force of guerrilla fighters, or bushwhackers, in 1861.

Attacking Union patrols and pro-Union civilians, the bushwhackers consistently stole money, jewelry, clothing, and other items from their victims. Quantrill later earned a commission as captain from the Confederacy as the head of a unit of Partisan Rangers.

Federal forces in Missouri ruled that Quantrill and his men should be given no quarter and treated as outlaws rather than enemy soldiers. Quantrill's forces frequently shot and killed any wounded Union troops they defeated in battle and often killed unarmed civilians they suspected of siding with the Union. Quantrill's force sometimes numbered as few as 18 or 20 men, and, at its largest, consisted of an estimated 320 to 450. Quantrill adopted classic guerrilla tactics, refusing to take on a unit larger than his own and dispersing when attacked by superior numbers. Many of his men carried several revolvers, and they used these rather than rifles or muskets as their primary weapon. Riding at full tilt toward Union troops who were armed with muzzle-loaded rifles, they frequently defeated the Union units that attempted to form a firing line. In effect, Quantrill anticipated the use of rapid-firing and repeating weapons by employing multiple revolvers rather than the slowly-loaded, single-shot rifled muskets of the era.

Quantrill led a notorious raid on Lawrence, Kansas, on August 21, 1863. His men had a list of pro-Union politicians and antislavery spokesmen that Quantrill had marked down for execution, and, in addition, he had ordered that all men and boys old enough to hold a gun be killed and the town burned. The citizens of the town were stunned to realize that men were taken from their homes and shot while trying to surrender. Although the raiders avoided killing women and small children, they murdered some 185 men and young boys and burned about 180 buildings, looting the town in a drunken rampage. Although pursued by regular Union troops and Kansas militia units, Quantrill's force escaped back into Missouri. When word of the atrocity spread, Union general Thomas Ewing issued an order to depopulate the border counties of Missouri that had harbored Quantrill and his guerrillas. Union forces forcibly evacuated 20,000 civilians from their homes in the region and methodically burned their farms and houses to prevent them providing a haven for Quantrill's bushwhackers.

After several other forays and the massacre of surrendering troops in what is now Oklahoma, Quantrill's unit began to break up, following other leaders who had been his lieutenants, in smaller, separate groups. At the end of the war, Quantrill took a remaining group of about 20 on a series of raids into Kentucky, where he was finally caught and shot by Union forces, six weeks after the surrender of Robert E. Lee. He died from his wounds on June 6, 1865. Most of the members of his former force surrendered in Missouri when offered amnesty.

Quantrill's name was frequently misspelled as "Quantrell" in some newspaper dispatches, military orders, and in some historical reports. Among the members of his raiders were several who became outlaw bank and train robbers after the war, including Frank and Jesse James and Cole Younger.

Semmes, Raphael (1809–1877) *Confederate commander of commerce-raiding cruisers*

Raphael Semmes was born in Maryland and was appointed as a midshipman in the U.S. Navy in 1826. He was promoted to lieutenant in 1837, and then to commander in 1855. He studied law between naval duties and was admitted to the bar in 1834. He served in the U.S.-Mexican War in the blockade of Veracruz. After the war, he settled in Mobile, Alabama, regarding himself as an adopted citizen of that state. When Alabama seceded from the Union, he resigned his U.S. naval commission and volunteered his services to the forming Confederacy. Even before the outbreak of war at Fort Sumter, Semmes worked for the Confederate navy in purchasing ships and military supplies in the north.

Semmes advocated the formation of a fleet of commerce raiders to attack and destroy Union merchant vessels. Confederate secretary of the navy Stephen Mallory supported Semmes's idea, and Semmes was placed in charge of a steamer at New Orleans. As the *Sumter,* under Semmes's command, the ship had a successful six-month cruise in late 1861 and early 1862, capturing and releasing 10 Union merchant ships and destroying another seven. The *Sumter* was decommissioned at Gibraltar, and Semmes awaited a new command. In August, he took passage to the Azores, and, with the rank of captain, took charge of a British-built cruiser, the *Alabama.* From August 1862 until June 1864, Semmes took the *Alabama* on a wide-ranging cruise, capturing or destroying a total of 66 Union ships, including whalers, clippers, and even a Union warship, the *Hatteras,* in an engagement off Galveston on January 11, 1863.

Semmes's exploits earned him accolades in Britain and the Confederacy, but gave him the reputa-

tion of a pirate in the North. From reports of released crews and passengers from ships he captured at sea, it was clear that he relished his role. According to some reports, he scrupulously obeyed the rules of warfare at sea, but many prisoners complained of harsh treatment, confinement on deck or in chains, and other offenses. Often Semmes and other cruiser commanders would "parole" a ship on promise that its owners would pay an indemnity to the Confederate government on the conclusion of the war. Semmes and his crew would be entitled to a proportion of that fee. Of course, with the defeat of the Confederacy, no such bounties were ever collected, yet during the war they provided an incentive for the crews of his and other Confederate sea raiders.

Semmes's *Alabama* was never able to come into a Confederate port, and he found it difficult to obtain coal and to conduct needed repairs. His crew included many volunteer recruits from England and Europe, and they were never as amenable to shipboard discipline as regular naval personnel. Facing these problems, in June 1864, Semmes put into the harbor at Cherbourg, France, for repairs. However, he soon learned that the Union ship *Kearsarge* was offshore, probably soon to be joined by other Union ships. Rather than surrendering his ship to French authorities, and not wanting to delay, Semmes ordered the *Alabama* out to engage the *Kearsarge.* He and his officers were surprised to learn that the *Kearsarge* was armored with anchor chains, which deflected most of the shots in the hour-long fight. Despite some well-aimed shots from *Alabama,* the Confederate ship soon foundered from shots that hit at its waterline.

When the *Alabama* was sinking, Semmes sent his wounded aboard lifeboats toward the *Kearsarge,* and then abandoned ship. He and some of his officers were picked up by a British yacht that was observing the battle, and he was taken to Britain. Controversy surrounded the battle, with some claiming he should have avoided the fight and that he had known of the armor of the *Kearsarge* before the battle. Others saw the battle as a fittingly gallant end to his cruise. He returned to the Confederacy and was given command of the small James River Squadron in the defense of Richmond. When Lee evacuated Richmond in early April 1865, Semmes ordered the fleet burned, and then led his sailors ashore to participate as ground troops. As Jefferson Davis retreated from Richmond to Danville, Virginia, he appointed Semmes acting brigadier general of the Confederate army. Semmes surrendered his troops with those of General Joseph E. Johnston to General Sherman.

After the war was over, Semmes was arrested and brought to Washington on charges of piracy and treason, along with other charges stemming from his treatment of prisoners. After being held three months, all charges were dropped. Semmes took up the practice of law in Mobile, Alabama. There, in 1869, he published *Memoirs of Service Afloat During the War Between the States.* He had earlier published a similarly titled work, *Service Afloat and Ashore During the Mexican War.* He died in Mobile on August 30, 1877.

Seward, William (1801–1872) *governor of New York, U.S. senator from New York, U.S. secretary of state*
Seward was born in upstate New York and attended Union College, graduating in 1820. After reading law, he was admitted to the bar and began practicing in Auburn, New York, in 1823. He was active in both the Anti-Masonic Party and the Whig Party. He served as state senator in the period 1830–34, and then as governor of New York State for two two-year terms, 1838–42. He angered some voters with his reform measures, which included prison reform and support for public schools that would teach immigrants in their own languages.

As a Whig, he was selected by the New York State legislature for the U.S. Senate in 1848 and there developed a reputation as a strongly antislavery senator with his opposition to the Fugitive Slave Act and his support for the admission of California as a free state during the debates over the Compromise of 1850. He served two terms in the Senate, from 1849 to 1861. While in the Senate, he shifted his allegiance from the Whig Party to the newly formed Republican Party at the end of 1855. Although he was regarded in the South as a firebrand in opposition to slavery, other antislavery politicians found his positions too moderate. They suspected that he ameliorated his antislavery views in hopes of winning the presidency with Southern or pro-Southern votes.

Seward was among the leading candidates for the Republican nomination for the presidency in 1860, but he lost on the third ballot at the convention to Abraham Lincoln. Seward campaigned vigorously for Lincoln in a speaking tour, and, partly as a reward for his help and as recognition for his prominent role in the party, Lincoln nominated him for secretary of state. However, Seward at first hesitated to accept the position, arguing for and against other nominees to cabinet positions. He finally accepted the day after Lincoln's inauguration. He immediately made efforts to dominate the new administration, even suggesting that he should play a role like that of prime minister. However, he soon recognized that Lincoln chose to make his own decisions and to implement them.

During the crisis over Fort Sumter, Seward argued for a quiet withdrawal and for compromise in order to avoid war, which would draw other states into the Confederacy. However, his position was outvoted in the cabinet. After the war started, Seward became aggressive in supporting the Union cause and worked to ensure that Britain and other nations did not recognize the Confederacy. He also pressured France to withdraw from Mexico.

Seward urged Lincoln to delay the preliminary Emancipation Proclamation until after a Union victory, and his advice appeared to influence Lincoln's decision to wait until after the Battle of Antietam before he announced his intention to free slaves still in regions under Confederate control as of January 1, 1863. Seward's moderating influence was well known, and some more radical members of the Republican Party hoped to get Lincoln to dismiss Seward.

On the evening when Booth assassinated Lincoln, another plotter, Lewis Paine (operating under the alias, Lewis Powell), accosted Seward in his sickbed and stabbed him in the throat. Severely wounded, Seward recovered and resumed his duties as secretary of state under Andrew Johnson. He supported Johnson in opposing congressional Reconstruction, further alienating congressional Radical Republicans. Under Johnson, he made several efforts to increase the territorial holdings of the United States. However, treaties to acquire Haiti, Santo Domingo, and the Danish Virgin Islands were defeated in the general opposition to Johnson-sponsored measures. Seward was able to secure, in 1867, Senate agreement to the purchase of Alaska for $7.2 million, as well as the annexation of Midway Island. Some funds from the Alaska purchase price were used to repay promoters who had lobbied for the purchase and bribed key senators. Seward left office with the inauguration of Ulysses S. Grant as president, and he died at his home in Auburn, New York, in 1872.

Seymour, Horatio (1810–1886) *Democratic governor of New York (1863–1865)*
Horatio Seymour was born in Pompey Hill, New York, and studied law at Utica. He was admitted to the bar in

1832, and then served as military secretary to New York governor William Marcy over the period 1833–39. He was elected to the state assembly in 1841, 1844, and 1845 and served as mayor of Utica in 1842. As a Democrat, he was elected governor of New York State in 1852, defeating the Whig candidate, Washington Hunt. As governor, he vetoed an alcohol prohibition bill, and that action led to his defeat for re-election when he was opposed by a strong temperance candidate. When the bill was later enacted, it was immediately declared unconstitutional. As a Democrat and a supporter of President Buchanan, Seymour advocated compromise with the Southern states, and he was widely regarded as one of the most prominent of the Peace Democrats, or Copperheads.

Seymour was elected governor in 1862 and soon emerged as one of Lincoln's most vociferous and powerful opponents in the North. He regarded the Emancipation Proclamation as unconstitutional and also opposed the federal draft on the grounds that it was an invasion of states' rights. Furthermore, when Lincoln ordered the deportation of Congressman Clement Vallandigham of Ohio, Seymour strongly protested this act as unconstitutional. During the draft riots in New York City in July 1863, he gave a speech to assembled rioters that was interpreted as an act of conciliation toward them. He argued that the draft law should not be implemented until its legality had been tested in court. That speech, combined with his resistance to other acts of Lincoln, was used by Republicans as evidence of disloyalty and led to his defeat for reelection in 1864. Republicans in New York regarded Seymour as a dangerous Copperhead, and many accused him of treason. He was considered as a candidate for the presidency at the Democratic convention of 1864, but George McClellan, the general and War Democrat, won that nomination. Seymour ran for president on the Democratic ticket in 1868 and lost that election to Ulysses S. Grant, winning only 80 votes in the Electoral College to 214 taken by Grant. At that point, Seymour retired from any active role in politics.

Sheridan, Philip Henry (1831–1888) *Union army officer*
Philip Sheridan's exact birthdate and place of birth are uncertain, but he noted in his memoir that he was born in Albany, New York. His family were Catholic pioneers in Ohio, and he entered West Point in 1848. He was expelled for a year due to a fight with a fellow cadet and graduated in 1853. After eight years of service on the frontier, he was still a second lieutenant at the outbreak of the Civil War. Due to his talents in command, he was repeatedly promoted through the war, achieving the rank of major general in the next four years.

He saw action at Perryville, Murfreesboro, Chickamauga, and Missionary Ridge outside Chattanooga. His men defeated Confederate forces under Braxton Bragg at Chattanooga, causing Bragg to request that he be relieved of command. Sheridan's leadership attracted the attention of Grant, who assigned Sheridan to supervise all the cavalry of the Army of the Potomac in the spring of 1864. After Jubal Early led a Confederate raid to the outskirts of Washington in July 1864, Sheridan was put in command of two army corps, three divisions of cavalry, and artillery forces, numbering over 40,000 troops. His orders were to close off the Shenandoah Valley, which had been the route through Virginia for attacks into Maryland and Pennsylvania, and to deny Confederates access to the food and other resources of the valley. Sheridan's cavalry took on Confederate cavalry under J. E. B. Stuart, who was killed as a result of wounds received at Yellow Tavern near Richmond in May 1864.

While Sheridan was reporting in Washington, Jubal Early attacked Sheridan's positions near Cedar Creek in October 1864. Sheridan arrived to find his men in full and disorganized retreat, and he rode at full speed from Winchester, Virginia, to the battlefront, where one division of his forces and some cavalry were holding the line. Sheridan reformed his troops, and his ability to convert the disaster into a victory won immediate national recognition. Grant praised him, and Congress voted an official thanks. Sheridan was then promoted to major general. Under his command, his troops laid waste to the Shenandoah, burning farms and destroying livestock to cut off this food and forage supply to Confederate troops.

Sheridan took a major part in the final battles that defeated Lee. At Five Forks, Sheridan's forces defeated a weakened Confederate right flank, and, at Sayler's Creek he took the surrender of a large part of the Army of Northern Virginia. His troops cut off Lee's retreat from Appomattox Court House, preventing Lee from linking up with Johnston.

After the war, Sheridan took over the Reconstruction military department of Louisiana, Texas, and Missouri. His policies there were regarded as so strict that President Andrew Johnson ordered his removal. When Grant became president, Sheridan was promoted to lieutenant general. He stayed with the army, and in 1884 he was promoted to commanding general of the army; in 1888 a few months before his death, he was promoted to the rank of general of the army. Sheridan ranked along with Grant and Sherman as one of the three most successful Union officers during the Civil War.

Sherman, William Tecumseh (1820–1891)
Union general

Sherman was born in Lancaster, Ohio, one of 11 children of a justice on the state supreme court. When his father died in 1829, the children were taken in by friends and relatives. Cump, as young Sherman was called, was raised in the family of Thomas Ewing, a U.S. senator and cabinet officer. Cump later married a daughter of Ewing. With his family connections, Sherman received an appointment to West Point, where he graduated near the top of his class in 1840.

He served in the U.S.-Mexican War, and in 1853 he resigned his commission to go into banking in San Francisco. When the bank failed, he entered law practice in Kansas. In 1859, he was appointed superintendent of the Louisiana State Seminary of Learning and Military Academy (which later became Louisiana State University). When asked to accept arms surrendered from the U.S. arsenal during the secession of Louisiana, Sherman declared his loyalty to the Union, resigned from the state position, and moved to St. Louis, where he briefly took a position as director of a streetcar company.

In May 1861, he accepted an appointment as a colonel in a new unit, the 13th U.S. Infantry, and in August was promoted to the rank of brigadier general of volunteers. In September 1861, he was ordered to Kentucky to help in keeping that state in the Union. In Kentucky, he estimated that with 60,000 troops he could clear Kentucky and with 200,000 troops he could win the war in the West. Although the estimates may have been realistic, newspaper reports that Sherman had requested 200,000 troops led to his being labeled as crazy. Rumors of his "insanity" spurred by this episode continued to plague him, and he was relieved of his duties. He reported to General Henry Halleck in St. Louis, and, soon afterward, was given command of a division at the Battle of Shiloh. He served under Grant at the Battle of Vicksburg.

In the fall of 1863, he was given command of the Army of the Tennessee, and in the spring of 1864 he was given command of the armies in the West. Grant ordered Sherman to destroy resources that might be of use to the enemy. After laying siege to Atlanta, he ordered its evacuation in September, explaining to Atlanta officials that the city had provided arms and resources to the insurrection and that those facilities were to be destroyed. On November 9, 1864, Sherman issued his orders describing the "March to the Sea," to create a swath of destruction some 60 miles wide through Georgia. Arriving in Savannah on December 21, he presented the city "as a present" to the president on Christmas 1864. In January 1865, he issued Special Field Order 15, which was intended to transfer abandoned plantations and lands near the sea to newly freed slaves. Although implemented briefly, most of the lands transferred under Sherman's order were later returned to their former owners.

Sherman led his army northward, and, some two weeks after the Battle of Appomattox, Sherman accepted the capitulation of Confederate forces under Joseph E. Johnston near Durham, North Carolina. Sherman was reprimanded by Secretary of War Stanton for initially offering terms that were too liberal and that touched on political matters. The final terms matched those offered by Grant to Lee at Appomattox. Sherman was later regarded as a general with a grasp of the military art that was far ahead of its time; however, most analysts agree that, at the tactical level, Sherman did not have a distinguished career. He was remembered in Georgia and South Carolina as a practitioner of ruthless total war.

After the war, Sherman remained in the army, becoming commander in chief of the army in 1869. He moved army headquarters to St. Louis and established a command school at Fort Leavenworth. He retired from the army in 1884 and was seriously considered as a possible candidate for the presidency in 1886. In that year he moved to New York City, where he died in 1891. His two-volume *Personal Memoirs* were published in 1875.

Smith, Edmund Kirby (1824–1893) *Confederate general, commander of the Trans-Mississippi Department*

Edmund Kirby Smith was born in St. Augustine, Florida, into a military family. His father, Joseph Lee Smith, had been a soldier in the War of 1812 and had attained the rank of colonel. A brother, Ephraim, was killed in the U.S.-Mexican War. A nephew of Edmund Kirby Smith, son of Ephraim, served on the Union side in the Civil War and was killed in the Battle of Corinth, having attained the rank of brevet colonel.

Edmund Kirby Smith graduated from West Point in 1845 and served in the infantry during the U.S.-Mexican War, where he received several commendations. He taught mathematics at West Point as an assistant professor, then joined the cavalry, serving in Texas in engagements with Native Americans. On the secession of Texas, he at first refused to surrender his command to Texas forces, but then resigned his U.S. Army commission and joined the Confederate army. He was wounded at the First Battle of Bull Run and then continued to serve through 1861 and 1862, achieving the rank of lieutenant general of the Confederate army in October 1862.

He was appointed to command the Southwestern Army in January 1863, and, in March, he was given command of the entire Trans-Mississippi Department. After Union forces closed the Mississippi, Edmund Kirby Smith effectively served as chief executive of the whole region, which operated almost as a separate country. His forces defeated those of Nathaniel Banks in the Red River expedition in 1864. As commander of the Trans-Mississippi Department, he had to manage the requisition of supplies, the operation of blockade-running through Mexico, and the destruction of cotton to prevent it falling into Union hands. Many of the military actions in his department were in the nature of guerrilla warfare. After the surrender of Lee in April, his forces remained undefeated, and he finally surrendered to the Union on May 26, 1865, the last substantial armed force of the Confederacy to do so.

After the war, he served first as president of the Atlantic and Pacific Telegraph Company (1866–68). He was later president of the Western Military Academy, chancellor of the University of Nashville, and professor of mathematics at the University of the South at Sewanee, Tennessee, where he taught from 1875 until his death in 1893.

Stanton, Edwin (1814–1868) *lawyer, United States attorney general, Union secretary of war*
Edwin Stanton was born in Steubenville, Ohio, and suffered acute asthma from childhood throughout the rest of his life. He graduated from Kenyon College in 1833 and read law under a local judge, being admitted to the Ohio bar even before reaching age 21, the legal age for practicing law. He ran a successful legal practice first in Ohio, later in Pittsburgh, and finally in Washington, D.C. He had been active in the Ohio antislavery movement, and, in 1857, he was appointed to handle California land cases. In 1859, he led in the defense of

Congressman Daniel Sickles, who had been accused of murdering his wife's lover. Stanton successfully adopted the argument that Sickles had been suffering from temporary insanity over discovering his wife's adultery, and Sickles's acquittal was one of the first uses of the temporary insanity plea.

James Buchanan appointed Stanton late in 1860 as attorney general. In that post, he quietly provided Republicans with information about White House and cabinet policy decisions in the period before Lincoln's inauguration. Lincoln's first secretary of war, Simon Cameron, was both inefficient and corrupt, so Lincoln finally removed him and appointed him minister to Russia. Secretary of State William Seward and Secretary of the Treasury Salmon Chase strongly recommended Stanton to replace Cameron, and Lincoln agreed. Stanton turned out to be an excellent administrator, not only ridding the department of corrupt contracting practices, but also establishing a system of assistant secretaries, who provided him with detailed staff reports on questions of personnel, intelligence, and supply. Stanton and his assistants focused on questions of logistics and supply, leaving matters of strategy and military operations largely to the military commanders. Bureau chiefs under Stanton provided General Henry Wager Halleck in the last years of the war with support, amounting to a primitive form of general staff, combining a focus on operations, intelligence, and logistics.

On the death of Chief Justice Roger Taney in October 1864, Stanton hoped to be named as his replacement. However, Lincoln believed that Stanton's work as secretary of war was too valuable, and Lincoln appointed Salmon Chase (whose resignation from the post of secretary of the treasury he had accepted a few months before) to the Court instead. On the assassination of Lincoln, Stanton was credited with the quote, "He now belongs to the ages." Stanton took the lead in organizing the investigation and the arrest of the conspirators associated with John Wilkes Booth.

Stanton continued to serve as secretary of war under Andrew Johnson, but he soon fell out with Johnson over Reconstruction policies. One of the issues in Johnson's impeachment was his effort to dismiss Stanton, who refused to leave office. He literally locked himself in his office until the Senate attempt to remove Johnson from office failed. Then, in May 1868, Stanton resigned his position and resumed the private practice of law. President Ulysses S. Grant appointed Stanton to the Supreme Court in 1868, but four days after his confirmation for that position by the Senate, he died, on Christmas Eve of 1868.

Stephens, Alexander (1812–1883) *U.S. senator from Georgia, vice president of the Confederacy, congressman from, governor of Georgia*

Alexander Stephens was born near Crawfordsville, Georgia, and lost both his parents as a child. He graduated from the University of Georgia at Athens in 1832, taught school, and then studied law, and was admitted to the bar in 1834. He immediately entered politics, serving as a Whig in the Georgia state house, 1834–41, in the state senate 1842–43, and then as a congressman from Georgia 1843–59. He was first a Whig, then a Unionist, and then joined the Democratic Party. Along with Howell Cobb and Robert Toombs, Stephens opposed secession. With the election of Lincoln, Cobb and Toombs changed their position and endorsed secession, but Stephens continued to oppose it at the Georgia state convention considering secession in January 1861. After the convention voted to secede, Stephens reluctantly accepted the decision. He was then selected by the convention as a state representative to the provisional government of the Confederacy. To his own surprise, he was then selected as provisional vice president of the Confederacy, as a way of representing the position of the Unionists and Cooperationists who had opposed immediate, state by state secession. He was later formally elected as vice president of the Confederacy.

Stephens served as Confederate vice president, but it was soon clear that his differences with Jefferson Davis, particularly over the issue of whether to have a strong central government (preferred by Davis) or a loose confederation of sovereign states (preferred by Stephens, by several state governors, and by many states' righters), meant that he was excluded from Davis's inner circle. He continued to advocate a negotiated peace and opened correspondence with several Northern leaders in the attempt to resolve the war through diplomatic negotiation. No doubt these efforts, as well as his reputation as a prominent Confederate who was a former Unionist, led President Davis to select Stephens as one of the representatives of the Confederacy at the Hampton Roads conference in February 1865. However, that conference could reach no compromise, and when the Confederacy was defeated, Stephens was among those arrested and held in prison in Boston. When the Johnson administration decided not to try the former leaders for treason, Stephens was released.

On his return to Georgia he was elected to the U.S. Senate under the Johnson Reconstruction constitution. Since the U.S. Congress refused to accept representatives of the Johnson-reconstructed states, he did not serve. However, with the formal end of Reconstruction, he was again elected to the U.S. Congress as a Democrat, serving from 1877 to 1882, when he was elected governor. Stephens never married. He served briefly as governor of the state from November 1882 until March 4, 1883, when he died.

He wrote an extensive defense of the Confederacy during the short period when he was absent from political office: *A Constitutional View of the Late War Between the States* (1868–70).

Stevens, Thaddeus (1792–1868) *Republican congressman from Pennsylvania, leader of the radical faction*

Thaddeus Stevens was born on April 4, 1792, in Danville, Vermont, the son of a poor shoemaker who was also an alcoholic. Like an older brother, he was born with a clubfoot, which led to his being taunted and ridiculed by other children. Despite their poverty, his mother insisted that the children of the family receive an education, and Thaddeus was sent to Peacham Academy, where he soon proved to be extremely bright. In recognition of his intelligence, he was admitted to Dartmouth College, where he excelled in literature and debating, qualifying for Phi Beta Kappa. However, due to his poverty, complete lack of social life, and infirmity, he was denied admission to the organization, perhaps partially accounting for his later distrust of those with wealth and those belonging to secret societies.

After graduation, he moved to the Gettysburg area of Pennsylvania, teaching in a school and studying law in the evenings. Within a year, he had learned enough law to be admitted to the bar, and he began practicing. He soon won fame for using the insanity defense for a man accused of murder and for winning other cases. He invested his earnings in real estate, soon becoming the largest landholder in the area. Stevens never married, but had a black housekeeper, Lydia Smith, and when rumors spread regarding the nature of their relationship he neither confirmed nor denied them.

He entered Pennsylvania politics, first as an anti-Mason. In the Pennsylvania legislature, he became famous for his defense of free public education, winning support for its establishment with a feat of oratory that shamed his opponents into supporting the bill. Pennsylvania was the first state outside of New England to establish a statewide system of free public education. Stevens served in Congress from 1849 to 1853, and then again beginning in 1858. Meanwhile, he had established a political machine in Pennsylvania, based on control of patronage and the dispersal of contracts for the building of a railroad. His opponents regarded him as power hungry and fanatical, but his supporters recognized him as a true proponent of equal rights. He put some of his fortune into an ironworks in Pennsylvania, where he insisted on retaining employees even when business declined. He was also a generous philanthropist, providing land and endowment both for Gettysburg College and for the school that became the Thaddeus Stevens College of Technology in Lancaster, Pennsylvania.

During the Civil War and Reconstruction, Stevens emerged as the most radical of the radical Republicans. His caustic speeches, his knowledge of parliamentary techniques, and his fixed commitment to political and social equality for all, including African Americans, soon earned him a host of enemies and a core of supporters. As chairman of the House Committee on Ways and Means, Stevens constantly pressured Lincoln to emancipate the slaves and to arm them. He opposed Lincoln's 10 percent plan, and he advocated enfranchisement of the freedmen, confiscation of planters' estates and redistribution of their lands and an extended disfranchisement of all the leading Confederate officials and military officers.

He became the House Republican floor leader and steered several key radical Reconstruction measures through Congress, including the Civil Rights Act of 1866, the Fourteenth Amendment to the Constitution, and the Reconstruction Act of 1867, which established military occupation in the South. He was one of the first to call for the impeachment of Andrew Johnson. He became popularly known as the advocate of "forty acres and a mule" for freedmen as part of the confiscation and land distribution he proposed. However, Stevens, as an intelligent and practical politician, was willing to settle for bills that only partially achieved the goals he set. He was one of the floor managers for the prosecution of Andrew Johnson before the Senate during the impeachment trial. At age 67, just before his death, he introduced a bill to establish free public schools in the District of Columbia.

After Stevens died on August 11, 1868, both blacks and whites flocked to the Capitol Rotunda to pay their respects, and his burial at Lancaster, Pennsylvania, was attended by 20,000. He insisted on being buried there in a quiet cemetery that allowed interment of both blacks and whites. He had a message inscribed on his headstone noting that he had chosen the spot to illustrate in his death the principles that he had advocated in life.

Stowe, Harriet Beecher (1811–1896) *antislavery fiction writer*

Born in Litchfield, Connecticut, Harriet Beecher attended school in Hartford in an academy established by her sister, Catherine. Her father, Lyman Beecher, was a respected minister, and the family moved to Cincinnati with him when he was appointed president of the Lane Theological Seminary there. In Cincinnati, she married Calvin Stowe, a professor of biblical literature at Lane and one of the first American students of the Bible to write of it as a historic document. While in Cincinnati, Harriet Beecher Stowe began writing and publishing short pieces for magazines and newspapers. In 1834, she published a collection of short stories. Living in Cincinnati, she learned of conditions under slavery across the Ohio River in Kentucky. Lane Seminary housed many abolitionist activists and she absorbed their ideas.

In 1850, she and her husband moved to Maine, where her husband took a professorship at Bowdoin College. Concern over the passage of the Fugitive Slave Act as part of the Compromise of 1850 spread through New England and other free states. Responding to the controversy, Harriet Stowe began writing an imaginary account of conditions under slavery, which she submitted to an antislavery newspaper published in Washington, D.C., the *National Era*. It was accepted by the editor, to be published in serialized form in 40 installments, and she was paid $300. With each section, published over the period June 5, 1851 to April 1, 1852 ending with suspense, readers eagerly anticipated the next issue and passed copies from hand to hand. Recognizing the story's success, a Boston publisher, J. P. Jewett, brought out the novel in a two-volume edition in 1852. Although Stowe received royalties from this American edition, which sold some 300,000 copies in the first year, she never received royalties from foreign editions nor from a sensationalized play that was widely performed across the North, with added scenes including barking bloodhounds chasing escaped slaves across stage. The book went on selling, with at least a half-million copies sold by 1857.

Partly because of the success and notoriety from this all-time best-seller, Stowe was immediately subjected to hostile criticism from defenders of slavery who claimed the story was entirely based on her imagination, that she had never visited the South, and that the incidents portrayed bore little resemblance to reality. In defense, she published in 1853 *A Key to Uncle Tom's Cabin,* in which she provided evidence from published accounts and eyewitnesses to substantiate the incidents she had pieced together into the novel.

Part of the novel's success derived from Stowe's ability to make the suffering of slave families facing separation or concern for their children real by placing herself and her readers into the thoughts and feelings of the victims. As a consequence of her work, hundreds of thousands of readers developed a sympathy for the plight of slaves that added an emotional and immediate urgency to the antislavery drive that mere appeals to logic or ideals probably could not have created. With some irony, during the civil rights era the term *Uncle Tom* evolved into a pejorative expression for a subservient black man, whereas in the novel Uncle Tom is a man who never abandons his dignity, even when he is sold down the river to die at the hands of a sadistic overseer.

Stowe's brother, Henry Ward Beecher, was a clergyman in Brooklyn, New York, and very active in the antislavery movement. He organized support and funding for the antislavery migrants to Kansas after the Kansas-Nebraska Act opened that territory to the possibility of slavery by popular sovereignty. However, Stowe's fame, based on her best-selling novel, far eclipsed that of her brother. Henry Ward Beecher was later accused by one of his parishioners, journalist Theodore Tilton, of having an affair with Tilton's wife. The resultant lawsuit and publication of private correspondence involving the famous Beecher family, was regarded as the scandal of the 1870s, if not of the century.

Harriet Beecher Stowe lectured extensively in the United States and Europe and continued her writing career. She wrote a second antislavery novel, *Dred; A Tale of the Great Dismal Swamp,* published in 1856. After the Civil War, Calvin and Harriet Stowe retired to Hartford, where they both continued writing. His work, the *Origin and History of the Books of the Bible* (1867), sold very well and was a major influence in the new approach of higher criticism or historical study of the Bible. In the same period, Harriet published numerous works of fiction and nonfiction, including *Oldtown Folks* (1869) and *Sam Lawson's Oldtown Fireside Stories* (1872), both based on Calvin's own reminiscences of his youth. He continued to support her in her writing career, reflecting a marital relationship rather rare in its time.

Sumner, Charles (1811–1874) *law professor, antislavery U.S. senator*

Charles Sumner was the son of an attorney and graduated from Harvard College in 1830. He attended and later taught at Harvard law school. He was admitted to the bar in 1834 and served as reporter for the United States Circuit Court. He published an edition of Joseph Story's decisions under the title, *Sumner's Reports.* Sumner traveled in Britain and France in the period 1837 to 1840, and he later published a 20-volume edition of *Vesey's Reports* (1841–46). During the 1840s, he became involved in the antislavery movement and in seeking educational opportunities for African Americans. He spoke out against the U.S.-Mexican War and was selected by a combination of Free-Soilers and antislavery Democrats for the U.S. Senate from Massachusetts in 1851, after the seat had been vacated by Daniel Webster on his appointment as secretary of state.

As an aggressive antislavery senator, Sumner denounced the Kansas-Nebraska Act of 1854. On May 19–20, 1856, he delivered an impassioned speech, "The Crime against Kansas," focusing his attack on Senator Andrew P. Butler of South Carolina by alluding to slavery as a "harlot" with whom Butler consorted. Butler, who was advanced in years, had not attended the session at which Sumner made the speech. Butler's nephew, Preston Brooks, a member of Congress, assaulted Sumner at his desk in the Senate, beating him with a gold-tipped gutta percha cane. Sumner was partially trapped under his desk, and, in attempting to rise and protect himself from the blows, he ripped the attached desk from the floor. The episode became one of the notorious political scandals of the period, as Southerners defended Brooks's actions as an appropriate thrashing for an insult to a gentleman's honor, while Northerners took it as evidence of the South's barbarism. Sumner was injured and perhaps psychologically scarred by the attack and did not attend the Senate for more than three years. However, during his absence, he participated in organizing the Republican Party and was reelected to the Senate. In 1861, he was elected chairman of the Senate Foreign Relations Committee in the Republican organization of the Senate.

In the Trent Affair in which U.S. Navy captain Charles Wilkes detained two Confederate commissioners to Europe, James Mason and John Slidell, Sumner advised Lincoln to release them in order to stick with American precedents and to avoid a clash with Britain. Sumner tended to be in advance of Lincoln on questions of abolition, favoring General John C.

Frémont's emancipation order in Missouri and the attempted enlistment of freed slaves into the army in South Carolina by General David Hunter before Lincoln accepted such measures. He approved the Emancipation Proclamation and emerged during the war as the leading Senate radical Republican on the slavery issue. He introduced the bill establishing the Freedmen's Bureau and also introduced into the Senate the Thirteenth Amendment that constitutionally abolished slavery in 1864.

During Reconstruction, Sumner in the Senate and Thaddeus Stevens in the House of Representatives became the advocates of a series of civil rights measures that would assist the former slaves in exercising the rights of citizens. Sumner argued that the seceding states had ceased to exist with their secession and that the Reconstruction of the states was a matter that should be decided entirely by Congress, not by the executive branch. Sumner took the lead in trying to obtain the conviction of President Andrew Johnson on impeachment charges; after the failure of that decision by one vote, he continued to advocate conviction when others abandoned the cause. Sumner pressed for claims against Britain due to its construction and sale of cruisers to the Confederacy in the *Alabama Claims* cases, eventually winning the United States a large cash settlement. He was so vehement in his opposition to President Ulysses S. Grant's proposal to acquire Santo Domingo that he was voted out of his position as chair of the Foreign Relations Committee in 1871.

In 1872, he assisted in organizing the Liberal Republican Party, supporting the candidacy of Horace Greeley for the presidency against Grant. The Liberal Republican Party offered him the nomination of governor of Massachusetts, but he declined for health reasons. He introduced a bill into the Senate that was passed after his death, the Civil Rights Act of 1875, which was declared unconstitutional in 1883. His many speeches and articles are collected in two editions of his works, published in 1870–83 and in 1900; an edition of his memoirs and letters was published in four volumes over the period 1877–93.

Thomas, George Henry (1816–1870) *Southern-born army officer, general in Union army*

George Thomas was born in slave country, near Newsom's Depot, Southampton County, Virginia. As a teenager during the rebellion of slaves under Nat Turner in 1831, Thomas helped his widowed mother and sisters find refuge in the woods. Graduating from West Point in 1840, he served in the artillery for 15 years. In the U.S.-Mexican War, he earned distinction at Monterrey and Buena Vista. In 1855, he was posted with the cavalry to Texas, where he served on the frontier until the outbreak of the Civil War.

He was given command of an independent force in eastern Kentucky, where he won the first important Union victory of the war at Mill Springs on January 19, 1862. That battle undermined the whole western defense of the Confederate army. After the Battle of Shiloh, General Halleck put Thomas in command of Grant's Army of the Tennessee, sidelining Grant to a nominal post as second in command under Halleck. Thomas led troops into Chattanooga, Tennessee, in September 1863. Along the Chickamauga Creek in Georgia on September 19 and 20, 1863, Thomas organized defenses after much of the Union forces had collapsed. Holding off many separate Confederate attacks until relieved, it was in this battle that he earned the nickname Rock of Chickamauga and was promoted to brigadier general of the regular army.

Thomas developed several strategic plans, some of them adopted and others rejected for poor reasons. He was an able administrator, recognized for his excellent use of the telegraph, for introducing map coordinates in planning for battles, and using remote fire control for artillery. He pioneered the introduction of folding pontoon bridges and developed specialized small blockhouses for railroad junctions and key points. His cavalry units made excellent use of Spencer repeating carbines. His espionage service was first-rate and supplied other units with battle intelligence. It was his secret service that uncovered the whereabouts of Jefferson Davis after the war had ended. In training, he emphasized advance by real-life sorties, rather than exercising at parade ground drills. He perfected a movable railway repair center and railway hospital cars and established an efficient hospital service that regularly utilized chloroform. A unit of African-American troops under his command played a key role in the Battle of Nashville. The Rock of Chickamauga earned further fame for succeeding in every battle in which he fought.

At the war's end, he served as military commander of most of the South, and then as military governor of five Southern states, out of his command post in Nashville. He worked to maintain order and to get the white citizens to accept African-American occupation troops. Eventually, he earned the respect of local people, and Tennessee granted him honorary citizenship. Because, as a Southerner, he had joined with the Union side, he lost his citizenship in the state of Virginia, and he was also disowned by his sisters.

Thomas supported the Reconstruction policies of Andrew Johnson and was probably the most effective of all of the military governors. However, in 1867 Johnson sought to have him supercede Grant in command of the army as part of Johnson's plan to move Grant into the position of secretary of war. Thomas refused to go along with the scheme, as did Grant. Thomas was transferred at his own request in 1869 to the Presidio in San Francisco to command the Division of the Pacific.

Although extremely innovative and successful during the war, he has remained relatively obscure in historical treatments of the war partly because he destroyed all of his personal papers and left no memoirs. He died of a stroke at age 54 while at his post in San Francisco.

Toombs, Robert (1810–1885) *U.S. senator from Georgia, Confederate secretary of state, Confederate general*

Robert Toombs was born in Wilkes County, Georgia. He entered the University of Georgia at age 14 but was expelled after an incident at cards. He entered Union College in New York and later studied law at the University of Virginia. He was admitted to the Georgia bar in 1830.

He soon became quite wealthy, building up a fortune in slaves and land. Successful as a lawyer, he was a popular figure, elected to the Georgia general assembly in 1837. In 1844, he was elected to the U.S. Congress, and, in 1853, the Georgia legislature chose Toombs as U.S. senator, and he served there until secession in 1861. He was a close friend of Alexander Stephens (later vice president of the Confederacy). Both men had been Whigs, then worked independently or through the Democratic Party as anti-secessionists. Toombs was a Southern supporter of the Compromise of 1850, defending it against secessionists during those debates. However, with the election of 1860, Toombs joined with others in advocating secession. With his long and distinguished political record, he was supported as a candidate for the presidency of the new Confederacy.

After Jefferson Davis was selected as president, he chose Toombs to be secretary of state in the provisional government. Toombs served only until July 19, 1861, resigning to accept a post as brigadier general in the army. He was also elected to serve as a member of the Confederate congress from Georgia. His unit saw action during the Seven Days battles, and he was criticized by General D. H. Hill for his performance in those engagements. Toombs treated the reprimand as an insult, absenting himself from the service temporarily, then returned to take up his command during Second Bull Run. He was slightly wounded at Burnside's Bridge at Antietam. Disgruntled over the formality of the chain of command, he was later quoted as remarking that the Confederacy "died of West Point." Passed over for promotion, he resigned on March 4, 1863.

Along with Vice President Stephens and Governor Joseph Brown, Toombs continued to criticize the administration of Davis during the remaining years of the war, focusing on Davis's use of conscription, his management of finances, and the confiscation of farm products. Toombs also spoke out against the proposal to arm slaves and free them to fight on the Confederate side.

After the war, he fled to Cuba and then to Europe to escape arrest. He returned in 1867 via Canada, but never took an oath of allegiance, remaining unreconstructed. Although he served in state conventions, he never again held public office, as his citizenship in the United States was never restored. His good friend Alexander Stephens died in 1883, as did Toombs's wife. Apparently devastated by the tragedies, he suffered from severe depression and died in 1885.

Tubman, Harriet (ca. 1820–1913) *escaped slave, Underground Railroad conductor, Union spy*

Harriet Tubman was born Araminta Ross in slavery in the year 1819 or 1820 in Bucktown, Dorchester County, Maryland. Both her parents were slaves, reputedly of pure African ancestry. Her father's name was Ross and her mother's was Harriet. At about the age of six she began work as a house servant; at about age 12, she suffered an injury to her head when a slave overseer threw a heavy weight at her when she refused to help him tie up a slave who had tried to escape. About a year later, she was transferred to work as a field hand. About 1844, she married a free African-American, John Tubman, but they soon separated.

Fearing that she would be sold from Maryland into the Deep South, she escaped to freedom in 1849. Leaving at night, she was given assistance by a white woman. Moving by wagon and on foot, and following the North Star, she found her way across the Pennsylvania state line and into Philadelphia. There she found work as a maid and began to attend the lively antislavery meetings conducted by African Americans in that city. In Philadelphia, she adopted the name Harriet Tubman, choosing her mother's first name.

After the passage of the Fugitive Slave Act in 1850, she joined the informal organization known as the Underground Railroad, as a conductor or guide on the routes from safe house to safe house from Maryland north. In 1851, she made her way to Baltimore and returned with her sister and her sister's children. Over the next decade, she made a total of some 18 trips south, bringing about 300 slaves to freedom in the North or in Canada. On one of the trips she found that her husband, John Tubman, had married another woman. Later, she escorted her own parents to freedom, taking them first to St. Catherines, Canada, and later to Auburn, New York. There she had met the former governor of New York and future secretary of state, William Seward, who provided a home both for her niece and for Harriet Tubman herself. She later purchased the home for a nominal sum and used it as her base of operations. She raised funds by speaking at abolitionist meetings and then used the donations to help arrange trips South.

She met other leaders in the African-American resistance movement, including William Still, who was something of a station master on the so-called railroad in Philadelphia. She also grew to know Thomas Garret who played a similar role in Wilmington, Delaware, and Frederick Douglass. All later praised her work, her bravery, and her intelligence in outwitting slave catchers and slave-state militias. Her renown spread through the South as well, with total rewards offered for her capture in the range of $40,000.

After the Civil War broke out, she served as a volunteer nurse and scout for the Union army, mostly in South Carolina. She also worked as a spy, reporting to Colonel James Montgomery, commander of a black unit, the 2nd South Carolina Volunteers. As William Still pointed out, she appeared to be an "ordinary specimen of humanity" and because of her experience at passing as a simple farm hand on an errand during her days escorting escaped slaves, she made an excellent courier, guide, and spy. At one point, General David Hunter asked her to help by guiding a raiding party behind enemy lines. On June 2, 1863, she led troops past Confederate picket lines, freeing over 700 slaves and destroying several million dollars worth of Confederate supplies. In South Carolina, she met Nelson Davis, whom she later married.

In the years after the Civil War, Tubman moved back to Auburn, where she established a home in 1908 for elderly African Americans, later known as the Harriet Tubman Home. After her death in 1913, she was given a full military funeral.

Vance, Zebulon Baird (1830–1894) *Confederate army officer, North Carolina governor, U.S. senator*

Zebulon Vance was born in Buncombe County, North Carolina, and briefly attended school in Tennessee. He studied law and moved to Asheville in 1852 to begin a law practice. He entered politics as a Whig at age 24, winning a seat in the North Carolina state legislature. He was elected to the U.S. Congress in 1858, at age 28, the youngest member of the House of Representatives. He was reelected in 1860, but on the secession of North Carolina he resigned his position and returned to North Carolina. He raised a company of troops in Raleigh and was later elected colonel of the 26th North Carolina Regiment. He led his troops for a period of 13 months, seeing action at New Bern and Richmond in 1862.

He ran for governor of North Carolina and handily won the election, taking office in September 1862 for a two-year term. He ran as a Conservative, opposing the Confederate party. Conservatives were largely made up of pro-Union Whigs. He was re-elected in 1864. Although pro-Unionists supported Vance, and some may have expected him to lead North Carolina back into the Union, Vance vowed to prosecute the war, while keeping the state government of North Carolina as an independent buffer between the Confederacy and the citizens of the state. Like several other Southern governors, Vance took quite seriously the idea that the Confederacy was not a central government, but a confederation of states. Because of his strong defense of states' rights, he was viewed then and later as an obstructionist. However, by supporting the Confederate cause and at the same time mitigating the effect of conscription by granting thousands of state exemptions from the draft, providing welfare to soldiers' families, and asserting North Carolina's independence, he may have found a compromise path, heading off discontent with the Confederacy.

The extensive coast and many small ports of North Carolina were natural leaks in the Union blockade. Vance insisted that goods imported through the blockade should be first available to North Carolina forces, and only after their needs had been satisfied could other states or the Confederate army get their share. The state continued to equip and clothe its own regiments throughout the war. Vance was also noted for his insistence that the writ of habeas corpus not be suspended in the state, and the state courts continued to operate during the war.

After the surrender of Lee and Joseph Johnston in April 1865, federal troops arrested Vance, and he was briefly incarcerated in the District of Columbia. At the end of 1865, he was paroled and returned to Charlotte, North Carolina, where he reentered the practice of law.

In 1870, the state legislature chose Vance for a U.S. Senate seat, but he had not yet received a federal pardon and could not take office. In 1876, he was elected for another term as governor, and, during that period, the last federal troops were withdrawn from North Carolina. He worked to increase state support for education. In 1878, he was again named U.S. senator and this time he was seated. He was reelected to the Senate in 1886 and in 1892, remaining in office until his death in 1894. In the Senate, he established a reputation as a moderate advocate of reconciling differences between North and South.

Van Lew, Elizabeth (1818–ca. 1900) *Southern-born Union spy*

Elizabeth Van Lew was born into the prosperous home of a hardware merchant in Richmond, Virginia. Her father was from Long Island, New York, a descendant of a Dutch family there, while his wife was from Philadelphia. After private tutoring, Elizabeth was educated in Philadelphia and returned to the family home in Richmond, where she lived with her widowed mother through the 1850s. The family continued to prosper, as her brother John operated the business.

In the 1850s, Elizabeth convinced her mother to free the family's slaves, and most of them stayed on as paid servants. Van Lew made no secret of her distaste for slavery, and, by the time Virginia seceded, she had already established a reputation as an eccentric spinster. Despite her obvious pro-Union sympathies, she was able to convince authorities to allow her to visit and bring aid to Union prisoners held in Libby Prison in Richmond. Soon she realized that they and the guards were great sources of information about the disposition of Confederate forces outside Richmond, and she simply wrote reports and mailed them to Union officers. As the war progressed, however, she developed far more sophisticated methods of communicating information, including systems of ciphers, concealed messages, and the use of couriers (including some of her own former slaves). One of her former slaves, Mary Bowser, secured a position in the home of Jefferson Davis and relayed details of overheard conversations, which Van Lew included in her reports. Some were sent to General Benjamin Butler at Fortress Monroe; later, she sent messages directly to General U.S. Grant.

Van Lew also provided sanctuary for escaped prisoners at her large home in Richmond and at a small country home on the outskirts of the city. Surprisingly, she never concealed her pro-Union sympathies, but, by exaggerating her reputation for eccentricity, she apparently convinced most authorities that she was harmless. Her nickname, Crazy Bet, suited her pretense perfectly.

Grant appreciated her information, later remarking that at times it was the best source of intelligence in Richmond. The full extent of her network is difficult to determine, because in order to protect participants who worked for the Confederacy from later retribution, she did not reveal their identities. However, from the quality of information she passed, it appears that her network became quite extensive by the end of the war.

As a reward for her work, General Grant ensured that she was given a federal appointment as postmistress of Richmond after the war. Even so, she was ostracized by Richmond neighbors and was locally regarded as a traitor to the cause. Her post office position was not renewed after 1877, and she lived out her remaining years on a small annuity provided by the family of one of the Union prisoners she had helped escape.

Welles, Gideon (1802–1878) *journalist, politician, secretary of the navy for the Union*

Gideon Welles was born in Glastonbury, Connecticut, and educated at the American Literary, Scientific, and Military Academy in Vermont (the predecessor of Norwich University). He began writing small romantic items for the *Hartford Times,* and in 1826 he became a part-owner and editor of the paper. He helped turn it into a leading supporter of Andrew Jackson and the Democratic Party. Welles served in the Connecticut state legislature as a Democrat in the period 1827–35. There he supported a change in the law that allowed witnesses to affirm, rather than swear, before God at trials, which earned him the enmity of the clergy and probably prevented his ever being elected to any state position in Connecticut after that. He also sponsored a general incorporation law, which became a model for business incorporation in other states.

Recognizing Welles's support, Jackson appointed him as postmaster at Hartford, and Welles held that position 1836–41, using it as a base to build a strong Democratic Party organization in Connecticut. Over the period 1841–45, he continued as editor on the *Hartford Times,* and in 1846 he received a patronage appointment in the Polk administration's Navy Department, as head of the Bureau of Provisions and Clothing.

An opponent of slavery, Welles joined the new Republican Party in 1856 and founded a newspaper, the *Hartford Evening Press,* to support the Republican positions. At the 1860 Republican Party convention, he served as a delegate from Connecticut and wielded influence to oppose the nomination of William Seward for the presidency. When Lincoln sought nominees for his cabinet, he chose Welles from among his supporters at the convention as a representative of New England, over Seward's objections.

As secretary of the navy, Welles established a reputation for energy, innovation, and avoidance of political favoritism. He oversaw the expansion of the fleet and the adoption of ironclads and new weapons and successfully supported both the blockade and the riverine activities of the navy, providing civilian logistic support while leaving military decisions to the admirals and other naval officers. He participated actively in cabinet meetings, often taking an independent position. Welles opposed Lincoln's suspension of habeas corpus in 1863 but supported Lincoln's plans for a moderate form of Reconstruction. He remained in his post under Andrew Johnson and supported Johnson during the impeachment proceedings. He left the cabinet in 1869, later publishing several articles of reminiscences, including *Lincoln and Seward* (1874). Welles revised his *Diary,* and it was published posthumously in 1911.

APPENDIX C
Maps and Tables

1. Emancipation, 1761–1962
2. U.S. Presidential Elections: Electoral Vote, 1848
3. U.S. Presidential Elections: Electoral Vote, 1852
4. U.S. Presidential Elections: Electoral Vote, 1856
5. U.S. Presidential Elections: Electoral Vote, 1860
6. Secession of the Southern States, 1860–1861
7. Confederate Cruiser Operations, 1861–1865
8. Emancipation in the United States, 1861–1865
9. Battle of Antietam, September 17, 1862
10. Battle of Fredericksburg, December 13, 1862
11. Battle of Gettysburg—Pickett's Charge, July 3, 1863
12. Battle of Chattanooga, November 23–25, 1863
13. Grant's Advance on Richmond, May–June, 1864
14. Battles of the Wilderness and Spotsylvania, May 4–20, 1864
15. Sherman's Advance on Atlanta, May 4–July 17, 1864
16. Siege of Petersburg, June 1864–April 1865
17. Jubal Early's Raid on Washington, July 9–11, 1864
18. March to the Sea, November 15–December 20, 1864
19. Battles of Franklin and Nashville, November 30 and December 15, 1864

EMANCIPATION, 1761–1962

(Year is shown for the official ending of slavery. Debt peonage replaced slavery in many areas, including the United States. In several African nations, chattel slavery persists to the present.)

Emancipation	Year	Slave Trade Laws and Treaties
Portugal (in Europe only)	1761	
Britain (British Isles)	1772	
Vermont	1777	
Massachusetts	1780–83	
Pennsylvania-gradual	1780	
New Hampshire	1783	
R.I.& Conn.	1784	
Northwest Territories (Ohio-Michigan)	1787	
Haiti	1791	
France	1794; reinstituted 1802	
New York-gradual	1799	
New Jersey-gradual	1804	
		Britain outlaws slave trade 1807 U.S. outlaws slave trade 1808
Argentina-gradual	1813	
		Sweden outlaws slave trade 1813
Colombia-gradual	1814	Holland outlaws slave trade 1814
	1815–1822	Portugal bans slave trade north of Equator 1815 France outlaws slave trade 1817 (–19?), effective 1826 Spain agrees to ban slave trade 1820 Britain-Zanzibar Moresby treaty bans slave trade to India and Persia (Iran) 1822
Venezuela-gradual	1821	
Santo Domingo (under Haitian rule) until 1844	1822	
British East India (Singapore)	1823	
Chile	1823	Supplants 1811 gradual emancipation
		Portugal bans slave trade anywhere 1823—extended to 1830
Central America	1824	
New York, permanent	1827	
Mexico	1829	
Bolivia	1831	
British Colonies	1834	
	1836	Portugal bans slave trade 1836 (Apprentice system until 1838)
Uruguay	1842	
		Ashburton Treaty U.S.-Britain, plans cooperation in anti-slave trade naval squadrons, 1842
Argentina	1843	
India	1843	
Swedish colonies	1847	(St. Barthelemy or St. Barts)

Emancipation	Year	Slave Trade Laws and Treaties
Franch & Danish colonies (in Carribbean)	1848	
French Senegambia (gradual)	1848	
		Brazil outlaws slave trading 1851
Colombia (final)	1851	
Ecuador	1851	
Boer South Africa	1852	Sand River Treaty
Argentina (final)	1853	
Angola (gradual)	1854	
Peru	1854	
Venezuela	1854	
Portuguese Colonies, incl Angola (with apprenticeship for 20 years)	1858	
Russia (serfdom)	1861	
United States of America	1861–65	See Table 7
Dutch colonies (Caribbean)	1863	
Portugal (colonies)	1869	
Paraguay	1870	Under Brazilian occupation
Cuba, Puerto Rico-gradual	1870	Moret Law at age 60; new babies to be held until 18
Brazil (gradual)	1871	Rio Branco Law—children of slaves freed
Puerto Rico complete	1873	
Turkey	1876	
Brazil	1885	all slaves over age 60
Cuba	1886	
Brazil	1888	all slaves
Belgian Congo	1889	
Madagascar (French)	1896	
Zanzibar?	1909	
China	1910	
Somalia	1920	
Nepal	1925	
Burma	1926	
Baluchistan	1927	
Sierra Leone	1927	
Persia	1928	
Liberia	1930	
Ethiopia	1932	
Saudi Arabia and Yemen	1962	

Source: Compiled by the author from international and United States records.

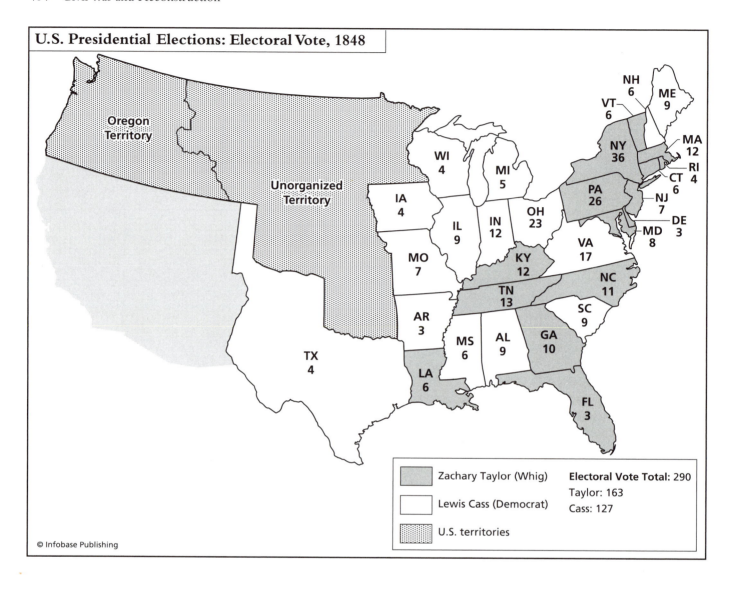

U.S. Presidential Elections: Electoral Vote, 1848

Oregon Territory

Unorganized Territory

NH 6

VT 6

ME 9

NY 36

MA 12

RI 4

CT 6

PA 26

NJ 7

DE 3

MD 8

WI 4

MI 5

IA 4

IL 9

IN 12

OH 23

VA 17

MO 7

KY 12

NC 11

AR 3

TN 13

SC 9

TX 4

MS 6

AL 9

GA 10

LA 6

FL 3

Zachary Taylor (Whig)

Lewis Cass (Democrat)

U.S. territories

Electoral Vote Total: 290
Taylor: 163
Cass: 127

© Infobase Publishing

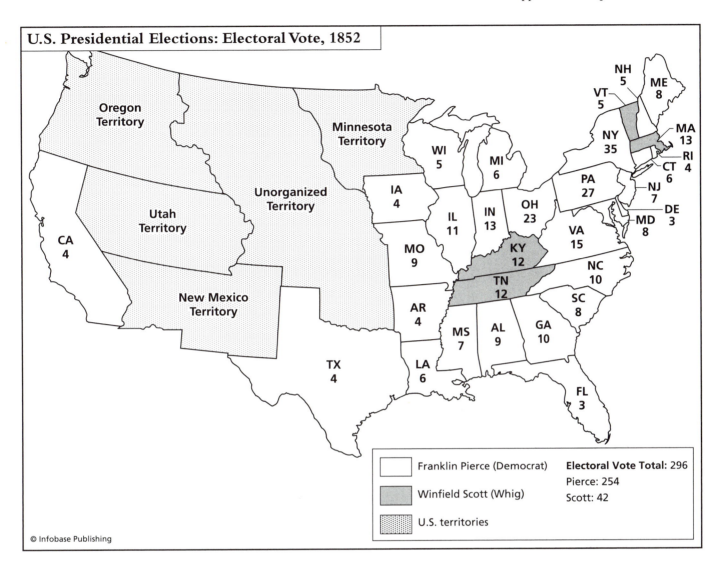

U.S. Presidential Elections: Electoral Vote, 1852

Franklin Pierce (Democrat)

Winfield Scott (Whig)

U.S. territories

Electoral Vote Total: 296

Pierce: 254

Scott: 42

Oregon Territory

Minnesota Territory

Unorganized Territory

Utah Territory

New Mexico Territory

CA 4

WI 5

MI 6

IA 4

IL 11

IN 13

OH 23

MO 9

KY 12

TN 12

AR 4

MS 7

AL 9

GA 10

LA 6

TX 4

FL 3

SC 8

NC 10

VA 15

PA 27

NY 35

VT 5

NH 5

ME 8

MA 13

RI 4

CT 6

NJ 7

DE 3

MD 8

© Infobase Publishing

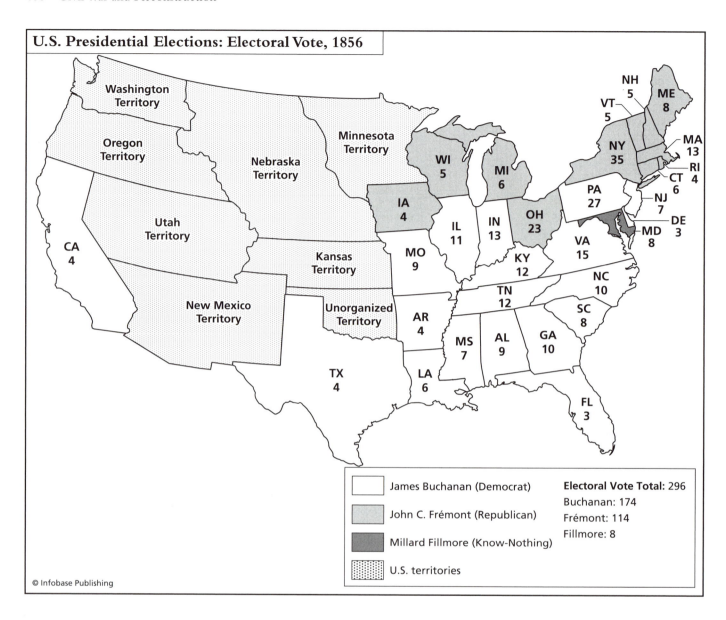

U.S. Presidential Elections: Electoral Vote, 1856

Washington Territory

Oregon Territory

Minnesota Territory

Nebraska Territory

WI 5

MI 6

NH 5

VT 5

ME 8

NY 35

MA 13

RI 4

CT 6

IA 4

Utah Territory

CA 4

New Mexico Territory

Kansas Territory

Unorganized Territory

IL 11

IN 13

OH 23

PA 27

NJ 7

DE 3

MD 8

MO 9

KY 12

VA 15

NC 10

AR 4

TN 12

SC 8

TX 4

MS 7

AL 9

GA 10

LA 6

FL 3

James Buchanan (Democrat)

John C. Frémont (Republican)

Millard Fillmore (Know-Nothing)

U.S. territories

Electoral Vote Total: 296

Buchanan: 174

Frémont: 114

Fillmore: 8

© Infobase Publishing

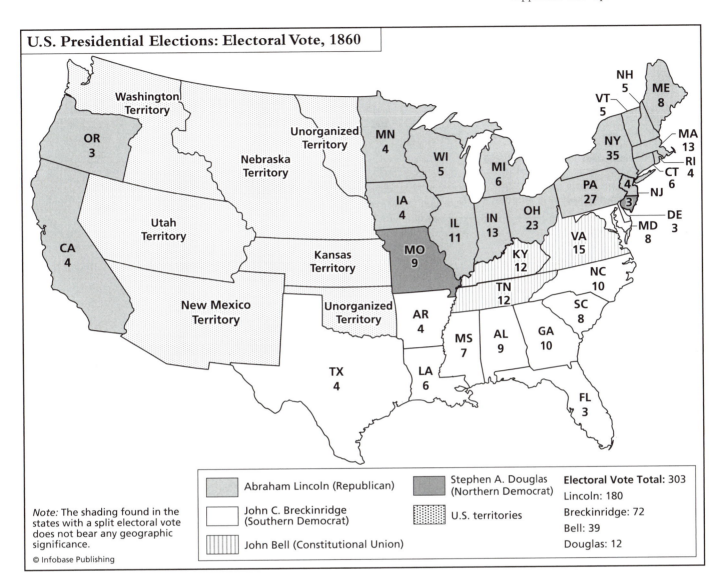

U.S. Presidential Elections: Electoral Vote, 1860

Washington Territory

OR 3

Unorganized Territory

Nebraska Territory

MN 4

WI 5

MI 6

NH 5

VT 5

ME 8

NY 35

MA 13

RI 4

CT 6

Utah Territory

IA 4

IL 11

IN 13

OH 23

PA 27

NJ 3

DE 3

MD 8

CA 4

Kansas Territory

MO 9

KY 12

VA 15

NC 10

New Mexico Territory

Unorganized Territory

AR 4

TN 12

SC 8

MS 7

AL 9

GA 10

TX 4

LA 6

FL 3

Note: The shading found in the states with a split electoral vote does not bear any geographic significance.

© Infobase Publishing

	Abraham Lincoln (Republican)
	John C. Breckinridge (Southern Democrat)
	John Bell (Constitutional Union)

| | Stephen A. Douglas (Northern Democrat) |
| | U.S. territories |

Electoral Vote Total: 303
Lincoln: 180
Breckinridge: 72
Bell: 39
Douglas: 12

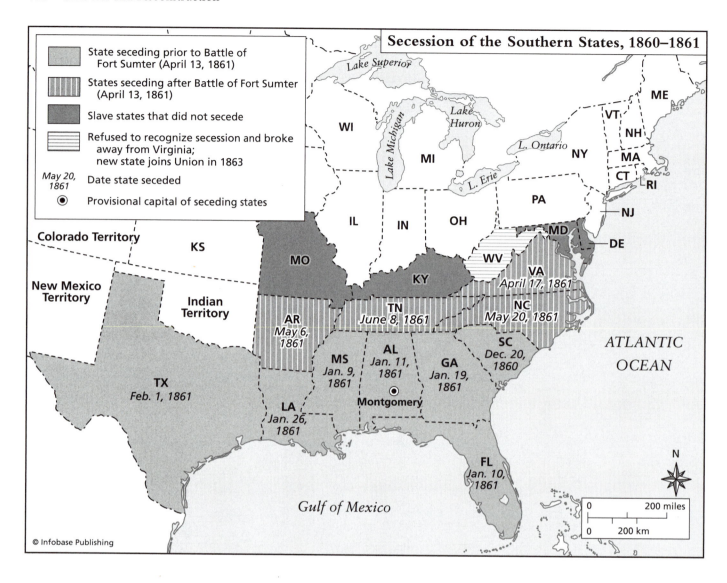

Secession of the Southern States, 1860–1861

State seceding prior to Battle of Fort Sumter (April 13, 1861)

States seceding after Battle of Fort Sumter (April 13, 1861)

Slave states that did not secede

Refused to recognize secession and broke away from Virginia; new state joins Union in 1863

May 20, 1861 Date state seceded

Provisional capital of seceding states

ME

VT

NH

MA

CT

RI

NJ

DE

MD

Lake Superior

WI

Lake Michigan

Lake Huron

L. Ontario

L. Erie

MI

NY

PA

Colorado Territory

KS

New Mexico Territory

Indian Territory

MO

IL

IN

OH

KY

WV

VA
April 17, 1861

AR
May 6, 1861

TN
June 8, 1861

NC
May 20, 1861

TX
Feb. 1, 1861

MS
Jan. 9, 1861

AL
Jan. 11, 1861

GA
Jan. 19, 1861

SC
Dec. 20, 1860

LA
Jan. 26, 1861

Montgomery

FL
Jan. 10, 1861

ATLANTIC OCEAN

Gulf of Mexico

N

0   200 miles

0   200 km

© Infobase Publishing

CONFEDERATE CRUISER OPERATIONS, 1861–1865

Year	Confederate Ship	Total Ships Captured or Sunk
1861	*Sumter*	16
	Nashville	1
1862	*Sumter*	2
	Nashville	1
	Alabama	26
1863	*Florida*	24
	Clarence-Tacony-Archer	21
	Alabama	37
	Georgia	9
1864	*Florida*	13
	Alabama	3
	Shenandoah	9
	Tallahassee	33
	Olustee (former *Tallahassee*)	6
	Chickamauga	7
1865	*Shenandoah* (including 25 after Appomattox)	29
Total		237

Source: compiled from Hearn, Chester G. *Gray Raiders of the Sea: How Eight Confederate Warships Destroyed the Union's High Seas Commerce.* Camden, Maine: International Marine Publishing, 1992.

EMANCIPATION IN THE UNITED STATES, 1861–1865

Date	Locations Affected	Action	Slaves Freed
Jan. 29, 1861	Kansas	Admission to Union	Kansas is admitted as a free state; slaves of owners who remain in state are free; some owners leave with slaves.
May 24, 1861	Virginia	General Butler's contraband principle	Those who had been employed by Confederates in the war effort and who escaped to Union lines
May 25, 1861– Aug. 5, 1861	Virginia	Contraband principle confirmed by War Department	The principle is applied inconsistently by different generals through the summer of 1861.
Aug. 6, 1861	Virginia, Missouri, parts Kentucky	1861 Confiscation Act	Those owned by disloyal owners and who had been employed by Confederates in the war effort
Aug. 30, 1861	Missouri	General Frémont	Orders all slaves of disloyal owners freed in Missouri.
Sept. 11, 1861	Missouri	Frémont reversed	Lincoln countermands Frémont's order and brings it in conformity with 1861 Confiscation Act.
Nov. 7, 1861	Sea Islands, Georgia	Union conquest by naval force under Dupont.	Slaves are abandoned; their status remains ill-defined until the 1862 Confiscation Act.
Dec. 1861	Less than 50 slaves in Territory of N. Mexico	Territorial constitution	Repeals 1859 black codes which sanctioned slavery; Karl Marx in N.Y. *Tribune* notes less than 50.
Dec. 1, 1861	Nationwide, but no effect	Secretary of War recommenda- tion	Simon Cameron recommends emancipation and employment of slaves as soldiers and military labor. Lincoln deletes recommendation from report.
March 13, 1862	in battle areas	Act of Congress	Amends articles of war of prevent soldiers from returning any slaves to their owners.
April 3, 1862	Sea Islands	Gen. Hunter request	David Hunter seeks authority to arm black units; without response, he begins to do so, but later he has to disband the unit.
April 10, 1862	Border states	Act of Congress	Congress pledges financial aid to any state offering gradual compensated emancipation.
April 16, 1862	District of Columbia	Act of Congress	Frees all slaves in the district; provides funds for colonization.
May 9, 1862	Florida, Georgia, S.C.	Order by Gen. Hunter	Frees all slaves in the three states; the order is coun- termanded on May 19 by Lincoln.
May 19, 1862	Border states	Lincoln request	Lincoln urges border states to take up gradual, com- pensated emancipation. They do not respond
June 7, 1862	Seceded states	Act of Congress	Provides for confiscation of lands whose owners failed to pay taxes.
June 19, 1862	All federal territories	Act of Congress	Frees slaves in Utah (including Nevada and Colorado), New Mexico, Nebraska.
July 12, 1862	Border states	Lincoln request	Lincoln again urges border states to adopt gradual compensated emancipation. On July 14, majority of congressmen from those states reject the suggestion.
July 17, 1862	All battle areas	1862 Confiscation Act	Declares free all slaves belonging to disloyal owners in areas in rebellion; authorizes military use of for- mer slaves.
Aug. 22, 1862	Louisiana	Order by Gen. Benjamin Butler	Prohibits return of slaves to loyal masters.
Sept. 22, 1862	Areas in rebellion	Preliminary Emancipation Proclamation	Lincoln announces Emancipation Proclamation to be effective Jan. 1
Jan. 1, 1863	Nowhere at first; as the war progresses, slaves are freed by its effect in Texas, the Gulf states, Virginia, and the Carolinas	Emancipation Proclamation	No immediate effect, as areas in Union control are specifically excluded; it is to have effect only in those areas still in rebellion as of January 1, 1863. No dis- tinction is made between loyal and disloyal owners.

Date	Locations Affected	Action	Slaves Freed
May 22, 1863	Black troops	Bureau of Colored Troops	War Department regularizes the recruitment and staffing of black regiments.
June 20, 1863	West Virginia	New constitution; admission to Union, constitution approved	
March 26	All born in West Va., after July 4, 1863, all others at age 25 or older.		
Oct. 1863	Maryland, Missouri, Tennessee	Army recruitment	Slaves recruited from loyal owners who receive $300 bounty; from disloyal owners, no bounty.
Mar. 16, 1864	Arkansas	New constitution	Prohibits slavery in the state
April 8, 1864	no immediate effect	Senate Approves Thirteenth amendment to Constitution	
June 7, 1864	Kentucky	Army recruitment	War Department pays $300 as compensation to loyal owners for slaves manumitted and who volunteer for service; slaves may enlist without consent of owners.
June 15, 1864	no effect	House of Representatives votes down Thirteenth Amendment to Constitution	
Sept. 5, 1864	Louisiana	New constitution	Prohibits slavery in the state.
Nov. 1, 1864	Maryland	New constitution	Adopted in October, the new constitution prohibits slavery after November 1, 1864.
Jan. 11, 1865	Missouri	New constitution	Frees all slaves in the state.
Jan. 16, 1865	S.C., Fla., Ga.	General Sherman Field Order 15	Sets plan for settlement of lands.
Jan. 31, 1865	no effect	House of Representatives approves Thirteenth Amendment to Constitution	Amendment is sent to states for ratification by legislatures.
Feb. 22, 1865	Tennessee	Tennessee constitutional amendment	Frees remaining slaves in the state.
March 3, 1865	All states; women and minors	Act of Congress	Frees all wives and children of any soldier; establishes Freedmen's Bureau.
March 13, 1863	no effect	Confederate Congress	Authorizes Jefferson Davis to recruit slaves for Confederate army.
June 19, 1865	Texas	Announcement of Emancipation Proc.	Slaves in Texas hear of Emancipation Proclamation; the date is later celebrated as Juneteenth.
Dec. 18, 1865	Kentucky, several counties in Va.	Thirteenth Amendment to U.S. Constitution	Frees slaves in Kentucky, in those counties of Virginia excluded from the effect of the Emancipation Proclamation, and a few hundred remaining slaves in Delaware. Some aged "servants for life" in New Jersey may have been affected; and some slaves older than 3 and younger than 25 in West Va.
April 9, 1866	All states	Civil Rights Act	Grants to former slaves all the rights of citizenship.
July 28, 1868	All states	Fourteenth Amendment to U.S. Constitution	Section 1 confirms the Civil Rights Act; Section 4 denies all outstanding claims for compensation for the emancipation of slaves.

Source: Compiled by the author from United States records.

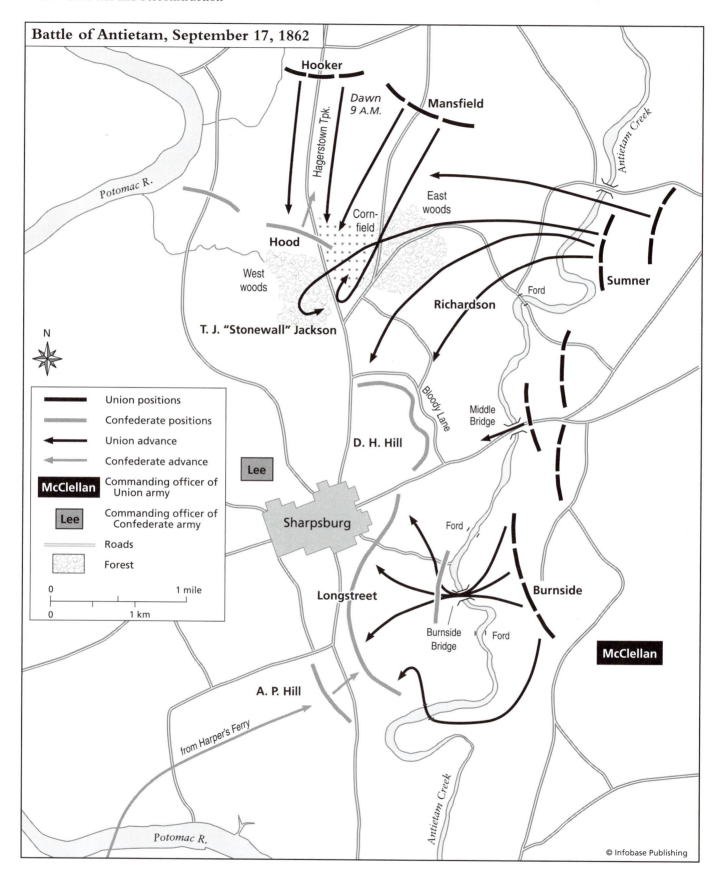

Battle of Antietam, September 17, 1862

Hooker

Mansfield

Dawn 9 A.M.

Hagerstown Tpk.

Potomac R.

East woods

Corn-field

Hood

West woods

Antietam Creek

Sumner

Ford

T. J. "Stonewall" Jackson

Richardson

Bloody Lane

N

Middle Bridge

D. H. Hill

Lee

Legend:
- Union positions
- Confederate positions
- Union advance
- Confederate advance
- **McClellan** Commanding officer of Union army
- **Lee** Commanding officer of Confederate army
- Roads
- Forest

0 — 1 mile
0 — 1 km

Sharpsburg

Ford

Longstreet

Burnside

McClellan

Burnside Bridge

Ford

A. P. Hill

from Harper's Ferry

Potomac R.

Antietam Creek

© Infobase Publishing

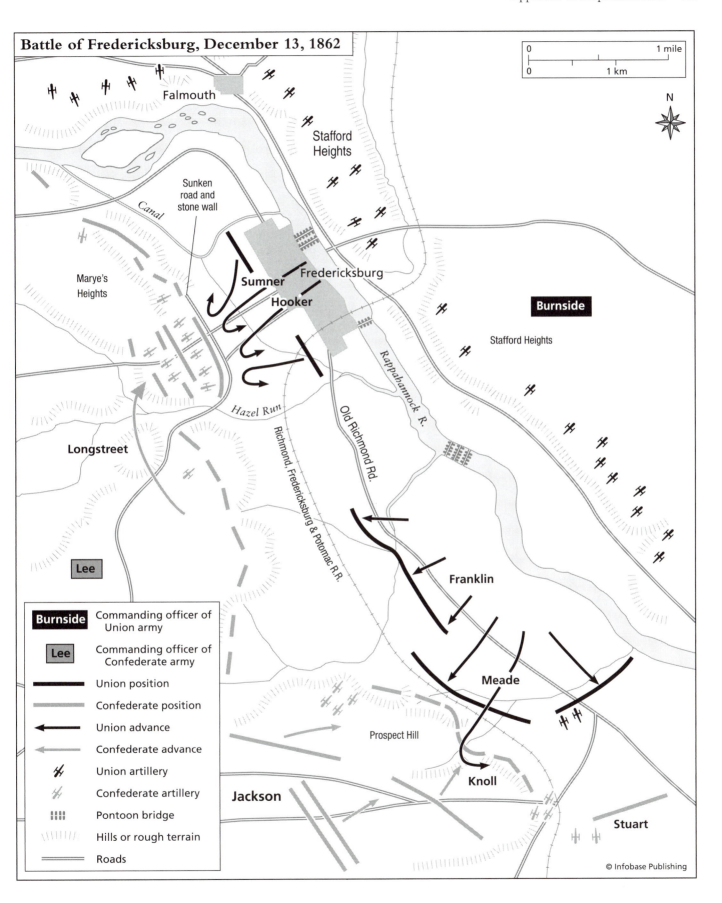

Battle of Fredericksburg, December 13, 1862

N

Falmouth

Stafford Heights

Canal

Sunken road and stone wall

Marye's Heights

Sumner

Fredericksburg

Hooker

Burnside

Stafford Heights

Rappahannock R.

Hazel Run

Longstreet

Richmond, Fredericksburg & Potomac R.R.

Old Richmond Rd.

Lee

Franklin

Meade

Prospect Hill

Jackson

Knoll

Stuart

Burnside	Commanding officer of Union army
Lee	Commanding officer of Confederate army
▬▬▬	Union position
▬▬▬	Confederate position
←	Union advance
←	Confederate advance
⚔	Union artillery
⚔	Confederate artillery
⁞⁞⁞⁞	Pontoon bridge
⁞⁞⁞⁞	Hills or rough terrain
═══	Roads

© Infobase Publishing

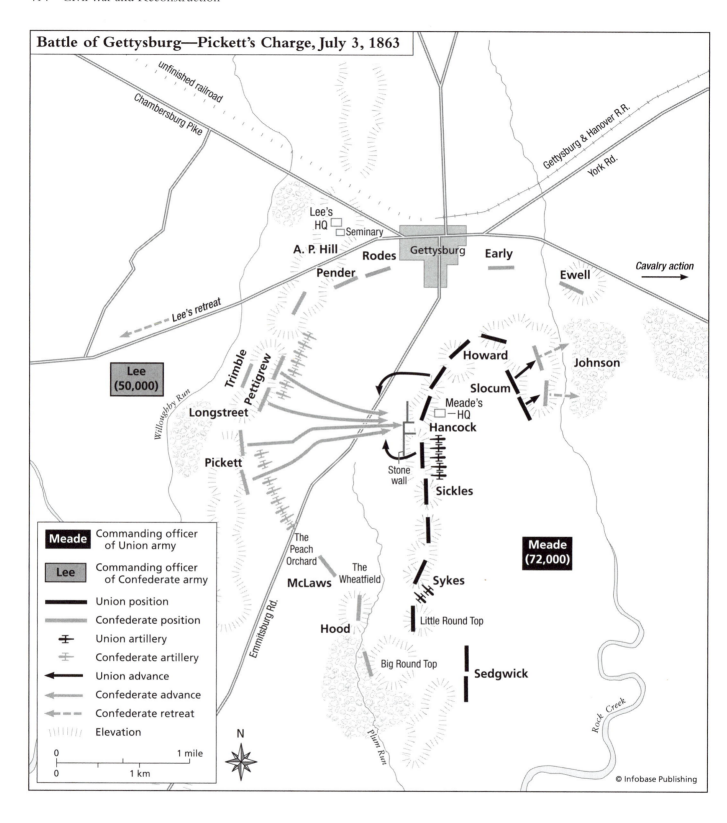

Battle of Gettysburg—Pickett's Charge, July 3, 1863

unfinished railroad

Chambersburg Pike

Gettysburg & Hanover R.R.

York Rd.

Lee's HQ

Seminary

A. P. Hill

Rodes

Gettysburg

Early

Cavalry action

Pender

Ewell

Lee's retreat

Howard

Johnson

Lee (50,000)

Trimble

Pettigrew

Slocum

Willoughby Run

Longstreet

Meade's HQ

Hancock

Pickett

Stone wall

Sickles

The Peach Orchard

The Wheatfield

Meade (72,000)

McLaws

Sykes

Meade — Commanding officer of Union army

Lee — Commanding officer of Confederate army

Union position

Confederate position

Union artillery

Confederate artillery

Union advance

Confederate advance

Confederate retreat

Elevation

Little Round Top

Hood

Big Round Top

Sedgwick

Emmitsburg Rd.

Plum Run

Rock Creek

N

0   1 mile

0   1 km

© Infobase Publishing

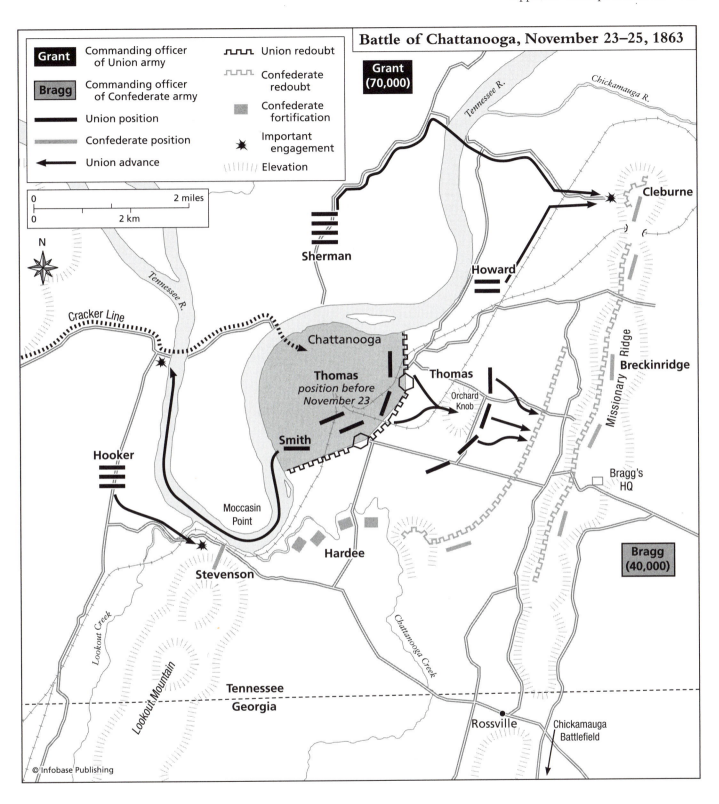

Battle of Chattanooga, November 23–25, 1863

Grant
Commanding officer of Union army

Bragg
Commanding officer of Confederate army

Union position

Confederate position

Union advance

Union redoubt

Confederate redoubt

Confederate fortification

Important engagement

Elevation

© Infobase Publishing

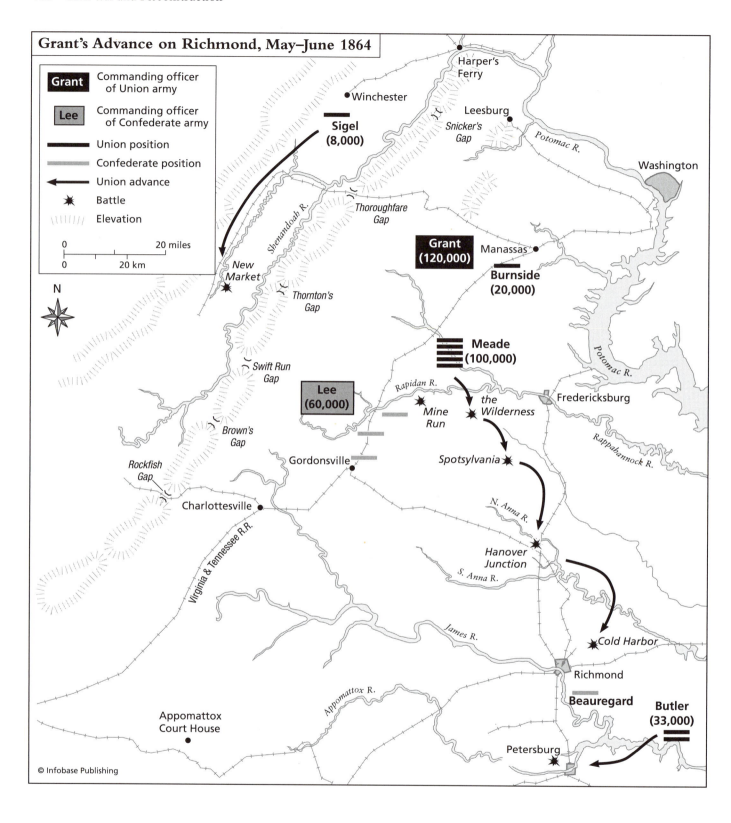

Grant's Advance on Richmond, May–June 1864

Grant Commanding officer of Union army

Lee Commanding officer of Confederate army

— Union position

— Confederate position

← Union advance

✸ Battle

Elevation

0   20 miles

0   20 km

N

Harper's Ferry

Winchester

Leesburg

Snicker's Gap

Potomac R.

Washington

Sigel (8,000)

Thoroughfare Gap

Grant (120,000)   Manassas

Burnside (20,000)

Shenandoah R.

Thornton's Gap

New Market

Meade (100,000)

Swift Run Gap

Rapidan R.

Fredericksburg

Lee (60,000)

Mine Run   the Wilderness

Rappahannock R.

Brown's Gap

Gordonsville

Spotsylvania

Rockfish Gap

N. Anna R.

Charlottesville

Hanover Junction

S. Anna R.

Virginia & Tennessee R.R.

James R.

Cold Harbor

Richmond

Appomattox R.

Beauregard   **Butler (33,000)**

Appomattox Court House

Petersburg

© Infobase Publishing

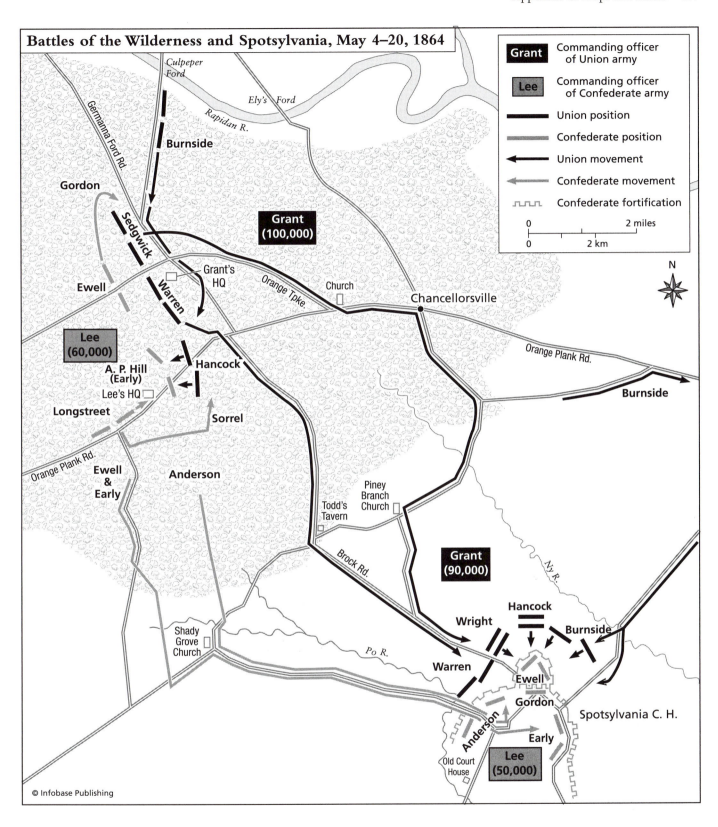

Battles of the Wilderness and Spotsylvania, May 4–20, 1864

Legend:

Grant	Commanding officer of Union army
Lee	Commanding officer of Confederate army
▬▬	Union position
▬▬	Confederate position
←	Union movement
←	Confederate movement
⌐⌐⌐	Confederate fortification

0   2 miles
0   2 km

N

Culpeper Ford
Ely's Ford
Rapidan R.
Germanna Ford Rd.
Burnside
Gordon
Sedgwick
Grant (100,000)
Warren
Ewell
Grant's HQ
Orange Tpke.
Church
Chancellorsville
Orange Plank Rd.
Lee (60,000)
A. P. Hill (Early)
Hancock
Lee's HQ
Longstreet
Sorrel
Burnside
Orange Plank Rd.
Ewell & Early
Anderson
Piney Branch Church
Todd's Tavern
Brock Rd.
Grant (90,000)
Ny R.
Shady Grove Church
Po R.
Wright
Hancock
Burnside
Warren
Ewell
Gordon
Spotsylvania C. H.
Anderson
Early
Old Court House
Lee (50,000)

© Infobase Publishing

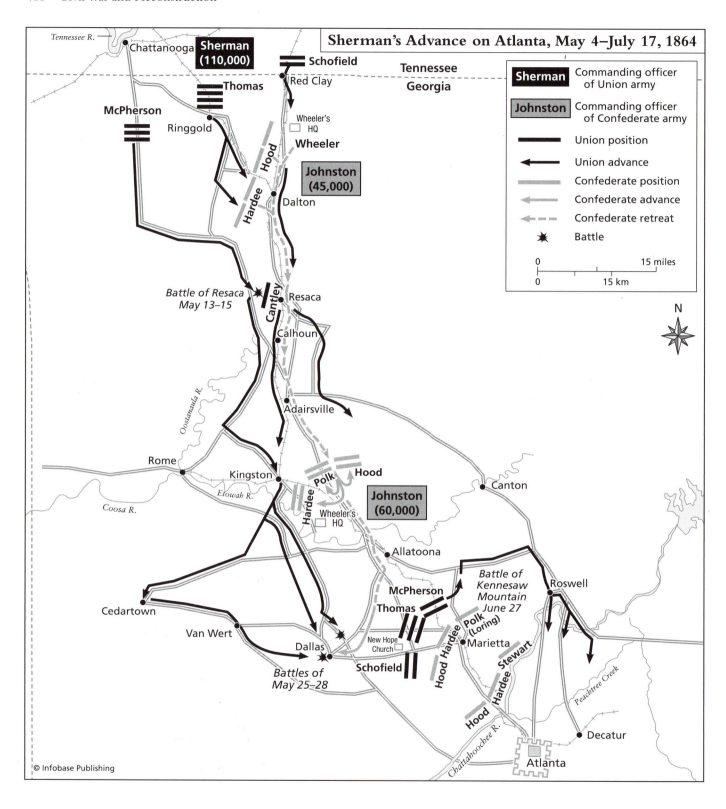

Sherman's Advance on Atlanta, May 4–July 17, 1864

Tennessee R.

Chattanooga

Sherman (110,000)

Schofield

Red Clay

Tennessee
Georgia

Thomas

McPherson

Ringgold

Wheeler's HQ

Wheeler

Hood

Hardee

Johnston (45,000)

Dalton

Sherman	Commanding officer of Union army
Johnston	Commanding officer of Confederate army
▬▬▬	Union position
◄───	Union advance
▬▬▬	Confederate position
◄───	Confederate advance
◄- - -	Confederate retreat
✴	Battle

0   15 miles
0   15 km

N

Battle of Resaca May 13–15

Cantley

Resaca

Calhoun

Oostanaula R.

Adairsville

Rome

Kingston

Polk

Hood

Canton

Coosa R.

Etowah R.

Hardee

Wheeler's HQ

Johnston (60,000)

Allatoona

Cedartown

McPherson

Thomas

Battle of Kennesaw Mountain June 27

Roswell

Van Wert

Dallas

New Hope Church

Polk (Loring)

Hood Hardee

Marietta

Stewart

Schofield

Battles of May 25–28

Hood Hardee

Peachtree Creek

Chattahoochee R.

Decatur

Atlanta

© Infobase Publishing

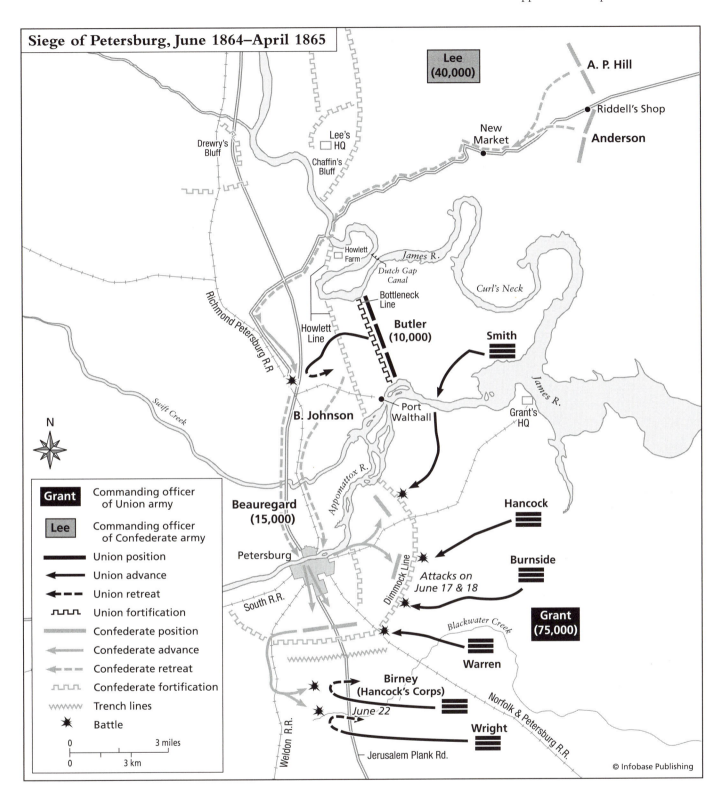

Siege of Petersburg, June 1864–April 1865

Lee (40,000)

A. P. Hill

Riddell's Shop

Anderson

New Market

Drewry's Bluff

Lee's HQ

Chaffin's Bluff

James R.

Curl's Neck

Howlett Farm

Dutch Gap Canal

Bottleneck Line

Howlett Line

Butler (10,000)

Smith

Richmond Petersburg R.R.

Swift Creek

B. Johnson

Port Walthall

James R.

Grant's HQ

Appomattox R.

Beauregard (15,000)

Petersburg

Hancock

Dimmock Line

Burnside

Attacks on June 17 & 18

Grant (75,000)

Blackwater Creek

South R.R.

Warren

Norfolk & Petersburg R.R.

Birney (Hancock's Corps)

June 22

Wright

Weldon R.R.

Jerusalem Plank Rd.

N

Grant	Commanding officer of Union army
Lee	Commanding officer of Confederate army
—	Union position
←	Union advance
←-	Union retreat
⊓⊔	Union fortification
—	Confederate position
←	Confederate advance
←-	Confederate retreat
⊓⊔	Confederate fortification
⋀⋀⋀	Trench lines
✸	Battle

0 — 3 miles
0 — 3 km

© Infobase Publishing

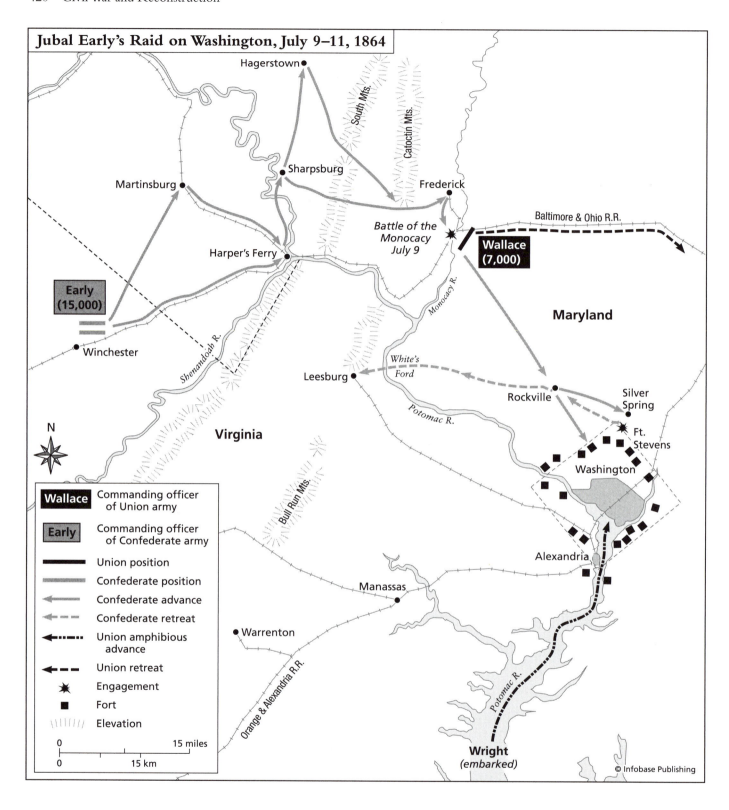

Jubal Early's Raid on Washington, July 9–11, 1864

Hagerstown

South Mts.

Catoctin Mts.

Sharpsburg

Frederick

Martinsburg

Baltimore & Ohio R.R.

Battle of the
Monocacy
July 9

Wallace
(7,000)

Harper's Ferry

Early
(15,000)

Maryland

Monocacy R.

Winchester

Shenandoah R.

White's
Ford

Leesburg

Rockville

Silver
Spring

Potomac R.

Ft.
Stevens

Virginia

Washington

N

Bull Run Mts.

| **Wallace** | Commanding officer of Union army |
| **Early** | Commanding officer of Confederate army |

Alexandria

Manassas

Union position

Confederate position

Warrenton

Confederate advance

Confederate retreat

Union amphibious advance

Union retreat

Potomac R.

Orange & Alexandria R.R.

Engagement

Fort

Elevation

0   15 miles

0   15 km

Wright
(embarked)

© Infobase Publishing

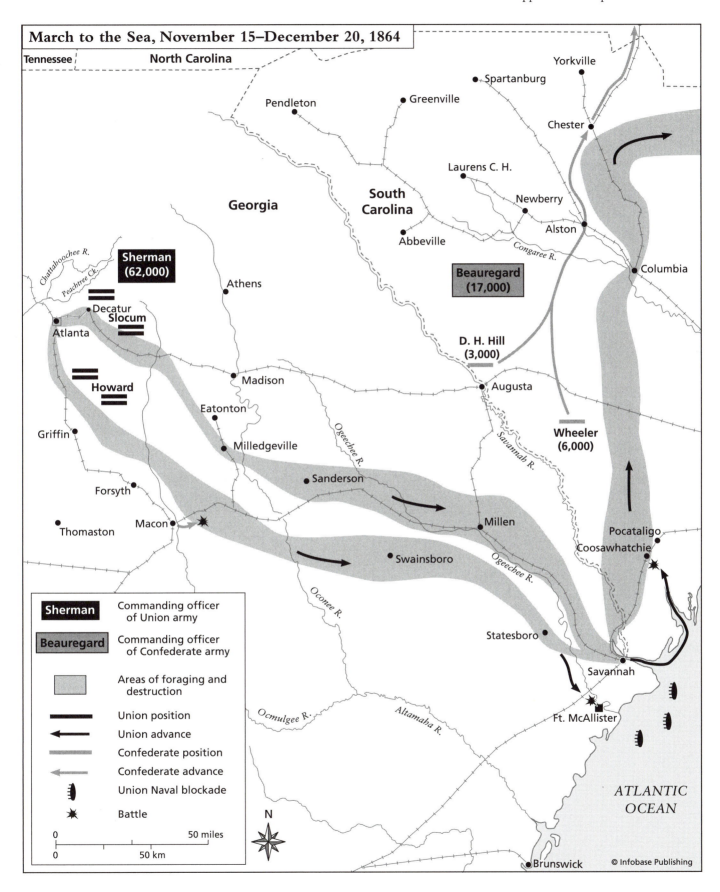

March to the Sea, November 15–December 20, 1864

Tennessee   North Carolina

Yorkville

Spartanburg

Greenville

Pendleton

Chester

Laurens C. H.

Georgia   **South Carolina**

Newberry

Alston

Sherman (62,000)

Athens

Abbeville

Congaree R.

Columbia

Beauregard (17,000)

Chattahoochee R.

Peachtree Ck.

Decatur
Slocum

Atlanta

D. H. Hill (3,000)

Madison

Augusta

Howard

Eatonton

Savannah R.

Wheeler (6,000)

Griffin

Milledgeville

Ogeechee R.

Forsyth

Sanderson

Macon

Millen

Thomaston

Swainsboro

Ogeechee R.

Pocataligo

Coosawhatchie

Oconee R.

Statesboro

Savannah

Sherman Commanding officer of Union army

Beauregard Commanding officer of Confederate army

Areas of foraging and destruction

Union position

Union advance

Confederate position

Confederate advance

Union Naval blockade

Battle

Ocmulgee R.

Ft. McAllister

Altamaha R.

N

0   50 miles

0   50 km

ATLANTIC OCEAN

Brunswick

© Infobase Publishing

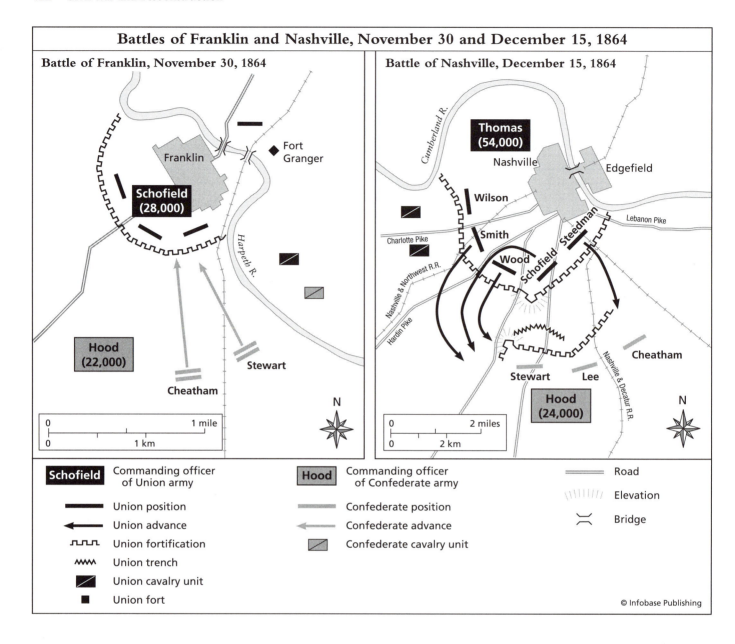

Battles of Franklin and Nashville, November 30 and December 15, 1864

Battle of Franklin, November 30, 1864

Battle of Nashville, December 15, 1864

Legend:

Schofield	Commanding officer of Union army	
Hood	Commanding officer of Confederate army	
←	Union position / Union advance	
Union fortification		
Union trench		
Union cavalry unit		
Union fort		
Confederate position		
Confederate advance		
Confederate cavalry unit		
Road		
Elevation		
Bridge		

© Infobase Publishing

NOTES

1. ULTIMATE AND PROXIMATE CAUSES

1. The difficulty of assessing the total number of fugitive slaves moved through the Underground Railroad is discussed in Fergus Bordewich, *Bound for Canaan: The Epic Story of the Underground Railroad, America's First Civil Rights Movement* (New York: HarperCollins, 2005), pp. 436–437.
2. Rendition cases: James M. McPherson, *Battle Cry of Freedom* (New York: Oxford University Press, 1988), pp. 78–89.
3. For a carefully considered evaluation of Stowe's work and its impact, see David Potter, *The Impending Crisis, 1848–1861* (New York: Harper and Row, 1976), p. 140.
4. Vote in May: Potter, pp. 166–167.
5. Lecompton: Potter, pp. 297–327.
6. Douglas chosen: Potter, p. 355.

2. SECESSION, BORDER STATES, AND FIRST BATTLES

1. Lincoln's defensive strategy: Clement Eaton, *A History of the Southern Confederacy* (New York: Free Press, 1954), p. 37.
2. For a thoughtful analysis of the difference between secession of the Gulf states and the border states, see Michael Holt, *The Political Crisis of the 1850s* (New York: John Wiley & Sons, 1978), pp. 253–257.
3. Duane Schultz, *Quantrill's War: The Life and Times of William Clarke Quantrill, 1837–1865* (New York: St. Martin's Press, 1996).
4. Merryman: Russell Weigley, *A Great Civil War: A Military and Political History, 1861–1865* (Bloomington: Indiana University Press, 2000), pp. 181–183.
5. Formation of West Virginia: Weigley, pp. 52–55.

3. FROM SLAVERY TO FREEDOM: BATTLEFIELD EMANCIPATION AND CONTRABANDS

1. Re contrabands: "Important Decision of the Government—Slaves of Rebel Owners Contraband of War," *The Liberator,* Vol. 31, No. 23 (June 7, 1861), p. 91.
2. Regarding the term entering the language: Allan Nevins, *Diary of the Civil War, 1860–1865* (New York: MacMillan, 1962), p. 192.
3. For Hunter's order and Lincoln's countermanding order, see Joel Williamson, *After Slavery: The Negro in South Carolina During Reconstruction, 1861–1877* (Chapel Hill: University of North Carolina Press, 1965), pp. 11–12.
4. For deportation plans during the Civil War, see Rodney Carlisle, *The Roots of Black Nationalism* (Port Washington, N.Y.: Kennikat 1975), pp. 87–92.
5. Sea Islands as an experiment: Philip Shaw Paludan, *A People's Contest* (Lawrence: University Press of Kansas, 1996), p. 203; see also Willie Lee Rose, *Rehearsal for Reconstruction: The Port Royal Experiment* (New York: Oxford University Press, 1964).

4. BLOCKADE SHIPS AND RIVER GUNBOATS

1. Raphael Semmes to Howell Cobb, January 26, 1861, in U. B. Phillips, *The Correspondence of Robert Toombs, Alexander H. Stephens, and Howell Cobb* (Washington, D.C.: American Historical Association, 1913), pp. 533–535.
2. Admiral D. D. Porter's account of the meetings November 12, 1861, in Robert Underwood Johnson and Clarence Clough Buel, *Battles and Leaders of the Civil War* (1894; reprint, New York: Thomas Yoseloff, 1956–58), Vol. II, pp. 23–24.

3. Fairfax's account of the incident, in Johnson and Buel, Vol. II, p. 136.
4. Mason and Slidell decision: James M. McPherson, *Battle Cry of Freedom* (New York: Oxford University Press), p. 391.
5. Failures of interservice cooperation: William H. Roberts: *Now for the Contest: Coastal and Oceanic Naval Operations in the Civil War* (Lincoln: University of Nebraska Press, 2004), pp. 37–38.
6. Donelson battle: Henry Walke, in Johnson and Buel, Vol. I, p. 431.

5. TWO BITTER YEARS

1. McClellan's information from Pinkerton: Bruce Catton, in *Bruce Catton's Civil War* (New York: Fairfax Press, 1984), pp. 74–75.
2. Peninsular Campaign: Catton, pp. 55–86.
3. Shiloh: Stanley F. Horn, *The Army of Tennessee* (Norman: University of Oklahoma Press), pp. 122–143.
4. Details of the lives and careers of the generals are confirmed from Ezra Warner, *Generals in Blue: Lives of the Union Commanders* (Baton Rouge: Louisiana State University Press, 1964) and from Warner's work on Confederate generals, *Generals in Gray* (Baton Rouge: Louisiana State University Press, 1959).
5. Of the many accounts of Gettysburg, one of the best is Russell Weigley, *A Great Civil War* (Bloomington: Indiana University Press, 2000), pp. 242–253.

6. EMANCIPATION AND THE MIND OF LINCOLN

1. There were many such requests for clarification. See, for example, General J. M. Schofield to Edward Stanton, July 17, 1863, in *Official Records of the War of the Rebellion,* Series II, Vol. 3, p. 525.
2. For the long-term survival of peonage, see Pete Daniel, *The Shadow of Slavery: Peonage in the South, 1901–1969* (Urbana: University of Illinois Press, 1990).
3. For plantation disrepair and the need for Northern initiative, see Rev. C. Nason, letter of February 5, 1863, in *Zion's Herald and Wesleyan Journal,* Vol. 34, No. 11 (March 18, 1863), p. 42.
4. Re Davis Bend, see Rodney Carlisle, *The Roots of Black Nationalism* (Port Washington, N.Y.: Kennikat, 1975), Carlisle, p. 91.

5. Nevins, *Diary of the Civil War, 1860–1865* (New York: Macmillan, 1962), pp. 335–337.

7. SEA DOGS AND SUBMARINES

1. Chester Hearn, *Gray Raiders of the Sea: How Eight Confederate Warships Destroyed the Union's High Seas Commerce* (Camden, Maine: International Marine Publishing, 1997), pp. 311–317.
2. Historic proportions, see Hearn, p. xv.
3. Tomb's story, see R. Thomas Campbell, *Engineer in Gray: Memoirs of Chief Engineer James H. Tomb, CSN* (Jefferson, N.C.: McFarland, 2005), p. 170.
4. David boats, see Campbell, pp. 65–75.
5. *Pioneer,* see Louis S. Schafer, *Confederate Underwater Warfare: An Illustrated History* (Jefferson, N.C.: MacFarland, 1996), pp. 104–112.
6. *Hunley,* see Schafer, pp. 113–125.
7. Trout boat, see Schafer, pp. 152–158.

8. THE TURNING OF THE TIDE

1. New York and Chicago, see John W. Headley, *Confederate Operations in Canada and New York* (New York: Neale, 1906), pp. 217–231, 264–283.
2. Measured retreat of General Johnston, see Stanley F. Horn, *The Army of Tennessee* (Norman: University of Oklahoma Press, 1993), pp. 305–340.
3. Hood's generalship, see Horn, pp. 341–390; James Lee McDonough and Thomas L. Connelly, *Five Tragic Hours: The Battle of Franklin* (Knoxville: University of Tennessee Press, 1998), pp. 3–18, 64–65.
4. The Bloody Angle, see Gordon C. Rhea, *The Battles for Spotsylvania Court House and the Road to Yellow Tavern* (Baton Rouge: Louisiana State University Press, 1997), pp. 267–307.
5. Defenses at Franklin, see McDonough and Connelly, pp. 80–81; Horn, pp. 394–397.
6. Confederate outrage at Richmond raid, see Headley, pp. 175–185.

9. PARTISAN POLITICS

1. For a thoughtful treatment of politics in the Confederacy, see Clement Eaton, *A History of the Southern Confederacy* (New York: Free Press, 1954), pp. 57–66.

2. Vallandigham, see Frank L. Klement, *The Limits of Dissent: Clement L. Vallandigham and the Civil War* (Lexington: University Press of Kentucky, 1970), pp. 138–296.
3. Impact of Atlanta victory, see George H. Mayer, *The Republican Party, 1854–1964* (New York: Oxford University Press, 1967), p. 121.
4. For 1864 results, see Mayer, pp. 115–123.
5. Regarding election fraud, see Jean Baker, *Affairs of Party* (New York: Fordham University Press, 1998), pp. 261–317.

10. TO APPOMATOX COURT HOUSE AND BEYOND

1. Jefferson as stubborn and difficult, see Clement Eaton, *A History of the Southern Confederacy* (New York: Free Press, 1954), pp. 56–57.
2. Fall of Richmond, see John B. Jones, *A Rebel War Clerk's Diary* (New York: A. S. Barnes, 1961), pp. 526–533.
3. Johnston-Davis meeting, see Stanley F. Horn, *The Army of Tennessee* (Norman: University of Oklahoma Press, 1993), p. 427.
4. For a close review of the terms offered to Johnston and Lincoln's consideration of terms to Virginia, see Russell Weigley, *A Great Civil War* (Bloomington: Indiana University Press, 2000), pp. 442–450.
5. Re trial, see Champ Clark, *The Assassination: Death of a President* (Alexandria, Va.: Time-Life Books, 1987), pp. 145–160.

11. RECONSTRUCTION

1. A good source for investigative reports on the progress of Reconstruction is Edward McPherson, *The Political History of the United States of America During the Period of Reconstruction, April 15, 1865–July 15, 1870.* (1871; reprint, New York: Da Capo Press, 1972).
2. Re Mississippi Plan, see Albert Morgan, *Yazoo; or On the Picket Line of Freedom in the South,* as reproduced in Glenn M. Linden, ed., *Voices from the Reconstruction Years, 1865–1877* (New York: Harcourt Brace, 1999), p. 240.
3. Vernon Lane Wharton, *The Negro in Mississippi, 1865–1890* (New York: Harper Torchbooks, 1965), pp. 181–215.
4. Protest regarded as "sauce," see LaWanda Cox and John H. Cox, eds., *Reconstruction, the Negro and the New South* (Columbia: University of South Carolina Press, 1973), pp. 4–5.
5. This perspective on the long-range consequences of Reconstruction is shaped by Kenneth Stampp, *The Era of Reconstruction: 1865–1877* (New York: Alfred A. Knopf, 1965).

BIBLIOGRAPHY

DOCUMENTARY COLLECTIONS

Official Records of the Union and Confederate Navies in the War of the Rebellion.
Washington, D.C.: Government Printing Office, 1894–1922.

The War of the Rebellion: A Compilation of the Official Records of the Union and Confederate Armies. [*Usually cited as "Official Records of the War of the Rebellion"*] Washington, D.C.: Government Printing Office, 1890–99.

BOOKS AND PERIODICALS

Albion, A Journal of News, Politics, and Literature. "North and South," Vol. 39, No. 8 (February 23, 1861), p. 90.

Anderson, Bern. *By Sea and By River: The Naval History of the Civil War.* New York: Alfred A. Knopf, 1962.

Baker, Jean H. *Affairs of Party: The Political Culture of Northern Democrats in the Mid-nineteenth Century.* New York: Fordham University Press, 1998.

Barrows, Rev. D. D. "The Freedmen of the South," *Christian Advocate and Journal,* Vol. 38, No. 46 (November 12, 1863), p. 362.

Beringer, Richard, and Herman Hattaway, Archer Jones, William N. Still, Jr. *Why the South Lost the Civil War.* Athens: University of Georgia Press, 1986.

Blackbridge [correspondent pen name]. "Political Affairs in Delaware. Action of the Union State Convention—The Nominations—The Military Movement." *New York Times,* August 27, 1862, p. 2.

Blassingame, John W., and John R. McKivigan, eds. *The Frederick Douglass Papers: Series One: Speeches, Debates, and Interviews, Vol. 4: 1864–80.* New Haven, Conn.: Yale University Press, 1991.

Blight, David W., and Brooks D. Simpson. *Union and Emancipation: Essays on Politics and Race in the Civil War Era.* Kent, Ohio: Kent State University Press, 1997.

Bordewich, Fergus M. *Bound for Canaan: The Epic Story of the Underground Railroad, America's First Civil Rights Movement.* New York: HarperCollins, 2005.

Brewer, James H. *The Confederate Negro: Virginia's Craftsmen and Military Laborers, 1861–1865.* Durham, N.C.: Duke University Press, 1969.

Butler, Benjamin. "General Butler on the Contraband Question" [letter to Secretary of War Simon Cameron, July 20, 1861], *The Liberator,* Vol. 1, No. 32 (August 9, 1861), p. 127.

Cameron, Simon. "The Contraband Question" [letter to General Benjamin Butler, August 11, 1861], *The Liberator,* Vol. 31, No. 32 (August 16, 1861), p. 131.

Campbell, R. Thomas, ed. *Engineer in Gray: Memoirs of Chief Engineer James H. Tomb, CSN.* Jefferson, N.C.: McFarland, 2005.

Canney, Donald L. *Lincoln's Navy: The Ships, Men and Organization, 1861–65.* Annapolis, Md.: Naval Institute Press, 1998.

Carlisle, Rodney. *The Roots of Black Nationalism.* Port Washington, N.Y.: Kennikat Press, 1975.

Catton, Bruce. *Bruce Catton's Civil War: Three Volumes in One: Mr. Lincoln's Army, Glory Road,* and *A Stillness at Appomattox.* New York: Fairfax Press, 1984.

———. *The Coming Fury.* Garden City, N.Y.: Doubleday, 1961.

Catton, William and Bruce. *Two Roads to Sumter.* New York: McGraw-Hill, 1963.

Chafin, Tom. *Sea of Gray: The Around the World Odyssey of the Confederate Raider Shenandoah.* New York: Hill & Wang, 2006.

Chase, Salmon. "Remarks of Chief Justice Chase," *The Liberator,* Vol. 35, No. 10 (March 10, 1865), p. 39.

Chesnut, Mary Boykin. Edited by Ben Ames Williams. *A Diary from Dixie.* Cambridge, Mass.: Harvard University Press, 1980.

Chesnut, Mary Boykin. Edited by C. Vann Woodward. *Mary Chesnut's Civil War.* New Haven, Conn.: Yale, 1981.

Clark, Champ. *The Assassination: Death of the President.* Alexandria, Va.: Time-Life Books, 1987.

Commager, Henry Steele, ed. *The Blue and the Gray: The Story of the Civil War as told by Participants,* 2 volumes. Indianapolis: Bobbs-Merrill, 1950.

———. *Fifty Basic Civil War Documents.* New York: Van Nostrand, 1965.

Cox, LaWanda, and John H. Cox, eds. *Reconstruction, the Negro, and the New South.* Columbia: University of South Carolina Press, 1973.

Daniel, Pete. *The Shadow of Slavery: Peonage in the South, 1901–1969.* Urbana: University of Illinois Press, 1990.

Durkin, Joseph T. *Confederate Navy Chief: Stephen R. Mallory.* Columbia: University of South Carolina Press, 1987.

D. W. B. [correspondent pen name]. "Our Washington Correspondence," *The Independent,* Vol. 15, No. 741 (February 12, 1863), p. 1.

———. *The Independent,* Vol. 29, No. 1474 (March 1, 1877), p. 18.

Eaton, Clement. *A History of the Southern Confederacy.* New York: Free Press, 1954.

Evans, Robert G. *The 16th Mississippi Infantry: Civil War Letters and Reminiscences.* Jackson: University Press of Mississippi, 2002.

Faust, Patricia L. *Historical Times Illustrated Encyclopedia of the Civil War.* New York: Harper and Row, 1986.

Frederickson, George M., ed. *William Lloyd Garrison.* Englewood Cliffs, N.J.: Prentice-Hall, 1968.

Friend, The, A Religious and Literary Journal. "Summary of Events," Vol. 38, No. 33 (April 15, 1865), p. 635.

Gallman, J. Matthew, ed. *The Civil War Chronicle.* New York: Crown, 2000.

Greeley, Horace. *The American Conflict: A History of the Great Rebellion in the United States of America, 1860–65.* Hartford, Conn.: O. D. Case, 1866.

Griffith, Paddy. *Battle in the Civil War: Generalship and Tactics in America, 1861–65.* Camberly, Great Britain: Fieldbooks, 1986.

Hattaway, Herman, and Archer Jones. *How the North Won: A Military History of the Civil War.* Urbana: University of Illinois Press, 1983.

Headley, John W. *Confederate Operations in Canada and New York.* New York: Neale, 1906.

Hearn, Chester G. *Gray Raiders of the Sea: How Eight Confederate Warships Destroyed the Union's High Seas Commerce.* Camden, Maine: International Marine Publishing, 1992.

Helper, Hinton. *The Impending Crisis of the South: How to Meet It.* 1857. Reprint, Westport, Conn.: Negro Universities Press, 1970.

Holt, Michael F. *The Political Crisis of the 1850s.* New York: John Wiley, 1978.

———. *Political Parties and American Political Development from the Age of Jackson to the Age of Lincoln*. Baton Rouge: Louisiana State University, 1992.

Horn, Stanley F. *The Army of Tennessee*. Norman: University of Oklahoma Press, 1993.

Hubbs, G. Ward, ed. *Voices from Company D: Diaries by the Greensboro Guards, Fifth Alabama Infantry Regiment, Army of Northern Virginia*. Athens: University of Georgia Press, 2003.

Independent, The. "How to Make a Great Campaign Meeting," Vol. 16, No. 829 (October 20, 1864), p. 4.

———. "Miscellaneous—Jeff. Davis under Bolt and Bar," Vol. 17, No. 860 (May 25, 1865), p. 8.

———. "Equal Rights," Vol. 27, No. 1363 (January 14, 1875), p. 27.

Johnson, Robert Underwood, and Clarence Clough Buel. *Battles and Leaders of the Civil War,* 4 vols. 1894. Reprint, New York: Thomas Yoseloff, 1956–58.

Jones, Archer. *Civil War Command and Strategy*. New York: Free Press, 1992.

Jones, John B. Edited by Earl Schenck Miers. *A Rebel War Clerk's Diary, by John B. Jones*. New York: A. S. Barnes, 1961.

Jordan, Ervin L., Jr. *Black Confederates and Afro-Yankees in Civil War Virginia*. Charlottesville: University of Virginia Press, 1995.

Klement, Frank L. *The Limits of Dissent: Clement L. Vallandigham & the Civil War*. New York: Fordham University Press, 1998.

Liberator, The. [Untitled article], Vol. 31, No. 22 (May 31, 1861), p. 87.

———. "Important Decision of the Government—Slaves of Rebel Owners Contraband of War," Vol. 31, No. 23 (June 7, 1861), p. 91.

———. "Colonization of the Blacks," Vol. 32, No. 38 (September 19, 1862), p. 150.

———. "Haytian Emigration," Vol. 36, No. 40 (October 3, 1862), p. 158.

———. "Major General Banks," Vol. 34, No. 36 (November 11, 1864), p. 182.

———. "Jeff. Davis on the Arming of Slaves," Vol. 34, No. 47 (November 18, 1864), p. 186.

———. "The Arrest of Secretary Seward's Assassin," Vol. 35, No. 16 (April 21, 1865), p. 63.

Linden, Glenn M., ed. *Voices from the Reconstruction Years, 1865–1877*. New York: Harcourt Brace, 1999.

Loving, Jerome M. *Civil War Letters of George Washington Whitman*. Durham, N.C.: Duke University Press, 1975.

Luraghi, Raimundo. *A History of the Confederate Navy*. Translated by Paolo E. Coletta. Annapolis, Md.: Naval Institute Press, 1996.

Massachusetts Anti-Slavery Society. *Annual Report—Vols. 18–24: 1850–1856*. Westport, Conn.: Negro Universities Press, 1970.

May, Samuel J. *Recollections of Our Antislavery Conflict*. 1869. Reprint, New York: Arno Press and New York Times, 1968.

Mayer, George H. *The Republican Party, 1854–1964*. New York: Oxford University Press, 1967.

McDonough, James Lee, and Thomas L. Connelly. *Five Tragic Hours: The Battle of Franklin*. Knoxville: University of Tennessee Press, 1983.

McKitrick, Eric L. *Andrew Johnson and Reconstruction*. New York: Oxford University Press, 1960.

McPherson, Edward. *The Political History of the United States of America During the Period of Reconstruction, April 15, 1865–July 15, 1870*. 1871. Reprint, New York: Da Capo Press, 1972.

McPherson, James M. *The Negro's Civil War: How American Negroes Felt and Acted During the War for the Union*. New York: Vintage Books, 1965.

————. *Battle Cry of Freedom: The Civil War Era*. New York: Oxford University Press, 1988.

Miller, Charles Dana. Ed. Steward Bennet and Barbara Tilley. *The Struggle for the Life of the Republic: A Civil War Narrative by Brevet Major Charles Dana Miller, 76th Ohio Volunteer Infantry*. Kent, Ohio: Kent State University Press, 2004.

Musicant, Ivan. *Divided Waters: The Naval History of the Civil War*. New York: HarperCollins, 1995.

Nason, Rev. C. [untilted eyewitness account, February 5, 1863], *Zion's Herald and Wesleyan Journal*, Vol. 34, No. 11 (March 18, 1863), p. 42.

New-York Daily Times. "The Slave Rescue at Syracuse." October 18, 1851, p. 2.

———— [untitled editorial]. May 31, 1852, p. 2.

————. "The Slave Trade and the South." December 6, 1854, p. 4.

———. "Fears and Hopes for Kansas." December 8, 1854, p. 4.

———. "Kansas and Slavery." December 11, 1854, p. 4.

New York Evangelist. "The Scene after the Surrender of Fort Donelson," Vol. 32, No. 10 (March 6, 1862), p. 7.

———. "Current Events," Vol. 36, No. 19 (May 11, 1865), p. 4.

———. "Current Events—Statement of James P. Ferguson," Vol. 36, No. 16 (April 20, 1865), p. 4.

New York Times. "The Question of the Forts." January 1, 1861, p. 10.

———. "The Delaware Legislature, Reception of the Secession Commissioner from Mississippi." January 4, 1861, p. 8.

———. "Our Washington Dispat[c]hes." January 14, 1861, p. 1.

———. "From Mobile—the Alabama Secession Flag—Sentiment of the People, etc." January 15, 1861, p. 1.

———. "The Ideas on Which Secession Is Based." January 15, 1861, p. 4.

———. "The Death of Col. Ellsworth, Full Particulars of the Assassination by an Eye-Witness—The Zouaves Swear That They Will Be Revenged—Singular Coincidences." May 26, 1861, p. 8.

———. "Government Policy on Slavery in the Seceded States." August 13, 1861, p. 4.

———. "The October Elections." October 6, 1861, p. 5.

———. "The Connecticut Mass Union Convention." January 9, 1862, p. 8.

——— [editorial]. "The Exploit of the Monitor—A Scientific Comment." March 13, 1862, p. 4.

———. "The Great Naval Victory" [from *The Norfolk Day Book*]. March 14, 1862, p. 8.

———. "The Naval Battle in Hampton Roads. Official Rebel Report of the Engagement." March 14, 1862, p. 8.

———. "The Planter and Its Colored Captors." May 25, 1862, p. 4.

———. "The Mob in New-York. Resistance to the Draft—Rioting and Bloodshed. Conscription Offices Sacked and Burned. Private Dwellings Pillaged and Fired." July 14, 1863, p. 1.

———. "Chicago Convention. McClellan Nominated for President. Pendleton, of Ohio, for Vice President. Vallandigham Moves to Make the Nomination Unanimous. A Peace Horse and a War Horse. Adjournment of the Convention." September 1, 1864, p. 1.

———. "Details of the Capture [of Jefferson Davis]." May 15, 1865, p. 1.

P. [pen name, probably Edward Pierce]. Letter to the *Boston Traveller,* July 10, 1861, in article, "The Contraband at Fortress Monroe." *New York Times,* July 20, 1861, p. 2.

Paludan, Philip Shaw. *A People's Contest: The Union and Civil War, 1861–1865.* Lawrence: University Press of Kansas, 1996.

Perry, Milton F. *Infernal Machines: The Story of Confederate Submarine and Mine Warfare.* Baton Rouge: Louisiana State University Press, 1965.

Phillips, U. B. *The Correspondence of Robert Toombs, Alexander H. Stephens, and Howell Cobb.* Washington, D.C.: American Historical Association, 1913.

Pokanoket [correspondent pen name]. "Rhode Island-Political," *Zion's Herald and Wesleyan Journal,* Vol. 35, No. 36 (September 7, 1864), p. 142.

Porter, Edward Alexander. *Military Memoirs of a Confederate.* 1907. Edited and with a new introduction by T. Harry Williams. Bloomington: Indiana University Press, 1962.

Potter, David M. *The Impending Crisis: 1848–1861.* New York: Harper and Row, 1976.

Redpath, James. "The Mississippi Plan," *The Independent,* Vol. 28, No. 1452 (September 28, 1876), p. 1.

Rhea, Gordon C. *The Battles for Spotsylvania Court House and the Road to Yellow Tavern.* Baton Rouge: Louisiana State University Press, 1997.

Roberts, William H. *Now for the Contest: Coastal and Oceanic Naval Operations in the Civil War.* Lincoln: University of Nebraska Press, 2004.

Rose, Willie Lee. *Rehearsal for Reconstruction: The Port Royal Experiment.* New York: Oxford Univesity Press, 1964.

Rozwenc, Edwin C., ed. *Slavery as a Cause of the Civil War.* Boston: D.C. Heath, 1963.

Schafer, Louis S. *Confederate Underwater Warfare: An Illustrated History.* Jefferson, N.C.: McFarland, 1996.

Schultz, Duane. *Quantrill's War: The Life and Times of William Clarke Quantrill, 1837–1865.* New York: St. Martin's Press, 1996.

Scott, Robert Garth, ed. *Forgotten Valor: The Memoirs, Journals, and Civil War Letters of Orlando B. Willcox.* Kent, Ohio: Kent State University Press, 1999.

Sears, Stephen W., ed. *The Civil War Papers of George B. McClellan: Selected Correspondence, 1860–1865.* New York: Ticknor and Fields, 1989.

Semmes, Raphael. Edited by Philip Van Doren Stern. *The Confederate Raider* Alabama: *Selections from Memoirs of Service Afloat During the War Between the States.* Bloomington: Indiana University Press, 1962.

Sherman, William T. *Memoirs of Gen. W. T. Sherman, Written by Himself.* New York: Charles L. Webster, 1892.

Smith, Gerritt. Letter to Montgomery Blair, Postmaster General, *The Liberator,* Vol. 32, No. 16 (April 18, 1862), p. 64.

Spear, Rev. Samuel T. Sermon of April 16, 1865, *The National Preacher and Village Pulpit,* Vol. 39, No. 5 (May 1865), p. 131.

———. "The President and Congress," *The American Presbyterian and Theological Review,* Vol. 5, No. 17 (January 1867), pp. 28–29.

Spencer, Warren F. *The Confederate Navy in Europe.* Tuscaloosa: University of Alabama Press, 1983.

Stampp, Kenneth. *The Era of Reconstruction: 1865–1877.* New York: Alfred A. Knopf, 1965.

Stern, Philp Van Doren. *The Confederate Navy: A Pictorial History.* New York: Bonanza Books, 1962.

Stiles, T. J., ed. *In Their Own Words: Civil War Commanders.* New York: Berkley, 1995.

Strong, George Templeton. *Diary of the Civil War.* Edited by Allan Nevins. New York: Macmillan, 1962.

Thomas, Emory M. *The Confederate Nation: 1861–1865.* New York: Harper and Row, 1979.

Tilton, Theodore. "Negro Suffrage—A letter from Theodore Tilton," *The Liberator,* Vol. 35, No. 3 (January 20, 1865), p. 10.

Unitarian Review and Religious Magazine, The. "The Editor's Note Book," Vol. 6, No. 6 (December 1876), p. 671.

United States Congress. *Report of the Joint Committee on Reconstruction At the First Session, Thirty-Ninth Congress.* Washington, D.C.: Government Printing Office, 1866.

Wagner, Margaret, et al. *The Library of Congress Civil War Desk Reference.* New York: Simon & Schuster, 2002.

Warner, Ezra J. *Generals in Blue: Lives of the Union Commanders.* Baton Rouge: Louisiana State University Press, 1964.

———. *Generals in Gray: Lives of the Confederate Commanders.* Baton Rouge: Louisiana State University Press, 1959.

Weigley, Russell F. *A Great Civil War: A Military and Political History, 1861–1865.* Bloomington: Indiana University Press, 2000.

Weiss, John. *Life and Correspondence of Theodore Parker. In Two Volumes.* 1864. Reprint, New York: Negro Universities Press, 1969.

Wharton, Vernon Lane. *The Negro in Mississippi, 1865–1890.* New York: Harper Torchbooks, 1965.

Wheeler, Richard, ed. *Voices of the Civil War.* New York: Thomas Crowell, 1976.

Williams, Robert C. *Horace Greeley: Champion of American Freedom.* New York: New York University Press, 2006.

Williams, T. Harry, ed. *Hayes: The Diary of a President, 1875–1881.* New York: David McKay, 1964.

Williamson, Joel. *After Slavery: The Negro in South Carolina During Reconstruction, 1861–1877.* Chapel Hill: University of North Carolina Press, 1965.

Wise, Stephen R. *Lifeline of the Confederacy: Blockade Running During the Civil War.* Columbia: University of South Carolina Press, 1991.

Wright, Henry C. "The Chicago Convention," *The Liberator.* Vol. 34, No. 37 (September 9, 1864), p. 147.

Wyandot [pen name]. "Correspondence of the New-York Daily Times." *New-York Daily Times.* January 8, 1855, p. 2.

Yacovone, Donald, ed. *A Voice of Thunder: The Civil War Letters of George E. Stephens.* Urbana: University of Illinois Press, 1997.

Younger, Edward, ed. *Inside the Confederate Government: The Diary of Robert Garlick Hill Kean.* New York: Oxford University Press, 1957.

Zion's Herald and Wesleyan Journal. "The Late Decision of the Supreme Court of the United States," Vol. 28, No. 11 (March 18, 1857), p. 42.

———. "President Johnson," Vol. 36, No. 17 (April 26, 1865), p. 66.

———. [untitled editorial], Vol. 36, No. 18 (May 3, 1865), p. 70.

INDEX

Locators in *italic* indicate illustrations. Locators in **boldface** indicate main entries/topics and biographies.
Locators followed by *m* indicate maps. Locators followed by *t* indicate tables.
Locators followed by *c* indicate chronology entries.